ECONOMICS for CONSUMERS
Seventh Edition

ECONOMICS for CONSUMERS

Seventh Edition

Leland J. Gordon
Denison University

Stewart M. Lee
Geneva College

 D. Van Nostrand Company

New York   Cincinnati   Toronto   London   Melbourne

Lovingly dedicated to
Doris Gilbert Gordon   Ann and Kathy Lee

D. Van Nostrand Company Regional Offices:
New York   Cincinnati

D. Van Nostrand Company International Offices:
London   Toronto   Melbourne

ISBN: 0–442–22242–4

Published by D. Van Nostrand Company
450 West 33rd Street, New York, N.Y. 10001

10 9 8 7 6 5 4 3 2 1

PREFACE

Consumer economics, consumer education, consumerism, whatever one wishes to call it, has come of age. The 1976 political platforms had their consumer planks. Neither major party dared to ignore the consumer. In the presidential election each party tried to capture the consumer vote. The results of the 1976 political campaign are now history. We shall see how much and what kind of action our elected representatives at the national, state, and local levels will take to improve the status of 215 million consumers.

Much has happened in the consumer movement since the Sixth Edition of *Economics for Consumers* was published. There has been continuing pressure to give the consumer more rights and protection in the market by expanding the scope of government regulations. At the same time, some individuals and organizations have complained that there is too much government action on behalf of the consumer. In this new edition our analysis of the consumer, the economy, and the market should help you decide how much and in what areas the government should be involved, and in what areas the government should allow the economy to operate relatively free of restraints.

This Seventh Edition of *Economics for Consumers* represents a major revision, updating the subject matter and making it relevant for our time. The changes in the text reflect the changes in consumerism. The chapter on the role of the federal government has been expanded to two chapters as the federal government, for better or worse, has become more involved in consumerism. The complex roles of such federal agencies as the Food and Drug Administration, the Federal Trade Commission, and the Consumer Product Safety Commission are examined, and the continuing expansion and activities of the state and local governments in the field of consumerism are described and evaluated.

Changing attitudes toward the free economy are investigated, especially the impact that inflation has had on the economy in general and the consumer in particular. There is hardly a facet of consumer activity that has not been touched by the spiraling inflation of the 1970s. Inflation has changed the spending patterns and investment plans of many persons; it has forced many prospective buyers of houses to question their ability to finance such a major purchase and spiraling prices have changed both the clothing and food-purchasing habits of millions of people. The impact of inflation, as it relates to such issues as consumer debt, insurance, and fashions and customs, is discussed throughout the text.

By the time you finish reading this book, you should have a better understanding of the marketplace, how it operates to serve you the consumer, and also how it operates at times to disserve and even defraud the consumer. In addition, each "consumer" of this book should have a better understanding of himself or herself as a consumer and some answers to the question of why one consumes in the way one does.

This is the first edition for which Professor Lee has assumed major responsibility and for which Dr. Gordon has assumed the role of consultant. All chapters have been largely rewritten, as have the Questions for Review and the Projects. An important feature is the Instructor's Manual, which includes an annotated bibliography of books, journals, and audiovisual aids, as well as a variety of test questions.

A continuing feature of *Economics for Consumers* is its thorough documentation. We have acknowledged our sources of information and our indebtedness to many researchers and writers. Business firms, trade and professional associations, government agencies, and individuals have answered questions, checked facts, and supplied materials. The librarians at Geneva College have been very helpful.

We wish to express our thanks to Ernest Morgan, one of the founders of the Continental Association of Funerals and Memorial Societies, for information used in Chapter 6; to Dr. Richard L. D. Morse, Chairman, Department of Family Economics, Kansas State University, for his help on Chapter 12; to Dr. Colston E. Warne, President of Consumers Union, for facts and judgments used in Chapter 16; to Leonard L. Chiappetta, realtor, for help on Chapter 17; to Joseph G. Bonnice, Assistant Vice-President, Insurance Information Institute, for checking the accuracy of the facts in Chapter 19; to Harold F. Wollin and Terrence Troy of the Office of Weights and Measures, National Bureau of Standards, for checking the facts in Chapter 23; to Wallace Janssen, historian for the Food and Drug Administration, who shared his years of experience with the FDA with us in checking the accuracy and current aspects of Chapter 25; to Commissioner Elizabeth Hanford Dole, of the Federal Trade Commission, for responding to many requests for information for Chapter 26; and to Nancy Steorts, Special Assistant to the Secretary of Agriculture, for supplying us with vital materials for Chapter 26.

Dr. Lee expresses special thanks to President Edwin Clarke and Dean William Russell of Geneva College for lightening his teaching load while the Seventh Edition was in preparation and without whose understanding this edition could not have been possible. In addition, he would like to express his appreciation to his colleagues in the Department of Economics and Business Administration at Geneva College for their patience and forebearance and to the department secretaries, Sue Snedeker, for her invaluable assistance in typing the manuscript, and Terri Hiltz, for her work on the indexes.

We also wish to thank Professor Lottie Tartell of Hofstra University and Professor Paul L. Ng of the University of Hawaii system, who provided us with helpful suggestions for the seventh edition.

Dr. Lee would like to thank his sister, Miss Rebecca Lee, whose expertise in linguistics was put to the test as she read every word from cover to cover and made many helpful suggestions.

For Dr. and Mrs. Gordon, this edition marks the culmination of seven editions and thirty-nine years of service to the consumer movement.

Leland J. Gordon
Stewart M. Lee

CONTENTS

PART

IS THE CONSUMER REALLY KING?

CHAPTER 1

THE CONSUMER IN A FREE ECONOMY

CAN CONSUMERS COPE WITH A FLUCTUATING ECONOMY?

"What do you think is the most important problem facing this country today?" In 1976 and 1975 a Gallup poll reported that the high cost of living and unemployment concerned respondents most.[1] The high cost of living is what economists call *inflation*. When the increase in the volume of money and credit exceeds the goods and services in the market, the general level of prices rises. As the general level of prices goes up, the purchasing power of the dollar goes down. For example, if $1.00 was worth $1.00 in the base year of 1967, it would have been worth $3.30 in 1913, and 58 cents in 1976.

Notice the qualifying adjective in the phrase "general level of prices." This means that while the prices of most goods and services go up during inflation, some prices may be stable, and some may actually decline. For example, in 1975 when the general level of prices rose 6.8 percent, the prices of twenty-two goods and services rose more than that percentage; the range in price increases among the twenty-two items was 7.2 percent to 55.8 percent. In the same time period the prices of sixteen goods and services rose less than the 6.8 percent average, with a range of increase from 0.1 percent to 6.4 percent, and the prices of eight items declined in a range from 1.3 percent to 56.9 percent.[2]

All the 215 million inhabitants of the United States are consumers. Of that number, 95.2 million comprise the total labor force. The employed — 87.8 million — are the ones who produce the goods and services that constitute the gross national product from year to year.* If all 95.2 million were at work and the general level of prices did not vary above or below 100 by more than 2 percent, the economy would be characterized as stable and a dollar would be worth a dollar year after year. Actually, in 1976, 7.4 million members of the labor force those able and willing to work — had no jobs. As is the case with prices, actual unemployment rates are higher in some

---

* Figures are for 1976.

3

geographical areas and among some potèntial workers, such as the young, the old, minority groups, and women. In some cities and among some groups unemployment may be as high as 20 or 25 percent.

When millions of consumers who have no income are faced with diminishing purchasing power (higher prices) for the few dollars they do have from savings, unemployment insurance, or welfare payments, their situation is critical. No wonder they consider inflation and unemployment their major concerns.

The actual goods and services that a dollar will buy is called *real income*. As dollar income increases during an inflationary period and prices also increase, the consumer makes no gain. This was the situation in the years from 1969 to 1975; real income was only $150 more per worker in 1975 than it was in 1969, although wages and salaries had risen considerably. According to the Bureau of the Census, the poverty income level is related to inflation. In 1973 the poverty level income for an urban family of four was $4,540, compared to $5,500 in 1976. Poverty, like unemployment, is divided unevenly among the 215 million persons making up the population. In 1974 only 9 percent of total whites in this country were below the poverty level, compared to 23 percent of the Spanish origin population and 31 percent of all blacks.

The chart on page 5 shows how much a family of four would need to have earned in 1975 to remain as well off as it was in 1965 and how much the family would have to earn by 1985 to be as well off as it was in 1965 if the rate of inflation for that decade were the same as for the previous decade.

Some Insidious Effects of Inflation

1. Inflation is a hidden tax. It takes away purchasing power without giving the consumer anything in return. Unless one's income increases, the inflation tax is roughly equal to the rate of inflation. Double-digit inflation in 1974 eroded income at the rate of 10 to 12 percent a year. The value of a dollar was reduced by 50 percent in just six or seven years.

2. Inflation encourages quality deterioration. Instead of or in addition to increasing prices, producers may reduce quality. When quality is reduced and prices are increased at the same time, the hidden effect is doubly bad.

3. Inflation encourages short measuring. Everything that is bought and sold has to be measured. In periods of increasing costs, producers can maintain prices by reducing quantity. This is usually legal if the smaller amount is declared on the label, but careless consumers who do not read labels will be unaware of this.*

4. Inflation upsets family financial planning. In 1974, when the rate of inflation was 13 percent, the U.S. Department of Labor's Bureau of Labor Statistics reported that a typical urban family of four needed an income of $14,300 annually to maintain a moderate level of living—that is,

* See Chapter 23.

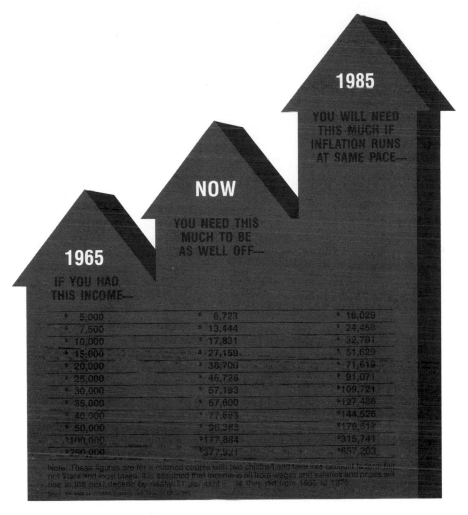

1965 IF YOU HAD THIS INCOME—	NOW YOU NEED THIS MUCH TO BE AS WELL OFF—	1985 YOU WILL NEED THIS MUCH IF INFLATION RUNS AT SAME PACE—
$ 5,000	$ 8,723	$ 18,029
$ 7,500	$ 13,444	$ 24,459
$ 10,000	$ 17,831	$ 32,781
$ 15,000	$ 27,159	$ 51,629
$ 20,000	$ 38,700	$ 71,618
$ 25,000	$ 46,728	$ 91,071
$ 30,000	$ 57,193	$109,721
$ 35,000	$ 67,600	$127,486
$ 40,000	$ 77,683	$144,526
$ 50,000	$ 96,383	$176,517
$100,000	$177,884	$315,741
$250,000	$377,021	$657,203

Note: These figures are for a married couple with two children and take into account federal but not State and local taxes. It is assumed that income is all from wages and salaries and prices will rise in the next decade by nearly 71 per cent — as they did from 1965 to 1975.

Reprinted from *U.S. News & World Report.* Copyright 1975, U.S. News & World Report, Inc.

$1,733 more than the preceding year because of inflation; by 1976, $15,318 were needed.

5. Inflation makes borrowing money cost more because interest rates are forced up. When inflation increases at a rapid rate, the Federal Reserve slows down the flow of money into the banking system. This has the effect of forcing interest rates up as the available amount of loanable funds is reduced. When the interest rate for mortgage money rises beyond customary rates, potential buyers and builders stop borrowing. The construction industry bears the brunt of this anti-inflationary measure, and building

drops to a minimal level. As a result of decreased supply, the market value of existing buildings rises.*

6.   Inflation diminishes the value of insurance coverage. A house that cost $30,000 in 1960 was worth approximately $68,000 in 1976. As a result, the insurance coverage in 1976 ought to have been more than twice what it was sixteen years earlier. Inflation creates similar problems with reference to other kinds of insurance, especially life insurance.†

7.   Inflation decreases the value of savings and investments. One of the requirements of a good monetary system is that money serve as a store-house of value. If a dollar were always worth 100 cents, a saver could be sure that the dollar saved in 1967 would be worth 100 cents in 1977. Instead, due to inflation, a dollar worth a dollar in 1967 was worth less than 60 cents ten years later.

In an effort to avoid such erosion (loss), some savers put their dollars into other forms of wealth, such as land and common stocks, whose value tends to rise as the general level of prices goes up. But small savers unfamiliar with real estate and the stockmarket, tend to keep their dollars in commercial banks or savings and loan banks. The maximum interest payable on such savings is approximately 7 percent. So if inflation amounts to 12 percent, the small saver loses all interest on his or her savings and approximately 5 percent of principal (that is, the amount invested).‡

Double Trouble — Inflation and Unemployment Together

Historically inflation has been concurrent with prosperity and full employment.§ In such a situation the evils of inflation are partially offset. But when 8 percent of the labor force is out of work and without income, as in 1976, the evils of inflation and unemployment are compounded.

The economic cost of unemployment can be estimated. The volume of goods and services lost in 1976 because of 7.4 million idle workers amounted to more than $100 billion. Add to that the transfer of money in unemployment compensation, welfare payments, and relief, and the total loss came to approximately $150 billion.

The noneconomic costs of unemployment — mental anguish, anxiety, disintegration of personality, loss of self-respect, feelings of inadequacy, helplessness, hopelessness, and powerlessness — cannot be measured, but they are very real. And the longer a person is idle and without income, the greater the physical and psychological cost.

Dr. M. Harvey Brenner of Johns Hopkins University testified before the Joint Economic Committee of Congress that "the rates of mental disorders, suicides, homicides, heart disease, and infant deaths have shown dramatic

* See Chapter 17.
† See chapters 18 and 19.
‡ See Chapter 20.
§ "Full employment" is taken to mean approximately 97 percent of the labor force at work.

Waiting in line for unemployment payments. (*Sybil Shelton, Monkmeyer*)

increases following periods of economic instability."[3] People in distress often turn to alcohol and consequently suffer the side effects of alcoholism, such as cirrhosis of the liver. It is not surprising that Dr. Brenner found a high correlation between coronary artery disease and unfavorable economic change.

Louis Harris, a leading pollster, made these remarks after polling a representative sample of the American people concerning their attitudes toward inflation and unemployment:

> If given a choice between seriously trimming their material life-styles or enduring more cycles of double-digit inflation and high levels of unemployment, they find that decision relatively easy. By 77 percent to eight percent they would opt for cutting back in their material life-styles. These are significant results, for they signal the enormous change that is taking place in our country. Simply put, it means in the future that the three bathtub and three car syndrome is disappearing from American life. . . . Instead, they are seeking, yearning, and even crying out for a different kind of existence.[4]

CONSUMERISM—A PEOPLE'S MOVEMENT

Consumerism Defined

Not very many years ago a person looking in a dictionary for a definition of the word "consumerism" would not have found it. Consumerism is a relatively new word, apparently coined in the business community in the mid-1960s as a term of derision used to encompass all the activities of the growing number of consumer advocates, both inside and outside the government, who were questioning the inadequacies of the marketplace and the reluctance of business to respond favorably to consumer needs and demands. It was not long, however, before the word assumed respectability. In 1969 the president, in a message to Congress, stated that consumerism is a healthy development that is here to stay.

The special assistant to the president for consumer affairs defined consumerism as nothing more and nothing less than a challenge to business to live up to its full potential – to give consumers what is promised, to be honest, to give people a product that will work and that is reasonably safe, to respond effectively to legitimate complaints, to provide information concerning the relevant quality characteristics of a product, to take into consideration the ecological and environmental ramifications of a company decision, and to return to the basic principle upon which so much of our nation's business was structured – satisfaction guaranteed or your money back.

Attitudes of the Business Community Toward Consumerism

A retired chairman of General Motors said that the ultimate aim of consumer advocates who criticize business is to alienate the American consumer from business and to tear down long-established relationships that have served both business and consumers so well.

Consumerism has also been attacked by business as an effort to cripple the free-enterprise system. On the other hand, some business managers look on consumerism favorably as an attempt to make business do what it should be doing, thereby making the free-enterprise system work as it is supposed to work, rewarding those businesses that serve consumers well and penalizing those that do not.

Dr. Drucker called consumerism "the shame of marketing."[5] He wrote that if those in marketing had looked at business from the buyer's viewpoint instead of the seller's viewpoint, there would have been no need for the consumer movement to develop.

When the words *consumerism, consumer movement,* and *consumer advocate* are mentioned, one name stands out, and that is the name of Ralph Nader. Ever since the publication of his book *Unsafe at Any Speed* in 1965, Nader has been in the forefront of the consumer movement, battling for the consumer and challenging American business when he believes it is not doing right by the consumer.[6] Nader was chosen as one of the ten most influential persons in the United States in a survey of 1,400 key Americans compiled by *U.S. News & World Report.*[7]

In the Watergate era, a time when many Americans had a low opinion of almost all public officials, 58 percent gave Nader a positive job rating, 18 percent a negative rating, and 24 percent not sure, for his efforts in attempting to protect the interests and safety of consumers.[8]

Much of what the term "consumerism" has come to mean is to be found in the varied activities of Ralph Nader as he has attempted to correct the shabby way that too many businesses have treated consumers for too long.

Consumerism Is Here to Stay

If the members of the business community think that consumerism is a passing fancy, they are mistaken. If they think that the consumer movement is idealistic or welfare oriented, they are mistaken. The consumer movement is the result of a great need on the part of consumers; it is not the result of political pressures; however, it has gained wide political acceptance. Consumerism means that the rising demands of consumers must be heard, that their views must be considered by business and government. Its real thrust and challenge is the demand of consumers that private and public agencies serve them to protect their basic interests.

WHO ARE CONSUMERS?

We All Are—You Are

As you read these words, you are a consumer. Not only are you consuming this book but at the same time you are consuming shelter, heat or air-conditioning, natural or artificial light, and furniture. The clothing you wear is being consumed. Perhaps you are wearing glasses. In all probability you have a pencil in your hand which you may use to mark certain portions of the book. Or you may have on the desk a sheet of paper on which you make notes as you read.

You have been a consumer every moment of your life, night and day. Indeed, from the moment of conception until after death the process of consumption continues.

As a consumer you have participated actively in the economy from the day you spent your first dime for candy. Later you spent quarters for such childhood delights as ice-cream cones and sodas. You did not know it, but your purchases, together with those of classmates and friends, reflected a demand for an increasing variety of goods and services. Your first contact with the economy began in a retail store. As your purchases depleted supplies, the retailer ordered new supplies from the processor, and the processor ordered more raw materials. The result was the production of things you and others wanted at prices that you were able and willing to pay.

Your consumer role as a college student is more significant. Your childhood purchases were the acts of an economic infant. Now you are mature and rational. Or are you? As a consumer you have an important role to play in the economy. The way you perform will in turn affect the performance of the economy. Buying is an act of faith—faith that the world will continue, that a major war will not begin, that prosperity will continue, and that your own life will continue. Consuming is more complicated than simply going to a store to buy food or clothing. It includes the purchase of housing and the services of banks and credit institutions. It includes purchases from public utilities of such services as gas, electricity, telephones, and water. In the years ahead you will probably buy insurance, medical and dental care, and hospital services. Throughout your lifetime you will pay over $200,000 in taxes for local, state, and federal government services. Your total expenditures will amount to $750,000 or more—three-quarters of a million dollars! In order to spend this money wisely you must know something about how our economy works.

HOW THE ECONOMY OPERATES

Demand

In the eighth decade of the 20th century there are 215 million consumers in the United States, and the number is growing at the rate of one and a half to two million a year. There are 56.1 million families of two or more persons living in the same household who are related by blood, marriage, or adoption. A household includes all persons who occupy a housing unit. Altogether there are 72.7 million households. Individually and collectively these households are the basic consuming units in the economy.

It is *family income* that gives family members the purchasing power with which to buy goods and services to satisfy their needs and wants. Collectively consumers had $1.2 trillion disposable personal income in 1976. If that income had been divided equally, each family would have had $21,390 to spend in a twelve-month period. If total disposable personal income had been divided equally among consumers, every man, woman, and child would have had $5,581 to spend.

Economists define money as a medium of exchange. To consumers money is something to be spent. In 1976 consumers spent about $435 billion for nondurable goods and $475 billion for services. In addition, they spent about $155 billion for durable goods. Year after year consumer expenditures constitute about two-thirds of total expenditures in the economy. If family incomes are steady or if they increase, family expenditures will either continue at the same level or increase. If they increase, the economy will continue to grow and family income will therefore grow.

After all their expenditures, consumers still have money left. This unspent money, called *savings,* ranges from 6 to 8 percent of total disposable personal income. In absolute figures, consumer savings amount to about $83 billion a year; money which is invested in a variety of ways.

The American economy might be described as a debt economy. All segments of the economy are in debt. The biggest debtors are business and farm enterprises, whose indebtedness amounts to $1.4 trillion. Government debt amounts to $745 billion, of which $525 billion is federal and $220 billion state and local. Personal debt amounts to $841 billion. Altogether this adds up to a debt of $3 trillion. Lest you become alarmed about the size of the private and public debt, it is well to remember that for every debtor there is a creditor. All of the $3 trillion owed by debtors are owed to other people or organizations in the economy who count this indebtedness as part of their assets.

The productive work of the nation is done by men and women over the age of sixteen In 1976 there were 95.2 million men and women in the labor force; of that number 87.8 million were gainfully employed. This figure includes all personnel in the armed forces. But it does not include the 30 million homemakers not employed outside the home, although their contribution to the economy is as important as the contribution made by those who are listed as gainfully employed. In their various jobs the 87.8 million employed people produce all the goods and services available for consumers.

Economists measure the performance and growth of the economy in terms of gross national product, net national product, national income, personal income, and disposable personal income. The total output of goods and services in a country is called _gross national product_, and in the United States in 1976 it amounted to $1.7 trillion. In the process of production capital goods wear out. This is known as _depreciation_. The figure resulting after depreciation is deducted from gross national product is known as _net national product_, which was $1.5 trillion for 1976. From net national product is deducted indirect business taxes to derive a figure described as _national income_ This amounted to $1.3 trillion in 1976.

Personal income consists of wages, rent, interest, dividends, transfer payments, and unincorporated net income. The national income items not included in personal income are undistributed corporate profits, corporate taxes, and social security tax payments. The resulting total personal income figure for 1976 was $1.4 trillion.

Disposable personal income is the amount left after deducting personal taxes from personal income. This is the amount of money consumers have for consumption and for savings; it was $1.2 trillion in 1976.

Per capita disposable income is derived by dividing total disposable personal income by the current total population figure For 1976 this amounted to $5,453. Of that amount, consumers spent on the average of $4,952 for personal consumption expenditures, with an average of $386 per person saved.

SATISFYING CONSUMER WANTS

What Makes Our Economy Go?

Men, women, and children must have food, clothing, and shelter to satisfy their minimum wants. In addition there are many other kinds of material goods and many kinds of services they wish to enjoy. The purpose of the economy is to provide these goods and services. It is important to keep this purpose in mind. There is a tendency to become so absorbed by particular aspects of our economy that one loses sight of the fundamental purpose. For example, some people seem to think that the primary purpose of the economy is to provide jobs for workers, or profits for owners of business firms, or to provide tax revenue for government. These are all desirable goals, but they are incidental to the primary purpose of satisfying consumer wants.

Engaged in hundreds of different kinds of occupations, those who are in the labor force work about 40 hours each week producing economic goods and services which, it is assumed, consumers will buy. These workers produce goods and perform services either in connection with the productive process or directly for consumers.

Consumers or Producers?

The 87.8 million people in the labor force who spend 40 or more hours each week in productive activity are also consumers every moment of the 168 hours in each week. While they work, they are consuming clothing, shelter, and food. When their working period ends, their consuming activities become more varied. Since all people are consumers 168 hours every week, and, only a portion of them are gainfully occupied, and for only 25 percent of that time, it is evident that economics must deal with the role of consumers in the economy, not just with the role of producers.

As we have noted, economic statistics do not include homemakers as a part of the labor force or as gainfully occupied. This is a serious defect in economic analysis. The 30 million women who manage the basic consuming units are vitally important in the economy. As homemakers they operate miniature hotels in which they provide food, shelter, and services for members of their family. If all women who are homemakers were to give up their jobs as homemakers, it would be necessary to rehire them or others to do the same work. They would then be listed as gainfully occupied, and the labor force would then total 118 million. The fact that homemakers do not receive salaries or wages does not alter the fact that they are engaged in productive economic activity and must be included in any study of consumers and of the economy.

In addition to those in the labor force and homemakers, there are about 97 million men, women, and children in the United States who are not engaged in productive enterprise but who are consumers. Some of these are older people living on incomes from savings accumulated during their working years. Others are children too young to be employed; and still others are men, women, and children who are incapacitated and for whom others in the economy must assume the responsibility of providing the necessary goods and services. And unfortunately there are those who want to work, but are unable to find a job. There were 7.4 million unemployed people in the United States in 1976.

Who Decides What Shall Be Produced?

Sometimes the most familiar aspects of daily life are the least understood. Ever since you spent that first dime in a candy store you have been able to find the goods and services you want readily available in various retail stores. Have you ever considered how those commodities came to be produced? How it happened that they were in the stores at the time you wanted them?

In the armed forces of the United States appropriate amounts and types of food, clothing, and shelter are automatically furnished for all military installations. The system by which this is accomplished is fundamentally different from that by which civilians are supplied with the things they want. The military establishment decides what kind of shelter shall be provided, what kind of food shall be served, and what kind of clothing shall be issued. Members of the armed forces must accept what they get, whether they like it or not. By contrast, civilian consumers must make their own decisions about which goods and services to buy. But, as in the armed forces, approximately the right amounts of consumer goods and services are made available for consumers, although in this case in stores.

Who are the supply officers for the civilian army of consumers? Most of them are self-appointed enterprisers or storekeepers. Many people make the decision to earn their livings by operating retail food stores. In the American system of free enterprise any person is able to make that choice if he or she has enough money to start a business. If the individual has judged the market correctly, some of the purchases made by consumers in that market area will be made in his store. Soon he will know approximately what quantities of goods to keep on the shelves every day. These estimates of what customers will purchase daily, weekly, monthly, and yearly are passed on to the wholesale suppliers in the form of orders. The wholesale suppliers in turn pass them on in the form of orders to the processors. Then the processors order the necessary raw materials. Notice this important fact: As a civilian consumer you are free to change your mind at any time about what you wish to consume. Although the retailer may have ordered bread, butter, and milk on the assumption that you and all of the other customers will buy the usual amounts today, you may cancel out and purchase nothing. That is one of many risks assumed by business firms. Your freedom to decide what you will or will not buy is an important freedom and carries with it certain consumer responsibilities.

CONSUMER SOVEREIGNTY?

The Classical Economists' Model Consumer

For analytical purposes economists construct models. This is necessary because the social sciences, unlike physical sciences, deal with people, whose actions and reactions cannot be predicted with the precision with which a physicist can predict a physical action or reaction. In the traditional economic model, the consumer is cast in the role of king or queen. The job of consumers is to guide the economy so that the goods and services they want will be produced. The model-maker passes no value judgments on the validity of consumer decisions, even if consumers demand goods and services that are detrimental to them. The model economy operates for the sole purpose of satisfying consumer wants. It is assumed that the production and consumption of goods and services automatically promotes consumer welfare, with no exploitation of consumers by producers or of producers by consumers.

In this model of a free economy the basic purpose, the promotion of consumer welfare, is accomplished by free persons engaging freely in productive enterprises to produce what consumers want. Consumers, exercising their freedom to choose, accept or reject what the market offers at the prices asked by sellers. Competition, defined as rivalry in buying and selling, is relied upon to assure good quality and full measure at prices equal to or close to the costs of production.

The Institutional Framework

In the model economy, the mechanism through which consumers' demands are registered is the price system. Free to make their choices, consumers register their decisions in retail stores by purchasing or refusing to purchase the goods and services available. If consumers demand more of a certain commodity or service, the price system supposedly reflects the increased demand in the form of higher prices. The higher prices encourage retailers to increase their supplies. Operating independently in the hope of making more profit, scores of business managers watch the reactions of consumers as reflected in the price system. If prices go down, production is presumably curtailed. If prices go up, production is increased. It is assumed that consumers reach decisions about what to buy or not to buy on the basis of full knowledge of the marketplace and rational choice.

The diagram on page 15 illustrates the organization and operation of a model economy, with emphasis on the functions of consumers. The outer border line shows the political and social institutions within which the economy functions. These are government, family, free press, free speech, church, and free public school. The representative democratic form of government in the United States is one cornerstone of American life. The family, operating as the basic consuming unit, is another cornerstone. A free church, uncontrolled by government, is basic to the American system. The free public school, a free press, and freedom of speech and assembly are all important in understanding the operation of the economy. The model-makers do not imply that all these institutions are perfect, but they do function and embody goals that the American people strive for.

Within the framework of political and social institutions, the diagram shows the framework of the economic system. The key concepts are free enterprise, profit motive, right of private property, free competition, and free contract. The profit system is the keystone in the classical model of the economy. Actually very few of the millions of workers in the labor force ever earn profit since they are employees, not owners, of the businesses. Most of them earn wages. All of them are motivated by a desire to earn more money. For this reason it might be better to use the term "money motive."

THE ORGANIZATION AND OPERATION OF A FREE ECONOMY

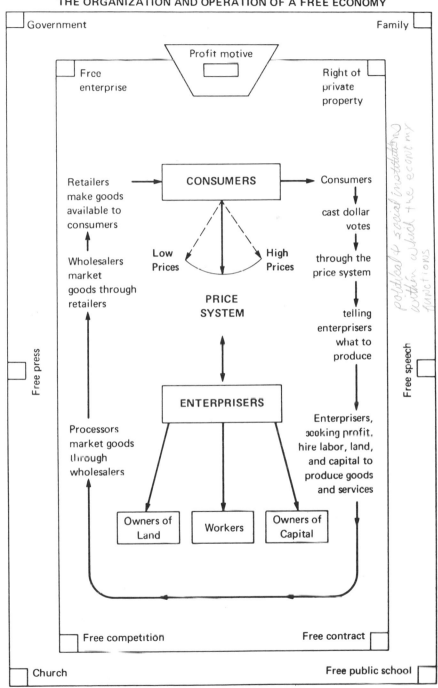

The term "free" as it is used in describing these economic institutions does not mean "absolutely unfettered." One of the functions of government, for example, is to prevent monopolies that might interfere with the rights of others to engage freely in enterprise.

The simplicity of this model is appealing. It is also deceptive.

Who Really Decides What Shall Be Produced: Buyers or Sellers?

Practically all sellers and some economists profess to believe that consumers are really sovereign – that they control and guide the production of goods and services. However, two Harvard Business School economists have said that this view of consumer sovereignty compliments consumers but is not real. "Given the complexity of many modern buying decisions, the marketer would like the consumer to be guided by manufacturer integrity and brand reputation, enhanced by advertising."[9]

Economist and psychologist George Katona of the University of Michigan Survey Research Center has written that "the consumer was never sovereign in the sense of being wholly autonomous, and he is not sovereign today." But "neither is he puppet or pawn."[10] After discussing the concept of consumer sovereignty, Katona says that consumers are sensible, discriminating buyers. They seek information and try to understand what goes on. They are not irrational, but sometimes they do act impulsively. They are not inclined to excessive behavior, and they are not pawns in the hands of sellers. They learn slowly and they change slowly. For these reasons, consumers are a stabilizing force in the economy.

The concept of the rational "economic man" was developed long before there was a science of psychology, however. Psychologists have made it clear that people are complex individuals who cannot be neatly fitted into a mold. After describing the economists' model of an "economic man," psychologist Charles K. Raymond stated bluntly that no such consumer exists.[11] Marketers James H. Myers and William H. Reynolds recognize that "consumers are vulnerable creatures." They were not born to cope with the modern market as buyers. The individual consumer's "senses often betray him, his powers of rationality fail him, and he often becomes confused. *And the seller knows it.*"[12]

Psychologist W. A. Woods divides consumers into six types:

1. Habit-determined, brand-loyal
2. Cognitive – sensitive to rational claims
3. Price-cognitive – decide mainly on basis of price
4. Impulse consumers – buy on the basis of physical appeal, insensitive to brands
5. Emotional reactors, respond to images
6. New consumers not yet classified

It has been estimated that only 20 percent of all consumers fall under the second classification, namely, sensitive to rational claims.[13]

Psychologist Sidney J. Levy calls attention to the fact that consumers today are not as functionally oriented as they were in earlier days. Consumers in a supermarket are not economic persons, nor can they be. They do not buy economically. They are often vague about the actual price they pay. They have few standards by which to judge quality. They cannot really make intelligent choices among competing brands. It is now recognized that consumer purchases are symbols of personal attitudes and goals, of social patterns and striving. If the symbols are appropriate, purchases will be made because consumers want to enhance themselves. Automobiles, houses, and mink coats are only a few of the symbols of social achievement consumers purchase.[14]

Economist John Kenneth Galbraith says that the accepted sequence of consumer demand and management response is no longer valid, but that this myth suits the technostructure and therefore continues to be taught in the colleges and universities.

> The initiative in deciding what is to be produced comes not from the sovereign consumer who, through the market, issues the instructions that bend the productivity mechanism to his ultimate will. Rather it comes from the great producing organization which reaches forward to control the markets that it is presumed to serve, and, beyond, to bend the customer to its needs.[15]

Significant Differences Among Consumers

The literature of economics is filled with misconceptions about *the consumer*. The myth of the economic man has given rise to the myth of the consumer. Actually each consumer is a person first and a statistic second. Each person passes through a life cycle that includes infancy, childhood, the teens, young adulthood, middle age, and old age. At any given time the total number of consumers consists of some who are infants, some who are children, some who are teenagers, some who are young adults, and some in middle age and old age. Obviously consumers in each of these groups have different interests and their interests change as they move through the life cycle.

Consumers over the age of sixty-five number 22.4 million. In 1975, 84 percent of all older people had adequate incomes, but 16 percent lacked enough to live in simple dignity. This brings up the question of distribution of income. Most households in this country are relatively affluent, and the economy is geared to these households. However, 23 million persons live on incomes below the poverty level. Who are the poor? Mostly they are people over age sixty-five, the disabled, nonwhites, members of one-parent families, small farmers and small businessmen, or low-wage workers. Approximately one-third of those classified as poor are nonwhite.

Aside from differences in income, other significant differences among consumers arise out of geographical location, national origin, race, religious affiliation, occupation, and place of residence, whether rural, urban, or suburban. All these differences affect consumer values, attitudes, choices, and practices.

Collective Consumption and Consumer Sovereignty

When analyzing the role of the consumer, it must be kept in mind that of the 215 million consumers, 87.8 million are employed as workers in the economy. Many are repeatedly faced with the question whether a policy or practice that may be beneficial to them as workers is detrimental or beneficial to other consumers.

More than 133 million consumers are influenced by their role as voting citizens. As citizens, consumers may, for example, favor or oppose rent controls in their states or the sale of alcoholic beverages in their local communities. Currently, military expenditures are the highest in our peacetime history. Decisions to spend billions of dollars for defense are made by people as citizens, not as consumers. No individual consumer makes a voluntary military expenditure in the market.

The federal budget is the "key instrument in national policy making." Through it the nation decides what the public sector shall do. "The budget is a major challenge to consumer sovereignty (which is) . . . a process of choice such that the society embodying it may be clearly seen as the result of that choice. Choice must be free, informed, responsible, and personal."[16] How can the individual consumer-citizen possibly express an intelligent and effective view that will influence budget-makers? Administrations are generally more concerned with remaining in office than with national goals and consumer sovereignty.

Public consumption expenditures for education, libraries, museums, parks, and highways are also made by people as citizens not as consumers. In contrast to individual, family, or group consumer expenditures, all of the expenditures listed above may more appropriately be described as *collective consumption.*

About 165 million persons belong to churches. Their roles as consumers are complemented and influenced by their roles as church members. Churches influence and even determine the actions of many consumers in the market. Churches determine certain values which are reflected in individual and group consumer purchasers or refusals to purchase.

Do Consumers Really Know What They Want?

Some economists hold that the best way to evaluate consumer wants is through the market. This assumes that the purpose of production is to produce what consumers want and that their wants are known by their behavior in the market. The first assumption raises this question: Are managers of business firms motivated by a desire to satisfy consumer wants or are they motivated primarily by a desire to make money? The second assumption is open to question also. Consumer choices in the market may not reflect their "real" or "true" preferences. Consumers do not buy direct satisfactions, except in the case of services. Before most products can be used, some home preparation is required. The economist John Hicks accepts the core of the concept of consumer sovereignty but adds that consumers need help in making the right choices and that their need for help increases as technology increases.[17]

Motivated by their desire to make money, managers of business firms use their ingenuity to create goods and to render services that they think they can make consumers want. For many years the makers of Geritol told consumers that if they were tired, felt a loss of strength, had a run-down feeling, or were nervous or irritable, these symptoms indicated a deficiency in iron that could be remedied by taking Geritol. According to the Federal Trade Commission, the Geritol advertising claims were without factual foundation.

There are numerous causes of the same symptoms other than a deficiency of iron or vitamins. These symptoms are common manifestations of almost any disease or disorder. Consumers have no way of knowing unless they consult a physician. This is just one case among many demonstrating that most consumers do not know what they need in order to maintain or regain their health and that some business firms try to take advantage of this ignorance.[18] In 1970 Geritol was still advertising as a remedy for iron deficiency. But in 1976 J. B. Williams Company, manufacturer of Geritol and Fem-Iron, paid fines totaling $302,000 for misrepresenting these products in advertisements.

The supply of goods and services in the world market is so extensive that millions of consumers do not even know of the existence of many commodities. In local shopping centers, food stores, variety stores, and department stores have thousands upon thousands of goods. How can consumers know which of these they want? How can they know which of these they need? How can they even know what is available?

Are there any consumers who have not had the experience of window-shopping and discovering some new item that evokes the remark, "That is just what I want"? At that moment the consumer is convinced that he or she wants a product which a moment before was unwanted because it was unknown. Who has not had the experience of leafing through the pages of a mail-order catalog and finding descriptions of hitherto unknown products? Such products may be called to one's attention by means of magazine, newspaper, radio, or television advertising. Of course the discovery of a new product does not always result in the creation of a want, but in many cases a new want is born. By contrast, is there anyone who has not had the experience of purchasing a commodity only to discover after possession that it is not wanted and is subsequently discarded or forgotten?

Many wants are derivative. This means that the purchase of one commodity makes it necessary to purchase another commodity or service in order to enjoy the first. An electric light bulb is useless without electricity. A gas furnace will yield no heat without gas. An automobile will not travel without gasoline, oil, and tires.

Can Consumers Determine Quality?

The quality characteristics of butter include percentages of moisture, curd, salt, fat, mold mycelia, and extraneous matter. In sixty-one samples tested in one month, the State Laboratories Department of North Dakota found moisture ranging from 8.2 to 18.4 percent; curd content ranging from 0.4 to 1.8 percent; fat content ranging from 79.1 to 90.2 percent; and mold mycelia ranging from 0 to 58 percent. There was no objectionable extraneous matter found in thirty-eight of the samples, but in the other twenty-three laboratory technicians found such objectionable matter as insect parts, mites, insect eggs, and rodent hairs.[19]

The quality characteristics for ice cream include protein content, fat content, total milk solids, Standard Plate Count bacteria per gram, coliform bacteria per million, and percentage of fruit and nuts. Laboratory tests showed significant differences among the quality characteristics of several brands of ice cream. Among twenty-five samples tested the Standard Plate Count bacteria per gram ranged from less than 1,000 to 180,000![20]

The quality characteristics of hamburger include moisture content, protein, fat, and bacteria count. Among forty-six laboratory samples the fat content ranged from 1.7 to 34.4 percent. Bacteriological examination showed that ten samples had a high bacteria count when received, that bacteria developed rapidly in storage, or that spoilage bacteria developed in storage.[21]

These examples should suffice to make it clear that consumers could not possibly determine the quality of such processed products by the old method of feeling, pinching, or smelling.

A food additive is a substance other than a basic food that is used by manufacturers to preserve, to aid in processing, or to improve the texture, appearance, or taste of food. Most food additives are chemicals. Obviously, consumers cannot possibly detect all the additives used or the amounts. In the United States the Food and Drug Administration and in Canada the Food and Drug Directorate employ technically qualified personnel to monitor the use of additives. Food processors and consumers were shaken when these two agencies banned the use of cyclamates as artificial sweeteners. The reason? Laboratory tests had shown that massive doses of cyclamates induce cancer in rats over the period of a lifetime. Saccharin was once regarded as harmless, but it was later placed on the FDA's restricted list.

Additional problems for the consumer are created by the new technology which makes it possible for manufacturers to construct synthetic food products out of processed materials and chemicals. The number of synthetic food products continues to increase at a rapid rate. Among dairy products very few consumers, if any, could distinguish between synthetic cream and cream obtained from the milk of cows.

The inability of consumers to determine quality goes far beyond the broad range of food products. They cannot determine the tensile strength of thread or rope; they cannot determine the fastness of dyes. They cannot distinguish among synthetic fabrics; they cannot possibly know the quality characteristics of gasoline, including the octane rating; nor can they know before making a purchase how an automobile or television set or an appliance will perform.

These are only a few of the illustrations that could be given to show the complexity and interdependence of our economic life. Every day consumers use products and services produced by people they have never seen. As the volume and variety of goods increase, consumers' ability to judge quality becomes progressively less. At the same time, the impersonal nature of the economy makes it easier for unscrupulous sellers to dispose of defective and dangerous merchandise. Instead of depending on their ability to judge quality, consumers must depend on the reliability and responsibility of the sellers from whom they purchase goods and services. They must trust those who prepare their food, those who are responsible for the purity of their water, and those who are responsible for the safety of gas and electrical installations. They trust their lives to operators of automobiles, airplanes, trains, and ships. Their daily life is an act of faith. Most sellers keep that faith. But some do not, and those sellers must be kept under continuing surveillance by government inspectors.

Can Consumers Be Sure It Is Pure?

Water is basic to human life and its purity is imperative. Yet a federal government survey of 446 community water systems found that 319, or 72 percent, failed to test an adequate number of water samples for bacterial contamination. In the same survey eighty-one of the water systems, or 18 percent, failed to meet the Public Health Service coliform (a type of bacteria) standards in two or more months in a twelve-month period.[22] The state of North Dakota will furnish an analysis of water for any individual for a nominal fee of $2.00 a sample. The North Dakota State Laboratories Department warns that nitrates in excess of forty-five parts per million can cause methemoglobinemia (blue babies); adults are not affected. The bacteriological examination of water samples includes a determination of the presence or absence of coliform bacteria.[23]

The National Commission of Water Quality has estimated that cleansing the nation's lakes and rivers of pollution will cost industry and government between $97 billion and $130 billion by 1983.[24]

Can Consumers Be Sure It Is Safe?

Twenty-five million products have been recalled by the Consumer Product Safety Commission because of safety defects or potential safety hazards. Millions of automobiles have been recalled because of safety problems, and the Food and Drug Administration has recalled many drugs. For example, 20,000 bottles of boric acid solution, often used as an eyewash, were recalled because they were contaminated with mold. A major manufacturer of ice-cream bars was found guilty of producing products that contained a bacterial count higher than that permitted by law. Poisonous industrial chemicals called PCBs have been found contaminating drinking water and fish.

Americans consume about 5 pounds of food additives per year. Some additives are beneficial, such as Vitamin D in milk. The iodine added in salt has eliminated goiter. Nitrates and nitrites added to foods prevent botulism, a form of food poisoning that is often fatal. Experiments have shown, however, that under certain conditions nitrates and nitrites can cause cancer in animals.

Even food prepared in one's home may be hazardous. If it is held at room temperatures for several hours, staphylococci or salmonellae bacteria may grow. These bacteria are not destroyed by normal cooking. A food may look, taste, and smell all right, yet it may cause a severe illness.

The range of hazardous products constantly increases. Automobiles, power mowers, and even toys kill consumers. Every year about 183,000 persons are injured in accidents involving glass doors and windows. About 5,000 are injured each year from space heaters and heating stoves.

These random illustrations emphasize the necessity of consumers being informed and alert. It also illustrates that no matter how informed or alert consumers may be, their lives are in danger every day because of hazards over which they have no control and of which they could not possibly know.

Can Consumers Check the Quantity?

Every purchase of a good or service involves measurement. Measurement involves weight, volume, or number. Meat is weighed in ounces and pounds, milk is measured in pints and quarts, and eggs are measured by size and by number, the usual quantity being twelve. Services are measured by time or piece. A worker may be paid by the hour, by the number of pieces of product produced, or by the job.

In all such transactions the classical economic model assumes that the purchaser is present at the time of measurement and is therefore able and willing to check the accuracy of the measurement. But in retail stores today most measurements take place before the purchaser reaches the store. Practically all meats are prepackaged, preweighed, and prepriced. When a buyer picks up a package of meat marked 1 lb. 13 oz., there is no practical way to check the accuracy of that statement. When a buyer puts a loaf of bread in a shopping cart, he or she has no way of knowing whether the declared weight on the label is accurate. When canned goods or products in carton boxes are bought, there is no way of knowing whether the cans or boxes are full or whether the net weight declaration is accurate. Today 90 percent of the products sold in retail food stores are prepackaged. More and more items in variety stores, hardware stores, and clothing stores are packaged. A buyer is not permitted to break a package, and there is usually no way of checking the accuracy of the contents until after the consumer has bought the product. If there are inaccuracies, there are then problems of exchange or adjustment.

The records show that there is a considerable amount of short-counting, short-measuring, and short-weighing. In addition, there is some short-changing at check-out counters. Since consumers cannot ascertain the accuracy of weighing and measuring devices or supervise their accuracy in use, local, state, and federal government inspectors must do these jobs for them. In the economists' model of the economy, competition was supposed to regulate this aspect of trade. In actuality competition may result in more rather than less short-measurement. The complicated and expensive measuring devices now in use require the supervision of trained and skilled inspectors. Chapter 23 deals in depth with many aspects of weights and measures.

Can Consumers Detect Fraud?

The economists' model economy makes no allowances for the possibility of fraud. The consumer today too often experiences evasions, half-truths, misrepresentations, deceptions, and outright frauds in his or her dealings with merchants. The prevalence of fraud in the market is so substantial that all of Chapter 14 of this book deals with it.

Can Consumers Cope With Pricing Practices?

Most consumers assume that a high price guarantees good quality and that a low price is evidence of inferiority. These assumptions give sellers a great advantage, and many sellers make the most of it. Sellers know that very few consumers have any idea of the expenses incurred in the production process, so it is easy to sell inferior products at high prices. This can go on indefinitely because consumers often have no way of comparing the quality of one article with that of a competing product.

The concept of fair price is relative, not absolute. In order to judge the fairness of the price of a commodity one must know what it cost to produce it. Among competing brands there may be real differences in quality with no difference in price. At the same time, there may be great differences in price with no difference in quality.

Does Competition Control Prices?

In the classical model of the economy it is assumed that *pure competition* exists. An economy of pure competition is one in which there are so many sellers and so many buyers that no one seller or buyer can control supply, demand, or price. Today practically all products are packaged and sold under brand names in retail markets. Each firm has a monopoly in the sale of its brand—there is only one Hammermill paper—but there may be many competing brands of the same product. These brands compete in price, quantity, and quality claims. Hence the term *monopolistic competition*. *Oligopoly* is a situation in which a few firms dominate production. In the retail market, price competition is frequently replaced by nonprice competition, mostly in the form of advertising. Oligopolistic prices are higher than competitive prices. Among the items families purchase that are produced under oligopolistic conditions are automobiles, appliances, matches, soap, heating oil, natural gas, cigarettes, sporting goods, and cameras. In the following industries the four largest firms produce from 75 to 100 percent of total output: motor vehicles, tires, cigarettes, chewing gum, breakfast cereals, flat glass, light bulbs, and aluminum.

The word *monopoly* means a single seller. A *natural monopoly* is one in which competition would be wasteful because resources would be needlessly duplicated. The result would be higher rather than lower prices under competitive conditions in such industries as railroads, telegraph, telephone, electric light and power, gas, and water. Today such industries are granted monopoly privileges on the condition that their prices be subject to control by government commissions.

It must be noted that competition may operate in oligopolistic industries in one of three ways. When the automobile oligopoly misread consumer demand, enough consumers purchased foreign automobiles to compel American producers to change their products. Substitute services may provide competition. In air transportation the nonscheduled airlines provided enough competition to force the scheduled airlines to reduce their prices. A third way in which competition may operate is by means of a government yardstick. In the electric light and power industry, the Tennessee Valley Authority provided competition that forced private companies to reduce their prices.

Does Market Price Measure Subjective Value?

When the model consumer goes to market and pays the asking price for goods and services, it is assumed that those prices reflect the subjective value for the consumer of the goods and services. If they did not, it is assumed that the purchases would not be made. These assumptions would be valid only if all consumers had equal purchasing power, were fully informed, and were equally well-trained buyers. In reality, family incomes differ greatly; not many consumers fully understand the operation of the economy; and there is much adulteration and falsification on the part of sellers. As a result, it is unrealistic to assume that if each of two buyers pays 60 cents for a loaf of bread, the subjective valuations of the loaves are identical.

If all families had equal purchasing power, the willingness of two homemakers to pay 60 cents would more nearly reflect their subjective evaluation of the bread. The _principle of diminishing utility_ applies to money, as well as to other goods and services. Families that have incomes amounting to hundreds of thousands of dollars a year value each additional dollar much less than families whose incomes amount to a few thousand dollars. The lower-income families, who value their 60 cents much more highly than the higher-income families, place a much higher use-value on bread. The uneven distribution of national income leads to waste in economic life because the wealthy few can purchase palatial houses, luxurious motor boats, and expensive racing stables while other consumers have only the bare necessities.

Even if all families had equal incomes, the assumption that price is a measure of subjective value would not hold. It is obvious that some consumers, as buyers, are much more shrewd than others. They know better how to judge quality and price. They are more skillful at bargaining, a practice from which many consumers shrink. Some consumers are businesslike in their buying, but their number is small. In our highly specialized economy, sellers are shrewder and better informed than consumers. Most of them are good practical psychologists; they know the weaknesses of consumers, and many of them exploit those weaknesses. The pricing of goods and services, described in Chapter 11, is an art, not a science. Sellers ask for what they hope to get, and many times they get it.

THE DUAL ROLE OF CONSUMERS

Consumer Spending Makes the Economy Go

Consumers spend $3.0 billion a day! They are the biggest spenders in the economy. A family may easily spend three quarters of a million dollars. It is this consumer spending that propels the economy. If spending is sustained at a high level, the economy operates at a high level.

The flow of money in the economy is illustrated on page 26. Since our concern is primarily with consumers, let us break into the diagram at the point marked "consumers" and follow the flow of money clockwise. Having a collective annual income of $1.4 trillion, consumers spend $1.1 trillion each year for current goods and services. Most of these expenditures are made in retail stores, which in turn spend the money to buy supplies from wholesalers. The wholesalers then spend the money to buy supplies from processors. And so the spending flow continues. Local, state, and federal governments take $190 billion of consumers' incomes for the services they perform. The remaining $83 billion is saved. Retailers, wholesalers, proces-

THE FLOW OF MONEY IN THE ECONOMY

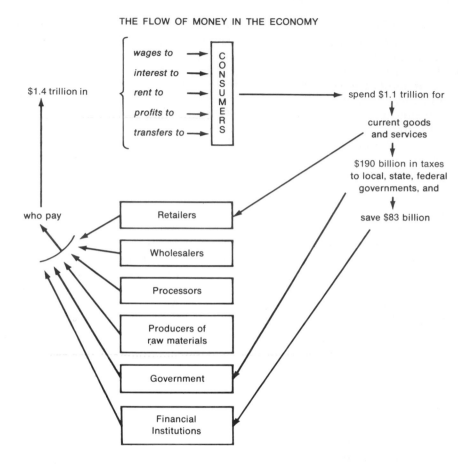

sors, producers of raw materials, governments, and financial institutions then spend the $1.4 trillion in wages, interest, rent, profits, and transfers such as Social Security payments. The recipients of these payments comprise the 215 million consumers for whose benefit the economy operates.

Consumer Rights

In 1962 the late President Kennedy sent a message to Congress devoted entirely to his "Consumers' Protection and Interest Program." That was the first time in the history of the nation that a president had considered consumers and their need for protection sufficiently important to submit to Congress a message devoted entirely to consumer interests.

In his message the president listed the following consumer rights:

- *The right to safety*—to be protected against the marketing of goods that are hazardous to health or life.

- *The right to be informed*—to be protected against fraudulent, deceitful, or grossly misleading information, advertising, labeling, or other practices, and to be given the facts needed to make informed choices.
- *The right to choose*—to be assured, wherever possible, access to a variety of products and services at competitive prices; and in those industries in which competition is not workable and government regulation is substituted, an assurance of satisfactory quality and service at fair prices.
- *The right to be heard*—to be assured that consumer interests will receive full and sympathetic consideration in the formulation of government policy and fair and expeditious treatment in the government's administrative tribunals.

President Johnson sent a message on consumer interests to the Congress in which he reiterated the four consumer rights enunciated by President Kennedy. And President Nixon sent a message to Congress in which he added consumers' right to register dissatisfaction and have their complaints heard and weighed. In 1975 President Ford stated that consumers should also have the right to consumer education.

The Congress of the International Co-Operative Alliance in London adopted an international declaration of consumers' rights. The declaration affirms that consumers have a right to:

- A reasonable standard of nutrition, clothing, and housing
- Adequate standards of safety and a healthy environment free from pollution
- Access to relevant information on goods and services and to education on consumer topics
- Influence in economic life and democratic participation in its control

In 1975 the Council of Europe adopted a charter of consumer rights that will be a determining factor in all European Economic Community policies.* This program establishes the framework of a genuine consumer policy and constitutes a consumer charter based on five fundamental rights patterned after those stated by the three presidents of the United States.

- The right to protection of health and safety
- The right to protection of economic interests
- The right of redress
- The right to information and education
- The right of representation[25]

Consumer Responsibilities

Where there are rights, there are responsibilities. A primary responsibility of consumers is to be aware of their role and function in the econ-

---

* The Council of Europe, a parliamentary institution of European nations that predates the European Community, gives advice and counsel to its members and the European Communities on any matters except defense.

omy. Anyone can spend money, but responsible consumers know that in spending money they are engaging in actions that, together with those of other consumers, influence what shall and shall not be produced.

A second consumer responsibility is to perform effectively. This requires training and knowledge, as well as independence of judgment and action. Consumers have an important job to do and must work at it conscientiously if they are to do it well. In the American economy consumers have an impressive freedom of choice. This freedom is not to be taken lightly or abused. Nor should it be abdicated.

Responsible consumers abhor needless waste. They have a sense of responsibility that embraces their own nation, consumers in other nations, and future generations. Many resources are irreplaceable. This fact lays a responsibility upon the responsible consumer to avoid waste. Consumers are now painfully aware that they have a heavy responsibility to avoid polluting air, water, and soil.

Consumers have a responsibility to avoid exploitation of those in the labor force who supply goods and services. At the same time they have a right to buy products and services that have been produced efficiently. This responsibility raises some difficult problems. Should consumers always buy in the cheapest market? What is the responsibility of consumers if goods and services are cheap because children, women, or men have been exploited to produce them? There have been times when some consumers and consumer groups have organized boycotts urging the public not to buy certain products when it was believed that the workers were being exploited. Such boycotts occurred against lettuce and grape producers during the late 1960s and early 1970s.

Consumers have a responsibility to be honest in all their dealings. Honest sellers and honest buyers have a mutuality of interests. On both sides of the counter there is a responsibility to give and to receive no less or no more than the exact quantity at the agreed price. Consumers have a responsibility to pay their bills. They have a responsibility to call attention to errors that are to their advantage, as well as to those that are to their disadvantage. One does not have to be antibusiness to be proconsumer, nor does one have to be anticonsumer to be probusiness.

In a free society consumers have the right and the responsibility to protest. The protest function may be exercised individually as well as in groups. Individual consumers may exercise their protest function by refusing to purchase. The collective effect of such action may bring about a change. Consumers may exercise their protest function in groups such as consumer cooperatives. If social control is necessary they may exercise their protest function by supporting or opposing proposed legislation.

Consumer Democracy

Democracy may be defined broadly as a society in which citizens are continuously creating the conditions under which they wish to live and work. The concept of economic democracy implies a share in the control of the economic system by the three groups of people most concerned with its operation—consumers, owners, and workers. Our immediate concern is with consumer democracy. This idea implies that consumers shall participate continuously in the economy to decide what goods and services shall be produced. If goods and services are produced that promote consumer "illfare" rather than consumer welfare, consumers share the responsibility. Many consumers have failed in their responsibility to make free and intelligent choices. They have permitted themselves to fall under the influence of habit, custom, fashion, and aggressive selling practices. As a result, their decisions are made for them rather than by them. If political democracy is to work, it must be supported by an understructure of economic democracy. If economic democracy is to work, consumers must exercise their right to make free choices intelligently and must assume responsibility for making the free price system operate effectively.

QUESTIONS FOR REVIEW

1. What are the problems of and how does the consumer cope with inflation?
2. What might be included under the term "consumerism"?
3. "People no longer aspire to sitting in front of a table and heaping more and more physical acquisitions onto a pile of things they own. Instead, they are seeking, yearning, and even crying out for a different kind of existence." What is your reaction to this assertion?
4. Write a brief outline of how our economy operates.
5. Is the consumer sovereign? Discuss.
6. How much influence do you as an individual have on determining what is produced?
7. As a consumer do you really know what you want?
8. What do you know about the purity and safety of the products you buy?
9. What is meant by "the dual role of consumers"?
10. What are the rights that three U.S. presidents have enumerated for consumers? To what extent are these rights being achieved?

PROJECTS

1. Select five significant products and/or services and trace their prices over the past decade, then draw conclusions from your research.
2. Debate the topic "Resolved: The consumer never has been and is not now sovereign."

3. Interview a retailer and ask him or her how the decision is made as to what to buy to stock the shelves.

4. Ask a business executive for his or her opinion concerning consumer rights.

REFERENCES

1. *St. Petersburg Times Parade*, 7 March 1976, p. 10.
2. *U.S. News & World Report*, 8 March 1976, p. 30.
3. *St. Petersburg Times Parade*, 28 March 1976, p. 11.
4. *Wall Street Journal*, 18 Nov. 1975, p. 26.
5. *Marketing/Communications*, Aug. 1969, p. 60.
6. Ralph Nader, *Unsafe at Any Speed: The Designed-In Dangers of the American Automobile* (New York: Grossman, 1965).
7. *U.S. News & World Report*, 19 April 1976, p. 25.
8. *St. Petersburg Times*, 26 June 1975, p. 9.
9. Raymond A. Bauer and Stephen A. Greyser, *Advertising in America: The Consumer View* (Cambridge: Harvard University Press, 1968), p. 386.
10. George Katona, *The Mass Consumption Society* (New York: McGraw-Hill, 1964), pp. 60–61, 333.
11. Charles K. Raymond, "The Economists' Mythical Consumer," in Steuart Henderson Britt, *Consumer Behavior and Behavioral Sciences* (New York: John Wiley & Sons, 1966), pp. 303–304.
12. James H. Myers and William H. Reynolds, *Consumer Behavior and Marketing Management* (Boston: Houghton Mifflin, 1967), p. 1. [Italics added.]
13. W. A. Woods, "Psychological Dimensions of Consumer Behavior," in Myers and Reynolds, p. 102.
14. Sidney J. Levy, "Symbols by Which We Buy," in James F. Engel, ed., *Consumer Behavior* (Homewood, Ill.: Richard D. Irwin, 1968), pp. 55–61.
15. John Kenneth Galbraith, *The New Industrial State* (Boston: Houghton Mifflin, 1967), p. 212.
16. Harold S. Diamond, "The Budget and Consumer Sovereignty," *American Journal of Economics and Sociology* 29 (1970): 163–170.
17. John R. Hicks, "Economic Theory and the Evaluation of Consumers' Wants," *Journal of Business* 35, no. 3 (July 1962): 256–263.
18. *Final Order (8547) in the Case of J. B. Williams Company and its Advertising Division, Parkson Advertising Agency, for the Drug Preparation Geritol*, Federal Trade Commission, Office of Information, Press Release, 7 Oct. 1965.
19. North Dakota State Laboratories Department, Food and Drug Bulletin no. 174, June 1974, pp. 32–36.
20. *Ibid.*, pp. 38–40.
21. *Ibid.*, pp. 61–65.
22. *Consumer Reports*, June 1974, p. 439.
23. North Dakota State Laboratories Department, Food and Drug Bulletin no. 174, June 1974, pp. 84–91.
24. *St. Petersburg Times*, 7 Sept. 1975, p. 7A.
25. The Commission of the European Communities, Information Memo, April 1975, p. 1.

CHAPTER

THE COMPLEXITY OF CONSUMER DEMAND

WHAT ARE THE BASIC GOALS IN LIFE?

The Search For Happiness

Each one of us is a bundle of physiological, psychological, and social wants. If these wants are satisfied, we are *more likely* to be happy than if they go unsatisfied. But notice the qualifying words in the preceding sentence. There are people who seem to derive more pleasure from deprivation than from fulfillment of wants. The explanation lies in the individual's philosophy of life. Some monastic orders elevate the practice of physical self-denial to a virtue; subsisting on locusts and honey can be rewarding. Such a philosophy elevates mind over matter. The time and energy spent by other people in acquiring material possessions is spent by ascetics in meditation on the mysteries of life and death and the world beyond.

The physical plane of life in many parts of the Orient is simpler than in the West. Yet there are many who believe that the millions of people in these countries are happy without the many services and goods we have in the West. For most people, however, the pursuit of happiness requires a basic minimum of goods and services to satisfy physical, psychological, and social needs. Wherever religious missionaries have gone, they have found that they cannot preach the gospel to people who are hungry and sick. It is true that we do not live by bread alone, but it is also true that we cannot live without bread.

If economic happiness is defined as a state of pleasurable contentment with one's condition in life, then we can inquire whether such a state is to be achieved by the acquisition of enough income to satisfy more and more of our unlimited wants or by limiting our wants to those that can be satisfied by our incomes. The first method leads to a *materialistic* philosophy of life, or the belief that the highest value is material well-being. Those who follow such a philosophy find satisfaction and their concept of happiness in

31

the acquisition and consumption of ever-increasing goods and services. Many critics believe that Western civilization in the twentieth century is motivated primarily by this materialistic philosophy. Such critics contend that we have lost our way and confuse the acquisition of goods and services with the pursuit of real happiness.

If an abundance of goods and services assures happiness, American consumers should be the happiest in the world. They have more goods and services than their fellow consumers in other countries. However, the results of an in-depth study of residents in four small towns in Illinois suggest that there is more to the achievement of happiness than the satisfaction of economic wants. The University of Chicago National Opinion Research Center researchers asked respondents this question: "Taking all things together, how would you say things are these days—would you say you are very happy, pretty happy, or not too happy?" To the extent that the responses are representative of those of consumers all over the country, they are very significant. Thirty-three percent of the respondents said they were very happy, fifty-four percent replied that they were pretty happy, and thirteen percent said they were not too happy.* Since 1975, when that research project was completed, conditions have changed significantly in the United States. One can only guess what the responses would be today, but it seems fair to conclude that increases in alcoholism, drug addiction, crime, and mental illness are evidences of failure in the pursuit of happiness.

Each individual has to make the decision as to how much prominence to give money and the acquisition of goods in life. One individual may decide that acquiring goods is the end-all of human activity; another may conclude that the chief end of life is not to glorify money, but to glorify God. Whatever the goal, each individual should be able to look back on his or her life and feel confident that the decisions made were the right ones. A proper attitude toward money and a proper use of money should help give an individual this confidence. But everyone will not agree on what this proper attitude is. Each individual has to decide what he believes to be best and then hope that he has made and will continue to make the right decisions.

The individual can choose to approach consumer economics in one of two basic ways. On the one hand, the tendency may be to emphasize ways of getting the best value for each dollar expenditure, with this becoming the overriding consideration in marketplace decisions—to get more for less. On the other hand, the emphasis may be on minimizing the importance of money and the material aspects of life, in which case the individual would pay little attention to marketplace decisions and would, therefore, be a careless and wasteful shopper. Neither extreme is an intelligent position to take; a proper balance between the two is the desirable goal.

---

* The National Opinion Research Center has conducted a general social survey each year since 1972, and the "general happiness" question is included in it. The figures above are for 1975.

Is There Any Limit to Consumer Wants?

Traditional economic analysis begins with one basic fact of life: *the insatiability of human wants.* It is presumed that the desires of consumers for goods and services are capable of indefinite expansion. Most economists accept this as a basic fact so obvious that it requires no demonstration. Consumers today want and expect to have goods and services that were unknown to their ancestors, or if known were considered luxuries to be enjoyed only by royalty and those who were very rich. The modern middle-income family lives in greater comfort than royalty enjoyed as recently as the turn of the century.

But this view that the human race has unlimited material wants is now being challenged. It has been suggested that our wants are limited and can, therefore, be satisfied. In other cultures, particularly in non-Western cultures past and present, there has been satisfaction with particular levels of consumption. Some economists contend that this unlimited-wants concept has been used falsely as the primary economic motivator in free-enterprise economics – unlimited wants continuously propelling the economy upward. During the youth counter-culture movement of the 1960s there seemed to be evidence of a reaction against a materialistic society. But the serious recession of the mid-1970s, combined with the high level of unemployment, seems to have changed attitudes rather quickly. We need only look around us to see that there are people who believe that their wants are unlimited and who strive to acquire more and more goods; and at the same time observe people who seem to be content because they feel that their wants have been adequately met.

Not All Wants Can Be Satisfied

Economics has been described as "the dismal science." With consumers clamoring for more and more, economists have told them that nature is niggardly. At any given time, increasing use of labor and capital combined with a fixed amount of land will produce progressively smaller yields. Economists call this *the principle of diminishing returns*. It is, in fact, a physical law, with far-reaching economic effects. In years past consumers have partially escaped the consequences of this principle through discoveries of new lands. This outlet is now closed, however, because there is no undiscovered land on earth and the moon has been found to be barren.

Another force that has offset the tendency toward diminishing returns has been the development of new and more effective ways of utilizing scarce resources. Historically scientists held that science and technology had replaced natural resources as a basis for economic growth. For years the gross national product steadily increased in this country, as the use of energy, in the form of electricity in particular, increased. For example, there is ten times as much horsepower per person per day available now as there was a century ago. But 1974 saw this pattern of an ever-increasing gross national product reversed. Much of the decline in gross national product for 1974 and 1975 was attributed to the "energy crunch." The full impact of this change and its effects on the satisfaction of our material wants will continue to be studied and debated. The attention of the government and the business community is now directed to finding alternate energy sources. Petroleum cannot continue to be used as it has been in the past, and its use cannot be increased almost exponentially as it has been. Greater attention is now being paid to coal, which there are vast amounts of in the United States, and greater emphasis is being given to the development of nuclear energy. Oil shale is being investigated. Solar energy, geothermal energy, and the harnessing of tides are being studied as alternate energy sources. The day of cheap energy has passed, and the satisfying of economic wants will be determined more and more by the availability of and accelerating cost of energy.

Many people contend that the human race will always find new methods of producing goods and services when the pressure becomes great enough. For example, as the demand for fresh water increases, business firms increase the supply by desalting sea water. The production of synthetic foods also increases every year. Even so, the supply of goods and services falls far below the volume required to satisfy all current consumer wants at prices all can pay.

Unlimited wants in the face of limited supplies creates the problem of scarcity. Since humans as producers cannot produce enough to satisfy their wants as consumers, the problem arises as to whose wants shall be satisfied. Scarce products and services are valued according to the expense of producing them. The power of individual consumers to acquire these scarce goods depends on their incomes. The central struggle of economic life is a contest to determine which of the unlimited wants of consumers will be satisfied.

Four Principles of Consumption

There are four principles of consumption which are useful to consider when examining and attempting to analyze buying behavior.[1] They are the principles of harmonious consumption, diminishing utility, variety, and satiety. The principle of harmonious consumption deals with the tendency to buy combinations of things, such as matching accessories and clothes. The principle of diminishing utility is the principle that having one of a certain item may be useful, but having two of the same item is not necessarily doubly useful. One portable record player is nice; a second is rather useless. The principle of variety concerns people's desire to have a variety of things. For example, we usually like to own clothing in different colors and styles. Variety overcomes diminishing utility for many people in many instances. The principle of satiety has to do with unlimited wants—people are just never satisfied. There is no end to the reasons people can come up with for buying something new.

These principles are almost always involved, in one way or another, in buying decisions. If you recognize the influence these four principles have on your buying decisions, you will be better able to control your buying habits and, therefore, able to make better use of your money.

WHY DO YOU WANT WHAT YOU WANT?

Needs, Wants, and Demand

Basic consumer _needs_ are limited to the necessities of life. These include enough food to sustain the physical strength necessary to work and the need for clothing and shelter. According to 1975 standards a family of four needs an income of about $9,838 to live at the minimum level. Consumers in that income level, like other consumers, have unlimited wants. These wants include comforts and luxuries. They may even include what moralists consider to be extravagances.

In the language of economists, _demand_ is defined as desire plus ability to pay. In addition to differences in income, economic demand is determined by differences in desire and by diminishing utility. Differences in desire are fairly obvious. The foods that some consumers want do not appeal to others. The art that delights some consumers leaves others puzzled and unsatisfied.

The principle of diminishing utility is a common-sense one. At any given time, as an individual consumes more and more of a given product or service, the ability of the product or service to satisfy his or her wants declines. In the consumption of food, for example, a first serving yields great satisfaction. A second serving, however, yields less utility, a third serving much less, and additional servings may yield none at all; in fact, they might yield disutility. Football fans can enjoy one or two games on television on New Year's Day, but many may switch off the third and fourth games.

These differences among needs, wants, and demand require further analysis. Consumers are not born with an intuitive sense that enables them to make the choices that will promote their welfare. Nor do they always acquire the wisdom to make such choices. Many consumers want goods and services that retard rather than promote their well-being. Many want goods and services that are not essential to life itself but are necessary for a more complete, abundant life.

Starting with the assumption that food, clothing, shelter, automobiles, and appliances are needs, the University of Michigan Survey Center surveyed consumer aspirations. Responses indicated that everything consumers want is a want, not a need. They want a house in the country, a vacation house, and plenty of land. They want higher education, and they want to travel to Europe.

In order to satisfy these wants, consumers do not buy food, housing, books, or washing machines as such. Basic needs and wants become consumer wants because goods and services must be purchased in order to satisfy them. They are hungry, so they buy food; they want protection from the elements, so they buy clothing and shelter.

The Complexity of Your Wants

If there were space here to give a capsule course in the history of economic thought, we would arrive at the conclusion that economists in the past have almost completely ignored consumers. It was assumed that the purpose of production was to satisfy consumer wants. What more was there to be said? The nature and origin of consumer wants and the factors influencing them were considered to lie largely outside the field of economics. For example, hunger is an observed fact, but what lies behind hunger is biological and therefore not included in the field of economics. Wants have psychological and social, as well as physical, origins. If you lived in Asia or Africa, your physical wants would be different because of differences in geography, climate, and social institutions. Yet the basic wants and needs are the same the world over. People get hungry, thirsty, cold, hot, and tired. They like certain sounds, sights, and tastes. A consumer in Africa may satisfy hunger by eating different foods than a consumer in North America, but in either place it requires food to satisfy the biological craving that we call hunger.

Psychological analysis is fundamental in determining consumer wants. The body is the instrument that reflects personality. The demands of individual consumers reflect differences in personality. The study of personality combines physiology, psychology, and social psychology. In choosing clothing people select specific items not only for the protection that the clothing may give but also for possible improvement in appearance. Appearance is improved by the selection of one kind of clothing for tall, thin people and another type for short, fat people. If a person is healthy, he has no desire for medicines or medical care. If an individual is a chronic dyspeptic introvert, however, he might succumb to the advertising of proprietary products, which promise to restore a sense of well-being.

Most people want pleasurable sensations and a sense of happiness. Pain and unhappiness are avoided. Pleasure is largely sensory, depending on the satisfaction of basic bodily appetites and a state of physical and mental health. Such pleasure is basic to happiness. But happiness also includes the aesthetic, moral, and intellectual satisfactions derived from objects outside the body.

The effects of the senses on the selection of goods and services are significant. Some people are tone-deaf and have no desire for music. Others are color-blind. There are obvious differences in taste, resulting in different demands for various kinds of foods. It is interesting to observe that we have no way of knowing precisely how an economic good affects the sense of taste or smell or the hearing or sight of another person. We assume that all people receive the same sensations, but we cannot be sure. Nor do we have any way of measuring the intensity of satisfaction felt by people when consuming a good or service.

Your Physiological Needs and Wants

In recent years psychologists have contributed significantly to our understanding of consumer needs and wants. The consumer is "a bio-psycho-sociological being" influenced by diverse stimuli. We know little or nothing about certain areas of influence, such as prenatal influence, but we do have significant knowledge about basic biological, physiological, psychological, and sociological influences.[2]

"Man is a wanting animal—as soon as one of his needs is satisfied, another appears in its place."[3] A *need* is a requirement of an organism that leads to action. It may be innate or learned; it makes no difference. The urge to satisfy a need is called a *motive,* or drive, and the subsequent action is called *consumer behavior.* Needs lead to drives, which produce tension until the needs are satisfied; then the organism returns to a state of mental or physical equilibrium.[4]

The basic biological needs, which require relief if the body is to survive, include the need for oxygen, water, food, elimination, sex, relief from pain, and protection from heat, cold, and fatigue. Although these needs are determined biologically, the physiological drives are subject to social influences. For example, consumers in one group may reject horse meat and insects because the group rejects them, whereas consumers in other groups may enjoy those edibles. Conversely, Americans like corn on the cob, but consumers in other groups consider corn acceptable only as chicken feed.[5]

Most of the basic biological needs are also consumer needs because individuals must, or may, be willing to purchase the satisfaction of them. We buy oxygen at the hospital, and we buy less-polluted air by paying higher prices for products such as automobiles equipped with catalytic converters and unleaded gasoline. We buy water if we live in a dry area, because of a dislike of tap water for drinking purposes, or for other uses where distilled or spring water is desired or needed. We buy food for nutrition; use a pay toilet for elimination; buy medicine and the services of a doctor for relief from pain; and buy clothes, air conditioners, and beds for relief from cold, heat, and fatigue.[6] All these consumer needs are based on the fundamental organic needs and drives listed below.

1. *Oxygen.* The need for oxygen is the most basic physiological need. Billions of dollars are currently being spent to purify our polluted air in many cities.
2. *Water.* Water is essential to the maintenance of life. It is such a fundamental need that the business of supplying water is a public enterprise in most communities.
3. *Food.* Families spend a large percentage of their incomes on food, and

the entire food industry, from farm to retail store, is organized to satisfy this need.

4. *Protection from the elements.* People need and want protection from heat and cold, wind and rain. This need leads business firms to build houses and transportation facilities that are warm when the weather is cold and cool when the air is hot. Consumers also need protection in the form of clothing, and the garment and fashion industries are based on this need.

5. *Health.* The desire to enjoy good health is the basis for the medical profession, hospitals, sanatoria, nursing homes, and the manufacture of the special equipment necessary in the medical field.

6. *Skin sensations.* In addition to the fundamental needs for food, water, oxygen, and so on, the senses and the desire for pleasurable sensations are the bases for many consumer activities. The cosmetics industry is organized on the need for pleasurable skin sensations and relief from itching, burning, and roughness, as well as on the psychological urge for beauty and social acceptability.

7. *Sound.* Many economic activities are based on the sense of hearing. The desire for pleasing sounds is the basis of the music industry, and for those whose hearing is defective, the manufacture of artificial hearing aids is an important industry.

8. *Sight.* The perception of color, like sound, taste, and touch, creates reactions that are pleasant or unpleasant, causing consumers to prefer goods of one color over another. Sellers are alert to the power of color, and it has been found that by changing the color of a package sales of a product can be increased by as much as 1,000 percent. Many people have defective vision, and the production of glasses and products to aid the blind are important industries based on the physiological sense of sight.

9. *Play.* The need for activity and play are also important human needs. Man is a playful animal. Children and young adults instinctively play, and almost all ages engage in games that require varying degrees of activity, physical or mental. Games such as football and baseball have become big business enterprises, and thousands of firms provide equipment for fishermen, hunters, skiers, and other sports enthusiasts.

Your Psychological Wants

Having noted the influence on economic wants of the basic physiological instincts and senses, we will now turn to some psychological influences. These include emotional responses such as fear and anger, love and hate, self-interest, and a desire for prestige or recognition. There are three main groups of drives, or motives. First are those, discussed above, that depend on internal bodily conditions. These are called *organic.* They include hunger and thirst, the need for oxygen and the removal of excess carbon dioxide, elimination, sex, activity, and rest. A second group of drives includes those that are aroused when events in the environment require quick and vigorous action. These are called *emergency motives.* They include escape, combat, efforts to overcome an obstacle, and pursuit. A third group includes those motives that are directed toward dealing with objects and persons in the environment. These are called *objective motives.* They include exploration, manipulation, and curiosity. An organic need operates in a cycle and subsides when satisfied, while the emergency and objective motives are continuous.

The three most important objective motives, as they relate to psychological wants and subsequent consumer behavior, are *love, gregariousness,* and *creativity, curiosity, and manipulation.* Love and the desire for the opposite sex and love of and the instinct to care for children are basic and universal human characteristics. Love of the opposite sex results in consumer demand for objects of display and a wide range of commodities to be used as gifts and tokens. Love of children leads to the consumption of many goods and services throughout life. Our inborn gregarious, or social, tendency also leads to a wide range of social activities and consumer demands. For some people this tendency can lead to conspicuous and lavish display for the purpose of attracting attention. In addition to being social creatures, human beings are curious and creative. We create buildings and transportation facilities, develop new foods and new fibers, create works of art, compose music, and write books and plays. Publishers of newspapers, magazines, and books and television writers and producers respond to consumer wants for information, news, and knowledge. The educational system is a response to consumer demand for knowledge.

Your Social Wants

Society may be regarded simply as a collection of people. A more useful concept, however, is one that regards society as an organized body of men, women, and children bound together by social customs and institutions. American society is characterized by religiosity; by achievement, which is highly esteemed; by the desire for security, which is highly valued; by conformity; by the sociable life; by an appreciation of leisure, which is taking preference over the Puritan preference for hard work; and by admiration for youthfulness, which is valued more highly than wisdom and age.

Every society includes a religious system, a political system, and an economic system. Social or group ideas tend to become institutionalized. The institutions then become the instruments through which society guides the consuming activities of the individuals. Within a society there are groups—such as farmers, labor unions, trade associations, political parties, and families—that have characteristics apart from the characteristics of the individual members. These groups exert influence on the economic wants of their members. Every society also has temporary groups, such as an audience, a crowd, or a mob, which have characteristics quite different from those of individual members.

Social and economic institutions change. They may be changed by individuals who are strong leaders or by groups that are in control. For example, the "laws" of economics prevailing in South Vietnam were changed when the Communists took over in 1975. When an economic system is changed, new "laws" of behavior arise that are, in psychological terms, "emergency laws." The fact of change is important. Social institutions may not be uprooted, but they are constantly pruned and trimmed. As a result the social and economic framework of the United States today, for example, is much different from what it was a generation ago.

People live in the culture of their time and place and, consequently, are products of it. Their culture includes the group attitude toward women and children, toward minority or racial groups, toward workers, the conditions of work, and labor unions. Also included are group attitudes concerning the types of food and clothing that are approved or forbidden and toward education, religion, medical care, and science. American society expects younger members to attend school, to get a job, to marry, have children and a home, and to conform to the community pattern of living. Deviants from these norms are given the social-pressure treatment.

All individuals face the problem of getting along in the society in which they live. One of the strongest guiding forces in civilized life is the desire for social approval. One way to gain such approval is to imitate the actions and the choices of group members. An individual who might never have a want for a specific good or service may realize a want by imitating another member of his or her group. Most people find it easier to get along with their group by doing as the group does. Sometimes individuals try to escape from a group in which they are unhappy, but usually they find it easier to conform.

While the pattern of consumer wants is definitely "set" for limited periods of time, it changes over longer periods. The underlying physiological and psychological bases of wants do not change, but the types of goods and services capable of satisfying such wants do change. This is well-illustrated by the changing pattern of food and clothing consumption in the United States.

Group Influence

The *culture* of a society comprises a complex of values, ideas, attitudes, and other meaningful symbols that were created by human beings to shape human behavior. Within this framework of attitude and behavior patterns, smaller entities, known as *reference groups,* take shape. "Culture" refers to learned patterns of behavior and symbolism that are passed on in a society from one generation to another generation. In a nation as large as the United States several cultures may coexist. A reference group is an interacting group of people that influences the attitudes or behavior of an individual.[7] It may be a group to which an individual belongs, to which he or she would like to belong, or to which he or she does not wish to belong. "Most social psychologists consider reference groups a person's major source of values, norms, and perspectives."[8] Obviously reference groups tend to produce conformity and an effort to keep up with the neighbors. In a research project, J. E. Stafford found that members of a group closely followed the brand preferences of the informal leader. Another researcher found support for the hypothesis that where there are no reference points or standards, consumers exposed to a group norm will tend to conform. In another study subjects were exposed to contrived incorrect decisions of a reference group. Even though the responses were obviously incorrect, 76 percent of the subjects gave the same response as the reference group.[9]

Social, or group, characteristics include language, religion, government, art, organizations, and the use of stimulants and sedatives. These may not be all the wants that should be included in this classification, nor is it certain that they are exclusively social, as distinguished from individual wants. It is clear, however, that group wants are social wants, as opposed to individual wants.

1.   If there is any single characteristic that distinguishes the human race from other animals, it is the ability to communicate thoughts by means of films, pictures, speech, and writing. Every human group has its language. The desire to communicate gives rise to consumer demand for instruments of communication. These include materials for writing and printing, for art and for commercial art, and for radio and television. The end products include newspapers, magazines, books, prints, and films.

2.   All peoples at all stages of development have a religion. Religions recognize a superhuman or mysterious power greater than man, and they include forms of worship, ranging from a sun dance to the elaborate ritual of the Roman Catholic church. Religious feeling is so strong that millions of consumers deny themselves material pleasures in exchange for the values of their religion. The money they spend for religion results in the satisfaction of a want for outward expression of religious feeling. A significant portion of our economic life is devoted to the creation of goods and to the rendering of services to satisfy these wants.

3.   When people live in groups, they need a government and social control. The larger a group becomes, the more complex are its interrelationships and the greater the need for social controls. Approximately 32 percent of the gross national product in this country is currently generated by the government sector of the economy—local, state, and federal. While this form of group want is satisfied primarily by direct personal services, the process of governing requires an increasing volume of goods. From a consumer point of view, one of the most important functions of government is the protection of consumers from unfair business practices.

4.   Recognition and appreciation of beauty is a group characteristic that finds expression in various forms of art. The more common forms of artistic expression are drawing, painting, sculpture, and architecture. From the crudely carved or painted stone of prehistory to the magnificent modern galleries of art, this form of group want has absorbed a significant portion of economic activity.

5. There are very few hermits in our nation. Most people are gregarious. They want to be with other people. They crave companionship and friendship. There are scores of organizations in every community to help fill this need. Some are open groups, such as political clubs, parent-teacher associations, or the League of Women Voters. Many organizations, however, are exclusive, which gives them a prestige value. Many of these are also secret societies. Clubs, fraternities, lodges, and sororities generate consumer wants for costumes, insignia, and regalia. The social activities of all groups result in consumer demand for decorations, gifts, and food.

6. An unusual group want is that for stimulants and sedatives. Many social groups condone the consumption of intoxicating drinks or narcotics. As the pace of life quickens and society becomes increasingly complex, many people in this country feel the need for stimulants or tranquilizers. Billions of dollars are spent for such products.

Group Ideas

The influence of the group in which one is born can be seen when one examines group taboos and concepts of survival value, prestige value, group welfare, and the conventional factor.

In every societal group, some wants are customary while others are taboo. For example, there may be certain food items or combinations of food that are shunned by group members because of a belief that such foods may cause illness or death. Some people will not eat mushrooms because of their similarity to the poisonous toadstool. Some people refuse to eat lobster and ice cream at the same meal. Others reject a combination of milk and fish in the same meal. Such notions are handed down from one generation to the next and become taboos. Usually, however, there are a few venturesome consumers in any group who are willing to risk group disapproval by eating the combination because they have found that they like it or because they wish to demonstrate the falsity of the taboo.

The influence of the *group concept of survival* is reflected in types of clothing, styles of architecture, and construction of buildings. In parts of the Orient it is customary for all children and most adults to wear a woolen band around the middle of the body. The purpose is to cover the stomach, in the belief that doing so gives protection against dysentary and malaria. In jungles houses are built on stilts. In earthquake areas houses are made of light, flexible materials. In all cases the influence of the group concept of survival is apparent.

In all societal groups certain wants are encouraged or discouraged on the basis of the *group concept of prestige value*. Many people like uniforms, and military dress uniforms have high prestige value in almost every society. In pre-World War II Germany, Italy, and Japan – nations dominated by militarists – the dress uniform provided high prestige value. Members of the American Legion gain prestige in the eyes of some people when they wear their distinctive uniforms. The Knights Templar and many other lodge groups gain satisfaction by parading in their colorful uniforms. The clergy of various denominations set themselves apart by the costumes they wear. High-ranking priests in the Catholic church are distinguished by their colorful robes. Judicial robes are considered to give judges an additional aura of dignity and prestige. The caps, gowns, and hoods worn by college professors yield a prestige value.

Other illustrations of consumer choice determined by group concepts of prestige will come to mind. It is easy to understand why individuals bow to a group edict; the gregarious tendency in most people is so strong that they will do almost anything to win admission to a group. But how shall we explain group acceptance of these ideas? And why does one group wish to set itself off from another?

Just as one individual tries to command the attention or respect of others by his or her exploits, so a societal group endeavors to command the admiration, respect, or envy of other groups. Society is stratified in several social and economic levels. Within each level there are scores of organizations having varying degrees of prestige. On a particular campus everyone recognizes that SiKA is the number-one prestige fraternity and that PiKA is the leading sorority. All prestige-seekers would like to belong to SiKA or PiKA. But prestige is achieved by exclusion, so SiKA and PiKA limit the number of members. Prestige-seekers then must turn to other groups. Sometimes, rather than join a low-prestige group, some students gain prestige by remaining independent. And some, of course, choose to remain outside the group altogether. The members of each group make a noble effort to give the impression that their group is superior. Badges become devices for advertising one's membership in a group. This has been called the *conventional factor* in determining consumer wants. Conven-

These college students wearing beanies to signify that they are freshmen illustrate the *conventional factor* at work. (*George Zimbel, Monkmeyer*)

tional utility replaces organic utility as a factor influencing consumer wants.

The *group concept of welfare* is broader than the group ideas mentioned thus far. A group's concept of what constitutes and promotes its welfare may include its attitude toward education, military strength, religion, artistic achievement, and economic productivity, to mention only a few. The German concept of group welfare, as reflected in national socialism, was in sharp contrast to the Russian concept, as reflected in communism. Nations and societal groups in the Orient place great emphasis on religion and philosophy in their scale of values whereas Americans place great importance on the production of economic goods and the accumulation of wealth.

OTHER WANT-INFLUENCING FORCES

Climate

Climate influences ideas and concepts, as well as economic wants. People who live in tropical and semitropical climates think of hell as a place of unbearable heat. On the other hand, people who live in frigid zones think of hell as a place of unbearable cold. People who live in frigid zones want fuel to heat their houses and warm clothing to wear out-of-doors. People who live where it is always hot want artificial cooling devices for their houses and very lightweight clothing. All these different wants lead to an increasing range of economic activity.

Natural Resources

The economic resources available to various groups limit the range of their wants. All people want and need food, but the kind of food they want is determined by what is available. American children want hamburgers; children in the Orient want rice; and Mexican children want tortillas.

All people want and need shelter, but the kind of shelter they want depends on the environment in which they live and the materials available. Some people live in houses made of stone, others live in houses made of bricks, and others use wood.

Almost all people want and need clothing, but the kind of clothing they wear depends on the climate and the materials available. Thermal underwear is worn in frigid zones; warm woolens are preferred in damp, chilly areas; and in the warmer sections of United States, cotton and lightweight synthetic materials are worn.

Beyond these life-sustaining essentials, other wants—for luxuries, ornaments, styles of architecture, religious ceremonies, and games—are also influenced by the materials available. The decorative headdress of the

American Indian was made of feathers, while the ornaments of the Eskimos consisted of bones, teeth, and tusks of fish, seals, and walrus.

As an economy develops, transportation facilities are expanded, opening the resources of other regions and nations to consumers in a specific area. This also widens the range of consumer wants.

Income

Income may be considered as the amount of money one receives, as the volume of goods and services the money will buy, or as the satisfactions that the goods and services will yield. The first is called _money income;_ the second _real income;_ and the third _psychic income_. Obviously income is dependent on the resources available. The United States is a "rich" country because it has an abundance of natural resources within its borders. As a consequence its gross national product is large and per capita incomes are high. The higher one's income, the more wants one can satisfy.

Within the United States personal income is divided unevenly. When the average income per person for the United States was $5,685, it was over $6,500 in Alaska, Connecticut, the District of Columbia, Hawaii, and New York. At the same time the average income per person was under $4,400 in Alabama, Arkansas, South Carolina, and Mississippi. Individual incomes vary even more sharply. _Business Week_ reported in 1975 that the total compensation for the fifteen highest paid executives in the United States ranged from $1,595,000 for the highest paid to $501,000 for the fifteenth highest salary.[10] A Bureau of the Census study reported the actual and projected distributions of families by money income for 1971 and 1980 as illustrated in Table 2-1.[11]

Not only are there great disparities in income in this country, but there are even greater disparities in _net worth_, which is the measure of all of

TABLE 2-1. Number and Percent Distribution of Families by Money Income for 1971

With Projections for 1980 in Constant 1971 Dollars by Selected Annual Compound Growth Rates

Money Income Intervals	Base Year, 1971	1980 Growth Rates		
		2.0	3.0	4.0
Total families (in millions)	53.3	61.3	61.3	61.3
Percent distribution	100.0	100.0	100.0	100.0
Under $4,000	13.0	10.0	8.6	7.4
$4,000 to $9,999	35.2	28.7	25.5	22.5
$10,000 to $14,999	26.9	26.4	24.8	23.0
$15,000 to $24,999	19.5	26.1	29.3	31.5
$25,000 and over	5.3	8.9	11.9	15.6
Median income (in dollars)	10,281	12,069	13,259	14,385
Mean income (in dollars)	11,583	13,673	14,928	16,284

one's wealth (*assets*) less all that one owes (*liabilities*). One study revealed that only .001 percent of the adult population has a net worth of $1,000,000 or more. Approximately 2.4 percent had a net worth between $100,000 and $1,000,000; 11.3 percent between $20,000 and $100,000; 23 percent between $5,000 and $20,000; and 63.2 percent had a net worth of less than $5,000.[12] It is obvious that the population in the United States ranges from the very rich to the very poor. The rich can satisfy all their economic wants, but some of the poor cannot even buy the basic necessities.

Occupation

As workers, many people engage in occupations that require special clothing. Agricultural workers want straw hats to protect them from the sun, heavy shoes for field work, and overalls made of durable denim to protect their bodies. Coal miners want warm, heavy clothing, waterproof shoes, and helmets to protect them from falling rock and to hold the necessary light bulb. Workers in flour mills and bakeshops want white clothing.

The nature of one's occupation gives rise to wants for a wide variety of supplemental equipment and facilities. Traveling sales representatives must have automobiles. Doctors and dentists must have waiting rooms equipped with furniture and reading materials, as well as equipment for diagnosis and treatment. Members of the clergy, lawyers, and professors need office space and equipment and libraries.

As these random illustrations show, an important group of wants is determined by the nature of the work in which people are engaged.

Taxes

Taxes are involuntary payments to local, state, and federal governments. As population and urbanization increase, society becomes more complex and citizens demand that government agencies provide additional services. Citizens, as consumers, must pay for these services. In a recent year a hypothetical family of four, living in its own home, having an income of $15,000 a year, and itemizing federal income tax deductions up to 15 percent, paid approximately $4,220, or 28 percent of its income, in taxes. The family tax bill was distributed among five kinds of taxes: federal income taxes, $1,655; social security taxes, $825; state income taxes, $300; local property taxes, $700; and sales and excise taxes, $740. In return for these tax payments citizens receive a wide range of services, most of which they could not provide for themselves, nor could private firms supply them. The money paid to government agencies cannot be spent for other goods and services. Taxes diminish personal income and reduce the freedom of consumer choice.

If the tax system were based on the principal of ability to pay, families having higher incomes would pay a higher percentage of their incomes in taxes. For the bulk of American tax payers, however, the tax structure is not *progressive*. One study showed that those people with incomes between $6,000 and $25,000 had a relative net tax burden of about 30 percent after taking into consideration who receives and who pays for various benefits made via government transfer payments such as Social Security and veterans' benefits, unemployment compensation, welfare, medicare and medicaid benefits, and public employee retirement and disability payments.[13]

For most Americans the burden of taxation is proportional; that is, taxes take equal proportions of the individual's income through a wide range of incomes. Total taxes paid through the $6,000 to $25,000 levels have a spread of only 1.2 percentage points. For the majority of Americans it seems that progressive taxes like the personal income tax are counterbalanced by regressive taxes like property taxes, leaving us, like it or not, with *proportional* taxation. If one excludes all government transfer payments to individuals, such as those listed above, then our tax system is highly *regressive*. This means that families having small incomes pay a higher percentage of their incomes in taxes than families with higher incomes.

In 1975 the Internal Revenue Service released its *Statistics of Income Report on Estate Tax Returns for 1972*. Ninety-three individuals with gross estates of $1 million or more paid no federal estate tax after their deaths. Two hundred and three individuals with gross estates of between $500,000 and $1 million paid no federal estate tax.[14] This is true in spite of the fact that the estate tax begins at $60,000. Legal loopholes make these escapes from taxation possible.

The number of millionaires and millionaire families in the United States is approximately 115,000, and many of them pay very low personal income taxes because of the various tax-avoidance measures built into the federal-personal income tax laws. For example, in sworn testimony before congressional committee hearings on Nelson Rockefeller's nomination to the office of vice-president, Rockefeller reported a total income of $2.4 million in 1970, yet he paid no federal income tax that year. His charitable contributions, interest, other taxes, and office and investment expenses were greater than his income. From 1964 through 1973 his total income was $46.9 million and he paid $15.3 million in federal income taxes.[15]

Former President Nixon paid $792 in federal income taxes in 1970 on an income of $262,942 and $878 in taxes in 1971 on an income of $262,384. An audit of his tax returns disallowed major deductions for contributions of his papers to the government, so back taxes with interest had to be paid.[16] Edward Kennedy paid $217,844 in federal income taxes on an income of $461,444 for 1973.[17] While governor of Pennsylvania, Milton Shapp, a millionaire, reported that he had paid no federal income taxes for at least one year while in office because of tax loopholes. More than 400 Americans with incomes over $100,000 did not pay any federal income taxes in one year.[18]

The wealthy can invest in state and municipal tax-exempt bonds. Owners of oil wells have used the oil-depletion allowance to reduce their taxable incomes. (A recent change in the law has limited this tax benefit.) "Gentlemen farmers" are permitted to charge off as losses thousands of dollars a year, while at the same time the value of their land increases. The effective rate of capital gains for the very wealthy goes up to a maximum of 32½ percent, instead of the 70 percent rate at which very high incomes would be taxed if treated as "normal" income.

Tax liability varies according to the state, county, and local community in which one lives. In 1975 only five states (Alaska, Delaware, Montana, New Hampshire, and Oregon) had no state sales tax. In some states the sales tax is as low as 2 percent; in others as high as 7 percent. Gasoline taxes range from a low of 5 cents per gallon to a high of 10 cents. In 1976 only Connecticut, Florida, Nevada, South Dakota, Texas, Washington, and Wyoming had no personal income tax. In the states that have an income tax the rate varies — from 2 percent to as high as 15 percent on incomes over $20,000. More and more local governments have introduced sales taxes and personal income taxes, while other communities (state and local) have either or neither. Local personal property taxes vary widely from community to community — from a tax rate of less than 1 percent of the value of the property to over 5 percent per year. Persons living in New York City are subjected to twenty-two different municipal taxes, probably the greatest variety of taxes levied by any American city.[19]

Tariffs   Tariffs may be levied by the federal government either to yield income or to protect selected industries. For most consumers the tariff is a concealed tax. Even though the duty on an import may be intended primarily to yield revenue, it operates in the same way that a sales tax does in reducing individual or family income. A tariff to protect a particular industry, such as textiles or shoe manufacturing, raises the import duty on such products in order to keep out competing foreign products. In doing so, it raises the prices of those products in the domestic market. Tourists returning from abroad are sometimes dismayed when customs collectors present their bills. They may find that some of the items they purchased abroad are taxed from 50 to 100 percent.

Quotas   Quotas differ from tariffs in that they limit the quantity of a product that can be imported. If no import duties are levied where a quota exists, the federal government does not collect any revenue. But the domestic price of the product is higher than it would be otherwise because the effect of the quota is to lower supply and lessen price competition.

QUESTIONS FOR DISCUSSION AND REVIEW

1. Does an abundance of goods and services assure happiness or consumer well-being?

2. How does the principle of diminishing returns affect how an individual spends money?

3. In your judgment, is the supply of consumer goods and services limited or unlimited?

4. Is it possible that our desire for the goods and services that money will buy increases more rapidly than our ability to increase our income? Why?

5. What are the implications of the four principles of consumption?

6. Differentiate between needs, wants, and demand.

7. How do your personal psychological wants affect your consuming activities?

8. What are the advantages and disadvantages for the individual of being either "one of the group" or standing "apart from the group" in consumption patterns?

9. What are possible problems that may develop within the United States due to disparities in family incomes both within the country and around the world?

10. Tax reform has been a perennial topic in Congress. Why has there been so much talk and so little reform?

11. What percentage of your income do you estimate you pay in local, state, and federal taxes?

PROJECTS

1. Write a paper showing how social and peer-group pressure guide your consuming activities.

2. In a short paper describe the ways in which your religious beliefs affect you as a consumer.

3. Analyze what your needs and wants might be if you had been born into a family whose economic position was much higher than yours; and a family whose economic position was much lower than yours.

4. Describe how the changing occupational opportunities for college graduates may affect your future consumption patterns.

5. Describe what taxes you or your family pay and what services the government provides in return.

REFERENCES

1. *Money Management* (Minneapolis: Paul S. Amidon & Associates, 1972). Note: This is a cassette series.
2. J. Markin, *The Psychology of Consumer Behavior* (Englewood Cliffs, N.J.: Prentice-Hall, 1969), p. 18.

3. Britt, p. 98.
4. Markin, pp. 9–11.
5. Harold H. Kassarjian and Thomas R. Robertson, eds., *Perspective in Consumer Behavior* (Glenview, Ill.: Scott, Foresman, 1968), p. 194.
6. J. U. McNeal, *An Introduction to Consumer Behavior* (New York: John Wiley & Sons, 1973), p. 37.
7. David T. Kollat, Roger D. Blackwell, and James F. Engel, eds., *Research in Consumer Behavior* (New York: Holt, Rinehart and Winston, 1970), pp. 355–356, 456.
8. J. E. Stafford, "Effects of Group Influences on Consumer Brand Preferences," in Kollat, Blackwell, and Engel, p. 458.
9. M. Venkatesan, "Experimental Study of Consumer Behavior, Conformity and Independence," in Kollat, Blackwell, and Engel, pp. 472–479.
10. "Executive Compensation: The Ups and Downs are Sharper," *Business Week,* 12 May 1975, p. 91.
11. *Current Population Reports: Special Studies Illustrative Projections of Money Income Size Distributions for Families and Unrelated Individuals* (Washington, D.C.: Government Printing Office, Feb. 1974) p. 2.
12. Allan J. Mayer, Rich Thomas, and Tom Joyce, "The Wary Consumer," *Newsweek,* 7 April 1975, p. 64.
13. Sterling E. Soderlind, "Whose Tax Burden Is Heaviest?" *Wall Street Journal,* 9 May 1972.
14. *St. Petersburg Times Parade,* 27 July 1975, p. 5.
15. *New York Times,* 24 Sept. 1974, p. 34.
16. *National Observer,* 22 Dec. 1973, p. 6.
17. *Washington Star News,* 20 May 1974, p. A9.
18. *Wall Street Journal,* 4 March 1974, p. 14.
19. *New York Times,* 18 May 1975, p. 6.

CHAPTER 3

ARE CONSUMERS THE GUIDES OR THE GUIDED?

ORGANIZING FOR CONSUMPTION: THE FAMILY

The Family as the Consuming Unit

The purpose of all productive activity in the economy is consumption, and the home, created by a family, is the center of almost all consuming activity. It is in the home that the routine of living takes place. In earlier times, the patriarchal family existed in a simple economic system. It was largely self-sufficient. Families produced and consumed a limited variety of goods. Whatever was produced was for the whole family and was shared by its members, according to their needs. This is still true, but the ways in which families operate have changed. The family has become almost exclusively a consuming unit. The production of most goods and services has been taken out of the home and assumed by business firms. One or more members of the family leave the home to work for a business firm. For their efforts they are paid money, which is then used to purchase goods and services in retail stores. The small single enterpriser has been replaced to a considerable extent by the large impersonal corporation.

While these changes were taking place, there was no comparable change in consuming activities. The family as a consuming unit has become less specialized, whereas business firms have become more specialized. Working parents have little time for traditional housekeeping activities. They depend increasingly on business firms to provide the goods and services that individuals formerly provided for themselves. If it were possible to develop a technique of consuming as efficient as our techniques of production, we could expand the satisfaction of our wants.

Family and Business Motives Compared

The welfare and preservation of the family are the goals of family members, particularly the parents. Instead of competing among themselves, family members practice the *principles of cooperation.* They share what the family has. The right of private property is essential to the maintenance of the family. In family life, the older and stronger members protect the younger and weaker members. If food is scarce, the weaker ones are fed first. If clothing is scarce, the warm, protective garments are given to those whose need is greatest. Parents generally strive to secure for their children more formal education than they themselves had. In times of danger, the older and stronger members protect the younger and weaker members of the family, at the sacrifice of their own lives if necessary. As children mature, they assume responsibilities in meeting the needs of their parents and grandparents. Typical family life exemplifies a high ethical level of living.

The transition from the self-contained economic life of the patriarchal family to the specialized interdependent economic life of the modern family has created complications. When production was taken out of the family and became a business, different motives were substituted and different standards of quality and action were adopted. Businessmen do not usually recognize the same responsibilities toward the members of other families as they do toward their own.

It is customary among economists to speak of *the profit motive* in business, but upon analysis it is found that the acquisition of money, by whatever means, is the basic motivation. Whether money is received as a wage, rent, interest, or profit, it is a means to economic security. People in business strive to accumulate all the money they can, so that they and the members of their families may have the goods and services they want. Included in their wants are provision for loss of money income resulting from accident, illness, unemployment, premature death, or old age. The notion still prevails that each family can achieve economic security by itself if it accumulates enough money. So the heads of families compete with one another in the business world. Whereas the family is a social organism of cooperating members, business is a social-economic institution whose members compete with one another.

The acquisition of money is not the sole motive of businessmen, however. Hard-headed business executives are also usually the heads of families. Their motives and actions are complex and mixed. Like other people, they were subjected to the social, religious, political, and economic views of their family when they were children. Their likes and dislikes, their loyalties and friendships, and their membership in various organizations all influence their activities and decisions.

Every individual is a collection of physiological and psychological drives and motives, no one of which can be singled out as the basic force. In normal day-to-day living every person reflects many motivating forces. Motives may be mixed and confused, some impelling individuals toward one action or decision and others impelling them to an opposite action or decision. If you attempt to analyze your own motives when making an economic choice, you will discover how difficult it is to disentangle the many influences leading to your decision.

Standards of Family Success

Families and firms have different standards by which they measure the success of their operations. Firms have a measurable standard: Will it pay? Their goal is to make all the money they can.

Families have no single standard of success. Their general goal is family welfare. Since this can be promoted if incomes are adequate, many families adopt the size of family income as an objective standard of success. Families with similar incomes tend to live in the same neighborhood. As one family's income increases, the family may move to a better neighborhood, thereby demonstrating its financial success. In each neighborhood there are gradations in status. There are a few families at the top, which set the plane of living that others in the neighborhood endeavor to emulate. In popular language this is known as "keeping up with the Joneses." Ability to keep up is a sign of success; inability to keep up is often considered a sign of failure.

Families in Transition

As a social institution the family is continuing and timeless. Individual families may die out, but the family as an institution continues. Ninety percent of the adults in any given society marry and establish homes. From the genealogical point of view, a specific family may be considered as continuing indefinitely over the years, but from the economic point of view, a family functions from forty to fifty years. During those years it passes through three stages. The first stage is preliminary and temporary. A man and woman marry, establish a home, are classified as a family, and constitute a new consuming unit.

The second stage is the most important. During this phase the family normally grows in size. Since the number of children varies among families, the length of the second stage varies. Dating from the birth of the first child, the second stage continues until the youngest child has reached maturity and left the home, probably to establish his or her own family. It is during this second stage that the family performs its most important functions as a social, economic, religious, and educational institution.

The third and final stage of family life dates from the time the youngest child has left home until one of the parents dies. It is then that this particular home is broken up and this family comes to an end. Out of it the children have joined with the children of other families to form new families and new homes to carry on the social process of continuing the human race.

WHO GUIDES CONSUMERS IN THE MARKET?

Parents Guide Minor Consumers

In family life children learn how to survive. One of the many things children must learn is how to spend money. In the first six years of a child's life parental influence dominates. From ages six to eighteen, parental influence is shared with church, school, advertisers, and the child's play-mates and friends. At a very early age children learn about money. They learn that 15 cents will buy a pack of gum or that 35 cents will buy a soft drink. As they grow older, they presumably learn how to spend their money so as to gain maximum satisfaction. Somehow, it is presumed, they will move from infancy to maturity. When they are infants, their parents supply them freely with the goods and services they need. As their horizons expand it is assumed that parents will teach them how to spend money. By the age of eighteen many of them marry and establish their own homes. Is it valid to assume that in the preceding years they have been educated as consumers? They may be able to earn money, but are they able to spend money wisely? Answers to these questions depend, in large part, on the training and education provided by parents. If the parents are *economic adults,* or rational informed consumers, the children learn how to spend family income so as to promote the welfare of family members. But if the parents are still *economic minors* — that is, irrational and uninformed consumers easily swayed by advertising — it is unlikely that their children will learn how to do their jobs as consumers. Anyone can spend money, but not everyone can spend money advantageously.

If a family's income is so small that it will not purchase adequate nutrition, sufficient clothing, proper housing, health care, and education, the needs of the children in such families will not be fully met. Their wants and their values are likely to be distorted. A common criticism of consumers in such circumstances is that they would not know how to consume wisely even if they had an adequate income. It is easy to cite cases of expenditures by poor families which, in the judgment of others, are foolish. If the money incomes of poor families are temporarily increased, it should not be surprising if some of them respond to advertising and to salespeople's efforts to sell luxury items, such as fur coats or color television sets. Never having had such luxuries, it is understandable that some people should spend part of their increased income for such items. However, not all so-called foolish expenditures are made by poor families. Some of the most foolish and wasteful consuming practices are to be found among the wealthy. There is ample evidence that rich parents do not necessarily choose wisely for their children and that poor parents do not necessarily choose unwisely for their children. Children reared in poor families may learn how to do their job as consumers better than children reared in rich families.

When Do Minors Become Mature Consumers?

The truth is that too many people never become mature consumers. It is assumed that children somehow grow into economic adulthood. It is also assumed that as people earn money of their own, they also learn how to spend it wisely. Neither of these assumptions is valid, yet American public schools have included very little, if any, training for intelligent use of income.

The family is the most important institution for educating children to become economic adults. It is in the family that children should learn that money is a valuable tool in reaching predetermined goals, not a goal in itself. Young children are remarkably alert and observant. They learn by listening to what their parents say and by observing what they do. They develop attitudes concerning money even before they know what money is and how it operates in the economy.

The allowance is a device used effectively by increasing numbers of families for the purpose of introducing children to the use of money. From a child's point of view, spending is very simple. All you do is go to a store and give the storekeeper money in exchange for the product you want. Among educators the prevalent view is that children are entitled to an allowance because they are members of the family. As members, they have the right to a share in the family income. As they grow older the allowance increases. More importantly, growing children learn that they can supplement their allowances by doing jobs for pay, which adds to their income. With parental understanding and guidance young people can learn how to use their money in ways that best promote their welfare. The habits they develop as children and teenagers will persist throughout their lives.

It is important that children know how much *they* cost their families and society. It has been estimated that it costs between $40,000 and $75,000 to rear a child from birth through college, and about $30,000 if the child does not attend college.

If a child has parents who are intelligent consumers, he or she will become a mature consumer. A child reared by parents who are still economic minors, however, is not likely to develop into a good consumer.

Who Guides the Parents?

Those who have goods and services to sell use advertising and salesmanship in an effort to guide consumer wants so as to benefit themselves. This process began with the increasing use of machines and with specialization. Business firms found that the economies of production on a large scale demanded steady maximum production. Since they could not afford to let expensive equipment stand idle while waiting for consumers to buy, they began to produce goods in anticipation of consumer demand. Then, as output increased, firms could not afford to let inventories accumulate while waiting for consumers to clear the shelves. Aggressive sellers found that they could increase demand for their products. Consumers have proved to be incapable of guiding producers and susceptible to suggestion from sellers, and the sellers now play a significant role in determining the choices of consumers.

Sellers have become increasingly skilled in the arts of persuasion, and neither the family nor the school has prepared consumers for the world in which they live. The principal school in which consumers learn is the "school of experience." The tuition is high and attendance does not ensure success. From birth to the age of six children are under the complete protective care of parents. If all people of all ages lived out their lives under the protective care of someone who "knows best," their bodies would be well nourished and healthy. Some adults do live in institutions where dietitians provide well-balanced, nourishing meals. This is accomplished, however, at the expense of freedom of choice. For most of us the fundamental issue we face is whether we can acquire the knowledge and develop the inner discipline that underlies real freedom of choice.

Who Makes the Buying Decisions?

The degree of influence members of a family have in making buying decisions varies from member to member and from family to family. In some families the buying is done almost entirely by the mother; in others by the father; and in some it is a joint decision by the mother and father. In some families the children play an active role in buying decisions; in others the children's desires are almost totally ignored.

One study of consumer patterns, "Purchase Influence Measures of Husband/Wife Influence on Buying Decisions,"[1] confirmed what one might expect with regard to what family member influences the buying of certain products. For example, wives initiated the purchase decision in buying vacuum cleaners 80 percent of the time. But in the case of automobiles, they initiated the purchase decision only 22 percent of the time.

How Much Guidance Should There Be?

The Federal Trade Commission has been given the responsibility by law to protect consumers. Since its origin in 1914 the FTC has struggled with the question of whether it has the task of protecting only sensible, intelligent consumers who conduct themselves carefully in the marketplace, or whether it also must protect consumers who are uninformed, careless, and wasteful. At times it has acted on behalf of the latter by invoking the "ignorant consumer standard." At other times it has been ordered by the courts to ignore these people and invoke the "reasonable consumer standard."*

How much guidance do consumers need? Who is to do the guiding? How much "interference" should there be between buyer and seller? These are just a few of the questions that must be asked when determining how

---

* For a more detailed discussion of these concepts, see Ivan L. Preston, "Reasonable Consumer or Ignorant Consumer? How The FTC Decides," *The Journal of Consumer Affairs*, 8:2 (1974), pp. 131–143.

the marketplace should serve the consumer and what degree of freedom
sellers should have in pursuing their goals.

There is a conflict within us as consumers—a conflict between the
desire for goods and pleasures and a sense of higher values. Consumers
are guided, pushed, or led. They are dependent or independent. But it is
up to each consumer to finally determine what his or her goals and aspirations are and then to follow them.

WHAT GUIDES DO SELLERS FOLLOW?

The Profit and Loss Statement

If consumers do not guide producers, what guide or guides do producers follow? How do they decide what and how much to produce? How
do they decide what standards of quality to use? How do they detect the
passing of old wants? How do they discover new wants? Answers to these
questions are found in the driving force that motivates modern business.
To the extent that business firms do guide production, the standard they
apply is "will it pay?" Business managers read their profit and loss statements, which are objective measures of success. If an established product
begins to show less profit, management must decide whether to discontinue
its production or whether to spend more on advertising. If the research
department comes up with a new product, management tests it in a limited
market area. This is a form of market research. If consumers in that area
buy the new product, their response is taken as evidence of acceptance not
only of the product but also of the package and the price. Management
may then decide to "go national," meaning that there is reason to believe
that the product will make a profit for the firm. Negatively, if consumers
in the sample area reject the new product, consumers in other parts of the
nation will never hear of it. Note this significant fact: *Producers propose
but consumers dispose.* Business firms take the initiative in developing
and advertising new products, but consumers collectively decide the fate
of a product by their acceptance or rejection of it. It has been estimated
that about 500 "new" products are brought into the marketplace each
month, and about 90 percent of these fail because they are rejected by
potential consumer-buyers. In a broad sense consumers do guide production, even though the guidance may be negative.

SOME CONSUMER CRITICISMS OF THE PROFIT SYSTEM

The basic assumption of the profit system is that it will pay business
firms to offer for sale only those goods and services that consumers want.
This in turn is predicated on the assumption that consumers know what
they want. These assumptions are not always valid.

Profit or Consumer Welfare?

"He profits most who serves best." Is this popular slogan true? For many business firms it is, but for too many it is not. One position many firms have taken on this issue is that it is not the business' concern if advertising and marketing corrupt society. "If what is offered can be sold at a profit . . . then it is legitimate." The businessman should not be concerned about any other considerations, moral, ethical, or religious. "It is true, you cannot as a businessman serve two masters, God and mammon. . . . I suggest you serve business and yourself."[2] Saving souls, stressing values, and helping consumers is the job of other people.

The desire for profit may supersede the service motive. Profits are greater in an economy of scarcity than in an economy of abundance. From a business point of view scarcity results in high prices and greater profits. From a consumer point of view more wants can be satisfied by having an abundance of goods and services at low prices. Sometimes business firms realize a profit by performing no service or by performing a disservice. Deliberate restrictions of output by managers of factories, farms, and mines can be explained only by the fact that such restrictions make it possible to limit supply and maintain or raise prices. Not many firms operate at full capacity. Management sets a profit goal and then sets prices and restricts production to achieve that goal. This practice began as long ago as 1925 when it was introduced by General Motors Corporation.

Typical profit targets are 20 percent to $33\frac{1}{3}$ percent on invested capital. Hoped-for targets and what is actually realized in profits and returns on invested capital can be very different and may vary greatly from company to company and from industry to industry. The medium net profit on sales for the 500 largest industrial companies in the United States in 1975 was 3.9 percent. The range was from a high of 23.2 percent for one company to no return for the companies that experienced losses. The medium net return on invested capital for the 500 was 11.6 percent, ranging from a high for one company of 60.2 percent to no return. The company with the poorest showing for the year lost $452 million. On an industry-wide basis, mining had a net return on sales of 12.3 percent while food had a net return of 2.3 percent. In net return on invested capital, pharmaceuticals had 19.4 percent while the apparel industry was lowest with 4.4 percent.[3]

The economy can produce many more goods and services, but these goods could be sold only if prices were reduced. Some firms find it possible to make adequate profits by producing to capacity and by setting prices at a level at which consumers will buy. But the predominant practice in the American economy is to administer prices and to restrict production in order to maintain those prices. It is easier for factory managers to restrict their production than it is for agricultural firms. Because of this we have such practices as the destruction of agricultural surpluses. Farmers have dumped coffee and bananas into the ocean or let oranges or potatoes rot in order to create an artificial scarcity that will maintain prices high enough to yield the profits they want.

Manipulation of Consumer Demand

In addition to restricting production, profit-seeking business firms try to control consumer demand. They attempt to persuade consumers to buy goods and services that will be profitable to the sellers, even though they may be detrimental to consumers. This leads business firms to spend more and more money on advertising and selling efforts. The purpose of such persuasive selling efforts is not primarily to help consumers find the goods and services they want, but to induce them to buy particular goods and specific brands. This results in competitive waste. Consumers are urged to drink more milk. If they respond, producers of other commodities, vitamin pills for example, find their sales diminishing. In turn, they then increase their advertising expenditures to urge consumers to purchase their pills. It is small wonder that consumers become bewildered!

Exploitation of Consumers

The desire for profit is so strong that it leads some sellers to resort to any practices, even fraudulent ones, that might yield a profit. When consumer economics as a science was in its infancy, it was difficult for a shopkeeper to defraud consumers because the market was so small that once the fraud was detected or had been worked to its limit its profit-yielding possibilities were ended. Today, with 215 million potential buyers, unscrupulous sellers need not concern themselves about repeat sales. In such a large market an operator can make a fortune before the fraud is detected. In fact it may never be detected. As a result there are many business firms that resort to practices such as adulteration, misbranding, mislabeling, and misleading or untruthful advertising.* To the extent that sellers make profits by these practices, the process of guiding the economic system is reversed. Consumers no longer guide by their power to buy or not buy a product. Sellers guide by selling.

DOES THE ECONOMY PRODUCE WHAT CONSUMERS WANT?

Demand First or Supply First

In the handicraft economy of the eighteenth century practically all goods and services were produced after consumers had ordered them. Such goods and services were described as custom-made. In the economy of the United States today there is still a significant volume of production of goods and services after buyers have placed their orders. Services are almost all rendered after an order has been placed. These include cleaning, pressing, papering and painting a house, barbering, hairdressing, and repair and

* For elaboration and evidence see chapters 10 and 14.

maintenance services in general. Some clothing is made to order. Some shoes are made to order, and all shoe repairing is custom work. Many houses are built after the buyer has placed an order. Automobiles may be semicustom-made. A prospective buyer may place an order, choosing the color and the equipment. He or she has several thousand variations to choose from. These are run through computers, and the particular choice is eventually produced on the assembly line.

But most goods in the United States are produced in anticipation of demand. Manufacturers and processors cannot realize the economies of large-scale production if they wait for consumers to express their demands in retail markets. In order to keep their large plants in operation continuously, they must estimate what and how much consumers will want. Then they produce those goods. If their estimates have been correct, the products are sold and profits are made. If the goods are new, sellers then use advertising to tell consumers why they should buy the new products. If consumer tastes are changing, sellers may use advertising in an effort to offset the declining demand for their products. Practically all food products, tobacco products, alcoholic beverages, and soft drinks are produced in anticipation of demand. Most large building operations are carried on by developers who anticipate demands for houses in an area where corn is now being grown. All public utilities are provided in anticipation of demand, as are household furnishings and clothing. Transportation by trains, bus, planes, and rental automobiles is provided in anticipation of demand. Billions of gallons of gasoline are refined and delivered to retail gasoline service stations in anticipation of demand by motorists. Medical and dental care, insurance services, banking, education, hotel and motel services, and the services of restaurants are made available in anticipation of demand.

The Economy Produces Enough and More

The real problem is that the economy produces many things consumers do not want or need and then puts pressure on them to buy. Instead of accepting the consumers' judgment that they do not want the goods or services, many sellers spend billions of dollars to persuade consumers to buy. This leads to waste. Waste results when any test other than utility determines the nature of things consumed.

It might be contended that the fact that the products and services offered for sale in retail stores are purchased by consumers is evidence that those are the goods and services they want. If consumers do not buy them, the sellers incur losses. These losses discourage further attempts to market such goods or services. On the other hand, if consumers buy what they find in the stores, sellers are encouraged to offer more. Within limits, this picture of what happens in the retail markets is valid. The real test is not whether consumers buy what they find in the market but whether business firms are constantly experimenting or testing for unknown demands for goods both old and new. If competition is really effective, business firms can survive only by producing what consumers want and by meeting the standards set by the marketplace. Competition means willingness to experiment to ascertain whether consumers will buy more at lower prices. This is the ultimate protection for consumers.[4]

QUESTIONS FOR REVIEW

1. "Typical family life exemplifies a high ethical level of living." Explain and illustrate.
2. Which descriptive term do you think is more accurate – "profit motive" or "money motive"?
3. By what standards has your family measured its success?
4. In your consuming activities, do you attempt to keep up with the Joneses?
5. Do you consider yourself a mature consumer?
6. "There is ample evidence that rich parents do not necessarily choose wisely for their children and that poor parents do not necessarily choose unwisely for their children." Do you agree? Explain.
7. Who guides you as a consumer? Who guides your parents?
8. Do you agree that "he profits most who serves best"? Explain.
9. To what extent do you agree with consumer criticisms of the profit system as presented in this chapter?
10. In what ways do consumers guide sellers?
11. What is economic waste? What causes it?
12. "If what is offered can be sold at a profit . . . then it is legitimate. The businessman should not be concerned about any other considerations, moral, ethical, or religious." Do you agree? Explain.

PROJECTS

1. In your family, which member has the greatest influence on buying decisions? Which the least? Explain.
2. Review your purchases during the past twenty-four hours, then list the reasons for making them and draw some conclusions about your buying habits and motives.
3. With the assistance of your parents estimate how much it has cost to maintain you from birth to college.
4. Ask ten businessmen or women what their motives are.

REFERENCES

1. *Advertising Age,* 17 March 1975, p. 52.
2. Theodore Levitt, "Are Advertising and Marketing Corrupting Society? It's Not Your Worry," in C. H. Sandage and Vernon Fryburger, *The Role of Advertising* (Homewood, Ill.: Richard D. Irwin, 1960), pp. 442–450.
3. *Fortune,* May 1976, pp. 339–340.
4. See Walter Adams, "Consumer Needs and Consumer Sovereignty in the American Economy," *Journal of Business* 35, no. 3 (July 1962): 268–269.

PART TWO

FORCES INFLUENCING CONSUMER DEMAND

CONSUMERS' FREEDOM TO CHOOSE

THE CONCEPT OF ECONOMIC FREEDOM

Freedom to Produce and Freedom to Consume

Producers and consumers in the United States have more freedom than producers and consumers in most other countries. Yet even in the United States there is not absolute freedom. The concept of freedom is relative. More than in any other country, men and women in the United States are free to choose their occupations. More than in any other country, consumers are free to choose the goods and services they want. These freedoms are a consequence of our economic, political, and social institutions and our abundance of natural and human resources.

The counterpart of free choice is free rejection. In a free society it is presumed that consumers know what they do *not* want as well as what they do want. Freedom of choice also includes freedom to choose badly. It implies a willingness to accept the consequences of a bad choice even though those consequences may be unknown or unknowable.

Wealth, Nealth, and Illth

If consumers are to make intelligent choices, they must know that some goods and services promote their well-being, that the consumption of other goods and services has harmful effects, and that some goods and services neither promote nor retard their well-being. Traditional economists consider wealth as all goods that have a monetary exchange value, whether they help or harm consumers. Consumer economists make a distinction between wealth, nealth, and illth. If goods and services promote the well-being of consumers, they are called *wealth;* if they have a negative effect that harms the consumer, they are called *illth;* if they have a neutral effect, which neither helps nor harms the consumer, they are called *nealth*. Although these concepts are very real and useful for individuals, they are difficult to work with objectively and in the aggregate. Who is to judge what is wealth, nealth, or illth? Not all the food one eats promotes one's well-being. Not all the beverages one drinks promotes one's well-being. One may eat or drink too much or too little. In either case, the result may be harmful to one's health. Overweight people who die prematurely because their heart cannot carry the load have not exercised their freedom of choice wisely.

What standard can we use to classify products and services as to whether they represent wealth, nealth, or illth? Would it be correct to conclude that any product or service that anyone wishes to sell and for which there is a willing buyer represents wealth, and further that all products and services in this category should be legal? If this line of reasoning is accepted, then prostitution and heroin should be legal and would represent wealth. Classifying goods and services as to their contribution to the well-being of the human race is both complicated and controversial. There are products and services, however, that are clearly harmful and represent illth. If one were to place examples of products and services on a continuum according to the way some people would classify them, it might look like this:[1]

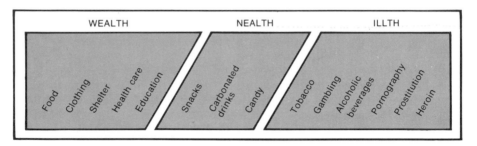

Various levels of government have already made numerous decisions about goods that are considered illth by either prohibiting or limiting their use, but each individual must decide which products and services to buy or not to buy.

Consumers are not born with an intuitive sense that enables them to choose the things that are good for them. They have to learn from others. In a free economy they may come under the influence of those who have their well-being foremost in mind or they may fall under the influence of those whose goal is personal gain, not the welfare of consumers.

The concept of economic freedom implies a standard or standards. The standard most commonly used is that of *welfare*. The dictionary definition of "welfare" mentions good fortune and prosperity. The implication is that if a person has an abundance of economic goods, he or she will enjoy a state of well-being. One has only to look around to observe that not all people with an abundance of worldly goods consider themselves to be in a state of well-being. Some of the "big rich" are unhappy or afflicted with ills. They worry about many things, including the possible loss of their money. Some consumers with little or no goods find happiness in the enjoyment of immaterial things. Obviously, the concepts of well-being and happiness are subjective.

Positive Versus Negative Freedom of Choice

Positive freedom of economic choice consists of two equally important elements. A consumer not only has the right to consume anything he or she wishes but also the purchasing power necessary to implement that right. Under negative freedom of economic choice, individuals have the right to consume anything they wish but lack the purchasing power needed to make that right effective.

The concept of freedom in an economy of relative abundance is very different from that in an economy of scarcity. Within an economy of abundance there are degrees of freedom. The very rich can live luxuriously in mansions. They can own yachts and airplanes, have libraries and art collections, and travel around the world. People in the very low income groups have the legal right to enjoy such luxuries, but they do not have the economic right because they lack the necessary purchasing power. For them freedom of choice is a negative right.

CONDITIONS NECESSARY FOR FREEDOM OF CHOICE

Free Entry

If consumers are to have freedom to choose, other people in the economy must have the freedom to supply. This implies freedom to enter a business or profession and to choose or to reject a job. Such rights are fundamental in a free-choice, free-enterprise economy.

Full Information

Uninformed choice is not really free choice. An educated, informed, rational consumer can and does engage in the process of free choice and free rejection. Economic minors, however, cannot really exercise their freedom to choose. Sellers have a responsibility to tell prospective buyers — by advertising and labels — the essential information needed to make an intelligent choice. Usually freedom of choice is restricted by a scarcity of goods and services among which to choose. There are also situations in which there are so many similar items among which to choose that one's freedom is negated by the abundance of goods. For example, buyers of 14 items of food in a supermarket were confronted with 246 possible choices. Such a situation represents a superabundance of brands and packages rather than an abundance of food.

A Price System

Who gets what? As long as human wants exceed the supply of goods and services to satisfy them, some system of allocation is necessary. If the goods and services on the market are not sold to those who have the money to pay for them, to whom shall they go? If producers are not to produce comforts and luxuries for those who have the money to pay for them, what shall they produce? In a free-enterprise, free-choice economy the price system has proven to be an effective device for regulating the volume and content of production. Though the price system is impersonal and may fail to provide for the welfare of consumers with small incomes, it does provide more goods and services for more people than alternative systems provide for consumers in other nations. Freedom of choice may not work perfectly, but it does work.

HOW MUCH FREEDOM OF CHOICE?

In our analysis of freedom of choice, let us move from the general to the particular by examining the restrictions on freedom of choice in the United States.

Natural Restrictions

The authority of nature restricts and determines consumer choice. What consumers want is influenced by climate, and what they can have depends on the resources available. Within the United States there are great differences among the states and regions in terrain, soil, water, and minerals.

The 1975 gas shortage in this country, when many gas stations limited the amount of gas each motorist could purchase, was an abrupt reminder to U.S. consumers that the world's supply of natural resources is not inexhaustible. (*Christy Park, Monkmeyer*)

Nature can be awesome and sometimes even destructive. Earthquakes, tornadoes, and floods kill and injure people and destroy their material possessions. Suddenly the supply of goods and services is limited. In such cases, the remaining goods are usually divided equitably among the survivors, not by means of the price system but by rational, authoritative control. Freedom of choice is restricted in these emergency situations.

Until the past decade little attention has been given to conserving what was thought to be an inexhaustible supply of natural resources. Recent recognition of natural limitations, however, has brought a new awareness of the significance of conserving our natural resources and of the threat of depleting our nonreplaceable resources. Conservation and/or the threat of running out of resources places an obvious, though indirect, limit on consumer choice.

Economic Restrictions

In a free enterprise economy producers of goods and services produce the things they expect will yield the greatest profit. The welfare of consumers is secondary rather than primary. As a consequence, considerable quantities of illth and nealth are produced. This reduces the supply of available wealth and diminishes consumer freedom of choice. A free-enterprise economy gives producers the freedom to produce what they choose, regardless of whether such production benefits people or not. It also gives consumers the freedom to buy the products they want, again whether or not the products benefit them.

In an "authoritarian" economy the government makes the decisions about what is to be produced and who will receive the products. If an "authoritarian" economy has a benevolent, paternalistic dictator, consumers might be reasonably well supplied, but their freedom of choice is denied.

Governmental Restrictions

In a free society government is the agent and servant of the people. The goal of responsible government is the greatest good of the greatest number of people. The larger the population of a nation and the more complex its economy, the greater the need for restrictions on the freedom of some business firms and consumers. For the sake of group welfare, individual consumers are restricted legally in the types of houses they may construct, in the way they may drive their automobiles, in the amount of liquor they may consume, and so on.

Governmental restrictions can be indirect as well as direct. Since the end of World War II the United States has been involved in two "limited" wars (limited, that is, when compared to World War II) in Korea and Vietnam. Although most citizens retain most of their freedoms, there have been and continue to be some indirect restrictions on consumer freedom; resources and productive power that could be used for the production of goods and services have been diverted to military use.

When a nation becomes involved in full-scale war there is a massive diversion of productive power to military uses. As a result government exercises extensive control in apportioning scarce materials. Items in critical supply may be rationed. Owners of automobiles may find that they can no longer buy tires or unlimited quantities of gasoline. They may find that it takes more than money to buy food. Under a rationing system consumers are given a limited number of stamps that, together with money, may be used to acquire rationed food products.

In a free-enterprise, free-choice economy the federal government has the primary responsibility for maintaining a high level of economic activity. Fiscal policy and monetary policy are the tools that modern government uses to encourage a lagging economy or to brake a too-active economy. In spite of government action, however, recessions do occur, and large numbers of people able and willing to work are unable to find jobs. Though they may receive unemployment compensation, the amount is much less than their normal income and as a consequence their freedom of choice is restricted.

The U.S. Government today takes more of consumers' income in taxes than it did in the past. As the gross national product has risen, the percentage of the GNP over which consumers have control has declined from 81 percent in 1929 to 70 percent in 1976. But for the past twenty-seven years it has been constant at 70 percent. Though government spending of tax money may reflect the will of the majority, the bureaucrats spend funds differently than consumers would. Government agencies are not infallible.

Social Restrictions

Compulsory public education is a prime example of authoritarian control in the United States. In most states children are required to go to school. The individual child has no choice. Economically one of the major resources of a nation is its people. If they are healthy, intelligent, and educated, they are more likely to be productive workers. Equally important is the fact that if a democratic nation is to be strong and to continue to vest political power in the hands of the citizens, they must be educated so that they can vote intelligently.

Society also restricts the freedom of those persons considered dangers to the community or dangers to themselves. Alcoholics and drug addicts are examples. Ultimately the excessive consumption of illth may incapacitate them and make it necessary for society to hospitalize them. In so doing, society deprives the individual of freedom to choose such consumer goods.

In a social group there are always individuals who cannot or will not abide by the rules and laws of society. Chronic and serious offenders are jailed. There they lose all freedom of choice. On any given day there are 360,000 persons in prisons in the United States.

The physically handicapped, the destitute, and the indigent are given the minimum necessities of life in institutions where some of them must live. Although they live in the midst of a free-choice economy, within these institutions they have practically no freedom to choose.

Group Authority

As a member of a group, every individual is restricted in his or her freedom of choice. Group authority is exercised through custom, mores, and law. Typical middle-class Americans today are other-directed — that is, they are controlled or strongly influenced by the people with whom they live in close association. Other-directed consumers have a strong psychological need for approval. They are easily influenced by their contemporaries and by advertisers.[2] Every individual faces the problem of getting along in the society in which he or she lives. The greatest guiding force in civilized life is the desire for social approval and respect.

Customs are such strong and pervasive restrictions on freedom of choice that they require the longer analysis found in chapters 5 and 6.

Religious Restrictions

Religious authority has been an important restrictive influence on the actions of consumers throughout recorded history. In this country the Protestant ethic extolled hard work, thrift, and competition. The American emphasis on economic competition can create an attitude of hostile tension. Tension produces fear of others and fear of failure. As a consequence one may find oneself in a dilemma. One must be aggressive and competitive at the same time as one attempts to live according to religious principles. Inability to reconcile the discrepancy between our theoretical freedom and the very real restrictions we encounter in attempting to exercise that freedom may result in a neurotic condition.[3]

Family Restrictions

The family has been described as the institution primarily responsible for converting children into responsible members of society. During the first six years of a child's life family influence is almost total. The child has very little freedom of choice. From ages six to eighteen children associate with other children in school, in church, and in Scouts, 4-H clubs, and other organizations. Through these associations they acquire new ideas and are subjected to group influence. The process of both group and family influence continues through the college years and throughout the lifetime of one's parents. Unconsciously the family exercises a strong and continuing restrictive influence on the freedom of its members. These restrictions reflect the wisdom of the centuries and their purpose is to promote individual as well as group welfare. But they also reflect the prejudices of the family and the group and may result in illth rather than welfare.

Discriminatory Restrictions

Discrimination on the basis of social class, color, creed, or origin restricts the individual's freedom to choose consumer goods and services. Though some members of a group that is discriminated against may have enough money to buy expensive houses in surburban communities, the dominant social group may attempt to deny them the right to exercise this freedom. Historically the pattern has been for people in privileged groups to reserve for themselves what they consider to be the good and choice things of life, while those in minority groups have to content themselves with what is left.

Physical and Self-Imposed Restrictions

There are millions of people in the United States whose freedom of economic choice is limited by physical handicaps. A boy with highly defective eyesight is not likely to take up stamp collecting as a hobby. A girl who is tone deaf is not likely to purchase a musical instrument.

Habit also limits the freedom of many individuals. Habitual patterns of consumption develop in childhood and often persist throughout life. A habit may be compulsive, such as smoking. It may be negative, resulting in refusal to purchase or consume certain goods or services.

Corporate Economic Restrictions

Individual and corporate employers exercise more control over the consuming practices of employees than is commonly recognized. One of the giants of advertising demanded that all employees of his agency and all his domestic employees use only the products whose advertising accounts he had. When an advertiser shifted accounts, the employees of the advertising agency were compelled to shift their consuming practices and their loyalties to the cigarettes, beer, or food product for which their firm was currently writing advertising copy.[4]

The corporate and military organizations of the nation determine almost all values for an increasing number of people. In the military members must live in housing according to their military rank, and in corporate organizations members must live in housing according to their income rank. No one may say so openly, but it is often true that junior executives live in one suburb and top executives in another. If the chairman of the board of a corporation drives a Cadillac, no one else in the corporation may own or drive a Cadillac.* Increasingly our society is creating a conformed consumer, one who conforms to the dictates of those exercising economic power.

CONDITIONS PROMOTING FREEDOM OF CHOICE

Political Freedom

The historical record shows that governments in the past have been predominantly authoritarian and often despotic. In every age there have been individuals who sought power for the sake of exercising power over others. Rarely have there been strong individuals who sought to exercise power *with* others. The breakthrough from political authoritarianism to political freedom occurred in the eighteenth century. A new nation emerged, dedicated to the proposition that all people are created equal and that they are free. Government was to be of the people, by the people, and for the people. In that climate of political freedom economic freedom also flourished. People were free to engage in the occupation of their choice. Consumers were free to choose and to consume anything they could afford. The United States became, and continues to be despite many problems, the nation in which the highest degree of freedom of choice prevails.

Economic Freedom in a Mixed Economy

The economy that has developed in the United States is best described by the word "mixed." It is an economy that combines unrestricted private enterprise, regulated private enterprise, private and public enterprise, and public enterprise. The combination works reasonably well to promote freedom of enterprise and freedom of choice. The complexities of economic life leave little room for completely unrestricted private enterprise. The owner of a store must have a license to sell milk, for example. The people, through their representative government, have imposed restrictions for the sake of their own welfare.

A large segment of the American economy may be described as "regulated private enterprise." The term "public utility" is descriptive and well known. Private firms are permitted to own and operate companies supplying electricity, gas, and transportation services. Complete or partial mo-

---

* An unmarried professor at a small college in a small community created a furor when he purchased a Cadillac. Townspeople talked; fellow faculty members were critical; and trustees objected to salary increases for a faculty whose members could afford Cadillacs! The professor soon sold his prestige car, even though he could well afford to own it.

nopolies are permitted in such fields because a single firm may provide the needed service more economically than two or more competing firms could. To protect consumers from monopoly prices, which would restrict their freedom of choice, state and federal government agencies regulate the quality of the service and the prices consumers pay.

Sometimes in a mixed economy the people prefer to permit private ownership of an enterprise operated by a public agency. More common is the type of enterprise owned by the public but operated by a private firm. An illustration of this would be the atomic energy industry.

Public ownership and operation are much more common in the United States than many people realize. Village, town, city, and county governments own and operate streets, water works, hospitals, airports, electric light and power plants, gas companies, housing, and transportation. They own and operate the public schools. They provide fire protection and police protection. Altogether local governments engage in some fifty such enterprises.

State governments engage in economic services such as the construction and maintenance of highways, hospitals, and penal and corrective institutions. They operate employment offices and liquor stores. They protect people and their property through law-enforcement; they provide education, medical care, and public health services.

The federal government is engaged in eighty-five economic operations ranging from surveillance of the purity of food and drugs to advertising. The property of citizens is protected and their lives insured. Consumers are protected against fraud by mail, and the sale of stocks and bonds is regulated. The federal government operates many businesses, from the Tennessee Valley Authority to the Government Printing Office.

FREEDOM OF CHOICE OR AUTHORITARIAN CONTROL?

In Which Direction Does Consumer Welfare Lie?

Just as parents guide the consuming activities of their children to promote their well-being, authoritarian officials might guide the "children" of the state. One can imagine such an economy dedicated to human welfare. A well-functioning system of authoritarian control might eliminate or at least reduce the waste found in a free-choice economy. Authoritarian control might serve consumers better — supplying them only with the goods and services conducive to individual and group welfare. The production of illth and nealth would be eliminated or reduced. Everyone would receive the basic necessities of life before being allowed to consume intoxicants, use narcotics, chew gum, or jump on a trampoline. With compulsory health care, quack health products and practices would disappear. There would be no need for advertising (but political propaganda would continue). Those in control presumably would not supply consumers with injurious drugs or adulterated foods, or obscene books, magazines, movies, or plays. In the absence of freedom of choice, there would be no market for bogus stocks or bonds. Candy and soft drinks might be taboo. High-pressure sales representatives, ambulance-chasing lawyers, and lobbyists would not be permitted to exploit consumers.

One might argue that in an economic system so well ordered and so dedicated to consumer welfare, consumers would have so many useful outlets for their energies that the various dissipations of the present system would be unnecessary. On the other hand, it might be argued that such a consumers' world would be so dull that its members would be compelled to seek release and excitement in dissipation. There is no point pursuing this argument, however, because such an ideal economy is beyond the reach and probably beyond the desire of consumers. Human beings the world over value freedom highly, often more than life itself. The continuing escapes and defections from communist countries illustrate the quest for freedom. People want the freedom to worship as they wish, or not to worship. They want freedom to govern themselves. They cherish the freedom to think, talk, and write as they choose. As consumers they want freedom to consume or refuse to consume whatever they desire. Many consumers place a higher value on freedom of choice than on their own welfare. If they must choose, there can be little doubt that they will choose freedom. To the extent that freedom of choice results in illfare rather than welfare, the problem is to find a way to economic welfare through freedom of choice. The task of the future is to educate consumers to make the best use of their freedom to choose.

QUESTIONS FOR REVIEW

1. What makes freedom of choice possible in the United States?
2. To what extent do you accept the concepts of wealth, nealth, and illth? What do you think these concepts add to your understanding of the economy?
3. Why do people continue to buy and use illth products when they are aware that they are illth?
4. How much money income do you think you need to be happy?
5. Do you consider your freedom to choose as positive or negative?
6. What are the conditions necessary for freedom of choice?
7. Can you think of restrictions on your freedom of choice that were not mentioned in this chapter?
8. What restrictions on your freedom of choice have you imposed on yourself?
9. What is a mixed economy?
10. What economic services are performed by your local government? By your state government?

11. Do you think consumer welfare is promoted better under authoritarian control, freedom of choice, or a combination of control and freedom?

PROJECTS

1. List five examples each of wealth, nealth, and illth.
2. Make a list of all the restrictions on your freedom of choice of which you are aware.
3. Ask your parents to tell you how World War II controls limited their freedom to choose.
4. Describe the ways in which the group or groups to which you belong restrict your freedom to choose.
5. Ask someone employed by a corporation in what ways, if any, his or her freedom to choose is restricted by corporate policy.
6. If you have served in the armed forces, write a report on the ways in which your freedom of choice was restricted.
7. Using the United States Government Organization Manual, prepare a list of the economic services performed by the federal government.

REFERENCES

1. Stewart M. Lee, "'Wealth,' 'Nealth,' and 'Illth' and the Responsibilities of the Consumer Educator," *Business Education World* 55, no. 4 (March–April 1975): 12.
2. David Riesman, *The Lonely Crowd* (New Haven: Yale University Press, 1950), pp. 22–23.
3. Leland James Gordon, *The Function of The Consumer In A Free Choice Economy* (Westport, Conn.: The Calvin K. Kazanjian Economics Foundation, 1958), p. 8.
4. John Gunther, *Taken At the Flood: The Story of Albert Lasker* (New York: Harper & Row, 1961), p. 173.

CHAPTER

CUSTOM-MADE WANTS

MEANING AND ORIGIN OF CUSTOMS

What Is Custom?

Customs are the long-established actions, conventions, practices, or usages that regulate the lives of a group of people. In consumer economics, *custom* is the tendency on the part of the *group* to consume according to a fixed pattern. *Habit* is a tendency on the part of an *individual* to consume in a fixed pattern. In a sentence, custom may be described as group habit.

In economic life, customary ways of consuming are transmitted from generation to generation. This is accomplished largely through the family by means of example and precept. This chain of transmittal results in control of economic choice by ancestors. The longer a custom prevails, the greater the aura of reverence surrounding it. Eventually customs acquire the force of law. If customs promote consumer welfare, they are good. But the development of new products and new services may be retarded by the heavy hand of custom. In that case custom may interfere with consumer welfare.

It is probable that many customs had their origin in utility. But once a custom becomes established, it may continue to control consumption long after the original justification for it has disappeared. The assertion that a custom originates and endures only because the populace desire it is based on an implied assumption that people are rational. People are not usually rational; individuals and groups represent a mixture of emotion and rationality, as amply illustrated in the literature of anthropology, psychology, and sociology.

Not many consumers are able or willing to disregard group customs. They may know that certain customs are silly and useless, but they hesitate to incur disapproval by flouting them. Anyone who violates custom too openly will be marked by the group as peculiar. If the violation is serious, the group has many ways of punishing offenders.

The power of custom is stronger in consuming activities than in occupational activities. Customary practices do develop in business firms. But in a dynamic economy competitors compel firms to abandon customary practices. The pioneer or the innovator in business is "smart," but the pioneer or innovator in consuming practices is labeled "eccentric."

One may find both good customs and bad customs in a group. The following discussion is intended to give the individual some basis on which to evaluate customs.

WHY DO CUSTOMS CONTINUE?

Inertia

Human nature is characterized by inertia. It requires positive action to experiment with new consumer products or services or to use familiar products or services in new ways. In business firms the prospect of monetary gain helps overcome inertia. But for consumers the prospect of greater satisfaction is too intangible to motivate them to change their habits.

Institutionalism

Group life is largely institutional, and institutions favor the establishment and continuance of customs. Social institutions such as the family, government, the church, and schools are essentially static. Once a group accepts monogamy or polygamy, democracy or communism, Christianity or Mohammedanism, compulsory free education or private schools, its consuming patterns are established. If changes do occur, they usually come slowly or as a result of a major upheaval, such as war.

Stratification

In every country people are grouped into classes. Politically there are liberals and conservatives; economically there are rich and poor; sociologically there are dominant and minority groups. Regardless of the basis of stratification those at the top enjoy a more abundant economic life than those in the lower classes. The favored ones can satisfy all their economic wants, and they can maintain the *status quo*. Because they fear that change may weaken their position or displace them, these small but powerful groups have a vested interest in the maintenance of customs that support the existing order.

Isolation

Whether isolation results from physical, political, racial, or linguistic barriers, the results are the same. Isolation perpetuates customs. Isolated groups are not exposed to new ideas or new practices. Until 1853 Japan was a closed country. Some of the customs that developed in the closed Japanese society became so firmly entrenched that they continue to influence the lives of those now living. In the free world the interchange of knowledge constantly challenges accepted customs. Air transportation has practically eliminated physical barriers to movement. Yet it is a curious fact that the beneficial effects of fast transportation and instantaneous communication are partially offset by the weapons of nationalism. The removal of a physical barrier is too often followed by the erection of an artificial political barrier, such as a tariff wall, a quota, or a ban on imports.

Racial distinctions are as old as mankind. When racial differences assume the force of prejudice, members of one group are isolated from other groups. In Europe, where some people live nearby yet speak different languages, their inability to converse freely operates as a barrier to the interchange of ideas. "Little Germanys" and "Little Italys" in large American cities illustrate the effects of linguistic isolation.

Private home life is a form of isolation that preserves custom. The family is a closely-knit unit whose consuming practices tend to become customary. These practices are transmitted from generation to generation, acquiring significance with each transmission. New consumer goods may be discovered, but families isolated in remote areas tend to be satisfied with the old familiar things. The power of custom, for example, in the selection and preparation of food is strong. A family is likely to have a nostalgic preference for certain dishes as mother or grandmother prepared them.

Illiteracy

In societies having high illiteracy, the power of the past prevails through customs and proverbs. Inability to read or write limits the experiences of groups to those attained by contact with family and neighbors. The only way a new idea can be communicated is by word of mouth. Illiteracy is often found in isolated geographic regions. Those who live in such isolation have little or no contact with the outside world. In these circumstances, customs change slowly, if at all.

WHAT CAUSES CUSTOMS TO CHANGE?

Communication

Radio and television have leaped the barriers of space, time, and illiteracy. In the most remote regions people can hear and see what is going on in the rest of the country and in other countries. Satellite communication has brought live news and entertainment to everyone having access to a receiving set. All people may not be able to read or write very well, but everyone can understand the spoken word and a picture. Simultaneous translation has broken the language barrier. Suddenly the world is one and it is smaller.

Transportation

In the United States the automobile has put people on wheels and made them mobile. Fifty years ago people did not have the time or money to travel. Now industries provide vacations with pay, making it possible for millions of people to broaden their horizons by taking the family on a summer trip. In their travels people see new sights and learn new ways of consuming.

Advertising

Using radio and television, advertisers have eliminated or weakened many customs. One of the functions of advertising is to tell people about new products and new services. Advertisers also tell prospective consumers of new ways to use known products. What the advertiser calls "sales resistance" is more likely to be resistance caused by custom. Most consumers have fun when they spend their money. They want the good things of life and advertisers help them break the shackles of custom.

Education

Formal education tends to break down customs. Even though the curriculum itself may be traditional, the educational process liberates people from the bondage of illiteracy. The free public school is an American institution. Children from remote regions are transported to a central school where they learn to read and write. Then they can read newspapers, magazines, and books. In the process their horizons are extended and the bonds of custom are weakened.

Competition

In a free economy competition among business firms results in new products, new services, and new ways of doing things. A competitive economy is a changing economy, and a changing economy challenges customs. Consumers no longer need to freeze in the winter or swelter in the summer. Industry has provided year-round air conditioning in workplaces, homes, and automobiles. The summer picnic with its flies and ants is giving way to the hygienic buffet out of the freezer and refrigerator, served in a cool and quiet house.

CUSTOMARY CONSUMPTION OF FOOD

Food Customs Vary Among Nations

Desire for food is a universal instinct. Food nourishes our bodies by supplying energy, by building and maintaining bodily structure, and by supplying necessary substances that regulate and coordinate life processes. No matter where one lives, certain minerals or inorganic elements are essential to life and health. These include iodine, iron, fluorine, sodium, potassium, calcium, phosphorus, and carbohydrates, fats, proteins, water, and six vitamins. Of the minerals required, only calcium, phosphorus, iron, and iodine are likely to be deficient in one's normal food consumption.

Food consumption is more than organically functional. The act of consuming food may be recreational and social. This is true of food eaten on festive occasions and also includes the evening meal and the Sunday dinner. It is customary to eat three meals a day. Breakfast may be hurried and lunch may be eaten wherever one is at the time, but the evening meal serves to bring many families together, not only to share the food but to share in conversation. The family dinner is an effective device for training children to eat properly. When guests are present, the consumption of food becomes a social function, a ceremony. Probably more people join together to enjoy food than for any other purpose. The food may be followed by speeches, by floor shows, by movies, by dancing, or by other forms of entertainment. When guests are entertained in the home, food sometimes becomes a means of demonstrating status.

These comments about the several purposes that food serves are applicable the world over. But the kinds of food eaten by people in the various nations are very different. Variations in national food customs depend, in part, on the foods available.

There is no society whose members deal rationally with food. Consumers do not select their foods on the basis of edibility, nutritional value, or easy availability. For example, in the United States, the flesh of dogs and horses is taboo. In South America, the flesh of the iguana is a choice morsel, but not in the United States or Europe. Toasted ants are a delicacy in Colombia, but frogs legs are rejected.[1]

Food Customs Vary Among Regions

In smaller countries food customs may be national in their influence. In larger nations, like China, Russia, or the United States, people in one region may consume and prefer foods that are very different from those consumed and preferred in other regions. In the United States people living on or near the seacoasts are likely to eat more seafood than those who live inland, although now that frozen seafood is available throughout the United States, this particular variation is disappearing. Boston housewives insist on brown-shelled eggs, while the women of New York insist on eggs whose shells are white. Boston brown bread is scarcely known by the white bread consumers of the Middle West or the cornbread devotees of the South.

Food Customs Vary Among Religions

A wide range of food products is avoided by consumers in many nations because of religious ideas concerning cleanliness and purity. In spite of the obvious food value of animal flesh, members of some religious groups refuse to eat it. In accordance with their views on the sanctity of life, the leaders in Buddhism and Hinduism demand vegetarian diets. The Hindu religion declares cattle to be sacred; they are not to be slaughtered, much less eaten. Pork is avoided by Muslims in the Middle East and by Orthodox Jews. Chicken and eggs are avoided in such diverse areas as Southeast Asia, some Pacific Islands, India, Tibet, Mongolia, and Africa because chicken bones are used for divining the future.[2]

Food Fads and Fashions

Odd and exotic foods appeal to some consumers. A fad among sophisticated consumers might develop into a custom. In some circles, Japanese fried grasshoppers are now a standard cocktail delicacy, to be consumed with a Russian Vodka stinger. French fried bees, fried ants, and chocolate-covered ants are among other popular delicacies.

Food Customs Are Acquired

Children should learn good food-consuming practices in the home and in the schools. Many of them do. But many do not. Later as adults they are subjected to the kind of advertising criticized by an official of the American Dairy Association who said that advertisements for dairy products should give accurate, dependable information because food advertising, together with advertising for vitamin pills and food supplements, is probably the leading source of information, good and bad, influencing food consumption and nutrition. Milk, for example, is not an elixir, but some advertisements have presented it as a cure-all and in so doing border on deception.

Sometimes parents compel children to eat a small portion of every dish on the table. Experiments have shown that repeated trials of previously rejected foods may lead one to develop a positive taste for them. Those who can and will experiment with various kinds of foods will find new gustatory delights. Moreover, the greater the variety of foods, the better the balance, and the better nourished you will be. To the extent that rationality replaces custom and habit in the choice of food, the area of freedom of choice is widened. The more an individual has traveled about the world, the longer the list of foods he or she is familiar with and whose pleasures are enjoyed.

CHANGING FOOD-CONSUMING CUSTOMS

New Food Customs for Old

Food-consuming customs do change. Counting infants, children, and old people, the average food consumption per person is 1,400 pounds a year. Two-thirds of that intake is water. This figure has scarcely changed in half a century, but the proportions of various kinds of foods consumed have changed. In the twenty year period ending in 1973, the average United States consumer ate more meat, poultry, fish, fats and oils, sweeteners, and processed fruits than ever before. In the same period fewer eggs and fresh potatoes, less flour and cereal products, and fewer fresh fruits and vegetables and dairy products were eaten. Consumption of processed vegetables was fairly constant.[3]

The inflationary food prices of the mid-1970s brought about some significant changes in food-consuming habits. The extreme increases in the price of sugar, in particular, found Americans buying and eating less sugar and products that used a lot of sugar, such as soft drinks, baked goods, and candy. The sale of convenience foods declined. Over one million new gardens were planted in 1975 in an attempt to offset the increasing costs of food.

Technological changes result in new food products and new ways of preparation and preservation. The frozen food industry continues to grow. We are on the verge of using atomic energy to increase the production of food and to preserve it. New chemicals improve the quality of foods and

During the mid-1970s many grocery stores asked their customers to limit their purchases of sugar. A worldwide shortage of raw sugar caused the price of sugar to increase by 400 percent in one year. (*UPI*)

preserve them better than refrigeration. To decrease the space taken up by supplies on atomic submarines, the Navy has developed specially processed foods that eliminate bulk and waste without sacrificing nutritional or taste value. The National Aeronautics and Space Administration has developed special foods for astronauts. These products, or variations of them, may very likely find their way into the food stores in the future. When they do, new food-consuming patterns will be established and present ones discarded.

An *analog* is something that is similar to something else but different in structure and origin. Increasing quantities of analogs of bacon, beef, milk, and cream are appearing in food stores. Surveys of housewives show increasing use of analogs. It is possible that sales of synthetic meat will account for 5 percent of total meat sales in the near future. Not only are analogs tasty and nutritious—they are less expensive than the products they replace. Synthetic milk, which fooled Arizona dairymen, cost 15 cents a quart, whereas cow's milk cost 35 cents.

In recent years there has been an increasing interest in "health foods" and so-called organically grown foods. There has been a reaction by many against the excesses in the processing of food, the many chemical additives, and the potentially hazardous preservatives. This interest has created a new demand for health foods, and manufacturers have responded by producing whole-wheat breads, granola, and other foods to satisfy this demand.

An increasing percentage of food store sales consists of convenience foods. These are the prepared, precooked food items that many people find so helpful in putting together a quick meal. Such foods are usually more expensive.

Changing food customs are not necessarily desirable. In spite of all that is known about the nutritional values of milk, green leafy vegetables, and fresh fruits, surveys of college students have shown deficiencies of such foods in their consuming patterns. High-school and college students have a tendency to eat between meals. They eat what they like, not necessarily what is good for them nutritionally. Between-meal items are often candy, cake, ice cream, cookies, sandwiches, or soft drinks.

FREEDOM OF CHOICE, FOOD CONSUMPTION, AND HEALTH

What Is Good Health?

The World Health Organization of the United Nations has declared that health is not merely the absence of disease or infirmity. It is a state of complete physical, mental, and social well-being. Total health exists when a person functions maximally as a physiological organism, as a thinking and feeling unit, and as part of the total social situation. Health is achieved by a well-balanced intake of food, adequate rest, and personal hygiene. In addition, good health requires a conscious development of self-discipline, to enable one to operate at maximum capacity within one's physical limitations.

Food and Health

Human life is sustained by oxygen, water, and food. We can live for only a moment without oxygen. The longest known survival without water is seventeen days. The body of a twenty-year-old male consists of 63 percent water, 20 percent proteins, 11 percent fat, and 6 percent minerals. At the same age, the body of a female consists of 57.5 percent water, 19 percent fat, 18 percent protein, and 5.5 percent minerals. Twenty years later, the water content of a male body drops to 57.5 percent, the percentage of fat increases to 19, the protein percentage declines to 18, and minerals constitute 5.5 percent. Comparable figures for 40-year-old females are: 48 percent water, 32 percent fat, 15.5 percent protein, and 4.5 percent minerals.[4] The amount of water we consume is controlled by a part of the brain called the _hypothalamus_. This operates like a thermostat to regular water intake.

There are two areas of the brain that operate as regulators of appetite. When more energy is needed, the feeding center is activated, leading to a sensation of hunger. In response to that sensation food is consumed. When enough food has been consumed to satisfy the energy requirements of the body, the satiety center is activated, telling one to stop eating. The sensation of hunger signals a real need for food. The current knowledge of body chemistry indicates that the hunger sensation is related to the amount of sugar available to the cells. The sensation of appetite is simply a desire for food—a desire associated with the psychological pleasures of taste and smell.

A person weighing 154 pounds "burns" 1,680 calories every 24 hours just to live. It takes that much energy to maintain body temperature and such vital processes as heartbeat, liver function, and respiration. This is the basic metabolic rate for a body at rest. An individual who engages in light activity needs 50 percent more calories. A _calorie_ is the amount of heat required to raise the temperature of a gram of water one degree centigrade. The heat, of course, is furnished by food, which functions as a fuel. The metabolic rate for women is lower than for men. After age 25 the calorie requirement diminishes. At middle age, adults need 5 or 10 percent fewer calories. The average adult in the United States derives 45 percent of his or her calories from carbohydrates, 40 percent from fats, and 15 percent from proteins.

Nutrition and Health

You are what you eat! Good nutrition is the basis for good health, body growth, and longevity. Preparation for an adequate old age begins with nutrition in infancy and continues through one's life.

At the beginning of the twentieth century, food was considered primarily as a fuel for supplying energy. Very little was known about nutrition.

In the last 50 years our knowledge of nutrition has advanced more than in all preceding centuries of recorded history. Yet the diets of American families have not improved with the increasing knowledge of nutrition. A wide variety of dietary changes have occurred since World War I. Our less physically active life has led to consumption of about 5 percent fewer calories, but the source of these calories (about 3,300 a day) is cause for some concern. Fat has increased from 32 to 52 percent of our caloric intake; carbohydrates have decreased from 56 to 46 percent; and protein has held fairly steady at 12 percent. Although the drop in total carbohydrate (starches such as potatoes, cereal grains, and sugars) consumption reflects decreased use of cereal products, a shift has occurred within the carbohydrate class itself. Before World War I only one-third of this class was consumed as sugar. Today over one-half comes from sugars, including refined sugars and those naturally present in food.[5] Many families are making poor choices from our food abundance. American families at all levels of income need guidance in meeting their nutritional requirements. The soaring price of sugar in 1974 encouraged many families to curtail their sugar consumption, and this, along with the use of sugar substitutes, helped to improve their nutrition, but increased sugar intake is still a problem.

It may surprise some readers to learn that, according to Senator Hollings, every survey shows that the poor are wiser than the affluent in their purchases of food.[6] In a nationwide survey it was found that about one-half of all U.S. households had adequate supplies of food meeting the Recommended Dietary Allowances of the Food and Nutrition Board for seven nutrients. Thirty percent of the households were rated as having fair diets, while twenty percent had poor diets that furnished less than two-thirds of the recommended seven nutrients.[7]

Good nutrition is achieved by the daily consumption of food that provides the nutrients body cells need for their health and functioning. It also involves the daily rejection of excess amounts of food. There is nothing sacred about eating three meals a day. Recent studies indicate that less fat will develop if daily food is consumed in several meals rather than in one large meal. Skipping breakfast or lunch or both and eating a big dinner is not a wise use of consumer freedom of choice.[8] Most special dietary foods are ineffective. They may even be detrimental, preventing the achievement of maximum health through well-balanced food consumption.[9]

HUNGER IN THE UNITED STATES

Although Americans have the most abundant food supply in the world and among the largest per capita incomes, many Americans are undernourished. In a 1969 Message to the Congress, the president said that the fact "that hunger and malnutrition should persist in a land such as ours is embarrassing and intolerable."

The Citizens' Board of Inquiry into Hunger and Malnutrition in the United States reported that "we have found concrete evidence of chronic hunger and malnutrition in every part of the United States where we have held hearings." Millions of people go without food for days each month. "To make four-fifths of a nation more affluent than any people in history, we have degraded one-fifth mercilessly."[10]

Undernutrition leads to a change in structure or function of cells because of a lack of one or more nutrients. Among the causes of undernutrition are lack of money, lack of knowledge, poor environment, living alone, fad diets, and absence of teeth with which to chew. (Some 97 percent of all persons develop cavities before reaching adulthood; 80 percent of those over fifteen suffer from some form of peridontal disease; and 26 million persons have lost all their teeth).[11]

Greater income and larger expenditures for food do not assure good diets. "Education and motivation are needed too."[12] The Peruvian Indians were long thought to be hereditarily small, but when children were given an adequate diet they grew to normal size.[13] The postwar generations of Japanese are taller, heavier, and healthier because they eat less rice and more milk and vegetables.

The United States Department of Agriculture (USDA) conducted a survey of food consumption in 1965 and reported that only 50 percent of American households had good diets, as compared to 60 percent in 1955. In 1965 there was a higher percentage of poor diets—20 percent compared to 15 percent in 1955. The president has declared 280 counties to be hunger areas. The direct relationship between income and quality of diet is shown in Table 5-1.

TABLE 5-1.   Quality of U.S. Diets by Income

	Good %	Fair %	Poor %
under $3,000	37	27	36
$3,000–$4,999	43	33	24
$5,000–$6,999	53	29	18
$7,000–$9,999	56	32	12
$10,000 & over	63	28	9

Source: Service: USDA's Report to Consumers, U.S. Department of Agriculture, Office of Information, March 1968. Note: The USDA expects to update these studies in 1979.

OVEREATING IN THE UNITED STATES

It has been estimated that as many as one-half of adult consumers in the United States are overweight. The Basal Metabolic Rate (BMR) is the amount of energy needed to maintain the continuing processes of life. BMR varies with body size, composition, age, and hormonal factors. One of the chief causes of excess weight is physical inactivity coupled with overeating. Unfortunately, we do not have an automatic control over our food intake. A USDA survey found that 16 percent of men in the twenty to thirty-four age group eat or drink six times or more a day. The White House

Conference on Food, Nutrition and Health declared that we have developed a society characterized by overconsumption of calories, with less than wise food choices, considering the nutritional information available. At the same time we have become more sedentary. The propensity to overeat results from social influence, advertising, frustration, boredom, and loneliness. When overeaters become fat, they are preyed on by commercial interests and encouraged to resort to fad diets.

Obesity impairs health and can kill. Food intake in excess of caloric requirements results in an accumulation of body fat. When a person eats more than he or she needs, the extra calories are converted to fat, which is stored in the adipose tissue. This is the one tissue that has practically unlimited stretch capacity. Half of the body fat is stored in the abdominal area. "The longer the belt line, the shorter the life line."[14] In individuals who are 20 percent above average weight, the mortality rate increases by 20 percent to 25 percent. The probability of heart attack is double. After the age of forty a person who is 10 percent over normal weight runs the risk of higher incidence of degenerative arthritis, varicose veins, gall bladder disease, hernia, diabetes, cardiovascular diseases, hypertension, and pulmonary disfunction.

The Council of Better Business Bureaus reported that because food is bound up with emotional satisfaction, reward and punishment, and in some cases with a kind of withdrawal from reality, there are enough customers for "fat melters" in the United States to make the production and sale of pills and esoteric diets very worthwhile for the producers. This business yields a profit of more than $100 million a year.[15]

The ordinary case of obesity can be cured by eliminating bad eating habits and by regular exercise. The key to weight control is to reduce one's intake of high calorie foods, fats, and carbohydrates. There is no other effective method of weight control. A daily twenty-minute walk at moderate speed will take off five pounds in six months, if one does not change food intake or other activities. A laboratory test in which rats were used showed that food-intake restriction alone reduced body weight 24 percent; exercise alone reduced body weight only 10 percent; but a combination of restricted food intake plus exercise reduced body weight 30 percent.[16] There is no evidence that manipulative machines or drugs have any effect on the distribution of fats. There are no over-the-counter drugs to help obesity, and prescription drugs are limited in effectiveness. Fraudulent operators cater to peoples' hopes that they can reduce their weight and still eat all the food they want. Calories do count and fad diets are ineffective. The use of such powerful drugs as thyroid extract, digitalis, and amphetamines, barbiturates, and prednisone is so ineffective and dangerous that the Food and Drug Administration has removed them from the market.

FOOD FACTS AND FALLACIES

"Probably most everyone holds some idea about a food that is not true. . . ." "No single food is essential to health."[17] As long as people think there is some magic shortcut to health, there will be those who prey on their weaknesses. Deluding people into believing that cancer, diabetes, arthritis, and other serious diseases can be cured by diet "is fraud of the worst possible sort."[18] By the clever use of words related to nutrition, some sellers are able to distort the facts so as to promote sales. "The medicine men of earlier times are still with us in the form of psuedo-scientists promoting products ranging from overrated foods at exorbitant prices to books the authors hope will make the best-seller list and line their pockets with big dollars."[19]

In an effort to combat widely held fallacies concerning food and nutrition, the American Dietetic Association published a thirty-four page pamphlet citing the facts about thirty-eight such fallacies. Here are some sample fallacies: so-called "organic" meats and poultry are safer sources of protein than regularly produced meat; white eggs are more nutritious than brown; raw eggs are better for you than cooked; oysters, raw eggs, and rare or raw meat increase sexual potency; fish is a brain food; our food supply is so deficient in vitamins that everyone needs vitamin concentrates; the nutritive value of foods raised on "depleted" soil is poor; foods sprayed with chemical pesticides are slowly poisoning us.

Who is to blame for the prevalence of these fallacies? According to one view we teach nutrition by fear. Also laws are inadequate and difficult to enforce, and so advertisers are able to communicate half-truths to millions of consumers. Many of the fallacies fall in the area of folklore handed down from generation to generation.

No one needs detailed knowledge of nutrition in order to eat properly. The basics of good nutrition are easily found in books and pamphlets in the nearest library. City, state, and federal governments provide pamphlets that inform consumers of current and recent developments in nutritional research. Single copies of *Nutritive Values of Foods* are available free from the Office of Communication, U.S. Department of Agriculture, Washington, D.C. 20250. This publication gives the nutritive values for household measures of 615 foods, a table showing the yield of cooked meat, and a table showing the recommended dietary allowances for individuals. It was prepared by nutrition experts in the USDA Agricultural Research Service. Armed with a working knowledge of good nutrition, consumers find greater enjoyment in their food because they know that while they are eating they are also building strong bodies and a high order of mental alertness.

Food and Nutrition

Nutrition researchers have made the following findings:

1. Grain products should provide the bulk of nourishment for most people. They are most helpful when eaten as whole grain or partly whole-grain products.
2. Mature legumes and nuts are rich in protein and thiamine.
3. Potatoes, especially sweet potatoes, are high in Vitamin A.

4. Green and yellow vegetables are rich in Vitamin A, and salad greens are rich in Vitamin C.
5. Citrus fruits and tomatoes are excellent sources of Vitamin C.
6. Other fruits and vegetables contribute to our vitamin needs and to the general balance of minerals. A good diet will include nine to eleven servings a week.
7. Milk and milk products, except butter, are the most important sources of calcium and riboflavin. They are also sources of protein.
8. Meat, fish, poultry, and eggs are basic sources of animal proteins. However, milk, cheese, soybeans, and peanuts are more economical sources.
9. Most people consume more carbohydrates than they need.
10. Sugar is another product that many people consume in excess. It would be better to secure our sugar intake in the form of fruit. Not only does fruit supply sugar but it adds to mineral and vitamin intake.

The United States Department of Agriculture recommends the food plan for good nutrition shown in Table 5-2.

This brief discussion of nutrition and health may be concluded by citing a source of authoritative and abundant information. The pamphlet *Con-*

TABLE 5-2. A Food Plan for Good Nutrition (Quantities for One Week)

Kinds of Food	Children Age 7 to 12	Women All Ages*	Men All Ages*
Leafy, green and yellow vegetables	½ to ¾ lbs.	¾ lb.	¾ lb.
Citrus fruits and tomatoes	2½ lbs.	2½ lbs.	2½ to 3 lbs.
Potatoes	1½ to 2 lbs.	1 to 1½ lbs.	2 to 3 lbs.
Other vegetables and fruits	6½ to 7½ lbs.	5 to 7½ lbs.	7 to 9 lbs.
Milk, cheese, and ice cream	6 to 6½ qts.	3½ quarts	3½ quarts
Meat, poultry, and fish	3 to 4 lbs.	4 to 4½ lbs.	5 to 5½ lbs.
Eggs	7 eggs	6 eggs	7 eggs
Dry beans, peas, and nuts	2 ounces	2 to 4 ounces	4 ounces
Cereals, flour, and baked goods (whole-grain or enriched)	2 to 3 lbs.	2 to 2½ lbs.	3 to 4 lbs.
Fats, oils	¾ lb.	½ lb.	¾ to 1 lb.
Sugar, syrups, and preserves	¾ lb.	½ to 1 lb.	1 to 1½ lbs.

* The smaller of the two quantities listed is for the age group over 55 years.
Source: Family Fare, Human Nutrition Research Branch, Agricultural Research Service, U.S. Department of Agriculture, Home and Garden Bulletin no. 1, pp. 14–15. (See also *Consumers All,* USDA Yearbook, 1965, p. 394.)

sumer Information, in the latest edition, is available free from Consumer Information, Public Documents Distribution Center, Pueblo, Colorado 81009. Along with a listing and annotation of a variety of government consumer publications, it includes about forty pamphlet listings under the heading of "Food." These pamphlets deal with food buying, preparation and storage, diet and nutrition, and vitamins and minerals. The pamphlets are either free or less than one dollar. The homemaker who makes use of these pamphlets will have information that will be helpful in making intelligent and rational purchases of food.

Don't Waste Food!

As a nation, the United States has an abundance of good food. Not many people know what it is to be really hungry. Too many people eat too much food, and many people waste too much food. It is estimated that every day on the average a household throws away food containing 200 calories. This amounts to 7 or 10 percent of all the calories in a household food supply. Some of the discarded food is fed to animals or used for nonfood purposes, but much of it is wasted. This waste reduces the 2,600 calories per person per day in the food supplies in city groups to 2,300 or 2,400. The greatest loss is in edible meat, poultry, fish, and milk products.[20]

CLOTHING CUSTOMS

Why Do We Wear Clothing?

Human beings are the only animals that have created and wear clothing. There is no known human group that does not wear clothing, ornaments, or body decorations. Throughout history people in different cultures have done various things to their bodies, such as cutting their hair or shaving it off, clipping their teeth, painting and tatooing their skin, piercing the ear lobes and nose, and hanging bracelets on the neck, arms, and ankles.[21]

Decisions as to whether to wear clothing, and if so how much and what kinds, are made largely by the group rather than by individuals. Since the conditions of life are similar for all members of a group, members become aware of certain needs not by imitation or by conscious decision but by group influence. Custom lies behind consumer choice for clothing. But what lies behind custom? Why do people wear any clothing? Why do costumes vary among groups? Any attempt to explain the use of clothing on the basis of physical need alone would be futile. And if utility alone were the guide, one would assume that in a given climate certain articles of dress would possess greatest utility, leading to their universal use. But this is not the case. Thoreau wrote that in choosing clothing "perhaps we are led

oftener by the love of novelty and a regard for the opinions of men, in pro-
curing it, than by a true utility."[22]

When we turn to anthropologists, sociologists, and psychologists for
an answer to the first question, we find several explanations. The anthro-
pologist Sumner held the view that "things were first hung on the bodies
as amulets or trophies, that is, for superstition or vanity, and that the body
was painted or tatooed for superstition or in play. The notion of ornament
followed."[23] Savages lying in ashes, dust, sand, or mud for warmth or
coolness discovered that protective layers guarded them from heat, cold,
and insects. The utility of certain attachments to the body was thus discovered. The prevalence of superstition led to copying by other members of
the group, thus developing group costumes. Any variations from these
clothing customs involved group reprisal, which few had the courage to
risk.

Others explain the origin of clothing as the result of imitativeness. In
those countries inhabited by fur-bearing animals, human beings discovered
the warmth and protection yielded by animal skins. In skinning trophies of
the hunt preparatory to eating, primitive humans may have experimented
by placing themselves inside the animal covering. When they found it
satisfactory, others imitated the practice and a custom based on original
utility was established.

The fact that clothing is not universally worn for the sake of modesty is
demonstrated by its total absence among some people. Experiments and
observation of results following the introduction of clothing among such
groups seem to justify the conclusion that clothing is not a result of shame,
but rather a cause. Among Christian women modesty requires covering the
greater part of the body except the face, but among most Moslem women
the face must also be covered.

Of all animals we are the most completely naked. This lack of a protective covering led us to supplement nature. For human beings clothing helps
to distinguish one person from another. At the same time clothing hides our
bare bodies, so that we partially resemble the people around us.[24] It is quite
possible that neither warmth nor modesty is a very important consideration
in the choice of clothing worn by most people. The well-dressed person of
today, psychologically speaking, wears clothing that gives security and
brings recognition, response, and new experiences.

A study of four thousand years of clothing history led Lawrence Langner
to the conclusion that clothing (including decorations such as jewels, furs,
and cosmetics) performs the functions of protecting the body, ornamenting
it, indicating rank and status, and stimulating sexual interest. Langner's
general thesis is that the human race has an inferiority complex and seeks
superiority in various ways, including the decoration of the body. According
to this thesis, the differences in clothing between males and females
developed from the wish of the males to assert superiority over females and
to hold them in their service.

In recent years there have been major changes in women's clothing
styles. Much of the change has been toward more casual and comfortable

clothing—an almost "anything goes" attitude toward the type of clothing worn. Slacks and the pants suit have become proper dress for almost any occasion. There are fewer and fewer places where men are required to wear suits and ties. Some fashion designers have attempted to develop a "unisex" look—a dress style that is similar for both men and women.

Pursuing the theme of superiority, Langner develops his theory that without the invention of clothing, with all its subsequent psychological consequences, civilization could not have progressed as far as it has. "It is clothes that make it possible for governments to obtain obedience, religion reverance, judiciaries a respect for law, and armies discipline," for the phrase "clothed with authority" actually means that clothing is an evidence of authority.[25]

Society has established standards of acceptable behavior, and we either conform or rebel. In either case clothing plays an important role. This is illustrated by the relatively staid clothing of the solid middle class in contrast to the often exotic clothing of the counter-culture. When dressed in a nonconformist style, people are advertising their desire to be different.

From these explanations of the reasons for wearing clothes, we may conclude that in the past clothing was adopted primarily as a means of protection. Its continued use is also to be explained, in large part, by its ability to protect the wearer. For example, much clothing is chosen to meet occupational requirements. Since 1900 the clothing worn by American workers has changed more than in any preceding period. The distinction between blue-collar and white-collar workers has almost disappeared. Probably the single most important reason for this change was the invention of synthetic fibers. Today all workers, manual and clerical, dress better and more comfortably than before, yet they spend a smaller percentage of their incomes on clothing. The functional clothing of earlier days has given way to the functional clothing of a nation centrally heated in winter and air-conditioned in summer—in houses, offices, factories, automobiles, trains, planes, restaurants, and theaters. The weight of winter suiting has dropped from sixteen ounces per yard of fifty-eight inches width to twelve ounces, and the weight of summer suiting has dropped from thirteen to ten ounces.[26]

In addition to the protective function of clothing, we must recognize the influence of individual and group concepts of beauty. Such concepts are reflected in harmony, color, and line. These decorative functions of clothing are considered more fully in a discussion of fashion in Chapter 8.

Variations in National Costumes

An interesting feature of the custom of wearing clothing is the development of a distinctive national dress. The main influences affecting national costume are religion, royalty, fashion, and war. The dress of Turkish people illustrated, until recently, a strong religious influence. The brimless fez (or hat) was worn to enable a devout Muslim to remain covered in the mosque and yet permit touching the forehead to the floor while praying.

Full-seated trousers were designed to permit the wearer to sit with legs crossed, while the slipperlike shoe could be easily removed upon entering the mosque.

The influence of royalty on national costumes was more pronounced in the past than it is at present. Under the leadership of Edward III Englishmen discarded long hampering robes for what was regarded as the more satisfactory dress of that period. The influence of royalty may be seen operating negatively through the once-numerous laws regulating the type of dress for different classes. In prewar Japan the clothing that people wore was regulated according to their inherited rank.[27]

The influence of war is apparent in the changing uniforms of military personnel. Serviceability, comfort, and camouflage have become increasingly important features. The influence of a long war and of changes in military uniform are often reflected in civilian costumes. Now we are in the space age and astronauts wear specialized, functional clothing.

After the two world wars there was a trend toward the adoption—by people all over the world—of western or American-style clothing. The colorful costumes to be seen at the United Nations are most often worn by representatives of the newer nations. Men and women from Europe, the Middle East, South America, and the Far East usually wear western-style clothing. The distinctive and beautiful clothing worn so long in Austria, Holland, Japan, Italy, and the Scandinavian nations, to mention only a few, has for the most part disappeared in everyday use. It is probable that in no case was the new costume superior to the one displaced in its ability to protect and decorate the wearer. A psychological explanation may be the wish to emulate the dress of nations that had achieved unprecedented economic progress. Perhaps the feeling prevailed in many countries, as it did in Turkey under the influence of its leaders, that the old costume was a mark of inferiority that set off the wearer as a member of an economically backward group. Strong pressure had to be used to break down the influence of religion and custom in national dress. The same forces that operate on individuals to secure conformity to group practice were apparently at work to secure conformity to the practices of larger and more economically powerful groups.

Ceremonial and Sports Clothing

Academic gowns, judicial robes, and the vestments of the clergy do not protect the wearers. There is no vestige of utility in such garb. In warm weather it is uncomfortable. Its only apparent purpose is that of setting the wearer off as a member of a prestigious group.

The influence of sports on clothing is a comparatively modern development. What we put on or take off to participate in a particular sport is a matter of serious concern to the group. When boys go fishing they simply get a pole, line, hook, and some worms. For their elders, however, custom demands that they first visit a sporting-goods store to secure a complete and approved outfit. From elaborate reel to wading boots, no detail is over-looked.

When country boys want to ride a horse, they emulate their ancestors by mounting a bareback animal. But to the urban or suburban dweller that is not riding. To be a proper horseman or horsewoman, the rider must have a riding habit made of the best materials, supplemented with genuine leather boots and an elaborate saddle.

Bathing costumes have passed through interesting cycles—from the days when men and women entered the water almost entirely clothed to the beach costume of today, obviously designed to expose the maximum legal limit of nakedness.

Whether at the seashore, in the mountains, or on the ranch; whether playing baseball, tennis, hockey, or golf; whether skiing, sailing, or hunting, the group requires that the participant be clothed in the approved manner. The costume may be ugly, stupid, useless, or expensive, but it is a coura-geous individual who will flout group authority by refusing to go along. As a result, the area of individual freedom of choice is restricted. Millions of dollars are spent on clothing, not because purchasers have an original desire for it but because the group demands conformity.

Vestiges of Former Customs

Why do vestiges of customs persist that have almost or entirely lost their original significance? Why do men wear trousers and women skirts? Why do men wear collars and ties, while women expose the neck? Why do men wear heavy felt hats and caps, while women wear fragile hats or no hat at all? Why does either sex wear any headdress at all? Why do men's coats have lapels and buttons on the sleeves? Why do men's coats button on the right, while those of women button on the left? Why do the trousers of men's business suits have cuffs, while it is considered improper to have cuffs on the trousers of formal evening clothes? Explanations may be found for some of these customs if one traces the development of group costumes sufficiently far back. Clothing is an area of our lives that is strongly in-fluenced by the customs of our culture and our reference group.

QUESTIONS FOR REVIEW

1. Do you agree that "not many consumers are able or willing to disregard group customs"? Give some reasons why this might be true.

2. Do you think the power of custom is as strong now as it was in the past? What forces are at work to bring about changes?

3. "There is no society whose members deal rationally with food." Do you think this is true?

4. Do your religious beliefs influence your consuming practices? If so, how?

5. To what extent is your selection of food influenced by custom?

6. "Increasing quantities of analogs are appearing in food stores." What does this mean? What is your reaction?

7. How prevalent is hunger in the United States? How does real hunger affect consumers?

8. "It has been estimated that as many as one-half of the adult consumers in the United States are overweight." Why? What are the results?

9. What is the key to weight control?

10. In terms of food consumption and health, how wisely do you use your freedom of choice?

11. "Probably most everyone holds some idea about a food that is not true." Cite some examples.

12. What is the meaning and significance of the phrase "clothed with authority"?

13. Why do you wear the clothing you wear to a formal party? For a job interview?

14. To what extent are you really free to choose the food you eat? The clothing you wear?

PROJECTS

1. If you have traveled abroad, write a paper describing your observations concerning differences in food consumption and differences in clothing.

2. Prepare a list of foods you consider to be repulsive; why do you reject them?

3. Choose three foods that you have never eaten. Whenever you can in the next three months, eat one or all of those foods. Then write a report on your experience and your conclusions.

4. If you are a person who experiments with exotic foods, describe the most interesting type of food you have discovered.

5. Keep account of the number of times you eat between meals in the next two weeks. Keep a record also of what you eat, why, and the amount of money spent. Draw some conclusions about your food-consuming habits from this data.

6. Describe and analyze the differences in customs in terms of food and/or clothing between your generation and your parents' generation.

REFERENCES

1. Marston Bates, *Gluttons and Libertines: Human Problems of Being a Naturalist* (New York: Random House, 1967), pp. 21, 23, 50; Mark Graubard, *Man's Food: Its Rhyme or Reason* (New York: The Macmillan Company, 1943), p. 93; F. S. Bodenheimer, *Insects as Human Food* (The Hague: W. Junk, 1951), pp. 7, 29. For additional illustrations of food choices among nations see Corinne H. Robinson, *Fundamentals of Normal Nutrition* (New York: The Macmillan Company, 1968), pp. 228–235.
2. Frederick J. Simoons, *Eat Not This Flesh: Food Avoidances in the Old World* (Madison: University of Wisconsin Press, 1961), chaps. 1–6.
3. Stephen Hiemstra, *Food Consumption, Prices, Expenditures*, U.S. Department of Agriculture Economic Research Service, Agriculture Economic Report 138, July 1968, pp. 56–57; and Supplement for 1973 to Agriculture Economic Report 138, p. 15.
4. Olaf Mickelson, *Nutrition, Science and You* (Englewood Cliffs, N.J.: Scholastic Book Services, 1964), p. 96.
5. Marilyn G. Stephenson, "The Changing Food Supply," *FDA Consumer* 8, no. 8 (Oct. 1974): 4–8.
6. Ernest F. Hollings, *The Case Against Hunger: A Demand for a National Policy* (New York: Cowles Book Company, 1970), p. 166.
7. Faith Clark, "A Scorecard On How We Americans Are Eating," in Rudolph Wurlitzer and Will Corry, *Food For Us All* (New York: Universal Publishing, 1970), p. 267.
8. Mickelson, p. 119.
9. *Ibid.*, p. 118.
10. Citizens' Board of Inquiry into Hunger and Malnutrition in the United States, *Hunger, U.S.A.* (Boston: Beacon Press, 1968), pp. 4, 16.
11. Robinson, pp. 415, 424, 434.
12. *Toward the New: A Report on Better Foods and Nutrition from Agricultural Research* (Washington, D.C.: Government Printing Office, 1970), p. 4.
13. Dale R. Lindsey, "Nutritional Considerations in Foods," *Food Drug Cosmetic Law Journal* 25 (1970): 40.
14. Robinson, p. 393.
15. *Be a Better Buyer*, Council of Better Business Bureaus, Washington, D.C., June 1975, p. 1.
16. *Toward the New*, p. 15.
17. Robinson, pp. 413, 415.
18. *Ibid.*
19. *Food Facts Talk Back* (Chicago: The American Dietetic Association, 1974), p. 2.
20. Sayde F. Adelson, et al., "Discard of Edible Food in Households," *Journal of Home Economics* 55 (1963): 638.
21. Bates, pp. 15–16.
22. *How American Buying Habits Change* (Washington, D.C.: U.S. Department of Labor, 1959), p. 127.
23. William Graham Sumner, *Folkways* (Boston: Ginn & Company, 1907), p. 429.
24. Ernest Dichter, *Handbook of Consumer Motivations: The Psychology of the World of Objects* (New York: McGraw-Hill, 1964), p. 78.
25. Lawrence Langner, *The Importance of Wearing Clothes* (New York: Hastings House, 1959), p. xiv.
26. *How American Buying Habits Change*, pp. 127, 131, 133, 141.
27. See Ruth Benedict, *The Chrysanthemum and the Sword: Patterns of Japanese Culture* (Boston: Houghton Mifflin, 1946).

CEREMONIAL CUSTOM-MADE WANTS

CEREMONIAL CUSTOMS

Events to Celebrate

Ceremonies are elaborate ways of satisfying important emotional needs. The primary events in life are birth, coming of age, marriage, and death. Each of these events is significant for individuals and for society, and ceremonial practices have developed to mark them. Birthdays, coming-out parties, weddings, and funerals are memorable ceremonial events. Secondary ceremonials center around graduation from high school and graduation from college. Tertiary ceremonials include induction into a church, a lodge, a fraternity, or a sorority. As an individual goes through life, there are other ceremonials marking his or her achievements, such as the awarding of honorary degrees and testimonial dinners.

All ceremonial events could be ignored, but life would be drab and dull without them. Through the years consumers spend a great deal of money celebrating various events and achievements. Their motivation is a matter of interest to psychologists and sociologists. The amount of money they spend attracts the interest of economists. Those who have ceremonial supplies and services for sale like to see consumers celebrate lavishly, without considering the cost.

DISPOSING OF THE DEAD

Human Beings Face the Unknown

The psalmist has written: "What man shall live and not see death?" Since death is inevitable, it is an event that commands universal concern. What lies beyond death? No one knows. Because no one knows, death instills awe, fear, superstition, or hope, according to the individual. Many people who have not found the meaning of life cringe at the thought of death. Some people contemplate death in a cavalier, almost flippant, way. Some are fatalistic, and many who are religious are hopeful. Most religions are based on a belief in the immortality of the human soul. Limited by the world in which they live, many people think of immortality as the resurrection of the body in identical physical form. Such people are willing to spend considerable sums of money to preserve the human body as long as possible.

When a person dies it is the responsibility of the family to arrange for burial. At such a moment many people discover that they have no real freedom of choice. The method of disposing of the body is prescribed by their religion, their lodge, and their community.

Practices vary among religions. An Orthodox Jew is given a starkly simple burial service. The body is not embalmed; there is no viewing at the services; there are no flowers and no music. The entire service is unostentatious.

Early Christians adopted equally simple practices. Burial was a communal ceremony. The body was laid out with lights around it. It was sprinkled with holy water and incense, and a cross was placed on the chest or the hands were folded on the chest. The body was buried in consecrated ground, with no coffin. White was the mourning color, although mourning was discouraged. In lieu of embalming, early Christians used spices and perfumes to counteract the odor of decay. Non-Christians disapproved of this practice because they considered it wasteful to use expensive ointments on the dead, which the survivors could use to better advantage. Burial was delayed at least eight hours, but not more than twenty-four. During that time one of the bereaved kept watch in case there might be signs of life. There was a common fear of being buried alive. Cemeteries were often on a hillside, where sepulchres were hewn out of solid rock. The catacombs in Rome contain the bones of many early Christians.[1]

The simplicity of early funerals eventually gave way to pomp and display. In the American colonies funerals had three functions: sociability, religiosity, and reaffirmation of the social status of the deceased. The latter led to extravagant burial practices which were deplored by the Puritans, who in the Massachusetts Colony passed a law in an effort to prevent excess and vain expenditures for burial and mourning.[2]

According to Fulton and Geis, attitudes toward death in the United States today are in a state of change. Urbanization and secularization of society have brought about changes in prevailing burial practices. The growth of retirement cities removes the aged from our midst. As a result the younger members of this generation do not experience the grief and anguish of death as directly as did their forebears.[3]

"The traditional belief in immortality of the soul does not seem to provide men with a sense of resource against the threat of death."[4] "There is a strong need in most of us to flee from the reality of death."[5] "Our rituals and ceremonies are characterized by a powerful flight from its presence."[6] Funeral practices are evasive because survivors feel a sense of inadequacy in the face of death. Our attempts to evade the reality of it through funeral practices are pathetic. Death is an event of such immensity that it is greater than our resources for coping with it. The rituals of today reflect disenchantment with church ceremonies. The attempt to cover up the reality of death is a disaster for the church; ministers avoid the subject in their preaching.[7] In a church-dominated age undertakers could not usurp control over funerals as they have in the secular city.

A completely different attitude toward death is envisioned by R. P. Arvio.[8] He describes a future society in which the bodies of the dead are used to benefit the living. They are put to use as needed body-part replacements and the remains processed into fertilizer, thus contributing to the life of others in a world threatened by international shortages of food. The threat of worldwide starvation will have forced society to rethink the whole death process. Speedy, useful, efficient, and inexpensive disposal of the dead will have replaced the elaborate, expensive ceremonies of the past — with a memorial service of friends of the deceased planned for a few days after death. This, says Arvio, is the alternative to our current attitude toward death, which has resulted in exploitation of the living.

> Our historic unwillingness to look at our death practices has contributed to the development of a multi-billion dollar industry, a private-profit, sales-and-service enterprise whose unchallenged preemption of an entire field of service may be unparalleled in human experience. Seldom have so few exploited so many, with so few critics and reformers, from either within or without.[9]

In present-day society the business ethic has partially displaced religion in the funeral service. Except for the reading of the Bible and the eulogy, which is the responsibility of the clergy, the modern-day funeral director is prepared to assume all activities associated with death. He finds himself in a dilemma. Survivors who have no theology to sustain them encourage him to disguise the reality of death. At the same time, as a businessman, he is impelled to call attention to his special service. "Thus he both blunts and sharpens the reality of death."[10] The bluntness stresses death; the made-up corpse in a slumber room denies the reality of death. In rejecting the reality of death, modern society embraces all the accouterments of the burial service and the grave, including artificial grass. Paul E. Irion calls attention to the avoidance pattern of modern funerals, which try to create the illusion of life and minimize the personal involvement of the survivors.[11]

"A successful funeral in any culture, in any society, in any religion — is the one that provides a dignified setting in which the bereaved can comfortably carry out their grief in a manner appropriate to the culture, the society, and the religion."[12] A funeral is a ceremony that disposes of the body of the deceased, helps the survivors adjust, and publicly acknowledges and commemorates the death. At the same time it demonstrates the viability of the group.[13] Another writer expresses the view that the funeral service is important for the survivors. It is "personal in its focus and is societal in its consequences."[14]

Death is a rite of passage not only for the deceased but for the survivors also. All those involved — the living and the dead — assume new roles, and funeral ceremonies are affected by this fact. "Funerals announce to the community that the bereaved are now in a new and unaccustomed status."[15] Funerals serve a function in keeping the community intact.

The secularization of the funeral service was summarized in a book sponsored by the National Funeral Directors Association (NFDA). The authors of that book wrote that it is the common consensus in the United States that the dead deserve professional service from a lay occupational group. That service includes embalming, preparation for viewing, and provision of a casket that is attractive and that will protect the remains. Convention demands burial in the earth. Finally, the bereaved must be satisfied "that they are acting in accord with their means."[16] Yet an opinion poll among the clergy revealed that 23 percent of the Protestant clergy and Catholic priests who were interviewed believed that "the funeral director takes advantage of his position for personal gain."[17]

Burials as a Business—Demand

The funeral industry defies economic analysis. Is it a business or is it a profession? More than most business firms, funeral directors operate within the limits of religion and custom. The demand is constant and the supply is fixed. There are nearly two million funerals a year. These are divided among 22,000 funeral firms. There is practically no free entry into the industry and there is no free market. Prospective buyers are normally in a state of shock. They do not shop around, nor do they bargain for lower prices. Because of the excess capacity there is a strong tendency to maintain prices. Prices are not based on cost and there is no marginal pricing. In many markets the price is what the traffic will bear. In most markets it is a customary price. The Federal Trade Commission staff estimated that consumers are paying some $2 billion a year for funeral services. Inclusion of the cost for flowers, cemetery fees, and other related charges brings the overall bill to about $4.2 billion, or an average of $2,000 a funeral.[18]

How do prospective buyers of funeral services make their choices? Hardly any of them have ever given thought to the purchase of a funeral service. Confronted with the need, they turn to other members of the family or to their friends. Rarely do they ask a member of the clergy for a recommendation. Sometimes they have no choice because there is only one funeral director in town.

Burials as a Business—Supply

Funeral directors have been described as ceremonial producers who stage a performance and see to it that the participants play their parts, that properties are provided, and that all arrangements are made. They are private enterprisers willing to do the unclean and distasteful job of preparing dead bodies for burial. As embalmers they close the staring eyes and gaping mouth and reinforce the dead muscles. As cosmeticians they perform the last toilette. All these services are rendered to soften the horror and the revulsion felt by the survivors. And for these services they collect a fee.[19]

The average number of funerals a year for all firms surveyed by the National Funeral Directors Association was 135, but 50 percent of the firms averaged only 5 funerals a month. At the other extreme, 9 percent of the firms averaged 411 funerals a year. Thirty-six percent of the firms are individual proprietorships. It might be more accurate to describe them as family firms that have been in the business for many years. Of the total firms, 13 percent are organized as partnerships, and 51 percent as corporations.

The average funeral firm has approximately $185,000 invested in buildings, equipment, and land. The range is from $117,000 for small firms having fewer than 100 funerals a year to $453,000 for large firms having more than 300 funerals a year. The average investment for a normal adult service is $1,574.[20]

As a service rather than a product industry the funeral industry has no national market. It consists of a composite of local markets characterized by oligopoly — (more than two but only a few producers) and a differentiated service. The proportion of fixed costs to total costs is high. There is considerable excess capacity. Demand is inelastic, and there is practically no price competition. A structure of legislative barriers, created and supported by the industry associations, have supported artificial price levels.[21]

All facets of the funeral industry are well organized. There are eight national associations of funeral directors. In addition there are associations representing cemeteries and crematories, manufacturers of burial merchandise such as caskets and burial vaults, manufacturers of monuments and markers, and manufacturers of embalming chemicals.

The largest association representing funeral directors is the National Funeral Directors Association, which has over 14,000 members. This organization is a federation of all state groups. A funeral firm or licensee must belong to a state association or to the District of Columbia association to be entitled to the services and facilities available from the NFDA. In some states individuals must belong to a metropolitan or district association within the state to qualify for membership in the state and hence the national association. The NFDA has a consumer information program that distributes twenty books and many brochures and pamphlets. The organization has also sponsored a number of films and illustrated lectures. The philosophy of the NFDA is that the place of the funeral and the role of the funeral director is to meet the needs, wants, and demands of those who survive a death. Its programs are built around funerals and are based on the belief that funeral directors serve the living through their care for the dead, and in the process give dignity to human life.

National Selected Morticians was established in 1917 by nine members of Rotary International. Their purpose was to operate on the Rotary noncompetitive principle. Accordingly, membership is limited to one firm in a city. Currently there are 850 member firms. NSM holds that the funeral industry is a business, not a profession, and that the relation of the mortician to a buyer is that of the traditional seller and buyer. NSM approves of advertising and of providing price information, practices which the NFDA opposes.

These trade associations effectively control the industry. They dominate the state boards of funeral directors. The laws of Ohio, for example, provide that the state Board of Embalmers and Funeral Directors shall consist of five members, all of whom must be licensed embalmers and practicing funeral directors with a minimum of ten consecutive years of experience in Ohio immediately preceding their appointment. These boards then establish the rules for entry. No one may be a funeral director or embalmer without a license.[22] By law the Illinois Board must be composed of five funeral directors. In thirty-three states all members of the regulating agency must be licensed funeral directors or embalmers. Thus the regulated are also the regulators. Only in California, Minnesota, and Massachusetts does a representative of the public at large serve on the board that regulates the funeral industry.

Pricing Funerals

According to economic analysis increased supplies of a good or service with demand remaining constant results in lower prices in a free market. But funeral firms do not operate in a free market. As a consequence consumers find that prices for funeral services have increased sharply in the United States in recent years.

The pricing of a funeral service represents a curious combination of cost, customs, and psychology. As a starting point the price of a funeral includes the cost of a casket, the cost of a cemetery plot or crematory, the cost of a grave marker or urn, and the costs for burial clothing, transportation, flowers, music, and other incidentals. A past president of the NFDA testified that funeral pricing practices are based on the cost of maintaining and operating the funeral home, staff services, and the price of the casket. It was asserted that on the average these expenses increase at the rate of 5 percent a year.

The casket is the key to the pricing of a funeral. Starting sixty-five years ago, when funeral firms were operated in conjunction with furniture stores in rural America, the practice of *casket pricing* has since become the custom. In the early days the casket manufacturer advised the furniture store owner to mark up the price of the casket three times — once to cover the cost of the casket; once to cover overhead expenses; and once for profit. Many funeral firms today mark up six or seven times, and in a few cases even more.

One of the best-kept secrets in the annals of American business is the actual manufacturing cost of a casket. There are fewer than 250 casket manufacturers in the United States, all of whom are members of the Casket Manufacturers Association of America. In 1974 the industry reported an average casket cost of $189.

Here is an example of casket formula pricing: The average casket cost of $189 is multiplied by 5.55 (the average markup), giving one an average funeral charge of $1,049. The $860 difference between the casket cost and the selling price covers the funeral director's expenses, such as wages, housing, automobiles, taxes, insurance, and depreciation and profit.

Basically there are three different materials employed in casket construction: cloth-covered soft wood, polished hardwood, and steel, copper, or bronze. Some caskets are made of eighteen-gauge steel with a gunmetal finish and include cotton mattresses and crêpe lining. There are varying degrees of quality and craftmanship in each of these casket types. Having most of these caskets in the display room, a funeral director uses applied psychology and the power of custom to persuade prospective buyers to choose the higher-priced caskets. Obviously a 560 percent markup on an expensive casket yields more profit than the same markup on an inexpensive casket.

The trade journals tell funeral firms how to use custom and psychology on buyers. Ideas and practices vary, but one popular device is to arrange the caskets so that the prospective buyer is first confronted with the highest-priced casket. If the buyer demurs, he is then moved along what is called "resistance lane." Subtly but effectively the salesperson suggests that the buyer would not wish to buy a "cheap" casket. In view of his status in the community and in order to show his devotion to the deceased, should he not select one of the "nicer" caskets? This play on emotion works. "You learn to know the people, to judge what they can afford. . . . There are subtle ways of selling you learn through experience. . . ."[23]

One way a funeral director can get a clue as to ability to pay is to ask, "How many copies of the death certificate do you need?" If the response is five or seven or ten the director knows at once that the family has several insurance policies, so when he takes the survivors to the casket room he shows them only the high priced caskets, and they usually choose one of these, without asking the prices of others.

A new method of pricing is called *functional pricing.* Under this method a buyer is charged a set price as soon as he walks into a funeral home, and the casket price is added on. The chart below illustrates this method of pricing:

Functional Pricing	
Professional services (assistants and all services in arrangement and direction of the funeral service)	$245.00
Preparation for burial (embalming, hair dressing, cosmetology, dressing and preparation of the body)	$175.00
Use of facilities and equipment	$210.00
Funeral coach (local)	$ 60.00
Total charge for services	$690.00
Bronze finish glass sealer casket	$700.00
Total Charge for Casket and Services	$1,390.00

In 1974 the median price for a funeral service was approximately $1,150. The industry reported the highest-priced funeral was $37,000. Those prices do not include cemetery plot, grave marker, transportation, flowers, or other services. Twenty percent of all funeral services are for children, welfare cases, and partial rather than complete adult services, all of which are lower in price. Funerals of this type yield only 7 percent of the income of funeral firms. As is true of the patients of doctors and the clients of lawyers, those "persons better situated in life generally help pay a portion of the funeral costs of the less fortunate."[24]

It might be assumed that in an industry operating on a 550 percent markup all firms would make substantial profits. According to the NFDA this is not true. In 1974 it was reported that the average profit per firm was $59 per funeral. The average salary owners of funeral firms paid themselves was $18,686.

Are funeral prices too high? Answering in the negative, an industry spokesman reasoned as follows: The ratio of bad debts to total costs for funeral services is less than 2 percent; "This proves that most people can afford to pay for the funerals they select."[25] He went on to say that no ethical funeral director would oversell a family because that would be bad for the director's public image and therefore would be bad business practice.

A different answer was given by another funeral director, who said, "In today's market, I can compete and provide a decent funeral for $200.00." At that price the body would be placed in a plain white box, without embalming, and taken to the cemetery the same day.

Two Florida cemetery owners have been offering funerals that look expensive but cost half the usual price. Following a funeral service, the body is transferred from an expensive metal or wooden display coffin to a cheaper fiberglass casket for burial. Predictably, funeral home owners are highly critical of the scheme since their biggest profit is derived from selling coffins.[26]

The Colorado Legislative Council concluded that the practice of tying the price of a funeral service to the price of the casket confuses the public and leads to abuses on the part of the funeral industry. The council recommended that funeral directors be required to itemize their charges for merchandise and services. Such a law became effective in New York State in 1964. This was a move toward providing prospective buyers with needed information, but it was no solution. It was shown in Colorado that an itemized list can be expanded to twenty-seven items involving sixty-one man hours. But some of the items are padding, as illustrated by the one described as "casketing and placing deceased in reposing room."

The Sordid Side of the Burial Business

The funeral industry operates in an aura of sanctity, behind which a few callous operators engage in reprehensible practices. As a group funeral directors are probably as ethical as people in other businesses. Yet the overcrowding of the industry leads to an unusual competitive situation. The large number of firms relative to the limited demand inevitably leads to abuses. In the Senate hearings on this topic a representative of the industry testified that 2,500 firms operating multiunit establishments that were strategically located could meet the total national demand for burial services. If this is correct, it means that nine out of ten funeral firms are unnecessary. In other industries such excess capacity would result in price wars and the elimination of many firms. Not so in the funeral industry. Funeral directors have succeeded in conditioning people to associate established funeral customs with all that is desirable in the "American way of life." The industry promotes the belief that a funeral service is a status symbol. So instead of reducing prices the industry has succeeded in raising prices to a level that is high enough to permit all firms in the industry to continue in business.

The concept of a "decent burial" is universal. It is even written into law. The corollary concept that one must pay a high price to secure a decent burial is almost universal. Insurance companies, the federal government, state governments, and unions provide increasing sums of money for funeral expenses.

Following a mine explosion in Hyden, Kentucky in which thirty-eight men were killed, a county judge denounced the outrageous charges made by funeral directors for their services. Each family received an allowance of $500 from Workmen's Compensation—an ample amount for a "decent" burial—but some of the funerals cost survivors over $2,000. In self-defense one undertaker said that he had provided only what survivors wanted. "I tried to keep them from buying the most expensive caskets, but you can't reason with people at times like this."[27]

William Manchester's description in *The Death of A President* of the undertaker's take-over of burial arrangements for President John F. Kennedy is almost incredible. "The funeral industry had attained a kind of metapsychic domination over all who dealt with death." The funeral director in Dallas is described as being straight out of Waugh's *The Loved One* or out of Huxley. His bill was $3,995 for a "solid double-wall casket and all services rendered at Dallas, Texas." When Robert Kennedy requested an itemized statement, the funeral director offered to reduce the price by $500. Inquiries at Elgin Casket Company disclosed that the Britannia model casket's factory cost was $1,150.

Although the assassinated president had been Commander-in-Chief of the Armed Forces, the military refused to prepare the body for burial when requested to do so by Robert Kennedy. Instead a colonel recommended one of the sixty-eight undertakers in Washington generally recognized as the aristocracy of the local industry. Because the Dallas casket had been damaged in transit, a second one was requested from the Washington firm. Influenced by Jessica Mitford's book *The American Way of Death*, Robert Kennedy requested a simple casket priced at $1,400. The one the firm used was priced at $2,460, and the total bill of the Washington firm was $3,160.

When Mrs. Kennedy and others in and close to the presidential family saw the cosmetized face of the slain president they were appalled. It looked like a wax dummy. Mrs. Kennedy had opposed exposure of the body to public viewing but had yielded to arguments that because he was a public figure mourners should be permitted to see his face. After seeing the body the family insisted that the casket be closed — an action that led to many rumors.

The $7,155 bill for the services of the two undertakers did not break the Kennedy family. What did break them — emotionally — was the attitude and manner in which the undertakers had crassly dominated arrangements.[28]

As we have noted, in all businesses and professions there are marginal operators whose practices are a discredit to the honest and conscientious firms and practitioners. In Detroit it was discovered that some of the clergy were accepting payments of $100 from certain funeral directors to whom they referred parishioners. One funeral director was reported to have taken nineteen ministers on a trip to Florida.[29] Some funeral firms use retired ministers as undercover solicitors. They call on families in their role as ministers and subtly direct bereaved persons to the funeral firm that pays them. Some funeral firms make secret payments to the employees of other firms who solicit burial business for them.

The National Selected Morticians conducted a survey that disclosed practices such as false and misleading price claims, deceptive selling, fictitious pricing, false invoicing, substituting of inferior products, and tie-in purchases.[30] Salespeople representing funeral firms offering preneed contracts took the license numbers of cars in a funeral procession and three days later called on the owners to sell them a preneed contract.[31] In California it was reported that operators of homes for older people were paid a commission of 10 percent by funeral homes for referrals of relatives of deceased persons.

Sometimes a funeral establishment installs a one-way window in the casket room through which a salesperson is able to watch the expressions and gestures of prospective purchasers. Some rooms are even wired for sound so that the sales representative can hear what the prospective buyers are saying. The salesperson then knows the psychologically correct moment to return and what sales talk to use. In the salesperson's absence it is hoped that the unsuspecting bereaved persons will be impressed with the firm's courtesy in giving them a few moments alone.[32]

Is It Unethical to Advertise?

Business firms in other industries spend billions of dollars to advertise their prices, their products, and their services. Some funeral directors are convinced that it pays to advertise, and some do advertise. The head of one large funeral firm in the national capital thinks that funeral directors should inform people about the funeral industry in order to help consumers exercise their freedom of choice intelligently. People should know what funerals cost. Advertising would eliminate the cloak of secrecy behind which the industry now operates.[33] But most directors consider themselves professionals. Like attorneys, the clergy, dentists, physicians, and college professors, they feel that advertising would be unethical.

The NFDA takes the view that funeral directing is a profession, therefore funeral directors should not advertise. A survey of funeral directors disclosed that a large percentage considered it appropriate to advertise their services but not their prices.[34] The NFDA justifies its ban on advertising on the basis that because of the nature of the industry advertising is uneconomical. Advertising cannot expand the market for funeral services, and advertising cannot and does not reduce prices. On the contrary, advertising increases funeral prices. In a typical year an average of $38 per funeral was spent on promotion. That amount "adds to the overall cost of funerals rather than reduces such costs." All advertising can do is shift the market or help firms maintain their percentage of the market.[35]

The NFDA, whose members do 75 percent of all funeral business, has a "code of ethics" that require members "to refrain from price advertising." Violation leads to expulsion. The code is in effect in practically all states, and expulsions have been made in California, Minnesota, Pennsylvania, Texas, Washington, and Wisconsin. In 1964 the Attorney General for the state of Wisconsin filed suit against the NFDA, charging restraint of competition by agreeing not to advertise funeral prices and by coercing those who do advertise. Three years later the circuit court ordered the NFDA to cease prevention of advertising and fined the national and state associations $250 each. The state had requested penalties of $5,000. In its presentation the state asserted that a funeral director could make a profit at a price of $195 per funeral. The court ruled that ". . . funeral directing is a business of a public or quasi-public nature, possessing attributes of a profession and related to the health, safety and general welfare of the community."[36]

The United States Department of Justice also filed an antitrust action against the NFDA, charging violation of the Sherman Antitrust Act because of its coercive actions to prevent members from advertising prices. A year later the NFDA agreed not to keep anyone from advertising the prices of funerals.[37]

In spite of these legal victories there is very little price advertising except on the West Coast. A funeral director in Daytona Beach, Florida who advertised funerals for $295 for which his six competitors charged prices ranging from $425 to $640 said that one of the alternatives to advertising is to call on hospitals, doctors, and nursing homes. This is what many funeral firms do.

Cemeteries for Profit?

Approximately one million acres of land in the United States are used as burial grounds. There are 87,000 traditional municipal or churchyard cemeteries, 12,500 cemeteries that are operated as business firms for the purpose of making a profit, 2,500 memorial parks, and 238 crematoria.[38] The number of publicly owned cemeteries is declining. Contrary to economic principles, the higher-priced cemeteries are driving out the lower-priced ones.

Prices for burial lots have a wide range. In Daytona Beach, Florida, for example, they cost from $80 to $2,300. Promoters have made fantastic profits with the promise of "perpetual care." A charge of $3.33 a grave for cutting the grass once in spring and once in fall yields a gross income of $4,000 an acre. It is estimated that one billion dollars has been paid by consumers to cemetery promoters for investment in "perpetual care" funds.

Clever promoters have made fortunes by capitalizing on grief and by taking advantage of tax exemptions. A promotional group may buy land at a price of $500 an acre, then sell 3,000 burial lots per acre at prices up to $300 each. Such a venture would yield $900,000. Salespeople are paid generous commissions. A popular nightclub singer says she earned $500 a week when she was only sixteen years old selling cemetery lots in Cleveland, Ohio. The cemetery is legally a nonprofit organization, but the promotional group operates it as a subsidiary of their land company and collects 50 percent of all revenue. The cemetery pays operating, selling, and maintenance expenses out of its tax-free portion of revenue. On a $200 investment a group of promoters in New York State made $1,600,000 profit in five years.

Although vaults are not required by law, more than half of all graves are lined with vaults. Grave digging is now done by machine in fifteen minutes. Yet the cost to open and close a grave ranges from $100 to $250 in commercial cemeteries. The standard markup is three times the direct labor cost. Current data for these costs is not available, so the above figures must be adjusted upward rather sharply for the inflation of recent years.

Psychologically the memorial park type of cemetery has proven to have profitable appeal. In many cases memorial parks are nothing more than the profit ventures of real-estate operators. The Colorado Legislative Council reported the story of Fremont Memory Gardens in Canon City, Colorado:

> These are the records of people who paid from a few dollars down to more than a thousand dollars in full for grave space and cemetery services and for vaults, markers, and monuments. The promoters are long gone. The cemetery has grown high with weeds. Some people are buried. Some have markers and memorials set. But the greatest number have nothing to show for what they paid.[39]

Individual speculation in cemetery lots is unwise, warns the Better Business Bureau of New York. Nevertheless, speculators, attracted by the lure of $1,000 gain per lot, purchase lots they do not need, purely for speculative gain. This in spite of the fact that cemeteries retain the right to repurchase the lots at the original selling price!

One of the most elaborate and widely advertised memorial parks is

Lullabyland in Forest Lawn Memorial Park. (*UPI*)

Forest Lawn in Glendale, California, where 5,000 funerals are conducted every year and two million tourists come to look and listen in awe and wonder. The promotional literature for Forest Lawn takes the reader into another world. There one finds the Great Mausoleum containing art treasures, the Church of the Recessional, the Little Church of the Flowers, The Wee Kirk o' the Heather, and the Hall of the Crucifixion. In addition there are the Courts of David and the Christus, the Garden of Memories, and many more. For $85,000 one may purchase a crypt in the Court of Freedom.

The operators of Forest Lawn advertise that Forest Lawn has everything, including a mortuary and a crematory. One may purchase an urn and a niche to hold the "cremains." The churches of Forest Lawn are advertised as places of romantic beauty for the "enchanted hour." It is reported that 50,000 weddings have taken place in the churches. The old ghost-infested cemetery has been converted into a garden of memories, where "songbirds trill only the melody of love," and soothing messages pour out of amplifiers hidden in the shrubbery. Over one million dollars are spent annually in advertising Forest Lawn. Its annual revenue is estimated to be from $14 million to $15 million.[40]

A twenty-story mausoleum was built in Nashville, Tennessee, that provides 129,500 crypts—a twelve million dollar skyscraper devoted to the dead. The builder stated that it takes 192 acres to bury 129,500 people, whereas the twenty-story mausoleum provides spaces for the same number on only 7 acres. It cost $1,900 to $2,500 for one of these crypts, with a discount of several hundred dollars if bought in advance.[41]

U.S. Government Death Benefits for Veterans

Responsibility for providing most federal benefits for veterans and their dependents is vested by law in the Administrator of Veterans Affairs. There are 117 national cemeteries in the United States and Puerto Rico. Of this number, 103 are administered by the Veterans Administration (VA), and 61 of these have gravesites available. Deceased military personnel, veterans, and their spouses and dependent children may be interred in these cemeteries. There is no charge for opening and closing a grave, and a headstone or marker is provided free. There are approximately twenty-nine million veterans who served in the armed forces of the United States, but only about one million gravesites are potentially available in existing VA cemeteries.

In addition to free burial in a national cemetery, the VA will pay an amount, not to exceed $250, toward a veteran's burial expenses. When a veteran is buried in other than a federally owned cemetery, a payment not exceeding $150 as a plot allowance may be authorized in addition to the $250 basic burial allowance. A headstone or marker may be provided without charge to a designated consignee for the unmarked grave of a veteran interred in a private cemetery. An American flag to drape the casket of a veteran is provided and presented to the next of kin at the conclusion of the service. Any VA office can render assistance in obtaining these services.[42]

Embalming for Display

Most American funerals are open-casket services. According to most funeral directors and many members of the clergy, viewing is a vital part of coming to terms with the reality of death. In addition it helps mourners retain a picture of the deceased. James Knight deplores the mounting criticism of the preservation of a dead body and its public display. He thinks "it is the misfortune of our time that we expend great effort attacking our traditions and ceremonials without understanding their usefulness to man through the ages."[43] Some people recognize the importance of viewing, but the value of the presence of the body of the deceased can reach a point of diminishing returns in a relatively short time. Long-term prevention of dissolution by embalming and burial vaults may weaken the sense of the finality of death. This is one reason why some people prefer cremation.

A society must decide whether a corpse should be preserved or not. Its decision involves custom and tradition. In the nineteenth century

American society first accepted the idea of corpse preservation, and this continues as a widespread practice in the twentieth century. The first patent for the injection of chemicals as body preservatives was issued in 1856. During the Civil War private contractors were hired by the federal government to bury the bodies of deceased servicemen. Although there was much experimentation with ice coolers as a means of preservation, chemical preservatives were preferred. Thus it was that embalming became an American custom.[44] An embalmer removes all blood from a corpse, drains all body cavities, and injects gallons of preservatives under the armpits, at the neck, and at the groin. Then the cosmetologist works to make the lifeless corpse look like a sleeping person.

Unless a body is to be shipped a long distance, embalming is unnecessary. It is not a health measure, nor is it required by law. Nevertheless, funeral directors often tell survivors that embalming is required, and they meekly agree to pay. In several states (for example, Arizona, Florida, and Pennsylvania) a body must either be embalmed or refrigerated if held for more than twenty-four hours. This is not required by law, but it is a regulation of the state health departments.

The practice of preserving a corpse by means of embalming or refrigeration increases funeral expenses because it creates demand for elaborate caskets in which to display the bodies. If a corpse is to be on display it must be made-up. Cosmetology is an important aspect of a funeral firm's operation. Embalming and the restorative arts are the chief trade assets of the mortician. Unless the subject can be made presentable for public exhibition, it is difficult to promote the sale of burial goods in desirable quantities.

Is Cremation A Better Way?

The early Christians and Jews outlawed the custom of cremation because of its pagan origins. Opposition to cremation among Christians today has diminished considerably. Christians believe that the body is the temple of the Holy Spirit, but once the soul departs at death the body is no more than an earthly shell. Episcopalians view cremation as an acceleration of the earth-to-earth, dust-to-dust process. Under certain circumstances the Catholic church will permit cremation. Special permission must be obtained from the bishop through the individual's pastor, and permission is granted only in certain situations. To Methodists and Lutherans cremation is not an issue; they consider it a matter to be decided by the survivors. Cremation is strictly forbidden in the Jewish faith, although many Jews do choose cremation.[45]

Many people shudder when they think of what happens to the bodies of their loved ones. Preservation of the body by embalming and burial satisfies a need on the part of people who believe in physical resurrection of the body. But a few prefer cremation. In Great Britain over two-thirds of all corpses are cremated, and more than one-third in Australia are cre-

mated. The Cremation Association of America reported that there were
112,298 cremations in the United States in 1973. This was an increase of
40 percent during the decade, but represents less than 6 percent of all
deaths that year. The Pacific Coast region accounted for 43 percent of all
cremations that year.

A rational observer might assume that cremation would be a less expensive method of disposing of a body, and it can be if the person in charge
of the funeral arrangements demands a simple cremation. A Miami, Florida
funeral home advertised a $137.50, no-frills, "cash and carry ashes" cre-
mation service that included the cost of a quart-size cardboard box for the
remains.[46] But the costs of cremation can be considerably more if the so-
called "traditional" funeral is purchased with cremation following. One
such funeral came to $798.75.[47] In a St. Petersburg, Florida survey it was
reported that the cost of the standard traditional funeral with the least
expensive casket (wood) was $465. Cremation with the standard-traditional
funeral and least expensive casket could cost as much as $835. However,
none of the fifteen funeral homes surveyed required caskets for the traditional cremation funeral.[48] In St. Petersburg, Florida, a complete funeral
including cremation was advertised for $299.[49]

To offset the loss of revenue from simple cremation services the funeral
industry tries to convince the public that a funeral service should be the
same up to the point of burial or cremation. This means that funeral directors insist that coffins be used, that the coffins be burned (even though
metal caskets will not burn), and that ashes be buried or deposited in an urn
in a crypt. The result is that cremation may be more expensive than customary earth burial. For example, one firm that charged $295 for a full-
service burial (which includes use of chapel, car, hearse, calling hours)
charged $100 more for cremation. There need be no ashes, and there are
none unless a relative requests them. What happens to the one thousand-
dollar metal caskets when cremation is requested? Of course they do not
burn; neither do the bodies burn. The bodies are baked, and the caskets
char and crack. The bodies are then removed and burned, and the caskets
are broken into scrap and taken to a dump. The executive director of the
National Funeral Directors Association stated that some members were
troubled by the trend developing in California, where families are arranging
for what he called "immediate disposition" and a memorial service later.[50]

"Say It with Flowers"

The advertising man who coined this phrase laid the foundation for
a one-and-a-quarter-billion dollar floral industry. So many people think that
the only way to "say it" is with flowers that an average of $375 is spent for
every funeral. Forty-five percent of the total annual revenue of the floral
industry is derived from the funeral industry. The other chief source of
revenue is weddings.

If survivors wish to discourage the expenditure of money on funeral flowers or if they wish to encourage the contribution of that amount of money to a worthy cause, they often find themselves blocked by the refusal of the newspapers to print a request to omit flowers. This is no accident. The Society of American Florists uses its advertising power to encourage newspapers to refuse to print a request to omit flowers or to contribute to a cause. A Pittsburgh, Pennsylvania consumer group charged the city's two daily newspapers with violating customers' rights by refusing to print "Please omit flowers" in paid death notices. The managements of both newspapers responded that their policy is not to accept negative advertising; that is, not to print advertising favoring a boycott of a legitimate product. Both papers stated that where such a request is made, they suggest instead that the bereaved family indicate where memorial contributions should be sent.[51]

"Rock of Ages"

What is more rare than an unmarked grave? A "suitable" marker or monument is an integral part of a "nice" funeral. Survivors may spend from one hundred dollars to thousands of dollars for elaborate tombstones. There are other ways to mark graves, but the tombstone custom is so firmly established that almost every family purchases one as a matter of course. Relating quality to price and expenditure to status, a family spending $2,000 on a funeral would not consider a mere $100 marker. Even in death differences in income are perpetuated. The graves of those whose families are in the high-income groups are located in the choice sections of the cemeteries and identified by expensive monuments or mausoleums. The graves of those whose survivors are in the lower-income groups will be found in a less desirable section of the cemetery, identified by modest headstones.

DO CONSUMERS HAVE ANY CHOICE?

A Manual of Simple Burial tells you briefly, but authoritatively, about a variety of choices open to consumers. In its forty-seven short sections and sixty-four pages you learn all you need to know about memorial societies, eye-banks, temporal bone banks, bequeathal of bodies to medical schools, and bequeathal of bodies for radiation research. Names and addresses of many organizations are given, enabling you to act individually or with a group. For those who wish to change the emphasis in burial practices to a positive, constructive direction this pamphlet is recommended.[52.]

Memorial Societies

The Continental Association of Funeral and Memorial Societies was created to promote the dignity, simplicity, and spiritual value of funeral rites and memorial services; to deepen understanding of the religious meaning of death in accordance with the religious, philosophical, and ethical beliefs of each individual; to reduce unjustifiable expenses of funeral services; and to promote the opportunity for every person to predetermine the price of the funeral or memorial service he or she desires.[53] There are 133 memorial societies in operation in the United States and 23 in Canada, representing a total of some half million members.

Memorial societies are not discount houses for the dead. Simplicity, dignity, and economy are emphasized. Advance planning is recommended. Memorial society services do cost less. The following services and prices were offered to members of the Rockland County (N.Y.) Memorial Society by one of the cooperating funeral directors: immediate cremation — $230 plus $75 crematory charges; immediate burial — $220 plus cemetery expenses; cremation with viewing and attendance — $405 plus $75 crematory charges; burial with viewing and attendance — $460 plus cemetery expenses; or delivery to medical school — $75.[54]

What About Preneed Contracts?

The managing director of National Selected Morticians favors preplanning as the act of rational persons who wish to spare survivors and to avoid excessive charges against their estates. The National Funeral Directors Association objects to preplanning because it is alleged that preplanning tends to lower the quality of funeral services. "If funeral directors insist on soliciting preneed funerals they are in fact prearranging the funeral of their profession."[55]

On the surface preneed arrangement appears to be a rational way to spare survivors and to reduce costs. How much simpler it would be for survivors to discover that all arrangements had been made and paid for. On second thought, however, it develops that preplanning can create problems instead of avoiding them. No one knows when, where, or under what circumstances he or she will die. Suppose the funeral firm has gone out of business. Suppose death occurs far away. These and many other unknowns can complicate the most carefully arranged plans.

The real problem with this type of arrangement, however, is that unscrupulous operators have found the psychological appeal of preplanning to be an easy way of exploiting people. A United States Senate committee investigated the topic of "Frauds and Misrepresentation Affecting the Elderly," and the Colorado Legislative Council investigated abuses of preneed burial planning. In New Mexico 80 percent of the contracts were found to be sold by high-pressure sales representatives to older people. A Colorado corporation with an intricate structure of subsidiaries operated under such names as "Our Chapel of Memories," "Order of Praying Hands," and "Lawn Haven Memorial Gardens." Their salespeople went from door to door selling on an installment plan. The purchase price of a contract was $637.50 for a casket costing $96.50. The contract did not include any services. The money collected was not deposited in a trust fund, and the seller collected the interest.

A Colorado state law requires that the full amount of money paid on a preneed contract be deposited in trust, under supervision of the state Insurance Commission. But the seller collects the interest! Preneed contracts in the amount of $10 million were sold in Colorado in one year. The sales argument for this practice is that funeral costs are certain to rise, so the buyer is purchasing a hedge against inflation. If a buyer defaults or moves from the state, the trustee is required to refund only 75 percent of the amount paid.

Bodies for Research and Transplants

There are many ways in which socially concerned people can arrange while they are living to serve the needs of their fellow human beings after they have died. Instead of burying or cremating a body, it may be given to a medical school for research. Many lives can be saved and health and sight can be restored to thousands through the intelligent "salvaging" of organs and tissues from persons who have died. In years past medical schools were given the unclaimed bodies from city morgues. Today our affluent society provides enough money for a decent burial for almost everyone. As a result there are not enough unclaimed bodies available. Thousands of bodies are needed each year for the training of future doctors and dentists. New medical schools are opening, and the supply of unclaimed bodies is steadily diminishing. Only the rapid increase in the practice of bequeathing bodies to medical schools has averted a serious crisis.

Lack of uniformity among state body donation laws created problems in the past. Whereas forty states permitted living persons to give their bodies in advance for medical research, only four states permitted donations of corneas. Moreover, state laws differed and body gifts in one state were often not recognized in another. In an effort to achieve uniformity, the American Medical Association, the American Bar Association, and the National Society for Medical Research jointly sponsored the Uniform Anatomical Gift Act as a model for reform.* Since all states have now passed the Uniform Anatomical Gift Act it is legally possible for any person of sound mind and eighteen years of age to donate all or part of his or her body to be used for medical research.[56] (Sale of one's body is illegal, however.)

All religious groups, except Orthodox Jews, encourage bequeathal. The Roman Catholic church permits cremation of a body after a medical school finishes with it, although it objects to the use of the word "cremation." It believes that the burning of the body must not be regarded as a religious rite.[57]

---

* A copy of the Anatomical Gift Act may be secured from the Legal Research Department, American Medical Association, 535 N. Dearborn Street, Chicago, Ill. 60610.

If one wishes to bequeath one's body to a medical school, it is suggested that arrangements be made with the aid of a family physician or by writing directly to the dean of the nearest medical school.

There are 350,000 blind persons in the United States. The number has doubled in a ten-year period. Approximately 10 percent of those who are blind can regain their sight by means of a corneal transplant. Forms for persons wishing to donate their eyes after death may be obtained from the Eye-Bank for Sight Restoration, 210 East 64th Street, New York, New York 10021. From the same source an explanatory pamphlet entitled *Every Day the Eye-Bank Helps More People See* may be secured.

Impairment of hearing is the single most prevalent chronic physical disability in the United States. More persons suffer from hearing defects than from visual impairments, heart disease, or other chronic disabilities. Over twenty million people in this country, including three million children, suffer from some degree of hearing loss, and the number increases every year. The temporal bones of a deceased person may be donated for research. Temporal bone banks are *not* like nerve or eye banks, where healthy parts are stored and later transplanted to the living; they are ear research laboratories where defective inner ear structures can be studied, together with the donors' medical and hearing records. Detailed information is available from the Deafness Research Foundation, 366 Madison Avenue, New York, New York 10017.

The Tissue Bank, United States Naval Medical School, Bethesda, Maryland 20014, is doing pioneering research. Many more bodies are needed, particularly under the age of thirty-five. One requirement of donation is that after the tissues wanted for research are used, the bodies must be buried or cremated at family expense.

The Living Bank is a nonprofit corporation organized in Texas in 1968 to help people who wish to donate all or parts of their bodies for transplantation, therapy, medical research, or anatomical studies. The Bank explains procedures and supplies a donor card, which is the only legal document required by the Uniform Anatomical Gift Act or similar laws. The Bank emphasizes that removal of organs or parts does not disfigure the body, nor does it interfere with funeral or burial arrangements. If a body is donated to a medical school, survivors can arrange a memorial service.*

Public Control

In Europe the general practice is to provide burial services as a public utility, controlled and regulated by the state. There is no such regulation in the United States. The state boards of funeral directors and embalmers have nothing to do with funeral costs, pricing practices, prepaid funeral practices, or types of funerals offered. They do not have the power to initiate complaints against a funeral director or embalmer. One might ask what

* For information, write to The Living Bank, 6631 South Main, P.O. Box 6725, Houston, Texas 77005.

do such boards do? The answer seems to be that they write their own codes of ethics and control entry to the industry.

The state of New York regulates so-called nonprofit cemetery corporations. A legislative committee decided that such control was needed because millions of dollars were being drained from the public every year by unscrupulous operators who exploited the bereaved.

In 1975 the Federal Trade Commission came to the conclusion that conditions in the funeral industry had reached a point where the commission was obligated to issue notice of a proposed rule to regulate the industry. This was necessary because, in the words of the commission, bereaved buyers are susceptible to and have been subjected to a variety of practices which exploit their disadvantaged position or which interfere with personal selection of funeral merchandise and services."[58] In addition, the commission felt the proposed rule was necessary to halt and prevent future use of unfair or deceptive practices. The proposed rule would place a number of prohibitions on what funeral directors would be allowed to do, such as prohibiting restraints on price advertising and other market impediments. It would prohibit bait-and-switch tactics; that is, the practice of advertising a low-price funeral as bait, then attempting to switch the consumer to a more expensive funeral once he or she responded to the bait by visiting the funeral home. It would prohibit the picking up or embalming of corpses without permission from the family. Those persons who choose to have the deceased cremated would not have to buy a casket. Funeral homes could not misrepresent the legal or public health necessity of embalming or the use of caskets or burial vaults, and they could not make disparaging comments about a consumer's concern for price. In addition the rule would prohibit the interference by the funeral home with the offering of low-cost funerals, direct cremation services, or other modes of disposition, preneed arrangements, or memorial society activities.

Under the commission's proposed rule, specific information would have to be given to consumers about funeral arrangements. This would include a fact sheet about the legal requirements for embalming, casket use, and burial vaults, a casket price list, an itemized list of prices for the services and merchandise offered for sale – with conspicuous disclosure of the consumer's right to select only the items desired – and a memorandum at the time funeral arrangements are made recording the items selected and their respective prices. Finally the rule also would require funeral homes that advertise to include in their advertisements a notice that price information is available and the telephone number to call to obtain such information.[59]

RELIGION AND CEREMONY

Religious Customs

One hundred sixty-five million people in the United States are church members. The range and diversity of convictions among religous sects are reflected in the customs influencing the economic lives of church members. From the extensive ceremonials characteristic of the Catholic faith to the simplicity of the Quakers, differences in customs and ceremony are largely a matter of degree.

In all religions the negative influence is as significant as the positive. The influence of religion on economic choice is seen in authoritative decrees as to what people shall or shall not wear, what they may or may not eat, how they may or may not act. Those most strongly influenced by religious regulations are officials of the church. In the most rigidly regulated faiths the vestments these officials wear set them apart from others in the group.

The influence of religious customs on economic choice is not limited to church officials. The 131 million church members in the United States require hundreds of millions of dollars' worth of economic goods prescribed by church regulations. Many of these members also avoid certain goods because of restrictions imposed by their faith. Members of a number of religious groups must abstain from alcoholic beverages and/or tobacco products. Some religious organizations require abstinence from coffee, tea, and cola drinks because they contain caffeine. Jews must eat certain foods and refrain from others. Similar restrictions regulate Moslems, who must never eat ham. Until 1966 Catholics were not permitted to eat meat on Fridays, but fish was permitted. As a result 90 percent of the weekly supply of seafood was sold on Fridays.

Obviously religious customs exert a significant influence on consumer choice. To ignore this influence by assuming that these millions of people act freely in choosing goods and services essential to their method of worship might simplify the problem of explaining choice, but it scarcely approaches reality. The fact is that church members are restricted in their freedom of choice.

Religious Holidays—Christmas Customs

In the West the anniversary of the birth of Jesus Christ is the occasion for one of the major ceremonial celebrations each year. Even in the Orient, and especially in Japan, the commercial aspects of Christmas celebrations have been adopted. Department stores in Tokyo are trimmed with decorations and the merchandise features toys and other traditional Christmas gifts.

In the United States the commercialization of Christmas increasingly overshadows the religious celebration. Non-Christians join Christians in the customary exchange of gifts. In the minds of many people the commercial aspect of Christmas is predominant. For many children the meaning of Christmas must be unclear. Is it a religious observance? Or is it an occasion for an abundance of gifts?

In the business world there is no confusion about the meaning of Christmas. Christmas means business. Weeks before December 25 business and trade journals are filled with news of the "Christmas trade." In the United States the "Christmas trade" involves the expenditure of billions of dollars annually. One-fourth of the sales of sporting goods, cameras, jewels, and watches are made in the Christmas season. For toys and games the figure is 60 percent. In addition the "Christmas trade" requires over $150 million for gift wrapping and over $155 million for natural and plastic Christmas trees.

Ironically the Christmas season is a bonanza for the liquor industry. Christmas holiday sales account for about 25 percent of the total annual liquor sales. An industry spokesman reported that "the holiday season could make or break a company's business for the entire year."

Christmas is not what it used to be. There is no requirement in the Protestant faith that Christians give presents to one another on Christmas Day. The origin of the custom is lost in antiquity, but its preservation is based in part on the profit that it generates.

MARRIAGE AND CEREMONY

Engagement Customs

Modern engagements are vestiges of the practice of signing and sealing formal contracts governing the economic aspects of the approaching marriage. Formerly this was a contract of vital importance to the families involved, as well as to the engaged couple, but the increasing tendency in this country is to regard the engagement as a contract between and affecting only the man and woman. The fact that engagements still have the binding force of a contract is demonstrated by the success of some lawsuits for breach of contract when an engagement is broken.

The engagement ring is an interesting example of a survival of custom. In former days, when most people were illiterate, the method of signing and sealing a contract was to affix one's mark by the use of a signet ring. Consequently, the ring came to be regarded as evidence of a contractual relationship. The signet ring has been replaced by the modern practice of wearing a diamond, a custom that serves admirably to sustain the diamond market. It is estimated that 80 percent of all engaged women receive diamonds. Many young couples spend money for a diamond ring that they cannot afford, but they feel that a ring must be purchased and worn by the fiancée for the sake of appearance and custom. The average engagement diamond is about a third of a carat and worth around $350.

An engagement is usually the occasion for an elaborate party at which the woman's parents announce the approaching marriage of their daughter. Then follow a series of "showers," which bolster the novelty business. There has been a noticeable tendency in recent years toward giving practical gifts on such occasions, but there still remains a high degree of uselessness and waste.

The Marriage Ceremony

The type of marriage service a couple chooses is dictated by custom. In this country a couple may be married by a representative of the church or by an official of the state.

Costumes worn at the bridal party are dictated by tradition. It is said that some of our customs are derived from the first Christians, who were Jews. Jewish brides habitually wore a gilt coronet, whose modern counterpart is an orange-blossom wreath. The use of orange blossoms is a carry-over from tropical regions where people regarded them as symbolic of fecundity. The bridal dress, together with the train, is also a product of custom.

During the 1960s student rebellion in the United States there was a reaction by many young people against tradition, and this included engagement and marriage customs. Brides and grooms wore jeans at marriage ceremonies and did not give rings. Individualistic marriage ceremonies were planned by many couples that were very different from traditional ceremonies. And some people rejected licensing or marriage procedures altogether and just started living together. These nontraditional patterns are the exception, however. In fact, formal weddings have increased in popularity since the late 1960s, when only 67 percent of first marriages were formal. Today the majority of first marriages—80 percent—are formal weddings.

About 97 percent of couples in their first marriage take a honeymoon trip. The average honeymoon expenditure is $833. Those who travel outside the United States (excluding Canada and Mexico) spend an average of $1,396.[60]

The Marriage Ceremony—Its Costs

Two sisters were married during the same year. The total cost of one sister's wedding was $4,000, while that of the other's wedding was only $210.[61] The one wedding was elaborate and professional, while the other was a small, informal, do-it-yourself ceremony.

Taken together, firms that cater to the marriage market gross about $8.5 billion per year, a figure that includes everything from bridal gowns to honeymoons. First National City Bank of New York reported in their *Consumer Views* newsletter that a small wedding for a bridal party of 5 plus 35 guests averages $2,000; a middle-priced wedding for a bridal party of 12 and 175 guests, $5,000; and a "big-big" wedding, $20,000.[62] The impact of inflation during the mid-1970s pushed these costs up 10 to 40 percent. One might conclude from this that wedding announcements should be listed on the financial pages of the newspapers instead of the society pages.*

---

* For a discussion of weddings and their costs see Marcia Seligson, *The Eternal Bliss Machine: America's Way of Wedding* (New York: William Morrow, 1973).

OTHER CEREMONIAL CELEBRATIONS

Mother's Day

This is a comparatively new occasion for celebration. Only fifty-five years ago a presidential proclamation designated the second Sunday in May as Mother's Day. Before long business promoters saw the potential gift-giving that could be generated. A promotional committee was created to persuade sons and daughters that the way to honor their mothers was to give flowers, send telegrams, give candy, and send sentimental cards. The amount of money spent for Mother's Day gifts now exceeds the amount spent at Easter. This is due, in part, to the fact that the giving has been expanded to include grandmothers, aunts, great aunts, and even cousins. Mother's Day proved to be so profitable that the promoters invented Father's Day.

Birthday Celebrations

Custom requires the celebration of the anniversary of the birth of every person. Regardless of the economic status of the family, custom demands that the birthday of each member be celebrated by a party and the presentation of gifts. Relatives, neighbors, and friends are invited to share in the festivities, and they are expected to bring gifts.

Graduation Ceremonies

Certain customs have developed in connection with the graduation of students from grammer school, high school, and college. In addition to ceremonial programs and speeches, graduation exercises require academic caps and gowns for high-school and college graduates.

An interesting graduation custom is the giving of gifts to those who have completed their course of study. Formerly these tokens of admiration were fairly simple and inexpensive, but today parents, grandparents, uncles, and aunts find the gift-giving custom increasingly expensive.

An important by-product of graduation exercises and ceremonial customs is the photograph. The custom of photographing individuals and groups in connection with ceremonial occasions accounts for a significant part of the photographic business.

One newspaper reporter made a study of the cost of high-school graduations in his community and found that it could cost either a pittance or plenty. The cost of cap, gown, and tassel was $6 to $7; rings were priced from $41 to $74; 100 announcements were $17 to $25; name cards cost $2 to $4; a yearbook cost $8 to $10; one black-and-white photograph cost $3.75, while the deluxe, color "varsity package" cost $75.[63] If a student were to choose all of these items, the cost would be about $75 to $200, and that does not include the cost of the prom!

The Phenomenon of Gift Giving

We have seen in the previous pages that there are many occasions at which gifts are given. Gift giving is a multi-billion dollar business. Many average-income families spend hundreds of dollars each year on gifts. Gifts are given for many reasons. They are given because it is the expected thing to do; as a means of showing off one's wealth; because gifts have been received; or because this represents a tangible way to show affection and love for another person.

There is a very significant difference between *reciprocity* and *exchange* in the transfer of goods and/or gifts between people, although they may seem alike. Boulding defined the difference as follows:

> In exchange, I give you something if and only if you give me something. In reciprocity, I give you something out of the sheer goodness of my heart and you give me something out of the sheer goodness of yours. Of course, if I do not get any return, the sheer goodness of my heart may depreciate. There is an uneasy division here between exchange and reciprocity, but they are not the same thing. Particularly, I would argue that it is reciprocity that holds society together; this is why we give Christmas presents, frequently reciprocally.[64]

In gift giving the giver has to decide on an amount to spend as well as on what to spend it. It may be that the choice will be something that the giver feels the other person would like but would hesitate to spend money on or he may buy something he likes hoping the recipient will like it also. It might be simpler just to give cash, but that carries with it a kind of coldness and detachment, so the sellers have come to the rescue with a gift certificate—something that is not as practical as cash but that does seem to carry with it a more personal touch.

QUESTIONS FOR REVIEW

1. To what extent can the principles of economic analysis be applied to the funeral industry?
2. Do you think the rendering of funeral services is a business or a profession?
3. Are funeral prices too high or too low?
4. What constitutes a "decent" burial?
5. Do you think it is unethical for a funeral firm to advertise its prices?
6. What is your attitude toward embalming? Cremation?
7. What is your reaction to donating all or part of your body for transplantation, therapy, medical research, or anatomical studies?
8. Analyze the regulations of the funeral industry as proposed by the Federal Trade Commission. Are they needed? Is this an attempt at over-regulation or is it too little regulation?

9. What religious customs do you consider to be important? Why?

10. How do you react to the commercialization of Christmas? Is there anything you can do about it?

11. When you marry, do you plan to have a big wedding?

12. What do you think of the commercialization of Mother's Day and Father's Day? How much do you spend on Mother's Day gifts?

13. Why are some people reluctant to give cash for gifts?

14. Should gift giving be looked at only as an economic activity?

15. Discuss what Boulding means by exchange and reciprocity in gift giving.

16. "All ceremonial events could be ignored, but life would be drab and dull without them." Discuss this statement.

PROJECTS

1. Think about what you have read in this chapter, then write a paper recording your general reactions.

2. Interview two or three funeral directors in your college or home area. Ask them questions suggested by this chapter. Summarize your responses and findings in a written report.

3. Visit one or two cemeteries in your home or college area. Ask the managers questions suggested by your reading in this chapter. Present your responses and impressions in a paper.

4. Interview five students about their attitudes concerning funeral customs.

5. Assume you have the full responsibility for making burial arrangements for a member of your family; explain in detail what you think you would do.

6. Survey five male and five females on attitudes toward small versus large weddings.

7. Write a paper on your attitude toward gift giving.

REFERENCES

1. Robert W. Habenstein and William M. Lamers, *The History of American Funeral Directing* (Milwaukee: Bulfin Printers, 1962), pp. 57–77.
2. *Ibid.*, pp. 216, 219.
3. Robert Fulton and Gilbert Geis, "Death and Social Values," in Robert Fulton, ed., *Death and Identity* (New York: John Wiley & Sons, 1965), pp. 67–74.
4. William May, "The Sacral Power of Death in Contemporary Experience," in Liston O. Mills, ed., *Perspectives on Death* (New York: Abingdon Press, 1969), p. 174.

5. Bernard Schoenberg, et al., eds., *Loss and Grief: Psychological Management in Medical Practice* (New York: Columbia University Press, 1970), p. 18.
6. May, p. 170.
7. *Ibid.*, p. 176.
8. Raymond Paavo Arvio, *The Cost of Dying* (New York: Harper & Row, 1974), pp. 1–11.
9. *Ibid.*, pp. 6–7.
10. Fulton and Geis, "Death and Social Values," in Fulton, pp. 67–74.
11. Paul E. Irion, *The Funeral: Vestige or Value?* (Nashville, Tenn.: Abingdon Press, 1966), chap. 3.
12. *Antitrust Aspects of the Funeral Industry,* Hearings Before the Subcommittee on Antitrust and Monopoly of the Committee on the Judiciary, U.S. Senate, 88th Congress, 2d Session, Pursuant to Res. 262, Part I, Funeral Directors, 7, 8, 9 July 1964, p. 257.
13. Fulton, p. 334.
14. Herman Feifel, ed., *The Meaning of Death* (New York: McGraw-Hill, 1959), p. 189.
15. Ernest Campbell, "Death as a Social Practice," in Mills, pp. 218–220.
16. Habenstein and Lamers, p. 4.
17. Robert L. Fulton, "Attitudes of Clergymen Toward Funerals and Funeral Directors in the United States," paper presented to the National Funeral Directors Association Convention, St. Louis, Mo., Oct. 20, 1959.
18. *Wall Street Journal,* 29 Aug. 1975, p. 3.
19. W. Lloyd Warner, "The City of the Dead," in Fulton, *Death and Identity,* pp. 360–381.
20. Vanderlyn R. Pine, *A Statistical Abstract of Funeral Service Facts and Figures of the United States* (National Funeral Directors Association, Milwaukee, Wisc., 1975), pp. 3–37.
21. Roger D. Blackwell, "Price Levels in the Funeral Industry," *The Quarterly Review of Economics and Business* 7 (1967): 75–84.
22. *Antitrust Aspects of the Funeral Industry,* pp. 14, 59, 62; Habenstein and Lamers, pp. 534–542.
23. *The National Observer,* 8 June 1970, p. 22.
24. Robert W. Habenstein and William M. Lamers, *Funeral Customs the World Over* (Milwaukee: Bulfin Printers, 1963), p. 753.
25. *Antitrust Aspects of the Funeral Industry,* p. 259.
26. *Newsweek,* 10 May 1976, pp. 95, 97.
27. *New York Times,* 9 Jan. 1971, p. 13.
28. William Manchester, *The Death of A President: November 20-November 25, 1963* (New York: Harper & Row, 1967), pp. 296, 381–383, 416, 430–435, 442–443, 634–635.
29. Continental Association of Funeral and Memorial Societies, News Bulletin, 3 June 1964, p. 6.
30. *Antitrust Aspects of the Funeral Industry,* pp. 8–9, 38, 220–229; Allan Earnshaw Backman, *Consumers Look at Burial Practices* (Columbia, Mo.: Council on Consumer Information, University of Missouri, 1956), pp. 12–16.
31. *Preneed Burial Service,* Hearings Before the Subcommittee on Frauds and Misrepresentations Affecting the Elderly of the Special Committee on Aging, U.S. Senate, 88th Congress, 2d Session, 19 May 1964.
32. Ruth Mulvey Harmer, *The High Cost of Dying* (New York: Crowell-Collier, 1963), p. 218.
33. *Antitrust Aspects of the Funeral Industry,* pp. 159–160.
34. See Harold H. Titus and Morris Keeton, *Ethics for Today* (New York: American Book Company, 1966), pp. 295–297, for the distinction between a profession and a business.
35. *Antitrust Aspects of the Funeral Industry,* 47, 117.
36. *New York Times,* 30 Nov. 1967, p. 17.

37. U.S. Department of Justice, News Release, 24 Nov. 1967 and 17 July 1968.
38. Habenstein and Lamers, *Funeral Customs the World Over*, p. 752.
39. Colorado Legislative Council, Denver, Colo., p. 18.
40. *Business Week,* 20 April 1974, p. 43.
41. *Wall Street Journal,* 12 June 1973, p. 1.
42. Letter received from National Cemetery System, Veterans Administration, 10 Oct. 1975.
43. Edgar N. Jackson, *For the Living* (Des Moines, Iowa: Channel Press, 1963), p. 11.
44. Habenstein and Lamers, *The History of American Funeral Directing,* pp. 311, 327, 338, chap. 8.
45. *St. Petersburg Times,* 11 Oct. 1975, p. 2D.
46. *St. Petersburg Times,* 7 Oct. 1974, p. 9B.
47. *Pittsburgh Post-Gazette,* 13 March 1974, p. 37.
48. *St. Petersburg Times,* 7 Oct. 1974, p. 9B.
49. *St. Petersburg Times,* 23 May 1976, p. 11D.
50. *New York Times,* 13 April 1973, p. 61.
51. *Pittsburgh Post-Gazette,* 29 Oct. 1975, p. 5.
52. Ernest Morgan, *A Manual of Simple Burial,* 7th ed. (Burnsville, N.C.: The Celo Press, 1975), $1.50.
53. Continental Association of Funeral and Memorial Societies, Proceedings, First and Second Annual Meeting, May 1963 and April 1964.
54. Arvio, pp. 43–44.
55. *Antitrust Aspects of the Funeral Industry,* p. 106.
56. Alfred M. Sadler, Blair L. Sadler, and E. Blythe Stason, "The Uniform Anatomical Gift Act: A Model of Reform," *The Journal of the American Medical Association* 206 (1968): 2501–2504; Russell S. Fisher, "Let the Dead Help the Living," *Today's Health* 47 (1969): 87–88.
57. Morgan, pp. 44–62.
58. *Funeral Industry Practices: Notice of Proceeding, Proposed Trade Regulation Rule, Statement of Reason for Proposed Rule, Invitation to Propose Issues of Fact for Consideration in Public Hearings, and Invitation to Comment on Proposed Rule* (Washington, D.C.: Federal Trade Commission, 29 Aug. 1975), p. 24.
59. *Federal Trade Commission News,* 28 Aug. 1975, pp. 1–2.
60. *Bride's Honeymoon Travel Market: A Report on the Honeymoon Travel of Bride's Readers,* Research Report no. 9166, Oct. 1974, p. 2.
61. *Money,* May 1975, p. 46.
62. *Consumer Views,* First National City Bank of New York Newsletter, March 1974, p. 1.
63. *St. Petersburg Times,* 27 May 1975, p. 1D.
64. Kenneth Boulding, "The Household as Achilles' Heel," *Journal of Consumer Affairs* 6, no. 2 (Winter 1972): 116.

CHAPTER 7

CONSPICUOUS CONSUMPTION AND EMULATION

CONSUMPTION IN THE GRAND MANNER

Little has been known about the private life of Seward Johnson, seventy-nine-year-old son and heir of Robert Wood Johnson, the founder in 1887 of the Johnson & Johnson empire. Johnson & Johnson manufactures surgical dressings, including Band-Aids, and an extensive line of related products. Seward Johnson is estimated to be worth at least half a billion dollars. What is known about his and his wife's consumption in the grand manner is fascinating. At the age of seventy-four he married a domestic from Poland, who was then twenty-eight years old. She apparently persuaded him to buy some fifty million dollars worth of eighteenth-century European furniture, paintings, and sculpture and then to build a mansion in which to house them. In the first years of construction, $12 million to $17 million were spent on the house. The final cost is not known. It has a Georgian-style main building and two adjacent wings, two cavernous art galleries, a vaultlike wine cellar, Grecian amphitheater, Olympic-size pool, a tennis pavilion, and a two-story, glass-walled, circular orchid house. All windows are bulletproof. Seven ironworkers were brought from Poland to do the bronze railings for the seventeen-foot-wide central staircase.[1] This is truly consumption in the grand manner.

When Aristotle Socrates Onassis married the widow of the thirty-fifth president of the United States in 1968, he emerged as the biggest spender of all time. To demonstrate to his wife Jackie, and to the world, his love for her, he is reported to have spent $20 million in the honeymoon year. The wedding alone cost $40,500, and $6.25 million worth of jewels, clothing, and furs were lavished on the bride. The sixty-two-year-old Greek shipping tycoon spent nearly $2 million on his various homes and over $1 million on his seagoing yacht. In that one year, the bridegroom spent $887,000 for works of art and $1.9 million for insurance premiums. At that time, Mr. and Mrs. Onassis were spending more money than any other couple on earth, exceeding the expenditures of Queen Elizabeth and Prince Philip by $18.8

Valued at $150,000 this car was custom made in 1961 for a movie star. Crushed diamond dust was used in the more than thirty coats of paint that were applied to the car. (*UPI*)

million.[2] At his death his financial empire was estimated to be worth one billion dollars.

If British royalty could not compete with the fabulous Onassis spenders, one might assume that no one could. But there are 115,000 millionaires in the United States whose assets range from $1 million to more than $1 billion. And there are more than 200,000 families whose assets amount to $500,000 or more. These are usually referred to as the "beautiful people," who live in a world all their own and spend money as if it were free.

Conspicuous consumption is the consumption of goods and services on a lavish scale. The purpose and effect of such lavish consumption is to demonstrate pecuniary power. Historically such lavish living was possible only among the nobility, but in the affluent economy of our time it is possible for large numbers of people to live in this manner.

Of course, not all rich people live lavishly; nor do all people with modest incomes consume inconspicuously. However, the urge to "show off" is pervasive. The degree to which one can show off depends on one's income. Those who cannot lead, follow by imitating the leaders. This is how conspicuous consumption gives rise to emulation.

DEMONSTRATING PECUNIARY POWER

The universality of the propensity to consume conspicuously is illustrated by a Chinese proverb: "In ordinary life you must be economical; when you invite guests you must be lavish in hospitality."[3] An advertising enthusiast believes that "our society does not put as much emphasis on buying things cheap as on conspicuous consumption."[4] And a social critic states that "the personal life of the rich, almost without exception, comes down to a sensory gratification on a grand scale. . . ."[5]

Food

If the supply of goods and services were unlimited, everyone could consume on a lavish scale. Even in the abundant economy of the United States, however, goods and services are limited in supply. Those who have great wealth can satisfy every wish and whim. Yet the essence of conspicuous consumption is more than scarcity; it is rarity. Rarity combines scarcity with distinguishability and demonstrability. Demonstrability requires pecuniary power.[6] Current illustrations of conspicuous consumption are easily found. Even in the consumption of food "man is more a peacock than either an economic or biologic animal."[7] He will even destroy food for the sake of prestige. The Trobriand Islanders decorate their choicest yams and display them until they rot, at the same time eating much inferior food. In North China, white rice and white flour were once considered more suitable for persons of social position and for those who had a formal education. When a student of humble origin attained university status, he would repudiate his diet of coarse, whole-grain cereals. When a family moved from the country to the city, they would substitute white flour for cornmeal. In the United States each income group has its prestige foods, embellished with foreign names such as *caviar* or *filet mignon*.

The Palace, a restaurant that opened in New York City in 1975, has a one-price dinner—$50 per person plus tax and an obligatory 23 percent tip, which brings the total to $65.50. Alcoholic beverages are extra. A *New York Times* columnist wrote that his check for two there was $196.50, and he chose the least expensive French wines on a list that ran to $300 a bottle.[8]

Clothing and Jewelry

A woman who wears a Dior gown and a fortune in jewelry obviously has superior pecuniary power. Women's millinery is another effective display device. At luncheons, bridge parties, teas, and cocktail parties, the relative wealth of a woman's husband is proclaimed. The real display takes place at dinner parties, at the opera, and at balls.

Compared with the clothing worn by women, men's clothing is relatively ineffective as a means of conspicuous display. One can hardly distinguish between the chairman of the board of a corporation whose income is a million dollars or more a year and a minor clerk in the same corporation whose income is below ten thousand dollars a year. Of course, the top executive probably pays much more for his suits and accouterments, but the difference in appearance between the two men would scarcely be noticeable to the casual observer. The similarity of male dress is found also in formal attire. The tuxedo and the evening suit are like military uniforms. The quality of the material may differ, but the overall appearance is very much the same.

In an affluent economy the goal of most men is to move out of the blue-collar type of clothing. Clothing that is obviously unsuited for manual labor acquires added meaning. The man who arrives at his office at nine o'clock wearing a gray flannel suit proclaims to all the world that he is not required to perform manual labor.

Because men's clothing is less conspicuous than the clothing of women, women may serve effectively to demonstrate the pecuniary power of their husbands by wearing evidences of great wealth, such as expensive furs and jewelry. Elizabeth Taylor's collection of jewels is reported to be worth $5 million. Ari Onassis sometimes gave Jackie a bracelet for breakfast. On one occasion when he was in Tokyo and she was in New York, he sent a bracelet of Mikimoto pearls by air, and it was delivered, encircling her morning roll, to the delighted Jackie as she ate her breakfast in bed.[9]

The catalogs of stores that cater to the rich show how the wealthy demonstrate their pecuniary power. A recent Abercrombie and Fitch catalog pictured a money clip for $850. Corum's catalog advertised an eighteen-carat gold watch with a peacock feather dial for $2,690, while Tiffany's catalog had as its most expensive piece of jewelry a diamond ring selling for $405,900.

Transportation

People of great wealth are always on the move. They go from estate to estate, from the city to the country, from the seashore to the mountains, and from country to country.

Before the days of the automobile, elaborate and expensive carriages were effective methods of demonstrating one's economic status. With the advent of the railroad, the private car became a mark of distinction. Surprising as it may seem, the private railroad car is still used by a few of the elite. The "Virginia City" is described as a roving palace that includes a Venetian marble fireplace, copies of murals from St. Peter's, six luxurious rooms, a Turkish bath, and a wine cellar. The price is $55,000.

When the automobile displaced the railroad as a means of passenger transportation, the British Rolls-Royce became the symbol of superiority, luxury, and pecuniary power. Its price—up to $90,000—puts it in a class by itself and puts the relatively few owners in a class by themselves. In the United States the Cadillac and the Lincoln Continental vie for first place as status symbols, although the makers of Chrysler Imperial are trying to challenge the Cadillac and Lincoln. It is considered a real achievement to own one or more such cars. Such an achievement is heightened by the ability to afford a chauffeur. The prestige of a chauffeur is enhanced if he is dressed in a uniform, decorated with the employer's crest. Ownership of two or three automobiles is also a status symbol. There are 30 million families in the United States who own two or more cars.

The airplane has become a means of conspicuous consumption. Fabulously wealthy consumers now own one or more airplanes. There is an added distinction in being able to fly one's own plane. But for real pecuniary power, one must have a personal pilot and crew – all dressed in uniforms bearing the coat of arms of the individual they serve. As airplanes change, the old ones lose their symbolic power. Currently one must own a jet.

In addition to a private railroad car, a Cadillac, and an airplane, current standards of conspicuous consumption require an ocean-going yacht. A yacht requires *real* money. Not thousands of dollars, but millions of dollars. The Onassis yacht *Christina* was valued at $5.7 million, carried a crew of sixty-five, and cost $1.1 million a year to operate and maintain.[10] The wealthy may properly sail their own boats, but the truly rich must have a captain and crew to maintain and operate the ship. Like chauffeurs and pilots, the yacht crew must wear distinctive uniforms whose markings demonstrate to all who see them that they are attached to the wealthy owner.

Housing

A mansion is an effective means of conspicuous display. Such mansions are usually made of splendid and expensive materials, some of which may be imported. Decorations and equipment are ornate. In the house of one Pennsylvania millionaire, solid gold doorknobs and bathroom fixtures demonstrate the pecuniary power of the owner. Only a few people actually see such evidences of wealth, but by word of mouth and through newspaper and magazine stories the information spreads. If a house is to serve as a means of conspicuous display, its size must be impressive. A small family would find it difficult to use a mansion having 142 rooms. Such complete disregard for space clearly demonstrates the owner's pecuniary power.

The setting for a mansion requires hundreds or thousands of acres of land. These acres are planted with grass, shrubbery, flowers, and trees interlaced with bridle paths. To own so many acres and to be able to afford to withhold them from agricultural use is an impressive evidence of wealth. To go one step further and actually use the land in such a way as to incur additional expense is evidence of even greater pecuniary power.

As the standard of conspicuous consumption is raised, possession of a mansion with a retinue of servants becomes inadequate to demonstrate the superior consuming power of the owner. A modern American potentate must also have a town house, a suburban estate, a home in the mountains, another at the seashore, a Georgia or California ranch, and a house in England, France, or South America.

Although there is no royalty in the United States, there are people who are so rich that they can and do live on a scale exceeding that of royalty in other countries. Helena Rubinstein made a fortune in the manufacture and sale of cosmetics. Living in the grand manner, she had seven homes — two in France, one in London, one in Mexico, one in Buenos Aires, one in New York City, and one in Greenwich, Connecticut. The top floor of each house was a showplace for her works of art. In her New York apartment, there was an English squire room, a Spanish dining room, a mid-Victorian room, a Georgian dining room, a Biedermeier room, a Dutch room, a French Second-Empire room, a Renaissance room, a Gay Nineties room, an Early American sitting room, a Queen Anne dining room, and an Austrian kitchen.

Kykuit, the Rockefeller family estate in Pocantico Hills, New York, is located on 4,180 acres of land. On the estate there is a fifty-room mansion, houses for each of the brothers, and scores of buildings for the staff of 350 and for maintenance. In addition, the brothers all have town houses, one has a ranch in Venezuela, another a plantation in Hawaii, and another has a working plantation in Arkansas.[11]

When Nelson Rockefeller was up for confirmation by the U.S. Senate as vice president, he released his personal income tax records for the previous ten years. His total income for the ten-year period was $48,884,030, for an average income of $4,888,403 per year. It should be pointed out that during these ten years, federal, state, and local taxes took $21,703,012 of the total income, leaving an average net income of $2,718,102 per year.

The Onassis properties included the island of Skorpios and all its buildings, a hacienda in Uruguay, villas in suburban Athens and Monte Carlo, an apartment on Fifth Avenue in New York City, and permanent hotel suites at the Pierre in New York City and Claridge's in London. Mr. Onassis had 202 persons on his payroll, to whom he paid $727,200 a year, plus $303,000 for food and lodging. Older employees and the disabled were pensioned, and the employer paid for all funerals.[12] At his death, it was reported that he provided his widow with an annual allowance of $250,000.

The advertisements for expensive homes and apartments found in the *New York Times* are revealing. The terms used to describe the apartments are themselves ostentatious. One luxury apartment house, The Sovereign, advertised palatial suites, powder rooms off the gallery, maid's room and bath, master bath fully encased in imported Italian marble, and an ultra-modern kitchen with adjacent butler's pantry. It also noted that "the Sovereign is situated at the very hub of one of the most exclusive yet exciting residential areas in the world." A three-bedroom apartment rented for $26,040 per year. Apartments in a full-service condominium in Miami were advertised for sale for $171,000 unfurnished; $183,000 custom-trimmed and ready for furniture; or $230,000 furnished.[13]

House Furnishings

A look at just one company's home furnishings catalog, *The Horchow Collection Pamper Book,* reveals what is available for the wealthy to buy to demonstrate their pecuniary power: a waste basket for $60; a vicuna throw blanket for $750; and a one-of-a-kind, museum-piece, Coromandel screen from the Ch'ien Lung period, A.D. 1736–1795, for $60,000.

Entertainment

Mrs. Merriweather Post, the cereal heiress, had a 115-room house in Palm Beach and a summer place in the Adirondack Mountains, to which she flew her guests in *The Merriweather*, a beautifully decorated jet. Each guest or couple was housed in a separate cottage, complete with maid and valet. For their entertainment a fleet of thirty boats, ranging from canoes to speedboats, was at their disposal. On her estate there were tennis courts, golf, fishing in two stocked lakes, swimming, water skiing, movies, bridge, dancing, and hiking.[14]

The really rich lavish hundreds of thousands of dollars on entertainment for their guests. Mrs. Post spared no expense when entertaining foreign dignitaries—in a style the government could never hope to duplicate. Over the years her guests have been treated to full Broadway productions of plays and The Ringling Brothers, Barnum & Bailey Circus. When the circus performed, the lawn was protected with carpets. At her death her will specified that the federal government was to be given her estate as a winter home for either the president or for foreign dignitaries, but neither the White House nor the State Department was interested because of the cost of upkeep. Salaries for twenty-two maintenance people and the costs of building supplies, utility bills, and minimal maintenance of the rest of the grounds were estimated to be $775,000 annually.[15]

Vacations

The amount of money that the wealthy can and do spend on vacations seems to be unlimited. The Mauna Kea Beach Hotel in Hawaii rents rooms for $100 to $125 per day per couple. A family of four can easily spend $2,000 on a week's holiday there, not counting air fare to the island. It is not unusual for guests to pay a bill of $10,000 or more when they check out after a long stay.[16]

The ultimate vacation was the "Premier World Cruise—The World in 80 Days" aboard the Queen Elizabeth II, which departed from New York on January 10, 1975. The lowest fare for this cruise was $6,950 for one adult. The highest price was almost $100,000 for the luxury-duplex penthouse suite. Cruise fare included cruise membership, stateroom accommodations, entertainment, and the services of the cruise staff.[17]

The *S.S. United States,* once the world's fastest ocean liner, was purchased from the U.S. Maritime Administration by a group that planned to operate her as a seagoing condominium for the ultra-rich. The ship was to be remodeled to provide 282 living units, to be sold at prices ranging from $650,000 for a single room to $2.5 million for an eight-room suite.[18]

CONTRASTS IN CONSPICUOUS DISPLAY

Inheritors of Fortunes

In other countries a select few inherit titles of nobility and fortunes that have been passed down from generation to generation. The United States is a young nation without a nobility. Some of the larger fortunes —like that of the Astor family—go back to the eighteenth century, but the foundations for the major well-known fortunes, such as those of the Duke, Field, and Rockefeller families, date from the nineteenth century. At least 60 percent of the top wealthy families in this country are inheritors; half are over the age of sixty-five, and one half are women. It is interesting to observe that greater prestige is accorded to the inheritor of great wealth than to the originator of a fortune. As a social group gains maturity, the position of those who inherit great wealth is more firmly entrenched than the position of those who are compelled to acquire it. Inheritors of wealth, having been reared in the grand manner, have learned how to consume wealth conspicuously without appearing to do so. They live in a closed society, and entrance to this world is very difficult for the newly rich. The social register was originally limited to 400 names because the originator of that exclusive group, Mrs. Astor, could accommodate only 400 in her ballroom.

The Newly Rich

In spite of high taxes, the rich are still with us. In fact there are more persons with an annual income of over $1 million today than ever before. And many of these became rich in the last fifteen years. *Fortune* reported that in the five-year period 1968 to 1972 thirty-nine individuals became extraordinarily wealthy. One acquired a fortune estimated to be between $500 million and $700 million; two more, between $300 and $500 million; three, between $200 and $300 million; five, between $150 and $200 million; four, between $100 and 150 million; fifteen, between $75 and $100 million; and nine, between $50 and $75 million.[19]

Inheritors of great wealth tend to look with disdain on these "intruders." They are downgraded as brash, gaudy, uncouth social climbers. They have not yet learned how to live conspicuously in the genteel manner. In this newly wealthy group, spending on a lavish scale is necessary to prove that one has arrived. Lacking tradition and not having grown up in the heady atmosphere of great wealth, such people are inclined to splurge. In doing so, they are likely to offend not only the inheritors of great wealth but also the rest of the population. Both groups are inclined to regard the frantic spending of the newly rich as vulgar. They do not yet have the prestige enjoyed by those who inherited their wealth.

Social Classes in America

The sociologist Warner has grouped Americans into six categories. The upper-upper constitute the aristocracy and comprise one-half of one percent of the total population. The lower-upper group includes the newly rich, comprising one and one-half percent of the population. Professionals and managers make up the upper-middle group of 10 percent. The lower-middle people are the "white-collar" workers, who total 33 percent, and the upper-lower "blue collar" workers, who comprise 40 percent. The last 15 percent is the lower-lower who are the unskilled workers. According to Kassarjian, a young lawyer on the make typifies the upper-middle professionals and managers. The typical lawyer spends more on housing in a prestige neighborhood, has expensive furniture, and dresses in high-priced clothing purchased from a "name" store. The lower-middle class typically includes an engineer who has a "nice" house in a lesser neighborhood, "good" furniture, a complete but not expensive wardrobe, and money in the bank. A truck driver illustrates the upper-lower group. He has a lesser house in a lesser neighborhood but probably has a bigger and later model car. He has more expensive appliances and spends less on clothing but more on sports equipment and events.[20]

The desire to consume conspicuously is found in all income groups. In this we are all alike. Where we differ is in our ability to spend conspicuously. Alfred Marshall, the leading economist in his time, was also a keen observer and commentator. What he wrote at the turn of the century is still valid:

> There is some misuse of wealth in all ranks of society. . . . [Y]et even among the artisans of England, and perhaps still more in new countries, there are signs of the growth of that unwholesome desire for wealth as a means of display which has been the chief bane of the well-to-do classes in every civilized country. Laws against luxury have been futile; but it would be a gain if the moral sentiment of the community could induce people to avoid all sorts of display of individual wealth.[21]

In the United States consumers are under heavy pressure to consume in order to command the respect of others in their group, as well as to maintain their own self-respect. The less people are able to excel or to command respect occupationally, educationally, or otherwise, the more likely they are to use the consuming process as a compensatory device. Stimulated by advertising and with the aid of installment credit, such people turn to automobiles and to appliances, which "become compensations for blocked social mobility."[22]

Men have traditionally placed the responsibility for conspicuous consuming on their wives and daughters. The wife of a small-town businessman or professional man is more than a wife, mother, and housekeeper. Together with the family home and automobile, she and her daughters help to demonstrate the man's pecuniary power by the clothing, furs, and jewelry they wear and by the parties they give at home and at the club. But as more and more women in this country work outside the home, these roles are changing and consuming is becoming a shared responsibility. Increasingly the young men of the family are also playing their role as conspicuous consumers.

At all income levels conspicuous consumption leads to competitive consumption. Whether among the very rich or among a college faculty, there are gradations in income that make it impossible for everyone to consume on the same scale. No matter how far down the scale a family may be there is usually a determination to put its best foot as far forward as possible.

INCONSPICUOUS CONSUMPTION

In Suburbia

In the fascinating field of consumer motivation one finds paradoxes and apparent contradictions. One apparent contradiction is the unwritten rule that a family must not spend beyond the income range of its group, no matter how much money it has. The social climbers and the show-offs are resented by their group, and the group finds effective ways of controlling such tendencies. The stability that characterized small towns and small cities a few years ago has been replaced by the instability of corporate families on the move. Suburbs are occupied by families whose heads are employees of a corporation, working their way up in the income status hierarchy. As they move from the trainee level to the junior executive level to the senior executive level, they move to more exclusive suburbs and adjust their spending practices to the standards already established. While living in Westmoreland Estates, they spend as others in that suburb spend. They all spend at about the same level; they keep up with one another. But the group rule is that no one must spend beyond the group level. If an individual has a larger income than his neighbors, or if one spouse's family is rich, the family must conceal such facts. Even if they can afford a prestige car, they drive a Ford, Chevrolet, or Plymouth.

Since the essence of competitive imitation in consuming is spending more than one's income justifies on things that other people can see, it follows that there must be a compensating economy in the use of things that other people cannot see. The financial strain of keeping up appearances may compel economy in the type and quality of household furnishings, which are not seen by most people, except in the living room and guest room. In these rooms all items must create the desired impression of being able to afford what others can afford. Throughout the household there are opportunities to skimp and save on items that are less commonly noticed.

Far more serious is the practice of driving an automobile without adequate insurance protection. The automobile is a lethal weapon. Its power to kill and maim is awesome. Most states require that owners of automobiles purchase insurance protection. The argument is that no one can afford to own and drive an automobile who cannot also afford insurance premiums to provide monetary payments to accident victims. Yet there are millions of cars on the highways whose owners cannot even afford garage rent, let alone insurance premiums. The car is a visible symbol of ability to pay, but the insurance premium and the policy it purchases are not visible.

EMULATIVE CONSUMPTION

What is Emulation?

Emulation is a human characteristic that causes individuals to wish to equal or excel others in some field of human activity. The word itself carries no connotation of desirability or undesirability. Church members may seek to equal or to excel others in Christian living, while gangsters may seek to equal or to excel the exploits of a notorious leader. The word is used here with special reference to consuming activities. Emulative consumption is a by-product of conspicuous consumption. Although the purpose of producing goods and services is to enable consumers to satisfy their wants and to enrich their living, the tendency to emulate has caused consumption to be regarded by many consumers as a means of invidious comparison. As a result, great wealth and large incomes are endowed with a secondary utility because they are in themselves evidence of ability to pay. The more expensive a commodity, the more utility in the second sense it possesses.

Competitive Consumption

Emulative and imitative consumption lead to and result in competitive consumption. Competition in buying takes a new form. Instead of rivalry among buyers to purchase at the lowest price, it becomes a rivalry in which buyers compete with one another to prove their financial superiority by paying high prices. This causes the economic buyer who haggles over price to lose social position. Only those who buy on a grand scale, and to whom price is no consideration, are able to maintain the desired social position. Emulators who do not have enough money to keep up the competitive pace sometimes borrow money to purchase on the installment plan.

The popular conception of competitive consumption is expressed in the phrase "keeping up with the Joneses." Much of family spending is for the purpose of bolstering family pride. The income earner struggles to equal or to excel the Joneses in the size of his or her paycheck, and the whole family struggles to equal or to excel them in the grandeur of their expenditures. If the family falls too far behind in this competitive race, another member of the family may take a job to augment the family income. This kind of competition leads to extravagance in using goods and services whose consumption is visible. Such items include automobiles, clothing, housing, furnishings, entertainment, club membership, and travel.

Automobiles Most emulators cannot afford private railroad cars or airplanes, but they can and do purchase prestige automobiles on the installment plan. While it is true that group pressure in suburbia controls the amount of money an emulator may spend for an automobile, there are communities in which individuals and families are free to indulge their desire to drive a prestige car in the latest model. The automobile-buying behavior of 300 blacks and 300 whites was compared in a block-controlled quota sample in Chicago. It was found that blacks owned higher priced cars than whites having comparable incomes.[23]

The threat of gasoline rationing and the sharp increases in the price of gasoline during the Arab oil embargo made many people reevaluate the automobile as a status symbol. Smaller cars that got better mileage per gallon were purchased in greater numbers. Detroit began producing smaller cars that gave better mileage and that were also luxury cars, both in appearance and price, thus still appealing to automobile status seekers. General Motors responded to these changes in two ways. It introduced a "small Cadillac," the Seville, with a list price of $12,000, and a truly small car, the Chevette, which was competitive both in size and price with Volkswagen and Toyota.

Clothing Because outer clothing is visible, it is an effective means of demonstrating family ability to "keep up." In years past tradition dictated that one dress according to one's social position. It was considered proper for factory workers and farmers to wear simple, sturdy suits, to be worn only on Sundays and on festive occasions and to last no less than five years. The tradition among office workers is different. The trainee and the junior accountant are expected to emulate the junior executive, who in turn imitates his or her superiors in the corporate structure. The woman office worker must wear a fur coat to demonstrate her ability to dress as well as the more highly paid women employees. If she cannot afford the expensive dresses they buy, she settles for less expensive imitations. The millions of consumers in lower-income brackets constitute a large market for inexpensive imitative clothing. Such clothing items are purchased not so much for their inherent utility as for their capacity to give the wearer added prestige.

Recently, however, significant changes have been taking place as people become more and more independent in their choices of attire. One may go to a reception and find women in miniskirts, knee- and calf-length dresses, long dresses, and pants suits. Formal dress for men has been changing— from the black tuxedo, white shirt, and black tie to colorful evening jackets, lace evening shirts, and a variety of sizes and colors in bow ties. But even so, there is peer group pressure to conform to the changes.

In the practice of competitive consumption the standard of high reputability requires that a woman have not only expensive clothing but considerable variety. It is a reflection on the family if a woman is compelled to wear the same evening gown more than once. Further down the income scale, the same standard prevails but necessity requires that a gown be worn an entire season.

Jewelry An interesting example of emulative consumption in jewelry is seen in the success of Wellington counterfeit diamonds. Wellington is the world's largest specialist in diamondlike gems.[24] The Wellington diamondlike gems are "flawless and fiery," and the difference between them and real diamonds is hardly detectable by the naked eye. The key difference is price. The Wellington counterfeit diamonds are priced at approximately $40 per carat, plus mounting. A one-carat real diamond in a mounting sells for around $1,200. The price for a one-carat Wellington diamondlike gem in a six pronged Tiffany mounting is $95. This is an example of emulative consumption at a low price.

Housing The house in which a family lives and its locality are additional ways of proving ability to keep up with the Joneses. All villages, towns, and cities have their poor sections and their swank sections. Leaders in each group live in the best house on the best street. Competitive imitators then place themselves in as favorable a location as their incomes permit. If a family cannot live in Morgan Manor, they can bask in the sunshine of reflected glory in nearby Morgan Manor Estates.

Address alone is not sufficient. The family home must conform to the standard of its location. If it has a $60,000 address, it must have a $60,000 house, and so on up or down the scale. Every town and city is zoned on this basis.

Apartments, like houses, are prestige symbols. Yet a six-bedroom apartment on Park Avenue does not command the respect or the envy of competitors nearly as much as a million dollar house on a two-thousand-acre estate. Apartment dwellers who park their prestige cars on the street find their automobiles also provide significance as income symbols.

House Furnishings When a family entertains competing members of its social group, its position in the consumer hierarchy is further determined by the elaborateness of its house furnishings. The best and most expensive furniture, rugs, dishes, silver, books, and pictures yield, in addition to direct utility, the peculiar satisfaction of demonstrating financial power.

Entertainment In all income groups entertainment provides opportunities for competitive consumption. Many people achieve distinction this way and are judged by their parties. "The hostess with the mostest" is in an enviable position. In each income group the lavishness of entertainment at luncheons, teas, dinners, bridge parties, dances, and weekend sojourns settles toward a minimum standard that must be respected by all who wish to retain membership in that social circle. The competitive process tends constantly to raise the standard, making it difficult for those near the lower margin to keep up with the pace. It may even result in their fall into the social pattern of the group below. Even among the wives of college professors, where one might expect to find more rationality in the consuming process, similar competitive standards prevail.

Club Membership Much entertaining takes place outside the home. Even in small towns and rural regions a family that does not belong to at least one social club is beyond the pale of social acceptability. There are thousands of clubs in the United States, each asserting its own degree of exclusiveness. The country club probably predominates. For an individual to be able to take his or her friends to a club for lunch is a mark of distinction. To be able to entertain lavishly in one's home is evidence of social success. But to be able to entertain in an exclusive club is evidence that the hosts are one rung farther up the social ladder. This sets new standards for imitators to copy and provides incentive for promoters to organize imitative clubs.

Travel The United States is a nation on wheels. There was a time when only the wealthy could take extensive automobile trips, garbed in their linen dusters. In recent years, the increase in the number of people who receive paid vacations has made the summer vacation trip to Yellowstone a must. The farther one goes, the greater the prestige because that indicates more vacation time and enough money to enjoy it. For people who live in the North, a winter vacation in the South is a status symbol. For people in the South, a summer vacation in the North serves the same purpose. The college students who spend their spring vacations in Florida are the envy of their classmates who must spend their vacations at home.

Emulation in Transition

The essence of emulation is the tendency of people in each socioeconomic class to choose as their goal the plane of living established by the next higher income group. If income distribution were more equal, conspicuous consumption might decrease because the pressure to spend for competitive consumption would be less. There would then be more money to spend on nonconspicuous and inconspicuous consumption. In this generation there has indeed been a considerable leveling of income distribution. There are not so many of the very poor. One result of this is the development of inconspicuous consumption. Blue jeans are worn by the sons and daughters of parents in all income groups. While all families have some of the same things, each family combines them in a pattern of its own. One family may stress music lessions, another the acquisition of antiques, another educational travel.

Is it possible that the so-called population explosion was a form of conspicuous or competitive consumption? A generation ago parents who had only one or two children were prone to be apologetic in the presence of a neighbor who had three or four or more. It costs money to raise children, so the more children one had the more money one also had to have. With the potential threat of over-population and the increasing cost of rearing children, there has been a reverse in this attitude. Now it is becoming a status symbol not to have children or to have only one or two. One reason for this change is the fact that rearing children in the "right" way, with all the "necessary" advantages, is too costly if a family has many children. The cost of rearing a child from birth to eighteen years of age varies considerably, depending upon the region where the family lives and the family income. The Agricultural Research Service of the Department of Agriculture has developed cost figures on raising a child that, when adjusted for inflation through 1974, illustrate these variations. The lowest cost was $17,000 for rearing a child in the North Central farm area on an economy budget. (The USDA measured costs according to three levels of budgets: economy, low cost, and moderate cost.) The highest cost was $48,000 for the Western rural nonfarm area with a moderate-cost budget.[25] In another study it was estimated that a middle-income family ($16,000 to $18,000) having a baby in 1975 could easily spend $70,000 to raise the child from birth through college.[26]

Large families are a thing of the past according to the United States Census Bureau. The bureau reported in 1975 that for the first time in history the average size of the nation's households dropped below the three-person level. A number of factors, including more effective birth control, later marriages, and women's liberation, have caused this decline according to the bureau.

Negative Emulation

The negative aspect of emulation is custom. Custom determines what consumers shall or shall not consume. Custom demands that consumers emulate their ancestors. If they do so, they must refrain from emulating contemporary violators of custom. The tendency to act customarily is constantly being combated by the tendency to imitate conspicuous and fashionable consumers. The latter course requires courage and financial power. The more income one has, the easier it is to flout custom. However, since so many people have small incomes, more consumers are controlled by custom than by the propensity to emulate.

Is Emulation Desirable?

The imitative tendency in itself is neither good nor bad. Its power is great in either direction. Our judgment of behavior based on emulation should depend on the form it takes. Whom do consumers copy? And why? We must have answers to these questions before we can decide whether emulation promotes or retards consumer welfare. The possibilities for beneficial emulation are numerous. Emulation in good taste, which results in a wider appreciation of the goods and services that do contribute to individual and to group welfare, is desirable. If the imitators cultivate a love for and an appreciation of music, art, literature, and drama, their lives will be enriched. If college students emulate the practice of purchasing and reading good books, they will benefit. If desirable trends in clothing are copied, those who copy may gain comfort and beauty. If they emulate styles of architecture that provide comfort, convenience, and health, they will benefit. If the house furnishings and equipment they copy include useful, labor-saving, health-conserving devices, not only the imitators but all members of the group will gain. As J. A. Hobson has said, "to copy good examples even if the copying is defective is an elevating practice."

Conversely, the practice of emulating may promote illfare. If false consuming standards are established, people will consume goods and services that do not promote their welfare. This is wasteful. It is here that pecuniary emulation takes its greatest toll.

The End of Affluence?

The recession of the 1970s, the food shortages that recently occurred around the world, shortages of other resources, and the problems connected with energy have raised serious questions as to whether western civilization, and the United States in particular, have come to the end of the age of affluence. Nothing in history compares with the cornucopia of the past three decades in the United States. Can it be sustained? Should it be sustained? "It can be argued that, next to freedom itself, a high and rising living standard is what Americans prize most about their country."[27] There is little doubt that the recession and the threat of a declining standard of living have sent shock waves through many Americans. This has brought on a time for reappraisal of our value system in America.

The internationally famous historian Arnold Toynbee saw a source for hope in this change:

> A society that is declining materially may be ascending spiritually. Perhaps we may be going to return perforce to the way of life of the first Christian monks in Upper Egypt and of their sixth-century Irish successors. The loss of our affluence will be extremely uncomfortable and it will certainly be difficult to manage. But, in some respects, it may be a blessing in disguise, if we can rise to this grave occasion.[28]

QUESTIONS FOR REVIEW

1. Do you have any desire to spend money lavishly?
2. Have you observed a "show-off" tendency in consumer behavior among any of your college classmates?

3. If you were a multimillionaire, do you think you would be a conspicuous consumer?

4. What is conspicuous consumption? What is its purpose? Is it something new?

5. What methods do people use to show off their wealth?

6. How do you explain the veneration most people feel for inherited fortunes?

7. Is emulation good or bad?

8. What are the status symbols on your campus, in order of importance?

9. How is the growth of inconspicuous consumption in recent years to be explained?

10. Do you consider long hair, blue jeans, and bare feet to be forms of conspicuous consumption?

11. How would you go about fighting conspicuous consumption in your own life?

12. Is it possible to go to an extreme in behavior that is anti-conspicuous consumption? Explain.

PROJECTS

1. Record and analyze your expenditures for a month. What percent was on competitive consumption to impress others? What percent was spent on emulative consumption to conform?

2. In the community in which your school is located, find out where the high-, middle-, and low-status neighborhoods are located. Discuss the observable differences in the neighborhoods that relate to the different levels of consumption.

3. With as much objectivity as you can, write an essay on the methods and manners of the status-seekers in your community or on your campus.

4. Ask ten or fifteen fellow students to what extent their consuming practices are geared toward impressing others. Tabulate your results and present them in class. (If all members of the class work on this project, a good sample of the student body could be secured.)

5. Ask ten students what part status and peer group pressure played in their decision to start smoking cigarettes.

REFERENCES

1. *People,* 3 March 1975, pp. 14–15.
2. Fred Sparks, *The $20,000,000 Honeymoon: Jackie and Ari's First Year* (New York: Bernard Geis Associates, 1970), pp. 49, 58, 64–67.

3. Alpha C. Chiang, "Religion, Proverbs and Economic Mentality," *American Journal of Economics and Sociology* 20 (April 1961): 258.
4. Britt, p. 412.
5. Ferdinand Lundberg, *The Rich and the Super-Rich: A Study in the Power of Money Today* (New York: Lyle Stuart, 1968), p. 843.
6. Dwight E. Robinson, "The Economics of Fashion Demand," *Quarterly Journal of Economics* 75 (1961): 385.
7. Graubard, p. 15.
8. *New York Times,* 6 June 1975, p. 21.
9. Sparks, pp. 75, 77–79.
10. *Ibid.,* p. 56.
11. Lundberg, pp. 848–849.
12. Sparks, pp. 52–56.
13. *New York Times,* 21 Sept. 1973, p. 47; 22 March 1975, p. 17; and 9 Nov. 1975, p. 61.
14. Betty Beale, "Washington Letter," *The Spokesman-Review,* 3 Aug. 1969, p. 37.
15. *Washington Post Parade,* 28 Sept. 1975, p. 8.
16. *Money,* May 1975, pp. 36–37.
17. *Wall Street Journal,* 24 Feb. 1976, p. 14.
18. *Pittsburgh Post-Gazette,* 7 Feb. 1975, p. 2.
19. Arthur M. Louis, "The New Rich of the Seventies," *Fortune* 3 (Sept. 1973): 170–173.
20. W. L. Warner, Marchia Meeker, and Kenneth Eels, *Social Class in America* (New York: Harper & Row, 1960), cited in Kassarjian and Robertson, pp. 373–374.
21. Alfred Marshall, *Principles of Economics,* 8th ed. (London: Macmillan, 1922), pp. 136–137.
22. David Caplovitz, *The Poor Pay More: Consumer Practices of Low Income Families* (New York: The Free Press of Glencoe, 1963), pp. 13, 41, 180, 181.
23. Fred C. Akers, "Negro and White Automobile Buying Behavior: New Evidence," *Journal of Marketing* 33 (1969): 81.
24. Wellington Jewels, 1120 Connecticut Ave., N.W., Washington, D.C. 20036.
25. *Cost of Raising A Child,* U.S. Department of Agriculture, Agricultural Research Service, Sept. 1971.
26. "What It Takes to Raise A Child," *Money,* Sept. 1975, p. 25. (Note that these figures have been increased to reflect a 4 percent annual rate of inflation.)
27. Edmund Faltermayer, "Ever Increasing Affluence Is Less of A Sure Thing," *Fortune,* April 1975, p. 92.
28. *National Observer,* 14 Sept. 1974, p. 14.

FASHION-MADE WANTS

THE LURE AND POWER OF FASHION

Fashion as a Dictator of Consumer Choice

Of all animals, humans alone have always been dissatisfied with their bodies. They have gone to great effort and expense to improve on nature. Many consumers follow fashion as the legendary children followed the Pied Piper of Hamelin. This leads them into curious and sometimes contradictory actions. They wish to conform and they wish to be fashionable. There are times when they must make a choice.

The blue jeans fashion has been a unique development. John Silber, president of Boston University, made an astute observation about this fashion:

> Consider a society in which artificially aged and worn blue jeans sell for more than new ones. . . . The younger generation finds a special value in the costumes of poverty and disarray simply because these aspects of life have become far scarcer for children of the middle class than good clothes and comeliness. Just as French aristocrats at the time of the French Revolution took great delight in dressing as peasants and cavorting in bucolic roles, our young people affect the costumes of poverty; in their horizon, the poor are little more than a romantic abstraction.[1]

In one year twenty-five and a half million dozen blue jeans were manufactured in the United States—enough to provide one and a half pairs for every man, woman, and child in the nation.[2] Although the jeans revolution at first glance seemed to signal the end of fashion, that has not been the case. Jeans have become just another fashion. People still take on roles in everyday life, and clothing is still a vital symbol of the roles we adopt.

WHAT IS FASHION?

A *fashion* is "the accepted way of talking, walking, eating, and dressing that is adopted by a group of people at a given time."[3] Automobiles, houses, house furnishings—in fact practically all consumer goods—are in or out of fashion. To be in fashion, they must be accepted by a majority of a group. Fashion serves to identify status. "The initiating spark is the social need of people to be like others and yet to be distinct from others."[4] For the individual, it expresses personality, defines status, and announces a role. For the group, it distinguishes occupational groups, identifies peer groups, and singles out prestige groups.

In an article on fashion in the *New York Times,* Isadore Barmash posed the question, "What is fashion?" His own answer to this question is that fashion is a subjective matter: ". . . Fashion is totally in the eyes of the beholder, sometimes, you can't see it; frequently, you can only sense it; and almost all the time, you're never quite sure you're in it."[5]

Barmash believes that fashion means innovation, change, and obsolescence, and that it therefore is not dependable—at least not for long. In the same article he asked several experts to define fashion. Their responses are both interesting and contradictory. "Fashion," said the president of a leading group of department stores, "is nothing but a lot of nonsense." "Fashion is nothing more than the extension of your personality," responded a professor of communications and chairman of the Advertising and Communications Department of the Fashion Institute of Technology in New York City. "Fashion no longer exists," was the response of Samuel Neaman, chairman of the McCrory Corporation. "Art on your back or in your home or personal life—that's fashion," asserted George Baylis, president of Bonwit Teller Specialty Stores.

In another article concerning fashion, syndicated columnist Sydney Harris wrote: "Reading about the new styles permeating from Paris and other chic centers, I am reminded of Wilde's wickedly accurate observation: 'Fashion is a form of ugliness so intolerable that we have to alter it every six months.'"[6]

Fashion is a volatile form of luxury, the essence of which is change in the design of things for decorative purposes. Functional irrelevance and symbolic significance for expression of the ego are implicit in fashion. The origin of fashion lies in social and sexual competition. The social elements are more obvious, while the sexual elements are indirect, or even concealed.[7]

A *fad* is a miniature fashion in some unimportant matter. Fads are usually associated with novelties, yet many things that come in as fads become fashions.

In contrast to fashion and fads, a *style* is a distinctive expression in some field of human endeavor, and it is permanent. It continues as a style even though it may be out of fashion. The styles that were in fashion when your parents were in college may be out of fashion now, but they are still styles because they still exist as distinctive methods of expression. It is not uncommon for styles to go through cycles of fashionability. The constantly shifting length of women's hemlines illustrates this fact. At one time long skirts may be fashionable. At another time, short skirts may be the fashion, followed by a recurrence of long skirts. In the 1970s fashion designers went back to the 1940s and even to the 1930s for ideas.

Custom is long-established group practice; it venerates the past, while fashion respects the present. The distinction among these terms may be illustrated in the case of clothing. In the United States it is customary to wear clothing—in contrast with some societies where little or no clothing is worn. Clothing styles in the United States, as a distinctive method of expression, are very different from clothing styles in some other countries, such as Japan where the kimono is worn. In both countries there is a distinctive style of dress, but in Japan the style has remained the same for many centuries, whereas in the United States the style is subject to frequent changes that are called fashions. In recent years, however, so-called western wear has become more and more prevalent in Japan.

Fashions are not necessarily progressive. They may introduce new styles or they may simply reintroduce old styles, with very little or no relation to utility. They may be described as *progressive* or *retrogressive*, according to the extent to which they promote or retard consumer welfare.

Taste is the ability to discern and appreciate that which is beautiful and appropriate. It requires real knowledge to exercise good taste. The fashion industry encourages the view that even though a style may be artistic, good taste forbids its use if it is not in fashion. Conversely, items in fashion may be ugly, but good taste adapts them in an effort to secure a pleasing effect.

THE PERVASIVENESS OF FASHION

Fashionable Clothing for Women

Although fashion dictates or influences consumer choice among many consumer goods, its power is probably greatest in determining the kind of clothing men and women wear at any given time. This is true because fashion depends on vanity and upon the efforts of people to transform and improve themselves. Many a survey has shown that when women purchase clothing for themselves, their first consideration is fashion, with price second, and quality third.

The influence of fashion on clothing is as old as the custom of wearing clothing. In considering the psychology of dress, Parsons concluded that people are always the same. Through the years and through the centuries they have the same vanities, the same hypocrisies, and the same absurdities.[8] In medieval times as now men and women followed the dictates of fashion. The frills and feathers worn by men were matched by the hoops and the flounces worn by women. Writers then as now were critical of the extravagance, the imitation, and the waste in clothing fashions.[9]

The chief difference between fashion in earlier centuries and fashion in the twentieth century is the rapidity with which fashions change. In earlier times fashions were in vogue for a generation or more. Now the average life of a fashion is two years. In that two-year period, it takes six months to introduce a fashion, then the fashion is in vogue for six months, and throughout the second year it diminishes in popularity. The annual edicts of New York and Parisian *couturieres* determine for millions of women whether skirts shall be long or short, high-waisted or low-waisted, tight or loose, made of wool, silk, cotton, or synthetic fabric, and whether the fashionable color shall be bright pink or subdued mulberry. There is some evidence that some male designers of dress hate women and delight in making fools of them. The "sack" or "shift" dress was a male joke because it made all women appear to be pregnant.[10]

If fashion designers decree that women's hair shall be long or short, straight or wavy, that heels shall be high or low, that shoes shall be white or black or colored to match the costume, that hose shall be decorated, that eyebrows shall be plucked or pencilled, millions of women will obey the decrees. If fashion demands that no hats be worn or that they be made of straw or wool or look like an inverted flowerpot, women for the most part accept the edict. If fashion decrees that winter coats be trimmed with fur and that women carry a matching muff, they comply. If it is fashionable to expose bare backs in the ballroom and on the beach, backless dresses and swimsuits will be purchased. Retailers of mass-produced clothing have representatives in Paris, New York, and Hollywood who send designs and specifications of new fashions by airmail. Within a few months, high-fashion, high-price items are on sale at popular prices all over the nation. Because volume and distribution are the keys to the fashion industry today, Sears, Penney, and Ward are fashion leaders because they promote the latest designs in the greatest quantity.[11] "The wearing of fashionable clothing by all classes of society is a modern American phenomenon."[12]

Public reaction to a new fashion varies. If it is ahead of its time, as the bare-bosom swimsuit was in 1964, it is rejected as being too extreme. (A decade later nude bathing was spreading on the East and West coasts.) If the timing of a new fashion brings it out a year ahead of public opinion, it is accepted by a few and is considered daring. When everybody accepts the new fashion, it is considered smart. Then the downgrade begins. Last year's fashion is dowdy. Fashions prevalent a decade ago are considered ugly, while those prevalent twenty years ago are ridiculous. After a fashion has been out for fifty years, it assumes a quality of quaintness. After a few more years, it is considered charming, and finally romantic. By that time the fashion will probably be reintroduced.

The pants suit for women has been the most "revolutionary" and widely accepted fashion change of the 1970s. The pants suit is now acceptable for practically any occasion—formal and informal. But even with the pants suits, fashions keep changing—from narrow pants to wide pants, from low heels to high heels. This fashion cycle confirms the observation that people "want newness within the bounds of conformity."[13]

Advertisers and merchandisers have helped to make teenagers fashion conscious. One researcher found that boys in the tenth and twelfth grades were as much concerned about high-fashion clothing as were girls. The boys, like the girls, were motivated by a desire to win attention and recognition.[14] In our affluent society millions of teenagers spend billions of dollars every year on clothing and accessories. Likewise, college students spend freely for high-fashion items. Fashion is a big business. Some magazines, such as *Vogue, Mademoiselle,* and *Seventeen,* are fashion handbooks.

Fashionable Clothing for Men

There was a time when the males of the human species dressed and strutted in peacock fashion. They curled their hair, wore wigs, pantaloons, and high-heeled shoes. Critics called them fops. The French Revolution changed everything, including male apparel. Calvin, Luther, and Protestantism introduced the drab costumes that have prevailed for the last 300 years. As commoners gained control of government, they continued to wear their work clothes. They were followed by white-collar workers whose clothing became even more colorless. Only the military, in their dress uniforms, continued to preen and decorate themselves. For businessmen conformity became a mark of superiority, and conservative blue serge or gray flannel suits gave them a sense of security.

The citadel of conformity was finally cracked in the early 1960s by the Beatles and fashion designer Pierre Cardin. By 1966 men eagerly accepted anything and everything suggested by designers and offered by clothing manufacturers. Now men have fashion shows and fashion magazines such as *Playboy, Esquire,* and *Gentleman's Quarterly.* Hemlines of coats and trousers rise and fall. Neckties expand and contract. Shirt colors follow the rainbow. Shoes take on color. High heels for men was a surprising fashion change that was quickly accepted by many youth. (High heels for men were also in vogue circa 1725–1750.) A classic example of a very rapid and extreme change in men's fashion took place in 1934 when Clark Gable took off his shirt in the film *It Happened One Night* and revealed a bare chest. Undershirt sales are said to have dropped 75 percent that year. Even military personnel search for color, comfort, and ways to rebel in clothing styles.

What caused men to go on such a wild fashion kick? Many forces were at work, but no one really knows the answer. One can speculate that television personalities have had an influence on fashion. For example, Johnny Carson is credited with catapulting the turtleneck sweater into high fashion. Rising salary scales have helped free men from their traditional practice of wearing clothing until it was thread-bare. A *Fortune* writer, with tongue in cheek, suggested that at one time when a woman married, she wanted her man to look like a bank clerk – symbolic of a good provider. But now she has her own money and the pill, so men have to compete in the peacock manner.[15]

In the fall of 1975 vests and gray flannel and pinstripe suits began to reappear. White shirts came back, belts narrowed, and collar points became shorter. In general the trend now seems to be toward a more regimented look, which runs counter to the "anything goes" peacock informality of the 60s, although some men still favor the more colorful styles of the 60s.

Fashion in Houses and House Furnishings

The current generation of homeowners has been exposed to the promotional pressure of the National Institute of Real Estate Brokers to move up from older middle-class housing to modern fashionable housing. In fact the institute urges a move up every four years. They suggest that owning a home without a mortgage is no longer fashionable.[16] A housing industry trade journal asks, "Who wants to live in a house a lifetime?" The journal expresses the view that the building industry must do as the auto industry did: find the equivalent of a little chromium and tailfins.

The recession of the 1970s and the resulting spiraling costs of houses has forced many potential homeowners to reevaluate houses as a status symbol. It also forced the housing industry to trim off the costly extras and build smaller and more economical houses.

Architectural styles in houses come and go with sufficient regularity to classify them as fashions. Whether the architecture of a house shall be Colonial, English, Spanish, Mexican, Italian, ranch, or one of many other possible styles depends on the period in which it is built. Builders do not have complete freedom of choice if they have respect for fashion. Even a very rich individual would be ridiculed if he or she were to build a house today in a mid-Victorian style. A few years ago two-story houses in wide-open spaces were out of fashion. Now they are coming back. Children who have never lived in two-story houses are fascinated by the stairways and the attics.

The furniture and furnishings of a house also reflect the influence of fashion. Surprising as it may seem, people reportedly consider fashion first, price second, and quality third when they purchase house furnishings, just as they do when buying clothing for themselves. Furniture for the living room will be leather, cane, plastic, bamboo, or aluminum, depending on the influence prevailing in the period when it is purchased. The influence of Louis XIV returns periodically to determine how bedrooms should be furnished, while the influence of Queen Anne determines the type of silver service used in the dining room. Styles in dishes range from gold and silver to china and glass.

Formerly kitchens and bathrooms were areas into which the power of fashion had not penetrated, but in recent years these rooms too have shown the fashion influence. Along with the very real utilitarian improvements in kitchen and bathroom design and fixtures, builders have learned that they can get a higher price for houses decorated with two-toned or contrasting colors.

Automobile Fashions and Obsolescence

Millions of automobiles are scrapped each year. In the automobile trade this figure is viewed with satisfaction. One of the best indications that automobile sales will continue to increase is the fact that increasing numbers of buyers have to replace the cars that they have scrapped. One reason for the high and rising rate of scrappage is the practice of *obsoletism* in the automobile industry. A former vice-president in charge of styling for General Motors Corporation proudly claims credit for introducing the concept of obsoletism in the 1930s. He stated that when the same models are produced indefinitely, the product becomes monotonous and people will not buy.[17] That was shortly before the Volkswagen appeared.

Planned obsolescence is the superficial redesign of a product for sales purposes only. *Built-in obsolescence* is deliberate under-engineering to give the product an unnecessarily short life span so as to require premature replacement. A team of economists estimated that the average obsolescence cost per automobile was $700. The aggregate cost of obsoleting automobiles was estimated at $5 billion annually.[18] Measured by today's dollar this figure would be considerably higher. But at the same time the degree of change that is being made in the model changeover each year has diminished, so the cost should be increasing at a decreasing rate.

It is significant that economists have concluded that "it seems likely . . . that . . . the car manufacturers were giving the public what it wanted, save perhaps for overshooting in some respects." This raises the question as to whether obsolescence is a virtue or a vice. The chairman of the board of an appliance manufacturing company is quoted as having said that the principal purpose of an engineer is to create obsolescence. The chairman

An example of an outmoded fashion in automobile design, fins were introduced in new car models produced in the 1950s. (*UPI*)

of the board of another company has written that obsolescence creates new business and makes jobs. Millions of people have to discard automobiles, appliances, and clothing because they are no longer in fashion. To drive obsolete cars, or use obsolete appliances, or wear obsolete clothes would make such people feel dowdy or out of fashion.[19]

In the automobile industry planned obsolescence has had a monopoly-creating effect. Regular and frequent model changes require expenditures that only the big three automobile manufacturers can afford. The smaller firms are driven out of business at no cost to the larger firms. The economics involved is that of the principle of diminishing costs per unit as production volume increases. General Motors Corporation can use a die two million times a year and then scrap it at the end of the second year. American Motor's smaller production would not scrap the die until the thirteenth year. If American Motors must scrap at the end of the second year, its costs per car are higher than those of General Motors.[20]

In the 1970s the automobile industry has been forced to reevaluate the practice of obsoleting its products. The high rate of inflation and the sky-rocketing price of gasoline have pressured the public into buying smaller cars and cars that get better gas mileage. The introduction of the 1976 model year occurred with little fanfare because most 1976 cars were similar to the 1975 models, except for minor face-lifts. One Ford executive predicted that by 1980 the "full-size" car will be two feet shorter and at least 600 pounds lighter. This happened sooner than predicted. General Motors reduced the length and weight of its "full-size" 1977 models.

There will always be a market for luxury cars, but the market is getting smaller. The American automobile industry finally has recognized the public's desire to buy smaller, more economical cars. In 1976 General Motors introduced the Chevette to compete directly with Volkswagen, Toyota, and Datsun. In the first year GM hoped to sell 250,000 Chevettes and regain some of the market that had been lost to the smaller foreign cars but only 150,000 were sold. The desire of many people to own flashy, sporty, large automobiles will not cease, but the economic realities of the marketplace have persuaded many people to settle for smaller, economical cars, which in turn has persuaded Detroit to produce to meet this demand.

The trend toward planned obsolescence has been general. Starting with automobiles, it spread to appliances, houses, hardware, and building materials. Many people have little or no concept of value. Consequently, they are easily persuaded to pay high prices. The lure of a liberal trade-in makes a price seem lower. And "easy credit" conceals the total payments. Obsolescence results in the production of shoddy products. This in turn leads to shoddy service and workmanship. Planned obsolescence involves a wasteful use of natural and human resources.

The service life expectancy of automobiles is six years. By contrast, the service life expectancy for sewing machines is twenty-four years; for vacuum cleaners, eighteen years; for electrical refrigerators and ranges, sixteen years; and for washing machines and television sets, eleven years.

These figures dramatize the differences among products built for durability and service and those built for obsolescence and scrappage.

Obsolescence may not be a total evil, however. A firm of industrial designers took the view that obsolescence is not bad because the birth of a new product may add some utility. Obsolescence is the mark of a free, expanding economy. These engineers did oppose what they called "phony obsolescence," defined as "doctoring up an existing product with chrome, gewgaws and meaningless gimcrackery" in order to make the current model of a product look new to prospective buyers. Their opposition was not based on ethical or moral considerations. They opposed it because they did not consider it to be good business in the long run. They favored style obsolescence, however, because "consumer tastes do change."

A panel of 375 marketing executives was asked several questions concerning obsolescence. Eighty-eight percent agreed that planned obsolescence does exist, notably in the automobile and appliance industries. Fifty-eight percent rejected the concept and practice of planned obsolescence, considering it a corruptive influence. Seventy percent considered planned obsolescence and its related prestige appeals undesirable because they emphasize trivialities and distort consumer values. What would happen if there were no planned obsolescence? One third of the panelists thought there would be fewer sales, fewer jobs, and less personal income. The majority expressed the view that consumers would then spend their money on products they really wanted rather than on superficial style changes.

Obsolescence may actually render a benefit to those individuals and families who have limited incomes. They might never be able to purchase new automobiles, new appliances, and new furniture. Since obsolescence encourages people who have the money to replace products before their useful life has expired, it also makes these usable products available to buyers at considerably lower prices than new products.

FACTORS FAVORING FASHIONS

Pursuit of Profit

The free, private enterprise, competitive economy of the United States is powered by men and women who wish to make money. There are many kinds of business firms, engaged in the production of raw materials, agricultural products, manufacturing, transportation and communication, banking and insurance, wholesaling and retailing. In the basic industries, style and fashion are scarcely involved in the production of goods and services, but change, based on improvements such as the computer, is a fact of life. In consumer goods industries styles and fashion changes are important. In the production and sale of clothing, automobiles, and appliances, fashion and obsolescence are devices which some sellers have found very profitable, so profitable that in their advertising they endeavor to persuade consumers to discard the old and buy the new. From a consumer point of view and from a social point of view, this may be wasteful. But from the individual point of view of the seller, it may be profitable.

Advertising

Fashion changes are introduced and spread in a variety of ways. Fashion shows display the latest in clothing and automobiles. Newspapers, magazines, and television contribute considerable coverage to the presentation of fashion changes. On a college campus or in a social group a leader may introduce a new fashion. But the mass spread of a fashion depends largely on commercial advertising. As a social animal, the consumer has an intense desire to be accepted by the group. If the group requires that the consumer wear clothing in the latest fashion and drive the newest model of an automobile, many consumers will do all they can to meet those requirements. It is easy for advertisers to use these observed propensities. Today advertising is so persuasive that many consumers cannot resist it. Subconsciously, if not consciously, many of us are influenced by the advertising theme that if we wish to be up-to-date, aware of what is being done, in the know, we must follow high fashion.

An Economy of Abundance

It takes money to stay in fashion. One cannot discard an automobile that still has several years of usefulness unless one has an adequate income. In the nineteenth century only the wealthy could follow fashion. In the twentieth century family incomes have increased at almost all levels. More and more people are now able to follow the dictates of fashion. The production of large quantities of fashionable goods or their imitations at low prices has made millions of consumers fashion conscious.

Transportation and Communication

Television has made the spread of fashion instantaneous. Sitting before the family television set, women see the fashion shows in Paris and New York. They see the gowns worn by women prominent in public life. The men see the new clothing styles for men and the new models of automobiles, the advertising of which is intended to propel them directly to the salesroom the next day. Television has shattered the former barriers of time and space. Supplementing television are high-speed planes that make transportation almost instantaneous. No longer does it take weeks or months for fashion changes to reach remote sections of the country. In conjunction with other factors, high-speed communication and transportation have made millions of consumers fashion conscious.

Leisure

Leisure time in which to display and use new fashions is essential to their continuance. If women spend most of their time in the kitchen or on a job, there is less opportunity to display their latest gowns or wigs. Among people of the middle-income group, women are the most faithful followers of fashions. Many years ago Thorstein Veblen suggested that men, wishing to consume conspicuously yet not having the leisure time to do it themselves, expected their women to do it for them. Consequently, luncheons and parties provide convenient opportunities for displaying the latest acquisitions in fashions. Ironically, the Sunday morning church service is a place where women display the latest clothing fashion. The importance of leisure is emphasized at resorts and playgrounds, where the influence of fashion is probably the strongest. At the more exclusive resorts the self-acknowledged elite of society introduce the newest styles. These are quickly imitated by various income groups, struggling to make an impression by consuming conspicuously and competitively.

Political Freedom

In nations where a caste system prevails there cannot be a broad base for fashion as we know it in the West. Not only do the mass of consumers lack purchasing power, there are also restrictions based on social position. In some countries this is fortified by legislation prohibiting the use of certain products by commoners. For example, the royal purple is reserved for royalty, and other products are available only to those in the ranks of nobility. On the other hand, in those countries where the ideal of political equality prevails, there is a desire for economic equality. Even though economic equality may not be attained, it can be simulated by the use of fashionable goods. In the United States anyone, regardless of race, creed, color, or national origin, may purchase and use any high-fashion product if he or she has the money to pay for it. In the United States there are probably more newly-rich than in any other country in the world. And in the democratic society that made it possible for them to acquire great wealth, they also have freedom of choice to spend their money as they wish.

A Philosophy of Change

Fashion changes thrive in a group that accepts change. Custom and tradition are powerful deterrents to change. If the members of a group believed that what has been or what is constitutes the ultimate in desirability, there would be little or no opportunity for fashion. This is illustrated by nations in the Orient where ancestor worship and religion combine with low income to maintain the status quo. Postwar Japan illustrates the eagerness with which consumers accept fashion as national income increases and the spirit of democracy grows. In Tokyo, now the largest city in the world, the kimono is rarely worn for everyday use. Women as well as men have adopted the Western style of dress and have embraced the annual cycle of fashion change. Yet the 80 million people living in mountain and seacoast villages in Japan still cling to the clothing styles of their ancestors. In the United States, as population has shifted from rural to urban areas, the willingness to accept change has accelerated.

One of the strongest forces causing change in patterns of living is war. And war invariably is the occasion for the introduction of changes in fashions. Under pressure of accepting new ideas in wartime, the group mind becomes accustomed to change. It is in such an atmosphere that fashion flourishes freely. But there are limits to the changes consumers will accept. In World War II civilian men rejected jackets without collars even though the appeal to accept them was based on the argument that the limited supply of wool would be conserved.

FACTORS RETARDING FASHIONS

Absence of Favorable Conditions

Fashions cannot thrive in underdeveloped economies or in underdeveloped areas of the United States. The composite picture of a society in which fashion flourishes may be turned over to see a society in which the absence of those conditions operates as a barrier to fashion. Underdeveloped economies are characterized by low income and the absence of high-speed transportation and communication. The struggle for subsistence leaves no time for leisure. The political-economic system in such countries often favors a small power group that exercises complete control.

Low Income

The essence of fashion is wastefulness. Consumers must have incomes large enough to permit them to discard usable products and purchase new, fashionable products. When incomes are so low that a woman buys only one dress a year and a man only one suit every three years, the items purchased may be in fashion at the time of purchase, but not for long. Long after double-breasted suits went out of fashion, some men continued to wear them because they could not afford a new suit. One could guess the income of a family by looking in its clothes closets.

Another indicator of family income would be the automobile. In the very low-income groups, there would be no garage and no automobile. Next, one would find an automobile fifteen or twenty years old. In many, one would find cars ten years old, and in still more, cars produced five years ago. The high-fashion consumers would be the ones in whose garage one would find two or three of the current models.

Advertising is not very prevalent in underdeveloped economies because people without money cannot buy, no matter how much they might wish to and no matter how appealing the advertisement might be. In the United States there are millions of low-income consumers who are unable to respond to the clarion call of the advertiser of high fashion to discard the old and buy the new.

A Static Society

It seems to be characteristically human that once a consuming pattern has been set, it becomes a personal habit and a group custom. Both habit and custom oppose change. Opposition to change is opposition to fashion. It is notable that men, who ignore custom and tradition on the job, have been more rigidly bound by customary consumption than women. In the matter of dress particularly, they have been less susceptible to fashion changes. On the job they work in an atmosphere where nothing is certain and change is common. The rapidity of change generates a sense of insecurity. Off the job, they enjoy the stability of customary consumption. They like things as they are. On the other hand, women who spend their days doing routine housework find the drab monotony so wearing on their nerves that they seek relief in the excitement of change. Perhaps this is why women are much more responsive to fashion change.

Religion and Tradition

Religion and tradition are almost synonymous. Religion, through the churches, is a guardian of group morals. Some fashions, such as the topless swimsuit and the micromini skirt, are regarded as immoral, so their adoption is actively opposed by religious leaders. The greater freedom of young people in each succeeding generation is usually a cause for concern on the part of older people and religious leaders. When fashion finally decreed that women might smoke in public, there was strong opposition among members of religious groups. When fashions in books, movies, and theaters condone practices and ideas that the churches consider immoral, they use their influence in an attempt to resist the trend.

In the Far East and in primitive societies ancestor worship is a form of religion. In such slow-changing societies the elders represent a storehouse of knowledge and wisdom, but in rapidly changing societies older people are "passé," "old fogies," "over 30." In the United States there is little respect for age; compulsory retirement, retirement homes and villages, which segregate the older citizens, and consequent erosion of the family group deprive elders of their function and authority. As a result, "Americans identify with their children, rather than with their parents."[21]

Sumptuary Laws

Sumptuary laws have two meanings and two purposes. One purpose is to regulate personal expenditures so as to prevent extravagance and luxury. A second purpose is to regulate consumer practices on moral or religious grounds. There was a time in England when the clothing that commoners might wear and the kinds of foods they might eat were regulated by royalty and nobility. Parliamentary restrictions on consumer freedom of choice in England curtailed and impeded the adoption of new fashions. In contrast to the present life span of two years in the United States, fashion in England in those days remained in vogue a generation or more.

Sumptuary legislation is comparatively rare in the United States. The illustrations that come to mind are those concerning indecent exposure. More common, and probably more significant, are the ordinances at beach resorts regulating the types of bathing costume. It is this kind of sumptuary law that prevented the spread of nude bathing.

WHO STARTS NEW FASHIONS?

Can Sellers Control Fashions?

The psychology of acceptance and imitation suggests that by means of advertising sellers can persuade consumers to adopt fashion changes whenever sellers wish to make a change. If this were true, those businesses whose product is fashion would be very successful. Without running a risk of loss, they would be able to produce those goods that would yield maximum profit, timing changes in styles so as to maintain a continuous market for their products.

Upon analysis it becomes evident that consumers are not sheep who follow the leader. Fashions are not forced on consumers; they are forced on designers by store buyers. If the time is opportune, consumers will accept the new fashion. Fad and fashion must appeal to consumer desire for novelty because "the basis for fad adoption is novelty alone."[22]

Even if sellers of fashions could control their acceptance, imagine the sharp conflict of interest among business firms. If one fashion group introduced the high hemline, the producers of dress and skirt materials would resist by endeavoring to lower the hemline. A change in fashion from cotton to synthetic fibers causes losses to cotton farmers and manufacturers.

Fashion is stronger than individual business firms. Indeed, there is evidence that it is stronger than trade associations representing groups of firms. In the United States' economy, most firms manufacture on a large scale in anticipation of demand. Such firms would lose more than they could gain by capricious changes in fashion. Losses in the clothing and the automobile industry have been heavy when a fashion change was rejected by consumers. Lacking effective control over consumer demand, business firms incur considerable risk in manufacturing fashion goods for which no demand is assured. They have large investments in equipment and materials, and if consumer demand has been incorrectly anticipated, the products they have produced can be sold only at a loss.

The year 1970 went into the fashion history records as the year the midi laid an egg, and the shoe industry misstepped on styling for women's shoes. Women flatly rejected the mid-calf length skirt but bought pants by the millions. They rejected Italian "monster" shoes and caused substantial losses to American importers. Women employees at Bonwit Teller bowed to an edict to wear midis on the job, but they did so reluctantly. *Women's Wear Daily* was determined that women should wear longer dresses, and women seemed equally determined not to do so. But gradually midis have come into their own and have become very popular.

Can Advertisers Control Fashion?

Can advertisers mold consumer demand? Is it possible to create demand? Some enthusiasts in the advertising business believe they can create and control consumer demand. If those enthusiasts were more conversant with the history of advertising, they would know that the record is filled with failures as well as successes. Advertising cannot manipulate people to make them buy. Neither can advertising stop a trend. Advertisers have endeavored to persuade all men to wear hats, but millions continue to go bareheaded. Sales of women's hats declined even as the number of potential women buyers increased. What advertising can do, and does, is to hasten the acceptance of goods already in fashion. This is a very different function. It may be likened to the practice of climbing on the bandwagon once the crowd has been attracted. Advertisers are prone to claim much more credit than the record justifies. It is doubtful that advertising has ever seriously altered any fashion trend. Fashions come in without a conscious effort, and they go out in spite of all efforts to retain them. There is much luck involved in advertising fashion goods which "take."

Nevertheless, advertisers continue to try. Their theme is that fashion is for the young, the under thirty-five. Ads depict the typical American woman as young, beautiful, slim, and well-dressed. Any woman who lets herself go beyond size 16 is outside the pale of fashion. Beauty contests accent youth; and thousands of contestants promote fashions in clothes, cosmetics, jewelry, and hairdos. Miss America receives over $100,000 for public appearances during her year's reign, as well as a $15,000 scholarship.

Do Consumers Start New Fashions?

Somewhere in the fashion cycle there must be an individual or a group with sufficient prestige and influence to decide whether a fashion change will be accepted. The process may be spontaneous, but someone or some group is in the lead. It must be concluded that ultimate control is exercised by consumers collectively. This does not mean that sellers do not exert considerable influence, and neither can it be denied that individual consumers sometimes influence the acceptance of a fashion change. What it does mean is that sellers suggest new fashions, but acceptance or rejection is exercised by consumers collectively. Once a new-fashioned product is offered on the market, its fate is beyond the control of the seller. Its acceptance or rejection depends entirely on consumers. If it strikes their fancy, they accept it, and the seller makes extra profit. If it arouses mild curiosity, it may enjoy a short vogue. If it does not please consumer fancy, it will be rejected. Each year there are about 200,000 dress models shown at the Paris openings. Out of that number not more than 200 find acceptance in the United States. Of the 200 accepted, perhaps 20 will be copied in all price ranges to become fashionable. Fashions in automobiles are equally unpredictable. Fashion-conscious buyers were delighted with the tailfins of one car, but flatly rejected the "horse collar" design of another.

Which Consumers Set the Fashions?

The decisions of royalty once were final in the realm of fashion. Whatever kings and queens adopted became fashionable. During the reign of King Henry VII of England, his mother established herself as the supreme arbiter of fashionable mourning attire. The lower the rank, the shorter and narrower the tippet, and the less fur one might wear. The approved costume varied after the first, second, and third months of mourning, and so on throughout the entire mourning period.

Since the United States has no royalty of its own, people of great wealth have assumed the role of fashion-setters. In a pecuniary society, the kings and the emperors are those who accumulate large fortunes. They are the successful people. They are the ones to emulate. The advertiser of a European fashion often endeavors to encourage its adoption by securing its approval by a duchess or a duke. An American advertiser seeks the same results by obtaining the endorsement of a very wealthy person, a movie star, or a popular politician.

One woman wearing a new design can scarcely start a fashion, but if many of the socially elite adopt the innovation it may very likely gain wide acceptance. Television has made millions of fashion-conscious women aware of the latest fashions worn by popular actresses. In order to promote new fashions, business firms or trade associations sometimes arrange promotional tie-ins with the producer of a film. The gowns, hats, and hairdos featured in the film are promoted by fashion magazines, movie magazines, trade papers, and newspapers and television. Unaware of the collaborative efforts of these representatives of business, many women flock to the stores to buy "what is being shown this season." Sellers of fashion goods sometimes give a college campus leader a new fashion item to wear, hoping that other students will be sufficiently impressed to adopt the new fashion. This method has proved successful. It has the added advantage that noncollege students and high-school students are impressed and influenced by the fashions college students are wearing.

The preceding analysis has been called the *trickle down theory,* the essence of which is that upper classes adopt fashions first, and in time the lower classes follow the leaders. Eventually the symbolic distinction is lost, and the leaders then turn to a new fashion. This may have been true in Veblen's time, but it is not true now, according to King, because mass communications and marketing practices "almost impede any systematic vertical flow process."[23] When designers introduce new fashions, the process of adoption is a form of social contagion. King's research leads to a mass-market, or *trickle across,* scheme of fashion adoption; the early buyers are not an elite esotery of upper classes, nor are they the influential force. Rather, the dominant influencers are found in the late-buyers group.

WHY DO FASHIONS CHANGE?

The Puzzling Cycle of Fashion

A puzzling fact about fashion is its rapid and increasing rate of change. Can fashion changes in clothing be explained as a search for beauty and perfection? According to one view, men and women dress and change styles in an effort to recapture what was lost in the process of evolution to the human level. Unconsciously they search for the absolute freedom, comfort, and suitability, and beauty of attire displayed elsewhere in nature. Displeased with ill-fitting, unsuitable, unlovely garments, each generation strives for the perfect human costume. Since perfection is unattainable, people continue to follow an elusive goal. This leads to the conclusion that the origin of every important style change is to be found in mental outlook. Psychologically fashion change may be explained by the principle of hierarchy of drives. "The search for satisfaction is always focused on the drive which is most prepotent at the moment. . . ."[24] When the drive is fulfilled, tension is released and other drives come to the fore. Whatever the product, the classic style is always in fashion to some extent. It almost never goes out of fashion. It is a compromise that gives satisfaction to people who are not swayed by fashion change.

The tempo of fashion change is influenced most by saturation. When the majority of people in a market promote a fashion, the saturation point is reached very quickly. The more a fashion is accepted, the quicker it declines. Television and jet transportation have shortened the life span of fashions.[25] The extremely mod fashion explosion of the early 1960s was introduced by a group of young English designers with the "Chelsea Look." Bright colors, daring stripes, gay designs, and offbeat materials were

"in," but today this fashion is completely passé. Fashions lose their unique-
ness quickly. As they become an old experience, users need fresh, new
experiences to satisfy their curiosity drive. The upcoming generation will
consider current fashions, such as the "Denim Look," as the products of
"squares." Even more significantly, some of the younger generation in the
1970s have rejected materialism and relegated fashion to a lesser role.[26]

Sex and Fashion

There can be little doubt that sex is a factor responsible for fashion
changes. In animal life decorative features reach their height at puberty.
This is one of the methods by which Nature draws the sexes together for
reproduction. A carry-over of this influence may subconsciously cause
humans to decorate themselves.

By following fashion a woman can proclaim and maintain her social
position, her rank, and her sexual attractiveness.[27] Males also dress to
attract feminine admirers. Men's clothes are by no means purely functional.
By following fashion a man also desires to proclaim and maintain his social
position, rank, and sexual attractiveness.

The fashions of the 1960s have been described as "a sort of gradual
national striptease."[28] Early in that decade an effort was made to persuade
women to wear topless swimsuits and topless dresses. The attempt never
went beyond the fad stage, but fashion designers made another try a few
years later with the "braless look." A student of the history of fashion may
predict that an effort to launch a bare-bosom fashion will be made again.
Actually the bare bosom was in high fashion thirty-five hundred years ago
among the women of Crete. Indeed there are many women in Africa and in
the South Pacific for whom the bare bosom is customary rather than
fashionable. With real insight one writer has noted that if a fashion is ten
years ahead of its time the public considers it indecent, and fifty years later
they regard it as quaint.[29] One researcher made a study of changing fashions
over more than a century, and his investigations indicate that fashion follows a century-long cycle, regardless of economic trends, functional considerations, or technological innovations.[30]

Pursuing the influence of sex in fashion change, Laver believes the
impulse to change lies in the impulse to seduction. The seductive impulse
is dormant in times of crisis, according to Laver, then emerges with pent-up
enthusiasm when the crisis has passed and people are free to enjoy themselves. After a major war women feel a sense of emancipation which they
try to express by adopting new fashions in clothing and hairdos.[31]

Fashion and Conspicuous Consumption

Early in this century Thorstein Veblen of the University of Chicago
emerged as a leading institutional economist. He was an astute observer

and critic of motivation and performance of the American economy. Veblen pioneered in bringing sociological and psychological insights to focus on economic behavior. His book *The Theory of the Leisure Class,* first published in 1899, is a classic. In that work, Veblen attributed changing fashions to their value in proving the wearer's freedom from the necessity of working. He contended that the standard of reputability in a pecuniary society requires that fashionable dress must show wasteful expenditure. He theorized that "changing styles are an expression of a restless search for something that will commend itself to our aesthetic sense."[32] This theory of style suggests that we shall ultimately attain perfection. It also reflects Veblen's European origin.

Europeans and Orientals have evolved national costumes that are beautiful and functional. Writing after World War II, Sumie Seo Mishima said:

> Japanese kimonos of good solid silk, easily adjustable to any individual size and practically free from the tyranny of fashion had a permanence and a universality which made them far more dependable as currency than the deflated paper money. Western clothes were also in good circulation, although fashion controlled their prices to a great extent.[33]

The stability of European and Oriental costumes may be explained by the fact that the various nationalities were relatively homogeneous, stable, and immobile. In the Orient competition in conspicuous leisure supplemented competition in conspicuous consumption. This led Veblen to the conclusion that "fashions are less stable and least becoming in those communities where the principle of a conspicuous waste of goods asserts itself most imperatively."[34]

What was Veblen's explanation of fashion changes? Although a pecuniary society requires conspicuous wastefulness in clothing styles, sheer wastefulness is abhorrent even to exponents of the doctrine of conspicuous waste. To overcome this abhorrence each innovation and style simulates some ostensible purpose, but the simulation is so obvious that the abhorrence soon causes a spirit of rebellion which then seeks satisfaction in a new style. To be acceptable in a pecuniary society, the new style also must be wasteful. It is not long, therefore, before followers of fashion seek refuge in another change. "Hence, the essential ugliness and unceasing change of fashionable attire."[35]

Fashion and Competitive Imitation

The psychological basis of fashion may be found in imitative reverence and competitive imitation. "Fashion is just the outcome of an ignoble desire to flaunt real or simulated superiority in the eyes of the world."[36] Competitive imitation is the desire to assert equality with the person or group being imitated. The motive behind such imitation may be hunger for companionship. "Dress is a nonverbal sign which helps to set the conditions of social interaction."[37]

A newcomer wishing to join a group looks for symbols that mark that group. Thus college freshmen imitate the dress patterns of upperclassmen. Those who are imitated are both flattered and offended. Their ambition is to differentiate themselves. Since they cannot do this by sumptuary laws in modern society, they change to another style of dress in order to maintain their leadership. Eventually the originality of fashion designers and leaders is exhausted, and they find it necessary to revive discarded styles. The flapper skirt of the 1920s, which failed to cover the knees of the wearer, was revived forty years later, and the pannier skirt of 1947 was revived in 1970 as the maxi. Fashion designers for men's clothing are limited by the basic permanence of a man's suit. They can and do switch from single-breasted to double-breasted suits, from suits with vests to suits without vests, from padded to unpadded shoulders, from three-button to two-button jackets, but that is about the extent of the changes. If men's clothing were as dependent on fashion changes as women's clothing is, we might see trouser lengths vary from ankle to knees! To be sure, walking shorts are popular, but they have not replaced the Brooks Brothers suit in the office.

Fashion Changes Linked to Seasonal Changes

For the many people who live in temperate zones, fashion changes are linked to seasonal changes. The closing point of any fashion is a change of season. When winter ends, the fashions of that season go out. When the next winter season arrives, new fashions are in vogue. This cycle is repeated in spring, summer, and autumn. Most people welcome the advent of a new season and change their wardrobe accordingly.

The weakness of this as an explanation for all fashion change is that people who live in areas where it is always summer nevertheless change their wardrobes with the season. When colleges reopen in the deep South in the autumn, many students return to their campuses attired in new fall fashions, even though temperatures may be in the 90s. In some regions seasonal changes also apply to other consumer goods and practices. While changes in season require changes in consuming practices, there is no basic reason why the same articles of dress and other goods might not be used year after year in their proper season. No reason, that is, except fashion. To fashion-conscious consumers nothing is older than last year's fashion. Nothing causes more embarrassment to a fashion-conscious consumer than to be compelled to wear clothing out of fashion or to have bare floors when the fashion is wall-to-wall carpeting.

Fashion Change and Profit

High fashion is big business in the clothing industry, in the automobile industry, in housing, house furnishings, and appliances. It is difficult to distinguish between change for the sake of change and change that reflects real improvement. The foregoing explanations of fashion changes in the clothing industry draw on anthropology, sociology, and psychology. But no explanation would be complete that did not include the artificial stimulation of fashion changes by business firms, which hope thereby to increase their profits. Motivation researchers know more about why consumers act as they do than the consumers themselves know. Sellers of fashion know that consumers will buy fashion items at high prices. Individual firms in the fashion industries, trade associations, advertisers, movie-makers, newspaper and magazine publishers, all have a profit stake in frequent changes in fashion. Knowing that people are more emotional than rational, sellers of fashion know that they can make more money by changing the fashions from season to season. Promoters of high fashion and obsoletism argue that consumers must be made to buy. If new commodities are not needed, artificial desires must be created.

"Fashion is the ingredient that sells things." A J. C. Penney official is reported to have said that his store formerly sought to meet consumer needs, but now finds it necessary to create wants. A few years ago "we relied heavily on basics, but now fashion change is the key to the whole thing."[38] This kind of merchandising may be profitable for some sellers, but its wastefulness and its cost to consumers are obvious. The inflation-recession of the 1970s has forced many retailers to shift back to stocking more of the basics.

Inflation and Changing Fashions

The magnitude of inflation during the 1970s has been great enough to have an effect in changing fashions. We saw earlier how sharp increases in food prices brought about changes in the kinds of foods being purchased. The increases in the prices of automobiles and the price of gasoline have made many people much less concerned about having the latest and the biggest car. They are buying smaller and more economical cars. The inflation in home construction prices has had an impact in reducing the size of many new homes being built. The sharp increases in the price of heating a home have also had an impact, encouraging the building of smaller homes. Smaller homes also require fewer pieces of furniture.

These changes in fashion are not necessarily made willingly by consumers, but they are being made because of the economic realities of the times.

FASHION AND WASTE

Whom Do Fashion Changes Benefit?

Those who gain from artificial stimulation of fashion are a few specialists who produce fashion goods. Large-scale manufacturers who produce in anticipation of consumer demand may incur heavy losses as a result of capricious changes in fashion. Such changes increase unused capacity and cause inventory losses. The literature dealing with the clothing industry is filled with examples of heavy losses. The turnover of firms in the industry is very high. Only the giants in the industry can stand the costs of annual model changes and the losses on models that consumers reject. Such losses must be anticipated and allowance must be made for them. This is why fashionable goods cost more than durable goods, which are produced for long service. In the automobile industry the classic example of the economy of a car that does not change every year was the Volkswagen.

The immediate loss in a fashion flop falls on the business firm, but the ultimate loss falls on consumers and on society. Fashion-minded merchandisers sometimes argue that fashion is the lifeblood of trade. Actually fashion increases the hazards and the uncertainties of business firms. One way to stabilize production would be to reduce or eliminate the annual fashion change. To which a fashion writer retorts: "If fashion were sensible, it wouldn't be any fun."

Should fashion be abolished? Not unless we want to go to uniforms, says Langner. Fashion is the enemy of the stereotyped individual, the mass-produced mind, and the unthinking product of the propaganda machine.[39]

Do Fashion Changes Contribute to Consumer Welfare?

Have you ever heard of an industrial sales representative trying to persuade the buyer for a business firm that he should buy new machines and new equipment because they are in high fashion? Managers of business firms depreciate their plant and equipment on a planned basis. If a machine becomes obsolete because of a real improvement, business accountants may accelerate the rate of depreciation. But there is no record of a buyer for a business firm discarding plant or equipment because it is out of fashion. Rational consumers might well emulate rational business executives. The satisfaction that some people gain from being in high fashion does not justify the social cost of fashion. In a dynamic economy characterized by initiative and inventiveness, improvements in consumer durable goods are made from decade to decade. When an appliance has served adequately for fifteen years, it may be time for a replacement. But appliances, automobiles, and clothing that have served only one year or two would not be discarded by a business firm. The constant goal for consumers might well be maximum utility. The essence of fashion is wastefulness rather than utility. Shakespeare saw this in his time: "All this I see, and I see that the fashion wears out more apparel than the man."[40] In the free-choice economy of the United States each consumer must decide individually which is more important: being in high fashion, being frugal, or an acceptable balance between the two.

QUESTIONS FOR REVIEW

1. "Fashion seems always to be making new demands on her slaves and they seem ready to obey her mandates no matter to what they may lead." Are you this kind of a fashion slave?

2. At what age did you become conscious of fashion in your clothing?

3. What is fashion? From the consumer point of view, what functions does fashion serve?

4. What are the differences among fashion, fad, style, and custom?

5. When you purchase clothing, which do you consider more important — price, quality, fashion, convenience, or comfort?

6. What is your reaction to the practice of obsoletism in the automobile industry?

7. Are automobile manufacturers making the kinds of cars you want? Do you believe that you have freedom of choice when purchasing an automobile?

8. Do you consider planned obsolescence to be good or bad?

9. As you survey the social scene, what forces do you see favoring fashions? What are the forces opposing fashion changes? Which set of forces do you think is stronger?

10. What is the meaning of the assertion that Americans identify with their children rather than with their parents? Do you think this is true? What are the implications for the future?

11. In the United States, which force do you think influences consumers more — custom or fashion?

12. Compare the trickle-down, trickle-across, and hierarchy-of-drives explanations of fashion change. Which theory do you find most persuasive?

13. Do you like to go along with changing fashions or would you prefer stability in fashions?

14. Do you think fashion contributes to consumer welfare?

PROJECTS

1. Look in a college yearbook of a generation ago and report on clothing fashions in vogue at that time.

2. Arrange a class debate on the topic "Resolved that planned obsolescence is desirable."

3. Ask ten friends whether they dress to impress or attract the opposite sex? Present their responses and your observations in a written report.

4. Read and report on key aspects of the writings of Thorstein Veblen in

his book *The Theory of the Leisure Class* that deal with fashion. Do you agree?

5. Analyze carefully a particular person's dress, hairstyle, and so on, and explain what that person may be attempting to project by such choices.

REFERENCES

1. *Wall Street Journal,* 23 July 1975, p. 14.
2. Cooperative Extension Service, University of Maryland, News Release, 10 April 1975, p. 3.
3. Karlyne Anspach, *The Why of Fashion* (Ames: Iowa State University Press, 1967), p. xi.
4. *Ibid.,* p. 3 and chap. 2.
5. *New York Times,* 16 Sept. 1973, p. 14F.
6. *Pittsburgh Post-Gazette,* 22 Nov. 1974, p. 27.
7. Dwight E. Robinson, "Economics of Fashion Demand," *Quarterly Journal of Economics* 75 (1961): 376–398.
8. Frank A. Parsons, *The Psychology of Dress* (New York: Doubleday, Doran, 1920), p. 148.
9. Frances Elizabeth Baldwin, *Sumptuary Legislation and Personal Regulation in England* (Baltimore: Johns Hopkins University Studies, 1926), p. 186.
10. Lawrence Langner, *The Importance of Wearing Clothes* (New York: Hastings House, 1959), pp. 294–295.
11. Anspach, p. 218.
12. Langner, p. 289.
13. Janet L. Wolff, *What Makes Women Buy?* (New York: McGraw-Hill, 1958), p. 54.
14. S. Evelyn Evans, "Motivations Underlying Clothing Selection and Wearing," *Journal of Home Economics* 56 (1964): 742.
15. Eleanore Carruth, "The Great Fashion Explosion," *Fortune* Oct. 1967, p. 217; Anspach, pp. 334–344; Langner, pp. 188–196; *New York Times,* 15 Dec. 1969, p. 62, 11 Sept. 1970, p. 38.
16. Joseph J. Seldin, *The Golden Fleece: Selling the Good Life to Americans* (New York: The Macmillan Company, 1963), p. 93.
17. Sigmund A. Lavine, *Kettering: Master Inventor* (New York: Dodd, Mead, 1960), p. 128.
18. Franklin M. Fisher, Zvi Griliches, and Carl Kaysen, "The Cost of Automobile Model Changes Since 1949," *Journal of Political Economy* 70 (1962): 433–451.
19. Walter Hoving, *The Distribution Revolution* (New York: Ives Washburn, 1960), p. 71.
20. John A. Menge, "Style Change Costs as a Market Weapon," *Quarterly Journal of Economics* 76 (1962): 632–647.
21. Anspach, pp. 278–280.
22. Chester R. Wasson, Frederick D. Sturdivant, and David H. McConnaughy, *Competition and Human Behavior* (New York: Appleton-Century-Crofts, 1968), p. 71.
23. Charles W. King, "Fashion Adoption: A Rebuttal to the Trickle Down Theory," in Engel, pp. 121–135.
24. Wasson, Sturdivant, and McConnaughy, p. 75.
25. Anspach, p. 219.
26. E. B. Weiss, "Youth Junks the 'Junk Culture'—Will Advertisers Follow?" *Advertising Age* 41 (1970): 35.
27. Langner, pp. 292–293.

28. Anspach, p. 285.
29. James Laver, *Taste and Fashion* (London: George C. Harrap, 1945), p. 202.
30. Dwight E. Robinson, "Style Changes: Cyclical, Inexorable, and Foreseeable," *Harvard Business Review* 53 (1975): 121.
31. Laver, pp. 201–202, 210.
32. Thorstein Veblen, *The Theory of the Leisure Class* (New York: The Viking Press, 1912), p. 174.
33. *The Broader Way: A Woman's Life in the New Japan* (New York: The John Day Company, 1953), p. 183.
34. Veblen, p. 176.
35. *Ibid.*, p. 177.
36. Ada H. Bigg, "What is Fashion?" *The Nineteenth Century* 33, p. 235.
37. Anspach, p. 240.
38. Carruth, p. 165.
39. Langner, p. 299.
40. William Shakespeare, *Much Ado About Nothing*, III, iii, 148.

SELLER-MADE WANTS: ADVERTISING

ADVERTISING AROUND THE CLOCK

Television Advertising

Ninety-nine point nine percent of all homes wired for electricity in the United States have at least one black-and-white television set. Television has developed into one of the most persuasive advertising media in advertising history. By the age of sixteen the average child has been exposed to over 640,000 commercials and has spent approximately 15,000 hours in front of the television. That is 4,000 hours more than the same child has spent in the classroom. Commercials on children's programs average twelve minutes per hour on weekends and as much as sixteen minutes per hour on weekday programs. These startling figures have been widely publicized by ACT—Action for Children's Television. ACT would like to see rigid Federal Communication Commission guidelines for advertising on children's television programs. Over $400 million are spent each year on television commercials aimed at children. The National Association of Broadcasters took notice of the public reaction against this and recommended that the commercial time on children's programs be reduced to ten minutes per hour on weekends and twelve minutes per hour on weekdays. This would not necessarily reduce the number of ads since one sixty-second spot ad could be replaced by two thirty-second ads, four fifteen-second ads, or six ten-second ads. Currently the length of ads has been reduced as the cost of ad time has increased. How many ads will be seen and how much time will the average person spend looking at ads by the time his or her alloted threescore and ten years are reached?

Ads Are Everywhere

From the moment you turn on your radio or television set for the morning news until you turn off the television after the late-late movie, you are

Each day consumers are bombarded by hundreds of advertisements—from roadside signs to TV commercials to ads in magazines and newspapers. (*Paul Conklin, Monkmeyer*)

subjected to repeated exhortations to buy. Newspapers and magazines are filled with ads. Buses and subway cars carry advertising cards. The mail carrier brings hundreds of direct advertising messages to you. Retail stores are filled with advertising messages and displays. Even the packages on the shelves silently plead to be picked up. Obviously you cannot absorb the contents of all these advertisements. "If people became full-time ad watchers they would not have enough time to use the products or to earn money to buy them."[1]

Advertising exposure has reached or even passed the point of saturation. Many advertisers feel that too many advertising messages have little value. There are so many ads that intended recipients develop a skill in blotting most of them out. If you are in the market for a product or a service you generally pay more attention to the ads. But when your purchase has been made or you have decided not to make it, you pay no more attention to the ads, unless it is an ad about a product you have purchased, in which case the ad is often viewed with reassurance that the right decision was made. This ability to block out the constant bombardment protects you from insanity, but it creates problems for advertisers, who are trying to reach consumers with their messages.

What Is Advertising?

The effort to influence sales by changing stimulus conditions is called *marketing*.[2] Advertising is only one ingredient of the marketing mix; other methods include personal selling, price policy, packaging, coupons, premiums, stamps, special price offerings, and many other practices.

The official definition of advertising recommended by the American Marketing Association is as follows: "Advertising is any paid form of non-personal presentation and promotion of ideas, goods, or services by an identified sponsor." Wright and Warner emphasize that, in addition to presentation and promotion, advertising *persuades*. They modify the definition to read: "Advertising is controlled, identifiable persuasion by means of mass communication media."[3]

An advertising executive has written:

> Advertising's objective is to enable people to imagine themselves as having a more fortunate lot in life, to realize the desirability of things they do not have, and to be willing to work hard to get them. It is this released energy which creates the wealth of nations and distributes it most broadly.[4]

And Stuart Britt comments that:

> All ads are psychological. Their purpose is to create a desired impression and to expand sales. This is accomplished by attracting attention, creating perception and interest, making the ad easily understood, arousing pleasant emotional feelings, and creating a favorable image.[5]

Advertising falls into three groups: soft-sell, hard-sell, and in-between. Soft-sell ads are usually simple announcements. Hard-sell ads are blatant, combative, and coercive. This is the type of advertising that irritates many television viewers/listeners. Practitioners of this kind of advertising contend that the more consumers are exposed to ads, the more they must be pressured by a unique selling proposition.[6] An illustration of a unique selling proposition is the story of the advertising agency that had an account for a brewery. When the copywriter, who knew very little about brewing, discovered that beer bottles were washed by steam, he chose that as his theme. The managers of the brewery protested, saying that all breweries wash their bottles with steam. "But do beer drinkers know that?" asked the copywriter. When the ads came out telling how the bottles of that brewery were washed by steam, sales did increase.

Word-of-Mouth Advertising

Word-of-mouth communication is important in consumer decision making. A survey in Texas showed that 60 percent of the people polled said that they relied on advice from their friends when making a major purchase.[7] Emulation becomes an ally of advertising. When one or two leaders in a neighborhood or a group purchase a new product, they are proud of it, talk about it, and show it off. But word-of-mouth advertising has negative as well as positive aspects. One study concluded that a negative report on a product or service is more likely to lead to a decision not to buy than a positive report is to lead to the decision to purchase.[8]

Not all word-of-mouth advertising is spontaneous or free. The company Word-Casters, Inc. had a network of 4,000 men and women around the country who would spread a good word about almost anything for a fee. For the modest sum of $2.00, each of the 4,000 would promise to say something good to at least five people about a new film, a television show, a book, a new product, or anything else.[9]

There is much so-called *tie-in advertising*. For example, when a movie is released, the producers may arrange for tie-in advertising of the clothing or the furniture or other items used in the movie. Some advertisers sponsor tie-in books on aviation, bowling, cooking, gardening, and travel. It is no coincidence that at most football stadiums only one brand of soft drink and one brand of cigarettes are available. In return for purchasing advertising space in the program, the advertiser is given exclusive selling rights.

How Much Money Do Advertisers Spend?

The estimate is $33 billion annually. By itself this figure does not mean much. When related to personal consumption expenditures, the $33 billion spent for advertising represents slightly more than 3 percent of the $1 trillion spent by consumers. Over the years this percentage figure has changed very little, having been 3 percent thirty-five years ago. It is estimated that 38 percent of all advertising dollars are spent at the local level and 62 percent spent for national advertising. This distribution of advertising expenditures varies according to the industry or the firm. For example, Sears, Roebuck & Co., the third largest national advertiser, spends $220 million annually advertising at the national level and over $250 million at the local level, making it the number-one advertiser in the nation when local and national advertising are combined.

It is estimated that about four million individuals and firms advertise. Their ads range from a simple announcement of a room for rent in the classified section of a local newspaper to the $360 million spent by Procter & Gamble for national advertising. The top one hundred advertisers spent $6.3 billion in 1975.[10] The top five advertisers – in order of size of expenditures – were Procter & Gamble; General Motors and Sears, Roebuck tied for second place; General Foods; and Bristol-Meyers. As a percentage of sales, advertising expenditures were 9.3 for Bristol-Meyers; 7.9 for Procter & Gamble; 6.8 for General Foods; 1.9 for Sears; and 0.6 for General Motors. It is interesting to note that the U.S. government was number ten in the top one hundred, with advertising expenditures of $113.4 million. Most of this money was spent on military recruiting, although some of it was spent for advertising for the U.S. Postal Service, Amtrak, and various U.S. agencies' public service programs. Of the top one hundred advertisers, twenty-three were food and soft drink producers, eighteen were drug and cosmetic firms, eight were automobile manufacturers, and six were breweries and distillers.

Where Do Advertisers Spend Their Money?

The main channels that advertisers use to contact consumers are newspapers, magazines, radio, television, direct mail, billboards, and store displays. In a typical year advertisers spend about 30 percent of their advertising dollars for newspaper ads; 18 percent for television; 15 percent for direct mail; 6 percent for magazines; and 7 percent for radio. These five mass media account for about 76 percent of all advertising expenditures.

Do Advertisers Call the Tunes?

To paraphrase an old proverb, the person who pays the fiddler is the person who calls the tune. The media used by advertisers are business firms operating for profit. For most of them the margin between profit and loss is their advertising revenue. In a typical year the one hundred leading national advertisers spend 55 percent of all money paid to the eight major advertising media. The television networks receive 76 percent of their revenues from the top advertisers; network radio 59 percent; magazines 47 percent; and newspapers 38 percent. It would be surprising if the small number of individuals who control such sizeable expenditures did not attempt to influence media editors and managers. A New York congressman reported that he had more than twenty case histories showing the efforts of advertisers to control advertising media. In 1970 militant housewives in significant metropolitan areas demanded that chain food stores reveal the secrets of their food coding practices so that buyers could tell whether the merchandise was fresh or stale. Two of the large retail food chains in Miami, Florida, stopped advertising in the Miami *News* because that newspaper ran a series of articles on food coding practices. Similar reports came out of Chicago and California.[11]

In his book *Since Silent Spring*, Frank Graham told how the Manufacturing Chemists Association threatened to withdraw advertising from gardening magazines and newspaper supplements if they gave favorable mention to Rachel Carson's *Silent Spring*. The association also mailed monthly attacks to news media. When CBS *Reports* was preparing a documentary on the issue of the use of chemical sprays, 60 percent of the sponsors of the program withdrew their support. Among them were some of the well-known food and drug producers in the nation.[12]

There have been, and continue to be, many illustrations of advertisers withdrawing ads when the media prints an article or broadcasts a program that offends the advertiser. A New York City newspaper lost $250,000 in movie advertising because its movie reviewer was too critical to suit the advertiser. During the Vietnam conflict one antiwar group ran an ad in the *Boston Globe* advocating a one-day shopping boycott to demonstrate opposition to the war. Two major department stores—Sears, Roebuck & Co. and Jordan Marsh—promptly cancelled seventeen pages of advertising, which represented a net loss to the *Globe* of $55,000.[13] Procter & Gamble withdrew its detergent commercials from the CBS News program "Is Mercury a Menace?" The program raised serious questions about pollution problems caused by chemicals, in this case mercury, which are dumped into our water system. Procter & Gamble thought this program might lead people to wonder about all the chemicals used in detergents, which also end up in our water system. This could have created negative thinking about detergents in general, and Procter & Gamble therefore withdrew its sponsorship. All four Chicago daily newspapers refused to run an ad sponsored by the Amalgamated Clothing Workers of America that explained why the union was picketing Marshall Field department stores. There seemed to be little doubt that the reason for the newspapers refusal was that Marshall Field, a major advertiser, might not like the ad. Six out of seven advertisers cancelled advertisements that were to have been shown on the CBS News program "The Guns of Autumn." This program was a documentary about hunting and killing animals. Sponsorship was withdrawn by the advertisers due to the pressure and threats of boycotts of their products by the gun lobby, led by the National Rifle Association. CBS went ahead and ran the program; but networks are in no position to lose many advertising dollars this way. The pressure to conform to the wishes of the sponsors is always present.

Based on his own experience in advertising, Samm Baker says that the primary and decisive factor in choosing a television program is the question "Will an advertiser sponsor this show?" When advertisers spend more than $100,000 for a thirty-minute program and a few commercials, they "demand and get rigid control of programming, directly or obliquely."[14]

The Washington editor of *Advertising Age* said that advertisers have discovered that "their ability to tamper with the content of a program varies inversely with the popularity of the program. The superstars frequently are able to demand immunity from interference from the advertiser and even, to some degree, from the broadcaster."[15]

IT PAYS TO ADVERTISE

Whom Does It Pay?

There is a widely held view, sponsored by advertising agencies and the media, that it pays to advertise. However, supporting evidence for this contention is meager. Those in the advertising business would like to have sellers believe that a clear relationship exists between the size of advertising expenditures and the size of or increase in sales. For many years Hershey and Woolworth did not advertise, and even now what little advertising either company does carry is primarily local, yet both are highly successful businesses. But it is also true that successful advertising campaigns on a crash basis can increase sales from 50 to 800 percent.

Much of advertising that does increase profits does so because it is persuasive and convinces enough consumers to switch brands. For example, consumers spend $300 million annually for toothpaste. If a company, through advertising, is able to increase its share of that market by just 1 percent, it will increase its annual sales by $3 million. Crest toothpaste was the first toothpaste to receive the endorsement of the American Dental Association, and this official support, along with a vigorous advertising campaign, garnered 34.5 percent of the market for Crest, with sales of well over $100 million.[16] Crest spends about $15 million annually on advertising. A twenty million dollar advertising and promotion budget was set by Armour-Dial in introducing its Tone moisturizing soap. In test markets in Dallas/Fort Worth and Kansas City it was able to achieve a 9 percent market share for Tone. On a national level a 9 percent share would mean retail sales of almost $40 million in the first year alone.[17] The Northwestern Mutual Life Insurance Company took a nationwide poll and found that when all the big insurance companies were listed in order of their name-familiarity scores, it came in thirty-fourth. Only two weeks later Northwestern came in third. Two weeks of advertising on television, at an expense of $2 million, as one of the sponsors for the summer Olympics increased its name-familiarity score dramatically.[18]

Alberto-Culver, a cosmetics manufacturer, is an example of what massive advertising can do to increase sales. It has grown tremendously by plowing over 25 percent of its sales revenue into advertising. Schick doubled its share of the electric razor market in six months with a highly controversial ad campaign. Sales increased from $42.8 million annually to $100 million. At the other extreme, sales of new cars declined sharply during the 1973 to 1975 recession in spite of the vigorous ad campaigns of the industry.

The simple truth is that nobody really knows how effective advertising is. Among the one hundred leading advertisers the amount of money spent on advertising as a percentage of sales ranges from 0.2 percent to 31.3 percent. Although the sales of the largest percentage advertiser amounted to $111 million, the sales of the smallest percentage advertiser amounted to $20 billion. Among the five major advertisers of tobacco products the advertising cost per carton of cigarettes ranged from less than 1 cent to 22.3 cents per carton, yet the smaller advertiser sold almost a billion more cigarettes.

Madison Avenue likes to believe that advertising stimulates economic growth, yet one of their favorite authors concluded that it was far more likely that increased economic activity caused the rise in advertising rather than the reverse.[19] Katona contends that advertising succeeds best when it conforms to trends in consumer wants. It cannot create demand, nor can it reverse demand.[20] Nevertheless, the fact that business firms spend $33 billion to advertise their goods and services is *prima facie* evidence that in the minds of most business executives it does pay to advertise.

Why Does Advertising Pay?

"The real test of ad creativity is the ring of the cash register."[21] The success of persuasive advertising is evidence that consumers are not sure of what they want. If they were aware of their wants, they would express them in the marketplace in the form of effective demand. The things they demanded would be produced. But that is not what happens. With the advent of production on a large scale in anticipation of consumer demand, sellers have been put under increasing pressure to create an expanding market to support maximum output and thus reduce the cost of production per unit. Their unexpected success in persuading consumers to buy what they have to sell has been responsible for the growth of advertising. Advertisers have found that it is more effective to appeal to emotions than to reason.

WHO REALLY PAYS FOR ADVERTISING?

Passing the Cost to Consumers

Every business firm that advertises considers expenditures for advertising as a cost of operation and includes that cost in the total price of its product or service. With gross advertising expenditures of $33 billion, the advertising cost per household is about $452, and per person it is about $153.

Who Pays the Postage?

When the United States Post Office was established in 1775, Congress deliberately subsidized the transportation by mail of newspapers and magazines because it considered it imperative to have an informed electorate in the new democracy. Once established, the practice continued for almost two hundred years. Newspapers, magazines, and direct-mail advertising were classified as second- and third-class mail. Second-class users paid less than 30 percent of the actual cost incurred by the Post Office Department. Users of third-class mail paid about two-thirds of the actual cost. First-class mail operations showed a profit, but not enough to offset the losses on the other operations. As a result the Post Office Department operated with deficits in the hundreds of millions of dollars year after year. The net effect was that users of first-class service and taxpayers in general were paying part of the postage for advertisers, who in turn subsidized newspapers and magazines. That put consumers in the position of helping to pay for advertising that was intended to persuade them to buy goods and services for the purpose of increasing the profits of the advertisers.

The continued and increasingly large deficits in the Post Office Department finally led to a change. On August 12, 1970, Public Law 91–375 went into effect. Its purpose was to improve and modernize the postal service and reorganize the Post Office Department. A new agency was created called the United States Postal Service, which immediately announced plans for postal rate increases. The preferential rates paid by profit-making organizations such as magazines and newspapers were to be phased out in five years, while preferential rates for nonprofit organizations were to be phased out in ten years. If the plan had gone according to schedule, users of first-class mail would not be subsidizing advertisers after 1975, but the increased rates in 1975 seem to be continuing this subsidy, although to a lesser degree.

Who Pays the Taxes?

The federal corporation income tax law permits firms to deduct advertising expenses as a cost of doing business for the purpose of calculating net taxable income. If company X spends $200 million to advertise its products, the $200 million can be deducted. If that amount were not deductible, the company would have to pay $96 million more in taxes because the corporation net income tax rate is 48 percent. In effect, consumers bear part of the cost of advertising, as in the case of the postal subsidy.

Who Pays for Radio and Television?

Each year the number of advertising dollars paid to owners of television and radio stations increases. Currently the figure is about 26 percent of the total advertising revenue. This amounts to more than $8 billion. Who really pays the bill? Not only those who buy the advertised products but all of the people—the real owners of the airwaves. Representing the people, the Federal Communications Commission has the responsibility of allocating the channels and issuing licenses for their use. A license to operate a television station is a very valuable asset. Advertisers pay billions of dollars to use the airwaves to sell their goods. One public policy issue is whether the monopoly of telecasting should be paid for entirely by commercial advertisers. The ultimate decision on this issue has not yet been reached, but government grants for public telecasting give viewers some alternative. They can now choose between commercially supported television and non-commercially supported television.

Other Ways to Pay for Television

When the moving picture industry was in its developmental stages, movie theaters followed the traditional practice of legitimate theaters in charging a price for admission. When the television industry was developing, it too could have used a pay-as-you-watch system. One of the problems was that of the mechanics of charging viewers. In the Netherlands television programs are financed by a nominal tax on each receiving set. Television viewers in the United States, however, have become so accustomed to "free" programs that it would be difficult for pay television to gain acceptance. Pay television is still in the developmental stage, partly because of the opposition of established commercial television. A Roper Organization poll of 1,995 people age eighteen and up reported that 84 percent felt that, everything considered, television ads were "a fair price to pay for being able to watch" television.[22]

A number of years ago the National Association of Broadcasters sponsored an opinion survey which was considered so alarming that the results were suppressed. It was found that 60 percent of the persons interviewed found television commercials annoying, and 63 percent said they would prefer television without commercials.[23] The NAB action in suppressing its own study seems to confirm the judgment of advertising man Fairfax Cone, who wrote in his memoirs that the "NAB is a bald-faced lobby, which pretends . . . to be acting in the public interest."[24] Its opposition to pay television is based on false premises. Nevertheless, all legal obstacles were cleared away and the Federal Communications Commission approved pay television in principle in December, 1968. Since that time there has been little development in pay television as a significant alternative to commercial television.

Another possible way of financing television would be through federal and/or state government sponsorship. This is the method that was adopted in Canada and Great Britain. Subsequently both countries permitted commercial television sponsored by advertisers. The British Broadcasting Company, sponsored by the government, presents programs without commercial advertising. In the United States educational television and public broadcasting continue to develop. More and more state universities are sponsoring noncommercial programs, and state governments are paying the bill instead of advertisers. Many local school districts also contribute to the support of educational television. In addition, millions of dollars are being contributed to the support of educational and public broadcasting by corporations that make contributions without advertising in the hope of improving the image of business and demonstrating corporate social responsibility. Commercial television continues to dominate the television screen in this country, however.

Commercial radio and television are almost completely dependent on advertising revenue. Magazines that accept advertising depend on advertisers for over 50 percent of their revenue. Newspapers depend on advertisers for over 70 percent of their revenue. Since all these advertising costs are passed on to the buyers of the advertised products, it is pertinent to ask what buyers get for *their* advertising money? In what ways, if any, does advertising promote their welfare? What are the specific services rendered by advertising?

DOES ADVERTISING HELP CONSUMERS?

Are Ads Informational?

One benefit of advertising is that consumers are informed about where they can buy specific goods or services. To a busy buyer who must purchase small amounts of a wide variety of goods, this type of advertising may be genuinely helpful. Its helpful possibilities are limited, however, to consumers' unusual requirements, for consumers know that the things they need from day to day can be found at various stores specializing in those goods. It requires no public announcement to inform consumers where they can find groceries, drugs, cosmetics, hardware, clothing, furniture, shoes, or any of the other numerous commodities they customarily want. There are times, however, when buyers may be uncertain as to where they can purchase less common commodities. Illustrations of this type of advertising are the store directories in large shopping centers and the yellow pages of telephone directories.

Informative advertising includes business and professional announcements such as those found in newspapers. The lawyer's shingle and the doctor's card or nameplate inform those in need of legal and medical services where they may be obtained. (It is considered unethical, however, for professional practitioners to inform the public how superior they are in the practice of their professions.) Other types of informative advertising include unadorned announcements of theater programs, newspaper notices of auctions, sheriff's sales, and some classified advertisements announcing houses for sale or rent and personal services for hire. A successful advertising copywriter says that informative advertising sells more goods than combative or persuasive advertising. This is true, he says, because "the more informative your advertising the more persuasive it will be."[25]

Advertising could be much more helpful and informative if advertisers would "debunk" one another's sales arguments. If this were done in the proper way it could be very educational. But the borderline between fact, fancy, and disparagement is hazy, and this kind of advertising could lead to greater competition and to trouble among the advertisers.

For years it was considered unethical for one advertiser to attack the product of another by name, and advertising codes prohibited such attacks. It was not illegal, but the codes were adhered to by advertisers. During the mid-1970s advertising codes were revised to allow the naming of a competitor's product in an ad, and comparisons of products were permitted. Ads soon appeared claiming that Schick Fleximatic electric razor was superior to Norelco, Remington, and Sunbeam; Ban deodorant superior to Arid Extra Dry, Right Guard, Soft & Dri, and Dial; and Avis superior to Hertz. The areas of superiority in comparison ads may be superficial or truly significant, and questions soon arose about the validity of comparison. Schick's claim was judged to be "false in some details" and "misleading in its over-all implications" by the National Advertising Review Board.[26]

Do Ads Tell About New Products and Services?

In our dynamic economy business firms are continually developing new goods and services. In a country as large as the United States the most effective and least expensive method of informing 63 million households is through advertising. Unless consumers are aware of new products, they do not constitute a potential market. In recent years industry has come forth with freezers, color television sets, and automobile air-conditioners, to mention only a few innovations. Word-of-mouth advertising would be too slow to develop a market large enough to sustain large-scale production of these items. Business firms feel justified in spending millions of dollars to tell consumers about their new products and to persuade consumers to buy them.

A defect of much of the advertising of new products and services is the advertiser's failure to tell prospective buyers anything significant about the product. In excited tones and glaring type consumers are told that there is a new product, but too often there is very little useful information concerning the product. Wrigley's advertised a new gum in 1975, called Freedent, that was truly a new product—a chewing gum that would not stick to dental work. Their ad for Freedent was an example of informative advertising, but most ads are neither reliable nor helpful.

The benefits derived by consumers from informative advertising also depend on the nature of the product. If it is real wealth, the service of informing consumers may be useful and desirable. If the new item is illth or nealth, consumers are not benefited by learning about it. Many consumers find it difficult to justify expensive advertising of a new brand of cigarettes or of cigarettes in general when the advertisements themselves must include the following: "Warning: The Surgeon General has Determined That Cigarette Smoking Is Dangerous to Your Health."

It has been argued that if advertising promises a benefit to the user and the consumer believes the promise, the value of the product has been increased. For example, if a girl buys an expensive cosmetic in the hope that it will make her as pretty as the girl in the ad and that romance will come into her life, then for her the advertising has served its purpose. Note the emphasis on belief rather than realization. What happens to the girl psychologically when she realizes that her trust was misplaced?

Advertising New Uses for Known Products

Sometimes new uses are discovered for products already on the market. This may come about accidentally or as a result of research or of contests among users. The advertising for Scotch Tape featured new uses for that product. To the extent that such advertising actually increases the utility of a commodity that is real wealth, this type of advertising is helpful. Consumer wants may be satisfied just as fully by discovering new uses for known products as by creating new products. Such advertising also benefits sellers if it increases the sales of their products. This kind of advertising is a good illustration of advertising that is both beneficial and economically desirable.

Advertising Prices

Advertisers claim that they provide a consumer service by telling prospective buyers what prices sellers are asking for their goods and services. Price advertising is found mostly in local newspapers, local radio ads, and direct-mail ads. National advertising in magazines and on television is much less likely to feature prices. In fact, it is more likely to emphasize emotional persuasion and quality assertions. At the local level advertising of special sales also emphasizes price. Food stores regularly announce weekend sales specials. Other types of stores advertise seasonal sales featuring reduced prices.

To the extent that price advertising enables consumers to compare prices among competing stores and competing products it is helpful. To the extent that price advertising helps prospective buyers by reducing the time required for comparative shopping it is genuinely useful. It is assumed, of course, that price ads are honest. Except for standardized products, comparative prices are not very helpful without information concerning quality and quantity. If such information is lacking or if it is inadequate, price advertising may be misleading.

Does Advertising Stimulate Competition?

One of the consumer benefits claimed for advertising is that it makes competition more effective. In a dynamic competitive economy the rivalry of sellers protects consumers from overpricing, short measuring, and inferior quality. If one store charges too high a price, short measures, or sells inferior merchandise, it is assumed that buyers will turn to competitors. As personal relationships among sellers and buyers have declined, advertising has become a method of helping buyers find stores whose products are fairly priced, accurately measured for quantity, and of good quality. In advertising parlance, retail stores and corporate manufacturers attempt to build a "favorable image." A retail store that has a good image converts casual buyers into customers. A manufacturer whose corporate image is good develops brand loyalty. This means that casual buyers become customers who never buy competing brands.

At the local level advertising does stimulate competition. If a food store advertises a special weekend sale price on bread of three twenty-ounce loaves for $1.00 while competing stores maintain the regular price of 48 cents a loaf, such advertising tends to compel the reduction of prices in all stores in the market area. The extent to which this happens depends on consumer response to the ad.

Much local advertising, however, is perfunctory and does not stimulate competition. Local merchants buy space in high-school annuals, college newspapers and yearbooks, theater programs, and village newspapers primarily to create and maintain goodwill. Rarely are the ads in such publications informative. It is doubtful whether such advertising pays the advertiser.

For many years cigarette smokers paid part of the publication costs for many college newspapers. The $5 million that cigarette makers spent annually for advertising in 1,000 college newspapers constituted one half of all college newspaper advertising income. That such advertising has little or no effect on competition was discovered when cigarette manufacturers discontinued these ads; there was no measurable change in sales volume.

Advertising can be used to prevent competition as well as to make it more effective. An established firm may use advertising to defend its position against new competitors offering similar goods or services. In such a case advertising becomes a defensive weapon.

Apparent competition is not always genuine competition. There are many holding companies whose subsidiary operating companies produce supposedly competing products. Holding company A may control companies B and C, which produce different brands of coffee. The intercorporate tie-up of these three companies is unknown to most consumers. Instead of combining companies B and C to secure the economies of large-scale production, which might be passed on to consumers in lower prices, company A may continue separate operations to give consumers the impression that the two companies are really competitive. Drinkers of brand B then continue their loyal devotion to the coffee that suits their taste, even though the price per package may be greater and the formula essentially the same as that for brand C.

Not many consumers are aware that there are major manufacturers that produce consumer products which compete with other products produced by the same company. General Foods manufactures the following different brands of coffee: Maxwell House, Maxim, Sanka, Yuban, Max-Pax, and Brim. Procter & Gamble produces Tide, Cheer, Bold, Gain, Dash, Oxydol, Duz, Bonus, Salvo and Era detergents. National Dairy advertises its Kraft margarine and Parkay margarine. Bristol-Myers does not care whether you buy Ban or Mum because it makes and advertises both products. An ad for Ultra Brite toothpaste said that it was the second least abrasive toothpaste among the six brands named in the ad. The ad did not state, however, that the least abrasive toothpaste, Colgate, was produced by the same company.

Price competition may be concealed when a processor advertises and sells a product under both a nationally advertised brand and a private-label brand. In such cases the nationally advertised brand price is higher than the private-label price for the same product. The Federal Trade Commission cited the Borden Company for selling its evaporated milk to wholesalers for $1.09 more a case than a private-label retailer paid per case for the identical product.

Competitive advertising may become *combative advertising,* with producers of substitute or supplemental products making claims of superiority for their product. Illustrations of this include gas versus electricity, butter versus oleo-margarine, milk versus vitamins, and rice versus potatoes.

Advertising may induce consumers to pay prices in excess of competitive levels. For most products wholesale prices are reasonably related to costs of production, and retail prices are reasonably related to wholesale prices. There are many commodities, however, whose prices are considerably above costs of production, and those prices are supported by advertising. Advertisers sometimes calculate advertising costs per unit of advertised product. The implication is that even though consumers do pay for the advertising, the amount that they pay is infinitesimal. One such advertiser calculated the advertising cost per package of his aspirin to be only 16/1000 of a cent. One might agree that this is really nothing to be concerned about. However, if the consumer pays more for an advertised product than for an identical unadvertised product, the real cost of the advertising may be much more. If buyers pay 25 cents for a package of twelve nationally advertised aspirins when they could buy the identical unadvertised product at a price of 99 cents for 1,000 tablets, the real cost of advertising is not 16/1000 of a cent but 23.8 cents. At the lower price of the unadvertised pills, twelve pills would cost only 1.2 cents.

Increasingly the purpose of much advertising is to switch consumers from one brand to another or from one product to another. This type of advertising is illustrated by the efforts of cigarette manufacturers to induce smokers to shift brands. No one makes any effort to inform consumers that they might dispense with both products. There is mounting evidence, however, that this kind of advertising has reached a point of diminishing returns. Consumers are not responding as strongly to such advertising as they did at one time. Advertisers are spending more dollars to maintain the same sales volume. If one firm increases its advertising appropriation, competing firms increase theirs proportionately. The result is that all of them stay in the same place on the treadmill. Almost all leading advertisers admit that advertising budgets are too big and that a small reduction in advertising expenditures would not decrease sales. One researcher found that cigarette advertising created goodwill and increased sales for individual firms, but only up to a certain point. To reach that point and to maintain it requires increasing advertising expenditures. A study of the six major cigarette companies led to the conclusion that they had all reached the point of diminishing returns in the period studied. The goodwill that had been created by advertising depreciated at a rate of 15 to 20 percent a year, even though advertising expenditures increased.[27]

The argument that advertising is beneficial because it makes competition more effective assumes that competition is always desirable. In some industries, however, competition may be the death of rather than the life of trade. Congress and the courts have long recognized that competition between natural monopolies is wasteful. Railroad, telephone, telegraph, gas, and electric companies have been given monopolistic privileges because experience showed that competition was wasteful of resources. Yet some firms in these industries advertise. Most of the advertising is institutional; that is, instead of advertising to increase sales of services, the advertising stresses the evils of public ownership and operation compared with the virtues of private enterprise. Although almost half a century has passed since Congress created the Tennessee Valley Authority and the Rural Electrification Administration, privately owned and operated electric companies still spend money for advertisements that attack publicly owned and operated companies. If competition itself is wasteful in some industries, it follows that advertising tending to promote competition is also wasteful.

There is very little real competition in the American economy if we compare it with the classical concept of competition, which assumed that there were so many sellers and so many buyers that no one seller or buyer could affect or influence the price of a product. Our economy is now characterized predominantly by monopolistic competition and oligopoly. Prices are administered by business firms, and competition stresses quality assertions in advertisements. Advertisers attempt to sell more of their products at the same price or at higher prices. In some cases advertisers hope to sell the same amount as before at a higher price. Such competitive advertising is not helpful to consumers, nor is it meant to be. It is intended to strengthen the entrenched positions of monopolistic and oligopolistic firms.

Do Ads Raise or Reduce Prices?

A former secretary of commerce said, "Advertising makes possible mass production and mass consumption through mass markets." A former president of Procter & Gamble, which spends $360 million annually to advertise its products, stated that advertising lowers prices. It is true, he said, that advertising adds to the cost of operation, but it results in savings that exceed the cost of advertising. This is accomplished by making mass production possible. Big volume lowers selling cost per unit, creates faster turnover, and makes possible lower-margin operation. In addition, advertising results in economies in buying materials and in financing. "Procter & Gamble has repeatedly made savings in excess of advertising outlay."[28]

The validity of this argument depends on the validity of the implied underlying assumptions:

1. It is assumed that advertising is responsible for the increase in sales. This may or may not be true. There is no way of demonstrating that advertising alone has caused increased sales. Advertising publications report many cases where sales declined even as advertising expenditures increased.
2. It is assumed that such economies as may be achieved by large firms are passed on to consumers by means of price reductions that offset or more than offset the cost of advertising.
3. It is assumed that the costs of operating large plants are lower than the costs of operating smaller ones. This is not always true.
4. The argument is valid only if the industry is one where costs of production per unit decline as production increases.

The validity of the argument as a whole has never been established. A generation ago a massive study of the economic effects of advertising was conducted under the supervision of a Harvard University professor. At the time advertisers hoped that the Harvard study would establish the validity of this argument. Some of them think that it did, but the controversy continues. The study showed that consumer demands for lettuce, sugar, green vegetables, and professional services increased with little or no advertising. Consumer demands for cigarettes, dentifrices, oranges, refrigerators, automobiles, radios, and electric washers were accelerated by advertising, but not created by it. The efforts of advertisers to combat the declining demands for cigars, smoking tobacco, furniture, wheat flour, and men's shoes proved futile. Professor Borden recognized that consumer demands are determined primarily by basic environmental conditions. "Advertising by itself serves not so much to increase demand for a product as to speed up the expansion of a demand that would come from favoring conditions or to retard adverse demand tends due to unfavorable conditions."[29]

There is adequate evidence to show that advertising can push the price of a product up for the consumer, and that it can also push the price down. The degree of competition in the marketplace will be the basic determinant of which way the price goes. Where the seller is selling in an oligopolistic market, advertising will primarily emphasize product differentiation and will rarely emphasize price, so prices will be higher. In more competitive market situations there will be more price advertising, and prices will be lower. What might well become a classic case of price competition at the national level among similar products took place between two nonaspirin analgesics, Tylenol and Datril. Tylenol, due to the absence of competition, was selling for $2.85 or more per 100 tablets. Datril was introduced to the public with a massive national advertising campaign emphasizing that the two products were the same except that the price was different. Datril was priced at $1.85 per 100 tablets. Bristol-Myers, manufacturer of Datril, said it captured the highest introductory share of the market of any analgesic in company history. The makers of Tylenol quickly reacted to this price competition by cutting Tylenol's price by 30 percent. In some stores Tylenol dropped to 79 cents per 100, and Datril to $1.00 per 100. The average price for these two products in 2,280 stores was $1.57 for Tylenol and $2.23 for Datril.[30] Price advertising played a dramatic role in lowering prices in this case.

The wide variations that existed in the prices of prescription drugs from one pharmacy to the next were due, to a considerable degree, to the prohibitions against prescription drug price advertising that have existed in many states. A significant study showed how the prohibition against advertising prices affected the prices of eyeglasses. In the states restricting advertising, the price of eyeglasses was 25 to 100 percent higher than in the states that imposed no such regulation.[31] In 1976 the United States Supreme Court ruled 7 to 1 that states may not forbid pharmacists to advertise the prices of prescription drugs. The court also ruled that advertising in general — even when it is "purely commercial," with the sole purpose of offering a product for sale — is entitled to at least some protection under the First Amendment's guarantee of freedom of speech. This ruling, though it applies specifically to prescription drugs, is being interpreted as invalidating laws in some states that prohibit advertising of two other major consumer items: funeral services and eyeglasses. In addition, prohibitions by professional associations against advertising by their members have been challenged.

Where advertising campaigns of major proportions are aimed primarily at emphasizing brand name and product differences and not price, they can be effective in restricting competition. A complaint filed by the Federal Trade Commission indicated that consumers were paying 15 to 20 percent extra for breakfast cereals because three companies (Kellog, General Mills, and General Foods) control 82 percent of the market. Other potential cereal producers, it was alleged, were effectively kept out of the cereal market because they could not compete against the enormous advertising campaigns of the big three companies, which spend 20 percent of their gross sales to promote their products.[32]

There is little question that where advertising creates greater demand and the fixed costs of production can be spread over more and more units of production the total unit cost of production will go down. Unfortunately all too frequently the competing products are well known so that advertising does not increase demand. In this situation advertising can only persuade consumers to switch from one product to another, and the economies of lower per unit costs due to increased demand do not materialize. Once a product is well known in the marketplace advertising tends to keep the price up because it tends to develop consumer loyalty for the specific product and the consumer is then willing to pay a higher price regardless of whether it is a better product or not. Widely advertised products, such as Bayer aspirin, cost considerably more than little advertised products, such as Revco aspirin. The only way manufacturers of private brands can hope to get a share of the market is to price their product below that of the na-

tionally advertised brand. Advertising is a double-edged sword in the marketplace; it can create effective price competition or it can insulate products
that are widely advertised from the rigors of price competition.

Does Advertising Tend to Reduce Production Costs?

In his study of advertising Borden claims that the answer to this question is indeterminate. There is some affirmative evidence, but it is impossible to show a clear causal relationship between decreased production
costs and advertising. On the other hand, "one cannot be certain to what
extent the *increased* distribution costs which have attended the growth
of industrialism are attributable to advertising." There is some evidence
that advertising has been partially responsible for the growth of some
business firms, but accompanying evidence also shows that large size does
not necessarily mean low marketing costs. On the contrary, some of the
larger firms have relatively high marketing costs.[33]

Those who support the view that advertising promotes large-scale
production ignore the fact that many industries and firms producing on a
large scale do not advertise at all or advertise only to a limited extent. On
the other hand, many of the best-known national advertisers are comparatively small-scale firms. There is simply no demonstrated or apparent
connection between the size of a firm and the extent of its advertising.

An interesting explanation of the huge advertising expenditures of
some large corporations is that the managements of those corporations
advertise to fulfill their need for security. Top executives want assurance
that their company will continue to grow. Multimillion dollar advertising
budgets reflect this need for security rather than a calculated estimate of
greater profit. An advertising man expressed the view that if the United
States Steel Corporation were to discontinue its advertising, it is unlikely
that even one ton less of steel would be sold.[34] It is tempting to speculate
about what would happen if all advertising were to be discontinued. Of
course no one knows the answer. No firm committed to advertising can run
the risk of experimentation. Perhaps its sales would not be affected, but if
sales did decline, the very existence of the firm might be jeopardized. After
a strike had deprived Detroit consumers of newspapers for four months,
seventy-five retail stores were asked what effect the lack of newspaper
advertising had on sales. One-third of the firms reported reduced sales, but
more than half reported that sales remained the same or actually increased.
A similar survey of New York City retailers who went through a Christmas
season without benefit of newspaper advertising because of a strike reported satisfactory sales volume. Any loss in sales volume was more than
offset by savings in advertising expenditures. Cigarette sales *increased*
when a law was passed prohibiting cigarette advertising on television. One
explanation for this may be that at the time cigarette ads were taken off
television, the anti-cigarette ads also ceased to be aired. There seems little

doubt that the anti-cigarette ads were having an effect on cigarette sales. The industry increased its ads in other media after this law was passed.

It is possible for a firm to grow so large that it becomes uneconomical. There are diseconomies of large-scale operations, as well as economies. Even if economies do result from large-scale operations, it does not follow that they are passed on to consumers in the form of lower prices. The director of advertising for a major oil company was reported to have said that "advertising does not necessarily or always lower prices."[35] One purpose and one result of advertising is advertisers hope that they can lift their products out of price competition. Advertisers have no answer when economists ask, "Does advertising reduce the prices of brand-name aspirin?"

With reference to their costs, business firms are classified into three major groups. *Extractive industries* are characterized by increasing costs as production increases. *Service industries* are characterized by constant costs as volume of business increases. *Manufacturing* and *processing firms* may have decreasing costs, up to a certain point, as volume of production increases. The argument that advertising increases sales and lowers prices does not apply to increasing or constant cost operations. Firms in these industries represent a substantial portion of American business enterprise. Some increasing cost industries advertise. The Bell Telephone Company, for example, insists that it is an increasing cost firm, yet it advertises extensively. Since advertising expenses are deductible for tax purposes, advertising may be used not so much for the purpose of increasing sales as for building goodwill and security. Whatever the reason for advertising, it cannot be argued that it reduces the prices of telephone services to consumers. In fact, advertising could conceivably increase prices because public utility commissions allow firms to base prices on costs, and advertising is a cost. The more costs incurred, the higher the price.

Something for Nothing?

Consumers are told that advertising reduces the prices of the goods and services they buy, that it reduces the prices for their newspapers and magazines, and that it provides free radio and television programs. It is asserted that advertising itself is entertainment. Some ads are clever, witty, informative, and provocative. Consumer polls have revealed that many consumers enjoy the ads. They read them and listen to them, even though they may never buy the product advertised. There can be no doubt that newspapers and magazines would cost much more if the publishers did not sell space to advertisers. During its earlier years the *Reader's Digest* carried no advertising. Faced with rising costs, management had to choose between a higher price to subscribers or selling advertising space. Now advertisers pay $54,080 for a one-time, one-page, black-and-white ad in *Reader's Digest*. In New York Marshall Field sponsored an adless newspaper, but the venture failed. In Chicago, Mr. Field sponsored the *Sun* as an adless newspaper, but eventually the *Sun* turned to advertisers for additional income.

Radio and television are free—in the sense that one does not pay a specific price for either service. All that is necessary is to purchase or rent a receiving set. The only price a listener pays is that of having to listen to the advertisements.

Borden estimated that one-fifth of total United States advertising outlay was returned to consumers in the form of lower prices for publications and free radio entertainment. If the same ratio is still valid, it would mean that consumers receive over $6 billion worth of free publications and radio and television programs. But are they really free? To the extent that newspaper readers buy other commodities, they pay more for those items in order to get their publications at a lower price. This can be illustrated. Consumers who do not use a headache remedy are able to buy newspapers at a lower price because those who do use the remedy pay a higher price for the advertised product. Radio listeners and television viewers who do not drink beer or buy analgesics get free radio and television at the expense of those who do purchase those products. It is well to remember that one rarely gets something for nothing.

Free Ads for Public Service

The Advertising Council is a private nonprofit organization supported by business and advertising firms. The council conducts national advertising campaigns on noncontroversial programs in national problem areas. This service is really free. Advertisers, advertising agencies, and media groups contribute the money for the operating budget. Thousands of television and radio stations contribute time, and newspapers, magazines, and billboard companies give free space. It is estimated that almost $530 million worth of advertising is given in a year to support such campaigns as Red Cross, Forest Fire Prevention, Aid to Higher Education, Keep America Beautiful, Peace Corps Volunteers, USO, and Mental Health.

QUESTIONS FOR REVIEW

1. How susceptible are you to the many ads to which you are exposed each day? Can you really know?

2. Do you find yourself paying more attention to ads when you are contemplating a purchase?

3. Do you agree with the assertion that "logic will not sell merchandise"?

4. Have you ever been influenced to make a purchase as a result of word-of-mouth advertising? Have you ever suspected that some apparent word-of-mouth advertising was actually paid for?

5. Among the several possible methods of paying for television shows

which one do you prefer—advertiser? Government? Individual by pay television?

6. Do you think it is unethical for one advertiser to disparage the product or service of a competitor?

7. Can you give an illustration of advertising that informed you of a new product or service?

8. Have you ever purchased products or services because you saw them advertised in one of your college publications?

9. Have you ever switched from one brand of a product to another or from the service of one company to another because of advertising?

10. Do you find advertising helpful to you as a consumer?

11. Do you think that advertising stimulates competition?

12. Do you think that advertising raises, lowers, or has no effect on the prices of advertised products?

13. Do ads tend to elevate or lower the moral tone of society?

PROJECTS

1. Count the number of ads to which you are exposed on a typical day. Classify these ads as to the degree of benefit you received from them.

2. Make up a list of ads you are exposed to that advertise nealth and illth. On what basis do you classify these?

3. Collect three ads from magazines, three from newspapers, and three from television that you think are helpful to you as a consumer. What standards did you use in deciding whether an ad was helpful?

4. Interview a retailer and get his or her views on the effectiveness, truthfulness, and competitive aspects of advertising.

5. Interview the public relations officer at your college and find out what the school's advertising budget is; in what media the school places its ads; and how the effectiveness of the ads is measured.

REFERENCES

1. Raymond A. Bauer and Stephen A. Greyser, *Advertising in America: The Consumer View* (Boston: Division of Research, Harvard University Graduate School of Business Administration, 1968), p. 334.
2. Joel N. Axelrod, "Attitude Measures That Predict Purchase," in Kollat, Blackwell, and Engel, p. 236.
3. Don S. Wright and Daniel S. Warner, *Advertising*, 2nd ed. (New York: McGraw-Hill, 1968), p. 8.
4. *Ibid.*, p. vi.
5. Britt, pp. 465–467.
6. Rosser Reeves, *Reality in Advertising* (New York: Alfred A. Knopf, 1961), chap. 13.

7. *New York Times,* 17 Feb. 1970, p. 44.
8. Engel, p. 570.
9. *Changing Times,* Nov. 1970, p. 43.
10. *Advertising Age,* 23 Aug. 1976, cover page.
11. *Advertising Age,* 3 Aug. 1970, p. 2.
12. Frank Graham, Jr., *Since Silent Spring* (Boston: Houghton Mifflin, 1970), pp. 58, 75.
13. *Changing Times,* Sept. 1971, p. 30.
14. Samm Sinclair Baker, *The Permissible Lie: The Inside Truth About Advertising* (Cleveland: World Publishing, 1968), p. 79.
15. *Advertising Age,* 5 Jan. 1970, p. 16.
16. *Advertising Age,* 20 Nov. 1972, p. 25.
17. *Advertising Age,* 9 June 1975, p. 3.
18. *TV Guide,* 9 Nov. 1974, p. 4.
19. Jules Backman, *Advertising and Competition* (New York: New York University Press, 1967), p. 36.
20. Katona, p. 60.
21. *Advertising Age,* 29 Dec. 1969, p. 35.
22. *Advertising Age,* 21 April 1975, p. 26.
23. *Advertising Age,* 4 Dec. 1967, pp. 1–6; 16 Dec. 1967, p. 16.
24. Fairfax M. Cone, *With All Its Faults: A Candid Account of Forty Years in Advertising* (Boston: Little, Brown, 1969), p. 317.
25. David Ogilvy, *Confessions of an Advertising Man* (New York: Atheneum, 1963), p. 186.
26. *Advertising Age,* 31 Dec. 1973, p. 1.
27. Lester G. Telser, "Advertising and Cigarettes," *Journal of Political Economy* 70 (1962): 471–499.
28. *Advertising Age,* 14 Nov. 1960, p. 111.
29. Neil H. Borden, *The Economic Effects of Advertising* (Chicago: Richard D. Irwin, 1942), p. 843.
30. *Advertising Age,* 14 July 1975, p. 1.
31. Lewis A. Engman, "Horseshoes, Eyeglasses and Milk: The Costs of Over-Regulation," address delivered to Federal Trade Commission, 12 Dec. 1974.
32. *Consumer Reports,* June 1975, p. 378.
33. Borden, pp. 851, 853.
34. Martin Mayer, *Madison Avenue, U.S.A.* (New York: Harper Brothers, 1958), pp. 24, 47.
35. *Advertising Age,* 17 Jan. 1963.

CHAPTER 10

A CONSUMER VIEW
OF ADVERTISING

SOME CRITICISMS OF ADVERTISING

Criticism from Outside the Industry

Public confidence in the institution of advertising has been at a low ebb in recent years. Some feel that this is due to the excessive amount of tasteless and objectionable advertising on television. Others contend that consumer expectations of product quality and satisfaction have been pushed too high by ads that promise more than they can fulfill, thus creating a general disenchantment with the product and the ad which promised so much. Poll-takers for George Gallup asked a cross-section of households what degree of confidence they had in eleven different groupings of society's leaders. Medical doctors ranked first and advertising executives ranked last.[1] In a survey of college students published by the Gallup poll, students were asked to rate the honesty and ethical standards of people in different fields. Only 6 percent rated advertising practitioners high-to-very high; 40 percent rated them average; and 54 percent rated them low-to-very low.[2] Members of a survey group were asked by Opinion Research whether they found advertising believable or not. Fifty-one percent stated that they found advertising believable, and forty-seven percent found it unbelievable. The scale, however, tips in the negative direction, against the advertiser, on the part of the young, the college educated, and society's thought leaders — that is, those people who tend to be in the forefront of public opinion.[3] Table 10-1 presents the results of this survey.

S. I. Hayakawa, expert on language, former president of San Francisco State College, and U.S. senator from California, had these critical comments to make about the role of advertising:

Each aspect of our world has an ethical goal. Government seeks to make us a law abiding citizenry; education aims to produce awareness; religion directs itself toward establishing morality. Advertising, however, has no ethical goal and attempts only to produce the dissatisfied man, whose dissatisfaction can be cured —

TABLE 10-1.   Survey Group's Opinion of Advertising

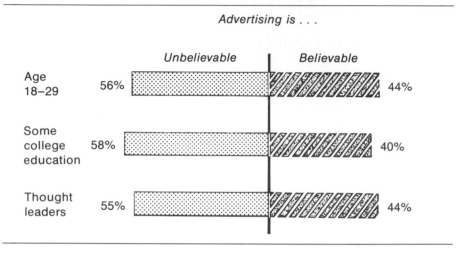

Advertising is . . .

advertisers hope—by the purchase of specific products; dissatisfaction so that people will buy more.[4]

Sydney Harris, nationally syndicated columnist, struck hard at advertising when he wrote:

> Excessive and inflated advertising claims are more "subversive" of the capitalistic system than any amount of radical propaganda—and more effective, too, in creating cynics and unbelievers out of young children who quickly learn to distrust Establishment voices.[5]

The late Arnold Toynbee, an eminent historian, in an address at Colonial Williamsburg suggested that "the destiny of our Western civilization turns on the issue of our struggle with all that Madison Avenue (i.e. the advertising industry) stands for more than it turns on the issue of our struggle with communism. That is a very controversial thing to say."[6] He felt that the American public is well aware of its external opponent—communism—and therefore on guard, but advertising is an inner adversary and therefore the degree of awareness of this adversary is minimal.

Dr. Jean Mayer, Tufts University president and nationally known nutritionist, contends that the number of dollars spent for food advertising tends to be in inverse relation to the nutritional value of the foods advertised. Alcoholic beverages, tobacco, soft drinks, and candy are widely advertised and have little nutritional value, while fruits, vegetables, dairy products, fish, and meat, which are highly nutritious, are advertised very little. In the case of cereals he pointed out that those cereals that are widely advertised are generally the poorest ones nutritionally, the sugar-coated and/or chocolate-covered ones, while the nutritional cereals, such as cream-of-wheat or oatmeal, are advertised very little. He also pointed out that the food industry spends $4 billion a year mainly to promote the sale of fabricated food and empty calories, and suggested that Americans would probably eat better if the $4 billion were not spent.[7] Action for Children's Television monitored children's programs on Saturday and Sunday mornings and found that nearly half the commercials were for cereals, candies, and sweets, and that 64 percent of the cereal products advertised were sugared.[8]

Some supporters of advertising contend that exposure to misleading commercials helps develop consumer skills in the young. However, a research project indicated that such evidence of allowable "institutional hypocrisy" actually causes conflict in children that may permanently distort "their views of morality, society, and business."[9] The children interviewed were divided into three groups: the five- and six-year-olds; the seven-to-ten age group; and the eleven- and twelve-year-olds. The youngest group is not badly affected by advertising because it is "insulated," and its members tend to believe that everything on television is entertainment, including the commercials. The oldest group seems not to be adversely affected because its members have already made "certain accommodations to the adult world and its values." It is the middle group that is "angry because they feel forced to accept practices that they believe are immoral." The ten-year-old's anger appears to reflect the first realization that advertising is an accepted part of society. Ads show the child that society allows for institutional hypocrisy, a fact that violates the moral precepts he or she has been taught. The authors contend that this anger of the ten-year-olds, as well as the tolerance of the older children, raises serious questions about the role of television advertising in the socialization of children.

A Harris poll showed that Americans, by 82 percent to 11 percent, would support measures to "sharply reduce the amount of advertising urging people to buy more products."[10] This public attitude could have a major impact on commercial radio and television, as well as on newspapers and magazines.

Criticism from Within the Industry

Criticism of advertising does not come solely from outside the industry. There are many people within the industry who are concerned about what advertising has done and is doing to harm the consumer, the economy, and the industry. A few statements show the degree of concern felt about the role advertising plays. Jere Patterson made the following comments while serving as president of the International Advertising Association:

> We in advertising are our own greatest foes. Not governments, not consumers, not educators. . . . It can be said that our worst enemies are (1) our own willingness on occasion to shade the truth—our tendency now and then to oversell inadequately designed, overpriced, hazily warranted, poorly serviced and perhaps even hazardous or unsafe products; (2) our reluctance to face up to the undesirability of pushing cigarettes until they are made safer; (3) our tendency to over-

encourage the gulping of pills and other drugs that are frequently useless, and sometimes harmful; (4) our eagerness to promote the consumption of alcohol to the point where at times our social occasions become saturated.[11]

One advertising executive stated that "too much advertising consists of mass waste instead of mass communications." And David Ogilvy, long-time president of his own advertising agency, gave a key reason for the growing animosity toward advertising:

> It is television advertising which has made Madison Avenue the arch-symbol of tasteless materialism. If governments do not soon set up machinery for the regulation of television, I fear that the majority of thoughtful men will come to agree with Toynbee that "the destiny of our Western civilization turns on the issue of our struggle with all that Madison Avenue stands for." I have a vested interest in the survival of Madison Avenue, and I doubt whether it can survive without drastic reform.... Advertising should not be abolished. But it must be reformed.[12]

People within the advertising industry and people outside the advertising industry are aware of the inadequacies of this major United States industry, which currently spends over $33 billion a year to influence consumers. How much of this influence is deceptive, misleading, or misdirected, and promotes fear and dissatisfaction?

Too Many Ads Are Deceptive

One deceptive ad is one too many, but no one will deny that some deceitful advertising will inevitably exist in a society containing as much commercial communication as ours and with a marketplace where more than $33 billion are spent annually for advertising.

The amount of overt deception in advertising is relatively small, and the number of "sins of commission" in advertising is relatively low. But a serious problem with advertising as a means of aiding the consumer in making intelligent decisions is the "sin of omission." What is stated in an ad is seldom false, but what is not stated can play a significant part in misleading the consumer. For example, some ads for annuities promised consumers that they would pay up to 10 percent yearly, but the ads failed to disclose that this high rate of return would be payable to the annuitant beginning at the age of eighty-six! Ford Motor Company ran an ad that stated that Ford had sold more small cars than anyone else in the world. The ad did not reveal that its claim was based on cars with a wheelbase of 111 inches or less. Between 1903 and 1933, 18,692,549 Model A's and Model T's were sold by Ford that measured 111 inches or less. Therefore all these Model T and Model A cars were counted.[13] Ford also advertised that its cars were quieter than a glider and stronger than a steel guardrail. The Federal Trade Commission alleged that these ads were misleading because a glider is not quiet. A glider is about as loud as a pneumatic drill heard from fifty feet away. In addition, the FTC alleged that the steel beams in the car's sides could not withstand the same lateral impact as highway guardrails. The Federal Trade Commission accepted a negogiated settlement of the complaint with Ford. Ford agreed to discontinue the ads, but did not admit that they were misleading.[14]

After sixteen years of litigation over the meaning of "tired blood," "that run-down feeling," and "iron power," the J. B. Williams Company, which makes and advertises Geritol and Fem-Iron, was fined $302,005 for flagrantly violating Federal Trade Commission orders. Listerine ads that claimed Listerine mouthwash could prevent and cure colds and sore throats were ruled to be false by an administrative judge of the Federal Trade Commission.

The National Advertising Division of the Council of Better Business Bureaus reported that 292 challenged ads were either discontinued or modified after they were challenged. In each case a word or words were used that the council felt to be misleading or deceptive.[15]

The use of a true statement to convey a falsehood is known as *co-opting the truth*. One illustration of this is the case of an insurance company ad that claims that its sales representatives are backed by computers to assure fast and efficient service, when in fact practically all insurance companies use computers.

Bait advertising is used to lure gullible consumers into a store. If a good or service is offered at a very low price but you find a salesperson unwilling to show it to you when you enter a store, be on your guard. Or if the salesperson tells you that the item is sold-out and then urges you to look at another more expensive item, you know that you are a potential victim of the *bait-and-switch technique*. If a salesperson downgrades the advertised product or tells you that the item can be ordered but that it will take a long time to be delivered, you know that you are the victim of bait advertising.

The ads for food specials may be deceptive to consumers who mistake the advertised prices as reduced prices. Of all the advertised food specials examined in a research project, at least 13 percent and as many as 25 percent of the specials advertised in newspapers were not reduced in price.[16]

Ivan Preston in his book *The Great American Blow-Up: Puffery in Advertising and Selling* discusses the types of falsity in advertising that legally produce no deception. Technically they are called *puffery, obvious falsity, social-psychological misrepresentations, literally misdescriptive names*, and *mock-ups*. Among the examples Preston gives are these: "We try harder" (Avis); "Bayer works wonders"; "Nestle's makes the very best chocolate"; "Get the best – get Sealtest"; "Kraft – the mayonnaise lover's mayonnaise"; "What's new for tomorrow is at Singer today"; "Breakfast of Champions" (Wheaties); "You can be sure if it's Westinghouse"; and "State Farm is all you need to know about insurance."[17]

Preston asks the simple question: "Why do laws exist that permit sellers to make false claims?" He concludes that puffery gives the seller a powerful tool with which to deceive the consumer. He believes that the great paradox of puffery is that the law defends it because it does not work, while the seller uses it because it does. In advertising what is legal is not automatically right, honest, and forthright.

In its efforts to protect consumers, the FTC uses a flexible definition of deceptive advertising. Under this definition, the sophistication and the educational level of the audience at which the ad is aimed are considered. The FTC is tougher on ads directed at people who are more vulnerable, such as children in low-income families.

Too Many Ads Promote Illth and Nealth

Some advertised products are positively harmful, some are potentially harmful, and others are innocuous. The distinction among wealth, nealth, and illth is an ambiguous one. Often it is subjective. Regarded objectively and on the basis of available evidence, narcotics, tobacco, and hard liquor are illth. The Post Office Department estimates that millions of advertisements for obscene publications are sent through the mail to school children every year. Postal authorities estimate that purveyors of such illth gross up to $500 million annually. A government report concluded that much of the advertising for tranquilizers and obesity cures is deceptive, misleading, and dangerous.

Two scientists charged that sleep aids and "calming" agents sold without prescriptions are too weak to relieve mild insomnia and tension but are potent enough, if overused, to harm or even kill, especially if the user is mentally disturbed.[18] In 1972, the latest year for which estimates were available, the producers of these products spent $9 million on television advertising and $1.2 million on ads in the print media.[19]

With three possible exceptions, dentifrices may be classified as nealth. Most dentifrices have no therapeutic value and are relatively unimportant adjuncts of toothbrushes. Yet a small number of dentifrice sellers spend millions of dollars every year in their efforts to persuade consumers to use their products.

There are literally scores of breakfast cereals on the shelves of food stores. According to Consumers Union only three of the forty-four breakfast cereals that it checked for nutritional quality earned top rating for being highly nutritious. These were Maypo 30-Second Oatmeal, Cheerios, and Special K. Twenty were judged of significantly lower nutritional quality than the top three, and the remaining twenty-one were judged of sufficiently low nutritional value to be considered deficient.[20] This means that almost half of the breakfast foods tested represented nealth. The number-one ingredient in many breakfast foods is sugar, and in some breakfast foods sugar makes up more than 50 percent of the contents. In an analysis of the sugar content of seventy-eight breakfast cereals only eight had less than 5 percent of the total content devoted to sugar. Twelve of the cereals contained 5 to 10 percent sugar; twenty-three contained 10 to 25 percent; twenty-four contained 25 to 50 percent sugar; and eleven contained more than 50 percent. One cereal, Super Orange Crisp, contained 70.8 percent sugar.[21]

American business has become increasingly aware, in selling many household and personal-care products, that how nice something smells may be more important than how well it does what it is supposed to do. This has transformed the obscure business of making fragrances for commercial products into a very profitable business. "Over the last five to six years, there has been a tremendous growth in the promotion of household products through their fragrance," said Alvin L. Lindsay, president of Roure-Bertrand DuPont, Inc., an international fragrance supplier. "It's a whole new concept that has totally revamped the marketing of these products."[22]

Too Many Ads Promote Dissatisfaction and Fear

The purpose of much advertising is to make consumers dissatisfied. If sellers can persuade consumers to discard what they have and purchase new clothing, new automobiles, or new houses, the sellers will make more profit. The doctrine of obsoletism is promoted. Artificial and competitive consuming practices are encouraged. False standards are suggested. The philosophy of materialism is exalted. In their pursuit of happiness consumers are persuaded that they must have more and newer material things. Advertising encourages consumers to live beyond their incomes. Many ads play on the average person's insecurity as a way of selling dentifrices, mouthwashes, dandruff cures, and products to eliminate body odors, as well as life insurance, fire insurance, and many other products.

Too Many Ads Miss the Mark

An advertising agency ran a two-page ad in *Advertising Age* stating, among other things, that "more than 90% of advertising is wasted."[23] A former president of General Motors Corporation wrote that "millions of dollars are spent each year for advertising without any valid way of determining its impact either before or after the campaign."[24] After analyzing 135 advertising campaigns, Professor Britt concluded that "most of the advertising agencies do not know whether their campaigns are successful or not."[25]

In attempts to sell magazines, magazine publishers send out tens of millions of pieces of promotional mail each year. If only 2 percent of those persons receiving these mailings subscribe, the mailing is felt to be quite successful. This means that 98 percent of these mail advertisements are wasted. Here is another much more significant illustration: The National Safety Council in conjunction with the Advertising Council spent $51,500,-000 to persuade automobile drivers to wear their seat belts. After the campaign was over, a marketing research firm interviewed drivers and found that 34 percent of those who had seat belts used them most or all of the time, as compared with 43 percent who said they never or practically never used them. A year earlier a similar survey disclosed that 35 percent used their seat belts and 39 percent did not. It would appear that the $51,500,000 were wasted.[26]

A former president of General Motors complained that many advertising campaigns are approved on the basis of subjective personal opinions instead of being subjected to scientific methods of determining in advance their probable effectiveness. No one measure is effective because there is no single answer. Even if an ad is remembered, what evidence is there that it causes readers to respond? A study made a decade ago by the American Association of Advertising Agencies suggested that the average person shut out some 1,400 ads a day and reacted to only 13 ads.[27]

Even though there is much "shooting in the dark," market researchers do attempt to measure the effectiveness of advertising. Starch Readership Service audits national consumer and business publications. For each issue a sample of 150 men and 150 women read a magazine page by page. The ads are then classified as being either noted, seen, and associated or read most. A measure of efficiency is then calculated. Although Readership Service is widely used by advertising agencies, the percentage of readers who claim to have noted an ad seldom exceeds 70 percent for the more popular products, and drops to 40 percent for such ads as insurance, finance, and pharmaceuticals.[28]

Gallup and Robinson use the aided recall test to measure the impact of an ad. Selected readers report what they can remember about the ads. They are assisted by being shown the name or logotypes of advertisers and non-advertisers in a magazine issue. Then follow-up questions probe the extent of recall of the advertising message.[29] For television commercials most of the industry depends upon the A. C. Nielsen Company. Using 3,500 audiometers, supplemented by telephone calls and diaries, Nielsen projects the national estimate of the number of persons listening to a particular program. Although there has been evidence presented showing the gross deficiency and inefficiency of this service, telecasters continue to use it. If the Nielsen audiometers show a rating of 26.5 percent, it is assumed that that percentage of all television sets in the nation were tuned in on the show. If the rating falls say to 10 percent, the show is likely to be discontinued. On the basis of these ratings one-half to three-fourths of the new shows each season fail.

It is irrational to assume that the more a company advertises the more it will sell because most companies set their advertising budgets as a percentage of their sales forecast. Consequently, an increased forecast causes an increase in advertising rather than the increased advertising causing the increase in sales. Also, although advertising is a stimulus and purchasing is a response, psychologists have not found that responses increase linearly or even continuously with more stimulation. Advertising agencies foster this irrationality on the part of advertisers because their income rises as advertising appropriations increase.[30]

Some advertisers are aware of the problem of waste in advertising, realizing that it does little good to advertise if the ads miss the mark. General Foods participated in a study in which the preliminary findings indicated that they could potentially save $100 million in the years ahead by eliminating wasteful advertising.[31]

Too Many Ads Are Useless

Much advertising is useless. Instead of supplying consumers with useful, reliable information, it is obviously biased. In some cases it is downright deceptive. One of the basic policies of many advertising agencies seems to be to minimize information and maximize emotional appeal.

Although matches "already have 100 percent distribution and 100 percent consumption," a well-known advertising agency official suggested that some smart manufacturer pre-empt the match market by adopting a distinctive trade name and spending millions of dollars in a national advertising campaign to convert all match-users to his product. This illustrates the individualistic outlook of advertisers in contrast with the social point of view. No more matches would be consumed, nor would better matches be produced. There would be no increase in the welfare of consumers. The net result would be a higher price to buyers for the purpose of swelling manufacturers' and advertisers' profits.

Too Many Ads Misuse Art, Science, and Language

Advertising has placed a dollar sign on art. Much advertising twists art for art's sake into art for the sake of profit. Promising artists are lured into commercial art by the attraction of high pay, and art is perverted to ulterior purposes. Sex appeal is overused in commercial advertising art. Much that passes for art in advertising is ugly. Touched-up photographs of pimply faces, portraits of sour-faced sufferers with jangled nerves caused by consuming the "wrong" brand of coffee or cigarettes are scarcely worth the efforts of potential artists. The vapid smile of a model to show teeth made white by using "Duzit" dentifrice represents a perversion of the artist's skill.

Pseudoscience is also used by advertisers for the sake of profit. Americans are impressed with efficiency and science. If advertisers claim that scientists have tested and approved their product, sales will probably increase. The mere assertion that two out of three doctors surveyed endorse the advertised product impresses many gullible consumers. For all they know, only three doctors may have been questioned. A scientist is always dressed in a freshly laundered white coat and holds a test tube in his hand. Chemists and physicists are paid to make tests, but producers reserve the right to publicize only those portions favorable to their products. In the lingo of the advertising agencies this is called "iceberg research," because the researcher is permitted to reveal only the favorable results of his research.[32]

Advertisers are destroying the meaning of words. With a bland disregard for truth, advertising copywriters assert that their brand is the best in the world. Obviously all brands of a particular product cannot be the best. When *The New Yorker* magazine asked advertisers to reduce their use of superlatives and exaggerations, the number of advertisers claiming that their product was the finest dropped from 312 to 103. The number who claimed that their product was the best in the world dropped from 281 to 79. The total number of unbelievable statements dropped from 698 to 206. Unfortunately most advertisers continue to overstate and to depreciate the meaning of words in the process of misrepresentation. Since advertising slogans often become a part of the language, copywriters have the responsibility to maintain the integrity of the English language.

In late 1975 Sears, Roebuck & Co. announced that it was removing most of the puffery and adjectives from its future general-merchandise catalogs. Instead of using such phrases as "this versatile casual shoe puts you right in step with fall," the text of the catalog would list only such information as construction, size, and color. Sears made this change because it believed that shoppers had become increasingly hostile to advertising claims.[33]

Too Many Ads Encourage Spenders

Advertising hails spenders and debtors as necessary to keep the economy going. According to Keynesian economics, the principal role of consumers, in the aggregate, is to spend money. Macroeconomists do not care what consumers spend their money for; the important thing is that they spend. This view coincides perfectly with the view of sellers that the function of the consumer is to buy whatever sellers advertise. It makes no difference whether the goods and services are wealth, nealth, or illth, or whether they are needed or not. When a recession starts, advertisers tell consumers that it is their "duty" to spend to keep the economy going. Spending for the sake of spending is likely to result in the purchase of aggressively advertised nealth or illth on credit. Economic stability and high-level employment are desirable goals, but the well-being of consumers is a desirable goal also. Spending for the purchase of wealth will maintain high-level employment just as effectively as spending for illth.

Too Many Questionable Testimonials for Sale

Many gullible consumers are impressed by what prominent people say and do. If a popular baseball player testifies that his success is due to eating an advertised brand of bread, many consumers, especially boys, will be persuaded to purchase that brand of bread. If a nationally known football player or golfer appears on television and speaks the words he has been told to speak by the advertiser, millions of consumers may be persuaded to buy "his brand" of product, from hair oil to razor blades, quite unaware that the athlete has been paid a great deal of money to endorse a product he may have used only once or several times because he was paid to use it. When Danny Thomas and Joe Dimaggio were giving personal testimonies in the media, each for a different brand of coffee, tens of thousands of people were persuaded to buy these products, unaware that payments were being made to these national personalities for their testimonials.

The purchase and sale of testimonials to be used in advertising became such a racket that the Federal Trade Commission felt it necessary to establish guidelines for the endorsement of products in testimonials. The goal of the FTC guidelines is to help consumers distinguish fact from fiction. Whenever an advertisement represents an endorser as an expert, he or she must actually be an expert. When an endorsement is based on a comparison, it must be based on actual evaluation. When an endorsement comes from an organization, it must represent the judgment of the group. In addition to the above, the FTC proposed a key guideline requiring that "every endorsement . . . reflect the honest views of the endorser" and that the endorser be a "bona fide user of the product."[34] Some advertising agencies, on the advice of their legal counsel, have for a long time required the celebrities they use to sign affidavits on product usage, and they frequently give them a year's supply of the product to make sure it is used and tested by them. The monetary return to a celebrity for a product endorsement can be substantial. One of the largest, if not the largest, fee ever paid was negotiated between football star Joe Namath and Fabergé. Namath signed a four-year contract at $250,000 a year to endorse Brut, the cologne for men, and other Fabergé products.

Too Many Ads Foster Monopoly

Large advertising expenditures have created substantial barriers to the entry of new firms in certain consumer goods industries, such as cereals, soap, liquor, cigarettes, and automobiles. In all but the automobile industry, the principal source of product differentiation has been advertising. "The Federal Trade Commission found a threshold level of industry advertising relative to sales does exist in food manufacturing; above that level, barriers created by advertising have a significant influence on profit."[35]

An assistant attorney general in charge of the Antitrust Division of the United States Department of Justice expressed the view that the relation between advertising and monopoly profits is significant and that advertising "probably accounts for monopoly profits in a significant number of cases." He cites aspirin as a good example. "Even though national and private brands of aspirin are the same physical product, national brands are sold at a substantially higher price. . . . There would be little prospect for monopoly profits in the aspirin business if all purchasers knew that the products of competing sellers were the same."[36] He went on to say that there can be little doubt that a company can violate the Sherman Act by the predatory use of advertising expenditures, just as it can by the predatory use of price cutting. In his judgment it would be appropriate to impose limitations on advertising expenditures.

In one consumer goods industry there are only four large sellers, and those sellers share 80 percent of the market. It is alleged that this concentration was developed by falsely advertising on television that their similar products were different.[37] The Supreme Court of the United States upheld a finding of the Federal Trade Commission that Procter & Gamble's acquisition of Clorox Chemical Company was illegal because "television can be a monopoly tool in the hands of a very large advertiser, who can get special discounts and other privileges unavailable to small advertisers."[38]

Does Advertising Really Add Value to a Product?

"What consumers believe to be true *is* true for *them.*"[39] In the view of some advertisers, consumers' right to the truth is matched by their right to buy an illusion.[40] If advertising says that a placebo will stop a headache, it will do so if the buyer has been persuaded by advertising that it will. The editors of *Advertising Age* have written that "Bayer advertising is carefully built around the theme that we consumers can place our complete confidence in the product; what we're really buying is confidence in a product and in the company that makes it, not just aspirin. To our way of thinking, this approach is perfectly valid and justified."[41]

This point of view has been contested by the Federal Trade Commission, which holds that physically identical goods should sell for the same price. Advertising that persuades consumers to pay a higher price for one brand over another, even though the products are identical, may be profitable to the advertiser, but it is a disservice to the consumer.

One result of expensive combative advertising is an upward pressure on prices. Sellers become trapped in a cycle of advertising expenditures in which an increase by one firm causes competitors to conclude that they must also increase their expenditures if they are to maintain their share of the market. This situation was illustrated by the competition in past years among cigarette manufacturers. This was especially true in television advertising, for which they were spending $225 million a year until a law stopped such advertising on January 2, 1971. The general view among advertising analysts at the time was that the sudden stoppage of advertising on television would have very little effect on cigarette sales for the simple reason that all the companies would stop advertising at once.

Another example of combative advertising is the competition among local gasoline stations in the placing of their identification signs. One Texaco station has an identification sign that towers twenty feet in the air. Across the street a Shell station erected a sign that rises thirty feet in the air, and an Esso station pushed its identification sign to an unprecedented forty feet. Some gas station signs now tower one hundred feet in the air!

After a three-year study of household detergents, the British Monopolies Commission held that Procter & Gamble and Unilever, which control 90 percent of the British market and whose detergents are almost chemically identical, are wasting money on advertising at the expense of consumers. Close to 25 percent of the retail price of their products consists of advertising and selling expenses. The commission recommended a 40 percent reduction in selling expenses and a 20 percent reduction in wholesale prices.[42]

ADVERTISING, CIGARETTES, AND CANCER: A CASE STUDY

Tobacco Is Illth

In 1940 a medical doctor named Jesse Gehman wrote a book about the health hazards of smoking entitled *Smoke Over America*.[43] When published, the book was given the silent treatment by all newspapers and magazines. No advertisements were accepted. No reviews were published. As a result the book never reached the public. Other doctors shared Dr. Gehman's concern. During the 1940s twenty-nine studies of the effects of smoking were made. By 1953 the massive research findings of the American Cancer Society were so authoritative that they could not be suppressed. In March, 1953, the *New York Times* published a full report that broke the barrier of silence, and Dr. Alton Ochsner's 1954 book *Smoking and Cancer: A Doctor's Report* went into a second edition. In 1963 Consumers Union published a 212-page book on smoking and the public interest.[44] In 1964 the Public Health Service of the United States Department of Health, Education, and Welfare published a report that substantiated the conviction that cigarettes are illth.[45]

From 1950 to 1960 twenty-one organizations in the United States and other countries issued statements declaring that smoking is a health hazard. By the end of 1964 the American Cancer Society reported that lung cancer was the chief cause of cancer deaths and that 75 percent of those deaths could be avoided if people did not smoke. In 1965 the Surgeon General of the United States estimated that 300,000 deaths would be caused by cigarettes. The American Public Health Association reported that if present trends continued more than one million children then in school would die before the age of seventy as a result of smoking.

Tobacco is a lethal product. It contains more than 400 times the safe level of carbon monoxide, 160 times the safe level of hydrogen cyanide, and from 0.5 to 2 milligrams of nicotine per cigarette. An injection of .70 milligrams of nicotine will kill a man of average weight within a few minutes.[46] Tobacco smoke is a heterogeneous mixture of 270 chemical compounds and 80 gaseous components, of which 15 are known to cause cancer. As it enters the mouth, cigarette smoke is an extremely concentrated aerosol with several hundred million to several hundred billion liquid particles in each cubic centimeter. When cigarette smoke is inhaled and held from two to five seconds, the retention of particles is 80 percent to 90 percent. If the smoke is held in the lungs thirty seconds, the retention is complete. A smoker who inhales usually gets 1 to 2 milligrams of nicotine per cigarette. Smoking one or two cigarettes increases the heartbeat up to 25 beats per minute and raises blood pressure significantly. The digital blood flow decreases, causing a drop in temperature of fingers and toes. "The risk of developing lung cancer increases with the duration of smoking and the number of cigarettes smoked per day and is diminished by discontinuing smoking."[47]

When one consumes the 270 chemical compounds in tobacco, a chain reaction is set off. Cigarette smokers may develop cancer of the larynx, and pipe smokers may develop lip cancer. Smoking is related to emphysema, a relatively new disease from which 7.5 million persons suffer. Emphysema is defined as a distention of the lungs and is related to heart disease. Smoking tends to thicken and harden the arteries. If ulcer patients continue to smoke, their chances of recovery are reduced. Smoking affects the cardiovascular system. Inhalers are more likely to die of coronary occlusion, a blood clot in the heart. Tobacco damages the digestive system. The heat from a burning cigarette reaches 884° Celsius when air is drawn through. This heat damages the taste buds. There is evidence that smoking can reduce night vision by as much as 10 percent. Smoking women have 20 percent more unsuccessful pregnancies than nonsmoking women, and unborn children are subjected to the adverse effects of tobacco.

If tobacco is such a killer, why do people smoke? Smoking tobacco is a habituation rather than an addiction. The habit originates in the search for contentment. Psychoanalysts compare smoking to thumb-sucking, a regressive oral activity related to an infant's pleasure at its mother's breast. They claim that thumb-suckers are very likely to smoke and drink in later years. This hypothesis that oral satisfaction accompanies smoking is supported by the observed fact that those who stop smoking eat more and chew gum.

The overwhelming evidence indicates that smokers begin and develop the habit for psychological and social reasons. Boys who start to smoke wish to appear tough, sophisticated, and, unmindful of conventional achievements, they seek to improve their self-image, as depicted in cigarette advertising.[48] From age twelve on, the number of smokers increases. By the twelfth grade, up to 55 percent are smokers. From the early teens to age twenty, 65 percent become smokers.

Until the explosion of adverse and damaging evidence that cigarettes are illth, cigarette advertisers directed their advertising appeals to teenagers and young people. Advertising associated smoking with pleasure, popularity, prestige, and beauty. Athletic stars were shown in television commercials as smokers and advocates of particular brands. Advertisers were convinced that if they could hook a teenager, they had a lifetime customer. On college campuses selected students were paid by cigarette manufacturers to distribute free samples.

State legislatures have become more and more concerned about the evidence showing the harmful effects of tobacco. Of the forty-nine states whose legislatures met in 1975, forty-eight introduced some form of legislation dealing with the control of tobacco products and smoking. Of the forty-eight states that considered such legislation, twenty-six passed a total of fifty antismoking laws.[49] Increasingly, state legislatures are beginning to deal with the issue of nonsmokers' rights by banning smoking in certain public places. Twenty states now have nonsmokers' rights on their law books. The federal government took action earlier in the field of non-smokers' rights with the Civil Aeronautics Board requiring airlines to provide no-smoking areas on airliners, backed up by possible fines of $1,000. One of the strongest antismoking laws was passed in Minnesota. Called the Clean Air Act, the law prohibits smoking in any public place. It provides that designated smoking areas may be established in public places and that such smoking areas be clearly defined by signs.

The Evidence Against Tobacco Continues to Grow

Cigarette smoking has been proven to be a contributing factor in lung cancer, heart disease, emphysema, and a multitude of other serious and often fatal illnesses. The Department of Health, Education and Welfare has developed a plan to be used in setting spending priorities for health programs through 1981. The plan identified smoking, alcohol abuse, over-eating, and poor diet as among the major causes of disease and illness.[50] The president of the American Cancer Society stated that lung cancer alone will kill about 75,000 annually – 60,000 men and 15,000 women.[51] The American Cancer Society asserts that one reason the incidence of cancer is not declining is that the number of women dying of cancer from smoking is increasing sharply. A lead article in the *Journal of the American Medical Society* stated that inhaling cigar smoke may be much more harmful than inhaling cigarette smoke. Literature and advertising lull people into believing that smoking cigars and pipes is not harmful or is less harmful than smoking cigarettes, but that is true only if you do not inhale.[52]

Advertising Illth

Following the publicity breakthrough about the health hazards of smoking in 1953, smokers were frightened, sales declined, prices of tobacco shares on the stock exchange fell, and the industry panicked. Recognizing the common danger, firms producing 99 percent of all tobacco products organized the Tobacco Industry Research Committee (TIRC), increased advertising expenditures, and developed filter-tip cigarettes.

The Tobacco Industry Research Committee hired a public relations firm to propagandize favorably for tobacco. The committee spent several million dollars on "research" to show that the increase in cancer was caused by smog and motor fumes, not by cigarettes. The economic importance of the industry was stressed – how many people are employed, how many tax dollars are collected by federal, state and local governments, and how important tobacco exports are to the American economy.

In the decade following the publicity breakthrough, advertising expenditures for cigarettes increased 134 percent. The 1970 figure was $240 million. All six of the big cigarette manufacturers were among the top twenty network advertisers. In one month in 1968 there were 13.3 billion exposures to cigarette ads on television alone. Each teenager was exposed to sixty-one ads, and each child was exposed to forty-five cigarette ads.[53] The purpose of these ads, of course, was to induce nonsmokers to smoke, smokers to smoke more, and to persuade all smokers to switch from one brand to another. The themes were aroma, flavor, pleasure, beauty, and fun.

No longer able to suppress the increasing volume of evidence that smoking is harmful to health and even to life itself, the tobacco industry, as its next strategy, developed the filter-tip cigarette. In their advertising the companies vied with one another in claiming reduction in the hazard of smoking. Lulled by the reassurance of the advertising, consumers resumed their smoking. Believing that the health hazards had been eliminated, or at least reduced, smokers increased their consumption of cigarettes. One reason for the increase was that smokers of filter cigarettes are deprived of the full "kick" to which they are accustomed. Not deriving their former satisfaction, they tend to smoke more. The smoker's dilemma is that if a filter works, the pleasure of smoking is diminished. If the filter does not work, the smoker's intake of nicotine, tars, gases, and compounds is greater. Not only did the advertisers exaggerate claims for their filters, but cigarettes were being made of lower grades of tobacco, which contain more nicotine, tar, and other deleterious matter. Nevertheless, in twelve years the proportion of filter-tip cigarettes rose from less than one-half of 1 percent to 55 percent of all cigarettes sold.

The Federal Trade Commission runs tests periodically to determine the nicotine and tar content of cigarettes. Carlton 70s were rated the least dangerous by the FTC, with 2 milligrams of tar and .2 milligrams of nicotine per cigarette. Players regular nonfilter were the highest in tar, with 31 milligrams per cigarette, and English Ovals king nonfilters were highest in nicotine, with 2.3 milligrams per cigarette.[54]

Cigarettes with a low tar and low nicotine content have been taking an increasing share of the market. This has stimulated more cigarette advertising emphasizing low tar and low nicotine content. In 1976 alone, $200 million was budgeted for advertising and promotion of just five of these brands of cigarettes.

The power of habit was on the side of the tobacco industry. Within a decade after 1953, 65 million smokers, of whom 25 million were women, were spending $7 billion a year for the purchase of 507 billion cigarettes, which averages out to a pack a day for each smoker.

The Tobacco Industry Code Failure

Unable to suppress the growing volume of evidence relating cigarettes to ill health and fearing that the states and the federal government would enact legislation regulating the advertising of cigarettes, the industry created the Cigarette Advertising Code, Inc. The purposes of the Code were to establish uniform standards for cigarette advertising and to provide methods of enforcing compliance.[55]

There are advertising codes in many industries, and the record shows that while the better elements in an industry may operate according to the code, there are always marginal operators whose actions tend to undermine a code. After the Cigarette Advertising Code had been in operation five months the chairman of the Federal Trade Commission said that "the cigaret advertising code under which the industry has been operating for some months has produced no material improvements in cigaret advertising."[56] In less than a year one major manufacturer withdrew from the Code, and after five years the Code quietly died.[57] In the words of an astute observer, ". . . self-regulation cannot practically be expected to extend to self-extinction."[58]

The Power Struggle in Congress: Phase I

Are cigarettes illth? Do cigarettes kill smokers? Do cigarettes impair the health of smokers? In the decade following 1953 the evidence supporting affirmative answers to these questions was repeatedly denied by the tobacco industry. If the truth were available, smokers had a right to know it. The United States Public Health Service, which is broadly concerned with the health of the American people, became increasingly conscious of its responsibility to answer these questions. The surgeon general appointed a committee of ten eminent scientists to review all the evidence and to provide answers. The committee's report was published in 1964. Immediately following, the Federal Trade Commission promulgated a trade regulation rule to go into effect July 1, 1965. The rule provided that in the sale of cigarettes it would be unlawful "to fail to disclose clearly and prominently, in all advertising and on every pack, box, carton, or other container in which cigarettes are sold to the consuming public that cigarette smoking is dangerous to health and may cause death from cancer and other diseases."

The tobacco industry responded in two ways. It came forth with the Cigarette Advertising Code, and its lobbyists went to Congress, seeking to nullify the FTC order. The tobacco industry and its representatives were willing to accept a show of public control, which would protect them from effective government control. Their first demand was that the FTC order be suspended. This was done. Their next demand was that attempts to regulate the advertising of cigarettes be stopped. This also was accomplished. The price the industry paid for these gains was acceptance of a law which required that the following statement appear on each package of cigarettes: "Caution: Cigarette Smoking May Be Hazardous to Your Health." The next section of the law states that "no statement relating smoking and health shall be required in the advertising of any cigarettes, the packages of which are labeled in conformity with the provisions of this act."[59] The law was effective January 1, 1966.

Critics were quick to point out that the law was contradictory. If cigarette smoking were hazardous to health, the sale of cigarettes should not be promoted. Yet the law not only permitted the continued advertising of cigarettes but also forbade the Federal Trade Commission or any state to impose any controls on cigarette advertising.

The industry was reasonably well pleased with this law. It had successfully prevented enactment of a more rigorous and effective law. The new law protected cigarette manufacturers from civil suits for damages claimed by smokers because the label on the package warned consumers that smoking may be hazardous to their health.

Phase II

It is doubtful that in 1966 anyone could have foreseen the abolition of cigarette advertising on television, effective January 2, 1971. Several incidents led to that unexpected action.

First the Cigarette Labeling Act of 1965 required that the Public Health Service of the Food and Drug Administration and the Federal Trade Commission submit annual reports to Congress on the effectiveness of the law and on recent developments in research on smoking. Year after year those reports added to the evidence that cigarette smoking is a serious health hazard.

In its 1968 report the Federal Trade Commission recommended outlawing cigarette ads on radio and television. In 1971 the surgeon general reported that the evidence confirmed that 1) cigarette smoking is a significant risk factor contributing to coronary heart disease and death; 2) cigarette smoking is associated with increased mortality from cerebrovascular disease; 3) cigarette smoking has been observed to increase the risk of death from nonsyphilitic aortic aneurysm; 4) cigarette smoking is the most important cause of chronic obstructive bronchial pulmonary disease in the United States; 5) it increases the risk of death from pulmonary emphysema and chronic bronchitis; 6) cigarette smoking is the main cause of lung cancer in men; 7) cigarette smoking is the significant factor in cancer of the larynx; 8) cigarette smoking is associated with the development of cancer of the esophagus; 9) likewise, it is associated with cancer of the urinary bladder among men and with cancer of the pancreas; 10) there is strong evidence that smoking mothers have a significantly greater number of unsuccessful pregnancies due to stillbirth and neonatal deaths as compared to nonsmoking mothers; and 11) cigarette smokers have increased prevalence of peptic ulcers. The mounting evidence in these reports played a large part in convincing Congress that the Cigarette Labeling and Advertising Act of 1965 had to be strengthened.*

* The HEW Reports were published under the following titles: *The Health Consequences of Smoking: A Public Health Service Review, 1967; The Health Consequences of Smoking: 1968 Supplement to the 1967 Public Health Service Review; The Health Consequences of Smoking: 1969 Supplement to the 1967 Public Health Service Review; The Health Consequences of Smoking: A Report of the Surgeon General – 1971.*

A second factor influencing Congress to strengthen the law restricting cigarette advertising was the attitude of the tobacco industry. After its victory in 1965, the industry as a whole became arrogant. In a three-year period cigarette advertising expenditures rose from $200 million to $300 million a year. In that same period the federal government spent $2 million to inform the public of the dangers of smoking.

A third incident having its effect on Congress illustrates how one person can influence government. In 1967 John Banzhaf, III, a professor of law at George Washington University and president of Action on Smoking and Health, requested the Federal Communications Commission to require television stations and cigarette advertisers to provide "a significant amount of time for anti-smoking ads." The FCC responded by passing a rule, based on the "equal time" doctrine, requiring one antismoking commercial for every three cigarette commercials. It was estimated that the ruling gave the antismoking forces about $75 million worth of free advertising time. The FCC ruling was challenged in court, but the FCC was upheld in 1968. The antismoking ads were credited with being the major factor in the subsequent decline in smoking and in cigarette sales. A study showed that one million persons stopped smoking; that 100,000 doctors quit smoking; and that 70 percent of the smoking population became aware of the hazards of cigarette smoking.[60]

Cigarette consumption began to rise again after the removal of most of the antismoking advertisements on television. In 1973 the United States led the world in the per capita consumption of cigarettes, with an average per capita consumption for all persons fifteen years of age and older of 1,812 cigarettes.[61] The next year per capita consumption of cigarettes dropped slightly—the first decline in five years—even though the industry spent more for advertising that year than it had in any year since 1970. At the same time, however, domestic sales of cigarettes were up by about 1.7 percent, or 594.5 billion cigarettes, which was a new record.[62] Americans bought a record 010 billion cigarettes in 1975, nearly 100 billion more than they bought in 1964, the year the surgeon general's report linked lung cancer with cigarette smoking.[63]

Even though cigarette consumption has increased, the percentage of adult Americans who smoked in 1975 declined. A survey of smoking habits for 1964 to 1966 showed that 52.4 percent of American men over the age of twenty-one were smokers. This dropped to 42.2 percent in 1970 and 39.3 percent in 1975. Among adult women, the trend was upward—from 32.5 percent in the mid 1960s to 42.2 percent in 1970—but then sharply down again to 28.9 percent in 1975.[64] Despite the declining percentage of adult American smokers, the total number of people who smoke is still on the increase, primarily because the total number of people in the population has been rising.

A fourth incident responsible for the changing mood of Congress was the breakdown of the attempted self-regulation of cigarette advertising by the National Association of Broadcasters. Congress was told that the NAB Code Authority would handle the problem, and the Code Authority was told that Congress would handle the problem, with the result being that no one regulated cigarette advertising. Outside critics referred to the NAB code as a "code in name only."[65]

A final factor influencing public and congressional attitudes toward cigarette smoking was the action of a major life insurance company which began offering lower premiums to nonsmokers. This represented a hard management recognition of the validity of the Surgeon General's report. After five years' experience the insurance company reported substantial growth of sales of the nonsmoker policy, and there were indications that other insurance companies might also offer lower premiums. As the expiration date of the 1965 Cigarette and Advertising Labeling Act approached, the tobacco industry and advertisers were not in as firm control of the situation as they had been five years earlier. With only token opposition, Congress unanimously passed the Public Health Cigarette Smoking Act of 1969.[66] The law requires the following statement on all packages of cigarettes: "WARNING: The Surgeon General Has Determined That Cigarette Smoking is Dangerous to Your Health." It further stipulates that "such statement shall be located in a conspicuous place on every cigarette package and shall appear in conspicuous and legible type in contrast by typography, layout, or color with other printed matter on the package."

The law also provided that after January 1, 1971, "it shall be unlawful to advertise cigarettes on any medium of electronic communication subject to the jurisdiction of the Federal Communications Commission." In 1970 television and radio income from cigarette advertising was $217.4 million. With the passage of this law their income from this source dropped to zero. The cigarette industry shifted its spending to ads in other media. In 1970 it spent $314.7 million on advertising, including television and radio ads. In 1974 it was again spending $306.8 million on ads, despite the decline to zero in radio and television ad expenditures. There were sharp increases in expenditures for advertising in newspapers, magazines, billboards and posters in outdoor transit, and direct advertising to consumers.[67]

The next step in controlling cigarette advertising was the requirement that the health warning be included in all advertising of cigarettes in newspapers, magazines, and other media. In 1975 the Department of Justice on behalf of the Federal Trade Commission filed six civil penalty suits against the six largest cigarette manufacturers in the country, charging them with violations of the requirements that clear and conspicuous health warnings be included in all cigarette advertising. The suits alleged specifically that Lorillard, Philip Morris, American Brands, Brown and Willamson, R. J. Reynolds, and Liggett and Myers had:

- Failed to disclose any health warning in numerous cigarette advertisements appearing on such point-of-sale and other promotional materials as vending machine panels, counter racks, shopping bags, and store signs. Philip Morris Inc. was also charged with failing to disclose any health warnings in numerous cigarette advertisements appearing in newspapers, magazines, and other periodicals.

- Failed in magazine and newspaper advertisements to disclose to the public the health warning in the precise type style, type size, and location prescribed by the orders.
- Failed to disclose the health warning properly in foreign language cigarette advertisements.[68]

The suits sought monetary penalties of up to $10,000 for each advertisement in violation of the orders and also the creation of a trust fund to pay for advertisements that would warn the public of the health hazards of smoking.

It seems reasonable to assume that there will be many more conflicts between the Federal Trade Commission and the tobacco industry over the regulation of tobacco advertising before this problem is solved.

The Future of Tobacco Advertising

Some countries – including Italy, Norway, and Sweden – have banned all advertising of tobacco products. The contention that cigar and pipe smokers run little health risk is being discounted as additional research is done on this topic. In the United States this has led to the proposal to ban all tobacco ads. A Swedish research team found that cigar smokers, if they inhale, run a greater risk of getting lung cancer than cigarette smokers and that pipe smokers are not much better off. The study showed that whether a person smokes a pipe or cigarettes, the risk of dying from lung cancer is the same – about seven times higher than for nonsmokers. The researchers found no evidence, however, that cigar smoking contributed to heart disease.[69]

Pressures continue to build in the United States to ban all tobacco advertising. In spite of the ban on cigarette advertising on radio and television and the warning on cigarette packages and in printed ads, Americans were smoking more cigarettes than ever before by 1974. The Department of Health, Education, and Welfare and the Federal Trade Commission spend $3 million annually warning the public of the hazards associated with smoking, yet the Department of Agriculture and other government agencies spend about $70 million a year to encourage the growth and marketing of tobacco. The Agriculture Department has been buying nearly $30 million worth of cigarettes each year to ship overseas as part of the U.S. Food for Peace program!

HOW TO INFLUENCE CONSUMERS

Psychology and Advertising

Psychology has become the supporting pillar in the temple of advertising. Advertisers have developed a psychology for selling, the potentials of which are awesome, even frightening. In the early days advertising was relatively crude and naive. Modern advertising began when copywriters dropped their rule-of-thumb methods and hunches and began to use the basic principles of psychology. They analyzed people to discover their weaknesses. Practitioners of the "dismal science" of economics, however, followed Adam Smith in assuming that consumers are "economic men." The mythical economic person is rational and omniscient. One hundred years after Adam Smith, the science of psychology began to develop. After World War I advertisers embraced psychology fervently, convinced that psychologists could guide them in their efforts to reach and to persuade consumers. Applied and theoretical psychologists and advertisers are right when they say that wherever decisions are involved, emotions are present. They are far ahead of economists, who still persist in using models based on an assumption of rational choice. The simple truth is that people cannot help but be influenced by some advertisers. Psychologists know that there are several distortion factors that interfere with our attempts to observe our motivations objectively. The most important distortion factor is our desire to appear rational to ourselves and to others. One applied psychologist cites many cases in which persons answered questions rationally, but when tested indirectly through their subconscious, exhibited responses that contradicted earlier responses.[70]

How Advertisers Use Psychology

Advertisers play on human impulses to spur the reactions they want. To make a sale they must attract attention, arouse interest, create a desire, or build confidence – all for the purpose of leading the consumer to a decision and to the action. To attract attention the advertiser thrusts into the thought-stream of consumers something that is sufficiently intense to drive out every other thought. Big billboards, blaring radios, violent action, and brilliant color are methods used to attract attention. Television commercials are effective because they often use these methods.

The applied psychologist assumes that the average adult ceases to grow in intelligence after the age of sixteen. So advertising themes and copy are beamed no higher than the sixteen-year-old mentality. The themes are emotional and the words are simple. Many people do not like the soap operas and westerns, but advertising realists know that such programs sell soap.

Motivation Research (MR)

This technique uses the analytical tools of psychology and sociology to uncover and evaluate motives underlying human behavior in the consumer market. Its purpose is to penetrate below the surface just far enough to ascertain what advertising appeals to us. MR is problem-centered rather than person-centered; it is interested only in group behavior. In addition to the in-depth interview, MR uses the open-end question, word association, sentence completion, and picture response methods of interpreting non-verbal behavior.[71] MR searches for hidden hopes and aspirations and for deeply imbedded anxieties and fears that advertisers can use to help sell their products. Instead of selling their goods and services directly, advertisers sell emotional security, a sense of power, reassurance of one's importance, and ego gratification. MR tries to find out why people behave as they do in given situations. It seeks to relate behavior to desires, emotions, and intentions. It focuses on what goes on in a consumer's mind after a stimulus is applied and before a response is made, and it capitalizes on the fact that consumers do not know what they want or why they act as they do.

There was a flurry of interest in MR in the early 1960s, but by the 1970s psychologists and advertisers were having second thoughts. According to Engel, the tools of MR are no more applicable to the measurement of motives than to the measurement of attitudes, personality traits, group influences, or other variables affecting consumer actions.[72] Britt regards the term "motivation research" as misleading. It is no panacea, nor are all its techniques or projections reliable.[73] According to Myers and Reynolds the literature on motivation research "seems to contain more semantic confusion than most other behavioral areas."[74] Markin thinks that it may take twenty-five to fifty years to correct the damage caused by the widespread adoption and misapplication of Freudian-based theories concerning consumer behavior. Freudian-based MR assumes that consumers are not very smart and that their behavior is guided by irrational forces.[75] Adam Baker says that researchers and psychologists would do better if "they knew a lot less and understood a lot more."[76]

Despite these arguments against MR, many advertisers continue to use MR findings. When MR discovered that 38 percent of the purchases in a supermarket were made on impulse, store managers rearranged their merchandise to take advantage of the discovery. When MR found that people who could not or did not brush their teeth after each meal had a sense of guilt, the makers of Gleem advertised that their product was made for just such people.

Can Consumers Be Manipulated?

Students and practitioners of advertising disagree in their responses to this question. For example, the president of an advertising agency told a conference that "our business *is* to manipulate people, to stir human yearnings, to use human motivations to sell goods. It is not only our business but everyone's business." In their effort to find "a universal handle on the consumer," his agency had discovered that "you can sell anything if you base your sales message on support, reassurance, reinforcement for a sagging ego."[77]

Psychologists are not so sure. Katona says that "much has been written but little is really known about consumers' reactions to advertising. . . . When genuine decisions are made, consumers are not marionettes that can be manipulated."[78] People seem to be able to screen out unwanted ads subliminally. Consequently the fear, or the hope, that ads can circumvent consumer powers of selective perception is without evidence. Engel says flatly that advertising cannot change consumer preferences; what it can do is to influence people already predisposed to the desired action.[79]

The American Association of Advertising Agencies put together a report based on the responses received from consumers concerning attitudes toward advertising and consumer manipulation.[80] Eighty-three percent of the consumers polled responded that they believed that advertising often persuades people to buy things they should not buy. Forty-three percent responded unfavorably toward the role of advertising because of the way advertising is used to manipulate consumers.

Obviously advertisers cannot make consumers do whatever advertisers want them to do. Consumers live in a cross-fire of advertising assertions and claims. They cannot possibly respond affirmatively to all of them. They must and do develop resistance and selectivity. People have an innate capacity to resist, even on the subconscious level. It is possible that they may even resist when the persuasion is in their own interest.[81]

Psychologist Alvin Rose declared that the public fear of being manipulated has no basis in psychological theory or experiment.[82] Nevertheless, psychologists at the University of Michigan remind their colleagues of their responsibility to resist the use of subliminal advertising for consumer manipulation. The first principle in ethical standards of psychologists is that "the psychologist's ultimate allegiance is to society." Psychologists must refuse to support or condone unjustified conclusions in the use of psychological techniques. "It is unethical to employ psychological techniques for devious purposes."[83]

CAN ADVERTISERS CONTROL THEMSELVES?

Can the Good Guys Control the Bad Guys?

The chairman of the Ethics Committee of the American Advertising Federation warned fellow advertisers that "advertising is not at the crossroads—it is past the crossroads. Much of the public has lost a good share of confidence in what we do."[84] An advertising agency executive also warned fellow advertisers that "advertising urgently needs self-imposed higher standards of practice, greater self-discipline, and greater sensitivity concerning the outer boundaries of public tolerance."[85]

Those who favor self-regulation of advertising face two problems: collusive action, or private agreements among advertisers, which is necessary, may run afoul of the antitrust laws; and there is no power of enforcement. In the words of one advertising executive, codes are "respected by the good guys and laughed at by the bad guys."[86]

Can Advertising Media Control Advertising?

Some newspapers refuse ads for X-rated movies. *Reader's Digest, Good Housekeeping, The New Yorker,* and *The Boston Globe* refuse advertisements for cigarettes. The major networks and most television stations have advertising review committees. Newspapers in general reject ads for matrimonial offers, fortune telling, guns by mail order, and computer dating. They also reject ads that discriminate on racial or religious grounds. They are likely to reject ads that may cause financial loss to their readers, injury to their health, or loss of their confidence in advertising and ethical business practices. Very few television stations will accept advertising for hard liquor, but a few radio stations will.

But for every newspaper and magazine that does exercise some control over advertising, there are scores of others that make no such attempt. Sometimes the most undesirable advertising can afford to pay the highest rates. Since newspapers and magazines are published for profit, their advertising managers cannot ignore the ability and willingness of deceptive advertisers to pay high prices. For these and other reasons, there is still much objectionable advertising in newspapers and magazines.

All three television networks and 62 percent of all on-air and licensed television stations subscribe to *The Television Code* written by the National Association of Broadcasters. The impact of combined network and station subscription is said to affect about 85 percent of all television stations nationwide because many noncode stations carry programming and advertising emanating from the networks that operate under the code guidelines. Also, much advertising, even that carried by noncode stations, is developed with code guides in mind. The original *Television Code* has been revised seventeen times. The code addresses itself to three areas: the content of programming; advertising approaches; and the amount and placement of nonprogram material. The code lists the types of advertising not acceptable, for example, tip sheets and racetrack publications that advertise for the purpose of giving odds or promoting betting. Advertising that appeals to viewers to purchase a product so as to support the program they are listening to is unacceptable. The "men-in-white" clause precludes the use of actors and actresses representing the medical professions, as well as medical professionals themselves, from the advertising of services or over-the-counter products involving health considerations. Additional rules concern the advertising of contests, premiums, and prizes. The code requires that great care be taken by broadcasters to prevent the presentation of "false, misleading or deceptive advertising." Ambiguous statements that might be misleading are also not acceptable. In both programming and advertising, "obscene, indecent or profane material," as proscribed by law, is unacceptable. The code also contains various provisions which address themselves to considerations of taste, rather than purely legal considerations. Testimonials, when used, must be genuine and reflect personal experience and may contain no statement that cannot be verified. The code states that if broadcasters have reason to question the integrity of an advertiser or the truth of proffered advertising they should reject it.[87]

In the three and one-half, high-viewing, prime-time evening hours for television, the Code stipulates that commercials shall not exceed nine minutes and thirty seconds in any sixty-minute period, or 15.8 percent of the time. Non-prime-time commercials are limited to not more than ten minutes in any sixty-minute period, or 16.7 percent of the time, on Saturday and Sunday, and to not more than twelve minutes in an hour, or 20 percent of the time, Monday through Friday.

It is the responsibility of individual code-subscribing broadcasters to screen the material that is carried on their stations. They are the first line of enforcement. The Code Authority is a quasi-autonomous department of the National Association of Broadcasters and is headed by a director. Those who subscribe to the code may display the Television Code Seal of Good Practice. If, subsequently, the station's activities constitute a "continuing willful or gross violation" of any of the code's provisions, the seal—and with it Code subscription—may be revoked after due process, as outlined in the "Regulations and Procedures" section of *The Television Code*. According to NAB records, no station has had its subscription revoked due to a "continuing, willful or gross violation" of code policy. However, a few have resigned because of disagreement over certain provisions of the code which they were unwilling to conform to.

Can Codes Control Ads?

The Advertising Code of American Business was jointly issued by the American Advertising Federation and the former Association of Better Business Bureaus International in 1964. It was subsequently endorsed in its approved form by the Association of National Advertisers and the American Association of Advertising Agencies. The code provides the following:

- *Truth*—Advertising shall tell the truth and shall reveal significant facts, the concealment of which would mislead the public.
- *Responsibility*—Advertising agencies and advertisers shall be willing to provide substantiation of claims made.
- *Taste and Decency*—Advertising shall be free of statements, illustrations, or implications which are offensive to good taste or public decency.
- *Disparagement*—Advertising shall offer merchandise or service on its merits and refrain from attacking competitors unfairly or disparaging their products, services, or methods of doing business.
- *Bait Advertising*—Advertising shall offer only merchandise or services which are readily available for purchase at the advertised price.

- *Guarantees and Warranties* — Advertising of guarantees and warranties shall be explicit. Advertising of any guarantee or warranty shall clearly and conspicuously disclose its nature and extent, the manner in which the guarantor or warrantor will perform, and the identity of the guarantor or warrantor.
- *Price Claims* — Advertising shall avoid price or savings claims which are false or misleading, or which do not offer provable bargains or savings.
- *Unprovable Claims* — Advertising shall avoid the use of exaggerated or unprovable claims.
- *Testimonials* — Advertising containing testimonials shall be limited to those of competent witnesses who are reflecting a real and honest choice.

A ten-page *Code of Advertising* was also issued by the Council of Better Business Bureaus as a guide for advertisers, advertising agencies, and the media. This code goes into great detail in specifically delineating the do's and don't's for advertising copy.

Codes tend to be exhortatory in nature. The nine principles of the Advertising Code of American Business cited above are both virtuous and obvious, but not very effective. Firms seeking to build permanent patronage are interested in self-control, but firms that cater to tourists or that are about to go out of business or to change location are much less concerned about deception. These are the firms that need to be controlled, but the concerned advertisers cannot control them. When a new provision was added to the NAB code, one advertiser boasted, "We'll have no trouble getting around this one *either*." Such advertisers steadily chip away at code provisions. The NAB Radio Code Board voted to lift the ban on advertising of feminine hygiene products because of pressures from code stations that wanted to get some of the millions of dollars in advertising expenditures. Then there are the advertisers who refuse to subscribe to a code. The efforts of reputable firms to achieve restraint and self-control are commendable, but a minority of 5 percent who flout the codes can wreck a program. Even more frustrating to good advertisers is the maverick who, though he uses sly deception, is the first to subscribe to a code, which he claims to follow to the letter, while he is at the same time deceiving the public.

A definitive statement concerning self-regulation versus government regulation was made by the Special Assistant to the President for Consumer Affairs in an address before the National Advertising Review Board's annual meetings.

Deregulation, or any perceived relaxation of government regulation, is a far greater threat and a far greater challenge to self-regulation than the most strident government involvement in an industry. As long as the fear of government regulation looms large in the consciousness of an industry, it will gladly support the alternative of more vigorous self-regulation. . . . But how do you prevent those same supporters from heaving a sigh of relief and forgetting about you, if they do not feel threatened from outside?[88]

What Can Better Business Bureaus Do?

More than sixty-five years ago responsible sellers throughout the nation organized to control "badvertising" and other objectionable retail selling practices. Bureaus were located in metropolitan areas in the United States and Canada, and each bureau had a staff to monitor local ads. Doubtful claims were investigated, and in some cases an investigation was enough to discontinue an undesirable ad. By means of bulletins, leaflets, radio and television appearances, and speeches to consumer groups, bureau representatives warned consumers to be on guard against current fraudulent practices and deceptive ads.

Through the years the bureaus have published a series of pamphlets as aids to consumers. Their tip sheets cover such topics as buying appliances, bait-and-switch advertising, and buying on time. There are over twenty information pamphlets concerned with such subjects as audio products, encyclopedias, home improvements, carpets and rugs, and home-study schools. The fact books discuss auto repairs, computer careers, health insurance, and a variety of other topics.

The better business bureau movement was a laudable effort, but its own officials finally admitted that it had never been very effective because of a lack of unified effort and lack of money. In an effort to revitalize the movement, the Council of Better Business Bureaus was incorporated in 1970. The intent was to provide the movement with one cohesive operation center on a national level to deal with national advertising problems and industry self-regulation in a variety of areas.

The bylaws of the new council declare that it

is a public service agency devoted to the protection of the consuming public and to the validity of the free enterprise system. It fulfills its purpose by fostering the highest standards of responsibility and probity in business practices, by advocating truth in advertising and by insuring integrity in the performance of business services, such objectives to be achieved through voluntary regulation and monitoring activities designed to enhance public trust and confidence in business.[89]

The Council consists of 142 better business bureaus in the United States, 14 in Canada, 2 in Israel, 1 in Mexico, 1 in Puerto Rico, and 1 in Venezuela. Voluntary membership fees support the programs of each bureau, and the headquarters of the council is in Washington. The council has a budget of about $2.5 million. When the council was formed in 1970 by merger of the Association of Better Business Bureaus and the National Better Business Bureaus it was hoped that a budget of $25 million could be reached. This hope has not materialized.

In 1971 four associations, the American Advertising Federation, the American Association of Advertising Agencies, the Association of National Advertisers, and the Council of Better Business Bureaus joined forces to establish the National Advertising Review Board (NARB). The primary purpose of NARB is to sustain high standards of truth and accuracy in national advertising. NARB works closely with the National Advertising

Division (NAD) of the Council of Better Business Bureaus. The NAD initially reviews and investigates all complaints, and most matters are settled at this level through negotiations with the advertiser. If, however, the NAD is unable to resolve a matter, it will refer it to NARB, which will then adjudicate it through a panel consisting of five of its members. During its first five years, a total of 1,054 complaints were filed with the NAD. If a complaint is referred to NARB by the NAD, the panel members evaluate the complaint. If they consider the complaint valid, they request that the advertiser make appropriate changes. If this is done and the basis for the complaint is removed, the matter is considered settled. If the advertiser will not or does not cooperate, the chairman of NARB will publicly refer the matter to an appropriate government enforcement agency. No advertiser failed to cooperate with and agree to NARB panel decisions in the twenty-seven cases adjudicated by the end of 1975. Consequently, no matter had to be referred to a government enforcement agency.[90] All NARB panel reports, whether favorable or unfavorable to an advertiser, are published.* This complaint handling service is not perfect, but it does put businesses against which an advertising complaint has been filed in an unfavorable public position if the decision of the NARB panel is rejected.† In some cases this procedure has brought an end to deceptive advertising faster than would have been possible through the legal processes of the Federal Trade Commission. The council has in recent years been establishing local advertising review boards patterned after NARB.

In addition the council has established nationwide, binding-arbitration programs in one hundred bureaus to settle disputes between consumers and business firms. The bureaus have used nonbinding mediation for many years, but the success of this method has been so limited that the establishment of these new binding-arbitration programs became a top priority.

Better business bureaus are organizations of business firms, financed by them and created to protect ethical firms and consumers from unscrupulous firms. A bureau, therefore, is not a disinterested spectator; it is a group of business firms that renders a service within its scope of interest, financial strength, and concern. Bureaus are neither panaceas nor public relations ploys.

CAN LOCAL GOVERNMENTS CONTROL ADVERTISING?

How Effective Are State Laws?

"If advertising cannot keep its own house in order, the government will have to." Almost half of the 2,400 business executives questioned by Greyser agreed with that statement.[91] Recognizing the ineffectiveness of volun-

---

* These reports are available from National Advertising Review Board, 850 Third Ave., New York, NY 10022.

† Complaints should be sent to the National Advertising Division, 845 Third Avenue, New York, N.Y. 10022.

tary controls, attempts have been made to compel acceptance of minimum standards by legal means. In 1911 *Printer's Ink,* an advertising trade journal, drafted a model law. Ohio was the first state to enact the model law in 1913. After thirty-two years the effectiveness of state control was re-examined. The law had several loopholes, which made it possible for some local advertisers to continue to deceive and mislead consumers. Consequently the model law was revised, in the hope that all states would enact the stronger version. Again Ohio led the way by amending its law in 1945 and by adding stronger enforcement powers. The penalty clauses provided for a $200 fine or twenty days in jail, or both. In addition the Ohio legislature added an injunctive clause. A false or misleading ad may be stopped at once by obtaining a court order. Not only does an injunction give immediate relief, it also carries severe penalties.

The *Printers' Ink* model law has been enacted by forty-seven state legislatures and the District of Columbia, but in seventeen states the law was enacted with the proviso that an intention to deceive must be proved. It is practically impossible to prove intent in a court of law, so a law containing such a proviso is useless.[92]

The Massachusetts and New York amendments to their advertising control laws provide that an ad can be judged illegal not only on the basis of what it says but also for failure to reveal material facts. The *Printers' Ink* model law declares that a false ad is a misdemeanor, whereas the amended New York law declares that false advertising is a civil offense, subject to $500 fine for each ad found to be false. The Massachusetts amendment includes an injunctive clause that could stop unfair and deceptive advertising within twenty-four hours.

Unfortunately no law is self-enforcing. If the law does not provide an enforcement agency, the responsibility for enforcement falls upon the Attorney General. An individual who considers himself a victim of deceptive advertising does not have much chance against an advertising agency or a large corporation. He must be willing and able to spend time and money and run the risk of legal action against him for false arrest or malicious prosecution.

A significant development in the enforcement of consumer protective laws at the state level has been the creation by ten states of consumer protection offices. The laws creating these agencies usually combine laws dealing with food and drug control and trade practices, including advertising. When a consumer protection office is established, its director is charged with the responsibility of enforcing all legislation under his or her jurisdiction, including the regulation of advertising. If other states follow this trend there may be more effective administration of laws regulating advertising at the local level.

A truth-in-advertising law passed in New York City provides that merchants who advertise prices at wholesale or less than cost must be prepared to prove that their prices are actually wholesale or less than cost. All statements about comparative savings must be substantiated when challenged by an inspector of the Department of Markets. Merchants cannot claim that a product costs less than a comparable item unless they include the standard of comparison in the advertisement.

Since 1975 Australian consumers have enjoyed some of the world's most straightforward advertising as a result of the passage of a Trade Practices Act that provides for large fines for advertisers who mislead the public. Newspapers there now carry ads from companies that want to "clarify" previous claims or that offer to reimburse customers who feel they have been cheated.[93]

CAN THE FEDERAL GOVERNMENT CONTROL ADVERTISING?

The First Attempt

More than half of all advertising is national in its coverage. It involves interstate commerce, over which the states have no control. Magazines having a national circulation are subject only to federal control. Radio and television advertising crosses state lines and so escapes state control. The Federal Communications Commission has no direct control over advertising, but it can refuse to renew a license if the advertising or programming of a station has been objectionable.

It was not until 1938 that Congress amended the Federal Trade Commission Act to include advertising. It is now unlawful to disseminate any false advertisement, by any means, or to induce the purchase of food, drugs, devices, or cosmetics. The commission may sue to stop the dissemination of an ad that it considers not in the public welfare until its hearings have been concluded and a decision rendered. Publishers, radio and television stations, and advertising agencies are exempt from the penalties of the law if they give the commission the name and address of the firm that caused them to disseminate a violative advertisement.

A false advertisement is one that is misleading in a material respect. In determining whether an ad is false, account is taken not only of representations made or suggested but also of failure to reveal material facts.

How the FTC Operates

One of the principal functions of the Federal Trade Commission is to protect consumers by preventing the dissemination of false or deceptive advertisements of food, drugs, cosmetics, and therapeutic devices and other unfair or deceptive practices. Its law enforcement work includes conducting formal litigation against offenders and obtaining compliance with the law by means of voluntary and cooperative action. The FTC may issue advisory opinions, trade regulation rules, and guides outlining legal requirements concerning particular business practices. If the Commission issues a complaint, the party concerned has the privilege of consenting to a cease-and-desist order without admitting any violation of law. If an agreement containing a consent order is not entered into, the Commission may then issue its complaint. The case is heard by a hearing examiner who issues an initial decision, which becomes final after thirty days unless the respondent appeals. If the respondent contests the decision, the full commission hears the evidence. After a commission review an order to cease-and-desist becomes final within sixty days, but the respondent may appeal to a United States Court of Appeals.

In addition to the regular proceedings by complaints and orders to cease and desist, the commission may bring suit in a United States district court to enjoin the dissemination of advertisements of food, drugs, cosmetics, and devices, whenever it has reason to believe that such a proceeding would be in the public interest. These temporary injunctions remain in effect until an order to cease and desist is issued and becomes final, or until the complaint is dismissed.

Whenever it is practicable to do so, the commission will furnish an advisory opinion as to whether a proposed course of conduct would be likely to result in further action by the commission. Also the commission may issue industry guides relating to a practice common to many industries or to specific practices of a particular industry.

How Effective Is the FTC?

In one of its annual reports the FTC stated as follows: "Cheating of consumers, principally by false advertising, is the evil for whose eradication the Commission's performance is judged by most Americans. If advertising can't be trusted and the public is being swindled by trick merchandising, the FTC fails in one of its major purposes." By 1969 there was a growing body of evidence that the FTC was indeed failing to perform its functions. Seven law students recruited by Ralph Nader studied the work of the commission and published a sharply critical report.[94] The students charged the FTC with failure to detect violations systematically, failing to establish efficient priorities, failing to use the powers it has with energy and speed, and failure to seek sufficient statutory authority to make its work effective.

Even more serious was the charge that "the Commission's behavior with regard to automobile advertising, drugs, automobile warranties, food and gasoline games, tires, medical devices and many other problem areas can be traced to purposeful delay aimed at protecting certain interests." As an example the students cited a report on automobile warranties that was shown to the big three automobile manufacturers but not to Consumers Union; then it was suppressed for political reasons. In addition the charge was made that "the FTC's public relations activities make for an image that is false and misleading." Here is an illustration: In a press release the commission said, "Deception is with us still, as it probably always will be. But the commission's alertness aided by ever more circumspect advertising media is making it tough for those who would mislead the public. . . ."[95]

Climaxing the barrage of criticism, a panel appointed by the American Bar Association advised the president that the Federal Trade Commission's performance was below what the public has the right to expect—so far below that it ought to be either abolished or drastically improved. The chairman of the ABA panel became chairman of the Federal Trade Commission, and drastic changes were made in the staff and procedures of the FTC. The commission has eleven offices located throughout the country, and the responsibilities that were formerly limited to Washington were subsequently delegated to field officers. They conduct field office investigations, recommend complaints to the Commission, try cases before hearing examiners in the field, and negotiate settlements; in effect they operate as small-scale FTCs.

An interesting innovation was the acceptance by the FTC of the idea that corrective ads were justified in some situations. The commission ruled that in unfair or deceptive advertising cases where it was deemed appropriate up to 25 percent of future ads run by the violators during the following twelve months would have to inform consumers that the earlier ads had been found to be deceptive by the FTC. In late 1975 the FTC ordered the maker of the nation's top-selling mouthwash, Listerine, to tailor its next $10.2 million in advertising to a confession that the product is not a cold remedy. The unanimous decision of the FTC represents the costliest corrective advertising order ever promulgated by the federal government. The order required the Warner-Lambert Company to include this message in roughly a year's worth of advertising: "Contrary to prior advertising, Listerine will not prevent colds or sore throats or lessen their severity."[96] A spokesman for the company said that the case would be appealed to the United States Supreme Court if necessary.

A second innovation has been a requirement that all advertisers submit, on demand by the FTC, documentation to support claims regarding safety, performance, efficacy, quality, or comparative price of the product advertised. The policy was first applied to seven domestic and foreign automobile manufacturers and has since been applied to a variety of advertised products. The FTC developed the principle that an advertising claim that is not substantiated—that the advertiser cannot prove to be true—may be adequate proof that the claim is in fact false. Enthusiasm tapered off for this approach, however, because once the FTC had all the documentation it was not quite sure what should be done with the data.

In another area dealing with advertising an FTC chairman took a strong stand. He favored "enforcement guides banning the advertising of premiums to children on television" and concluded that "under some circumstances at least, the use of 'hero figures' in children's television advertising may constitute an unfair practice within the meaning of the Federal Trade Commission Act."[97]

Divided Responsibility

There are several federal agencies that exercise some control over advertising. These include the Federal Trade Commission, the Food and Drug Administration, the U.S. Postal Service, the Federal Communications

Commission, and the Securities and Exchange Commission. Because their basic laws result in overlapping jurisdiction, the FDA and FTC operate under a voluntary agreement that specifies the areas of authority of each agency. In the advertising of drugs, for example, the FDA is responsible for surveillance of prescription drug advertising, and the FTC is responsible for over-the-counter drug advertising. With pharmaceutical firms spending nearly a billion dollars a year advertising to doctors, the FDA has been concerned about half-truths and inadequate disclosures in prescription drug advertising because these ads provide a significant source of information for the medical profession. In June, 1969, the FDA issued new regulations to provide precise guidelines to drug companies "so that advertising aimed at physicians and other health professionals will be truthful, fairly balanced, and informative."[98] The regulations list twenty specific practices that would make an ad false, lacking in fair balance, or otherwise misleading. For example, it is forbidden to advertise that a drug is better, more effective, safer, or has fewer or less serious side effects than can be supported by chemical experience or other evidence.

In 1965 Congress extended federal control over advertising by banning billboards within 600 feet of federal interstate and primary highways. Within two years *Business Week* reported that "a powerful lobby at work on Congress is well on its way to success in weakening the billboard control section of the 1965 Highway Beautification Act before the first billboard comes down." In addition, some state legislatures have passed bills "blatantly written by the billboard lobby which would declare nearly everything along the highway exempt from the federal law."[99] This type of thinking was expressed by one lobbyist, a former major general who now has his own firm in Washington: "My experience has been that the best way to get legislation or federal regulations that you can live with is to help write it."[100] One effective way to counter the encroachment of billboard advertising on the interstate highway system is for the federal government to reduce the percentage of highway construction costs that it will pay if a state government does not meet federal standards for such advertising.

WHAT CAN CONSUMERS DO?

Close Your Mail Box

If you object to receiving pornographic materials through the mail, all you have to do is to go to the post office and ask for Form 2201, on which you indicate your request not to have such materials delivered to you. It then becomes the responsibility of mailers to remove your name from their mailing lists. In upholding the constitutionality of a 1967 federal law giving you this power, the Supreme Court said:

> Today's merchandising methods, the plethora of mass selling subsidized by low postal rates, and the growth of the sale of large mailing lists as an industry in

itself, have changed the mailman from a carrier of primarily private communications, as he was in a more leisurely day, and has made him adjunct of the mass mailers who send unsolicited and often unwanted mail into every home. Whether measured by pieces or pounds, Everyman's mail today is made up overwhelmingly of material he did not seek from persons he does not know. And all too often it is matter he finds offensive.[101]

Demand Proof of Ad Claims

As an individual and as a member of a consumer organization, write letters to the manufacturers and advertising agencies requesting proof to support their advertising claims.

Fight Back!

The Federal Trade Commission published a four-page leaflet with the striking title *Fight Back! The Ungentle Art of Self-Defense As Recommended by the Federal Trade Commission*. Here are some of the points covered:

- Shop before you buy. No government agency is as effective as chin-pinching purchasers who are willing to shop for what they want and who are intelligent enough to judge what quantity and what quality they should receive for the price they pay. Just plain old cold-blooded shopping makes it tougher on the gypsters.
- If you have a complaint, make it directly to the seller. It could be that the practice you are complaining about was a mistake or unintentional Give the seller a chance to make restitution. If they shrug you off, take your complaint to the Better Business Bureau and to the advertising media.
- Take your complaint to your local government. This is important because most of the things you buy are marketed locally, and the seller is engaged in intrastate commerce. This means that the seller is not subject to federal laws. Some cities and some states have fraud bureaus, some form of consumer counsel, or a consumer council. If you do not have such agencies, it is your responsibility to work with other consumers in your city and state to secure them.*
- Alert consumers perform a valuable service for the FTC by reporting deceptive practices. Simply write a letter to the Federal Trade Commission, Washington, D.C. 20580. In your letter give facts and supporting evidence, such as a copy of a misleading ad. The FTC will then investigate, and it will not be necessary for you to be involved any fur-

---

* For a comprehensive listing of local, state, and federal government consumer agencies, plus additional help on seeking redress of consumer complaints, see Joseph Rosenbloom, *Consumer Complaint Guide*, published annually (New York: Macmillan Co.), approximately 500 pages.

ther. After investigation the FTC might issue a consent decree under which the violator of the law would agree to stop the violation. If it is more serious, the FTC will issue a cease-and-desist order prohibiting the offender from engaging in the illegal act. If the offender should violate the cease-and-desist order, the FTC could secure a court order, resulting in a fine of up to $5,000 per day for each violation of the order.

As long as consumers permit themselves to be influenced by misleading and emotional advertising, it will continue to be profitable for advertisers to use that type of advertising. It is difficult to enact legislation that unscrupulous advertisers cannot circumvent. When such advertisers find that false and misleading advertising no longer sells their product or service, then and only then will they advertise truthfully and factually. In the final analysis, control of advertising must be exercised by consumers in cooperation with private and public agencies.

QUESTIONS FOR REVIEW

1. Do you think advertising promotes values that are too materialistic?
2. Would you go so far as to say that advertising insults your intelligence?
3. Do you believe that the critics of advertising have overstated their case?
4. Have you or members of your family ever been subjected to bait-and-switch advertising? Explain.
5. Do you think that advertising tends to foster monopoly?
6. What do you think of this statement: "The advertising industry can control itself through self-regulation"?
7. Do you think that advertising adds value to a product? Can you give an illustration?
8. Do you feel an obligation to spend in order to "keep the economy going"?
9. What is your reaction to the factual evidence that cigarettes are illth? Should they be allowed to be advertised?
10. How effective do you believe government control of advertising is?
11. After reading about motivation research, what is your reaction to it?
12. Have you ever purchased a product because of a testimonial ad? Why?
13. What can you as a consumer do to protect yourself against bad advertising?
14. What is your responsibility as a consumer in the effort to control advertising?

PROJECTS

1. Present a review of Ivan L. Preston's *The Great American Blow-Up: Puffery in Advertising and Selling.*

2. Write an essay on what you thought of advertising before and after reading chapters 9 and 10 of this book.

3. Read, view, and listen to a series of ads and list all the valuable or useful information contained in them that might help you make intelligent choices in the marketplace.

4. Ask ten friends if they have ever purchased advertised products because of a testimonial by a prominent person. Tabulate the answers and record the comments.

5. Ask ten smokers if they have read the caution label on their packages of cigarettes. Then ask them whether they believe the statement. If their answers are affirmative, ask why they continue to smoke. If their answers are negative, ask for their reasons. Tabulate your responses and report additional comments.

6. Collect six ads that you consider to be deceptive and give your reasons for classifying them as deceptive.

7. Write an essay on the following questions: Can consumers be manipulated by advertising? Are you manipulated by advertising? Are you and "Consumers" different?

8. Check the advertised specials in food store ads in a local newspaper and then go to the store or stores. Were all the advertised specials available?

REFERENCES

1. *New York Times,* 22 Aug., 1976. p. 32.
2. *Ibid.*
3. Harry W. O'Neill, "On Being Credible to an Incredulous Public," address given at workshop of the Association of National Advertisers, New York, N.Y., 26 March 1975.
4. *Advertising Age,* 28 Sept. 1959, p. 2.
5. *Pittsburgh Post-Gazette,* 22 Nov. 1974, p. 27.
6. Arnold J. Toynbee, "The Continuing Effect of the American Revolution," address given at Williamsburg, Va., 10 June 1961.
7. Remarks of Dr. Jean Mayer at President's Consumer Advisory Council meeting, Washington, D.C., 14–15 July 1975.
8. *New York Times,* 16 Dec. 1975, p. 71.
9. Martin L. Smith, et al., "Young Viewers' Troubling Response to TV Ads," *Harvard Business Review* 53 (1975): 109–120.
10. *St. Petersburg Times,* 4 Dec. 1975, p. 22A.
11. *Advertising Age,* 29 Sept. 1969, p. 1.
12. Ogilvy, pp. 163–164.
13. Letter received from Dennis G. Prunkard, Corporate Advertising and Sales Promotion, Ford Motor Company, dated April 26, 1974.

14. *Federal Trade Commission News Summary,* 21 June 1974.
15. *Advertising Age,* 9 Feb. 1976, p. 46.
16. J. B. Wilkinson and J. Barry Mason, "The Grocery Shopper and Food Specials: A Case of Subjective Deception?" *Journal of Consumer Affairs* 8, no. 1 (Summer 1974): 30.
17. Ivan L. Preston, *The Great American Blow-Up: Puffery in Advertising and Selling* (Madison: University of Wisconsin Press, 1975), pp. 16, 18–19.
18. *St. Petersburg Times,* 30 Oct. 1975, p. 3A.
19. *Ibid.*
20. *Consumer Reports,* Feb. 1975, pp. 76–82.
21. *Pittsburgh Post-Gazette,* 1 Dec. 1975, p. 17.
22. *St. Petersburg Times,* 16 Nov. 1975, p. 6E.
23. *Advertising Age,* 16 March 1970, pp. 53–54.
24. *Advertising Age,* 12 Jan. 1970, p. 58.
25. Steuart Henderson Britt, "Are So-Called Successful Advertising Campaigns Really Successful?" *Journal of Advertising Research* 9, no 2 (June 1969): 9.
26. *Changing Times,* Jan. 1970, p. 31.
27. James H. Myers and William H. Reynolds, *Consumer Behavior and Marketing Management* (Boston: Houghton Mifflin, 1967), pp. 72, 139.
28. *Ibid.,* pp. 68–70.
29. *Ibid.,* pp. 70–71; *Advertising Age,* 21 April 1975, pp. 57–58.
30. Edward H. Vogel, *Journal of Advertising Research* 10, no. 1 (Feb. 1970): 42–44.
31. *Advertising Age,* 17 Nov. 1975, p. 4.
32. Samm Sinclair Baker, *The Permissable Lie: The Inside Truth About Advertising* (Cleveland: World Publishing, 1968), p. 29.
33. *Wall Street Journal,* 18 Nov. 1975, p. 15.
34. *Federal Trade Commission News,* 20 May 1975, pp. 1–2.
35. *Economic Report on the Influence of Market Structure on the Profit Performance of Food Manufacturing Companies* (Washington, D.C.: Government Printing Office, 1969), pp. 11, 29.
36. *Advertising Age,* 20 Feb. 1967, p. 186.
37. *Antitrust Law and Economic Review* 2, no. 4 (Summer 1969): 15–16.
38. *Consumer Reports,* July 1967, p. 360.
39. Britt, p. 573.
40. Allen R. Dodd, Jr., "The Barnum Principle: Let'em Buy Dreams," *Journal of Marketing* 33, no. 2 (April 1969): 85.
41. *Advertising Age,* 25 Jan. 1971, p. 12.
42. *Business Week,* 20 Aug. 1966, pp. 34–35.
43. Jesse Mercer Gehman, *Smoke Over America* (East Aurora, N.Y.: The Roycrofters, 1943).
44. Ruth and Edward Brecher, et al., *The Consumers Union Report On Smoking and the Public Interest* (Mt. Vernon, N.Y.: Consumers Union, 1963).
45. *Smoking and Health: Report of the Advisory Committee to the Surgeon General of the Public Health Service,* U.S. Department of Health, Education, and Welfare, Public Health Service Publication no. 1103, 1964.
46. Harold Diehl, *Tobacco and Your Health: The Smoking Controversy* (New York: McGraw-Hill, 1969), pp. 41–45.
47. *Smoking and Health,* passim.
48. *Public Health Reports* 85, no. 4, 1963, p. 333.
49. *St. Petersburg Times,* 11 Nov. 1975, p. 6D.
50. *New York Times,* 6 Aug. 1975, p. 32.
51. *Christian Statesman,* May–June 1975, p. 6.
52. *St. Petersburg Times,* 30 June 1975, p. 33.
53. *Washington* (D.C.) *Evening Star,* 9 June 1969, p. 10.
54. *St. Petersburg Times,* 7 Nov. 1975, p. 3A.

55. Cigarette Advertising Code, Inc., 51 Madison Avenue, New York, N.Y. 10010.
56. *Advertising Age,* 17 May 1965, p. 113.
57. *New York Times,* 13 Nov. 1970, p. 17.
58. *Harvard Law Review,* 80, no. 1151, 1966.
59. Public Law 89–92, 89th Congress, S. 559, 27 July 1965.
60. Task Force for Smoking and Health, *Report to the Surgeon General* (Washington, D.C.: U.S. Department of Health, Education, and Welfare, Public Health Service, 1908), p. 14.
61. *New York Times,* 8 June 1975, p. E7.
62. Federal Trade Commission, News Release, 28 Aug. 1975.
63. *St. Petersburg Times,* 15 Jan. 1976, p. 13A.
64. *New York Times,* 16 June 1976, p. 45.
65. *Washington* (D.C.) *Evening Star,* 9 June 1969, p. 1; Baker, p. 116.
66. Public Law 91–222, 91st Congress, H.R. 6543, 1 April 1970.
67. *Advertising Age,* 1 Sept. 1975, p. 4.
68. *Federal Trade Commission News,* 17 Oct. 1975.
69. *New York Times,* 17 May 1975, p. 36.
70. Dichter, p. 63.
71. Markin, pp. 74–75.
72. Engel, pp. 69–70.
73. Britt, pp. 43–45.
74. Myers and Reynolds, p. 80.
75. Markin, p. 34.
76. Baker, p. 124.
77. *Advertising Age,* 22 Feb. 1971, p. 130.
78. Katona, pp. 290, 295.
79. Engel, pp. 110, 224.
80. Rena Bartos, "The Consumer View of Advertising – 1974," address given at Dorado, Puerto Rico, 22 March 1975.
81. Raymond A. Bauer, "Limits of Persuasion," *Harvard Business Review* 36 (1958): 110.
82. Alvin Rose, "Motivation Research and Subliminal Advertising," *Social Research* 27 (1960): 271.
83. James V. McConnell, Richard L. Cutler, and Elton D. McNeil, "The Ethics of Subliminal Influence," *American Psychologist* 13 (May 1958): 237–239. Reprinted in C. N. Sandage and Vernon Fryburger, eds., *The Role of Advertising* (Homewood, Illinois: Irwin, 1960), pp. 466–469.
84. *Advertising Age,* 5 Oct. 1970, p. 10.
85. E. B. Weiss, *A Critique of Consumerism* (New York: Doyle, Dane, Bernback, 1967), pp. 27–28.
86. *Advertising Age,* 5 Oct. 1970, p. 10.
87. *The Television Code,* 18 ed. (Washington, D.C.: National Association of Broadcasters, 1975).
88. Address by Virginia Knauer at the annual meeting of the National Advertising Review Board, New York, N.Y., 12 Nov. 1975.
89. Bylaws of Council of Better Business Bureaus, Inc., 1970, p. 5.
90. *News & Views* – a publication of the Council of Better Business Bureaus Inc., Summer 1976, pp. 1–2.
91. Stephen A. Greyser, "Businessmen Re Advertising: 'Yes, But . . . ,'" *Harvard Business Review* 40 (June 1962): 186.
92. "Developments in the Law of Deceptive Advertising," *Harvard Law Review* 80 (1967): 1005.
93. American Council on Consumer Interests, Newsletter, Sept. 1975, p. 2.
94. Edward F. Cox, Robert C. Fellmeth, and John E. Schulz, *The Nader Report on the Federal Trade Commission* (New York: Richard W. Baron, 1969), p. 39.
95. *Ibid.,* pp. 75, 99; Federal Trade Commission, Press Release, 14 March 1965.

96. *New York Times,* 19 Dec. 1975, p. 9.
97. Lewis A. Engman, "Children's TV," address before the American Advertising Federation, 2 June 1975.
98. Food and Drug Administration, Press Release, 16 May 1969.
99. *Business Week,* 17 June 1967, pp. 106–107.
100. *Advertising Age,* 6 May 1968, p. 108.
101. *Daniel Rowan, American Book Service, et al., v. United States Post Office* 4 May 1970.

PART THREE

THE CONSUMER GOES TO RETAIL STORES

CHAPTER 11

THE MARKETING AND PRICING PROCESSES

THE MARKETING PROCESS

The Flow of Goods From Producers to Consumers

The production of consumer goods begins with raw materials supplied by the extractive industries. Agriculture is a basic extractive industry that provides food and fiber for consumers. Raw materials are transported to processing and manufacturing plants where value is added by converting them into finished products for consumer use. The finished products are then transported to wholesalers and finally to retail stores. There the purchasing agents for millions of families find daily supplies of the goods they want. The productive and marketing processes are so smooth and continuous that they provide a fifteen-day supply of food in retail stores for each person in continental United States. A day's supply is considered to be 2,000 calories. Three-fourths of total production of 3½ million agricultural workers flows through the marketing process to feed 215 million consumers.

Farming efficiency in the United States is so high that one farm worker provides enough food for himself and sixty other consumers. By contrast, one farm worker in Europe produces enough food for only ten consumers, and a major problem of developing nations is the prevalence of "subsistence farming," where each farmer is able to feed only his own family with little surplus to market in the newly industrialized urban centers. It takes 1.3 acres to produce the cereals, vegetables, and fruits necessary for each con-

THE FLOW OF GOODS FROM PRODUCERS TO CONSUMERS

Extractive Industries
Farming · Fishing · Mining

Transportation → Processing
Manufacturing

→ Transportation → Wholesaler → Transportation → Retail Store

Consumers

sumer and another 1.3 acres to produce an individual's supply of meat and poultry. The marketing process now makes fresh fruits and vegetables available to almost all consumers in all regions throughout the year. Ten million people are employed to transport, process, finance, store, sell, and deliver the flow of goods that makes up the marketing process illustrated on page 235. This chain of activity raises the value of raw products by 300 percent.

Marketing Costs

Today consumers spend on the average of only 17.1 percent of their take-home pay for food, but those whose incomes are below $3,000 a year spend about 40 percent on food. Twenty years ago it took 10.4 hours of work to buy a week's supply of food for the average household; today it takes only 8.2 hours.

As the productive and marketing processes have become increasingly specialized the percentage of each farm food dollar received by farmers has declined. As of 1975, out of each dollar spent by consumers for food, 58 cents pays for marketing and 42 cents goes to farmers. For example, on the 35.2 cents average price paid by consumers for a loaf of bread, the farmer gets 7.0 cents, the retailer 4.0 cents, the baker and the wholesaler 20.9 cents, the miller 0.6 cents, and those who provide transportation and storage services 2.7 cents.

The following is a breakdown, prepared by the Federal Energy Administration, of where the consumer's gasoline dollar goes:

Percent	To
33.2	Producer
25.0	Refiner
6.7	Wholesale distributor
14.3	Retailer
6.8	Federal taxes
14.0	State and local taxes
100.0	

What Is A Market?

A *market* may be defined as a place where the forces representing *demand* and *supply* meet. This may be a place where buyers and sellers meet regularly, such as a retail store or a commodity exchange. It may also be a place where buyers and sellers meet irregularly, as at an auction. It is not necessary that buyers and sellers meet in person, although this is more common.

Markets may be local, regional, national, or worldwide in scope. The local type of market is the one with which consumers are most familiar. It is illustrated by a retail store to which consumers usually go to purchase the many items that enter into the family budget. Within a local market there are usually two or more food stores whose prices are influenced not only by the actions of competitors in that market but also by the actions of potential competitors in adjoining market areas. If food prices were to rise in one market area by an amount greater than prices in adjoining market areas, plus the expense of round-trip transportation, consumers would have a choice of buying in one of the other markets. This choice limits the degree of price difference among markets. For many goods, consumers can shop in more distant markets by purchasing from mail-order stores.

The United States is divided into several regions, such as New England, the Middle Atlantic States, the Southeast, the Southwest, and the Pacific Northwest. In each region one would find regional markets. The nation as a whole is the market for certain types of merchandise.

It is important to recognize that buying and selling are two aspects of an *exchange transaction*. In a monetary economy the buyer sells money and buys merchandise, while the seller sells merchandise and buys money. Obviously there cannot be a purchase without a sale or a sale without a purchase.

Types of Market Situations: Buyer's Side

1. *Pure competition*. Competition exists when there is rivalry in buying and selling. In a purely competitive market there are so many sellers and so many buyers that the action or inaction of one or a few cannot have any noticeable effect on market price. Although there are many sellers, the products they supply are homogeneous and standardized. No portion is distinguishable from any other portion. As a result, a uniform price prevails.

This type of market situation is rare. It has never been as common as generally supposed and seems to be growing less common. If there were pure competition in all markets or in most segments of the economy, consumers would be automatically protected from high prices and inferior quality. Sellers would be protected from prices too low to recover expenses. There are times when selling prices do not recover expenses; such a situation is known as *cutthroat competition* because it leads to the insolvency of some or all of the competing sellers.

2. *Monopolistic competition*. A second type of market is one in which competition operates imperfectly. The term used to describe this situation is monopolistic competition. In such a market there are still many sellers, but not as many as in a purely competitive market. While the products each offers for sale are essentially alike, they are made to appear different by brand names, distinctive packages, and advertising that represents each product as possessing unique qualities. To the extent that the seller is able to convince the buyer that his or her product is different and unique and the only one that will satisfy the buyer, the seller has a monopoly.

A great deal of monopolistic competition may be found in retail stores. In each store there may be several brands of bread. Each seller has a different name for his product, yet the only distinguishing mark may be on the paper wrappers. There may be no difference in price and not much difference in quality. There may, however, be differences of one or several ounces in weight. As a result of advertising, many consumers are convinced that significant quality differences exist. Exercising their freedom to choose, consumers divide their purchases among the several brands of bread. Sometimes their conviction that the bread they buy is superior is so strong that it amounts to a loyalty, giving the seller a monopoly of that portion of the market he represents. This type of market situation is common.

3. *Oligopoly.* A third market situation is one in which there are more than two sellers, but not very many more. This is known as oligopoly. Because there are only a few sellers, the action of any one seller is likely to affect the actions of the other sellers. This is the feature that distinguishes oligopoly from pure competition. Products may be homogeneous, but they are more likely to possess distinguishing differences. There is usually not much competition in price. Most of the so-called competition takes the form of advertising. The market for automobiles is an illustration of oligopolistic competition.

4. *Duopoly.* A fourth type of marketing is one in which there are only two sellers. In the language of economics, this is known as duopoly. The action of one of the two sellers is certain to affect the action of the other. Although their branded or trademarked products may be basically identical, they are differentiated to the extent that the buyer thinks of them as different and distinctive. It is comparatively easy for the two sellers to agree on production and price policies. The resulting price is almost certain to be higher than it would be under purely competitive conditions.

5. *Monopoly.* A fifth type of market is one in which monopoly prevails. This means that there is only one seller, a situation which is relatively rare. When it does exist, the one seller has the power to set a price that he or she thinks will yield the greatest net profit in the long run. Monopoly prices tend to be higher than competitive prices, and the amount of a good or service offered for sale would be less.

While absolute monopoly is rare, monopoly power is not uncommon. Monopolistic power prevails in a market in which a number of firms have achieved control over the supply of a large part of an industry by means of ownership or by agreement to control supply and to fix prices. The Antitrust Division of the United States Department of Justice is constantly on the alert to protect consumers from monopoly power.

This brief description of price and market situations may be concluded with the generalization that neither pure competition nor absolute monopoly is characteristic of the American economy. The most common situation is a combination of monopolistic competition and oligopoly; instead of monopoly, a situation in which two or three firms are dominant is much more likely.

Types of Market Situations: Seller's Side

1. *Pure competition.* The five market situations in which buyers find themselves have their counterpart in the market situations that sellers find themselves in when offering goods and services for sale. From the sellers'

point of view, the most desirable situation is that of pure competition. Technically this might be described as *multiopsony*. It means that there are so many buyers that they compete with one another to purchase the sellers' products. Such competition tends to raise selling prices. If a single seller is one of a few among whom there is no price competition selling to large numbers of buyers among whom there is keen competition, he has a market situation that should yield substantial net profits. For most items in the family budget multiopsony is the most common market situation. There are many more consumer buyers than there are sellers.

2. *Monopsonistic competition.* This counterpart of monopolistic competition is not common. Where it does exist it means that there are relatively large numbers of buyers, but fewer buyers than in the case of multiopsony. This type of market situation might be illustrated by collectors of stamps, coins, and rare books.

3. *Oligopsony.* This is the counterpart of oligopoly. The word describes a market situation in which there are only a few buyers. From the sellers' point of view, it is not a common situation. It might be illustrated by collectors of original paintings, tapestries, and period furniture.

4. *Duopsony.* This would be a situation in which there would be only two buyers. From the point of view of the seller of consumer goods or services, this situation is rare on a national or regional scale. But it is found more frequently in local markets. In many small communities someone at some time has built a very large house. When the builder dies and the property is put up for sale, it is found that there may actually be only two potential buyers because other members of the community cannot afford the initial price or the upkeep. This is an example of duopsony. In the milk market a duopsony situation is found in many areas where only two processors are the dominant buyers to whom dairy farmers may sell their fluid milk.

5. *Monopsony.* This is a situation in which there is only one buyer. An illustration would be the purchase of personal stationery with the buyer's name and address printed on it. Once the paper has been printed, it can be sold only to that individual. Similar situations include those in which buyers have their names or initials printed or engraved on glassware or silverware. The government as the only buyer of such items as aircraft carriers and atomic weapons represents a monopsony.

BOTH SIDES OF THE COUNTER: DEMAND AND SUPPLY

Consumer Demand

There is an important difference between the concepts of want and demand. *Demand* may be defined as an amount of a good or service that will be purchased at a specific price. Demand implies a combination of desire plus ability to pay. A *demand schedule* represents a series of amounts of a good or service that will be purchased at a series of prices at a given time in a given market.

As a general rule the demand schedule shows that people will buy larger quantities of a good or service as prices decline. In a given market consumers might purchase 10,000 quarts of milk if the price were 40 cents, compared with 20,000 quarts if the price were 30 cents. Usually sellers know that if they are to sell more goods or services, prices must be lower. This is due to differences in desire for every product and involved with the *principle of diminishing utility. Utility* is the power of an economic good or service to satisfy a human want; *quality* is what makes a particular good or service desirable. The concept of utility is subjective and consequently not measurable. It is impossible to tell how much utility two different people enjoy when consuming a pint of milk. It may be equal or it may be unequal. What is known is that the satisfaction yielded by a second pint of milk immediately after consumption of the first pint is noticeably less. This diminishing utility continues until an additional pint of milk has little or no utility. Even if milk were free, the principle of diminishing utility would involve a maximum amount of milk that the families of any community could or would consume in a given day. This leads to the *principle of variety in consumption.* Rather than spend their limited income on duplicate purchases of goods or services, most individuals and most families prefer to spread their purchases so as to increase the satisfactions they gain. The fact that most families have limited incomes also leads them to spread their purchases.

The responses of consumers to price changes are measurable. The degree to which purchases increase or decline as prices decline or increase indicates *elasticity or inelasticity of demand.* Many family incomes are so small that they are spent chiefly for necessities. If there is any surplus after purchasing necessities, it may be spent for comforts or luxuries. The elasticity of demand for a particular product depends upon the extent to which that product alone can satisfy a want. It also depends upon the importance of that product in the standard of living and the income of the group to which it appeals. Sellers must determine their price policies on the basis of their estimates of the elasticity of demand for their product. A few consumers have so much money that they do not respond to lower prices. Some consumers, even with limited incomes, have established consuming habits that cannot be broken by price reduction. Consumers often have a notion as to what is the proper relation between quality and price. They may look with suspicion upon a good or service whose price is low. In a period of falling prices, a price reduction may not increase sales because consumers will wait for still further price reductions. In a period of rising prices, consumers may actually purchase more because they may expect prices to rise still further. For all these reasons, many sellers believe that the demands for their products are relatively inelastic. As a result they follow a policy of maintaining at a constant price nationally advertised branded or trademarked merchandise. Surpluses are sold under another brand name and perhaps in different types of stores, such as discount stores.

A real increase in demand occurs when consumers are willing and able to purchase more of a good or service at the same price or the same amount at a higher price. As family incomes increase, demand for some goods and services will increase. In a dynamic economy new goods and services are offered for sale, and demand for them may represent an increase in demand resulting from a change in desire. Population changes result in changes in demand. The composition of the population also influences demand changes. Young people with children demand quite different goods and services than do older people who are retired.

When a consumer-buyer enters a store, his or her demand represents a composite of many factors. A buyer does not have to be convinced of the need for food. What sellers try to do is to influence buyers to purchase certain kinds of food and certain brands. Sellers are aggressive and usually more effective in their efforts to secure higher prices than are consumer-buyers in their efforts to secure lower prices. Sellers can measure the effectiveness of their selling efforts by the profit they make or the loss they incur. Buyers do not have such precise standards of measurement. Consumer demand represents not only physiological and psychological factors but also the influence of sellers, family, group, church, and school.

In a food store demands for food in general are translated into specific quantities at specific prices. There are different individual and aggregate demand schedules for each one of the other several thousand items in the store. The elasticity of demand for food products as a whole is very slight in the middle- and upper-income groups, but demand for such items as fruits, vegetables, dairy products, and meat is very elastic in the lower-income groups. Demands for coffee and bread are relatively inelastic, but for most of the other items in a food store, the manager knows that sales will respond to changes in price. If the store is located in an area where family incomes are low, the manager knows that he must carry low-priced food items, while a grocer located in a higher income neighborhood will carry goods at higher prices. The grocer knows that buyers want more than a selection of foods. He knows they like displays of new items; they want wide, open aisles and background music; they want the candy on higher shelves out of the reach of children; they like games and trading stamps; they appreciate the "halo" effect created by friendliness and courtesy.[1]

Four types of shoppers emerged in a sample survey of women shoppers on the north side of Chicago. The *economic* shoppers, comprising 33 percent of the group, were sensitive to price, quality, and assortment of merchandise. The *personalizing* shoppers, comprising 28 percent of the group, formed strong personal relations with store personnel; they wanted personal treatment. The *ethical* shoppers (18 percent) were willing to forego lower prices so as to help small stores, and the *apathetic* shoppers (17 percent) considered shopping a burden so they ranked convenience of location as most important.[2]

Seller Supply

Psychologists have researched consumers and have reported to sellers what it is that makes consumers buy. Prospective buyers want to pick up merchandise, handle it, and inspect it. Buyers are attracted by colorful displays. They can hardly resist new items or reduced prices. Many of them cannot distinguish between real and apparent price reductions. For many commodities, laws require sellers to mark on their packages the quantity and the price of the contents. Laws do not require sellers to show differences in quality on package labels. Sellers prefer to have buyers depend on brand names as assurances of quality.

In most markets there are many buyers (multiopsony) and a few (oligopoly) sellers. Theoretically every family within a market area is a potential buyer in each store, but in practice this is not true. Some people will rarely buy in a chain store. Others nearly always buy from independent store A, although store B next door is also an independent. Because families in an area tend to attach themselves to various stores, pure competition among buyers does not prevail. Those who buy all their merchandise from one store do not compete with those who buy regularly from another store. Store managers know that some shoppers are unaware of prices elsewhere and take advantage of this knowledge to price their products higher, even though they may be identical in quality and weight.

In most market areas there are several stores competing with one another. The competition is imperfect, however, which means that each seller has more control over price than would be possible under conditions of pure competition. As a result, identical merchandise can be purchased in all stores, but not at identical prices. Prices vary among sellers because they sell different services. Even though all stores in a market area may sell the same brands of bread, coffee, and flour, they offer different conditions, such as convenience of location, organization and layout, reputation for fairness, courtesy, and efficiency. Some stores take orders by telephone, deliver merchandise to the buyer's home, and give credit. Such services are expensive and result in price differences.

Every store manager endeavors to convert shoppers to customers. This word describes buyers who customarily or habitually make all their purchases in a certain store. In popular language, the terms for customer and buyer are likely to be synonymous, but in retail trade there is an important difference between the casual buyer and the regular buyer. To the extent that a store manager succeeds in establishing a clientele of customers, he or she achieves a monopoly so far as these customers are concerned. In this situation the store owner's monopoly position is not very strong, but it does enable him to secure higher prices for his goods and services.

In attempting to convert buyers into customers, noneconomic factors are important. Family and friends are likely to patronize a store operated by a member of the family or a close friend. If only one grocer belongs to a small church, there is a tendency for all members of that church to buy their groceries from him. Likewise if there is only one grocer in a lodge or a club, the members are quite likely to patronize him. *Reciprocity* is a common business practice. For example, if there is a flour mill in a small town and only one store carries the brand of that mill, it is quite likely that all the family buyers of the employees of the flour mill will purchase their groceries from that store even though its prices may be higher than those of other stores in the same market.

A significant fact disclosed by price surveys is that no one store has lower prices on all merchandise. An independent store that offers telephone orders, delivery, and credit service may have lower prices on some items than a cash-and-carry chain store. In times of scarcity independent stores' sales tend to increase because independent store managers favor regular customers by reserving items that are difficult to secure. In such a time consumer incomes are higher, and consumers are less concerned about prices than they are about availability. In recession periods chain stores' sales tend to increase or decrease proportionately less than the sales of independent stores because consumers are more price conscious. During the double-digit inflation of the mid-1970s there was a shift in spending patterns as consumers sought out those stores where prices seemed to be going up less rapidly.

THE PLACE OF THE RETAIL STORE IN THE ECONOMY

Where Buyers and Sellers Meet

The retail store is an integral part of the American economy. In the stream of economic activity it is a connecting link between consumers and producers. It is the last step in the process of production and the first step in the process of consumption. Consumers go to retail stores to buy most of the goods and services they want. Retailers play a significant role in the marketing function. They have a dual responsibility, that of acting as buying agents for consumers and as selling agents for manufacturers.

Retail Store Functions

The managers of retail stores are the purchasing agents for consumers. Having chosen to go into the business of operating a food store, a particular manager must estimate the demand for the hundreds of commodities that consumers expect to find on the shelves of a well-stocked store. The manager then orders supplies from wholesalers and processors. When the merchandise arrives, the retailer unpacks it, puts part of it on the shelves for the convenience of shoppers, and stores the rest near at hand. In addition to making merchandise available, retailers perform such supplemental functions as financing the enterprise, determining quality, securing market information, and assuming risks.

Retailers' profit consists of the money that remains after paying for the merchandise and the expenses of operating the store. If monthly sales amount to $100,000 and a store manager pays $80,000 for merchandise and $18,000 for expenses of operation, the remaining $2,000 may be described as a profit of 2 percent of sales. Some stores do not make a net profit, and some incur losses that compel them to go out of business.

TYPES OF RETAIL STORES

There are all kinds of consumers and many kinds of stores to serve them. Some stores cater to upper-income families. Most families are in the middle- or lower-income brackets and most stores cater to these people. Some stores cater to racial or national groups, others to armed forces personnel or other special-interest groups. Some stores serve consumers in a neighborhood area. With the increasing numbers of older people, the neighborhood convenience store is having a revival. For families without automobiles, telephone and delivery services are available.

The Independent Store

The Mom and Pop Store   This type of store is found chiefly in large towns and cities. Often the store occupies space that was formerly the parlor or front room of a family home. Such stores are usually open twelve to sixteen hours a day, including Sundays. This type of store is an extension of the family into the business world. In the front part of the house the family conducts a small business, while it carries on its consuming activities in the rest of the house. Such stores are necessarily small and are not usually well managed. As a result their expenses are high, their prices are high, their volume of sales is small, and their mortality is high. Many of these small stores are operated as a sideline by the family. Often the family head has an outside job. While the father is at work, someone else in the family runs the store and he tends the store during his off time.

The Neighborhood Store   The chief difference between this and the Mom and Pop store is that the neighborhood store is operated in a room or building detached from the house. The store may be on the same lot or in a separate building, but it is still essentially a small family enterprise. In fact it is not so much a business as it is a way of life. Seventy-five percent of the customers of this type of store live within walking distance. Like the Mom and Pop stores, neighborhood stores are open seven days a week and twelve to sixteen hours each day.

The Main Street Store   This may be a family enterprise in the sense that the money invested represents family savings and family members do the work. It is a business in the sense that it is closer to other types of retail stores. Usually it is larger in size and has a larger volume of sales, and it is often well arranged and well stocked with quality merchandise. Independent Main Street stores usually supply their customers with telephone ordering services, delivery, and credit services. Instead of charging separately for these services, the expense of providing them is included in the price of the merchandise. For this reason independent store prices are often higher than those of cash-and-carry stores.

Semichain Stores (Voluntary Chains)   These are independent stores that
have organized to compete with the chain type of store. Outwardly they usually have distinguishing exterior markings and colors that show that they
are affiliated with a voluntary chain such as Red and White, I.G.A. (Independent Grocers Alliance), or National Food Stores. The interiors of these
stores are very similar to those of any other independent store. But on the
shelves one is likely to find private-label brands of merchandise as well as
nationally advertised brands. As chain store competition became increasingly keen at the retail level, some wholesalers sought to save their markets
by helping out the retail storekeepers who purchased from them. Such a
voluntary chain includes a varying number of retail stores whose merchandise is largely purchased through a single wholesaler. This kind of cooperation makes possible many economies for participating retailers and assures
a market for the wholesaler. Other services included in the voluntary chain
system are the establishment and supervision of accounting records, assistance in arranging the merchandise for display and sale, and advice on
general policies, with special reference to price policies. The result is that
voluntary chains have many of the advantages of corporate chains, yet at
the same time they preserve the advantages of independent stores.

Chain Stores

The twenty largest retailers in the nation are all chain stores. The ten
largest, each with annual sales in excess of $3.2 billion, are Sears, Roebuck
& Co.; Safeway Stores; J. C. Penney; S. S. Kresge; Great Atlantic & Pacific
Tea; Kroger; Marcor (Montgomery Ward); F. W. Woolworth; Federated
Department Stores; and American Stores.[3] The largest food store chain,
Safeway Stores, has sales of almost $10 billion a year. In the grocery busi-
ness corporate chains and semichains have been squeezing out many
independent stores, but at the same time the Great Atlantic & Pacific Tea
chain shut down hundreds of its stores in the mid-1970s because of major
financial losses. Many of the stores that were shut down were bought out
and reopened by small regional chains that thought they could operate the
stores at a profit. W. T. Grant, which was the seventeenth largest retail chain
in the United States in 1974, went bankrupt in 1975. All Grant stores were
liquidated. Over 20 percent of all retail stores sales are made by the fifty
largest retailing companies, which represented sales of $121 billion in
1975.[4]
The exteriors of chain retail food stores are usually distinguishable by
color as well as by conspicuous signs. The interior of a chain store is usually
distinguishable by the brands of merchandise on display. The larger chains
have their own brands as well as the brands of nationally advertised products.
Chain-store prices tend to be lower than the prices of other types of
stores. This does not mean that the price of every item is cheaper in a chain.
But it does mean that on merchandise as a whole, chain prices tend to be

lower. This is because of economies achieved in buying, marketing, processing, and merchandising in large quantities. A small sampling of identical items priced in different types of chain stores will generally reveal chain-store prices lower than those of semichains, while the prices of independent stores will be slightly higher than those in chain and semichain stores. Price differences may range from about three to ten percent.

The chain method of marketing is less expensive than the independent method. If a processor can sell his entire output to one chain he reduces or eliminates the expenses of sales representatives advertising, duplicate accounting records, and the granting of credit. Depending on the relative bargaining powers of the parties, the processor will quote prices to chain-store buyers which are lower than the prevailing prices by a margin that represents all or a portion of the savings in the expense of selling. Chains perform their own wholesaling functions. After chain-store buyers have purchased merchandise from many processors, the chain moves it directly through its own warehouses to its retail stores.

Chains have developed another economy at the processing level. They contract with processors and manufacturers to pack merchandise in their own private brand containers. For example, flour may be processed by an independent firm, but packed in packages supplied by a chain. Some chains have acquired their own processing plants and operate them. Some have their own bakeries, dairy processing plants, and canneries.

Corporate chains have developed economies in the operation of their retail stores. Chief among these is the rapid turnover. Chain merchandise sells faster because prices are lower and because slow-selling items are not stocked. Moreover, chains are leaders in developing and adopting new merchandising methods. Trained managers plan the arrangement and display of their merchandise with care and skill. The expenses of operation have been reduced by eliminating all services except the basic service of providing merchandise in a place convenient to the consumer-buyer. There is no telephone ordering, no delivery service, and no charge accounts. In the retail trade a "free" service is one for which no separate charge is made. Telephone, delivery, and credit services are expensive and stores that provide them must mark up the prices on their merchandise to cover those expenses. All buyers are required to pay the higher prices even though they do not use the services. Chains have found that there are many consumers who are willing to come to the store, make their own selection of merchandise, pay cash for it, and carry it to their homes in their automobiles. On the other hand, some chains use trading stamps, games, and other promotional methods that raise their costs and partially offset their economies.

Supermarkets

The old-fashioned general store which sold food, drugs, clothing, and housewares, and even operated the post office in a corner is back in the form of a streamlined supermarket with a general line inventory. There are

The modern supermarket, with display shelves at the end of each aisle and in front of the checkout counters to attract last-minute impulse buying. (*UPI*)

31,000 supermarkets, which account for 72 percent of all food sales. A typical supermarket stocks 9,000 different food products; 20 percent of its merchandise consists of nonfood products. The practices of open display and self-service have been adopted by almost all stores, regardless of size or type of merchandise handled. The dynamic nature of merchandising is indicated by the fact that one-half of the items bought in a modern supermarket did not exist ten years ago. There are 500 new products available to managers of food stores every year. For every new item on the market, two never reach the shelves of retail stores, and many of them do not survive more than one year. Supermarkets have proven to be an important countervailing power against giant processors, not only in price but also in private brands.

The location of supermarkets in less congested areas where parking facilities are provided followed the increased use of automobiles. A modern supermarket must provide five times as much parking space as selling space. Many shoppers are willing to travel a number of miles to shop at the supermarket of their choice.

Supermarkets generally have several thousand square feet of space at street level. The walls are lined with shelves, with more shelving arranged in rows and aisles in between. Merchandise is displayed attractively, and prices are marked on the shelves and usually on every item. Shoppers may take their time to examine the information contained on the packages. Carts are available for those who plan to purchase many items.

There are no salesclerks in supermarkets today, as there were in the old general stores. There are employees who unpack, mark, and shelve the merchandise and others who serve as check-out clerks. As a result of the large sales volume and rapid turnover, payroll expense per unit of sale is lower than for other types of stores.

It is important to emphasize that the self-service practice can be and is used by independent, semichain, chain, and consumer cooperative types of stores. The self-service supermarket climaxes a gradual change in methods of retail marketing that altered the functions of the retail store manager. In a sense the manager still serves as the purchasing agent for customers. He or she still orders the merchandise and provides the other services necessary for the convenience of shoppers. But it can scarcely be said that he anticipates their demand, as store managers did in earlier years. This is because of extensive use of national advertising by processors of food products. Also practically every item in a self-service supermarket is packaged and branded. The processor advertises his products to consumers all over the nation, seeking to create a demand for them. To the extent that the processor succeeds, the manager of a retail store is simply an order taker. When shoppers enter his store most of them have already made up their minds that they want certain brands. They expect to find them on the shelves, and if they are not there, they call for them or go elsewhere.

In years past shoppers depended on storekeepers for advice and suggestions when choosing merchandise. It was assumed that storekeepers were experts and their judgment was respected. This is still true of some independent store managers, especially those who operate the deluxe service type of store. In chain stores and self-service supermarkets employees know little or nothing about the merchandise. As a result the principle that the buyer should beware assumes new importance, for it is presumed that the buyer can make a free selection voluntarily and with full opportunity to examine the merchandise. If the merchandise proves unsatisfactory, the store manager can say truthfully that he did not urge the buyer to make the purchase, nor did he recommend that particular brand. Nevertheless, some chain store managements follow the policy that the customer is always right. Consumer-buyers in such stores are promised satisfaction or their money back. For stores not following such a policy, any adjustment must be made by the processor, but the impersonal relation between processor and consumer does not include the practice of the principle that the customer is always right. The customer is not always right. As an individual dealing with a giant firm, the customer is in a weak bargaining position.

The trend in marketing food is toward precleaning, precooking, prepackaging, and preselling by the processor. The retail store has become no more than a marketing center. Retailers can perform their traditional functions for consumers or they can serve primarily as selling representatives for processors. They cannot do both. Merchandising studies show that chain self-service market operators spend more time and effort thinking up new ways of luring shoppers to purchase high-profit items than they do in helping shoppers purchase low-priced items that would serve their needs just as well. This means that consumer-buyers must be alert and informed.

According to Consumers Union alert buyers can save up to $200 a year. The secret is to buy the private brands of chain supermarkets.

Discount Stores—What Are They?

A discount store is a retail store. A discount store is not a wholesale store, regardless of what it calls itself, as long as its sales are to the ultimate consumer. Since retail stores of all varieties call themselves discount stores, it is impossible to give a definition that adequately defines all types of discount stores, but in general a discount store is a retail store whose major reason for existence is to attract customers by selling merchandise at prices below the prevailing prices in the competing market area. Whether a particular discount store actually meets this definition may be ascertained only by shopping at different types of competing retail stores and comparing prices of identical merchandise.

If a discount store were defined as simply any store that sells some merchandise at reduced prices, all retail stores would fall into this category. All stores sell merchandise at reduced prices, some more frequently than others, but true discount stores do so on a continuing basis. A retail store falls under the definition of a discount store if its major appeal to the buying public is low prices—discounted from the manufacturer's suggested list price or the prevailing prices in its competitive marketing area.

There are many types of discount stores: the department store, the warehouse store, the appliance store, the gift store, the cut-rate store, the bargain-basement store, and the closed-door membership store. The last "restricts" its sales to persons who are government employees, employees of educational institutions, ex-servicemen, employees of industries working on government contracts, or employees of nonprofit institutions, all of whom purchase annual or lifetime memberships for a fee of a few dollars. The restrictive feature has some status appeal and for the store the membership fee makes available some ready cash and a mailing list to whom advertising may be directed with generally better results than the "shotgun" approach of much of the advertising done by retail stores.

Are Discount Store Prices Really Lower? There is abundant evidence to support an affirmative answer. Evidence can be obtained by the consumer who does some comparison shopping. Comparison shopping will show, however, that no particular type of retail store has a monopoly on low prices. It will also show that true discount stores will have more lower prices than a traditional retail store.

To a considerable degree pricing at retail is best characterized by change. What the price situation was yesterday may vary considerably from that of today, and today's prices may be quite different from tomorrow's prices. Some price checks made between traditional retail stores and discount stores showed the following results. The writer purchased thirty-six items from discount stores. These ranged from a child's playpen to a television set. If the items had been purchased in other types of stores, which were selling them at the list prices indicated by the manufacturers, the buyer would have paid $1,972.49. The price paid was $1,443.18, a saving of $529.31, or 26.8 percent.

Discounting has become prevalent in health and beauty aids. Actual price comparing is the best way to find out what are truly discount prices. In one shopping area prior to the introduction of discount health and beauty aid stores, the variety stores and supermarkets sold health and beauty aids at prices similar to those in the independent drugstore. The independent drugstore prices in most cases were the manufacturers' suggested list prices. Some time after the discount health and beauty aid stores opened, the variety stores and supermarkets began discounting to meet this new competition. Thus the discount stores not only offered reduced prices but they also stimulated other retailers to reduce prices. The benefits of lower prices are available now from many stores other than those whose main attraction is selling at discount prices.

The consumer should be aware that the fact that a retail store calls itself a discount store is not always proof that its prices are the lowest in the shopping area. Many traditional retail stores are meeting the discount store price competition. Some industry spokesmen even contend that there is more discount selling by traditional retail stores than by discount stores.

The buyer should also be aware that the manufacturer's suggested list price, or the price that is being discounted, may be set artificially high in order to make the discounted price look better. This was found to be particularly true in a survey of catalogs of discount catalog stores. The biggest illusion found by the surveyers was the so-called "list price." In 88 percent of the cases, the "list price" was higher than the price the item was selling for in the competing market area.[5] Two researchers found that 11.3 percent of the 275 persons surveyed complained that they learned after buying that the "special discount price" they paid was as high or higher than the regular price of other sellers.[6] The Federal Trade Commission attempts to police this deceptive type of pricing by enforcing its *Guides Against Deceptive Pricing.*[7]

What About Quality?   Neither the traditional retail stores nor the discount stores have a monopoly in selling either quality products or inferior products. Both types of stores sell both. Stores will be found in both categories which seem to "specialize" in products that are inferior, while some stores in both categories make a definite policy of handling quality products. The consumer must know the store well to know the quality of goods it handles.

Most warranties of quality and use are given by the manufacturer, not the retailer. A reputable manufacturer cannot afford to damage his name by not honoring his warranty. The wise manufacturer is not going to honor his warranty at one type of retail store and fail to honor it at another type of retail store. Whatever degree of consumer protection is offered by a warranty is dependent on the integrity of the manufacturer and the seller than on the type of retail store through which the sale is made.

What About Service? "The inability to offer service ultimately will eliminate the current menace of the discount store."[8] It has been said that price appeal does not last long and that services then reappear as a part of competition. This early prophecy for the demise of the discount store has proven wrong, but many discount stores have increased their free services for consumers, while at the same time many conventional retail stores have reduced their services or charge extra for certain services. Thus the price differential between many of these competing types of stores has narrowed.

Because discount stores' prices are not always lower than the prices of other stores it is important to shop around, comparing model numbers, warranties, credit terms, and service policies as well as prices. Which is the better buy—a refrigerator priced at $339 in a local store, a price which includes delivery and installation, or a refrigerator bearing the same brand at $309 at a discount store thirty miles distant for which the buyer pays delivery and installation charges and must depend solely on the manufacturer for his warranty?

Discount Store Pricing Policies The discount store has evolved primarily because of the competition among sellers to attract buyers and the aggressiveness of more and more buyers to get price concessions from sellers. The relatively inflexible markup policy of many traditional retail stores in the past in maintaining the manufacturer's suggested list price attracted competing sellers who saw the possibility of making a profit by cutting prices, getting a more rapid turnover of merchandise, locating in low-rent areas, offering fewer free services, and operating on a self-service and cash-and-carry basis. In addition, national brand advertising, and not the salesclerk, has been persuading many people what to buy. Prospective buyers have been presold, so the lowest price became for many buyers the determining factor as to where to buy.

The growth of the U.S. economy called for an expansion in mass marketing at the retail level. National brands, national advertising, and nationally advertised prices helped set the stage, and discount stores moved in. The rise of discount stores is an example of the competitive free enterprise system at work.

Discounters introduced a new pricing formula. Instead of adding markup to invoice costs to determine selling prices and then figuring profit as a percentage of sales, the new method stresses lower markups, larger sales, and more profit per dollar invested. The consumers' acceptance of discount stores has shown that price elasticity of demand is greater than traditional retailers had realized. If nationally advertised brand-name goods are offered for sale at prices substantially below the manufacturer's suggested list prices maintained by many traditional stores, consumers will buy more.

Significant differences do exist in gross margins from one type of store to another. A number of the country's largest department stores operate on gross margins of 44, 46, and 48 percent, while the Mass Retailing Institute (a trade association made up of discount stores) reported that its members' gross margin averaged 28.5 percent.[9]

The consumer's image of the various discount department stores will vary. Some discount stores like K-Mart go in for storewide discounting and limit their merchandise mostly to nationally advertised brands. Other discount chains handle large quantities of unfamiliar brands, and still others will be selective as to which products will be discounted. Careful comparison shopping is necessary to become aware of the type of policy followed by a particular discount store.

The growth in the number of discount stores has paralleled the growing congestion of cities, which has led to the decline of downtown stores and the rise of the suburban shopping centers. The operating expenses in some outlying districts have been less, and ample parking space for customers can be provided. The phenomenal success of the supermarket type of food store encouraged operators of other kinds of stores to adopt the supermarket method of merchandising: self-service, no-pressure selling, and cash-and-carry.

Discount Stores Stimulate Competition   Most of the established stores have reacted to the discount-type store by attempting to meet this competition. Food supermarkets have added profitable nonfood items, an action to which some discount stores have responded by adding some profitable food items. Some department stores have attempted to meet and are meeting the price competition of discount stores. Department stores in general are not attempting to compete on all items. Some have discontinued the sale of appliances, while others have resorted to warehouse sales. Some department stores have adopted their own brands, and some have leased departments to discount-store operations.

The discount stores have brought more competition into our competitive free-enterprise system. Competition at the retail level tends to be either 1) sales-promotional, which generally adds to the cost of the goods being sold; 2) quality competition, which adds to the ultimate price but offers additional value; 3) price competition; or 4) quantity competition—that is, the price is maintained but the quantity reduced. The discount store is stimulating price competition.

If a consumer has been presold on a product through advertising, if he prefers to deliver it himself, if he prefers to pay cash, and if he is willing to shop in lower rent areas in unpretentious stores, certainly he should be able to buy from those stores that have lower operating expenses. For the same reason the store that prefers to offer these services is free to do so, and the consumer is free to buy there if he wishes.

When a manufacturer is able to reduce his prices because of lower costs of production, society feels he is rendering a service to the economy.

Should not the same attitude prevail when a retailer is able to reduce his costs of marketing and pass the savings along in the form of lower prices?

Consumer Reaction to Discount Stores: Qualified Acceptance   Millions of price-minded consumers have accepted the discount store because they have found that they can buy name-brand merchandise at lower prices. In some cases they have been willing to forego some of the services traditionally rendered by other types of stores. But consumer acceptance is less than complete. Many consumers are able and willing to pay for the services offered by other types of stores. They prefer to buy from local stores and to depend on them for services. Unsophisticated buyers fear that they may be the victims of unfair or deceptive practices. There is no evidence that such practices are more prevalent in discount store operations than in other types of stores, but some people are suspicious of strangers and prefer to deal with local merchants whom they know.

Discount Food Stores

There are two basic types of discount food stores. One type is reminiscent of the 1930s, when sellers let buyers serve themselves directly from the cartons, buy in quantity lots, do their own sacking, and carry their purchases to their cars. Some stores of this type even provide the shopper with a pencil or crayon with which to mark the prices on purchases; this saves the store the expense of price marking. This type of discount food store may be a barn-type or warehouse-type structure located away from the high-rent commercial districts. These stores carry a smaller variety, and a large percentage of their sales consists of nationally advertised brands. Their stores are larger, their parking lots are larger, and their selling areas are larger. They open later in the morning, and close later in the evening.

The other type of discount food store is represented by regular supermarkets that have made the decision to "go discount." Often the competitive pressures on these stores were such that, in order to maintain their percentage of the market, something had to be done. That something for a number of national and regional chains has been to emphasize discount prices. Such price competition forces other food stores to advertise as discount stores. In Ohio a law was enacted that required discount stores and discount supermarkets to use the word "discount" only if they sell at least 75 percent of their merchandise for at least 10 percent below the regular market prices.

Convenience Stores

There are over 20,000 convenience stores in this country and their numbers continue to grow. Operated or franchised by corporate chains, they include such stores as Stop 'n' Shop, Minit Market, Fast 'n' Friendly, and 7-11. They are small—2,400 square feet—and typical sales are about $4,000 a week. Their big sellers are bread, milk, soft drinks, candy, and snacks. According to the United States Department of Commerce convenience stores experienced a sales growth of 24.2 percent from 1973 to 1975. They are usually conveniently located near apartments, motels, and heavily populated neighborhoods. They do not offer stamps or games, nor do they use other promotional methods. They stock national brands almost exclusively, and their prices are higher than those in supermarkets. Prices in convenience stores in one study averaged as much as 45 percent higher than those in supermarkets. On individual items the difference was as much as 86 percent for identical products. Similar surveys have shown convenience store price averages ranging from 14 percent to 35 percent above the local supermarket prices.[10] Even though prices are higher than those in supermarkets, patrons are willing to pay more for the convenience of longer store hours, nearby location, and quick check-outs. Convenience stores are especially popular with young single people who work and with families where both the husband and wife work.

Military Commissary Stores

The federal government operates the seventh largest food retailing chain in the United States. Its 279 commissaries operating on military bases had sales totaling $2.2 billion in 1974—an average of almost $8 million per unit.[11] These stores serve military personnel in the armed forces, retired military personnel, and civilians in the Defense Department. The Federal Office of Management and Budget reported that commissary customers pay an average of 22 percent less for their purchases than they would pay at supermarkets. The government appropriated $324 million to subsidize commissaries in 1975. The General Accounting Office of the federal government stated its opinion that military commissary stores are not justified in major metropolitan areas. Locating commissaries in these areas, the GAO said, violates Congress's intent that these stores only be located in remote stations that are not adequately served by commercial food stores. It is doubtful, however, despite the GAO's statement, that Congress will eliminate this significant fringe benefit for the military.

PX Stores

The Army, Air Force, Navy, and Marine Corps operate approximately 500 post exchanges (PX) at United States military installations around the world. They serve 6.5 million active duty and retired military personnel, dependents of both groups, reserve component personnel in a training status, and U.S. civilian employees of the military departments serving overseas or in isolated locations. Patrons pay no sales taxes and the stores

are exempt from income taxes, pay no rent, do not advertise, and are subsidized by Congress. Their average markup is only 22 percent, and they
sell at about 20 percent below list prices. (A $50 order in a private store
would cost $40 in a PX.) They earn a profit of about 5 percent on sales of
$3.6 billion a year. Annually the exchanges contribute about $100 million
from profits to build and finance libraries, sports centers, bowling lanes,
swimming pools, and other recreation facilities. The type and scope of items
sold by exchanges located in the United States have been limited to a list
authorized by Congress. Overseas exchanges have no such restrictions.
A PX is a miniature department store.[12]

Catalog Shopping

Catalog shopping-by-mail originally developed because many people
were far removed from retail stores. Today this century-old practice is still
booming, now using high-technology methods, attracting consumers of all
income levels, and selling goods and services that satisfy many consumer
demands. Buying by catalog through the mail is a $15 billion business. The
current boom in catalog buying is attributed to four factors: the fact that
more women are working today and so have less time to shop in stores; the
retreat of shoppers from crime-plagued urban shopping areas; high gasoline prices; and the lack of sales help encountered in cost-pinched stores.
The proliferation in the kinds of goods and services sold through the mails
has made it a convenient way for many people to do some of their shopping,
particularly for the elderly.

Catalog Showrooms

Even though three out of four Americans do not know what a catalog
showroom is, catalog showrooms are a thriving and expanding business. A
catalog showroom is a retail store that uses a catalog as its prime form of
advertising, drawing customers into the showroom where nationally-
known, brand-name merchandise is displayed and sold. Unlike other retailers, catalog showroom operators put only one of each item on display.
Customers fill out a form listing the products they wish to purchase, and
the order is filled at the counter in the store. The basic appeal of catalog
showroom stores is their image of selling at discount.

Consumer Cooperative Stores

In some rural and urban areas consumers have organized their own
stores, according to the pioneer Rochdale (England) principles. These
stores are owned by consumers and operated by them for their benefit. They
are not operated for profit. If there is any surplus, it is divided among the

patrons of the stores and called a patronage refund. Instead of voting according to the number of shares of stock owned, as in profit-making firms, each member has one vote. Consumer co-ops are frequently distinguished by the emblem of twin pines in a circle. Although relatively unimportant nationally—representing only $600 million in gross sales, or .6 percent of retail sales—the number of this type of store has recently increased. Co-op bookstores operate on many college campuses.

The double-digit inflation in food prices during the mid-1970s stimulated renewed activity in consumer cooperative food stores. More than 3,000 small cooperative food-buying clubs opened during this period. In a food co-op, a dozen or so families pool their purchases and buy in quantity at food warehouses at wholesale prices. The overhead is kept at a bare minimum by operating out of a member's basement or garage with volunteer labor. The economies realized in operating a cooperative food store make it possible for the cooperative to sell goods at prices considerably below the prices charged by supermarkets. Buying cooperatively can save a family 15 to 50 percent on food bills. Perishables are the items that are marked up the most in supermarkets, while packaged groceries, with their high-volume turnover and long shelf life, are marked up the least. The greatest savings in cooperative buying, therefore, are on fresh fruits and vegetables, while packaged goods involve the least savings.[13] A 10 percent surcharge added to the wholesale price is all a co-op may need to cover its operating expenses.

THE PRICE SYSTEM

Functions of the Price System

In our economy the price system is the device by which it is decided how scarce resources shall be used and how limited supplies of goods and services shall be divided among consumers. On the supply side, if the expenses of a firm exceed income over a period of time, the firm has no choice but to go out of business. On the consumer side, if the prices of goods or services are higher than people can afford, they have no choice but to do without things. In a competitive economy the impersonal forces operating behind demand and supply are brought to the surface in the market, resulting in prices that balance supply and demand. Although consumers may not be satisfied with a particular price, they at least have the assurance in a competitive economy that a high price usually reflects a shortage of supply and that no one producer has undue influence in determining that price. The record shows, however, that some sellers continually endeavor to restrict competition. To the extent that they succeed, prices are established arbitrarily, and such prices are higher than they would be in a purely competitive market. As a consequence some consumers are priced out of the market. In such a situation the price system is still functioning, but it is a controlled rather than a free system. The more rigid prices become, the less satisfactorily the price system performs its functions.

PRICING POLICIES AND PRACTICES

Traditional Price Theory

Objective exchange value is the power of a commodity or service to command other goods or services in exchange. If a loaf of bread exchanges for a package of oatmeal, the value of the bread is a package of oatmeal and the value of a package of oatmeal is a loaf of bread. Long ago the barter system of exchange was replaced by the use of money. Under a monetary system the values of bread and oatmeal are measured in terms of money.

Since the days of Adam Smith, theoretical economists and business executives have insisted that the consumer is king. This means that consumers supposedly guide the economic system. Consumers are presumed to be omniscient—that is, they are fully informed about quantity, quality, and price. Acting on the basis of such assumed knowledge, they express their choices in a completely competitive market. According to this analysis, if consumers wanted more of certain goods or services, the prices of those goods and services would rise. Those higher prices would induce producers to increase supplies. Conversely, if consumers wanted less, prices would fall and supplies would be curtailed. If prices were to rise in response to increasing demands or decreasing supplies, consumers would be discouraged from buying. As prices began to fall sellers would be warned to curtail output and consumers would be encouraged to buy more. In the long run such a rhythmic swing of market forces was presumed to result in an equilibrium of supply and price.

In the short run traditional price theory held that demand would be the active determining factor. Price would be determined by the willingness of consumers to buy. If the supply of bread were limited on any given day, its price would be determined by the importance of the last loaf to the buyer whose purchase would clear the market. In a freely and fiercely competitive market the price of bread would rise sharply if an emergency reduced the supply. A flood or a fire might curtail the supply of bread in a particular town temporarily. According to traditional theory, market prices would rise sharply in such a situation. In practice sellers rarely raise their prices to take full advantage of an emergency shortage. Over a period of time supplies of goods and services are variable. Store managers usually sell their inventory at the same price as long as it lasts. As new supplies come in they may then raise or lower prices.

The inflation in food prices during the mid-1970s saw products on the shelf being repriced again and again. This created a good deal of animosity between the store and the shopper. To reassure and appease buyers a number of supermarkets eventually advertised that they would not raise prices on items already priced and on the shelves. When double-digit inflation began to abate, many goods were repriced at lower prices.

Food manufacturers adjust to increasing and decreasing costs of production at times by reducing or increasing the quantities in packages. While sellers will take temporary losses, in the long run the prices they receive must cover total cost of production. Otherwise those sellers on the borderline who cannot meet expenses are priced out of business. This would diminish supplies, and if demand remained constant, prices would rise.[14]

Does Price Measure Value?

Traditional price theory assumes that price does measure value. The assumption is invalid, however, because there are significant differences in the market information available to consumers, differences in their bargaining ability, and differences in their purchasing power. In large segments of the retail market nonprice competition has replaced price competition. Many consumers are unable to judge the quality of merchandise. Many consumers do not check the quantity contents of packages, and in many cases it is not feasible to do so. As a result they may not receive all they pay for. Sometimes, as we have noted, consumers are positively attracted by higher prices. Those who cannot judge quality often depend on price as an indication of quality. Knowing this, some store managers raise their prices. There is a widely held belief that "you get what you pay for." People who hold this belief are often attracted by high prices. If buyers expect to pay high prices, one can hardly expect store managers to disappoint them. Marketing journals are filled with illustrations of increased sales after prices were raised.

Convenience sometimes takes precedence over price. Buyers choose stores according to the convenience of their location. Store managers know that prospective buyers rarely shop around. Buyers often know little or nothing about comparative prices. In many cases the only limit to a retailer's markup is the retailer's judgment of what the traffic will bear. There is an impressive amount of evidence that the traffic will bear a very heavy load.

The One-Price System

In the United States the one-price system prevails in retail food stores and, with some exceptions, it predominates in most other retail stores.* Under this plan the retail store manager is the active participant in setting a price. The usual practice is to charge as much as consumers are willing to pay. This does not mean, however, that retailers can set the price wherever they wish. Considering all the factors of demand, a retailer will set his

* See pp. 395–397, Chapter 16.

price at the highest point at which he can move his merchandise. He must recover the cost of his merchandise and the expenses of operating his store. Whatever he can get above those expenses represents net profit. If he pays 70 cents for an article and estimates that it will cost him 28 cents to resell it to a consumer-buyer, his minimum price will be 98 cents. That would be 40 percent above the price he paid. If he thinks he can get more, he will mark it up still higher. The only choice the individual consumer has is to buy or to refuse to buy. If enough shoppers refuse to buy at the asking price, the seller may subsequently lower his price to one that will clear his shelves. This is the way competition is supposed to operate under the one-price plan.

Retail pricing methods comprise strategy, policies, and specific decisions. *Strategy* deals with location, store size, and store image. A firm's prices are set to achieve total objectives, some of which may be nonmonetary. *Policies* refer to the number and frequency of special sales; the types of items to run as specials; the days of the week to run specials; whether to meet competitors' specials; what prices to feature in advertising. Also a store manager must decide whether to maintain the level of prices above, below, or similar to other stores. *Specific decisions* include such questions as what items to offer on special sales and what level of prices to maintain.

In practice, retailers use different margins, margins vary among departments, and margins are usually higher on private brands than on nationally advertised brands. Specials vary from season to season, are often developed by the processor, and are substantial enough to attract attention.

ADD-ON PRICING

Fixed Expenses

The expenses of operating a store fall into two main classifications: those that remain constant regardless of the volume of sales, and those that vary directly or closely with the volume of sales. The first type of expense is sometimes called *fixed* or *overhead*. Even though there are no sales, such expenses continue. Some of them continue even though the store may be closed. There is no escaping them.

Among the fixed expenses is interest on money invested in store equipment. A second fixed expense is depreciation. Equipment decreases in value from week to week as a result of use and also because of obsolescence. If a store is opened with new equipment, its value depreciates rapidly in the first six months. Another expense that is constant is rent. This is usually stated as a fixed number of dollars per month or per year. If the rent is related to the volume of sales, it then becomes a variable expense.

At any given time a store has a supply of merchandise, which is called *inventory*. This represents an investment of money, the interest on which must be considered as a fixed expense. If the money were not invested in inventory, it could be invested in some other way so as to yield an income. Like equipment, merchandise depreciates the longer it remains in stock. It becomes shopworn or shelfworn or out of date. In any case it must be sold for less than the price the manager had hoped to receive.

Expenditures for air-conditioning in summer and heating in winter do not vary with sales. Expenditures for electricity for refrigeration and for lighting remain the same, regardless of sales. Charges for telephone and water services are fairly constant, regardless of the volume of sales. Expenses for repair and maintenance of buildings and equipment are relatively fixed.

Insurance premiums are fixed expenses. A firm needs protection against loss by fire, burglary, breakage of display windows, liability for employees and the public, damage to merchandise while being delivered, and life insurance payable to the firm. Property taxes also are constant.

The wages of the manager and his assistants, together with those of some of the office workers, are the same whether sales are high or low. There may be some variation as a result of commission or bonus payment plans, but usually the basic wage is constant. Expenses of maintaining and operating the office and warehouse are relatively constant. The same is true of delivery service, if that is provided. Social security taxes and fringe benefits, such as supplemental retirement plans, accident, health and life insurance, and paid vacations, are relatively constant for permanent personnel.

Independent merchants and store managers are expected to be joiners, so membership dues are fixed expenses. These include the businessman's association, service clubs, and trade associations.

Even with a good cost-accounting system it is impossible to allocate fixed expenses precisely. The more a person knows about his expenses, the more intelligently he can manage his business. If he has a system of allocating fixed expenses, he then charges each department or category of merchandise in the store with its proportionate share. In case of losses or unsatisfactory profits it is then possible to discover which departments or types of merchandise are unprofitable. The manager who knows and studies his fixed expenses may find it possible to cut some expenses or to spread them over a larger number of units. This is one reason for advertising. The larger the number of units sold, the less the fixed expense per item.

Add-on pricing is less general than it was in the past. Alert managers now recognize that the value of the things they have to sell depends on demand, supply, and competitive conditions. Sometimes prices far above cost of merchandise do not deter buyers. Sometimes prices below cost of merchandise do not attract buyers. Neither average costs for an entire store operation or a particular department have any real relevance to pricing specific items. *Dynamic pricing* is based on a recognition of the fact that consumer demand is generally elastic and that demand may be increased. Chain stores and discount stores generally follow dynamic pricing policies.

The principle of fixed and variable costs explains why you cannot assume that "you get what you pay for," and why price alone cannot be taken as a guide to quality. It explains why an identical private-brand item can be sold at lower prices, why air-line travel is cheaper on night flights, and why a restaurant can charge only $3.50 for a luncheon and $7.00 for the same meal at dinner time.

Variable Expenses

Traditionally the wages of most employees have been considered variable expenses. As business increases seasonally and at Christmas time, more workers are employed. When business declines, some workers are laid off. For most retail stores selling expenses are variable. These include advertising and the promotional expenses of sales departments. When business is good many firms advertise, but when a recession starts sales begin to decline and store managers reduce appropriations for sales promotion. Those in the advertising business argue that the procedure should be reversed. As business declines they say that promotional expenditures should be increased. However, a store manager struggling to stay in business sees such expenses as variables that can be reduced or eliminated.

Probably the major variable expenditure is that for merchandise. In accounting terms the "cost of goods sold" means the invoice price less the discount, plus transportation charges. If a store manager can reduce his cost of goods by purchasing at a lower cost, he has more gross margin with which to cover expenses. Those stores that grant credit incur losses on bad debts that vary with sales. Some stores use the figure of one half of 1 percent of sales to cover such losses. Shoplifting is an expense that in some cases amounts to over 3 percent for discount stores and self-service stores and slightly over 1 percent for conventional stores. Paper bags, other wrapping materials, and laundering of clerks' uniforms and aprons are also variable expenses.

Gross margin is the difference between net retail sales and the net cost of merchandise sold. When expressed as a percentage, it is a percentage of sales, not of cost. It is the price consumers pay for the cost of operating the store plus the cost of merchandise to the store. A 1 percent increase in total gross margins of food retailers would involve $1.2 billion. In the 1930s supermarket gross margins were as low as 10 percent. Since that time they have doubled. The 1974 to 1975 average, as reported by Cornell University, for fifty-three food chains was 21.15 percent. Margins have risen because utility costs have risen, wages and fringe benefits have increased, advertising and promotional expenses have increased, stores provide more space and have more and improved facilities, and because more consumer services are provided.

Table 11-1 shows typical markups for twelve types of retail stores. It is margins like some of these that make it possible for a buyer to bargain for lower prices. Such margins also make it possible for discount stores to undersell other types of stores and still make a profit. These margin figures also explain how retail store managers can reduce prices drastically and still recover the cost of the merchandise. A buyer could not reasonably expect to bargain for lower prices in food stores or gasoline filling stations. When

TABLE 11-1. Typical Markups

Type of store	Percentage markup over invoice price	Percentage margin
Grocery	24	19.3
Gas Station	34	25.3
Drug	46	31.5
Variety	48	32.4
Department	58	36.7
Gift	76	43.2
Furniture	78	43.8
Radio	84	45.7
Fur	100	50.0
Jewelry	102	50.5
Bakery	124	55.4
Florist	146	59.3

Source: Changing Times, Family Success Book, p. 15 (shows markups on twenty-five items).

markups approach 50 percent, there is room for bargaining. As markups increase to a 100 percent and on up to almost 150 percent, there is ample room for bargaining and for price differences.

When a store manager adopts a margin policy, it does not mean that every item in the store is marked up that much. For example, in the J. C. Penney chain the markups vary from store to store, and the markups within a store vary from department to department. In one J. C. Penney store the highest average markup was 53.1 percent in the floor coverings department, while the lowest was 25 percent in the health and beauty, personal care, appliances department. The average markup for this particular store was 43.5 percent. Penney's storewide average markup is about 44 percent to 45 percent. This overall margin yielded a profit after taxes of 2.5 percent on sales and 11.1 percent on stockholders' equity.[15]

THE PRICING PROCESS: HOW MUCH WILL CONSUMERS PAY?

Step One: The Wholesale Cost of the Merchandise

In the long run consumers must pay retail stores prices that will reimburse stores for the cost of the merchandise. Unless retail store managers can pay wholesale suppliers, processors, and manufacturers for their merchandise they cannot stay in business very long. On the average about 78 cents to 80 cents out of every dollar spent by consumers in the retail food stores is passed on by the store managers to suppliers for merchandise.

When prices are rising, managers can, and many do, make an extra profit. For example, the FTC found uniform markup policies on bread among grocery retailers in Baltimore, Chicago, Denver, Milwaukee, New

York, and Seattle. If the wholesale price of a one-pound loaf were 20 cents, the markup of 25 percent would result in a retail price of 25 cents, for a gross margin of 5 cents. Then if the wholesale price were to rise to 22 cents, retailers would not only pass on the 2 cents, but would add 1 cent to their margin, making the retail price 28 cents, for a gross margin of 6 cents a pound.[16]

Step Two: Add-On Store Expenses

Managers of food stores know that the overall expenses of operation, including a profit, range from 20 percent to 25 percent. Expenses of operation for other types of stores are higher because of slower turnover and the larger amounts of money invested in inventory. In marking prices on specific items managers take into consideration the expenses and set a price that they hope will recover a proportionate share of the overall expense of store operations.

Leakages

The term *leakage* as used in the retail trade includes two distinct categories of costs to the retailer. One category covered by the term includes normal and expected losses due to spoilage, breakage, and damage to merchandise. These losses have to be covered in the markup. The other category includes stealing by customers and employees, losses on bad checks, shopping cart losses, armed robberies, and burglaries. These losses also have to be covered in the cost of goods sold. All these leakages are estimated to cost stores as much as 7 percent to 8 percent of sales, with stealing costing 2.5 percent of total sales. The National Retail Merchants Association estimates that stealing by employees and shoplifters costs retailers over $2 billion annually.[17] In one four-year period stealing increased by 43 percent.[18] The NRMA estimates that about half of the stealing is done by employees and half by shoplifters. Another estimate indicated that shoplifters were responsible for only one-fifth of the total.[19] About four million shoplifters are caught annually, but the majority get away.[20] Shoplifters come from all age groups and all social and economic groups. Teenage girls comprise the largest group of shoplifters. The Florida Crime Commission reported that the figures showed that 53 percent of the shoplifters in Florida are under the age of eighteen, with 58 percent of that total composed of girls. A growing number of shoplifters are elderly persons who, caught in an income crunch, usually steal essentials such as food and clothing.[21] Most shoplifters who get caught have been found to have enough money on their person to pay for the goods stolen. The commission reported that more than 50 percent of shoplifting losses each year occur during the Christmas season, with the back-to-school sale period coming in second.[22]

Shoplifting increased 221 percent from 1960 to 1973, according to the

National Council on Crime and Delinquency. The Federal Bureau of Investigation calls shoplifting "the fastest-growing larceny in the country"—up 23 percent since 1973.[23] Supermarkets report loss and damage to carts amount to $10,000 a year for a single store. Supermarkets cash more checks than banks, and their losses from bad checks amount to over $450 million annually. Many stores do not make as much in net profit after taxes on sales as thieves steal. All leakages present a serious problem for retailers and place a significant cost burden on the paying consumer.

Because of the magnitude of losses from shoplifting more and more retail stores are instituting a "get-tough" policy and are setting up numerous measures to control stealing. More store detectives are being employed, there is greater control in fitting rooms, customers are made aware of the stricter security measures adopted by stores, moral persuasion is being used through community cooperation, and rewards are being given to employees to motivate them to be more active and aware of the problem. In addition, more mirrors, closed circuit television, cameras, turnstiles, and electronic merchandise sensing devices are being used.[24]

Competitors' Prices

Regardless of general markup policy, store managers find that if their prices on specific items are much higher than those of other stores, their merchandise will not be sold. Directly and indirectly, competitive store managers watch the prices their competitors are quoting for the same items. They read the advertisements of other stores and agree to meet a lower price if an alert shopper tells the salesclerk that the item can be purchased elsewhere at a lower price. In metropolitan areas department stores often employ shoppers to compare prices in other stores. Then if a prospective buyer tells a salesclerk that he or she can purchase a particular watch for $19.95 at another store, the $24.95 price tag will be scratched and the watch sold for $19.95. Some stores advertise and have signs throughout the store saying, "We will not be undersold." In spite of all such activity market surveys have shown repeatedly that substantial differences in prices for identical merchandise can continue indefinitely in a retail market area.

Suggested Prices

Manufacturers, processors, and wholesalers frequently suggest a retail price that store managers should charge for their product. Sometimes strong pressure is exerted to compel store managers to conform to suggested retail prices. In such cases the line between mandatory minimum resale prices and voluntary minimum resale prices is a thin one. National advertisers of brand products wish to maintain uniform prices throughout the country. Obviously it costs more to ship breakfast cereals from Battle Creek,

Michigan to distant points than it does to nearby points, but instead of such differences being reflected in the price consumers pay, they are absorbed by the manufacturers and processors. In such cases retail store buyers and consumers in nearby areas pay more than the actual freight charges while stores and consumers located far away pay less. Store managers who follow recommended and suggested prices usually find those prices high enough to cover expenses of store operations and yield a substantial profit. Store managers who think that consumer demand is elastic and who follow a dynamic pricing policy refuse to accept artificially high suggested prices.

Nationally Advertised Prices

Nationally advertised prices are usually closely related to suggested prices. Sometimes manufacturers whose products are sold all over the nation advertise uniform prices for every region.

Often there are marketing tie-ins in which local stores feature displays of merchandise with a sign reading, "As advertised in *Time*." As a general rule nationally advertised prices are high enough to assure all retail stores a profit. They may be so high that some store managers decide they can make more sales and more profit by charging less than the advertised price.

Price Lines

It is common practice among retail stores to maintain variously priced lines of merchandise. There will be one line for low-income buyers, another for middle-income, and still another for upper-income buyers. Some stores cater exclusively to one of the income groups. Those stores that attract shoppers from all income classes have found that price lines make it easier to sell. In department stores, for example, the price lines for panty hose may be 89 cents, $1.29, or $1.97. Price lining is not often used in food stores.

Seasonal Prices

When the first shipments of seasonal merchandise are received, they are priced considerably above the average markup. As the season advances and the supplies of merchandise increase, prices will be reduced. At the height of a season prices are usually much less than they were at the beginning. Food store managers adjust the prices of seasonal products so as to secure substantial profits when supplies are limited and demand is strong and to dispose of surpluses when demand diminishes and supplies are abundant.

Stores handling fashion merchandise adjust their prices in the fashion season. Sellers of automobiles start off the new car model season by charging the full nationally advertised suggested or sticker price, then as stocks become more plentiful price reduction begins, and toward the end of the model year bigger discounts follow. At the end of the model year, as the next year's models are being introduced, the old models' prices are discounted quite sharply in order to make way for the new models.

Clearance Prices

Seasonal pricing and clearance pricing are similar. The prices for fruits, vegetables, and bakery products may change several times in a single day. Early morning buyers pay the highest price. By mid-afternoon, if the stock is still large, prices may be reduced. Just before closing time on Saturdays prices may be reduced drastically for final clearance. Refrigeration and chemicals retard spoilage of perishable products and so reduce the losses that store managers incur. This lessens the pressure to reduce prices.

Not all stores use clearance pricing policies. Some of them prefer to maintain the original asking price even though it means throwing away or giving away the unsold portions. As a general rule chain store managements use clearance prices. The United States Department of Agriculture priced 230 items and found that Tuesday prices averaged from 7 to 10 percent higher than weekend prices. Supermarkets mark down selected, in-demand items for weekend sales so as to attract shoppers to their stores. Markdowns range from 10 percent to 50 percent under the original shelf prices. Chain stores change prices more frequently than semichains and independents, and semichain stores change prices more frequently than independents. The timing of price changes reflects the weekend special practice. Nelson and Preston found more than one-half of Friday price changes by chains and semichains were decreases, but among independents one-half of the price changes were increases on both Tuesday and Friday.[25] By changing prices often, up and down, large chain stores may gain a reputation for price reductions without actually making a permanent change in the level of prices in the market.[26]

Variable Pricing

This tactic is used by many large grocery stores. Under this plan, when the prices of some items are marked down, the prices of other items are raised. In a long time period the average price of any one item and the average level of all items in a store can remain the same.

Variable pricing is related to store layout and arrangement of merchandise. Advertised specials are tucked away here and there so the shopper has to really hunt for them. The store manager hopes that while shoppers are hunting they may see and select other items on which prices have been raised. It is possible for both an alert shopper and store management to gain, the one by searching out real bargains, and the other by establishing a reputation for reducing prices.

Cents-Off Pricing

Sellers like this idea because a "ten cents off" sale draws attention to a particular product and package. Also the retailer can reduce prices on a few products for a limited time period and tie it in with his advertising. It helps to smooth out low seasonal production periods and to meet competition.

Cents-off pricing has increased in volume in recent years and has come under sharp consumer criticism, with some resulting government regulation, as a result of abuses. The question is "ten cents off" what? Section 5 of the Fair Packaging and Labeling Act authorizes the Food and Drug Administration to promulgate regulations to control cents-off pricing. For one thing, the seller must prove that a ten cents-off deal is actually ten cents below a price that has been in effect for at least a year.[27]

Loss-Leader Pricing

Loss-leader pricing is the practice of pricing some products in a store so low that the store makes no profit on these items. Some store managers use loss-leaders to attract shoppers to their stores. It is hoped that while shoppers are in a store to purchase one or more loss-leaders, they will purchase enough other high markup items to offset the loss taken by the store on the loss-leaders. It is difficult to give a precise definition of loss-leader pricing. It may be anything below normal markup. A loss-leader may be priced to recover no more than the cost of the merchandise or it may be priced at less than the merchandise cost to the store. Loss-leader pricing was one reason for resale price maintenance legislation. Such legislation was designed to protect the majority of stores against the competition of loss-leader merchandisers.

Consumer-buyers can save money by purchasing loss-leader items. But unless they know the prices of merchandise they may think that all prices in a store advertising loss-leader items are lower than in other types of stores. One survey of shoppers disclosed that 80 percent of them did not know the specific prices of sixty highly competitive items in a food store. Store managers were then told that one way to take advantage of consumer ignorance is to arrange special displays at *regular prices*. To unknowing shoppers, the displays imply low prices. Tests have shown that sales from special displays at regular prices were nearly as great as from similar special displays at reduced prices.[28]

Quantity Discounts

For some types of consumer goods, prices may be lower if more than one item or package is purchased. In the trade this is known as "pricing according to size of purchase." Large packages are usually, but not always, lower in price per ounce than small packages. Two or more items may be offered at prices lower than if purchased separately. Canned goods may be priced at 35 cents each or three for 99 cents. Hose may be priced at 69 cents a pair or three for $1.98. It is known that there are economies in quantity sales, but it is impossible to measure them accurately.

From a consumer-buyer's point of view nothing is a bargain if it is not needed. If the larger quantity cannot be used within a reasonable time or stored, there is no real advantage in the quantity price. On the other hand buyers for large families can and do realize substantial savings by purchasing in large quantities.

Odd-Number Pricing

It is common for stores to quote prices in odd numbers, such as 89 cents, 99 cents, or $99.95. Retailers are convinced that they get better results with odd prices than even prices. Shoppers tend to think of the price of an item as being about 90 cents when it is priced at 99 cents, rather than thinking of it as a dollar item. The 88-cent price has been used successfully because many shoppers think of that as being a discount from a higher price. Even prices would make it easier for the shopper to make price comparisons and easier to calculate the unit price of a product—that is, the price per pound, per hundred, or per unit. Yet a survey of retail store managers found that shoppers favor odd-number prices two to one over even-number prices.

Multiple Pricing

Market researchers have found that consumer-buyers are easily influenced by multiple pricing. For example, sales of a forty-six-ounce can of tomato juice priced at 33 cents increased by 70 percent when the price was changed to three cans for 99 cents! Shoppers prefer multiple pricing, whether there is or is not a fractional saving. Within the one dollar price range multiple pricing increases sales.[29]

Customary Prices

As a retail store manager marks prices on merchandise, he or she must keep in mind prospective buyers' notions as to what is fair and customary. People as a rule are willing to pay what they are accustomed to paying. Consumers are likely to accept a drop in price without question, but will be critical of price increases above those to which they are accustomed. When store prices are increased, managers sometimes find it necessary to offer explanations. The usual justification for a price increase is an increase in the cost of merchandise and an increase in expenses of operating a store. As a rule a store manager will wait a long time before changing a customary price, except during periods of rapid inflation when the manager has little choice.

Manufacturers are also aware of the power of custom. In a period of increasing prices they are likely to reduce quality or quantity rather than attempt to change the price. While customary prices tend to diminish profits in a period of rising prices, they also tend to increase profits in a period of falling prices. As a result of national advertising of brand merchandise there is a tendency for the prices of such items to remain stable. Once stability has been maintained for a long time customers regard the established price as customary and retailers find it difficult to make a change. Five cents for a candy bar and five cents for a package of chewing gum were the customary prices for decades. The candy manufacturers varied the weight instead of varying the price until the costs of production, including raw materials, rose so sharply that they had no choice but to raise the price. The gum manufacturers were forced to raise prices also. Now instead of having one customary price of five cents for these products, there are various prices based on the weight of the candy bar and the number of sticks in a package of gum. A customary price can be continued for some time even after costs of production go up by diluting the quality. One candy bar manufacturer reduced the amount of chocolate in his candy to zero, substituting cheap, artificial chocolate-flavored material and artificial coloring. Until products are fully labeled only consumer-financed testing agencies will be able to ascertain and report to consumers whether quality has been diluted.

Convenience Prices

Within the geographic area it serves each store has a spatial monopoly. Shoppers may choose to buy in a nearby store even though prices are higher rather than take the time and incur the expense of traveling to a lower-price store farther away. An alert store manager considers his location when marking prices on his merchandise. A University of Indiana study revealed that when people shop for food they are more likely to be influenced by the location of the store than by its prices, service, or quality of merchandise. Again and again the people surveyed said that they chose a store on the basis of location rather than any other factor.[30] In one case 60 percent of the regular customers of a store patronized it because of its convenient location, as compared with 28 percent who said they were attracted by quality and 12 percent by low prices.

Cash Versus Credit Prices

Cash-and-carry stores do not have to add a percentage markup to cover the costs of credit or losses on bad debts. These two items alone would make a difference of 3 or 4 percent of sales. Stores that provide credit and delivery service do not usually make a separate charge for those services. Credit cost is included in the general markup, although some stores show cash prices and credit prices separately on the price tags.

Discriminatory Pricing

How much do shoppers know about retail prices? Are they able to do the mathematical calculations when shopping to make the right decisions? How important is this to them? For how many products that they buy on a fairly regular basis can they give the exact price? The results from the first national assessment of mathematics made by the Education Commission of the States showed many consumers' inability to solve very simple mathematical problems concerning pricing. In a key problem the persons surveyed were asked to choose the lowest priced product from a group of five cans that had different weights and different prices. Only 25 percent of the thirteen-year-olds were able to give the correct answer, only 34 percent of the seventeen-year-olds, and only 39 percent of the adults.[31] A shrewd manager may take advantage of this lack of information and mathematical ability on the part of consumers by increasing prices a little here and a little there and by quoting prices in odd numbers.

Many studies have been made that indicate that there is discriminatory pricing. One of the earliest and most significant studies was conducted by David Caplovitz.[32] Caplovitz describes discriminatory pricing practices in Harlem, an area in New York City whose inhabitants are predominantly black, with a considerable number of Puerto Ricans and a smaller number of native whites. Low-income families have to pay higher prices for lower-quality appliances. They pay more in the neighborhood in which they live than those living outside that neighborhood. Most of them buy on credit and pay a much higher price for the credit. White buyers of television sets, record players, and washing machines paid lower prices than the Puerto Ricans, and black buyers paid prices in between. There are very few one-price stores in Harlem. There are no price tags. Prospective buyers must ask "how much?" The answer depends on the seller's judgment of the prospective buyer's ability to pay and his probable credit rating. If the buyer has been referred to the store, the quoted price is increased enough to cover the commission that must be paid to the merchant or customer who may have sent the prospect to the store.

A system of pricing by numbers is prevalent in East Harlem. A one-number item means a markup of 100 percent. If the wholesale price of an appliance were $75, a one-number markup would add $75 for a total of $150. Two-number and three-number markups are common.

There is a noticeable absence of name-brand merchandise in East Harlem stores. Prospective buyers rarely shop around. A merchant can sell almost without any upper limit on price. The only limit is the seller's own willingness to sell on credit. The peddler is a part of the marketing system.

Door-to-door peddlers help merchants find prospects, evaluate them as credit risks, and help collect the payments. For these services merchants must pay commissions or the peddlers set their own prices. Under this system a $5 item may rise in price by six numbers to $30.

The so-called "turnover system" is used. This means that when one salesman is unable to complete a sale, he turns the prospect over to the "assistant manager." The "assistant manager" is a practical psychologist who plays on the vanity of the buyer. He will find some reason for reducing the original asking price by a small amount. The customer then feels flattered and agrees to buy. A variation of the turnover system is the referral of a prospective buyer to another store where a more liberal credit policy is practiced.

The FTC found that a major factor in the 1968 riots in Washington, D.C. was the feeling of nine out of ten blacks interviewed that they paid more for goods and that quality was lower. Checking on advertised specials, the FTC found 23 percent not available, compared with 11 percent in higher income areas. Moreover, it was found that prices on special sales were as likely to be high as they were to be low. Far too often investigators found items mispriced or incorrectly marked.[33]

Another study showed that due to a lack of mobility the poor are confined to shopping within inner-city areas, which are characterized by smaller, more expensive stores, and as a result, they are charged higher prices.[34] This was supported by another study which found that only 23 percent of the St. Louis inner-city sample had automobiles and 42 percent stated that they were limited to shopping within walking distance of their homes.[35] Alexis, Simon, and Smith have shown that consumers in the lowest economic group are more likely to patronize independent neighborhood stores than consumers in the middle-income and upper-income groups. The reasons for this are lack of mobility and less education.[36] The "selection of goods and services in these (inner-city) neighborhoods is believed to be relatively limited in scope, lower in quality, and higher in price than in other neighborhoods."[37]

Monopoly Pricing

Bread baking and marketing over the years has been a conspiracy-prone industry because there are only a few sellers in local markets. In the space of ten years the FTC found and broke up nine conspiracies to set monopoly prices for bread. In Washington State the conspiracy raised prices 20 percent over the national average, but when the FTC took legal action, bread prices fell abruptly to the national average. While the conspiracy was effective, bread-buyers paid $35 million a year more for their bread; on a national basis the Washington conspiracy would have cost consumers $200 million a year.[38] In another case the Department of Justice charged ITT Continental Baking with having dropped the price of Wonder Bread in one part of the country to the point where it was taking a loss, but covering the loss by increasing the price in other areas where competition was limited. Once the competing bread manufacturers were forced out of business, the former price of Wonder Bread was restored.

A national survey conducted by the Conference of Consumer Organizations (COCO) revealed some interesting information about the prices of bread and milk indicating the existence of monopoly pricing practices.[39] The bread unit priced nationally was the standard one-pound loaf of sliced white bread. The price ranged from 25 cents for a regional chain's loaf to 65 cents for a private label loaf at an independent store. In some states price patterns for brand name breads were evident—the selling price being the same throughout a state. In some states price patterns for private label bread were apparent, with the bread selling at the same price throughout the chain's stores in the state. The private label bread of chain stores sold at 15 to 20 cents less per pound than national brands, yet the quality difference was minimal.

The COCO study also showed that the price spread across the country in one-half gallon cartons of grade A whole milk ranged from a low of 59 cents to a high of 97 cents. In a few states, such as Nevada and Pennsylvania, minimum retail prices for milk are set by the state government. Again, as in the study of bread prices, monopoly price patterns appeared. In some states name brand labels of milk sold at the same price statewide, as did the house label milk in a number of states. The report concluded by stating that it is difficult to understand why the Federal Trade Commission and the Anti-Trust Division of the U.S. Department of Justice have not taken steps to end the uniform pricing practices in the bread and milk industries in this country.

"Fair-Trade Pricing" (Resale Price Maintenance)

From the time the first state "fair trade" law was passed in California in 1931 until Congress repealed the federal "fair trade" laws in 1975, resale price maintenance laws were used by many manufacturers to limit price competition among retailers selling their particular products. At one time forty-six of the fifty states had such laws in force. The federal statutes, the Miller-Tydings Act of 1937 and the McGuire Act of 1952, permitted "fair trade" pricing in interstate trade when goods moved into a state that had a "fair trade" law in force.

A "fair trade" or resale price maintenance law permits the manufacturer, processor, grower, or distributor of a commodity identified by brand name or trademark to set the price at which it may be sold in the retail market. The manufacturer may compel all sellers to advertise and to sell his product at the established price by making a contract with one seller in the state. The moment one seller signs a contract agreeing to sell only at the stipulated price, all other sellers, *whether parties to the contract or not,* are bound. This is known as the "nonsigner clause." It is the heart of the law and has been one of the key legal issues in subsequent court interpretations. One section of the law legalizes contracts vertically between producer and retailer if the commodity covered "is in fair and open competition with commodities of the same general class produced by others." On the other hand, another section of the law specifically states that any contract between two or more producers, wholesalers, or retailers is illegal. In the language of the trade, vertical contracts are legal but horizontal agreements are illegal.

Under the "fair trade" law, anyone who willfully advertised, offered for sale, or sold a commodity at a price below that stipulated in the resale price maintenance contract was guilty of unfair competition and could be sued by any person who had been damaged by this action. This was the only penalty provision in the law. The violator of a resale price maintenance law, unlike violaters of other laws, was not guilty of an offense against the state; consequently there was no provision for fine or imprisonment. Neither was there any provision for enforcement by state officers. Violation of a contract could have resulted in a damage suit by another retailer or by the producer. In most cases it was producers who sought monetary damages or a court order to discontinue the violation.

Under resale price maintenance a manufacturer would almost certainly establish resale prices on the basis of the expenses incurred by the store that needed the highest margin rather than by the stores with the lowest costs of operation if he wanted broad distribution of his products. This is illustrated in the following diagram.

HOW RESALE PRICE MAINTENANCE TENDS TO RAISE PRICES

Store number 1, a nonservice supermarket type, could sell an item for 80 cents and make a profit. It would sell at that price if it were free to set its own prices. Store number 2 would normally charge 90 cents for the same item, while store number 3 would charge $1.00. In a price-free competitive market these three prices would be found, and shoppers could decide whether it was worth while to pay cash at store number 1 or use the credit, delivery, and other services of store number 3. When a manufacturer decided to set a minimum resale price, he would set it to cover the expenses of store number 3. If the price were set below $1.00, store number 3 would not handle his product. As a result, store number 1 could not legally sell the item for 80 cents and would have to charge $1.00 for it. Thus patrons of lower-price, limited-service stores would be paying higher prices for goods under resale price maintenance than they would pay in a free market.

Artificially high prices in "fair-trade" states cost the buying public an estimated $1.5 billion a year according to a 1969 report of the President's Council of Economic Advisers. In the ensuing years the number of products sold under "fair-trade" prices declined, and the number of states in which resale price maintenance was legal decreased, so the cost to the consumers also declined.

There have been many legal challenges of resale price maintenance laws. In many states these laws were repealed or ruled unconstitutional in whole or in part, but it was not until 1975 that a major momentum developed to repeal "fair trade" laws. In 1975 fifteen states repealed such laws, and bills were introduced into both the House and the Senate to repeal the Miller-Tydings Act and the McGuire Act. Both of these laws permitted states to have resale price maintenance laws without antitrust interference. By a vote of 380 to 11, the House voted for repeal. The Senate voted for repeal by voice vote. The president signed the repeal measure—the Consumer Goods Pricing Act—on December 12, 1975. With this action, a forty-four-year history of legal price fixing ended. Now all retailers are free to determine for themselves what price they wish to charge for the merchandise they handle. The repeal of the federal resale price maintenance laws was a victory for price competition.

Merchandise Turnover

Markup and profit are related to the rate of turnover. If the price of an item to a store manager is $1.00 and she marks it up to $1.50, at which price it stays on the shelves for twelve months before being sold, the net profit will be less than that made on another article marked up to $1.40 but sold three or four times during the year. As a general rule, items that move rapidly are marked up less than those that sell slowly. One way to sell merchandise more rapidly is to mark it up less.

The overall turnover rate of Colonial Stores was 27.7. But only 536 items out of 4,729 sold more than one case of twenty-four packages per week. Only 250 items moved fast—that is, two cases a week. In order to increase turnover, store managers exposed shoppers to as many items as possible. They used every device—departmental grouping, shelf locations, displays, point-of-sale promotion—to maximize sales and profits. On merchandise that turns over quickly a manager keeps his prices competitive. He "ekes out an extra fraction of margin on less competitive items."[40]

Staple groceries usually turn over ten to fifteen times a year, meat about two times a week, or one hundred times a year, and produce once a week. Milk and baked goods turn over daily.

Store-Image Pricing

Different stores project different images to prospective buyers. A discount store operating in a barn with unshaded light bulbs projects an image of economy to some people and cheapness to others. At the other extreme, a luxury store presents a decor of carpeted floors, pastel colors, soft lighting, and elegant furniture. People who patronize such stores expect to pay higher prices, and store managers live up to such expectations by using high markups.

Unit Pricing

In retail food pricing, unit pricing is a break for the buyer, and a boon for the images of chains that adopt it. Unit pricing shows prospective buyers the price of a given item by the pound, ounce, quart, or other standard measure. Unit pricing is the result of fractional pricing and fractional measuring, the effect of which, if not the intent, is to confuse buyers into

A consumer checking the unit price label on the shelf of a supermarket. (*Dr. Lilly Bruck, Director, Consumer Education, New York City Dept. of Consumer Affairs*)

paying more than they think they are paying. In many cases fractional pricing makes it practically impossible for shoppers to calculate the price per unit without pencil and paper or a calculating gadget. Gummed unit-price labels are posted on shelf edges where packages are displayed, showing the name of the produce, the contents, in ounces or other appropriate measures, the price of the item, and the price per pound, as illustrated below.

```
15 oz. Special K
Price per box.............$0.95
Price per pound.........$1.01
```

This information enables the shopper to see at a glance that the price per pound of Special K cereal is $1.01, and that figure becomes the basis for comparing prices per pound of competing and alternative packages.* The Commonwealth of Massachusetts was the first state to enact legislation requiring unit pricing for 80 percent of all food retail stores. Low volume, family run stores were exempted from this ruling.

One study showed that where unit pricing had been adopted, only 14 percent of the shoppers were actually using it on a regular basis; 29 percent said that they sometimes looked at it; and 57 percent reported that they rarely used the unit pricing shelf signs. Forty-one percent of the shoppers said that they did not use unit pricing because it takes too long; 48 percent said they did not understand it because it was too confusing. Others said that they did not use it because they could not be bothered, were not aware of it, used their own shopping methods, or could not see the signs.[41] Unit pricing is a valuable aid to those consumers who use it. The cost of food can be reduced 3 percent when used regularly.[42] With more stores adopting unit pricing and with greater consumer awareness of its benefits, more shoppers will use unit pricing.

Boom and Recession Pricing

In a period of rising prices, if a store manager has purchased his stock of merchandise at low prices, he may be able to mark it up according to the higher prices, and thus make more profit. As noted before, consumer-buyers are likely to increase their purchases in a period of rising prices if they expect prices to rise still higher. Conversely, in a recession, when prices are declining, consumer-buyers may defer purchases in anticipation of still lower prices. In a recession store managers may find it necessary to

---

* Special K is one of only three cereals that *Consumer Reports* found to be "far and away the most nutritious." The others were Maypo 30-Second Oatmeal and Cheerios. *Consumer Reports,* Feb. 1975, pp. 76–82.

mark up less or mark down more. If the recession is severe, consumer-buyers are likely to shift their purchases to low-margin items.

IS PRICING A SCIENCE OR AN ART?

Are Retailers Economic Persons?

Pricing merchandise is a combination of art, psychology, expense analysis, guesses, and hunches. Retailers attempt to operate their stores so as to make as much profit as possible. In that sense they might be called "economic people." Retailers are not completely informed about all costs, however, nor do they really know very much about the way a prospective buyer will react to certain prices. There is abundant evidence that retailers are motivated by noneconomic as well as by economic factors. Very few managers of retail stores engage in theoretical calculation of the optimum level of operation by comparing marginal revenue and marginal costs. Their methods are better than rule of thumb, but they are by no means as perfect as marginal analysis. Our analysis of retail store operations in this chapter seems to justify the conclusion that chain-store prices *do* result from careful calculation and a profit maximizing markup, and that pricing by managers of semichain stores is based increasingly on careful calculation of percentage markup. Pricing in independent stores, however, generally reflects trial-and-error and "guesstimates" at least as much as it reflects rational calculation.

Are Consumer-Buyers Rational?

When buyers and sellers meet in a retail store, sellers have an advantage. They are full-time specialists whose primary goal is to make money. Consumer buyers are part time amateurs, motivated by a variety of forces. One of those forces may be economic, but many of them are noneconomic. Even their goals are mixed. Basically they wish to satisfy their wants and those of their families but they may, in addition, be seeking status or prestige.

Amateur part-time buyers cannot possibly be as well-informed as sellers. Why is it that sales in food stores increase 20 percent when a display shelf is full, compared with a shelf normally depleted by sales? Would a full shelf make any difference to rational buyers? Why is it that a placard placed at right angles to a shelf increases sales by as much as 152 percent? Why is it that a shelf-extender—a rack attached to a shelf—attracts attention and increases sales on small-margin nonfood items in a food store by as much as 2,033 percent? Why is it that when items are raised from floor level to eye level sales increase 78 percent? Why do sales decline 40 percent when items are changed from waist level to floor level? Why is it that consumer-buyers do not recognize selective price increases, which increase store profits by as much as 20 percent? Are these consumer responses rational?

Why Prices Differ

Having considered the many factors entering into the price of a specific item in a retail store, it is not surprising to find price variations among stores. If we were to compare prices in two stores, the managers of which paid the same prices to wholesalers for their merchandise and who used the same percentage markup, more likely than not we would still find price differences. One reason for this is that the two managers might differ in the way they convert general markup into specific prices. This may explain the lower prices sometimes obtainable in the deluxe service stores on merchandise selling at higher prices in chain stores.

In one J. C. Penney region that encompasses fourteen stores there are wide variations in margins in the same department from one store to another. In one department grouping that included candy, foods, tobacco products, stationery, records, luggage, watches, and fine jewelry, one store had the lowest margin—28.2 percent—and another store the highest margin—43.7 percent. The health and beauty, personal care, and appliances grouping had an average margin of 25 percent in one store and 66.7 percent in another store. The product mix (that is, the percentage of each type of product in a broader category) would play a part in explaining these wide differences. In women's dress departments the margin differential was much narrower, varying from a low of 47.4 percent in one store to a high of 49.0 percent in another store. On a storewide basis the store with the lowest overall margin had 42.8 percent, while the highest for any one store in the region was 45.3 percent.

Another reason for price differences is that it is well recognized that chains generally vary their prices from community to community, depending upon competitive conditions. If a chain is dominant in a local market, its prices may be found to be higher than prices for identical products in other market areas. Chains also charge different prices in different stores in the same community.[43]

Prices also vary regionally. U.S. government figures show that the same cartfull of groceries for a family of four that costs $26 in Cedar Rapids, Iowa and Austin, Texas will cost $33 in New York City and $35 in Honolulu, Hawaii or Anchorage, Alaska.

The FTC found three basic pricing policies among chains. One is *area-wide pricing*, under which prices are the same for all products in all stores in an area. Another is *zonal pricing*, where prices are the same on all items except dry groceries and frozen foods. Food Fair, for example, has two price structures on meat and three on dry groceries and frozen foods. Finally there is the "my-store" policy, where prices vary greatly from store to store.[44]

How Informed Consumer-Buyers Can Benefit

The more a shopper knows about the pricing process, the better able he is to play the game of shrewd buying. He knows comparative prices in competing stores and is alert for selective price increases. He passes by high-price items displayed next to items on sale. Like the store manager, he has a goal. That goal is to buy as much merchandise for his money as he can.*

QUESTIONS FOR REVIEW

1. What is involved in the flow of goods from producer to consumer?
2. What all goes into marketing costs and why do marketing costs take such a large proportion of the consumers' dollar?
3. Define each of the kinds of market situations. In which one is price highest and in which one is price lowest. Why?
4. Why are there relatively few examples of oligopsony, duopsony, and monopsony?
5. Define and distinguish the differences among the terms demand, desire, and utility.
6. Which kind of shopper would you classify yourself as being – economical, personal, ethical, or apathetic? Why?
7. What pattern, if any, is there in the kinds of stores at which your family chooses to shop?
8. Why do different stores have different prices for identical products?
9. Do the major chains stimulate competition or stimulate movement away from competition?
10. Why is there such a variety in the types of stores where one may purchase food products?
11 Do you look at shopping from a catalog positively or negatively? Why?
12. What is the basic function of the price system in our economy?
13. Price and value are synonymous. True or false? Why?
14. What are the pros and cons of the one-price system?
15. Differentiate between fixed and variable expenses.
16. Should loss-leader pricing be illegal?
17. Should federal "fair trade" laws have been repealed?
18. Is unit pricing the answer to the problem of odd measures and weights and odd prices?
19. Are retailers economic persons? Are consumers rational buyers?

PROJECTS

1. Interview five students and five professors to find out whether they believe the economy would operate better under Adam Smith's con-

* See Chapter 16 for details on intelligent buying.

cept of the "invisible hand" or with the government directing economic activity.

2. Interview a retailer to find out what his or her costs of production are, what has happened to these costs during the recent inflation, and what this means for the retailer.

3. Interview a retailer and ask him if he would prefer more government control if it would bring less competition from other retailers or if he would prefer less government control.

4. Find out if there are any retail monopolies, duopolies, or oligopolies in your community.

5. Take one shopping area and list all the stores by kind of goods sold and type of operation. Then determine the market structure that exists for each store in that competing area.

6. Interview a retailer concerning the store's pricing policy or policies and find out why the retailer follows these policies.

7. Shop in one supermarket. List the various kinds of selling techniques you observe that are used to stimulate the shopper to buy.

8. Shop in a supermarket that has unit pricing and a supermarket that does not. Do you think that unit pricing is helpful to the shopper?

9. Interview a group of shoppers as to whether they use and like unit shopping.

REFERENCES

1. *Progressive Grocer Colonial Study: A Report on Supermarket Operations and Customer Habits* (New York: Progressive Grocer, 1965), pp. 97–120.
2. G. P. Stone, "City Shoppers and Urban Identification: Observations on the Social Psychology of City Life," *American Journal of Sociology* 60 (1954): 36–45, cited by Engel, p. 459.
3. *Fortune,* July 1976, p. 210.
4. *Ibid.*
5. *Con$umer New$week,* 8 Dec. 1975, p. 1.
6. Ralph L. Day and E. Laird Landon, "Collecting Comprehensive Consumer Complaint Data by Survey Research," *Advances in Consumer Research* 3 (1976).
7. *Guides Against Deceptive Pricing* (Washington, D.C.: Federal Trade Commission, 1964).
8. "Lack of Service Seen Eliminating Discount Operator," *Retailing Daily,* 12 Feb. 1956.
9. *Fair Trade Laws,* Hearings before the Subcommittee on Antitrust and Monopoly of the Committee on the Judiciary, U.S. Senate, 94th Congress, 1st Session, 18, 19, 20, 21 Feb., 9, 10 April, 1975, pp. 70–71.
10. *Christian Science Monitor,* 10 Dec. 1975, p. 30.
11. *Supermarket News,* 2 June 1975, p. 2.
12. Letter received from Deputy Assistant Secretary of Defense, dated 4 March 1976.
13. *The Food Co-op Handbook* (Boston: Houghton Mifflin, 1975), pp. 1–3.
14. Ralph Cassady, Jr., *Competition and Price Making in Food Retailing: The*

Anatomy of Supermarket Operation (New York: Ronald Press, 1962), chaps. 1, 2, 3, 4.

15. *Fortune,* July 1976, pp. 210–211.
16. The Federal Trade Commission, *Economic Report on the Baking Industry* (Washington, D.C.: Government Printing Office, 1967), p. 61.
17. *New York Times,* 9 Nov. 1974, p. 16F.
18. *New York Times,* 4 July 1974, p. 40.
19. *New York Times,* 29 Dec. 1974, pp. iv, 9; 9 Nov. 1975, p. 16F.
20. *New York Times,* 17 March 1974, pp. iv, 8.
21. *St. Petersburg Times,* 3 Nov. 1975, p. 12B.
22. *Ibid.*
23. *Pittsburgh Post-Gazette,* 8 Dec. 1975, p. 29.
24. Fact Sheet, issued by the National Retail Merchants Association, New York, N.Y., 1975.
25. Paul E. Nelson and Lee E. Preston, *Price Merchandising in Food Retailing: A Case Study* (Berkeley: Institute of Business and Economic Research, University of California, 1966), p. 59.
26. *Ibid.,* p. 101.
27. *Federal Register,* 21 May 1970, p. 7811; 30 June 1971, pp. 12288–12290; *HEW News,* 21 May 1970; Lawrence Friedman, "Psychological Pricing in the Food Industry," in Almarin Phillips and Oliver E. Williamson, eds., *Prices: Issues in Theory, Practice and Public Policy* (Philadelphia: University of Pennsylvania Press, 1967), pp. 198–201.
28. *Progressive Grocer Colonial Study,* p. 106.
29. Friedman, pp. 128–129.
30. *St. Petersburg Times Parade,* 7 Sept. 1975, p. 7.
31. *Consumer Math—Selected Results from the First National Assessment of Mathematics* (Denver: Education Commission of States, 1975), p. 1.
32. David Caplovitz, *The Poor Pay More: Consumer Practices of Low Income Families* (New York: The Free Press, 1965), pp. 16–18, 25, 28, 88, 90–93.
33. *Economic Report on Food Chain Selling Practices in the District of Columbia and San Francisco,* Staff Report to the Federal Trade Commission, July 1969, pp. 1–5.
34. George H. Haines, Leonard S. Simon, and Marcus Alexis, "Maximum Likelihood Estimation of Central-City Food Trading Areas," *Journal of Marketing Research* 9 (May 1972): 155.
35. Carl E. Block, et al., *The Badge of Poverty: The St. Louis Report* (Columbia: University of Missouri Press, 1970), pp. 67–68.
36. Marcus Alexis, Leonard S. Simon, and Kenneth Smith, "Some Determinants of Food Buying Behavior," in Marcus Alexis, Robert Holloway, and Robert S. Hancock, eds., *Empirical Foundations of Marketing Research Findings In the Behavioral and Applied Sciences* (Chicago, Ill.: Marcham Press, 1969), pp. 20–32.
37. Donald E. Sexton, Jr., "Black Buyer Behavior," *Journal of Marketing* 36 (Oct. 1972): 36.
38. Willard F. Mueller, "Can the Antitrust Laws Prevent Monopolistic Food Prices?" paper presented at Chicago, 21 April 1969, pp. 3–6; Russell C. Parker, "The Baking Industry," *Antitrust Law and Economic Review* 2 (Summer 1969): 117–120.
39. *Report: COCO National Bread and Milk Price Survey,* Conference of Consumer Organizations, Tucson, Arizona, March 1975.
40. *Progressive Grocer Colonial Study,* pp. 48, 81–82.
41. Nassau County Office of Consumer Affairs, Mineola, N.Y., Consumer News, 9 Sept. 1975.
42. *New York Post,* 22 Oct. 1975, p. 38.
43. Mueller, p. 23.
44. *Economic Report on Food Chain Selling Practices,* pp. 21–22.

CHAPTER 12

CONSUMER DEBT – A WAY OF LIFE?

THE DEBT SYNDROME

A Way of Life

U. S. News & World Report headlined an article, "$3-Trillion Debt – Is It Out of Control?"[1] The article stated that "the mountain of debt that has piled up in this country in recent years is beginning to cause trouble on all sides." From 1970 to 1975 corporate debt increased 65 percent to $1.3 billion; farmers' indebtedness was up 60 percent to $94 billion; state and local government debt was up 52 percent to $220 billion; federal debt was up 54 percent to $525 billion; and personal debt increased by 59 percent to $841 billion. The recession of the 1970s and its aftereffects have made debt much more of a burden. The debt problem was so severe that in 1974 there were 254,484 bankruptcy cases filed, of which 224,354 were nonbusiness bankruptcies, with 184,178 of these employee bankruptcies.[2] The dilemma for many families is how to close the gap between earnings, on the one side, and living expenses plus repayment of debt on the other.

Debt for many does become a way of life. One couple, both twenty-seven years old, were working and each was earning $13,000, yet they got themselves deeply in debt. They contracted to buy a house and took out a $26,500 mortgage, on which the monthly payments were $257. They then contracted to buy two cars – both on the installment plan. In addition, they ran up a bill of $2,500 on their Master Charge card; an additional $2,100 was borrowed from Household Finance, a small loan company; and $1,000 was owed to the May Department Store, $600 to Sears, and $350 to Penney's. Their debts including the mortgage totaled $41,500.[3] A bank employee living alone had a take-home pay of $700 a month; living expenses totaled $650. This left $50 to give the six creditors the monthly $600 she owed them.[4] Before long both the couple and the single person would have ended up in bankruptcy court if they had not gone to financial counselors who helped them untangle their debt situation.

According to the Family Service Association of America, the principal family financial problem is overindebtedness. Many consumers are economic minors. Like children, they cannot resist the pressure to buy. As a result, some get themselves in a condition of virtual bondage. There is abundant evidence that loan sharks deliberately keep their victims in debt. And there is some evidence that many cash lenders and installment sellers fail to check a prospective buyer's total commitments before granting additional credit. The credit addict has no self-restraint. Some installment sellers tempt consumers with the bait of "no down payment, only $7.50 per month." Childlike buyers never ask for or figure total prices, credit costs, or rates of interest. If they can squeeze another payment out of their incomes, they succumb to the pressure, and before they realize it are hopelessly in debt.

What Is Buying?

Buying implies the exchange of goods and services for cash. But a buyer may give a promise to pay in lieu of cash. This may or may not create a *net debt*.* If it is a promise to pay out of future income, a net debt is created. The practice of purchasing goods on open account illustrates the first type of credit, while the method of purchasing on the installment plan illustrates the second. In both cases, the buyer is securing from the merchant not only the merchandise he or she wants, but also the credit he or she needs. The merchant in turn may borrow from a banker or a finance company the necessary money to carry these accounts.

Historical Use of Credit

In colonial America, where there was a shortage of money, the use of credit for consumption purposes was more common than the use of cash. Credit was used by all economic and social groups – by the wealthy for convenience, by others out of necessity. By present standards, losses on bad debts were high – as much as 10 percent, compared with 2 or 3 percent today. Nevertheless, it has been argued that the extensive use of credit had beneficial effects in that it helped to increase the productivity of the country.

In earlier years, consumer cash lending was carried on almost entirely by lenders who violated the general usury laws, which set the maximum interest rate too low to cover the expenses of making small loans. Moral usury was defined as "taking advantage of the ignorance or necessitous

---

* If one has $2,000 invested in securities or real estate those assets could be sold to get cash with which to purchase a new automobile. But if, for various reasons, one does not wish to sell the assets, one may borrow $2,000. Such a loan, being offset by equivalent assets, does not create a net debt; a loan of $2,500 would create a net debt of $500.

conditions of the needy borrower." Those guilty of this practice were called *loan sharks*, a descriptive term still in use.

The sale of houses on the installment plan by mortgages, using the house as security for repayment of the loan, has long been accepted. But the selling of consumers' durable goods on the installment plan, using the chattel mortgages (also known now as "security interest" in a majority of states) on the goods as security for repayment of the loan, is comparatively new. The rapid growth of population and development of a large-scale, impersonal market provided the modern need for a new merchandising method. As production of automobiles and appliances exceeded effective demand, the solution was to lend buyers the money with which to buy.

Attitudes have changed. Consumers are encouraged to buy now and pay later. The word "debtor" is no longer a disparaging term. In times of recession it becomes almost a patriotic duty to spend in order to spur recovery of the economy. A generation of boom and inflation has created increasing numbers of willing consumer-borrowers. Never having known depression, they are optimists, confident that their incomes will increase so that they can repay their loans. They are realists who know that the value of the dollar may depreciate, making it easier to pay debts with more numerous, cheaper dollars.

Present Use and Volume of Consumer Credit

About 50 percent of all families in this country have installment debt. Twenty-nine percent of the families with incomes under $3,000 have installment debt. Forty-six percent of the families in the $15,000 and over income group have installment debt. Of the families having installment debt, the majority of them make payments on this debt that are under 10 to 20 percent of their disposable income. A small percentage of families in each income group makes payments that are over 40 percent of their disposable income.[5]

Total outstanding consumer installment credit was $164 billion by 1976. This included $55 billion for automobile loans, $12 billion for loans on other mobile homes, $12 billion for revolving credit, $8 billion for home repair and modernization loans, and $77 billion for all other loans.[6]

Installment debt now equals almost 15 percent of all disposable personal income. Obviously the use of credit makes it easier to agree to buy by promising now to pay in the future. Extension of retail credit has become a popular means of temporarily expanding the market for consumer goods and services. This development constitutes a significant force affecting consumer demand. No longer is it necessary for a buyer to have cash in hand to make a purchase. Tempted by the comforts and luxuries forced on our attention by advertising, salesmanship, and peer group pressure, we as consumers are told that we can have whatever we want by paying nothing now or a few dollars down and then a few dollars each week or month.

Formal Sources of Consumer Credit

Commercial Banks Bankers once regarded personal loans as nonproductive because they are not self-liquidating, as most loans to business firms are. With a business loan a firm can buy raw materials that can be processed and sold within thirty or sixty days, yielding cash with which to pay off the loan. Consumer loans were considered bad risks because most of them were incurred to meet emergency situations or to pay off other debts. This attitude has changed within the past generation, however. Commercial banks now have personal loan departments, which currently make over 61 percent of all loans for repair and modernization of houses, over 25 percent of all loans made for automobile purchases by individuals, 71 percent of loans made for mobile homes, and 28 percent of all other installment credit loans.[7]

Finance Companies There are financial institutions that buy installment credit contracts from retail merchants. When one buys an automobile on credit, the contract one signs is usually sold by the retailer to a sales finance company for cash. The finance company then has title to the car and collects the monthly or weekly payments. In case of default, the sales finance company repossesses the car, hoping to resell it for enough to cover the unpaid balance on the loan. Finance companies supply 25 percent of the retail automobile credit, 28 percent of the mobile homes credit, and 28 percent of all other installment credit.[8]

Credit Unions Credit unions are consumer cooperative lending agencies. The credit union is based on the principle that the funds necessary to meet the credit needs of any group can be found within that group. These funds are made available for cooperative use by pooling them in a credit union for loans to members. Credit unions extend about 15 percent of all consumer installment credit and about one-third of the money lent is for automobile purchases. Credit unions had more than $26 billion of loans outstanding at the end of 1975.[9]

Consumer Finance Companies Such companies are also called personal finance companies or small-loan companies. They operate under regulatory laws in forty-nine states (excluding Arkansas and the District of Columbia). In 1916 the Russell Sage Foundation cooperated with the National Federation of Remedial Loan Associations to draft a model law regulating interest rates and practices in making small loans. The original maximum loan permitted was $300, but legislative action has increased loan limits in keeping with price and wage increases. Today most states permit consumer finance companies to make loans of $2,000 or more.

Passage of the Uniform Small Loan Law by the states constituted recognition by society of the need for making consumer credit available at prices high enough for successful business operation, but no higher. The New York State law provides for a charge of 2.5 percent a month on loan balances of $100 or less, 2 percent a month on the next $200, 1.5 percent a month on the loan balance to $900, and 1.25 percent on the remaining loan balance to the maximum of $2,500. Compound interest is not permitted. Loans of up to $300 may not exceed a twenty-four-and-a-half-month maturity in New York State, and not over forty-eight and one-half months on loans of over $1,400. Most of the loans made by consumer finance companies are secured by chattel mortgages (or security interest), although consumer finance companies do lend on an unsecured basis. These financial institutions are now the largest suppliers of personal installment cash loans, which are loans incurred for purposes other than the purchase of durable goods. Companies operating primarily under small loan laws account for about 37 percent of the personal installment cash loan business through more than 23,000 licensed offices.[10]

Other Financial Institutions and Retailers   Other financial institutions and retailers hold 19 percent of the outstanding consumer installment credit. They extend credit primarily for personal loans and automobile loans. Retail outlets themselves supply almost half of the credit for the purchase of consumer durables other than automobiles. This grouping includes department stores, mail-order stores, furniture stores, and appliance stores.

Pawnbrokers   The role of pawnbrokers as a source of loan funds is relatively small. Their basic operation is to lend money for goods deposited and to charge a rate of interest that is within the usury laws of the state in which they are operating. If the loan is not paid back, an attempt is made to sell the goods to recover the loan. Many states have very restrictive laws supervising pawnshops. Pawnshops generally spring up in low-income neighborhoods and around military bases. In general a pawnshop is just about the last place to go to borrow money. The rates allowed are generally high. Pawnbrokers traditionally charge 10 percent per month, or 120 percent a year. In California pawnbrokers may legally charge interest at an annual rate of 160 to 240 percent for loans of up to $200 that have to be repaid within ninety days. Florida sets no limit on the interest that pawnbrokers may charge. In Ohio interest rates on such loans are limited by state law to 36 percent a year.

Credit Cards   Few innovations in consumer credit have made quite the impact in as short a time as credit cards have. The better known, more widely used credit cards that have been available for years have been those of major department stores in metropolitan centers. Credit cards were adopted originally merely to facilitate buying without the necessity of carrying cash. Items purchased were paid for at the end of the month and no interest or carrying charges were levied. Stores were willing to sell this way because it developed customer loyalty to the store. For example, Sears, Roebuck & Company has 14 million active credit card holders, the largest number for any retail chain.
     In the past few years there has been a revolution in the credit card field.

It is estimated that there are more than 500 million credit cards in use in the United States today, and that eight out of every ten adults carry at least one card. The variety of goods and services that may now be purchased with credit cards is almost unlimited.

In the past decade a major impact in the entire credit card field has been the introduction of bank credit cards, such as BankAmericard and Master Charge. In 1967 the idea of a bank card was just gaining wider acceptance and distribution. By the end of 1975, bank credit cards were held by at least 64 million Americans, issued by over 10,000 banks, and accepted by over 1.5 million retail outlets. By the end of 1975, consumers owed $10.5 billion on credit card charges, but this still was only a little over 6 percent of all outstanding consumer debt, not counting home mortgages. The acceptance of the bank credit cards by sellers of goods and services has been phenomenal. Even doctors, lawyers, churches, and the Internal Revenue Service have been accepting them.

Sellers like credit cards. Specialized credit cards build up brand and company loyalty. "Credit customers are your customers. Cash customers are anybody's customers." One oil company reported that 75 percent of its credit card customers ask the station attendant to "fill'er up" as compared to 40 percent of the cash customers. American Express estimates that patrons of restaurants spend as much as 51 percent more when they charge meals to their American Express card. Even barbers and hair stylists have found that credit cards "turn misers into big-time spenders."[11] The owner of the service station where the writer trades reported that the average cash purchase was about $5 to $6, while the average purchase by credit card customers was almost $9.

Possession of a credit card may indeed stimulate a greater use of credit; however, there is one study that indicates that people with higher incomes are more likely to have credit cards and that customers with travel and entertainment credit cards may pay more for a meal than cash customers not because they have a credit card, but because they have higher incomes.[12]

The major problem for consumers in the use of credit cards is that they may accumulate charges more rapidly than they realize and so may live beyond their means because of the ease of saying, "Charge it." The delinquency rate as a percent of outstanding credit in the United States for Bank-Americard is 4.03 percent, and one-fourth of this is charged off as uncollectable. Past-due accounts of thirty days or more for Master Charge totaled 3.5 percent, or $184 million. During 1973–1975 as inflation and unemployment put more people under financial pressure, the number of credit cards repossessed increased as people found it more difficult to meet their debt obligations. The legal principle is well established that the cards serve as credit devices only at the pleasure of the grantor. Some credit cards bear the notation: "This card remains the property of the issuing company." There are companies in the business of retrieving credit cards. Credit card issuers usually come to these companies after bills are delinquent for ninety days. In one month one credit card recovery company received orders to repossess 37,000 cards.[13]

Another disadvantage of credit cards is that it costs more to service credit accounts than cash transactions even when the account is paid within the specified time limit to avoid paying interest charges. No definitive study has been made of how much the use of credit cards cost consumers when they pay immediately and avoid interest charges, but the merchant participating in the credit card plan pays approximately 6 percent for the service.

The advantages of using credit cards include the ease of charging purchases and elimination of the need to carry large sums of cash, particularly when traveling. On trips credit card billing may be so slow as to give the individual the use of the bank's money for up to three months—interest free. The same advantages and disadvantages that apply to the use of credit in general also apply to the use of credit cards.

A serious problem in the use of credit cards has to do with lost and stolen cards. One estimate of losses incurred from the illegal use of lost and stolen credit cards is $350 million annually.[14] These losses have to be covered in the interest rates charged the honest credit card user. The greatest credit card company losses are due to unscrupulous merchants or their employees.[15]

Travel and Entertainment Credit Cards   In 1950 Diners Club produced the first of what became known as "Travel and Entertainment" or T & E cards. Diners Club later was joined by American Express and Carte Blanche.

The owner of this restaurant not only honors various travel and entertainment credit cards but also makes an appeal to customers who do not use the "eat now, pay later" plan. (*UPI*)

T & E cards provide their holders with credit at specified hotels, motels, restaurants, airlines, car rental agencies, service stations, and gift outlets. Their use is limited to goods and services associated with the travel and entertainment business. The annual membership fee is $20. The Diners Club card is accepted at tens of thousands more places than American Express — with Carte Blanche a distant third — but American Express has 6.5 million cardholders, as compared to about 2 million for Diners Club and 700,000 for Carte Blanche.[16] T & E charges are expected to be paid in full when billed. They do not serve as revolving charge accounts. The ownership of a T & E card is thought by some to be a status symbol because there is an attempt to make them more prestigious than bank cards. In 1974 Carte Blanche had a sales volume of about $425 million; Diners Club $575 million; and American Express $5.5 billion. These figures compare with about $7 billion for Bank Americard and $8.4 billion for Master Charge.[17]

The Unsolicited Credit Card During the late 1960s when the expansion of credit cards was at its peak literally millions of unsolicited credit cards were distributed through the mail. One bank card system distributed four million unsolicited credit cards in its first few months of operation. The abuses, losses, and thefts accounted for by this indiscriminate distribution of unsolicited credit cards called for remedial legislation. In 1969 and 1970 congressional hearings were held on this topic, and in 1970 Congress passed an amendment to the Truth-in-Lending Act which became effective in 1971. The law bans the issuance of unsolicited credit cards, and limits to $50 a cardholder's liability for unauthorized use of a lost or stolen credit card. The cardholder's liability ends, in any case, when he or she has notified the issuer. This practically negates the need for credit card insurance protection.

The Fair Credit Billing Act of 1974 has provided credit card holders with additional legal protection under certain provisions that went into effect in 1975. Under the regulations, credit card users can hold the issuer of the credit card accountable for the quality and serviceability of the goods purchased. This regulation eliminates in certain transactions the "holder-in-due-course" doctrine, under which customers could be held liable for bills to creditors, even when the credit was used to buy goods that turned out to be unserviceable. This means, assuming certain conditions of the law are met, that the customer may cease further payment to the credit card issuer for a specific transaction if the product is unserviceable. Alleged errors in billings for credit cards or open-end credit, such as checking account loans, are subject to specific procedures for resolution. Customers have sixty days to notify the lender of a contested billing. The lender must correct or challenge the alleged error in ninety days or forfeit the amount in dispute. The regulations also provide that credit card companies may not restrain merchants from offering discounts to cash customers. The discount would stem from the fact that credit card companies impose service charges on merchants, usually from 2 to 5 percent of the total volume of business transacted with the cards in a given period. A discount for cash payment does not have to be given by the seller, but the credit card issuer may not prohibit a discount from being given for a cash purchase if the seller so desires. In addition, a credit card issuer may not cancel a customer's account or file an adverse report on the customer's credit rating while a dispute is in progress. Finally, under the Fair Credit Billing Act credit issuers must notify customers of their rights under the law.

As is true in the case of all contracts, you should read credit card contracts very carefully *before* signing them. In this way you will be aware of your liability, rights, and finance charges and rates of interest before buying.

WHAT DOES IT COST TO BUY ON CREDIT?

Consumer Credit Costs

"I'll lend you $5 this week if you pay me $6 next week." A low rate of interest? A 20 percent rate of interest? No. The annual rate on this transaction is an astonishing 1,040 percent. If the credit charge had been at the rate of 6 percent per year, the interest on this loan for a week would have been just a little more than half a cent.

The market for consumer credit is one in which there are comparatively few sellers (oligopoly) whose services differ. The product is the same—money—but imperfect competition exists because of differentiation in the services offered. Some of the differences are in the length of the loan, the type of security required, the size of the loan, and the cost of the loan. In addition there are differences in state loan laws. Consumer borrowers pay over $15 billion a year for credit, and many do so without a full realization of how much it costs. They do not know the various rates and sources of credit, and they do not shop around.

The imperfection of the marketplace is indicated by the range of charges for cash loans and credit shown in Table 12-1. For a loan of $100 for one year some consumers pay 8 percent and some pay up to 42 percent.

The rates quoted here are general. You should check lending agencies

TABLE 12-1. Credit Rates Commonly Charged by Different Lenders

Lender	Annual Percentage Rate (%)
Retail dealers (including mail-order companies)	
Revolving or budget charge accounts	8 to 18
Installment purchase of appliances or furniture	12 to 20 (or more)
Banks	8 to 16
Bank credit cards	
Cash loans	12
Merchandise and service loans	12 to 18
Credit unions	9 to 15
Small loan companies	18 to 42
Auto-finance companies	12 to 24

in your area to obtain specific rates. An illustration of the fluctuations in rates in the various states is seen in the charges for revolving credit. Eighteen percent is the legal annual percentage rate in forty-two states, but in Pennsylvania it is fifteen percent; in Connecticut, Hawaii, Minnesota, South Dakota, and Washington it is twelve; in Arkansas it is ten; and in Missouri it is eighteen percent on the first $500 and nine percent on any amount over $500. These rates are not necessarily permanent. Lenders in Pennsylvania have been trying for years to have the legal rate raised to 18 percent, but have been unsuccessful. In Wisconsin the rate was raised from 12 percent to 18 percent after a successful campaign by retailers and other extenders of credit.

There are marked differences in rates charged within a competing commercial area as well as across the country even among the same types of lenders. For example, in 1975 in the Dallas–Fort Worth area among commercial banks, one bank charged the lowest rate of 7.51 percent for a car loan while another bank charged the highest rate of 11.52 percent; for a consumer goods loan the lowest rate was 10.68 percent and the highest rate was 14.68 percent; and for a personal loan the lowest rate was 10 percent and the highest rate was 17.97 percent.[18] All rates, as required by law, were quoted as annual percentage rates. Nationally the lowest rate quoted for an automobile loan was 7.51 percent while the highest rate was 14.55; the lowest rate for a consumer goods loan was 10.22 percent and the highest rate was 19.02 percent; and for a personal loan the lowest rate was 10 percent and the highest rate was 17.97 percent.[19] Rates may have changed since 1975, but *Consumer Reports* states that *relative* differences tend to remain constant.

It is possible to borrow on your life insurance policy at a rate of about 8 percent. This is possible because there is practically no risk and administrative expenses are small.* Commercial banks and consumer finance companies on the other hand, which deal with prospective borrowers whose credit has not been established, must investigate the credit standing of the applicant, issue bills, record payments, incur collection expenses, assume the risk of nonpayment, and earn a profit besides recovering interest on the money loaned.

The total cost of borrowing includes all finance charges and fees that have to be paid in order to get the loan or buy the item on credit. From the borrower's point of view it makes no difference whether credit costs are considered as interest charges or as interest charges plus service costs. The Internal Revenue Service ruled in 1971 that all interest costs, fees, and finance charges paid on borrowed funds may all be treated in the same way and deducted as interest when filing the personal income tax form 1040. The net result is that the total credit price is considerably more than the cash price. Is this differential too much? Who is to decide? It may be argued that if buyers need or want goods badly, their willingness to pay a considerable differential is in itself evidence that the price is fair, for other-

---

* For an explanation of insurance policy loans see p. 474.

wise the installment purchases would not be made. This assumes, however, that the buyer is aware of the costs involved.

Even though the annual percentage rates and dollar finance charge costs are cited in the contract, many consumers are not as aware of these costs as they should be to shop effectively for credit terms. For all too many consumers the only two points of concern in buying on credit are the amount of the down payment and the amount of the monthly payment; little thought is given to rates of interest or dollar charges.

Since the Truth-in-Lending Act went into effect on July 1, 1969, borrowers know when they borrow money or buy goods on credit what the annual percentage rate and dollar finance charges are, and it is no longer necessary for them to do the arithmetic to calculate the annual percentage rate.* For persons who wish to calculate an approximate annual percentage rate, however, the following simplified procedures and formula are provided.† This is found by dividing the credit charge by the average amount of money borrowed for a year. The average amount borrowed can be approximated by assuming that the debt is reduced by equal amounts with each monthly payment. For example, if a borrower from a bank or an installment buyer were to borrow $240 for twelve months, repayable in twelve installments of $20 each, he would pay interest of $14.40. The first month he would owe the full $240; the second month $220; and so on until the twelfth month, when he would owe only $20. By totaling the balances owed each month ($240 + 220 + 200 + 180 + 160 + 140 + 120 + 100 + 80 + 60 + 40 + 20 = $1,560) and dividing the total by twelve, the annual average amount owed is found to be $130. Now, if the credit charge were figured on the beginning balance ($240 in this case) at what creditors like to refer to as an "add-on" rate, in this case $6 per $100 per year (or 6%), the credit charge would be found by multiplying the beginning balance by 6 percent (6 percent × $240 = $14.40). The credit charge is then divided by the average yearly payment $\left(\dfrac{\$14.40}{\$130}\right)$, giving an annual interest rate of 11.08 percent. We now can see why many consumers are misled into believing they are getting a 6 percent rate when in fact the rate is close to double that. (Under the Truth-in-Lending Act it is illegal to quote an add-on rate as the annual percentage rate.)

An easier and shorter way to calculate the average amount borrowed is to add the first and last balance owed and divide the total by two $\left(\dfrac{\$240 + \$20}{2}\right.$ $= \$130\left.\right)$. You will note that $130 is in the middle, between the sixth and seventh payments.

If the loan is to run six months, divide $240 by 6. This equals $40, the

---

* See pp. 304–307 for a discussion of this act.

† Two excellent resources for persons interested in the mathematics of interest rates and in a more precise determination of interest rate are: Richard L. D. Morse, *Truth in Lending* and *Consumer Credit Computations* (Columbia, Mo.: American Council on Consumer Interests, 1966).

amount to be repaid each month. Then $\dfrac{\$240 + \$40}{2} = \$140$ and $\dfrac{\$7.20}{\$140} = 5.14$ percent for six months, or 10.29 percent on an annual basis.

If the loan were for eighteen months, one would divide $240 by 18. This equals $13.33 to be repaid each month. Then $\dfrac{\$240 + \$13.33}{2} = \$126.66$, the average amount on loan. Dividing $21.60 (the credit charge) by $126.66 (the average amount owed) yields a rate of 17.05 percent, two-thirds of which is 11.37 percent on a yearly basis. This method of figuring the average balance is implicit in the following formula frequently used to estimate the annual percentage rate:

$$ r = \frac{2\,mi}{p\,(n + 1)} $$

r = the approximate annual percentage rate
m = the number of payment periods in a year (12 monthly, or 52 weekly)
i = the finance cost in dollars
p = the amount of credit advanced
n = the number of installment payments you will make

For example, you are offered a $300 freezer for $60 down and the balance in six monthly installments of $42 each. You finance $240 at a cost of $12. In the formula, m would be 12, i would be $12, p would be $240, n would be 6. And r turns out to be 17.14 percent.

PROS AND CONS OF CONSUMER CREDIT

Reasons for and Advantages of Buying on Credit

Buyers Can Enjoy the Goods While Paying for Them Installment credit breaks the total price of a commodity into fractional payments. This makes it possible for persons receiving small incomes to purchase relatively high-priced durable goods. The alternative to this method of purchasing is to save first and pay cash at the time of purchase. It may be contended that the alternative is much wiser, since the buyer not only does not pay any interest or finance charges, but actually could receive interest on savings accumulated for the purchase. This assumes that buyers are sufficiently patient to forgo immediate enjoyment of the things they want. Some consumers are indeed willing and able to wait for the enjoyment of economic goods until they can purchase for cash, but others are neither willing nor disciplined enough to accumulate cash. In between is a third group of potential buyers who would be willing to wait a reasonably long time, but whose incomes are so small that enjoyment of certain goods would have to be postponed too long a time awaiting their accumulation of the purchase price. It is obvious that they cannot save any faster while using the commodity than while anticipating its acquisition. In fact, they cannot save the full purchase price as quickly because they pay interest instead of receiving it. But many people find the incentive to save less effective than the necessity of meeting an installment payment.

Installment buying has long been used in the purchase of houses. Very few families could pay the full price of a house at the time of purchase. If it were not for mortgage credit, many families could not own their homes. Until automobiles were offered for sale on the installment plan, the number of buyers was relatively small because the price of a new car was and still is equal to 25, 50, or even 75 percent of a family's yearly income. As a consequence, almost two-thirds of all car sales are on credit.

Widening the field of consumer credit to include household appliances was a logical development of a merchandising method that had proven its worth. Down payments, which range from 10 to 40 percent of the purchase price, are equal to or in excess of the rental charge for such items. This means that the purchaser is, in effect, paying rent for the use of the commodity, the rent being applied to the purchase price so that ultimately he or she becomes the full owner. Whether or not the satisfaction of present use is worth the added cost depends on the cost of credit. No objective standard can be applied since a charge that may seem too high to one buyer may be acceptable to another, depending on individual subjective satisfactions. What the average buyer on the installment plan sees and understands is that by deducting a few dollars per week or month from her income, she will be able to acquire at once the article she desires. Surveys show that many borrowers fail to pay much attention to comparative cash and credit prices. If previous commitments leave enough dollars to make an additional purchase, the purchase will be made regardless of the interest rate and finance charges. If the price of the article is $25.92 a month that is understandable. What is not fully appreciated is the cost of credit when the rate is, say, 18 percent. Even if this were understood, some buyers would still be willing to pay it because of their desire for immediate satisfaction.

Borrowing increases current spending, but it decreases future spending by more than it increases current spending. For example, assume a family has a perfectly adequate black-and-white television set, but the pressure is mounting to purchase a color set. The color set desired costs $600. The family has the choice of purchasing the set today for a $120 down payment and twelve monthly payments at 18 percent, equaling $43.90, or of saving $50 a month and putting off the purchase for one year and making do with the black-and-white set. The total cost of the color set purchased on credit would be $643.90, while the net cost of the set purchased for cash could be $585, assuming that the savings earned 5 percent interest from the day of deposit to the day of withdrawal. So the net difference in this illustration between cash and credit is $58.90. The satisfaction of obtaining the set a year earlier costs 10 percent more, or it costs sixteen cents a day to get the set one year sooner!

In buying on credit one has the additional costs of the interest charges paid, the lost interest on savings, and the loss of a possible savings from a discount for cash payment.

Installment Credit Purchases Compel a Form of Saving Persons who would otherwise fritter away their incomes are disciplined by incurring obligations that must be met regularly. It is not likely that buyers responsible for the billions of dollars' worth of annual installment loans and purchases would voluntarily save enough in advance to enable them to pay cash. Amounts going to installment collectors might be used for temporary satisfactions. But one must remember that buying on credit is *not* saving.

Installment Credit May Encourage a Wiser Use of Income Credit buyers do acquire automobiles, washing machines, television sets, and many other goods that enrich their daily living. Moreover, a car eliminates bus fares, and a television set makes it unnecessary to spend money on movies. Account must also be taken of the psychic satisfaction a family or an individual derives from the ownership of such things when their neighbors also have them.

Many Credit Transactions Are for Convenience This is true of open-account buying, the oldest form of credit. The traditional form of open-account credit with retail merchants usually grants the buyer a month in which to pay the bill. This practice is based on the customary method of paying wages and salaries; the expectation being that buyers will pay their bills when they get their paychecks. Many customers who could pay cash out of current income or out of savings each time they buy something find it more convenient to make periodic payments.

Open accounts are based almost entirely on personal credit. The buyer is not usually asked for any tangible evidence of indebtedness or for any form of security. As the system operates, a person who pays cash at a store allowing open accounts is at a disadvantage because he or she probably pays higher prices yet receives fewer services. For example, if a purchase proves unsatisfactory, an open-account buyer enjoys an advantage over the cash buyer in securing adjustment. At the same time this practice invites abuse by unscrupulous buyers who seek to return merchandise after using it.

Credit Is Useful to Help Meet Emergencies Illness, accident, and death involve unexpected expenses, while unemployment eliminates anticipated income. Families with little or no reserve have to use credit. After using their savings, they turn to merchants in the hope of receiving merchandise or services on open account, it being understood that when the emergency has passed the account will be paid. Then they turn to whatever lending institution will be willing to extend credit.

Credit Protects Savings Often people who could pay cash prefer to buy on credit because they do not have to withdraw their money from a savings account. They fear that they might not replace their savings if they spent them, but they know that they have to pay their debts or their purchases will be repossessed.

Credit Influences Budgeting   Others use credit because it makes them budget their incomes and encourages them to spend their money for more durable goods.

If all consumers were well-educated buyers, installment credit would be less widely used. But we must take consumers as they are, and we must keep in mind their limited incomes in relationship to their almost unlimited desires. Borrowing to buy may encourage the purchase of useful durable commodities, but this should not blind us to the abuses of installment selling.

Free Use of Someone Else's Money   Any credit that is used and paid for before interest has to be paid allows one the free use of someone else's money. A simple open account at a department store will allow the borrower to use the store's money up to a month without charge to purchase goods. The time lag between buying on credit and being billed and having to pay before interest is charged can be as long as ninety days. Credit card purchases made while on summer vacations may not be billed for three months. Airline tickets purchased on bank credit cards may not be called for payment for two or three months. In order not to overspend, or forget the indebtedness one has incurred, the consumer should keep careful records of credit purchases and retain all charge slips.

Credit Abuses by Sellers

Overextension of Credit   Installment credit is the handmaiden of advertising and high-pressure selling. As the economy develops new products, the task of selling is not only one of creating desire but also of providing the money or credit with which to buy. Before the widespread use of credit the last defense of consumers against high-pressure selling was inability to meet the purchase price. Installment selling has broken down this barrier, making it still easier for sellers to dispose of their wares. This is not an altogether undesirable development, but when unsuspecting and trusting consumers are enticed to incur too much debt they are in trouble.

Personal Bankruptcies   The overextension of credit has led more and more families into bankruptcy. In the year ending June 30, 1975, an estimated 183,051 personal bankruptcies were filed in United States courts.[20] Of all bankruptcies filed in court almost 90 percent are personal or family bankruptcies. Personal bankruptcies have increased by 41 percent in the past two years. Personal bankruptcies are more prevalent in states that permit garnisheeing or wage assignments.* Some employers fire employees who have had one or two garnishments, practically forcing them into bankruptcy. After bankruptcy, a borrower is a better credit risk because he or

* Garnisheeing is a legal proceeding whereby the creditor secures a court order directing the employer to withhold wages from the debtor-employee and to pay the withheld funds directly to the creditor.

she cannot go bankrupt again for six years and is thus an attractive customer for credit merchants.

Debt Consolidations and Debt Adjusters Of all the consumer credit inventions, the consolidated loan can be the most deadly. Yet it is widely used. The honest debt consolidators or adjusters take all, or almost all, of a client's income and apportion it among creditors. They are not loan companies. This service is performed without charge by certain counseling groups and for a fee by others. The fee of a reputable debt adjuster is about 10 to 12 percent of the indebtedness. Unfortunately, some debt consolidation operators try to keep their victims in virtual bondage. Abuses have been so bad that commercial debt adjusters are not permitted to operate in twenty-nine states. Eighteen states regulate this type of business.*

If a person's debts get beyond his ability to manage them, he should consult the Legal Aid Society. If a debtor is a union member, he should consult the Community Service Activities of his union. If he is a member of a credit union, he should consult its financial counselor. A national trade association of consumer finance companies, the National Foundation for Consumer Credit, Inc. (NFCC), has established offices across the country for the purpose of extending financial counseling services. One might well question the idea of creditors counseling debtors — whether for free or for a fee. Charles Neal, who has had experience in both bankruptcy proceedings and private debt counseling, stated: "There is a serious conflict of interest in my opinion. It may be similar to asking the Tobacco Institute to help us curb our smoking. Those who helped you get into trouble in the first place qualify poorly as experts to help you get out."[21]

There is a real difference of opinion concerning consumer credit counseling services that are sponsored entirely or in part by extenders of credit. On the other hand, the National Foundation for Consumer Credit, Inc. (NFCC), founded in 1951, whose financial support comes from banks, insurance companies, credit unions, family service associations, Better Business Bureaus, credit bureaus, large retail chains, and consumer finance companies, has played the leadership role in the establishment of nearly 200 Consumer Credit Counseling Services offices in 42 states, the District of Columbia, and Canada. The NFCC has established a target of 800 offices by 1980. These counseling services are locally owned and managed. They are sponsored by the NFCC, with support and cooperation coming from NFCC members, who are the principal firms in the consumer credit field

* The following information was made available in a letter from the Conference on Personal Finance Law, dated Jan. 26, 1976. States prohibiting debt pooling as a commercial business: Arkansas, Delaware, Florida, Georgia, Hawaii, Kansas, Kentucky, Louisiana, Maine, Maryland, Massachusetts, Mississippi, Missouri, Montana, New Jersey, New Mexico, New York, North Carolina, North Dakota, Ohio, Oklahoma, Pennsylvania, Rhode Island, South Carolina, Tennessee, Texas, Virginia, West Virginia, and Wyoming. States regulating this type of business: Arizona, California, Colorado, Connecticut, Idaho, Indiana, Illinois, Iowa, Michigan, Minnesota, Nebraska, Nevada, New Hampshire, Oregon, Utah, Vermont, Washington, and Wisconsin.

and other national organizations such as the Family Service Association of America, the American Home Economics Association, the AFL-CIO, the National Legal Aid and Defenders Association, and the National Urban League. Any counseling service sponsored by the NFCC must provide free counseling services and nominal fees may be charged if a program of debt liquidation is required. In addition, at no time shall any counselor be employed by any creditor of the person or family being counseled.

This NFCC-sponsored counseling service exists in addition to other consumer counseling services provided by such organizations as the Community Services Committee of the AFL-CIO, the Conference on Personal Finance Law, the Subcommittee on Personal Bankruptcy of the American Bar Association, the Legal Aid Society in many of its community branches, the Family Service Association, several Referees in Bankruptcy, and the legal services provided through the Office of Economic Opportunity.

What a Counseling Service Can Do.[22]

- Reduce the number of personal bankruptcies by providing sound alternative programs
- Minimize the garnishment and assignment of wages and salaries
- Relieve employers of bothersome and expensive participation in these procedures
- Assist individuals and families in credit difficulties by recharting their financial program, returning their accounts to current status, and preventing loss of credit standing
- Restore self-reliance, confidence, and family well-being; at the same time as strengthening the economic fabric of the community
- Reduce absenteeism and accident risks and generally increase worker efficiency and self-respect
- Educate consumers, including the consumers of tomorrow, in the intelligent use of credit

Revolving Credit Plans   Although revolving credit plans and revolving check loans are legitimate and serve a need when properly used, they offer an irresistible temptation to consumers who are not economic adults. Not only is credit made available but borrowers are pushed into debt and kept in debt because lenders make money this way. Both of these plans are designed for the small buyer on credit. A revolving check loan sets a limit on credit, such as twelve times the agreed monthly payment. The borrower is given a book of checks and charged 25 cents for each check written. Each month the borrower repays one-twelfth of the credit limit, plus interest at the rate of 1 to $1\frac{1}{2}$ percent per month. A store using a revolving credit plan opens a line of credit for a customer, who agrees to repay a minimum amount each month plus interest. These plans make it possible to purchase almost anything on credit.

Concealed Charges Unwary installment credit buyers of automobiles, household appliances, and home improvements may be the victims of the worst credit abuses. These include such practices as concealing charges, adding extra charges, charging for insurance when none is provided, overcharging for credit, and many others. In some states step-rate or split-rates have been set by law, such as 36 percent per year for the first $150 borrowed and 24 percent per year for the next $150 borrowed. Lenders will sometimes grant two $150 loans at 36 percent per year each instead of one $300 loan at the step-rate plan.

The Federal Trade Commission has promulgated rules for the retail installment sale and financing of automobiles. Under these rules there shall be no misrepresentations of insurance coverage, rates, or financing costs; the dealer may not require the buyer to place his or her automobile insurance with a specified company; and dealers may not use deceptive rate charts, nor may they induce a buyer to sign a blank contract. On the positive side, dealers are required to give buyers an itemized breakdown of installment finance charges. Unfortunately, most of these rules are not very helpful because they apply only to interstate sales. Since most sales are intrastate, buyers have no effective protection until the states also make these rules effective.

Misuse of Credit Life Insurance The use of credit life insurance, in itself a valid protective device, has led to such abuses as requiring excessive insurance, overcharging, and the nonpayment of claims. The basic purpose of credit life insurance is to pay off the creditor in case of the death of the debtor during the life of the credit contract. Credit unions absorb credit insurance costs. Other lending institutions charge 30 to 65 cents per $1,000 per month and up. Lenders profit from tie-in sales of insurance. Hearings and court records have shown cases in which 80 percent of the premiums paid by borrowers for credit life, accident, and health insurance are kicked back to the lenders.

Under the Truth-in-Lending Act, premiums for credit life and disability insurance need not be included in the finance charge if the insurance coverage is offered to the customer on an optional basis and the customer voluntarily elects to take the insurance. The Federal Trade Commission became concerned when it discovered that almost 100 percent of the borrowers with the option-to-buy were buying credit insurance. The commission stated that such a high rate indicated that some creditors were circumventing the act's disclosure requirements through practices that led borrowers to believe that the purchase of this insurance was necessary to obtain the loan, despite disclosures to the contrary. The commission recommended that the act be amended to require premiums for such insurance to be included in the finance charge, despite the fact that insurance may nominally be offered on an optional basis.[23]

One-Sided Contracts Another abuse associated with installment selling involves the powerful legal instruments used by the seller. The laws and the courts are on the seller's side. A conditional sales contract is so complicated that few if any buyers read or understand it. Indeed, it would do them little good if they did. Buyers who are able to meet their payments regularly have no difficulty. But buyers who are unable to meet payments due to illness or unemployment feel the legal power of the contract they have signed. Even though all but one payment may have been made, if the purchaser then defaults, the merchandise may be repossessed with all previous payments forfeited. There is no escape from a purchase that has proven unsatisfactory if at the time of sale the unwary buyer gave the seller a warrant of attorney. This instrument may be used—in states permitting it—to turn over wages due an employee to the creditor until the amount is paid. Moreover, such wage assignments are valid against all subsequent employers.

Holder-In-Due-Course "The single factor most responsible for consumer injustices is the holder-in-due-course doctrine. A New Jersey judge called it 'the mask behind which fraud hides.'"[24] Under this doctrine merchants who sell goods or services on an installment payment plan may get their money immediately by selling the contract to a finance institution. The new holder of the credit contract has no responsibility for the product that has been sold. He is solely interested in receiving payments from the consumer. In the event of a defect or any problem with the merchandise the consumer has little recourse. He or she must continue to make payment to the finance institution while attempting to resolve the product problems with the merchant and/or manufacturer, who has already been paid in full by the finance company. If the consumer defaults in payments, the product may be repossessed by the finance company without consideration of the "extenuating" circumstances.

The Federal Fair Credit Billing Act—along with legislative action in about forty states—has placed some restrictions on the use of the holder-in-due-course clause. And in 1976 the Federal Trade Commission issued a rule barring holder-in-due-course clauses under most conditions. The rule requires that the following clause be inserted in all installment contracts:

> Notice: Any holder of this consumer credit contract is subject to all claims and defenses which the debtor could assert against the seller of goods or services obtained pursuant hereto or with the proceeds hereof. Recovery hereunder by the debtor shall not exceed amounts paid by the debtor hereunder.[25]

This rule means that any party, such as a finance company or bank, that buys an installment contract from a selling party will be liable in case the dealer fails to deliver agreed-upon satisfactory goods or services. Under the holder-in-due-course clause the finance company or bank has no such responsibility to the consumer. However, the rule applies only when the dealer or seller arranges for the financing. On loans that an individual arranges for himself with a lender, he does, of course, have to pay back the loan even if the purchase is misrepresented or defective. In addition, the rule does not completely assure the consumer of dependable service or merchandise. The consumer still needs to get a written, rather than just a verbal, statement of the seller's promises. The rule makes it possible for the buyer to raise against the third party (the lender) any legal complaint he or she may have of breach of contract or warranty, of defective merchandise, or of misrepresentation by the seller. One further benefit of this rule is that it makes finance companies and banks more cautious about financing high-pressure or "fly-by-night" sellers.

Confession of Judgment   Legally called a *cognovit note*, a confession of judgment clause in a credit contract stipulates that by signing the contract the customer waives the right to defend himself or herself in a court of law. By signing the confession of judgment contract the debtor, for all practical purposes, has pleaded guilty in advance. When the confession of judgment was legal in Pennsylvania, the Supreme Court of Pennsylvania described such a contract as:

> Perhaps the most powerful and drastic document known to civil law. The signer deprives himself of every defense and every delay of execution, he waives exemption of personal property from levy and sale under the exemption laws, he places his cause in the hands of a hostile defender.[26]

The confession of judgment contract is not legal in all states. The Federal Trade Commission has promulgated a ruling that would make confession of judgment illegal in all states.

Debt Collection Deception   Many ruses are employed by debt collectors to obtain information on debts and debtors. The Federal Trade Commission found this to be a serious enough problem to issue *Guides Against Debt Collection Deception.* "The primary objectives of these guides are (1) the prevention of deception in connection with collection or attempted collection of debts and (2) the maintenance of fair competition among those engaged in the business of collecting debts."[27]

There can be no doubt that a great many installment buyers permit themselves to be victimized by legal chicanery rather than suffer the embarrassment and humiliation of reporting their case to a legal aid society. Few purchasers have the necessary funds to fight a case in court, but the seller can afford a skilled attorney.

American shoppers run up bills at the rate of $150 billion a year. There is an obvious need, therefore, for collection agencies. Most are reputable agencies performing an unpleasant but necessary task. In 1974 they collected more than $3 billion in past-due accounts.[28] There would be no problem if all persons paid their debts on time; since they do not, there is a need for debt collectors, but this does not give the debt collectors the right to harass, threaten, or intimidate debtors.

Sex Discrimination in Lending   For decades women seeking economic independence have been handicapped by the hidden sex discrimination of lending institutions. Women have been denied full participation in obtain ing credit. For example, they frequently needed a cosigner for a note, whereas a man would not; divorced women found it difficult to get credit; a wife's earnings would not be taken into consideration in determining the soundness of a request for a home mortgage; and some lenders would even ask a couple about their birth control plans. In 1975 the Equal Credit Opportunity Act went into effect. This act makes it illegal for banks, retailers, or other lenders to deny or terminate credit on the basis of sex or marital status; applicants are now judged on their personal merits and not on the basis of sex or marital status. In 1976 the act was amended to prohibit discrimination because of age, race, color, religion, or national origin, or because one is on welfare.

Loansharking   In the extension of credit to the debtor there are a number of legal actions available to the creditor that place the debtor in a undesirable position. Loansharking, on the other hand, is the act of lending money at rates of interest and under conditions of repayment that are strictly illegal. "Interest rates charged by loansharks vary from 200 to 2,000 percent per year, depending on the relationship between the lender and borrower, the intended use of the money, the size of the loan, and the repayment potential. The classic '6-for-5' loan, 20 percent a week, is common with small borrowers."[29] The 6-for-5 rate means that the borrower pays back $6 per week for each $5 borrowed, or the equivalent of 1,040 percent interest per year.

Loansharking tends to evolve when one or both of two conditions is present: a chronic shortage in the supply of loanable funds, particularly for personal loans, and/or the establishment of legal rates of interest set too low to attract loanable funds. Thus it might make more sense to set a legal rate of interest of 36 percent per year on small loans up to $150, as is done in Pennsylvania, and have loanable funds available than to set the rate at 12 percent for such a small loan and have no loanable funds available, thus practically forcing the borrower to the loanshark. In New York and Illinois it is now a felony to lend money at interest rates in excess of 20 and 25 percent respectively. No set interest rate has evolved that will assure an adequate supply of loanable funds and that will block loansharking.

It is a tragedy that all too often it is the person least able to afford usurious interest rates who in desperation borrows from a loanshark. Often the threat of physical violence keeps the debtor from going to the police to expose the illegal activity. "A loan-shark organization's reputation for violence and ruthlessness is the most important factor inducing borrowers to repay their loans."[30] Loansharking is one of the main stays of the underworld in its illegal operations. After gambling, loansharking is the second highest source of revenue for organized crime.[31]

Credit Abuses by Buyers

Not all buyers are honest. Some of them abuse the use of credit deliberately. These include the ones who fail to pay or refuse to pay for the money or goods they have received. Some people buy goods on the installment plan, make a minimum down payment, and then fail to pay any more until the goods are repossessed, thereby securing the use of the merchandise for what is, in effect, a small rental. Another abuse is that of excessive wear and tear on goods, as a result of which they have a smaller repossession value. Actually, losses such as these constitute one of the expenses of the credit business for which all users of credit must pay in the form of higher prices.

CONTROLLING CONSUMER CREDIT

Problems of Regulating Prices and Practices

The first problem in controlling credit is regulating cash lenders. Consumer borrowers in most states are protected by varying versions of the Uniform Small Loan Law, which sets a maximum interest rate on the unpaid balance of 3 percent per month on the first $100 and 2 percent per month on $100 to $300, with no further charges permitted. The Uniform Small Loan Law specifies the method to be used in computing charges on unpaid balances, permits loans to be repaid faster than the time agreed upon, and requires the lender to give the borrower a written statement of the terms of the loan. This law forbids judgment notes, salary buying, and tie-in sales of merchandising, and it outlaws misleading and fraudulent advertising. In addition, it forbids certain other practices.*

Every state, except Arkansas, has statutory maximum small-loan rates, but some states, such as Mississippi, South Carolina, and Tennessee, have little small loan protection for consumers. Oregon has no maximum rate for revolving credit. Maryland has no maximum rate for home repair loans, while Connecticut and Kentucky have no maximum rate for loans on goods other than automobiles and no maximum rate for revolving credit plans. All other states have regulations that establish the maximum rates that can be charged for installment sales of automobiles, revolving credit plans, and other goods.[32]

Good legislation recognizes the greater expenses incurred in making small loans by permitting monthly charges on unpaid balances up to 3 percent. The Pennsylvania law, for instance, permits charges of 3 percent a month on the first $150, 2 percent up to $300, and 1 percent up to $600. The rate drops to 6 percent a year twenty-four months after the date of the loan. Legal rates that are too low tend to cause legitimate lenders to leave a state. The vacuum thus created is filled by loansharks, whose charges are excessive and whose practices are unethical.

The second problem is that of regulating the prices and practices of installment sellers. The courts have ruled that the extension of credit by a retailer is an integral part of the sale of merchandise and not a loan of

* See Barbara A. Curran, *Trends in Consumer Credit Legislation* (Chicago: University of Chicago Press, 1965), pp. 144–157, for the entire draft of the Uniform Small Loan Law.

money. Consequently, installment credit sales are generally not covered by usury laws or small-loan legislation. Indiana and Wisconsin were the first states to deal with this situation by enacting legislation in 1935 designed to control retail installment selling and financing. Other states were slow to follow, but an increasing number of abuses led to the enactment of regulatory laws in every state, except Arkansas. Thirty-one states and the District of Columbia have enacted the Uniform Commercial Code, which provides additional protection for the consumer. On one significant subject the code states, "Regulatory statutes have long been concerned with the abuse of the consumer through the continuous consolidation of separate purchase obligations and the retention of title or a security interest of all goods purchased until all debt is paid, so that the consumer never acquires absolute ownership even of his earliest purchases."[33] Although the code does not prohibit this practice, there must be a "conspicuous disclosure" of such a clause in the contract, and there are strict limitations on its enforcement.

Today the state of New York has the most comprehensive and stringent sales-financing law of all the states. New York is also one of the few states that effectively regulates installment sales of automobiles. The New York law requires full disclosure of the terms of sale and sets upper limits on credit charges. On new cars the limit is $7 a year per $100 of principal balance, $10 for used cars not more than two years old, and $13 for all other used cars. Buyers may purchase their insurance wherever they wish, premiums are controlled, and the contract must specify what coverages are included. Buyers are informed of their rights in case of repossession and are told how and to whom to make complaints.

Truth-in-Lending Legislation

Paul Douglas, former senator, professor of economics, and past president of the American Economic Association, introduced a bill into the 86th, 87th, 88th, and 89th Congresses known as the "Truth-in-Lending Bill." The bill's full title was "A Bill to Assist in the Promotion of Economic Stabilization by Requiring the Disclosure of Finance Charges in Connection with the Extension of Credit." Hearings were held before a subcommittee of the Senate Committee on Banking and Currency in 1960, 1961, and 1963. The testimony and exhibits presented at these hearings fill 3,962 pages.[34] Hearings held in 1967 added another 1,221 pages of testimony.[35] The opposition from lending institutions, retailers, and their trade associations was so strong that these bills were blocked year after year until finally, in 1968, Congress passed and the president signed into law the Consumer Credit Protection Act, Public Law 90–321, more popularly known as the Truth-in-Lending Act.

The first and major provisions of this act became effective July 1, 1969. All lenders of money and sellers of goods on time who charge interest and/or finance charges must give to the lender or buyer in writing the full cost of finance charges in both the dollar amount and the true annual percentage rate of interest. A major exemption was made allowing the home mortgage industry not to disclose the full dollar cost of the mortgage. Full disclosure — the truth — it was felt, might be too much of a shock to the home buyer. On some mortgages the buyer would then be made aware of the fact that the interest was equal to or greater than the price of the house. A special exemption is also provided for installment purchases on items costing $25 or less; items costing $25 to $75 are exempt if the finance charge is less than $5 and up to $7.50 in finance charges are allowed on purchases of more than $75 without requiring disclosure of the interest rate and other credit charges.

On July 1, 1970, another provision of the act became effective. The first 75 percent of a debtor's take-home pay became exempt from garnishment, and a weekly pay check of $48 or less, after deductions, no longer could be garnisheed. In addition, the law stipulates that an employee may not be fired the first time his or her pay has been garnisheed.

In 1975 additional protection was given to the credit card user. Regulations under the Truth-in-Lending Act spell out the procedures that must be followed by the creditor in making prompt correction of billing mistakes. These regulations require the creditor to acknowledge all letters pointing out possible errors in billing within thirty days of receipt. No finance charges are to be made on the disputed amount if the creditor has made a mistake. In addition, if the credit buyer has a problem with property or services purchased with a credit card, she has the right not to pay the remaining amount due if she first tries in good faith to return the item or give the seller a chance to correct the problem.

A problem that has developed since the passage of the Truth-in-Lending Act has to do with revolving charge accounts. Revolving charge accounts are open accounts, usually carried with stores and used with bank or store credit cards, to which a person may add charges as he or she is paying off previous charges. Revolving charge accounts are also referred to as "open-end credit" and are characterized by a plan that has the three following aspects: first, the creditor may permit the customer to make purchases (or loans) from time to time, usually by means of a credit card; second, the customer has the privilege of paying the balance in full or in installments; and third, the finance charge may be computed by the creditor from time to time on an *outstanding* unpaid balance.[36]

It is this third aspect of open-end credit that has confused many consumers. Creditors can compute finance charges on revolving charge accounts by one of three methods. The "previous balance method" is traditionally used by retailers and is the most costly to the borrower. The finance charges are imposed upon the amount of the "previous balance" and do not take into account any payments, returns, or purchases during the billing cycle. For example, if you receive a bill for $100 and pay part of that amount ($50), your next month's bill (assuming no other purchases) will show finance charges of $1\frac{1}{2}$ percent computed upon the "previous balance" of $100 ($1.50). This will be added to your balance remaining unpaid ($50.00) for a "new balance" of $51.50. This is clearly permissible according to the Truth-in-Lending Act. The act does not prohibit or require any particular balance computation method; it simply requires that the consumer be informed of what method is being used.

The "average daily balance" method is used by some creditors. More than two-thirds of the banks using BankAmericard and Master Charge cards use the "average daily balance" method, having switched from the "adjusted balance" method in an effort to raise revenue. This method relates the finance charge only to an amount which is the sum of the actual amounts outstanding each day during the billing period, divided by the number of days in the billing period. Payments are credited on the exact date of receipt. By this method, early payment of one's account or a payment larger than the "minimum payment due" will result in a smaller finance charge.

Some creditors calculate finance charges by using the "adjusted balance" method, which relates the rate of finance charges to the balance remaining in the account after deducting payments and credits. This is the least costly for the borrower.

The method used by the creditor may mean that the borrower is paying anywhere from a 0 to 36 percent finance charge, even when the quoted rate is 18 percent per year. The 18 percent per year rate may run as high as 66 percent per year, depending on the method of computing it.

The basic purpose of the Truth-in-Lending Act is to give to borrowers of money and the buyers of goods and services on credit the information to which they have a right. Nothing has been included in the act that sets rates of interest. It was hoped that with full disclosure of credit terms and costs consumers would be motivated to shop around for the best credit deal. A 1970 survey made by the Federal Reserve Board showed the degree of success the act has had in accomplishing this purpose. In comparing the 1970 survey with one made just before the act went into effect, the board reported to Congress that "significant improvement" in the knowledgeability of consumers was not indicated. Table 12-2 shows the percentages of re-

TABLE 12-2. Survey of Consumer Borrowers' Awareness of Interest Rates

Type of Loan	Percent Not Aware of Interest Rate Paid	
	1969	1970
First mortgages	26.7	12.7
Home improvement	35.0	27.3
New automobiles	26.6	21.4
Used automobiles	40.4	33.8
Appliances and furniture	57.7	41.6
Personal loans	42.6	27.8
Retail charge accounts	48.1	32.2

Source: Annual Report to Congress on Truth in Lending for the Year 1970, Board of Governors of the Federal Reserve System, Washington, D.C., Jan. 4, 1971, Appendix B.

spondents who said they did not know what interest rates they were paying after the act was passed in 1969, but it also showed a measurable improvement in consumer awareness from 1969 to 1970.

Education of the consumer is vital. The Truth-in-Lending Act sees that the consumer is given the needed information, but many consumers apparently do not care enough to use the valuable information made available to them, or they are not aware of its significance.

Uniform Consumer Credit Code

The National Conference of Commissioners on Uniform Laws has drafted a Uniform Consumer Credit Code (UCCC). The UCCC is a proposal for an overall regulatory law to replace all existing state consumer credit laws. The code would fix the same maximum rates for all types of consumer credit grantors. For example, the maximum code rates for installment credit (loans and sales) are 36 percent per year for the first $300, 21 percent on the next $700, and 15 percent per year on the remainder. But when these graduated rates yield less than 18 percent per year, the maximum allowed is 18 percent. The rates for open-end credit sales (revolving credit) are limited to 24 percent per year on the first $500, and 18 percent on the remainder.

This code has received mixed reactions. When it was first proposed, the president's special assistant for consumer affairs and his Consumer Advisory Council approved it. Consumers Union and the Consumer Federation of America, however, opposed the code. The complexity of the code is a factor against it. One important criticism is that the Code would raise the maximum finance charges considerably in many states. For example, in Massachusetts, if enacted, the maximum annual interest rate on small loans up to $300 would go up from 28 percent to 36 percent, and on revolving credit accounts the rate would go from 18 percent to 24 percent for the first $500.[37] The code's rates are generally higher than existent rates. One reason given for this is that code rates include charges that have traditionally been extra charges for such items as credit investigations, services, and brokerage expenses. In general, lenders have supported the UCCC while consumer groups have opposed it. The UCCC has been introduced into many state legislatures and has become law, in its entirety or in a modified form, in Colorado, Idaho, Indiana, Kansas, Oklahoma, Utah, and Wyoming.

Credit Bureaus

Credit bureaus exist throughout the country to collect information about persons who are interested in establishing credit and about persons who have already established credit. The basic purpose of credit bureaus is to disseminate information to lenders of money and sellers of goods and services on credit about persons seeking such credit. Credit bureaus perform a useful function in protecting the dispensers of credit from being "taken" by the unscrupulous and those who inadvertently or carelessly overextend themselves by going too far into debt. Unfortunately, many abuses have grown out of consumer credit investigations. Errors have been made on occasion, and a person's credit standing ruined without due process. The establishment and maintenance of a good credit rating are important, and anything that jeopardizes one's credit rating is a serious matter.

The serious problems that many persons encountered with regard to consumer credit reporting agencies brought enough public pressure to bear on Congress that the Consumer Credit Reporting Act was passed. It was signed into law in 1970 as Public Law 91–508, and it went into effect in 1971.

IS IT WISE TO BUY ON CREDIT?

The Consumer Must Decide

Whether it is wise to buy on credit depends. Obviously it depends on the size of one's income. There can be no doubt that those whose income is large enough to permit them to buy all necessities and a reasonable number of comforts out of income and savings should pay cash. The cash buyer gets more merchandise for his or her money. If an individual's income and rate of impatience are so adjusted as to make it possible to save the purchase price in advance, he or she gains in several ways. Instead of paying interest, the consumer receives interest on savings. Having cash, the consumer can buy in larger quantities and at opportune times. Instead of paying 10 to 40 percent for the privilege of immediate use, the cash buyer, purchasing with his savings, may save from 10 to 30 percent.

Dropping to the next income group, where maintenance of a cash reserve in the form of a bank deposit is either impossible or uncommon, the answer is somewhat different. In this group family heads often carry fairly substantial amounts of life insurance. Ordinary life (whole-life) and other permanent life insurance contracts carry a loan provision. As a general rule it is unwise to borrow on life insurance contracts, for they are primarily a means of protecting dependents against loss of income. But there are circumstances in which a loan on an insurance policy is justified. A family sufficiently provident to use this means of providing for its future is less likely to fall prey to installment salesmen. Nor is it likely to jeopardize the insurance by borrowing too much or for unnecessary commodities. If such a family finds that the time has come for an addition to household equipment or to replace a car whose expense of operation is increasing because of age or wear, it would be wiser to borrow enough cash on a life insurance policy than to make the purchase on the installment plan. This is a matter of simple arithmetic. An insurance policy loan can be negotiated at a rate of about 8 percent a year. This would be 4 to 10 percent less than the lowest installment credit rate.

There is one serious weakness in this procedure, however. Under an installment plan buyers are bound as tightly as legal instruments can tie them to repay the amount of the loan with interest at regular intervals. Borrowers on a life insurance policy, however, are under no compulsion to repay the loan. It is easy to permit a loan to run indefinitely. In such a case interest charges would mount and the advantage would be lost.

Dropping to the next income group, where the weekly income is so small as to prevent the purchase of very little, if any, life insurance if an adequate plane of living is to be maintained, there are few alternatives to the expensive method of installment buying. Membership in a credit union or a savings and loan association makes it possible to borrow at a rate not exceeding 12 percent. The personal loan departments of commercial banks charge from 12 to 18 percent on declining balances. Consumers in this income group should compare these various rates with finance charges on the installment purchase plans. For any credit transaction, the borrower or buyer of goods and services on time, since the passage of the Truth-in-Lending Act, has the necessary information to decide where he or she can obtain the financing at the lowest interest rate.

A large volume of installment sales is made to this last group. And it is for this group that it is most difficult to answer the question as to whether it is wise to buy on credit. It must be recognized that installment buying, even though expensive, is often helpful to consumers in this lower-income group, particularly those who find it psychologically difficult to save in anticipation of a purchase. For such buyers the installment plan combines immediate satisfaction with incentive and a method of so-called "forced saving."

ECONOMICS OF CONSUMER CREDIT

Does Installment Buying Increase One's Income?

Economists are not agreed on whether credit does or does not expand purchasing power. One writer contended that it merely accelerates it. There is no magic in this form of credit, he pointed out, that would enable buyers to spend more than they receive. It is a device that makes it possible for consumers to use the income they do have to buy what they want sooner than they otherwise could. Another writer, on the other hand, stoutly defended the idea that "installment credit . . . does not simply advance purchasing power; it may augment purchasing power."

A borrower may work harder so as to meet his or her payments. But many worker-borrowers are paid wages and salaries that cannot and do not fluctuate with degrees of effort. And one may well ask, "How can purchasing power be increased by charging prices in excess of cash prices?"

For most buyers, the installment credit plan is a means of mortgaging future income. With the first installment loan the consumer is ahead in his store of goods, but from that point on he is paying on the loan, which limits his purchases in the future. If he were able to make that first purchase for cash, then save instead of having to make payments, he would be ahead instead of behind in his financial position. This means that what is spent now cannot be spent for something else in the future. Installment buying simply advances purchasing power at the time. This is very important for consumers to realize. As individuals and as a group, consumers are prone to magnify the importance of goods in the present, while at the same time underestimating the importance of cash in the future. It is well to remember that after the first thrill of possession has passed, the burden of paying for a good or service for one, two, or three years is likely to grow from month to month.

For every consumer who buys on the installment plan, the days of reckoning come with monotonous regularity. Unless an individual can be reasonably sure of an increasing income in the future, he or she had better balance carefully the present utility of the desired goods or services with the future utility of the cash exchanged for them. A generation ago a business economist said, "It is too bad that we have not had as much money spent in instructing the *consumer* in reasons why he or she should not get entangled in installment buying. If every dollar spent in urging installment buying were met with another dollar to point out the disadvantages, I am sure a great many prospective installment customers would be guided away from the pitfalls of installment buying."

Does Consumer Credit Cause Recessions?

Affirmative and negative responses to this question are included in a massive study published in six volumes by the Board of Governors of the Federal Reserve System.[38] The view that overextension of consumer credit can cause a recession may be summarized in four parts. First, consumer credit adds to the amount of money in circulation. The $164 billion of consumer installment credit greatly exceeds the total cash in circulation. Second, credit is extended to those most likely to be laid off early in a business decline. This would cause a further decline in production, especially in durable-goods industries. In other words, a decline in the rate of debt increase could cause a decrease in production. Third, there is no effective control by government. Fourth, there is no effective control by the market.

Some business managers and business-economists believe that the influence of consumer credit on economic stability is slight and that the market provides adequate self-correcting controls. Three staff members of the Board of Governors concluded that "consumer installment credit has often been a factor in changes in the level of business activity, but it has not been the principal cause of such changes." It has, however, been a leading and an amplifying force in economic fluctuations. The major influence of consumer credit has been to accelerate booms. It has less often been an aggravating factor during recessions.

The board decided on the basis of their study not to ask for standby control powers. Critics said this decision rested on such ancient arguments as these: industry self-regulation is adequate; consumers have a right to spend as they wish; and the market will automatically correct for any excesses. During World War II the Board of Governors did regulate the volume of consumer credit by establishing high minimum down payments and a shorter time period for repayment. Some economists think such controls should be restored. Then they could be used, if necessary, without having to wait for Congress to enact legislation under pressure of an emergency. A debate also centers around the question of whether the Federal Reserve System should restrict total credit available during prosperity periods and/or should have and use selective credit controls at such times.

The answer to the question, "Do movements in consumer installment borrowing make the economy significantly more unstable?" appears to be "Not significantly." They are a source of changes in general business conditions but not a major part of the problem. Since World War II they have been markedly less important than, for example, swings in inventory accumulation during reversals of business activity.

QUESTIONS FOR REVIEW

1. Why might the United States have developed a "debt syndrome"?
2. In earlier years, what was the attitude toward debt in this country?
3. What are the sources of consumer credit? Which source tends to be most expensive and which least expensive?
4. What are the pros and cons of using credit cards?
5. What are the differences between travel and entertainment credit cards and bank credit cards?
6. What problems have been caused by unsolicited credit cards?
7. What protection does the Fair Credit Billing Act give the borrower?
8. What does it cost to buy on credit? Why is there no one answer to this question?
9. What are reasons for using credit?
10. What are reasons for not using credit?
11. What are some problems of debt consolidations?
12. If a person gets over-extended with debt, what steps should be taken to correct the problem?
13. What does the Equal Credit Opportunity Act provide for the borrower?
14. What protection does the Truth-in-Lending Law give a borrower?
15. What is the purpose of a credit bureau?
16. What is the Consumer Credit Reporting Act?

PROJECTS

1. Interview a loan officer at a bank, a small loan company, or a credit union about slow payers, nonpayers, and repossessions.

2. List all the places one may borrow money in your community and find out what each lending agency charges for a $300 loan for one year to be paid back in monthly installments.

3. What credit cards are available at the banks in your community? What interest rates do the banks charge for the use of the credit cards and what line of credit will be extended?

4. Survey ten different kinds of retail outlets and find out what credit cards, if any, they will accept.

5. Discuss one of the consumer credit acts mentioned in the chapter with an officer of a bank, a small loan company, a credit union, or a retail outlet and get his or her opinion about it.

6. Complete Table 12-1 for your community.

7. Have a debate in class on the pros and cons of consumer credit.

8. Find out all you can about the consumer credit counseling services available in your community.

9. Interview ten students who have borrowed money or purchased goods on credit. Find out if they knew the rate of interest charged, and whether they shopped around for the lowest interest rate.

10. Interview one credit retailer and ask how important selling on credit is to his or her business.

REFERENCES

1. *U.S. News & World Report,* 24 Nov. 1975, p. 63.
2. *Bankruptcy Filings by Class,* Administrative Office of the United States Courts, Washington, D.C., 1975.
3. *The American Legion Magazine,* Sept. 1975, p. 18.
4. *McCall's,* May 1975, p. 104.
5. George Katona, et al., *Survey of Consumer Finances* (Ann Arbor, Mich.: Survey Research Center, University of Michigan, 1972).
6. "Installment Credit—Total Outstanding and Net Charge," *Federal Reserve Bulletin* 62 (July 1976): A46.
7. *Ibid.*
8. *Ibid.*
9. Letter received from Credit Union National Association, Inc., dated 9 Dec. 1975.
10. Letter received from National Consumer Finance Association, dated 16 Dec. 1975.
11. *Media & Consumer,* March 1975, p. 4.
12. L. Mandell, *Credit Card Use in the United States* (Ann Arbor, Mich.: Institute for Social Research, 1972), pp. 22–29.
13. *The National Observer,* 5 April 1975, p. 9.
14. *Business Week,* 22 June 1974, pp. 102–104.
15. *Science Digest,* June 1975, pp. 58–65.

16. *The Washington Post,* 8 June 1975, p. F1.
17. *Business Week,* 4 Aug. 1975, p. 53.
18. *Consumer Reports,* March 1975, p. 175.
19. *Ibid.*
20. See *Tables of Bankruptcy Statistics, June 30, 1975,* Administrative Office of the United States Courts, Washington, D.C., 21 May 1976.
21. Charles Neal, *Sense with Dollars* (New York: Doubleday, 1965), p. 10.
22. *Consumer Credit Counseling Service: Plans and Working Suggestions* (Washington, D.C.: National Foundation for Consumer Credit, Inc., 1968), p. 5.
23. *Annual Report to Congress on Truth in Lending for the Year 1974,* Board of Governors of the Federal Reserve System, 3 Jan. 1975, pp. 11–12.
24. Warren G. Magnuson and Jean Carper, *The Dark Side of the Marketplace* (Englewood Cliffs, N.J.: Prentice-Hall, 1968), p. 118.
25. *Federal Register,* 18 Nov. 1975, p. 53506.
26. *Cutler Corp. vs. Latshaw,* 374 Pa. 1, 97 A.2d 234 (1953).
27. *Guides Against Debt Collection Deception* (Washington, D.C.: Federal Trade Commission, 30 June 1965, as amended 14 June 1968), p. 1.
28. *St. Petersburg Times Parade,* 28 Sept. 1975, p. 6.
29. Lawrence J. Kaplan and Salvatore Matteis, "The Economics of Loansharking," *American Journal of Economics and Sociology* 27 (1968): 239.
30. John M. Seidl, "Let's Compete with Loan Sharks," *Harvard Business Review* 48 (1970): 69.
31. *The Challenge of Crime in a Free Society,* Report by the President's Commission on Law Enforcement and Administration of Justice (Washington, D.C.: Government Printing Office, 1967), p. 189.
32. *Consumer Loan and Sales Finance Rate and Regulation Chart,* compiled by National Consumer Finance Association, Washington, D.C., April 1975.
33. Sidney Rutberg, "The New York Law Has Built-In Protection For Consumers," *Home Furnishings Daily* 37 (23 Dec. 1964): 2.
34. *Consumer Credit Labeling Bill,* Hearings Before a Subcommittee of the Committee on Banking and Currency, U.S. Senate, 86th Congress, 2d Session, S. 2755, 1960; *Truth-in-Lending Bill,* U.S. Senate, 87th Congress, 1st Session, S. 1740, 1961; *Truth-in-Lending Bill,* U.S. Senate, 88th Congress, 1st and 2d Sessions, S. 750.
35. *Consumer Credit Protection Act,* Hearings Before the Subcommittee on Consumer Affairs of the Committee on Banking and Currency, U.S. House of Representatives, 90th Congress, 1st Session, H.R. 11601, 1967.
36. *Consumer Credit Policy Statement No. 4,* Federal Trade Commission News Release, 7 May 1970.
37. Roger Spooner Barrett and Christian T. Jones, *Summary of State Consumer Credit Laws and Rates* (Chicago: Household Finance Corp., 1976), pp. 12–13, 30.
38. Board of Governors of the Federal Reserve System, *Consumer Installment Credit, Part I, Growth and Import I, II; Part II, Conference on Regulation I, II; Part III, Views on Regulation* (Washington, D.C.: Government Printing Office, 1957).

CHAPTER 13

DO HIGH PRICES AND BRAND NAMES ASSURE TOP QUALITY?

BRANDS, PRICES, AND QUALITY OF PACKAGED GOODS

Why Brands?

Consumers want to have confidence in the products they buy. The variety and complexity of products makes this a difficult want to satisfy, so consumers have become dependent upon brand names, whether they wish to be or not. Where our grandparents would have purchased ten pounds of sugar from a barrel packaged in a brown paper bag, today we must decide whether to buy Jack Frost, Domino, Godchaux, Great Western, or Franklin sugar packaged in a variety of container sizes, shapes, colors, and prices.

The consumer has become dependent upon brand names, and the manufacturers have accentuated and stimulated this dependency by spending billions of dollars on advertising that keeps brand names constantly before the consumer. In some respects, what has developed is a Pavlovian response: consumers buy Brand X because the ads tell them to buy Brand X.

Brand name terminology may be a little confusing, but in general there are four types of brands:

1. *National brands.* These are nationally advertised, sold in a wide variety of stores, generally near the top of the price line, and found in most areas. Examples would be Del Monte canned fruits and vegetables, Heinz ketchup, Tide soap, Motorola television, Chrysler cars, and Wrigley chewing gum.
2. *Private or in-store brands of major national retail chains.* Nationally advertised but to a lesser degree, generally priced below national brands, sold only in the chains' own stores, and their stores are found in most areas. Sears, Roebuck & Co. and the Great Atlantic and Pacific Tea Company sell a wide variety of products under their own store brand name.
3. *Private or in-store brands of regional retail chains.* Similar to the brands of the major national retail chains, but distribution is limited to

its own stores in its region; for example, in western Pennsylvania there are the Revco health-and-beauty-aid store chain and the Golden Dawn food store chain.

4. *Private brands.* Manufactured and distributed primarily emphasizing low price with no advertising; the products may be found in a variety of types of stores, with the prices nearly always lower than the prices of the national or regional brands; the brand name is generally unfamiliar to the consumer.

The national brand tries to get consumer attention and loyalty through a vast network of national advertising; the private in-store brand of the national chains tries to get a high degree of store loyalty; while the "off brand" or unknown brand tries to get the consumer to buy at the point-of-purchase because of its low price. It is important for the consumer to understand the types of brands, the methods used in selling the brands, the pricing of brands, and—the most difficult task—quality comparison of the brands.

The manufacturer and/or seller does not want you to buy just any product. It is essential to him that you buy his product; and he cannot be sure this will be done unless his product has a distinct identity in your mind. Therefore, each manufacturer differentiates his product from his competitor's products. In a number of cases a single manufacturer will produce differentiated products himself which compete with each other, hoping in this way to get an even larger share of the total market. This has brought about a great deal of brand proliferation. The Minnesota Pollution Control Agency reported a 282 percent increase since 1971 in the number of brand selections of hair coloring products, a 261.5 percent increase in the number of stomach relief preparations, and a 260 percent increase in the number of antiseptics and deodorants.[1]

What Is in a Package?

When consumers shop for packaged merchandise the guides they use to measure quality in relation to price are a mixture of experience, tips from friends, advertising, slogans, brands, trademarks, labels, and comments from salesclerks. The buyer cannot see, smell, or feel the contents of a package until after purchase. In the absence of quality grades on labels, buyers must rely to a considerable degree on price as a measure of quality. This makes it easy for sellers to capitalize on consumer ignorance by the simple process of raising prices. Without a word of misrepresentation on the part of sellers, many consumers conclude that high price is an indication of quality. Which would you buy—an RCA color television for $595 or a Georgetown color television for $495? This lack of confidence and consumers' lack of knowledge make them lean heavily on the familiar, the heavily advertised, and generally higher priced products.

Current marketing practices are designed to create in the minds of consumers an association of quality with a particular brand name. By repetitive advertising consumers are told that the advertised brand assures high quality; but rarely are they given any factual evidence. Consumers simply cannot rely solely on brand names as guides to quality. The quality of a product is determined by the producer, and the producer can improve or deteriorate the quality as he or she sees fit and still continue to use the same brand name. Nor can consumers rely on their own judgment. Price is no indication of quality. As a result consumers are engaged in a game of blindman's buff in which they pay a high price for the privilege of playing.

Are Brand Names Dependable Guides?

If a buyer were to purchase by brand name, which brands should she buy? Knowledgeable consumers know that the private brand merchandise sold by giant retailers has been made by large processors who also sell their own nationally advertised brands. These private brands are competitive in quality and in price with the brands of most of the manufacturers. Nationally advertised brands are likely to be overpriced partly because of the expenses incurred in advertising. The majority of the merchandise sold by Sears, Roebuck is sold under Sears' brands, although the merchandise may have been made by national brand manufacturers.

Although individual consumers cannot make laboratory tests to ascertain the quality of packaged merchandise, testing organizations such as Consumers Union and Consumers' Research can and do. The results of these studies always lead to the same conclusion, that there is no dependable correlation among brand, price, and quality.

There is a reluctance on the part of manufacturers who make both national and private brands and retailers who sell private brands to let the consumer know which company makes the private brands. The government does not require that this information be on the label; it requires that either the name of the manufacturer or the name of the distributor be on the label, but not both. Rarely does the consumer know who is the manufacturer of the private brand. Even if the consumer is able to find out what company makes a particular private brand, there is no assurance that a manufacturer's national brand and private brand are the same. There may be only superficial differences between the products or there may be substantive differences in quality.

What Do Brand Names Cost?

It is relatively simple for consumers to make their own price comparison studies of national brands versus private brands. The following illustrations are just a few of the types of studies one may make. It must be understood that the comparisons are between *comparable* not necessarily *identical* products.

The Great Atlantic and Pacific Tea Company (A & P) ran a series of advertisements in which price comparisons were shown between national brands and comparable A & P brands. One advertisement listed thirty-seven products of a wide variety with the following results: The total price for the national brands was $23.85, while the A & P price total was $18.90. The savings were $4.95, or 20.75 percent.

In a Thorofare supermarket one gallon of the national brand of laundry bleach, Clorox, was priced at 75 cents; the regional brand, Auston A-1, at 69 cents; and the store brand, Thorofare, at 67 cents. The label of each product listed the ingredients as $5\frac{1}{4}$ percent sodium hypochlorite and $94\frac{3}{4}$ percent inert matter.

A 3.5-ounce bar of glycerin soap proved to work as well in keeping mirrors and eyeglasses steam and fog free as Everclear, a national brand. The glycerin soap cost 28.5 cents an ounce, and Everclear cost $7.00 an ounce.[2]

A price comparison of thirty grocery items showed the average total cost of the items—priced in ten different food chain stores—to be $14.43; the store brand total of the same thirty items was $12.19, a savings of $2.24, or 15.5 percent.

While Kroger brand pure petroleum jelly was selling at 79 cents for a 16-ounce jar, the national brand petroleum jelly, Vaseline, was selling in the same store for 99 cents for a 12-ounce jar, or $1.32 for 16 ounces, which is 67 percent higher than the store brand. The prices of private brand appliances produced by national brand appliance manufacturers have a differential of anywhere from 14 to 17 percent, depending on the deal, in favor of the private brand customers. The president of a supermarket chain said that an attractive price spread between private and national brands is crucial in spurring sales of the private brands, and if prices are brought too close together, sales of the private brand will drop off appreciably.[3]

Again it must be emphasized that these price comparisons are based on comparable, not necessarily identical, goods. Manufacturers of national brands attempt to defend their products as being superior on the bases of quality, quality control, and just general, greater "know-how." When products have the identical percentage of the same ingredients, this makes one wonder how they can be different; but manufacturers seem convinced of their own products' superiority. So, with little or no quality information or grade labeling, consumers must judge for themselves in areas where they are without the expertise needed to make intelligent choices.

There was growth in the private brand business during the mid-1970s because the recession made people more concerned about prices. Households having annual incomes of $15,000 increased their private-brand grocery dollar spending from 26 percent in 1971 to 40 percent in 1974. One study showed that in ten major categories of packaged goods, private-brand merchandise accounted for 13 percent of total dollar expenditures, and some 60 percent of all U.S. households purchased private-brand products in at least one of the ten categories.[4]

Food   There was little correlation between price and quality in a comparative testing and rating of frozen chicken pot pies conducted by Consumers Union. Of eight brands rated in *Consumer Reports*, the prices ranged from 3.4 cents to 8.6 cents per ounce.[5] A better measure of their value than the price per ounce is the cost of their protein content. The daily allowance of protein recommended for many persons is 60 grams; the cost for one-third of that amount (20 grams) was 79 cents for Stouffer's and 52 cents for Swanson's.[6]

The results of the test of the quality of frozen chicken pot pies based on sensory judgments by Consumers Union consultants showed that among the two rated "Good" to "Very Good" the price per ounce was 5.5 cents for the one and 8.6 cents for the other, with one costing 56 percent more than the other. Only one was rated "Good," and it cost 3.5 cents per ounce. Three were rated "Fair" to "Good" and cost 3.4 to 4.6 cents per ounce. One was rated "Fair" at 3.4 cents per ounce, and one was rated "Variable—from Fair to Good" at 3.4 cents per ounce.

Nutritionists agree that there is not enough nutritional difference among the various kinds of orange juice to matter; however, prices for orange juice vary a great deal. In one price survey, fresh orange juice cost 6.70 cents for a 4-ounce serving, chilled cost 4.36 cents, canned cost 4.36 cents, and frozen cost 3.35 cents, just half as much as fresh orange juice. Eighty percent of all orange juice shipped out of Florida is frozen concentrate. In one price check the six-ounce can of frozen concentrate varied in price from a low of 20 cents for a private brand to a high of 35 cents for a national brand, or 75 percent higher than the private brand. The Florida State Department of Citrus insists that all frozen concentrate has the same nutritional value.[7]

In a price survey made by Geneva College students in Beaver Falls, Pennsylvania, students found that a one-pound loaf of sliced, white bread could sell for as low as 37 cents or as high as 68 cents. Milk, in one-half gallon cartons, Grade A white, was selling for a low of 60 cents and a high of 89 cents.

Two additional illustrations emphasize price variations. A check of sugar prices in one area found sugar selling for a low of 35 cents a pound and a high of $1.05 a pound. Proctor & Gamble's Pringles, a potato chip made from dried potatoes, sold for $1.71 a pound, while traditionally made potato chips were sold for 93 cents a pound.

Cosmetics   The consumer's propensity to follow price as a guide to quality has been profitably used by the sellers of cosmetics. Buyers are unable to judge quality on the basis of performance. The satisfaction derived from using such products may be, in part, the result of ideas implanted in consumers' minds by advertising. Large sums of money are spent for competitive advertising by the sellers of cosmetics. The margins between cost of manufacture and selling price are high; one face cream, which costs $1 to make, sells at retail for $6. Note the wide spread in price between famous brand cosmetics and the private brands. Expensive cosmetic products like those made by Borghese may sell for $10 to $20, while comparable products with the Revlon name sell for $2.50 to $4.00. Few people know that Revlon owns Borghese and that ingredients, according to Revlon, are for the most part the same in all Revlon-made products.[8] Inexpensive cosmetics "often work better, and are safer than expensive, complicated ones."[9] The hormones and chemical thinners used as moisturizers in some high-priced cosmetics may be dangerous. Lanolin oil, a common face-cream in-gredient, varies in cost from 10 cents to $1.60 a pound.[10] One after-shave lotion sells for $10 for six ounces, while another sells for 99 cents for the same size, and both serve the same purpose adequately. One company has made a specialty of copying the fragrances of famous brand perfumes. For example, it sells a fragrance similar to Shalimar for $14 per ounce, as com-pared to $35 an ounce for the Shalimar brand.[11]

Cosmetics are basically similar. Many private brands are made by com-panies that produce the expensive nationally advertised brands. But retail sellers have learned that lower prices do not necessarily increase sales. This is because national brand advertising has succeeded in convincing many buyers that a high-priced brand assures high quality.

It is not necessary to pay a high price to obtain good cosmetics. Many products selling at low prices contain pure, high-quality ingredients and are skillfully blended. Manufacturers of paraffin and petrolatum blends manu-facture the basic cream for face cream by the ton. Except for differences in perfuming and packaging, high-priced and low-priced creams may come from the same batch. But until cosmetics are adequately labeled, it will continue to be difficult to compare them.

Dentifrices Millions of Americans dutifully brush their teeth after every meal. They spend millions of dollars for toothbrushes and more than $350 million annually for toothpastes and toothpowders. For many years the American Dental Association (ADA) has assured consumers that a simple solution of salt and soda is as effective a dentifrice as most products available in retail stores, with the exception of the toothpastes that contain fluoride. But the ADA is no match for the dentifrice-makers who spend millions of dollars telling consumers that if they use a particular product they will have gleaming, white teeth, no mouth odors, and fewer cavities. The ADA emphasizes that many dentifrices are essentially scouring agents. There are no significant differences among brands, except for those few that the ADA certifies as having therapeutic properties.

In Table 13-1 the results of a survey of toothpaste prices at just one drugstore are shown. The store stocked nine different brands of toothpaste in nine different sizes and eleven different prices. The price per ounce varied from a low of 9.6 cents for Revco Stannous Fluoride, 7-ounce size, to a high of 27.9 cents per ounce for Close-Up, in the 1.4-ounce size. These prices indicated nothing about quality; in many ways prices tend to confuse rather than help as indicators of quality.

TABLE 13-1. Toothpaste Price Survey

Brand	Price Per Ounce (in cents)								
	1.4	1.5	2.7	3.0	4.6	5.0	6.4	7.0	8.0
Aim			.57		.74				.99
Close-Up	.39		.63		.72		.84		
Colgate		.39		.63		.84		.84	
Crest		.39		.63		.84		.99	
Gleem II		.39		.63		.84		.99	
MacLeans								.99	
Pepsodent				.53				.99	
Revco									
Super White								.99	
Stannuous Fluoride								.67	
Ultra Brite				.63				.75	

Note: Prices checked Jan. 15, 1976, at Revco Drugstore (regional chain), Beaver Falls, Pennsylvania.

Drugs Brand names for drugs have created a serious problem for consumers in the market. Consumers' lack of medical knowledge, the emotional impact of sickness, and price variations create a situation in which it is difficult to make an intelligent decision. The *brand name* of a drug is the manufacturer's proprietary name, for example Schering's Chlor-Trimeton. The *generic name* is a nonproprietary name, or "public" name, applied to specific compounds. The generic name for Chlor-Trimeton is chlorpheniramine maleate. One might call Chevrolet the proprietary name, while the generic name would be automobile. The sellers of drugs try to persuade the consumer to buy by the proprietary (brand) name not the generic name.

Aspirin might properly be called the first real "wonder drug." It is an effective and inexpensive palliative. In addition to relieving the national headache, it provides relief for arthritic pains and many other pains. Long ago the federal government established a definition and standard for aspirin. The product is usually sold in 5-grain tablets, the contents and potency of which must meet the standards specified in the United States Pharmacopoeia or the National Formulary. As a result, consumers may buy any brand of aspirin or unbranded aspirin with assurance that there are no differences in formulas. The differences are in the prices. Yet the sellers of some brands have been successful in persuading consumers that their brands are superior to other brands.

The Federal Trade Commission requested the American Medical Association (AMA) to make a comparative study of two brands of aspirin and three brands of products containing aspirin plus other ingredients. The brands compared were Bayer, St. Joseph, Bufferin, Excedrin, and Anacin. The AMA reported that they found no significant difference in the pain relieving effects of the five products, that price was no measure of effectiveness, and that the less expensive brands compared favorably with the expensive ones.

In one price check a bottle of 100 Bayer aspirin tablets sold for 92 cents.

In the same store the store brand sold for 27 cents for 100 tablets, and the store brand bottle of 1,000 aspirin tablets sold for $1.99.

An unusually wide price spread was found by the author in one case where the brand name drug Chlor-Trimeton sold at a conventional drugstore for $3.85 per 100 tablets. It was priced at a discount mail-order prescription service store for $3.25 per 100. Then a medical friend procured it under its generic name, chlorpheniramine maleate, at a net cost of 15 cents per 100. This was an unusual case, but it indicates the magnitude of the price spread for the same generic drug.

The 1962 drug amendments to the Food, Drug, Cosmetic Act are an enduring monument to the late Senator Estes Kefauver. They were enacted as a result of patient and painstaking investigation by the senator and his staff. In the hearings on the proposed legislation, drug company pricing policies and practices were made public.[12] There was a time when physicians writing prescriptions used the generic names of drugs and the quantities to be included in a compound. That method of writing and filling prescriptions has almost passed out of use. Today pharmaceutical firms put together combinations of drugs under trademarked brand names. Potassium penicillin G, a widely used antibiotic, is marketed under several brand names. The firms then hire salespeople, whom they call "detail men," to call on physicians for the purpose of persuading them to prescribe the brand name products of a particular firm. One of the leading pharmaceutical firms had 5,700 employees of whom 1,000 were sales representatives. The pharmaceutical firms have given themselves the attractive name of "ethical drug" firms; the only meaning the word "ethical" has here is that in the trade it refers to trademarked brand name products. An estimated $500 million, or $2,500 per doctor per year, is spent on promoting prescription drugs.

Under the "ethical drug" system of marketing, there is no relation among prices, quality, and brands. The cost of producing a leading mild tranquilizer was found to be seven-tenths of a cent, the price to the retail druggist was 6.5 cents, and the price to the consumer was 10.8 cents. The cost of material, manufacture, and bottling another product was found to be 1.567 cents a tablet, for which the druggist paid 18 cents and the consumer 30 cents.

Several years ago it was found that pharmaceutical firms were selling their products in other countries at prices considerably below the prices being paid by U.S. consumers. For example, Chloromycetin, for which American consumers paid $5.10 for a bottle of sixteen 250-milligram tablets, was sold in other countries for $2.19. Senate committee investigators delved into the prices paid by large nonprofit buyers. It was found that the Military Medical Supply Agency paid $23.63 for 1,000 prednisone tablets for which the commercial wholesale price was $170. Investigators found that prednisone and prednisolone tablets were priced at $17.90 for one hundred 5-milligram tablets. Under the generic drug name the price was $4.50.

More recently, F. Hoffman-LaRoche & Co., a Swiss-based pharmaceutical manufacturer, reported that it sold its Librium tranquilizer, 100 10-

milligram tablets, to wholesalers in Great Britain for 14 cents, in West Germany for $4.38, in Switzerland for $4.75, and in the United States for $5.80. The Monopolies and Mergers Commission of Great Britain had forced LaRoche to reduce the price it charged wholesalers in that country.[13]

The *Fortune Directory* showed the median return on stockholders' equity for the top 500 industrial corporations in 1975 as 11.6 percent.[14] For the pharmaceutical industry, which was third, it was 16.2 percent, or a 40 percent higher return than the median of the 500 largest industrial corporations. For five of the past ten years the *Fortune Directory* has listed the pharmaceutical industry as number one on net return on stockholders' equity, number two for three years, and number three for two years.

A classic case of overcharging on prescription drugs was exposed in a United States government case against five drug companies. They were accused of conspiring to monopolize the market and to restrain trade of certain antibiotics, thus overcharging consumers. Before going to trial, the firms agreed to a cash settlement of the suit, while admitting no wrong-doing. Since that time more than $20 million has been refunded to 888,371 antibiotic purchasers.[15]

A 694-page volume published by the staff of the Federal Trade Commission presents a revealing study of the drug industry and the price variations of prescription drugs.[16] Total prescription drug sales were reported as being $6.8 billion for 1973. Price checks for 418 prescription drugs were made throughout the country, and these checks showed wide variations in the prices of identical drugs. For example, for one drug, Raudixin, the lowest price found was $2.50 and the highest was $11.75, or 370 percent higher. In some cases the highest price for a drug was more than 650 percent higher than the lowest price. For 220 of the 418 drugs the highest price was 150 to 249 percent higher than the lowest price. The report stated, "The observed price dispersion for retail prescription drugs is not an isolated phenomenon — it is a persistent, pervasive, nationwide occurrence."[17]

Additional support for price savings through buying prescription drugs under generic names is shown in Table 13-2, which represents the results of a random-sample study of thirty chain pharmacies and thirty independent pharmacies. The researchers concluded that:

> The results obtained in this investigation tend to confirm the impression that prescriptions written and dispensed generically are cheaper to the patient than those written and dispensed for brand name products of the same drug. As the generic drugs' share of the total retail drug market increases, it is possible that consumer prescription prices will decline. It is also evident that the pharmacists included in this investigation pass on the savings, from lower generic drug costs to the patient.[18]

A number of states have passed laws to help consumers find their way through the maze of prescription drug prices. For example, New York State law requires each pharmacy to have on display a large chart on which must be listed the 150 most frequently prescribed drugs with their usual quantity and prices. Ironically there are a few states with laws prohibiting such

TABLE 13-2. Consumer Prices Per Unit for Selected Items

Product	Mean Generic Price	Mean Brand Price	Lowest Generic Price	RANGE Lowest Brand Price	Highest Generic Price	Highest Brand Price
Tetracycline	$0.095	$0.126	$0.059	$0.060	$0.175	$0.212
Penicillin G	0.085	0.124	0.047	0.059	0.142	0.192
Prednisone	0.066	0.071	0.032	0.040	0.123	0.152
Meprobamate	0.074	0.096	0.044	0.065	0.112	0.155
Reserpine	0.038	0.069	0.022	0.043	0.073	0.103
Digoxin	0.024	0.024	0.015	0.014	0.049	0.041
Chloral hydrate	0.078	0.096	0.048	0.072	0.124	0.154

Source: American Journal of Public Health, 64(1974), p. 980.

display of prices.[19] Some states also prohibit the advertising of prescription drug prices, but the Federal Trade Commission has drafted a rule that will make it illegal for states to have such prohibitions.

Research shows that wide price differences exist between the same brand name prescription drugs. In addition, price differences exist between the same drug under different brand names, and between the same drug under its brand name and its generic name. One price comparison showed that the prescription drug erythromycin sold for $11.40 for 100 tablets under its generic name, but under brand names the prices were $20.30 for SK-Erythromycin, $23.66 for Ethril, and $31.74 for Erypar.[20] The Pharmaceutical Manufacturers Association (PMA), an organization whose 110 member companies account for approximately 95 percent of all prescription drug sales in this country, claims that products that are chemically equivalent (that is, contain the same amounts of the same active ingredients in the same dosage form) may not be *therapeutically* equivalent; that is, they may not be equally effective in treating the patient's disease.* If two drugs have the same bio-availability (the amount of the product's active ingredient that is absorbed into the bloodstream to perform its function), then they are termed bio-equivalent and are therefore therapeutically equivalent.

In 1975 the U.S. Department of Health, Education, and Welfare introduced a plan to set price ceilings on prescription drugs covered by Medicaid and Medicare and produced by more than one company. The program was designed to cut the price of drug reimbursements by prodding doctors to prescribe bioequivalent generic drugs when they are available rather than prescribing by brand name. This plan was expected to save the government about $60 million by 1978, two years after the program became effective. Both the American Medical Association (AMA) and the PMA fought the ruling. The secretary of HEW stated that in 1975, 10 percent of all prescriptions were being written generically, authorizing the pharmacist to

* For a defense of brand name selling see *Brands, Generics, Prices and Quality: The Prescribing Debate After a Decade* (Washington, D.C.: Pharmaceutical Manufacturers Association, 1971).

select the source of the product to be dispensed, and that in major teaching hospitals the selection was delegated to pharmacists about 85 percent of the time. In addition, the secretary pointed out that the frequency of drug recalls made by the Food and Drug Administration was no greater for generic drugs than for brand name products, despite the steady increase in the marketing and use of generic drugs. He emphasized that drug quality is not necessarily a function of price, and that many millions of dollars would be saved without compromising the quality of health care.[21] Thirty-seven states have laws forbidding pharmacists to substitute chemically identical generic drugs for the brand name drug listed on a doctor's pre-scription. The HEW order overrides all such laws, but only for prescriptions purchased under Medicaid and Medicare. The Drug Research Board of the National Academy of Sciences adopted a resolution that pharmacists should be allowed to substitute unless the prescription specifically indicates that they may not.[22]

The Food and Drug Administration has the responsibility to see that generic drugs are equivalent to brand name drugs. If it does its job right, there should be no differences between generic and brand name drugs. In many countries drugs are prescribed only by generic names. A forceful statement on the dispute was made by the chairman of the Council on Drugs of the AMA who testified that, "the question . . . is not should we abolish brand names and use generic names, but when? The sooner the better. It can be done, and it will be a step forward in medicine."[23]

Appliances   Among fifteen clothes dryers, all of which were tested and rated as acceptable by Consumers Union, prices ranged from $150 to $180 for electric dryers and $180 to $290 for gas dryers. For one identical electric dryer model the prices ranged from $170 to $280, and for a gas dryer the prices ranged from $196 to $280. Knowing this price information ahead of time should make it possible for the shopper to compare prices and shop more intelligently.[24]

Differences in prices for no-frost, top-freezer refrigerators among twelve major metropolitan shopping areas "gives the American market-place something of the aspect of a Near East Bazaar."[25] The widest spread in prices from low to high for the identical model was $130. If shoppers had bargained, the price differences might have been even greater. The price range for Gibson was from a low of $399 to a high of $529. The price range for a Frigidaire was from $380 to $474. A Sears Coldspot ranged from $399 to $480 and a Montgomery Ward Signature from $370 to $440.[26]

BARGAINING FOR AN AUTOMOBILE

Should One Pay List Price?

Unlike many other products, automobiles are sold exclusively under brand names. There are three major and one minor U.S. automobile manufacturers whose names are known to nearly everyone. Their products are essentially the same and their list prices are almost the same. But when consumers decide to purchase a car, they soon discover that they are in a maze in which it is difficult to secure dependable information on the basis of which to make rational price comparisons. In the absence of significant price differences, sellers rely on personal selling appeals, discounts, and over-allowances on trade-ins. Price cutting has become the usual practice. This leads to deception and unethical practices. Because of the deception in automobile pricing practices, the Federal Trade Commission instigated an investigation for the purposes of correcting abuses. Testimony given at hearings held by the FTC revealed the following as the most flagrant forms of deception:

- Gimmicking new car prices by deleting "standard" equipment and making it optional from one model year to the next without explaining the change.
- Implying that a customer may purchase this year's model X at a price below last year's without disclosing the difference in equipment between the two.
- Raising prices indirectly by reducing warranty coverage and not disclosing the changes to prospective customers.
- Quoting prices for cars in advertisements without fully explaining the cost of equipment on the car pictured.
- Posting prices that are fictitiously high in order to allow trade-in values far above actual values and give the customer the illusion of a bargain.[27]

The purchase of a new car tends to be an individual bargaining process. The Federal Automobile Disclosure Act requires every seller to attach to the left rear window of each automobile a schedule showing the list price and the prices of all extras, such as freight charges and accessories. That price is the starting point for bargaining. One can estimate a dealer's cost for domestic cars fairly closely by deducting from the "sticker" price 12 percent for subcompact and compact cars, 17 percent for intermediate size cars, 20 percent for full size cars, and 23 percent for high-priced cars.*

For example, the dealer's cost for a new 1976 Chevrolet Impala with no optional equipment was $3,595. The suggested retail price was $4,507. The dealer's cost was 20 percent below the suggested price, or the suggested price was 25 percent above the dealer's cost.[28]

Naive consumers who believe that the published, or sticker, price is the real price may agree to pay the full list price. In addition, they may

---

* *The Consumer Guide Auto Quarterly* gives dealers' costs and manufacturers' suggested retail prices for each model and all optional equipment. This is available at newsstands, along with other automobile price magazines. Car/Puter International, Inc., 1603 Bushwick Ave., Brooklyn, N.Y. 11207, will send you a computer printout showing dealer cost and list prices of any car, with whatever options the buyer wants, along with the name and address of the dealer closest to the buyer who will sell the car at $125 to $200 above cost. This service costs $10.

agree to pay for freight charges that have not been incurred; they may receive a minimum trade-in allowance for their old car; and they may receive few or no accessories. Other consumers who are more knowledgeable and who know how the industry operates know that the list price is a point of departure for bargaining. The author purchased a 1975 Chevrolet Impala V-8 with a selected list of accessories that carried a sticker or manufacturer's suggested list price of $5653.30. The actual price he paid was $4,650, without a trade-in. This was a discount of 17.7 percent.

There seems to be no direct correlation between price and quality. Buyers purchasing the identical car from the same dealer will frequently be charged different prices depending upon their bargaining ability. The Opinion Research Corporation surveyed thirty-four automobile dealers in ten major cities to find the actual selling prices of new automobiles. The survey covered five large-selling models in different size and price classes. Data was provided on the selling prices for the 298 cars in the five models chosen. The discounts on the identical models ranged from 0 to 13 percent for the subcompact; 0 to 15 percent for the compact; 0 to 17 percent for the intermediate size; 1 to 20 percent for the full size; and 0 to 32 percent for the luxury car. Only about six out of every hundred car buyers paid the full sticker price.[29]

The automobile industry has brought upon itself many of the problems of bargaining, discounting, and questionable deals by unrealistic markups. One dealer cited the Oldsmobile 98 as having an unrealistic markup. The sticker price would have given him a gross profit of $1,700 to $1,800, but competition forced him to sell it for a profit of only $300, which he felt was adequate. He said, "I'd like to see Detroit cut prices and then mark cars up realistically."[30]

As to quality, *Consumer Reports* and consumer advocate Ralph Nader and his staff have found that defects in new automobiles crop up almost as frequently in the luxury line as in the economy line.[31]

The most economical way to buy a car is to pay cash, since you save the interest on the loan and you may get a better deal. And yet approximately six out of every ten new automobiles are purchased on some credit plan. This provides another variable in the retail price. After agreeing to a price for the car he or she has chosen, the consumer then enters another never-never land in which the seller has the advantage. Even if the transaction is honest, the cost of credit adds considerably to the price of the automobile. If the buyer has the misfortune to be dealing with an unscrupulous seller, he may agree to pay excessive credit charges without even knowing it.

BRANDS, PRICES, AND QUALITY OF GASOLINE

What Consumers Do Not Know about Gasoline

There are no established federal standards for gasoline. There are hundreds of brands of gasoline, but the brand names are not dependable quality guides. One may buy a local brand at a low price and get a good product or one may buy a nationally advertised brand at a high price and get a product that is no better. When a buyer drives up to a gasoline pump, the forces behind his or her decision to purchase a particular brand of gasoline are a combination of faith and hope, with little actual knowledge. Only a few buyers know the meaning and significance of such terms as "octane rating" or "volatility." Gasoline companies present very little reliable information in their advertising or through their salespeople that might aid the consumer in making the proper choice of gasoline.

What Is Good Gasoline?

The quality characteristics of gasoline include volatility, corrosive effect, gum content, and sulphur content. The antiknock quality of gasoline affects only the detonation and preignition. Volatility influences vapor lock, starting, evaporation loss, warm-up, stalling, acceleration, fuel economy, crankcase oil dilution, and engine cleanliness.

The octane rating of a gasoline is a number that indicates its antiknock qualities. If the octane rating is too low, the gasoline will cause the motor to knock, while a higher octane rating practically eliminates knocking. There are two methods of measuring octane numbers: 1) the research method, which gives higher numbers because the test conditions are less severe; and 2) the motor method. The research octane number is usually higher by six to ten units than the motor octane number. The octane number that the federal government requires to be posted on gasoline pumps is the sum of the research octane number and the motor octane number divided by two $\frac{(R + M)}{2}$ Thus, the number posted on the pumps is about three to five points lower than the research octane number, and three to five points higher than the motor octane number. Generally, it is referred to as the average octane number, or antiknock index.

Testimony presented by W. J. Tancig, head of the chemical division of Consumers Union, before the Federal Trade Commission at the hearings on the FTC proposal for the posting of octane ratings on gasoline pumps emphasized the following points:

1. It is generally agreed that the research octane relates most reliably to the octanes the motorist requires.
2. The prime job of gasoline is to provide octanes which will satisfy that engine.
3. Of all the factors that go into the performance of gasoline octane rating is the single most important factor.
4. If you buy a gasoline for anything else but octanes you are deluding yourself. If you need a mechanic, go to a mechanic. Don't buy gasoline to cure your engine's ills.[32]

In general, gasolines are so standardized that the one basic difference is the octane rating, and even here the "regular" gas of all service stations tends to be quite standardized. There are some differences among gasolines with regard to pollution—from completely lead-free gasolines, to low-lead gasolines, to the regular leaded gasolines. Here the consumer's problem is to be sure that his or her car is equipped to benefit from the use of a no-lead or low-lead gasoline. Beginning with the 1975 model year, all cars are required by the federal government to be equipped with a catalytic converter, which reduces the pollution emissions. Cars thus equipped can use only unleaded gasoline.

There are no objective quality grades of gasoline. In the trade the following eight terms are used to distinguish gasolines according to their octane rating: super premium, premium, subpremium, economy premium, high quality regular, medium regular, regular, and economy regular. In addition, the pollution problem has encouraged petroleum companies to introduce a variety of lead-free, partially lead-free, and supposedly lead-free gasolines, which adds to consumer confusion. The major marketers have brand names for these various "grades." The $\frac{(R + M)}{2}$ octane ratings among these "grades" range from a high of 85 to a low of 95. The higher the compression ratio of a motor, the higher the octane rating requirement.

New automobiles are required by law to be designed to operate effectively using unleaded gasoline with an octane rating of 87 $\frac{(R + M)}{2}$. Most cars built prior to this requirement will operate effectively on regular gasoline with an octane rating of 87 $\frac{(R + M)}{2}$, but many motorists do not know this. Influenced by advertising and the sales talk of a filling station attendant, they buy higher octane gasoline than is needed for their motors.

The secret of maximum gasoline mileage lies in the way a motorist operates his or her car. Buying a higher octane gas than your car's engine requires is a waste of money and increases air pollution. In general the higher the octane, the higher the pollution emissions. The average motorist who buys a higher octane gasoline than he needs pays $50 to $75 a year extra.

The Federal Energy Administration (FEA) has stated that the principal difference between gasoline grades is the ability to resist knock during combustion in an engine. The FEA recommends that motorists buy one or two tanks of gasoline of a lower octane than they are currently using to see if they can economize. If the engine knocks, they should go back to buying the higher octane fuel. If it does not knock, they can keep trying the next lower grade until the car begins to knock, then move back up to the next higher grade. One or two tanks of gasoline that is too low will not hurt a car's engine; damage is done only under sustained knocking conditions. The motorist may notice that, as the car becomes older, the engine's antiknock requirement may increase.[33]

The weight of a car is a very significant factor in how many miles it will travel per gallon. For every 100 pounds of added weight, gas mileage can drop by as much as 4 percent. Each year the Environmental Protection Agency (EPA) publishes the comparative fuel economy ratings of all models of all cars sold in the United States. The EPA tests cars for city and highway driving and then averages these results for a third measure called the city-highway figure. In the 1976 tests, Chevrolet Chevette, Datsun B-210, and the Suburu came in first, getting a city-highway rating of 33 miles per gallon. The Jaguar and Rolls-Royce came in last with an average of 11 miles per gallon. EPA figures showed that the overall mileage for 1976 cars improved to an average 17.6 miles per gallon. The 1975 models averaged 15.6 m.p.g., while the 1974 models only averaged 13.9 m.p.g.[34]

There are no inexpensive additives or "juices" that will make any gasoline give more mileage. Unnecessary idling, excessive low or high speeds, and jack-rabbit starts and stops burn up gasoline. Braking a car to a stop from a speed of 30 miles per hour wastes two and a half times as much energy as when braking to a stop from 20 mph. From 60 mph the loss is nine times greater. A steady speed of 50 miles per hour is 25 percent more economical than varying speeds from 30 to 70 mph. The most economical cruising speed is 55 mph. Dragging brakes, underinflated tires, an out-of-tune engine, and a too-heavy motor oil are other causes of low mileage per gallon of gasoline. By maintaining one's car properly and driving at reasonable speeds a motorist can get 5 miles more per gallon and save $100 or more in a year, based on 10,000 to 12,000 miles of driving per year.

Do Brands of Gasoline Really Differ in Quality?

Gasoline is fairly uniform in quality. There is no special or secret process that makes one gasoline better than another. There are no secrets in the industry. The FTC hearings verified the fact that "it is commonplace in the marketing of refined gasoline for the identical product to be sold to competing retailers at widely disparate prices." The rationale for this is that it saves the expense of cross-hauling. Each refiner receives a supply of gasoline in an area where it markets but does not have a refinery or a pipeline.

Another practice unknown to many consumers is that practically all of the gasoline sold by so-called independent stations at a price 4 to 8 cents below the price of regular gasoline in that market comes from the big-name nationally advertised brand refiners. The major oil companies prefer to dispose of their surplus gasoline by selling anonymously to independent stations rather than by reducing prices at their own stations. According to testimony presented at the FTC hearings, "the sale of excess gasoline to so-called 'unbranded' or independent brand dealers or jobbers at prices substantially below those quoted by a refiner to his regular branded outlets is a pervasive industry practice which frequently is responsible for price wars. . . ." Armed with a wholesale price as much as 6 to 8 cents below that of the branded stations, unbranded retailers are tempted to increase their volume by dropping their prices below the usual 4-cent differential between unbranded and branded gasoline.

The people who write advertising copy for the major brand gasoline marketers have a real problem. Knowing that there are no significant differences among the various brands, what can a copywriter say? They often take refuge in ambiguity. The copywriter tries to give the impression that this particular brand will perform in a special way, without letting the consumer know that all the other gasolines perform in the same way. The attempt is to create a product differentiation in the mind of the buyer where there is basically no such thing. Standard Oil of New Jersey (Esso) spent $100 million for station facelifting to change the signs at its more than 25,000 stations and to put its new corporate name, Exxon, on its letterheads, gas pumps, and trucks. In addition, it spent $25 million advertising the name change.[35]

In the few states where motorists are protected against the meaningless ambiguity of gasoline marketers' claims, standards are established and samples are regularly tested. Inspectors take samples of gasoline, test them, and prosecute violators. The Florida law has an effective device for controlling octane rating claims: Marketers may claim any octane rating they wish, but their products must then pass the inspector's test. In addition, gasoline samples are tested for volatility, gum residue, sulphur, corrosion, and vapor pressure. In a typical year only 0.4 percent of 50,000 samples were in violation. The independent marketers' products proved to be as good as those of the major marketers, or even a little better.

Are Gasoline Prices a Quality Guide?

Price is no guide to quality in gasoline. One will find the same brand of gasoline selling at different prices at different stations in the same city. In such cases, the buyer should ask, "What is the octane rating for the gas coming from this pump?" In some states the weights and measures inspectors may enforce the octane rating posting requirement.

Table 13-3 shows the range of prices for gasoline in the same competitive market. There was a 13 cents per gallon price spread between the station charging the highest price and the station charging the lowest for regular, unleaded, and premium gasolines. On a 23-gallon tank that is a spread of approximately $3.00. The price spread for the same national brand of gasoline, Exxon, was 6 to 8 cents per gallon.

Many gasoline tank trucks of both national brands and private brands of gasoline are filled from the same common pool storage tanks at terminals. National brand companies often trade gasoline among themselves depending on which one has a refinery serving the area. This, again, is an example of why national brands tend to be the higher-priced products.

On the basis of the information presented in this section owners and operators of motor vehicles should now know that they are reasonably safe

TABLE 13-3. Gasoline Price Comparison Survey

Gasoline Station	REGULAR Price Per Gallon (in cents)	REGULAR Octane Rating $\frac{(M + R)}{2}$	UNLEADED Price Per Gallon (in cents)	UNLEADED Octane Rating $\frac{(M + R)}{2}$	PREMIUM Price Per Gallon (in cents)	PREMIUM Octane Rating $\frac{(M + R)}{2}$
Amoco	52.9	90	57.9	87	60.9	95
Boron	55.9	90	57.9	87	61.9	95
Exxon	54.9	89	58.9	87	61.9	95.5
Exxon	56.9	89	58.9	87	61.9	95.5
Exxon	62.8	89	65.1	87	66.8	95.5
Falcon	51.9	89.3	53.9	87	55.9	95
Gulf	57.9	89.5	58.9	87	61.9	95
Highway Oil	49.9	89	51.9	87		
Pennzoil	54.9	89.5	55.9	87	58.9	95
Solo*	49.9	89	51.9	87	53.9	95
Sunoco	54.9	89	58.9	87	61.9	95
	57.9	90			63.9	97.5
	59.9	93				

* Self-service

Source: This survey was made by Geneva College students Jan., 1976, in the Beaver Falls, Pennsylvania area.

buying gasoline from independent stations at a price 4 to 8 cents a gallon below the administered prices maintained by the refiners of nationally advertised major brands. If you switch from a branded gasoline sold at a regular price to an independent gasoline sold at cut-rate, you can save about 6 cents per gallon. That adds a savings of $42 a year for 700 gallons, which is about the national average gas consumption per car per year.

Since price is not a guide to quality in buying gasoline, the buyer should choose a gasoline with an octane rating that is best suited for his or her particular car. The FEA has attempted to help the buyer by requiring that the octane ratings be posted on all gasoline pumps in a clear and conspicuous manner. The FEA also ruled that the posted rating had to be the $\frac{(M + R)}{2}$ octane number. The enforcement of this regulation has been relatively weak, however, so consumers are still not always able to find the octane number posted on the pump when buying gasoline.

QUESTIONS FOR REVIEW

1. Do you think you usually get what you pay for?
2. Can you list as many as ten nonbrand items available in stores?
3. Is the consumer's welfare enhanced or retarded by the use of brand names?
4. What would the marketplace be like without brands?

5. Why do national brand product manufacturers who also make private brands not want consumers to know who manufactured the private brand? Are their reasons defensible?

6. What are problems in the brand name versus generic name prescription drug controversy?

7. Why do prices vary so much between national and private brand products?

8. "Basically all products of the same type are so similar it makes little difference which one you buy." Discuss.

9. Does the price of a pound of meat measure its nutritive value?

10. Why do you buy the brand of soap you do?

11. What gasoline does your family buy, and why?

12. What can a driver do to get better gasoline mileage?

13. Would you like a market without brand names? Why?

PROJECTS

1. See how many private brand name products you can find that have the identical ingredients as national brand name products. Compare the prices.

2. Survey a group of friends and see how many can give the brand name of each piece of their wearing apparel.

3. Get the prices for five national brand name prescription drugs and the prices for these prescriptions under their generic names and compare.

4. Interview a pharmacist and a doctor concerning the generic-brand name controversy. Summarize their opinions.

5. Make a price and octane survey of gasoline stations in your area.

6. If there is a refinery in your area ask the manager what filling stations are served by his refinery. Then visit the gas stations and ask the managers where their gas comes from. Summarize your findings.

REFERENCES

1. *NRTA Journal,* July–Aug. 1975, p. 8.
2. *St. Petersburg Times,* 22 April 1975, p. 1D.
3. *Supermarket News,* 26 May 1975, p. 4.
4. *Advertising Age,* 22 Sept. 1975, p. 71.
5. *Consumer Reports,* Aug. 1975, p. 471.
6. *Ibid.*
7. *New York Times,* 7 March 1975, p. 28.
8. *Money,* Oct. 1975, p. 14.
9. *Ibid.*
10. *St. Petersburg Times,* 20 July 1975, p. 1-E.

11. *Wall Street Journal,* 18 Sept. 1975, p. 21.
12. This material is taken from Richard Harris, *The Real Voice* (New York: The Macmillan Company, 1964), pp. 30–40, 72–79, a very readable and authoritative account of the congressional hearings conducted by Senator Estes Kefauver.
13. *Business Week,* 16 June 1975, p. 53.
14. "The Fortune Directory of the 500 Largest Industrial Corporations," *Fortune,* May 1976, p. 339.
15. *Consumer Reports,* Oct. 1975, p. 586.
16. *Prescription Drug Price Disclosures* (Washington, D.C.: Federal Trade Commission, 1975).
17. *Ibid.* pp. 120–121.
18. Ashok K. Gumbhir and Christopher A. Rodowskas, Jr., "Consumer Price Differentials between Generic and Brand Name Prescriptions," *American Journal of Public Health* 64 (1974): 980.
19. *Ibid,* p. 38.
20. *Consumer Reports,* Jan. 1975, pp. 50–51.
21. *Wall Street Journal,* 28 July 1975, p. 7. Note: This information was contained in a letter to the editor from the Secretary of Health, Education, and Welfare.
22. *Consumer Reports,* April 1975, p. 208.
23. Richard Burack and Fred J. Fox, *The New Handbook of Prescription Drugs,* rev. ed. (New York: Ballantine, 1975), p. xxi.
24. *Consumer Reports,* Nov. 1975, pp. 686–689.
25. *Consumer Reports,* Sept. 1975, pp. 564–567.
26. *Ibid.*
27. *U.S. Consumer,* 1 Oct. 1969, p. 2.
28. *Consumer Guide Auto Quarterly,* Winter 1976, p. 162.
29. *Money,* May 1975, pp. 30–31.
30. *Business Week,* 10 March 1975, p. 73.
31. Ralph Nader, Lowell Dodge, and Ralf Hotchkiss, *What To Do with Your Bad Car* (New York: Grossman, 1971), pp. 130–131.
32. *Hearings on Posting Octane Ratings,* Federal Trade Commission, 14 Oct. 1969, pp. 179–204.
33. *Fact Sheet on Octane Rating,* Federal Energy Administration, 2 May 1974.
34. *St. Petersburg Times,* 21 Oct. 1975, p. 5D.
35. *Time,* 22 May 1972, p. 93.

CHAPTER 14

THE PROFITABLE PRACTICE
OF FRAUD

WHAT IS FRAUD?

Let the Buyer Beware

In 1776 a Scotsman, Adam Smith, wrote, "Every man, as long as he does not violate the laws of justice is left perfectly free to pursue his own interest his own way, and to bring both his industry and capital into competition with those of any man, or order of men."[1] In an economic system organized on the assumption that every individual will seek to promote his or her self-interest by acquiring as much profit as possible, there will always be those who attempt to secure profit by any possible means, and those who do violate the laws of justice. Deception, fraud, and swindling are the outcome of the operation of self-interest (selfishness) and the profit motive. It makes no difference to some individuals whether profit results from the rendering of a service or disservice, just so long as a profit is made.

Traditional economic doctrine holds that consumers are protected from fraud by competition. Consumers are supposed to act as economic persons —that is, it is assumed that in a given market area they will shop in all stores, comparing prices, quantity, quality, and service, and make purchases at the stores offering the highest quality and the greatest quantity at the lowest price. If by any chance this assumed economic person should be defrauded, theory holds that he or she will refuse to patronize the same merchant again. The assumed result is that dishonest dealers are driven out of business and only the honest merchants survive. Business executives have repeatedly said that a business cannot continue if it defrauds buyers. But the reports of their own better business bureaus, of state consumer protection bureaus, of the Federal Trade Commission, the Justice Department, and the Food and Drug Administration provide contradictory evidence. If the fraudulent operators constitute only 1 percent of all business firms, in absolute numbers that equals more than 50 thousand firms that prosper by cheating.

In real life, however, consumers are not economic persons, so competition fails to operate as a completely protective device. *Caveat emptor* — let the buyer beware — is the rule governing relations between sellers and buyers all too frequently. Out of the abundance of available evidence the following pages present a sampling of practices against which buyers must be on guard.

Large-Scale Fraud

Today fraud is not only impersonal but is perpetrated on a grand scale. The impersonality of the modern market frees fraudulent practitioners from the necessity of facing their victims and thus eases their consciences. To the dealer in fraud, every consumer is a possible victim. In a market of 215 million potential buyers, many businesses need not be concerned about repeat sales. Once the market has been exhausted, some new trick or device offered under a new corporate name holds all the possibilities of a fresh start.

In a message to Congress in 1971 the president enumerated six major areas of government concern. One of these was a "national attack on consumer fraud." He stated that "consumer fraud and deception jeopardize the health and welfare of our people. . . . Efforts to eliminate these unethical business practices have not been successful enough."

Every year the Antitrust Division of the Department of Justice and the Federal Trade Commission bring firm after firm to court for illegal price-fixing that costs consumers tens of millions of dollars. The following are just a few examples of this practice.

Tetracycline is an important antibiotic used regularly by many people. In the late 1960s the FTC charged five major drug companies of unfair competition designed to monopolize the antibiotic market and fix prices. After this conspiracy was uncovered, the price of tetracycline fell in 1969 from $40.60 per 100 capsules to $4.25, a price reduction of 86 percent. Over the next decade the companies had to pay settlements of almost $230 million to many private concerns, to forty three states, and to numerous municipalities that had sued for damages, as well as to tens of thousands of private citizens.[2] In six states alone nearly a million citizens received more than $20 million in refunds during 1975 from the five companies involved in this price-fixing conspiracy.[3] Six sugar companies were charged with illegal price-fixing. They pleaded, "No contest," which means they did not admit guilt but would not contest the case. They each paid $50 thousand per charge against them, which is the maximum fine allowed under the antitrust law. Total fines collected amounted to $400 thousand.[4] This fine, however, was less than $100 thousand per company, as compared to the millions of dollars collected. In addition, a case of this magnitude costs the federal government tens of thousands of dollars. Three of New York City's famous women's clothing stores (Bergdorf Goodman, Saks Fifth Avenue, and Bonwit Teller) were fined $50,000 each for conspiracy to violate the antitrust laws by adopting uniform markups for retail clothing prices and inducing manufacturers to impose them on other stores as "suggested retail prices."[5]

In 1976 the FTC began a nationwide investigation into the possibility of price-fixing in the multibillion-dollar women's apparel industry. The commission said pricing violations could cost the public as much as $1 billion a year.[6] The magnitude and complexity of this case are such that it will take years to resolve it in the courts, at a cost of tens of thousands of dollars to the taxpayers.

Many times it has been said that fraud is perpetrated on the consumer only by the "fly-by-night" concerns. It would be fortunate for consumers if that were the truth, but time after time consumer frauds are publicized that have been perpetrated on the consumer by some of the largest and best-known companies in America.

Not All That Deceives Is Fraudulent

Just what constitutes fraud is a matter of definition. If it were defined in law, as it is in the dictionary, as "any artifice by which the right or interest of another person is injured," consumers would have more protection and fraudulent sellers less. Actually, laws and courts have so defined fraud as to restrict it to deliberate deceit. This means that the buyer-plaintiff must prove that the seller intended to deceive him, and it is very difficult to prove such intent. As a result, the sellers of much merchandise which is fraudulent are protected by the law.

This situation is aggravated by the freedom of any person to go into almost any business he or she chooses. In some cases the law recognizes the need for protecting consumers from fraudulent practitioners — licenses are required, for instance, before one may practice medicine or compound drugs. Yet a person without training in medicine or chemistry may set himself or herself up as a company for producing some "marvelous" cure. Direct damage suits by injured consumers are comparatively uncommon and unsuccessful. Lung cancer victims have sued cigarette manufacturers for advertising that their products were safe, but so far the courts have refused to hold manufacturers liable even though one court held that the smoking of a manufacturer's cigarettes had caused cancer. State and federal laws are inadequate to give the degree of protection for consumers that is needed. This situation protects individuals in their acquisitive actions, but leaves consumers the victim of their own weakness and of the dishonesty of sellers.

AREAS OF FRAUD

The entire range of human wants presents opportunities for fraud. The sale of food and clothing has long been a profitable field for such forms of fraud as adulteration, misbranding, misrepresentation, short-changing, short-measuring, short-weighing, and overpricing. (See Chapter 23 for a more detailed discussion of these problems.) Charlatans also cater to the natural human desire for health, wealth, and beauty. Even religion is subject to fraudulent practice. Charity schemes exploit the generous and humane impulses of people. Dream books, horoscopes, and lucky charms are palmed off on those who are credulous and naive. In our culture overweight people are objects of ridicule, and they spend well over $100 million a year on reducing frauds. The press releases from the Federal Trade Commission are filled with cases involving false advertising of accident and health insurance, batteries, tires, cookware, perfume, hair-growers, weight-reducers, vitamins, television sets and service, watches, food freezers, and pianos. The FTC states: "The kinds of deceptive practices are as varied as the ingenuity of hucksters can devise."

Better business bureau surveys have shown the following ten consumer fraud schemes as the most frequent: bait-and-switch advertising, home improvement swindles, chain referral sales plans, charity gyps, phony credit certificates, business opportunity schemes, debt consolidation gouging, victimizing the aged, health quackery, and work-at-home gyps.

A breakdown of 439,486 complaints by type of business, received by better business bureaus throughout the nation during a twelve-month period, ranked complaints as shown in Table 14-1. These fifteen major complaint groupings accounted for 57.1 percent of the total, with all other complaints accounting for the remaining 42.9 percent.

TABLE 14-1. Formal Complaints Processed by Better Business Bureaus

Type of Business	Rank	Number	Total
Mail-order companies	1	67,359	15.3%
Auto dealers (cars and trucks)	2	26,076	5.9%
Miscellaneous service establishments	3	20,047	4.6%
Miscellaneous retail stores/shops	4	16,721	3.8%
Home furnishings stores	5	15,997	3.6%
Department stores	6	14,359	3.3%
Magazines (ordered by mail)	7	12,368	2.8%
Miscellaneous home maintenance	8	12,265	2.8%
Television servicing	9	10,233	2.3%
Appliance stores	10	10,210	2.3%
Auto repair shops-transmissions	11	9,986	2.3%
Home remodeling contractors	12	9,621	2.2%
Appliance service	13	9,148	2.1%
Real estate sales/rental companies	14	8,378	1.9%
Dry cleaning/laundry companies	15	8,270	1.9%
Subtotal		251,038	57.1%
All other complaints		188,448	42.9%
Total		439,486	100.0%

Source: Statistical Summary of BBB System Activity, Council of Better Business Bureaus, Washington, D.C., 1976.

EVIDENCES OF FRAUD

Food Frauds

Food poisoning is commonly, though not necessarily, associated with food frauds. Scientific data concerning food poisoning is still meager, but the number of cases is increasing rather than decreasing. This increase is surprising in view of improved food-preservation methods and is to be explained by gross mishandling and carelessness. It is estimated that there are two thousand cases of salmonella poisoning in the U.S. every year. Over one hundred passengers on a Japanese international airline were struck down with food poisoning; all recovered, but the head of the catering service that had provided the food committed suicide.* Fortunately the majority of cases of food poisoning are mild; most are not even reported to a doctor.[7] The sources of infection are rarely established, but foods derived from animal sources—meat, poultry, and egg products—lead the list of foods containing salmonella. The Food and Drug Administration has developed a means of detecting staphylococcal poisoning in food. The FDA described this as a major step forward, permitting the identification in food of the specific staphylococcal toxin that is responsible for most of the food poisoning outbreaks in the United States.

The need of consumers in the low-income groups for low-priced food and the practices of some producers in attempting to meet that demand by using cheap ingredients or substitutes lead to such food frauds as passing off horsemeat as beef and selling the flesh of animals that have died from natural causes. It should be added that horsemeat is an acceptable food when packed under federal inspection and sold as horsemeat at horsemeat prices. But selling horsemeat tenderloins, which cost the meat store 50 cents a pound, as beef tenderloins for $2.00 a pound is fraudulent. Fortunately the FDA has developed a test to detect the presence of horsemeat in hamburger. As a result, the former large-scale frauds involving "horseburgers" have been stopped.

A summary of "Notices of Judgment" actions taken by the FDA, published in the *FDA Consumer*, gives a fair indication of the size of the problem. A total of forty-one actions to remove from the consumer market food products charged to be violative were reported in two months.[8] These included twenty-nine seizures of foods: for contamination, spoilage, and insanitary handling, which included swollen cans, metal fragments in food, decomposed foods, and insect and rodent filth; one case involved charges concerning a poisonous and deleterious substance; four cases involved economic and labeling violations; and two cases involved products containing nonconforming food or color additives. There were three notices of judgment on criminal actions, and two on injunction actions. The criminal and injunctive actions were taken against firms that had not corrected problems or were unwilling to without legal pressure. In addition to the

---

* This would never happen in the U.S.; it is part of Japanese tradition.

food notices, there were nine notices regarding animal feed, drugs, and medical devices. This is typical, month after month and year after year. One can only guess what the volume of fraudulent adulteration would be in the absence of FDA inspectors. The FDA assures us that, fortunately, only 2 percent of the firms in the business are responsible for these types of violations.

"Health" for Sale

Every year Americans spend about $4 billion for do-it-yourself relief from all manner of ailments—mental, physical, and biological.[9] One might suppose that when people become ill, they would go to doctors for treatment, but the prices charged by most doctors, clinics, and hospitals seem too high for those in low-income brackets, so they turn to patent medicines and quack doctors who promise wonders at low prices. Those in higher income brackets who turn to charlatans do so because their doctors have told them they can do little or nothing for them. The FDA reports that sick people are so anxious to believe in quick, easy, miraculous cure-alls that reputable practitioners find it almost impossible to convince them that a product is worthless or harmful.

According to the FDA there are three major kinds of health frauds that violate the Federal Food, Drug and Cosmetic Act: 1) quackery in the promotion of so-called therapeutic devices; 2) quackery in the marketing of food supplements and so-called health foods; and 3) false claims for drugs and cosmetics.

Many people fall for fraudulent therapeutic devices sold by companies offering instant or easy cures. Weird medical devices are dreamed up and sold at fantastic prices. Out of scores of examples, a few may be chosen to illustrate the problem. The "Slim-Twist Exerciser" is a mechanical device consisting of two pieces of wood, each about one-foot square, connected to each other by a ball-bearing swivel joint, which permits the wood squares to rotate individually. The device is used as a pedestal; the user stands on the top piece of wood and simulates dancing the "Twist" in place, gyrating from side to side or back and forth. There are no electrical connections. Labels on the device suggest that it is an effective treatment for body weight reduction, heart or vascular trouble, arthritis, diabetes, emphysema, chronic fatigue, aching legs, soreness, and stiffness, and that the use of the device will result in good health and physical fitness and will stimulate circulation. The devices and promotional literature were seized by the FDA on charges of misbranding.

The Arthritis Foundation reports that desperate sufferers of arthritis are swindled out of $408 million a year by promoters of misrepresented remedies and worthless "cures." This is going on even though no specific cure is known. Medicine today can prevent severe crippling in some cases through a combination of early diagnosis and prompt treatment. The foundation reports that almost half the nation's 20 million arthritics are sold fake and exaggerated products and treatments each year. These range from "miracle-ray" lamps, copper bracelets, electric gadgets, and high-priced pills with nothing useful in them but aspirin, to worthless diets and radiation treatments. More serious than the waste of money is the patient's loss of faith in legitimate treatments that offer genuine hope for relief.

These and other fraudulent devices account for a large part of dishonest medical practices, but food faddism and nutritional quackery rank as the biggest racket in the health field today. Millions of people fall for food fads to the tune of hundreds of millions of dollars a year. Diet foods are also big business—over $700 million a year. Diet foods generally cost a good deal more than regular food. *Chain Store Age,* a trade publication, stated that the gross profit margin on diet foods in supermarkets is 23 percent. This compares with 15.6 percent for pet products, usually considered a high markup category; 13.9 percent for breakfast foods; 12.4 percent for soaps and detergents; and 10.2 percent for baby foods. Diet soft drinks alone represent about $400 million worth of annual business.[10] Special "low calorie" foods can be helpful. They will give you a bit more food with fewer calories, and the non-caloric sweeteners and low calorie dressings may make your food more interesting, but their nutritional value is negligible. Buying and eating less of standard food will not only save money but will help reduce weight.

A frightening fact is that only one-fourth or perhaps one-third, of these frauds are detected and stopped by FDA inspectors. Protective agencies like the federal Food and Drug Administration do not have enough money to hire enough inspectors. Compared to the $114.9 billion called for in the President's budget for the Department of Defense for fiscal 1977, the FDA's budget was set at $226 million.

The sale of various drugs and cosmetics under false claims is a third area of medical fraud. The FDA says that enormous profits are made by counterfeiting legitimate drugs. These defraud consumers, but worse is the fact that counterfeit drugs may endanger the health or life of the consumers. Some counterfeit drugs are produced and marketed under independent labels; some are marketed under counterfeit labels of reputable pharmaceutical firms. In addition to counterfeit drugs, various other drug-related products are sold under false pretenses. For example, consumers are persistently bombarded with misinformation by sellers of prepared dentifrices. Advertisers try to persuade consumers that an advertised dentifrice will prevent tooth decay or cure oral diseases. Such preparations are not likely to do any good, or any harm. This is an illustration of nealth. The FDA warns consumers to beware of claims made by advertisers that their products will prevent cavities. Only a few dentifrices now advertised have any curative or preventive powers.

Mouthwashes are among the most useless of modern frauds. The American Dental Association says flatly that the commercial preparations advertised and sold in stores have no medicinal value. If they are strong enough to destroy germs, they will destroy delicate tissues also. Most mouthwashes are so weak as to be useless. One widely advertised product is composed chiefly of alcohol and water with a little boric and benzoic acid. The market for mouthwashes has been estimated by the FDA to be over $250 million annually.

The FDA recently took action to ban claims by the manufacturers of nine mouthwashes (constituting the greater part of the market) that their products had medical usefulness in destroying bad breath or germs or for relieving sore throats of the common cold. As a result of the FDA action, the FTC started an investigation of the advertising of mouthwashes. In 1975 the FTC ordered the makers of Listerine mouthwash to run $10.2 million worth of "corrective advertising" carrying the statement: "Contrary to prior advertising, Listerine will not prevent colds or sore throats or lessen their severity." The FTC ruled that the preponderance of evidence failed to support Listerine's anticold claims.[11]

Buying Beauty

The buying of beauty is a multibillion-dollar business based on advertising claims that beauty can be bought in bottles, jars, or packages. In return for their money, buyers get tons of cleansing cream or skin lotion in formulas that are fairly standard and that are available to every manufacturer. It might be supposed that every firm making cosmetics would employ a manufacturing chemist, but such is not the case. In fact, some so-called manufacturers do no manufacturing, but instead have their products made by an independent manufacturing chemist. This means that the only difference among some cosmetics is the container or label. But consumers do not know this, unless they have inside information or depend on a consumer testing agency for guidance. Teenagers suffering from social ostracism because of pimples, chafed hands, or body odor are told that they can surround themselves with admirers by purchasing and using an ordinary soap priced at 25 or 50 cents for a small bar. There is probably no field in which advertising claims are more extravagant, misleading, or fraudulent. Not only are the claims made for many cosmetics grossly misleading, but the ingredients in some may be harmful. Moreover, practically all preparations are greatly overpriced. Advertising and fashion have been used to bolster an artificial demand at ridiculous prices. Some cosmetic companies spend 25 to 30 percent of sales on advertising.

Consumer protection is difficult. As fast as the regulatory agencies catch up with and stop one fraud, another springs up. It is a never-ending process. The quacks have been peddling concoctions like these: a cosmetic containing chick embryo extract to regenerate cells to prevent wrinkles and sagging skin; pig-skin extract and horse blood serum as skin rejuvenators; and shark oil to revitalize aging skin.

Medical and cosmetic quackery has some well-defined characteristics. The FDA suggests that if your answer is "yes" to any of the following questions, it is very likely that you are one of the thousands of people who are being victimized by quackery.

- Is the product or service being offered a "secret remedy" or not available from other sources?
- Does the sponsor claim that he is battling the medical profession, which does not accept his wonderful discovery?
- Is the remedy being sold from door to door, by a self-styled "health adviser" or promoted in lectures to the public, from town to town?
- Is this "miracle" drug, device, or diet being promoted in a sensational magazine, by a faith healer's group, or a crusading organization?
- Does the promoter tell you about the wonderful miracles the product or service has performed for others?
- Is the product or service good for a vast variety of illnesses, real or fancied?[12]

Medical and Surgical Frauds

Unfortunately some presumably reputable doctors practice frauds such as fee splitting and performing unnecessary operations. Appendectomies, tonsillectomies, hysterectomies, and caesarians are the most common needless operations.

The findings of various studies concerning unnecessary operations are shocking. In testimony presented before the House of Representatives Oversight and Investigations Subcommittee, the Public Interest Research Group estimated there are 3.2 million unnecessary operations performed each year, with 16 thousand patients dying, at a cost of about $5 billion.[13] The number of operations performed for persons who are covered by health insurance is twice that of those uninsured.[14] The Public Interest Research Group estimated that the probability for all women in the United States having a hysterectomy was 45.3 percent, and 16.8 percent for women in prepaid health group plans. Other probabilities reported included: tonsillectomy, 30.1 percent for the entire population versus 10.5 percent for members of health group plans; prostate operations, 17.5 percent for the entire population versus 7.7 percent for members of health group plans.[15] Hysterectomies are performed two and a half times as often in the United States as in England and Wales, and four times as often as in Sweden, which has a national health care plan so that doctors stand to gain very little financially by performing more hysterectomies.[16] Another study showed that under the fee-for-service basis there were sixty-nine operations per one thousand persons, but in prepayment plan groups thirty-three per thousand persons had surgery.[17] Where a second opinion was paid for by a union for its members, the consulting surgeons recommended against the surgery proposed 17.5 percent of the time.[18] The consensus of the witnesses testifying before a congressional committee, regardless of their attitude on unnecessary surgery, was that anyone who has been told that surgery is needed should get a second opinion from another physician.[19]

After long considering the incompetent or careless doctor as a rare aberration of minor consequence, the American medical profession is beginning to regard unfit physicians as a serious problem that may account for tens of thousands of needless injuries and deaths each year.

While most authorities emphasize that the majority of the country's 320,000 doctors are competent and conscientious, they estimate that as many as 16,000 licensed physicians, or 5 percent of the profession, are unfit to practice medicine. These doctors, they say, should have their licenses revoked, be required to undergo further training or practice only under close supervision.

The incompetent doctors, who treat an estimated total of 7.5 million patients a year, include some who are mentally ill or addicted to drugs as well as others who are simply ignorant of modern medical knowledge or careless in their use of it.[20]

A Pennsylvania state study showed that doctors were drawn to areas where people are more inclined to spend more for medical services, and their fees are based on "what the traffic will bear."[21] On the basis of the study it was concluded that the average gross income for a physician in an affluent resort area county was $132,631, and that residents paid an average of $149 a year for private medical care. In a neighboring county, the average gross income for a doctor was $32,854, with the residents spending an average of $29.90 for private medical care. The study concluded: "As with other goods and services, when the price of physicians' services increases, the quantity demanded will decrease. . . . physicians themselves generate demand whenever physician supply is relatively slack, through unnecessary surgery."

In its "Statements on Principles" the American College of Surgeons included the following statement about fee splitting.

Any form of inducement to refer a patient to another physician, other than the superior care to be secured, is unethical. Fee splitting is one form of unethical inducement. Other forms of inducement, referred to as "indirect" fee splitting, are equally unethical. Violation of this tenet disqualifies an applicant. If a Fellow, it is a cause for expulsion from Fellowship.

About half of the states have laws which forbid any form of fee splitting, and there is no state which sanctions it. Additionally, federal law makes illegal any form of rebate, kickback or splitting of fees which include any federal money. Thus, such illegal inducement cannot be considered an item of deductible business expense.[22]

The U.S. Department of Justice investigated three Tampa, Florida firms because "referral fees" allegedly were paid to osteopaths and chiropractors. The firms, two laboratories and an inhalation therapy service, would bill Medicare and then remit fees to those doctors who referred business to them. The doctors interviewed said that they had been advised by the firms' sales representatives that the plan was legal.[23] In California a medical laboratory, without admitting guilt, agreed to pay $180 thousand in civil penalties and costs and $255 thousand in restitution after being sued for raising its fees and splitting them with doctors who referred patients to the lab.[24]

Fraud in Selling Automobiles

There are many traps to avoid when buying a new or used car. A sizable portion of automobile advertising is unethical. In addition to bait advertising, many sellers of automobiles use such gimmicks as "high-balling," "low-balling," "bushing," "packing," "macing," "double dipping," blank contracts, and turning back odometers on used cars in order to sell them as new cars. Some of these gimmicks are illegal, but effective enforcement of the law in these cases is difficult, if not impossible.

"High-balling" is a way of turning a shopper into a buyer. When a sales representative finds a shopper, an extra high price is offered on a trade-in. This is "the high ball"—a price much in excess of the real value of the used car. Of course no legitimate dealer can or will meet such an offer, so shoppers return to the high-baller and buy, paying high prices for extras that they may not really want but that are part of the deal. One shopper was offered prices ranging from $400 to $1,000 for his old car.

On a "low-ball" deal there is no trade-in. A new car buyer is offered a price just $100 over the factory list price, compared with the $200 to $500 a legitimate dealer must get to cover his operating expenses and profit margin. When a prospect decides to buy after comparing prices, the salesman then says he made a mistake in his figuring and the car will cost $400 more. Many times the prospect will go ahead and buy it. "Bushing" is the practice of including unordered accessories, such as power steering at $150. When a buyer calls for her car she is told that the only way the dealer could get the car immediately was to take this one and that they "figured you would want power equipment anyway." Many buyers, though they complain, will pay. "Bushing" is common, as is the signing of blank orders, although both these practices are illegal. Another fraud is the practice of overcharging installment buyers for insurance coverage.

"Packing" involves adding extra charges, such as special fees and exorbitant finance-insurance fees, on top of the quoted purchase price. "Macing" is a racket in which unsuspecting individuals sell their used cars to used-car dealers and receive only a small cash payment, with the rest of the purchase price paid in notes or a post-dated check. At the due date, the note or the check turns out to be worthless, and the dealer has skipped town. "Double dipping" is a legal but questionable credit arrangement, used most often when the buyer has little if any down payment or no trade-in. Three-fourths of the price of a car may be financed at a bank at a reasonable rate of interest, and the remainder financed at a loan company at a high rate of interest since the bank would not finance a larger percentage of the purchase price. The buyer then finds that he or she has two payments to make on the car each month.

A former car salesman enumerated a number of the deceptive practices used by some car salespeople.[25] For example, there is the "T. O. man" technique. The T.O. man "takes over" from another salesperson who has been successful in getting the customer to sign a "little-or-no-profit" contract. The T. O. man then encourages the addition of extras at high prices, credit insurance at a high price, and credit terms at high interest rates, and what began as a "little-or-no-profit" contract for the dealer becomes a lucrative deal. Dealer license plates on dealers' demonstrators do not necessitate having the car registered, so after the car has been used as a demonstrator for many months, the odometer can be rolled back, new tires put on the car, a clean-up job done, and the used car can be pawned off as a new car with an original registration certificate.

It was revealed that some major truck makers have been recalling unsold vehicles, stamping them with current model numbers, and selling them to unwary customers as the latest models. One truck manufacturer official stated that his company's truck division followed the industry practice of "redesignation" of truck products.[26]

In 1958 Congress passed legislation requiring every new automobile to have a manufacturer's suggested price posted conspicuously on the automobile.[27] The suggested price is not the price the customer must pay; it is the price at which bargaining begins. This legislation was aimed, in particular, at stopping the "price-pack." In a "price-pack" a dealer quotes an exceptionally high figure for a trade-in. For example, a dealer might offer $300 more in trade-in value than any other dealer in the area would offer and then "packs" the price of the new car by $300. There is no question that the posting of the price on the car has lessened certain kinds of deceptive practices, but others continue to plague the consumer.

Odometer tampering has created problems for many automobile buyers. This form of deception has been almost universal. The author traded a six-year-old car, which he had purchased new, for a new car. His used car showed 99,817 actual miles on the odometer. A week after the new car was purchased he took it back to the dealer to have some work done on it. While there he wandered back to the used-car lot and checked his old car. The odometer had been turned back 54,000 miles and showed 45,817 miles. Pity the unfortunate consumer who trusted the dealer and believed that he or she was getting a car with only 45,817. When the author confronted the salesman about this, the salesman said that that was the only way he could make a profit in the automobile business. This is a very sad indictment of the ethical and moral level of a large and important industry in the United States.

This episode took place prior to the passage in 1973 of the Motor Vehicle Information and Cost Savings Act (Public Law 92-513). This law requires a written mileage disclosure statement for all vehicles except those that are twenty-five-years-old or older, not selfpropelled, or exceeding 16 thousand pounds. The law stipulates that the seller must provide the buyer with a written statement of the registered mileage. The law also requires written notice of odometer servicing and prohibits any act that would cause the odometer to indicate incorrect mileage. If a buyer believes there is a violation of the law, he or she must prove that there was intent to mislead and defraud and must also know who committed the violation. The penalty for odometer tampering is fines up to $50,000 and/or imprisonment for up to one year. Unfortunately enforcement has been a problem. A National

Highway Traffic Safety Administration study disclosed that less than half
of the nation's used-auto dealers complied with the law and that fewer
than 10 percent of all private sellers met the requirement.[28]

Automobile Repair Swindles

Not many of the people who own the 100 million automobiles in the
U.S. understand the mechanics of car operation, and still fewer can or do
service their cars. They have to trust operators of garages and filling stations, but their trust may be misplaced. The tourist who has a breakdown
away from home is fair game for the repairman who can charge excessive
prices for work not done or not needed and for parts not supplied or not
needed.

> Automobile mechanics are not tested in this country, nor do they serve five years
> of indentured apprenticeship as mechanics do throughout most of the civilized
> world, nor are they controlled by any trade organization or by any state or federal
> government agency. In other words, anyone can become an automobile mechanic
> tomorrow, simply by calling himself one and by persuading some overworked and
> understaffed garage owner to employ him.[29]

A Senate investigation found that of the $30 billion spent on automobile
repairs every year, $10 billion, or a third, is wasted on repairs that either are
not done or are not needed. That represents an average of $80 per year per
vehicle in the United States.[30] During the Senate investigation criticism
was leveled at the so-called "flat rate books" used by repair shops, which
tell mechanics how much time should be charged for each of several thousand repair operations. The rate books thus become a form of price-fixing
arrangement and tend to encourage heavy use of replacement parts instead
of minor repairs to old parts.

The *New York Times* in conjunction with the Suffolk County Department of Consumer Affairs conducted an investigation in which they asked
twenty-four repair shops to fix a car with a minor and easily detectable
mechanical fault. Thirteen of the repair shops either diagnosed the problem
incorrectly or performed or recommended expensive and unnecessary
work. One shop made the repair without charging. Another shop recognized that there was no internal transmission problem and recommended
that the car be taken to a nonspecialized repair shop. Eight shops made
nominal charges of $5 to $19.79 for the repair job. Five shops charged from
$27 to $80.25. Seven of those that made the wrong diagnosis estimated repair costs ranging from $199.95 to $345. Two shops made a completely
wrong diagnosis and did not attempt to do the repair job.[31]

The licensing or registering of automobile mechanics or repair shops
is a reasonable step for the government to take to lessen the fraud in automobile repair work and to improve service. Such licensing should not be
so restrictive as to block entry, but should be such that those licensed could
lose their license for fraudulent practices or incompetency. The increasing

number of automobiles make it imperative that the number of skilled mechanics be increased. In addition, manufacturers should take steps to lessen high repair costs by making it easier to make repairs and less costly to replace parts.

A few states and municipalities have passed laws attempting to police auto repair shops. The California law has been particularly successful. This law established a Bureau of Automotive Repairs in the Bureau of Consumer Affairs. The bureau is empowered to license (register) almost every automobile repair and diagnostic business in the state, except those shops that perform only minor maintenance functions and those that repair only trucks and tractors. An annual registration fee of $50, paid by some 35,000 shops, largely underwrites the cost of running the bureau. Under the law the bureau has the power to refuse and revoke registrations, without which a repair shop governed by the law cannot operate in the state. The source of the bureau's power is this right to revoke registrations.

An attempt was made to improve automobile repair service by the establishment of the National Institute for Automotive Service Excellence, a independent nonprofit organization dedicated to the goal of bettering automotive service. It is a voluntary, nationwide program for testing and certifying the competence of automobile mechanics. The written tests are developed and administered by the Educational Testing Service of Princeton, New Jersey. Approximately 83,000 mechanics have voluntarily taken and passed one or more of the institute's tests.[32] Identifications are issued to the mechanics who pass the tests. Car owners may check to see if the mechanic working on their car has such identification.

Television Repair Frauds

A television set is a complicated electronic instrument, and a color set is especially complicated. When it needs to be repaired, it may be either a minor repair or a major overhaul, including a new picture tube. This presents the fraudulent repair shop with a real opportunity. Some unscrupulous television repair shops advertise a complete repair job on any set for $24.95; then once the repairman gets into the person's home he indicates that the price will be much higher, but that he can fix it right then and there in the home. It is then up to the owner whether to get the set fixed immediately at the higher price or to wait. Charging for parts that are not replaced and for parts that have been replaced but that were unnecessary are widespread frauds. The Florida Bureau of Electronic Repair received 1,523 complaints about television repairs in one twelve-month period.[33] The National Electronics Service Dealers Association started a program for certifying electronics repairmen. There are only about 8,000 certified electronics technicians in the country. Unlike the certification program for automobile mechanics, which is supported by automobile manufacturers, there is no strong support from the television manufacturers for this certification program.[34]

Something-for-Nothing Frauds

A Louis Harris poll revealed that 23 percent of all Americans regularly bet on football games, in amounts ranging from thousands of dollars to one dollar and less. This means that one out of every four Americans willingly and knowingly breaks the law on a regular basis, since laws prohibiting betting on football games exist in all states except Nevada.* The U.S. Department of Justice estimated that $29 billion to $39 billion are wagered illegally each year in the United States. One witness familiar with nationwide bookmaking operations told the National Gambling Commission that it is conceivable that as much as $100 billion is wagered illegally in this country each year. Parimutual wagering is a legal form of gambling in many states and generates more than $4.9 billion in bets, with attendance at race tracks topping 78 million people each year. In spite of the amount of gambling that goes on in this country, 58 percent to 34 percent of Americans oppose legalizing betting on professional sports, except horse racing, according to a Louis Harris poll.

Gamblers Anonymous estimates that there are more than ten million persons in the United States who lose upwards of $30 billion a year in gambling. Compulsive gamblers are virtually unrecognizable. Like the cocktail hour alcoholics they are nameless faces who look no different than the average citizen.

Legalized gambling is increasing across the country. Many states have legalized lotteries. In 1963 New Hampshire introduced the first legal lottery of this century, and other states soon followed. In many states an attempt has been made to give the state gambling operations the appearance of respectability by earmarking the revenues collected from gambling for such worthwhile purposes as education. For example, in Pennsylvania part of the state gambling revenue goes for education and part goes directly to low-income, elderly persons who qualify for a refund on their real estate taxes.

State operation of gambling is expensive. In New Hampshire it costs the state an average of 30 cents to gain one dollar in net revenue from its lottery, compared with about two cents to collect one dollar of tax revenue. Revenues from state lotteries have fallen far short of projections, in some cases by as much as 50 percent.[35] In New York City the Off-Track Betting Corporation contributed $58 million to the city and $18 million to the state, but this amounts to only a minute contribution in solving the financial woes of the city and state.[36]

Congress has outlawed national lotteries, even if the money made through the lotteries is to be used for worthy purposes, because it judges lotteries to be gambling devices and therefore "seldom pure and rarely simple." From 80 to 90 percent of the money put into slot machines is clear profit for the operators, who fix the machines to pay out whatever small

* The source of much of this material is an in-depth, seven-part series on gambling published in the *St. Petersburg Times*, May 11–17, 1975.

return they choose. The odds on winning on the numbers is 999 to 1, although the payoff is only 600 to 1.

Interstate Land Sales

Each year Americans contract to buy an estimated $5 billion worth of recreation-oriented land, retirement homesites, development plots, and small tracts of raw acreage. While many buyers are dealt with ethically and fairly, far too many are defrauded, gypped, or pressured into buying totally worthless property by the land hustlers – the best trained group of high pressure salespeople since the snake-oil men.[37]

Too often vacation and retirement sites are sold to eager out-of-state buyers who have not inspected the property. The fact that lots may be paid for in small monthly installments tends to make buyers casual about checking on the properties. Generally this informal method of land purchase has been satisfactory. But in a significant number of cases, buyers did not receive what they thought they were buying. Many purchases were based on inadequate or misleading information.

> A development might be described as "10 miles from Rainbow City," without any indication that the 10 miles leads through an impassable swamp, and that it is 34 miles via passable roads.
> Land advertised as "a home site" may have no good drinking water available.
> A lot may be described as "readily accessible" when it can be reached only by footpath or a car with four-wheel drive.
> Information about liens against the property, soil conditions and the type of title the buyer will receive may be omitted from promotion materials.
> In most cases misleading information results from half-truths rather than outright misrepresentation. Since such statements do not constitute provable fraud, court redress has been difficult to obtain.[38]

To protect the public in interstate land transactions, Congress passed a law in 1968 requiring those engaged in the interstate sale or leasing of land to register the offering with the Department of Housing and Urban Development. The law went into effect in 1969. It is designed to afford the prospective buyer a full and fair disclosure of the facts about a subdivision offering. But if the buyer ignores or fails to read and understand the property report, the consumer protection aspects of the law are virtually negated. "The law will light the threshold but not unlock the door."[39]

The law gives some protection, but land frauds continue. In 1975 a real estate group was indicted on accusations of a two hundred million dollar swindle in the public sale of undeveloped, semi-arid desert lots in New Mexico. The eighty-count federal indictment alleged it to be one of the most massive land swindles in history and charged that more than 45,000 people from thirty-seven states had been defrauded. According to the indictment, the defendants bought more than 91,000 acres of desert grazing land for about $180 an acre and then sold individual lots for prices that ranged up to $11,800 an acre for "home-site" lots and more than $25,000 an acre for

Members of the New Mexico Undevelopment Commission erected this billboard to show prospective out-of-state land purchasers the kind of barren land unscrupulous developers might try to sell them as "developed" homesites. (*UPI*)

"commercial" lots. The company officials called the charges "wholly unwarranted and legally and morally unjust."[40]

Before a person buys land from one of the land development organizations, he or she should obtain the Department of Housing and Urban Development (HUD) property report from the developer and should read it carefully before signing anything. HUD neither judges the merits of an offering nor the value of the property, but it does require that the developer spell out in detail any information that might give potential buyers protection against fraudulent claims.

Education Frauds

An area in which one might not expect to find fraud is education, but frauds are perpetrated on consumers of education as well as on consumers of almost every other kind of good or service. The Education Commission estimates that there are approximately 14,000 institutions and programs comprising the range of post secondary institutions, including traditional higher educational institutions, post secondary vocational and technical institutions, and other private and proprietary schools. While the actual number of institutions and programs with questionable, unethical, or fraudulent practices may be small, the leeway for such practices may be greater, and estimates suggest that unsuspecting consumers may be defrauded of millions of dollars each year.[41] The commission estimated that there were about 110 "degree mills," essentially providing no training or education but selling degrees for a price. For example, a Jackson State

University, with addresses in a number of states and no connection with the accredited Jackson State University in Jackson, Mississippi, in its 1975 to 1976 "External Degree Program" catalog offered degrees on the basis of the submission of a résumé or biographical sketch of one's experience. High-school diplomas were sold for $100, an associate of arts degree for $150, a bachelor's degree for $175, a master's degree for $200, and a Ph.D. for $250. A 20 percent discount was allowed if one applied for more than one degree at the same time. The catalog stated that many applicants apply for two or more degrees at the same time and are totally satisfied with their service.[42] Action has been taken against this and other "diploma mills" in a number of states, but as long as there are people willing to pay to get degrees without working for them, there will be people willing to sell such degrees. The lax chartering laws in some states permit the existence of correspondence schools whose practices amount virtually to the sale of degrees.

Proprietary schools—schools established as profit-making operations—which include a wide variety of vocational schools, present another problem. For example, a school for computer technicians in New Mexico solicited American Indians to enroll in courses and promised them careers as highly paid computer programmers. Would-be students borrowed thousands of dollars in federally insured student loans through the same company that offered the courses. They never saw the money, and since they were academically unprepared for the field they had to withdraw after the first class meeting. The school offered no refunds and charged interest on the loans, which no longer received federal subsidy.[43] Another computer school consented to a Federal Trade Commission order requiring it to refund nearly $750,000 to students because the school had not fulfilled its contractual obligations.[44]

The academic community was shocked when a student sued the University of Bridgeport in Connecticut. She had received a grade of A in the course she was taking, but she claimed that the course was an insult to her intelligence and had taught her nothing. She sued to have the $350 enrollment fee refunded.[45] This case has already made colleges and universities more aware of their responsibilities to their "customers." The U.S. Office of Education has inventoried twenty-five possible educational abuses, ranging from degree mills to the use of outdated or obsolete equipment, textbooks, or laboratories.[46] Because of the mounting problems in the education field, the FTC initiated a proceeding for the promulgation of a "Trade Regulation Rule Concerning Proprietary Vocational and Home Study Schools." Action is currently pending on this rule.

Charity and Religious Frauds

The 215 million Americans together contribute over $25 billion annually to charitable, philanthropic, and religious causes. Most of us are humane and sympathetic; when appeals for money are made on behalf of people in distress, our response is usually generous. It is therefore easy for dishonest operators to capitalize on our charitable instincts.

One so-called charity, using the come-on of being "Red-Cross sponsored," charged $50 a seat for a Liza Minnelli concert, took in about $200,-000, but turned over only $3,600, or 1.8 percent of the proceeds, to charity.[47] A Baltimore-based Pallottine Mission Office raised some $20 million in two years from its mail campaigns but sent only about $500,000 in cash to overseas missions.[48]

A key measure of any charitable solicitation is what percentage of the money collected actually goes to benefit those for whom it is collected. The president of the American Association of Fund-Raising Counsel stated that if the charity's cause is worthwhile, if it has committed leadership, if it uses volunteers to solicit funds, if its constituency is aware of the agency, and if it has a professional staff, then fund-raising costs for this kind of operation should range between 10 and 25 percent of all monies collected.[49]

The National Health Council reported on the financial operations of a number of charitable groups. The Epilepsy Foundation had the highest expenses of the groups checked, with only 48 percent of its receipts going to charitable work and the rest spent on expenses; the American Cancer Society reported 78 percent for its programs, with expenses of 22 percent; and the National Kidney Foundation had expenses of 21 percent, with 79 percent spent for programs.[50]

One of the biggest charity rackets ever investigated involved a professional fund-raising firm that sent circulars through the mail to millions of persons throughout the country year after year, seeking funds to help cure a crippling disease. Investigation disclosed that of the approximately $22 million contributed by the public, nearly $11 million were earmarked for salaries and expenses, with illegal kickbacks for the charity's officers.[51]

Defrauding the Elderly

The elderly are particularly susceptible to fraudulent practices. The National Retired Teachers Association and the American Association of Retired Persons surveyed some eighty-eight attorneys general and consumer protection agencies throughout the country to determine what kind of consumer complaints they received most often from older persons.[52] None of the fifty-five respondents categorized consumer complaints by age, but the most prevalent problems reported affecting the elderly were as follows:

1. Home repair and improvement schemes
2. Deceptive sales practices
3. Hearing aid sales practices
4. Land sales schemes
5. Automobiles (purchase and repair)

6. Credit problems (including incorrect billing and credit cards)
7. Pyramid schemes and franchises
8. Mail order
9. Health foods and medical quackery
10. Insurance frauds

Older consumers are victimized by some of the most extreme forms of exploitation and commercial indignity. For example, one company sold a "Solarama Board," an electronic bedboard that salespeople recommended for arthritis, tension, nerves, sleeplessness, sore muscles, burns of all sorts, frostbite, post-operative healing, and hemorrhoidal pain and shrinkage. A small board sold for about $80 and a large one for about $130. A Florida health department official said that it was nothing more than an expensive hot water bottle being sold primarily to the elderly.[53]

Extensive hearings were held by a Special Committee on Aging of the United States Senate in the areas of health frauds and quackery, deceptive or misleading methods in health insurance sales, interstate mail-order land sales, and pre-need burial service. A few pertinent items presented at these hearings emphasize some areas of fraud which confront all consumers, but to which the aged are particularly susceptible.[54] An American Dental Association study showed that the public pays more than $20 million each year to unqualified persons who operate contrary to state dental laws. The average cost of complete upper dentures obtained from dentists was 26 percent higher than those obtained from the "quacks." The averages for complete lower dentures were 39 percent higher from dentists than from "quacks." In this case, for an illusory savings, people subject themselves to nonprofessional care and risk injury to their oral health. The hearings on health insurance showed that economic pressures on older persons are causing many to turn to mail-order health insurance offered by marginal companies that distort or omit facts in order to suggest that the policy gives more protection than it really does.

The elderly are particularly susceptible to fraud. They seem to be more willing to trust a person who pretends to show real concern for their welfare. They do not get to the marketplace very often and, being at home most of the time, are readily accessible to unscrupulous door-to-door salespeople. They tend to be more fearful both for their own health and the condition of their homes. They have fewer contacts with the public and become less aware of what is going on in the "outer" world. It is a tragedy that when people become less able to care for themselves, when their incomes are usually considerably less, they have to be more wary of fraudulent operators.

Defrauding the Poor

Frauds are perpetrated on persons at all levels of income, but the poor are particularly susceptible to fraudulent operators and are also least able to afford being defrauded. The President's Commission on Civil Disorders, reporting on the causes of rioting in ghettos, stated: "Many residents of disadvantaged . . . neighborhoods believe that they suffer constant abuses by local merchants." The ignorance of many of the poor when in the marketplace is pathetic. The lack of knowledge of what to do creates real hardships for them and makes them easy prey to the fraudulent operator. They do not read contracts. They do not save contracts, sales slips, receipts, or guarantees. They do not understand the intricacies of buying on credit. They place their trust in the merchant, and too frequently this has been a misplaced trust.

Mail Frauds

The Inspection Service of the United States Postal Service estimates that fraudulent mail schemes represent a potential annual loss to the public of nearly $400 million. Of the endless variety of fraudulent schemes the most vicious is the sale of worthless medicines and therapeutic devices. The worst schemes advertise quick cures for cancer, tuberculosis, arthritis, diabetes, and other serious illnesses. "Prophets," soothsayers, and fortune-tellers promise love, money, long life, and good health – until postal inspectors catch them. Mailings of pornographic matter are on the increase in spite of the efforts of the inspectors.

In 1975 Postal Inspection Service processed 127,044 complaints alleging mail fraud. Many of these did not, of course, constitute criminal mail fraud, but as the result of investigations undertaken by this service, 1,260 persons were convicted of criminal mail fraud during this period. Fines assessed by the courts in these cases totaled $1,345,061 and restitution (both voluntary and court ordered) totaled $9,336,917. In spite of such vigilance, the fleecing continues year after year. People can help the Postal Service detect frauds by returning suspicious matter to the local post office or notifying the Postal Inspection Service.

In general, the mails are used for the same types of frauds as are found in face-to-face or telephone contacts. The Postal Inspection Service lists the following as major areas in which consumer frauds are perpetrated through the mails: chain-referral schemes; fake contests; low-price traps; home improvements; debt consolidation; auto insurance fraud; retirement homes; missing heir schemes; charity rackets; and unordered merchandise.[55]

Section 3009 of the Postal Reorganization Act of 1970 has resolved the problem of unordered merchandise. The law stipulates that anyone receiving unordered merchandise by mail may do whatever he or she wants with it and no payment need be made. Thus, the law is very clear and relieves the recipient of any responsibility.

The avalanche of unsolicited pornography that has been sent through the mails to persons of all ages in the last few years has created such resentment that Congress passed a law (39 U.S. Code 3010) to stem this flow of sexually oriented material. The law went into effect in 1971. This law protects all persons from receiving pornographic advertisements through the mail. A family can now list the names at the local post office of those members of the family who do not wish to receive such advertisements. These names are compiled, and any mailer who sends out sexually oriented advertisements to persons whose names appear on the list is subject to both civil and criminal legal action by the government.

Advertising Fraud

False and misleading advertising costs consumers hundreds of millions of dollars a year. This topic is treated in detail on pages 196–198.

White-Collar Fraud

"It is better," C. Wright Mills once observed, "to take one dime from each of ten million people at the point of a corporation than $100,000 from each of ten banks at the point of a gun. It is also safer."[56] It is estimated that forty billion dollars is lost each year through so-called "white-collar" crime in America. Consumers indirectly pay for this form of fraud because businesses add the cost of it to the prices consumers pay for goods and services. Much of white-collar crime consists of employees stealing from their employers, but it also includes "respectable" businessmen stealing from consumers. Illegal price-fixing is one example of this. Another example came to the public's attention when the FTC forced four retail department stores to return unclaimed balances to their charge customers. According to the FTC staff, the stores kept a total of at least $2.8 million in customer funds over a five-year period. The stores wrote off the balances from the accounts when the customers failed to use them or to ask for refunds.[57] Illegal political contributions and the millions of dollars in payoffs and bribes paid by major corporations to foreign government officials are additional "costs of doing business" that are paid for indirectly by consumers in the prices of the goods and services that they buy from these companies.

WHY DOES FRAUD PERSIST?

Gullible Consumers and Greedy Sellers

Fraud is as old as the human race; it changes only in form and amount. Frauds of a generation or a century ago have given way to newer frauds, which are probably no more clever, for very few frauds are or need to be clever. The country is full of people who will believe almost anything. For predatory producers such people are easy prey. Craving health, wealth, beauty, or power, people like to believe that a simple mixture of water and alcohol will cure an incurable disease, that an advertised remedy will make them thin. They do not stop to analyze such propositions; if they did, the fraud would be apparent. Rather, they act on emotion, a dangerous guide in the marketplace. Such persons as selfishly seek something for nothing as the sellers of the worthless preparation or product.

All consumers are ignorant in varying degrees. Some are aware of their ignorance, but many are not. Evidence presented throughout this book demonstrates the inability of most consumers to be wary in the marketplace. Only chemists can analyze some products, and sometimes even they have difficulty. Even though merchandise may be represented honestly, few buyers have any way of judging the validity of its price. Some dealers keep this in mind as they set the retail prices for their merchandise and services.

Not all sellers, of course, are greedy, but many of them are. Nor are all greedy sellers devoid of conscience, but many of them are. Persons who make poisonous products that kill or injure their users may be operating within the limits of law, but not within the restrictions of any code of ethics. The growth of a large, impersonal market has made it easier for conscienceless producers to ply their trade, not only because detection is more difficult but because personal relationships with their victims are unnecessary.

Impotent Laws

Caught between the horns of this dilemma, consumers need protection from their own ignorance and from the avarice of predatory sellers. It is futile to talk about educating consumers adequately. No one person can ever be sufficiently trained in all fields of knowledge to combat the specialized skill of such sellers. The best that can be done is to develop a body of more wary consumers. This needs to be supplemented by law. Consumer ignorance, however, makes it difficult to enact and to enforce legislation. The problem of consumer protection is further complicated because many such laws are defective and authority is divided among local, state, and federal governments. Effective legislation is difficult to secure not only because uninformed, unorganized consumers fail to demand it but also because well-organized and well-informed groups of business executives oppose it. In the view of business, the right of free enterprise carries with it the right of exploitation. The punitive provisions of such laws as are on the statute books are absurdly lenient. Rarely is the vendor of a fraud committed to jail, and fines are so small as to be only an additional cost of doing business.

ARE CONSUMERS HELPLESS?

Consumers cannot do much as individuals. To be sure, the better informed they are, the more they can be on guard. Anyone who has graduated from high school should know enough to see through fraudulent schemes and reject them. Yet people continue to sign blank contracts and then complain when they are cheated. Every individual would do well to ask questions and to investigate before making a commitment. Inquiries can be made at the Better Business Bureau or the local chamber of commerce in communities not served by a Better Business Bureau.

The Federal Trade Commission has a consumer complaint office in Washington, D.C., and has established twelve field offices throughout the nation as a part of its campaign against consumer frauds. The FTC has specific jurisdiction over unfair trade practices in the District of Columbia, but elsewhere it has authority only in cases involving interstate commerce. In addition, the following federal agencies are ready to assist the consumer when called upon:

Consumer Product Safety Commission, Washington, D.C. 20207
Food and Drug Administration, Rockville, Md. 20852
U.S. Postal Service, Washington, D.C. 20260
Federal Trade Commission, Washington, D.C. 20580
Federal Housing Administration (contact the field office nearest you for complaints where FHA or VA financing is involved)
U.S. Securities and Exchange Commission, Washington, D.C. 20549 (for problems concerning the selling and purchasing of stocks and bonds)
President's Special Assistant for Consumer Affairs, Office of Consumer Affairs, Washington, D.C. 20201

The attorney generals' offices of many states have also established consumer fraud divisions to render protection to the public.

Consumers Are Not Angels

All fraud is not perpetrated by the seller on the buyer. Unfortunately there are some consumers who perpetrate fraud on the seller. Sellers have had to counteract customer fraud by making it more difficult for consumers to be dishonest.* In addition to outright shoplifting, retailers have found that some shoppers switch price labels from a low-priced item to a high-priced item. Because of this we now have to contend with price labels that seem almost impossible to get off. Some shoppers have been found switching a high-priced item into a carton with a low price marked on it. Lid switching is another problem. To prevent shoppers from switching a lid with a low price marked on it to a bottle with a high-priced lid sellers invented hard-to-open tops. Small products such as razor blades are packed into large "bubble" packages to make them harder to steal.

"Refund reapers" create another problem for retailers. They purchase an item at discount, then take it to a store selling it at list price and request a

* See Chapter 11, pp. 263–264 for additional details on shoplifting.

refund, in cash if possible. They state they have no sales slip because the item was a gift. If the store gives them a refund slip instead of cash, they can take the refund slip, buy new merchandise, then have a confederate return in a few days with the item and the sales slip for a cash refund. It is important for consumers to realize that such losses are covered in stores by the prices they charge.

QUESTIONS FOR REVIEW

1. Why does fraud exist in the marketplace?
2. Where and how does the practice of fraud fit into the traditional economic theory of the competitive free enterprise system?
3. Why should, or should not, the government protect the consumer from fraud?
4. Why do you think fraud exists in some areas more than in others?
5. Why is the health care field particularly susceptible to fraud?
6. Why should fee splitting be ruled an evil practice?
7. Why are there so many questionable practices in the selling of automobiles?
8. How does one find a reputable repair shop?
9. "All gambling should be illegal." Discuss the pros and cons of this.
10. What are the results of white-collar crime?
11. Why are perfectly good products frequently sold in a fraudulent manner?
12. Do you believe that honesty is the best policy in business? Does it always pay?

PROJECTS

1. Write a report on the tetracycline price-fixing case.
2. Write a report on the FTC versus Listerine case.
3. Interview a doctor or dentist about medical or dental fraud.
4. Interview a group of students to see if any of them have ever been trapped by a repair swindle.
5. Interview a group of students and find out what kinds of frauds they are aware of that consumers have perpetrated on sellers.
6. What is being done by your local better business bureau or chamber of commerce to combat fraud?
7. Interview ten students who use mouthwashes and find out if they are aware of the American Dental Association's position on mouthwashes.

REFERENCES

1. Adam Smith, *The Wealth of Nations* (New York: Modern Library, 1937), p. 651.
2. *New York Times*, 15 Aug. 1975, p. 5.
3. *New York Times*, 9 July 1975, p. 47.
4. *New York Times*, 20 Jan. 1976, p. 45.
5. *New York Times*, 13 Aug. 1975, p. 41.
6. *New York Times*, 14 Jan. 1976, p. 1.
7. *Changing Times*, Aug. 1975, p. 36.
8. *FDA Consumer*, July–Aug. 1976, pp. 35–40.
9. *New York Times*, 10 Dec. 1975, p. 76.
10. *New York Times*, 30 May 1975, p. 36.
11. *Advertising Age*, 22 Dec. 1975, p. 1.
12. Food and Drug Administration, Consumer Memo March 1974, p. 1.
13. *New York Times*, 7 Aug. 1975, p. 19.
14. *New York Times Magazine*, 21 Sept. 1975, p. 34.
15. *New York Times*, 6 Aug. 1975, p. 28.
16. *Ibid.*
17. *Harper's*, May 1975, p. 30.
18. *New York Times*, 7 Aug. 1975, p. 19.
19. *New York Times*, 6 Aug. 1975, p. 28.
20. *New York Times*, 26 Jan. 1976, p. 1.
21. *News-Tribune* (Beaver Falls, Pa.), 20 Nov. 1975, p. A-8.
22. *Bulletin of the American College of Surgeons*, Jan. 1975.
23. *St. Petersburg Times*, 26 Aug. 1975, p. 1B.
24. *Newsweek*, 15 Dec. 1975, p. 80.
25. Anthony Till, *What You Should Know Before You Buy A Car* (New York: Sherbourne Press, 1968), pp. 81–95.
26. *New York Times*, 27 Aug. 1969, p. 47.
27. Public Law 85-506, 85th Congress, S. 3500
28. National Highway Traffic Safety Administration, Department of Transportation, News Release, 18 Feb. 1975.
29. Anthony Till, *What You Should Know Before You Have Your Car Repaired* (Los Angeles: Sherbourne Press, 1970), p. 12.
30. *Consumer Survival Kit: Auto Repairanoia* (Owings Mills, Md.: Maryland Center for Public Broadcasting, 1974), p. 1.
31. *New York Times*, 8 Dec. 1975, pp. 1, 50
32. *N.A.D.A. Official Used Car Guide* (Washington, D.C.: National Automobile Dealers Association, Jan. 1976), pp. E2, E3.
33. *St. Petersburg Times*, 19 Aug. 1975, p. 1D.
34. *Changing Times*, Nov. 1975, p. 20.
35. *Business Week*, 4 Aug. 1975, p. 68.
36. *Ibid.*
37. Morton C. Paulson, *The Great Land Hustle* (Chicago: Henry Regnery, 1972), p. 2.
38. *Consumer Protection: Interstate Land Sales*, Office of Interstate Land Sales Registration, U.S. Department of Housing and Urban Development, Aug. 1970, p. 2.
39. *Ibid.*
40. *New York Times*, 29 Oct. 1975, p. 1.
41. *Model State Legislation: Report of the Task Force on Model State Legislation for Approval of Postsecondary Educational Institutions and Authorization to Grant Degrees* (Denver, Col.: Education Commission of the States, 1973), pp. v–vi.
42. External Degree Program Catalog, 1975–76, Jackson State University, Nashville, Tenn.

43. *Toward a Federal Strategy for Protection of the Consumer of Education* (Washington, D.C.: U.S. Department of Health, Education, and Welfare, 1975), p. 9.
44. Federal Trade Commission, News Summary, 25 July 1975.
45. *Washington Star News*, 14 Jan. 1975, p. A6.
46. "An Overview: Consumer Protection in Higher Education. Why? For Whom? How?," address by Sandra Willett, Director of Consumer Education, Office of Consumer Affairs, before the annual meeting of the Association of American Colleges, 12 Jan. 1975.
47. *People*, 3 March 1975, p. 64.
48. *New York Times*, 19 June 1976, p. 1.
49. *U.S. News & World Report*, Oct.–Nov. 1974, p. 1.
50. *Con$umer New$week*, 15 April 1975, p. 3.
51. *Mail Fraud Laws Protecting: Consumers, Investors, Businessmen, Patients, Students* (Washington, D.C.: U.S. Government Printing Office, 1971), p. 5.
52. Frederick E. Waddell, "Consumer Research and Programs for the Elderly: The Forgotten Dimension," *Journal of Consumer Affairs* 9 (1975): 169–170.
53. *St. Petersburg Times*, 30 Sept. 1975, p. 8D.
54. This material is derived from the *Hearings before the Subcommittee on Frauds and Misrepresentations Affecting the Elderly of the Special Committee on Aging*, United States Senate, 88th Congress, 2d Session, 13 Jan., 9, 10 March, 6 April, 18 May, 19 May, and 20 May, 1964.
55. *Mail Fraud Laws Protecting: Consumers, Investors, Businessmen, Patients, Students*, pp. 1–5.
56. *Consumer Reports*, Aug. 1974, p. 583.
57. *Ibid.*

PART  FOUR

MAKING CONSUMER CONTROL EFFECTIVE: A RATIONALE FOR CONSUMERS

CHAPTER 15

PLANNING AND RECORDING EXPENDITURES

SPENDING WITHOUT RESPONSIBILITY

Bankrupt Consumers

In the ten-year period ending in 1975, there was a 34 percent increase in the number of individuals filing personal bankruptcy petitions, despite the fact that personal income rose 133 percent and per capita personal income rose 111 percent during the same decade. A supposedly better educated public was making no headway in slowing down the growing number of personal bankruptcies by handling its money better. Sound money management is a skill, an art. Without it, consumers may suffer economic, sociological, and psychological injuries; using it, they may greatly benefit.

One out of every two families has some form of consumer installment debt, the average debt being over $4,000. In 1949 consumers used 8 percent of their take-home income to meet payments on their installment debts. By 1973 the percentage of take-home income used to repay installment debt had more than doubled, to 17 percent. Many families use 30 percent, 40 percent, or more of their income to repay consumer debts.[1]

A survey of American families concluded that 54 percent argue about money, and in families hard pressed by money problems, the percentage arguing over money increases to 64 percent.[2] Admissions to mental hospitals go up during recessions and decline during periods of prosperity. Psychiatrists attribute much of this increase to worry over financial insecurity. It is apparent that the American family needs guidance and education in personal money management and spending with responsibility.

RESPONSIBLE SPENDING

"The problem of managing our money will be with us all of our lives. Money management is not an option. We do not have any choice about whether or not to manage money. Our only choice is between effective and ineffective management."[3] How one thinks about money may be more significant in terms of money management than how one spends money. A family's living standard and financial stability may be dictated more by the way it spends money than by the size of its income. The individual's or family's goal in personal money management should be to keep its purchases within the limitations of its income.

Consumer Life Cycle

Patterns of spending change rather dramatically as an individual progresses through the life cycle. Each stage in the life cycle presents a unique set of conditions affecting the consumer's ability and willingness to consume various items and to undertake the financial burdens involved in their acquisition. The stages of the life cycle for most persons include the following: 1) the bachelor stage – the young, single person living alone; 2) young married couple with no children – generally with both earning an income; 3) young married couple with small children; 4) older married couple still with dependent children at home; 5) older married couple with no children living with them or dependent upon them; 6) older married couple on retirement; 7) solitary survivor – older single or widowed persons. Intelligent budgeting has to take into consideration the important changes that take place in spending patterns as one moves from one stage of life to another.

Spending According to a Plan

In a traditional marriage partnership the wife is the primary purchasing agent for everyday items. Women purchase 90 percent of the food, kitchenware, draperies, curtains, and clothing consumed by families. Men are usually the chief buyers of insurance, automobiles, and automotive supplies. Few women or men are trained for their responsibilities as purchasing agents. A business firm is established to make profit and employees are hired for their skill, but a family is established for noneconomic reasons. Men do not usually marry women because they are efficient and careful spenders. Nor do women choose mates on the basis of their consumer intelligence. Moreover, the task of purchasing for a family is different from that of purchasing for a business firm. Purchasing agents for a business firm perform one task in which they specialize. The range of commodities they buy is limited to those required by the firm. The purchasing agent for a family finds that his or her task of buying is only one of the many tasks that must be accomplished in the full stride of a day's work. The range of commodities to be purchased covers the whole field of human wants and includes everything ready for final consumption. Women and men do not approach their task of buying in a professional spirit. In business, survival depends on efficient operations throughout the firm. In many cases survival of a marriage also depends on rational and efficient purchasing. Spend-thriftism can destroy a family as well as a firm. One ingredient of success-ful family living is cooperation in spending the family income. Family members must work together to secure maximum utility. The planned budget, supplemented with a record of expenditures, is the key to coopera-tion in spending family income so as to achieve maximum well-being.

Benefits of a Budget

The family that does not somehow plan expenditures must be rare. Most families plan their expenditures after a fashion. This includes the un-conscious planning of recurring expenditures and deliberate planning for larger nonrecurring expenditures. But only a few families actually prepare a complete budget. Real budgeting is the act of putting on paper a complete plan of spending for a definite period, such as one year. The following are some advantages of budgeting:

1. Budgeting encourages the rational use of income. The very act of preparing a budget requires evaluation and reexamination of con-suming practices. This tends to elevate the importance of utility in allocating income and in choosing goods and services. At the same time it minimizes the influence of custom, conspicuous consumption, emulation, fashion, and advertising.
2. Budgeting makes it easier to adjust irregular income to regular expend-itures. A family that receives a regular monthly salary or income has fewer problems in planning expenditures than a family whose income is intermittent. Wage earners, salespeople on commission, business executives who are dependent on profits, and professionals can never be certain of their annual income. The minimum amount of money neces-sary to maintain the desired plane of living is fairly regular for all fam-ilies. But for some families the amount and the time of receiving annual income are uncertain. A family budget based on past experience will help to meet the problem of uncertain income.
3. Budgeting is helpful when family income increases or decreases. When the economy is booming, a family may have an unexpected increase in income. It is much easier to increase family expenditures than to curtail them. Failure to budget may lead a family into a scale of living that it cannot maintain in the lean years that may follow. Salaried men or women who find their real incomes reduced as money prices rise, as well as workers whose incomes decline in recession periods, are better able to adjust themselves to such reductions if they operate on a budget.
4. Another service that budgeting can perform is helping one to plan ex-penditures over a period of years. Professional athletes earn their maxi-mum income from the age of twenty to the age of thirty-five. Although it is customary to speak of a fifty-year-old man as being middle-aged,

actually a man is middle-aged at thirty-five. Athletes and many other workers may find their incomes declining after middle age. In preparation for the later years, budgeting is a helpful device in allocating income for savings and investment.

5. Adjustments to increases and decreases in family size are accomplished more easily when a family operates on a budget. In the first year or two following marriage, the family usually consists of only two. A modest income may be budgeted to include some comforts and a few luxuries. As children begin to arrive, family expenses are increased. Unless the family income increases proportionately, a reallocation of expenditures must take place. Estimates of the cost of rearing children were presented on page 55. These costs usually continue for twenty-five years — a quarter of a century. As the children establish their own homes, the size of the family reverts to two. With a larger income the parents then have diminished expenses, leaving more to spend in other ways. Finally, when the head of a family retires, family income is likely to be diminished by as much as 50 percent, and the retired couple must again revise their budget. In all phases of the family cycle the use of a budget facilitates adjustment to change.

6. The process of preparing a budget requires a reexamination of family goals and values. The very act of putting anticipated expenditures on paper makes the important ones stand out more sharply than the less important. With a budget spread out on the family dining room table it is possible to compare various items. After such comparisons, it is much more likely that essential goods and services will be given priority.

7. Budgeting can be helpful in allocating *discretionary income,* which is that portion of family income in excess of necessary expenditures and contract commitments. It is the uncommitted income that a family can spend as it pleases. It can be frittered away, spent on luxuries, or saved. In the decade ending in 1976, discretionary income increased by more than 75 percent. When a family finds itself with increasing discretionary income, a budget will help to plan the expenditure of that portion of family income rationally and beneficially.

8. Another advantage to be gained from a budget is that it makes possible a comparison of expenditures for selected items. This in turn makes it possible to determine whether the allowance for each item is more or less than the approved minimum standard; for example, whether enough money has been allocated for food. A correct budgetary allowance for food and for certain kinds of food will help promote health. The same generalization applies to other items in the budget. By comparing sample budgets a family may learn how much of their income should be budgeted for clothing and how much should be allowed for specific items of clothing.

9. Finally budgeting helps to discover and plug leaks in family expenditures. It is a common experience to discover that within a short time after receiving one's paycheck it is impossible to recall where or for what it was spent. If money is spent as planned in the budget, the

records will show where every dollar went. If any money has been spent foolishly, the record will show it and help the budgeters to prevent a recurrence.

Why Don't All Families Budget?

It has been estimated that only four out of ten families operate on budgets. When there are so many demonstrable advantages to budgeting why is it that families that budget their incomes are in the minority?

1. Perhaps the basic reason is that most American consumers believe that the way to raise the family plane of living is to increase income. They ignore the possibility of increasing *real income* – that is, the amount of goods and services their money will buy – by planning expenditures and buying intelligently.
2. Closely related is the fact that very few adult consumers were exposed to good consuming practices when they were children. There has been very little consumer education in the public school system. In some families children are taught to handle their money intelligently, but in too many families children are exposed to spendthriftism. Habits developed in childhood tend to persist in later years. Economic infants may never grow up.
3. The beneficial results of budgeting are intangible. The careless spender can see a 10 percent salary increase in his or her paycheck, but if he or she manages the family income so as to make it yield a 10 percent increase in real income, the latter increase is much more difficult to see or to measure.
4. Inertia is a deterring force. It takes time and effort to prepare a budget and to keep a record of expenditures. For many people even a simple system of financial records is too difficult.
5. It is easier to budget a regular income than it is to budget an irregular income. Although the task is more difficult for the family with an irregular income, the advantages are likely to be greater.
6. One sometimes hears this comment: "There is no point in budgeting our income because it is so small. It takes all we earn just to live." When people who hold this view are converted to the use of a budget they discover that planning and recording expenditures help them use their limited incomes in such a way as to increase their real incomes.
7. Effective budgeting requires the cooperation of all members of a family. If either one of the parents in a family enterprise refuses to cooperate, budgeting is impossible. As the children grow older, their cooperation is also necessary. Budgeting is essentially a family project. Each member of the family should have a voice in determining the amount to be spent for all items, whether he or she contributes to the money income or not. And each member of the family must cooperate in keeping a record of expenditures.

THE ABC'S OF BUDGETING

Prior to budgeting for expenditures, it is necessary to make as accurate an estimate as possible of all income. This may be done on a weekly, bi-weekly, or monthly basis, depending on the frequency of the paydays. The income record should include the gross income less all deductions with-held from the paycheck, thus indicating what remains available to use for budgeted expenditures. Individuals who do not receive the bulk of their income from wages and salaries must be particularly careful in estimating their income. After recording all income, you are ready to budget for expenditures.

There are three steps in the planning and recording of expenditures. The way to start is to put on paper a weekly or monthly expenditure plan. This is supplemented by a written record of actual expenditures week by week or month by month. The final step is a comparison of actual expenditures with anticipated expenditures.

Step One: Planning a Budget

Families and individuals wishing to increase their real incomes by budgeting will need some guidance in planning expenditures. Those who have never budgeted may not know how to set up accounts. For such consumers the budgets shown in Table 15-1 will be helpful. These three budgets — lower, intermediate, and higher — were prepared by the Bureau of Labor Statistics of the U.S. Department of Labor and show typical costs for an urban family of four.

TABLE 15-1.   Three Budgets for Four-Person Families

Expenses	Low Budget $9,198	Intermediate Budget $14,333	High Budget $20,777
Food	30.1%	24.7%	21.4%
Housing (includes shelter, household operations, and house furnishings)	19.1	22.6	23.6
Transportation	7.0	8.2	7.3
Clothing	8.3	7.6	7.7
Personal care	2.5	2.2	2.1
Medical care	8.0	5.2	3.7
Other family consumption	4.6	5.5	6.2
Other expenses (gifts, charitable contributions, life insurance, and occupational expenses)	4.5	4.6	5.4
Social security and disability payments	6.0	5.4	3.8
Personal income taxes	9.9	14.0	18.8
Total	100.0%	100.0%	100.0%

Source: U.S. Department of Labor, News Release, 9 April 1975.

A budget is more satisfactory if it has eighteen to twenty items. Up to a certain point the greater the number of items, the more accurate and the more useful the budget will be. Table 15-2 presents a suggested budget form. It is difficult to say whether some expenditures are essential and others less essential or nonessential, but an effort has been made to group the items in the approximate order of importance. This does not mean that if budget restriction becomes necessary certain items should be discontinued completely, but rather that expenditures on some of the essential items might be reduced while less essential items might be cut drastically. Then, if necessary, nonessentials could be eliminated. Certain items, such as social security payments and personal taxes, obviously cannot be reduced.

TABLE 15-2. Sample Budget Form

Item No.	Item	JANUARY	FEBRUARY	MARCH	APRIL	MAY	JUNE	JULY	AUGUST	SEPTEMBER	OCTOBER	NOVEMBER	DECEMBER
1	A. Food												
2	Housing												
3	Household operation												
4	Household furnishings												
5	Clothing												
	Father												
	Mother												
	Son												
	Daughter												
6	Transportation												
	Automobile												
7	Taxes												
	Income (withholding)												
	Sales												
	Property												
8	B. Personal care												
9	Medical care												
10	Dental care												
11	Insurance (life, social security, disability)												
12	Savings												
13	C. Vacation and recreation												
14	Newspapers, magazines, Postage												
15	Education												
16	Dues												
17	Contributions												
18	Gifts												
19	Miscellaneous												

Figures showing the monthly budget as a percentage of income should be filled in by each family, according to its own budget. There are so many variables, such as size of income, size of family, and others, that it is not feasible to suggest specific figures. Beginning budgeters might use the percentages shown in Table 15-1 as guides. Adjustments can be made with experience. In Table 15-2 the monthly columns are reserved for recording the amounts actually spent. By having all figures on one page, you can compare the amount allocated for each account with the amount actually spent. At the end of the year this provides a condensed summary of your financial record.

Step Two: Keeping the Records

After planning a budget and putting it into operation, the next step is to keep a record of expenditures. The method of keeping such a record will vary with circumstances and experience. When bills are paid weekly or monthly by check, the stub is a convenient record, but some people do not maintain bank accounts. It is usually advantageous to pay cash for frequently recurring purchases. For these reasons a system for recording daily cash expenditures with a minimum of effort is necessary.

How detailed a record should be kept? The more detailed the record, the more useful it will be. The classification of food items, for example, serves not only as a record of expenditures for food, but also as a means of testing the adequacy of your diet. Also you can compare the amounts spent on meat, milk, butter, eggs, and cheese to see if the proportions conform to the recommendations in approved family diets. Equally detailed records may be kept for all items, and from time to time it may be desirable to do so in order to ascertain where the family money is going and to detect leaks. Once this has been done for several months it may be unnecessary to continue. For the experienced budgeter the burden of keeping a detailed record of expenditures may outweigh possible gains.

How accurate should the record be? Let it be said at once that record-keeping is not bookkeeping. Accounts need not balance to the last penny. The family is not a business. It is a consuming unit, using the budget as a guide to better living. Budgeting and record-keeping are a means to an end.

A simple method of recording daily cash expenditures is shown in Table 15-3. One of these sheets is prepared for each month in the year. Together with the budget itself these sheets can be kept in an $8\frac{1}{2} \times 11$ inch notebook at a convenient location in the kitchen. If a pencil is attached to the notebook, as members of the family come home after a shopping tour or at the end of the day, they can go to the budget book and record all the expenditures they have made.

The column marked "Date" is a device for helping to recall whether a certain expenditure has been recorded. It will be noted that the columns to the left are too small to allow space for comment. For the food items the only necessary notations are date, quantity, and price. The other columns

TABLE 15-3.   Suggested Form For Recording Daily Cash Expenditures

								Date	(2) Housing	Date	(5) Clothing
											January, 19
Date	(1) Food							Date	(2) Housing	Date	(5) Clothing
	Butter	Date	Bread	Date	Fruits and vegetables	Date	Groceries				
	Milk										
											(6) Transportation
	Eggs		Meat						(4) Household furnishings		
	Cheese										
											(12) Savings
	(3) Household Operation			(14) Newspapers, etc.					(7) Taxes		
											(9, 10) Medical, Dental Care
	(15) Education			(16) Dues					(8) Personal Care	2	Doctor $10
											(13) Vacation and Recreation
	(17) Contributions			(18) Gifts					(11) Insurance		
											(19) Miscellaneous

carry items for which some notation is frequently desirable. For example, in the medical dental account the sample entry shows that on the second of the month $10 was spent for a doctor's visit. Such records are also useful in preparing income tax returns.

Step Three: Comparing the Record with the Plan

At the end of each month the figures in each column are totaled and transferred to the proper column on the budget sheet, shown in Table 15-2. At a glance the budgeter can compare the amount actually spent with the amount budgeted. For example, if the amount spent for food in January was a few dollars more than the amount budgeted, the budgeter knows that the amount spent in February will probably be a few dollars less. January has three more days than February and the budgeter knows that the monthly average can be maintained. If excess expenditures show up in the several successive months the budgeter knows that some expensive items must be reduced in amount or eliminated.

In the same way the monthly expenditure for each item is recorded and compared with the amount budgeted. If overdrafts appear they must be reduced in subsequent months or the budget for that item must be increased, with a corresponding reduction in the budget for some other item. If the comparison shows some accounts for which expenditures have been less than the amount budgeted, the surplus may be transferred temporarily to one or more of the other items.

If expenditures for one account consistently fall below the amount budgeted, the budget should be revised to allow more for another account which consistently falls in arrears.

TAKING AN ANNUAL INVENTORY

Determining Net Worth

At least once a year assets and liabilities should be listed to show what financial progress is being made. Budgeting and record-keeping show the annual net acquisition of permanent wealth as well as annual operating expenses. A suggested form of financial statement is shown in Table 15-4.

Family assets should be classified as "liquid" and "nonliquid." A liquid

TABLE 15-4.   Suggested Form For a Family Financial Statement

Liquid assets
    Cash on hand   _____
    Cash on deposit in checking account   _____
    Savings account   _____
    Market value of listed stocks   _____
    Market value of listed bonds   _____
    Cash surrender value of life insurance policies   _____

Nonliquid assets
    Market value of house   _____
    Market value of furniture and furnishings   _____
    Resale value of automobile   _____
    Cash value of annuity contracts   _____
    Cash value of retirement fund   _____
    Bid prices on unlisted stocks   _____
    Bid prices on unlisted bonds   _____
    Market value of land owned   _____
    Market value of buildings owned   _____
    Money loaned on mortgage   _____
    Accounts receivable   _____
    Other assets   _____
      Total assets $_____

Liabilities
    Mortgage on house   _____
    Loan from bank   _____
    Loan on life insurance   _____
    Bills payable at stores   _____
    Installment debt   _____
    Other liabilities   _____
      Total Liabilities $_____

Net Worth December 31, 19___ $_____

asset is cash or an asset that can be converted to cash quickly. If the family has a checking account in a commercial bank, checks may be written or cashed on demand. Some savings banks require thirty, sixty, or ninety days notice, but many of them permit depositors to withdraw cash on demand. Corporation stocks that are listed on one of the exchanges can be converted into cash quickly at current market prices. Likewise for bonds. Life insurance companies, like savings banks, usually require advance notice of an insured's wish to borrow on a contract or to cash it in. In practice, however, most companies are so liberal as to justify listing the cash value of insurance contracts as a liquid asset.

Nonliquid assets cannot be converted to cash quickly. There is no continuous market for them. In a booming market a house may sell quickly, but in a depressed market a seller may have to wait months before finding a buyer. The same is true of furniture and furnishings, unless they are offered for sale at an auction. There is no continuously stable market for used automobiles. They may sell quickly at one time and slowly at another time.

Annuity contracts usually contain a clause denying to the annuitant the right to borrow on the contract or to cash it in. He or she must wait until reaching retirement age. In case of premature death the cash value is paid to the beneficiary. The same is true of funds or pension plans. There is no continuous market for unlisted stocks or bonds. In calculating net worth one may secure the bid prices and use those figures as approximations.

An older family in the upper-income brackets may have invested savings in undeveloped land or in buildings for income purposes. There is no continuous market for such assets, but one can estimate their market value for purposes of ascertaining net worth. An affluent family may have loaned money to others on mortgage. No matter how secure the loan may be, the money cannot be retrieved until the mortgage matures. Of course, if the mortgage is amortized, the lender will receive periodic repayments on the principal.

A family may have other accounts receivable, and it may have other assets, such as shares in a building and loan association. There are so many ways in which savings may be invested that it is not feasible to attempt a complete listing. Each family may adapt the form shown in Table 15-4 to its own assets.

The major liability of most families is the mortgage on its house. Money may also have been borrowed from a bank. Instead of cashing in life insurance contracts an insured may borrow an amount equal to the cash surrender value, keeping the insurance in effect. Many families have open charge accounts at stores, which are usually due in thirty days. And many families owe money on installment contracts for the purchase of an automobile, furniture, or furnishings.

The difference between total assets and total liabilities represents the net worth of the family on the date of the financial statement. A well-managed family, like a well-managed business firm, should show an annually increasing net worth.

A BUDGET FOR COLLEGE STUDENTS

Nine Million College Consumers

There are approximately 9 million men and women in American colleges and universities. Some of these students live at home, but many of them live on or near college campuses in dormitories, boarding houses, fraternities, or sororities. Families of students should include the student's expenditures in the family budget, and each student should also operate on an individual budget.

Student budgeting is helpful in several ways. For one thing, it enables a student to give an account to his or her parents of money received and spent. Budgeting is also likely to help insure the careful use of money. If a student is paying for his own college education, budgeting helps him plan ahead for expenses.

In many private colleges the tuition that a student pays does not cover the full cost of the services provided. The rest of the college's operating expenses are paid for by endowments or gifts from supporters or alumni(ae) of the institution. Students in state and municipal universities pay only nominal fees for educational services. Most such public institutions receive their money from general tax revenues. The fact that the student is being fully or partially subsidized, that someone else is paying all or part of the tuition, should be taken into account when contemplating an expenditure of doubtful utility.

A further advantage of budgeting by college students is that it helps educate them in rational spending and consuming practices. These practices may become habitual and will be helpful to the student throughout his or her life.

A Sample Budget Form

The advantages of budgeting are essentially the same for college students as for families and the technique is the same. The only difference is in the accounts. Table 15-5 presents a suggested budget form for college students. The table lists many items that are specialized student expenditures. Such expenses as tuition, board, room, books, and dues are fairly constant. Many colleges provide medical and dental care at a flat rate. If the student uses a train, plane, bus, the family car, or his or her own car to travel to and from school, the cost involved should also be included in the budget.

The amount of money spent on the items listed under personal expenses in this table will be an indicator of the values and wealth of an individual student. Differences in the amount of money budgeted or spent for nonessential items will appear, for example, in expenditures for membership in fraternities or sororities. For some this will not be an expense at all, since many schools do not have this type of club. Automobiles are a

TABLE 15-5. Suggested Budget Form For College Students

Account	For College Year	S E P	O C T	N O V	D E C	J A N	F E B	M C H	A P R	M A Y	J U N
		For Each Month									
I. Anticipated expenses 　A. College: 　　　Tuition 　　　Fees 　　　Board 　　　Room 　　　Books, supplies 　　　Fraternity or sorority 　　　Honorary societies, clubs 　　　Transportation to and 　　　　from college 　　　Other (specify)											
Subtotals:											
B. Personal: 　　　Clothing 　　　Cleaning, pressing 　　　Laundry 　　　Dental care 　　　Medical 　　　Barber or beauty shop 　　　Toilet articles 　　　Telephone, telegraph 　　　Postage 　　　Newspapers, magazines 　　　Donations 　　　Gifts 　　　Recreation (movies, 　　　　theater, dances) 　　　Beverages 　　　Snacks 　　　Insurance (life, accident, 　　　　health, auto) 　　　Automobile (gas, oil, 　　　　repairs) 　　　Local transportation 　　　Bank charges 　　　Other (specify)											
Total expenses:											
II. Anticipated income 　　　Gifts from parents 　　　Gifts from others 　　　Drawn from savings 　　　Current earnings 　　　Scholarship 　　　Prizes 　　　Other (specify)											
Total income:											

common additional expense for many students, as are vacation trips or entertainment. One study showed that most college students spend more than $75 a month for the items included in part B of the budget form — that is, the things that are not included under tuition, room, and board. Almost 12 percent of all students were found to spend $250 or more each month for expenses other than tuition, room, and board.[4]

Many students carry insurance policies, and insurance should thus be included in their budgets. In these days of increasing direct and indirect taxation, students should include taxes in their budgets. In recording expenditures for gasoline, for example, the amount actually paid for the merchandise could be recorded in one place and the amount superimposed as a tax separated and recorded under the tax account.

Six items are included under anticipated income. Many students also receive supplemental income in the form of scholarships, awards, and wages for part-time work. All such income should be included in the budget.

Budgeting and Inflation

The annual rate of inflation increased considerably during the first half of the 1970s. Between 1965 and 1970 the Consumer Price Index increased an average of 4.26 percent annually, but from 1970 through 1975 the Index increased an average of 6.4 percent per year. In 1974 inflation was at an annual rate of 10.97 percent. Inflation of this magnitude can play havoc with a family's budget unless the family income increases at the same or a faster rate. In fact, the family income must increase more than the increase in inflation if that family is to remain in the same financial bracket.

For example, if the wage earner in a family of four with an annual income of $15,000 had received an 8 percent raise in 1975, as against the 6.4 percent rate of inflation in that year, the family could have been confronted with this financial picture:

8 Percent Increase in Salary		*$1,200*
Additional income taxes	$264	
Increased social security taxes	$70	
Increased state and local taxes	$36	
Cost of inflation at 6.4 percent	$960	
Total increased expenses		$1,330
Net loss		$130

An increase of 8.87 percent would have been needed just to remain at a par with the previous year. This means that those persons and families whose incomes have not been increasing at that rate must reevaluate their expenditures and reduce their level of living, draw on savings, or go into debt. If the individual or family does not wish to draw on savings or go into debt, they must become more careful consumers. (A brief description of how a careful shopper operates so as to reduce expenses is to be found on pages 387–402).

QUESTIONS FOR REVIEW

1. Why do you think there are so many personal bankruptcies?
2. What constitutes responsible spending?
3. What do you think might be the key to responsible spending?
4. Outline the advantages of maintaining a budget.
5. If there are so many advantages to be gained from budgeting, why doesn't everyone operate on a budget?
6. How do the percentages shown for various items in the typical budget for a family of four on page 368 compare with the percentages allotted to those items in your family budget?
7. What training have you had in how to spend money?
8. Do you know the income and net worth of your family? Do you think you should?
9. Discuss the significant differences in budget preparation for a college student and budget preparation for a family.
10. "Keeping a budget does not increase your income; therefore, there is no point to budgeting." Discuss.
11. If your income does not increase and inflation continues to rise, what will you do?
12. Do you think that planning and recording expenditures and calculating net worth are worth the time and trouble required?

PROJECTS

1. List the significant changes that take place in spending patterns as one moves from one stage of the life cycle to the next.
2. Let each member of the class ask ten students on campus whether they budget and record expenditures and whether they know their net worth. Record the combined responses, including a summary of comments.
3. Keep a budget for the duration of this course, following the suggestions in this chapter. At the end of the course outline the advantages and disadvantages you found in maintaining this budget.
4. Make an inventory of your assets and liabilities as of the present. Did you find any surprises when you took this inventory?
5. For one month keep a record of every cent you spend. At the end of the month evaluate your spending. Were you a responsible spender?

REFERENCES

1. David Caplovitz, *Consumers in Trouble: A Study of Debtors in Default* (New York: Free Press, 1974), p. ix.
2. *Money*, Jan. 1976, p. 24.
3. Michael L. Speer, *A Complete Guide to the Christian's Budget* (Nashville: Boardman Press, 1975), p. ix.
4. *New York Times*, 17 July 1975, p. 45.

CHAPTER 16

HOW TO BECOME
A BETTER BUYER

SPENDING THE FAMILY INCOME

Spending Money

Money is not something to hoard; only misers gain pleasure from watching their money accumulate and counting it. Most people like to exchange their money for the goods and services that they want and that will give them greater satisfaction and pleasure. Researchers Rich and Jain studied women shoppers in Cleveland and New York and found that most people "enjoyed shopping, regardless of [their] social class."[1]

In the act of exchanging money for goods and services consumers are converting their money incomes to real incomes. Economists define *real income* as the quantity of goods and services that one's money will buy. *Psychic income* is the satisfaction gained in consuming the goods and services purchased. Psychic income may be temporary, as in the case of consuming food, or it may be long term, as in the case of consuming (enjoying) a painting in one's home.

For some people spending is a form of escape. They refuse to face up to the reality that their money incomes are limited. Even though they do not have enough money, they spend as if they had a lot. Such spendthriftism has resulted in expressions like "he spends money as though it were going out of style," or "they spend money as if they think it grows on trees." People who do this use their credit to the limit. When the limit is reached, they face the reality of bankruptcy.

Psychologists tell us that people sometimes make a purchase to offset a frustration. A woman may indulge in a spending spree, perhaps purchasing a handbag with shoes to match; a man is more likely to go on a drinking binge. One psychologist suggests that the act of spending money creates the illusion that one can control one's destiny.[2]

Most people love a bargain. Bargain-hunters are constantly on the search for good buys. When stores advertise sales, crowds of prospective buyers line up on the street waiting for the doors to open.

Buymanship Versus Salesmanship

The literature of advertising and salesmanship is filled with suggestions to sellers, telling them how they can break down sales resistance. In reality, however, there is very little sales resistance; consumers need and want goods and services. Better buymanship substitutes rational for emotional consumer responses. Better buyers develop resistance to high-pressure selling methods used by some firms. It is as important for consumer-buyers to get the most they can for their money as it is for sellers to get as high prices as they can for their goods and services. Remember, however, that the consumer is the amateur while the seller is the professional. Better buymanship will help make the contest more equal.

BE PREPARED WITH INFORMATION

The first step in developing better buymanship is to fortify oneself with information. This is what professional purchasing agents do. After learning all they can about the products to be purchased, they draft quantity and quality specifications. In the same way, but not to the same degree, rational consumer-buyers can obtain as much information as possible about the products they need. They can acquire knowledge about devices for measuring or ascertaining quantity and quality characteristics. With this information at their disposal, retail buyers know enough to ask salespeople the right questions. They also know enough to judge whether a salesperson is qualified to give helpful answers.

There are several sources to which consumers may turn for specific, technical, preshopping information. One of these, and the oldest, is Consumers' Research, Inc. (subsequently referred to as CR), Washington, New Jersey 07882. Another is Consumers Union, which is a nonprofit organization in Mount Vernon, New York 10550.

Consumers' Research Magazine

In 1927, *Your Money's Worth,* a book by Stuart Chase and F. J. Schlink describing the plight of consumers attempting to get their money's worth, caught popular fancy and became a best-seller. Growing consumer consciousness of the need for help was rendered articulate by lively revelations of quackery, fraud, misrepresentation, and disparities in quantity, quality, price, and cost of production. The latter part of the book was devoted to a general discussion of agencies for assisting consumers. After reading the book many consumers wrote to the authors asking how or where they could get more specific technical information to guide them in buying merchandise. These expressions of widespread consumer interest resulted in the formation in 1929 of a nonprofit corporation — Consumers' Research, Inc., — to serve as a research agency and clearinghouse for consumer information. On the basis of tests made in its own and outside laboratories, supplemented by information from other sources, CR issues *Consumers' Research Magazine*, where widely used products are listed by brand name as recommended, intermediate, or not recommended. The subscription rate is $9 a year for 12 issues.

The following quotation from *Consumers' Research Magazine* is probably the best indication of the ideological approach of CR.

> Consumers' Research firmly believes that nothing is gained by hell-raising, militancy, and strident anti-business attitudes. CR is against lobbying and litigiousness as means for consumer protection. It does not urge the passing of a multitude of laws and regulations, the setting up of more government agencies, enormously increased power of government agencies over business, industry, and consumers' freedom of choice.
>
> CR believes that an alert and informed consumer is his own best friend and needs no militant "advocates" or "world savers" to protect him. The informed consumer needs no protection from "big, bad business," which is, incidentally, the producer of the largest variety and best quality of goods and services in the world. Consumer products are always best and most plentiful in countries where governmental regulation is held within reasonable and traditional limits. Products mass-produced in U.S. factories have given Americans, even the so-called disadvantaged persons, a standard of living so abundant that it is unequalled in any other country. Consumers' Research firmly believes in the value of free enterprise as the best-in-the-long-run protection of consumer interests and to that end CR aims to provide the information the consumer needs to make wise and economical choices in the marketplace.[3]

CR's aim is to educate buyers rather than to limit or control sellers or manufacturers.

There are certain problems confronting consumer testing and reporting publications such as CR in getting helpful information to consumers. The size of the United States is one obstacle. In discussing custom in chapters 5 and 6 it was shown that consumer practices vary geographically. Similarly, certain brand products available in one section are not available in another. Another basic limitation to consumer product testing and reporting is dependence on the structure of trademarks and brands. In many cases unmarked and unbranded merchandise or local brands may be superior or acceptable, but there is no practical way of discovering or providing such information. But even with these limitations CR performs a vital service for consumers.

Consumer Reports

Consumers Union (256 Washington Street, Mount Vernon, New York 10550) was chartered in February, 1936, as a nonprofit corporation. Its purpose is to provide consumers with information and counsel on consumer goods and services, to give information on all matters relating to the expenditure of the family income, and to initiate and to cooperate with individual and group efforts seeking to create and maintain decent living standards.

CU's basic publication is *Consumer Reports*. From January through November of each year, eleven regular issues are published. In December an enlarged issue, the *Buying Guide*, is published. The *Guide* summarizes the results of the tests made in that year and in previous years, and it also contains buying advice not included in the other issues. The *Buying Guide* contains about 416 pages and is pocket-sized. CU's publications contain reports of laboratory tests, controlled-use tests, expert opinion or experience, or a combination of these. No test products are accepted as gifts or loans from manufacturers; all are purchased in retail stores by CU's shoppers, who do not identify their CU affiliation. CU's product ratings are usually based on estimated overall quality without regard to price. Models are check-rated (✔) when CU judges the samples tested to be of high overall quality and appreciably superior to non-check-rated models tested for the same report. A rating of one model is not to be considered a rating of other models sold under the same brand name unless so noted. "Best Buy" ratings are accorded to products that are not only rated high in overall quality but also priced relatively low; they should thus provide more quality per dollar than other "Acceptable" products in that set of ratings. *Consumer Reports*, including the *Buying Guide* issue, costs $11 a year.

Like *Consumer's Research Magazine*, *Consumer Reports* contains much useful information. In addition to general articles, each *Report* on specific products is prefaced with a statement telling consumers what they need to know about those particular products when shopping. CU has become famous for its *Reports* on new and used automobiles. In addition to point-by-point technical comparisons of brands, readers learn much about how automobile companies operate, what goes into their products, and what buyers should know about an automobile. As the year progresses, a regular reader of the *Consumer Reports* will find that he or she accumulates a compendium of information about nearly 2,000 product brands or models.

Consumers who use CU test results can save themselves substantial sums of money. Morris and Bronson have calculated the potential difference between "best" choice and "worst" choice to be 25 percent; the arithmetic mean difference was 27.4 percent. "This constitutes a rough estimate of the typical maximum loss of money income the public may incur through haphazard (as distinct from scientific, well-informed) buying."[4] The potential loss ranges from 10 percent off the price paid for autos and automotive equipment to 85 percent for drugs and cosmetics.

CU, like CR, has the problem of convincing readers of its reliability, technical competence, and integrity. How can one be sure that good ratings are not paid for? The business-oriented *Wall Street Journal* has written that "Consumers Union owes much of its present broad appeal to the reputation for honesty and technical accuracy it has maintained since its birth."[5] Further evidence of CU's competence and impartiality is the fact that a study of its ratings over the years will reveal that one company's product may receive a low rating one year and the next time it is rated receive an "Accepted" rating. Such changes in rating indicate significant improvements in the product. In some product lines one company's product may consistently be "Check-rated," or in the runner-up category. This has been the case with Maytag washers.

Another evidence of CU's integrity is the publication of its annual financial report, which is certified by a registered public accounting firm. In a recent year CU's income amounted to $16 million, and its assets totaled $10 million. No comparison can be made with CR because that organization does not publish its financial statements.

The $8 million that CU spends on testing and publishing each year is miniscule when compared with the advertising expenditures of the firms whose products are tested. CU has over 355 employees and more than 101 shoppers in 67 cities. All types of stores are shopped to obtain prices but no attempt is made to bargain for lower prices. Test samples are purchased from retail stores. Eighty percent of the testing is done in CU laboratories. Writing in *Fortune*, Philip Siekman concluded, after a study of CU, that its testing is adequate, with some qualifications. The laboratories are staffed by eighty men and women, thirty-seven with college degrees in engineering or science. Most of them were employed in industry previously. Siekman writes that industry engineers who have been skeptical about CU's technical adequacy usually change their minds after a trip through the laboratories. When industry critics sometimes complain about the limited number of test samples, CU's answer is that they buy as the individual consumer buys.[6]

CU, like CR, is dependent on the structure of brands and trademarks. Nationally advertised and available brands have an advantage over local brands and unbranded products because favorable ratings may lead readers to purchase them, even though regionally produced products may be as good or better. Moreover, CU's point system of grading a product is subjective, and its limited funds restricts the number of products that can be purchased for testing.[7]

Over the years CU has developed into much more than a technical testing agency. In its *Reports* a notable feature is the department dealing with health. Another far-ranging section deals with broad problems of national concern, such as consumer credit, grading of meat and poultry, and the prices of drugs. CU has sponsored significant research and such independent organizations as the Weights and Measures Research Center and the American Council on Consumer Interests. The CU special publications list includes ten titles, ranging from a publication on life insurance to *Weights and Measures and the Consumer*, all of special interest to consumers and at low prices. CU has become the voice of organized consumers in the United States. In addition, CU took the lead in organizing the International Organization of Consumers Unions, with its headquarters in The Hague, The Netherlands. IOCU is composed of consumer organizations in forty-five nations plus the Consumer Federation of America, a national consumer organization.

How to Use *Consumers' Research Magazine* and *Consumer Reports*

As sources of reasonably objective preshopping information both CR and CU publications are helpful. For an expenditure of $20 a year one may receive both publications. The $20 investment may pay for itself on a single purchase. On purchases of expensive products such as automobiles or electrical appliances subscribers may save enough to pay their subscriptions for many years. Intelligent consumers will use their recommendations as guides, not as mandates. And even if they do not follow the recommendations of either agency, they will learn enough in reading the reports to enable them to make better buys.

U.S. GOVERNMENT BUYING GUIDES

Consumer Information Catalog

Consumer Information Catalog is a sixteen-page pamphlet published quarterly by the U.S. Government Printing Office. Each issue lists about 250 publications dealing with automobiles, clothing, consumer education and protection, food, health, housing, leisure activities, and money management, and it includes a listing of items for older persons. The *Catalog* is also available in Spanish. Almost half of the pamphlets listed are free, and the others range in price from 25 cents to about $3.00. Copies of *Consumer Information Catalog* are available free from Consumer Information Center, Pueblo, Colorado 81009.

Consumer News

Consumer News, an eight-page newsletter, is published twice a month by the Office of Consumer Affairs, Department of Health, Education and Welfare, to report on federal government programs for consumers. It is packed with current consumer information from federal agencies; it lists new federal consumer publications, calls to the attention of the reader products that have been recently recalled by government agencies, and alerts the reader to other consumer activities and information. Four pages of each issue are devoted to "Consumer Register," a listing of regulations that have been issued by Federal agencies, alerting consumers to proposals that may affect them, and it indicates where consumers can send their opinions on proposed regulations. *Consumer News* is available for $4.00 a year from Consumer Information Center, Pueblo, Colorado 81009.

Product Tests and Brand Name Information

A major breakthrough in providing consumers with federal government product test results occurred when the President signed an executive order releasing such information. For years consumer advocates had argued that government test results belong to citizen-consumers as much as to government agencies. In a test case Consumers Union sued the Veterans Administration under the Freedom of Information Act to compel the release of test results on hearing aids. That suit was won by the CU and it opened the door "to mountains of test data on thousands of products. . . ."[8]

The first three booklets based on National Bureau of Standards test results were published by the U.S. Department of Commerce in 1970 and are available through the Office of the Special Assistant to the President for Consumer Affairs. They contain consumer do's and don't's for fabrics, adhesives, and tires. In the words of a CU official, "They are better than nothing," but they do not contain brand information. The Bureau of Standards followed up these booklets with other publications on hearing aids, care and preservation of books, documents, prints and films, the metric system, and three publications dealing with energy conservation in heating and cooling homes.

Brand name information was made available to the general public in 1972 when the General Services Administration* was required to publish a listing of products purchased and tested for use by the federal government. This listing, in the annual publication *Brand Names*, contains all brand name products available to the consumer which were certified by suppliers during the previous calendar year as being the same as those tested and accepted for purchase by the federal government during that year. Since the General Services Administration does not perform comparison tests, the list does not constitute a rating of products. The brand names listed do not necessarily represent top quality since the government buys that product that will serve the needs of federal agencies at the lowest competitive cost. The needs of the government relating to performance and quality sometimes differ from those of the individual consumer.

OTHER BUYING GUIDES

CBBB Booklets

The Council of Better Business Bureaus (1150 17th Street, N.W., Washington, D.C. 20036) publishes a variety of materials, including tip sheets, fact books, and information pamphlets. Among the titles are: *Buying by Mail*, *Guarantees and Warranties*, *Life Insurance Companies*, *Shopping for Food*, *Home Study Schools*, and *Sales Contracts*. Single copies are free if the request is accompanied by self-addressed, stamped, business-size envelope. A complete list of the CBBB's fifty-five titles is available free from the council.

Those who live in or near a metropolitan area should use the services offered by their local better business bureau. Many bureaus publish

---

*The General Services Administration (GSA) establishes policy and provides an economical and efficient system for the management of federal government property and records.

monthly bulletins that contain preshopping information. Consumers are warned against misleading advertising and against fraudulent selling practices. Individual consumers may telephone or write to their local better business bureaus for reports on the number of complaints, if any, that they have on file concerning a particular firm.*

Money Management Booklets

These are published by the Household Finance Corporation, Prudential Plaza, Chicago, Illinois 60601. Household Finance is the largest personal loan company operating in the United States and Canada. Years ago the company learned that borrowers who were delinquent were usually people who simply did not know how to manage their money. In an effort to help such borrowers, and thereby reduce losses on loans, Household Finance established a department to provide information about money management. For $3.50 one may purchase a set of twelve booklets. Three of the booklets deal with budgeting. The others treat such topics as the purchase of food, clothing, housing, home furnishings, and equipment. *Your Shopping Dollar* presents techniques for developing skills. The one on automobiles discusses aspects of owning, maintaining, and operating a car. *Your Health and Recreation Dollar* suggests ways to plan a health and recreation program, with a special section on health insurance. Finally, *Your Savings and Investment Dollar* contains information to assist in planning a savings and investment program.

Changing Times

Changing Times (Kiplinger Magazine, 1729 H Street, N.W., Washington, D.C. 20006) is written for middle- and upper-middle-income consumers. For their benefit the monthly issues carry articles on such topics as stocks and bonds, income taxes, life insurance, housing, retirement income, and the wisdom of investing in real estate. New subscribers should ask for the *Family Success Book*, which contains ideas on money, jobs, and living. The subscription rate for the magazine is $9 a year. Like *Consumer Reports* and *Consumers' Research Magazine*, *Changing Times* does not accept advertising. Unlike CU and CR, however, *Changing Times* does not rate products.

Books for Consumers

The careful reader of this volume will find many useful books cited in the reference sections at the end of each chapter. In addition, Sylvia Porter

---

* For more information concerning better business bureaus, see pp. 220–221.

presents a wealth of material the consumer should know about in her encyclopedic *Money Book,* including information on how to earn money, spend it, save it, invest it, borrow it, and use it for a better life.[9] In *The Consumer's Guide To Better Buying* Sidney Margolius draws on a life-time of experience to give tested advice about a wide range of goods and services.[10] *Shopper's Guide, 1974 Yearbook of Agriculture* is useful for its sections on food, equipment, gardening, services, and recreation, all written by experts.[11] *Consumer Survival Kit,* adapted by John Dorfman from a television series, provides the consumer with dollar-saving ideas on anything from buying pets to buying funerals.[12] Christopher and Bonnie Weathersbee combine consumer suggestions with information on costs to the buyer and to the environment in their book *The Intelligent Consumer.*[13] A good way to keep informed about new books of interest to the consumer is to read the section on consumer resource materials each month in the newsletter published by the American Council on Consumer Interests.[14]

HOW A CAREFUL SHOPPER SHOPS

A careful shopper is one who takes the job of purchasing seriously. Whether mother, father, or older child, he or she endeavors to operate intelligently so as to get the most for his or her money. Here is a brief description of how a careful shopper operates.

How A Good Shopper Uses Advertising

It is common practice among food stores to use local newspapers to advertise special prices on certain articles over the weekend. Other stores advertise the prices of a wide variety of merchandise from day to day and announce special sales. The wise buyer, supplied with factual information making possible some comparison of quality, will save many steps and considerable time by comparing the newspaper advertisements of competing stores. You will find frequently that identical trademarked or branded merchandise is offered at a lower price in one store than in another. It is much easier to discover this by reading advertisements than by going from store to store. By comparing prices in mail-order catalogs and the catalogs of discount houses, the careful buyer is better able to judge whether prices are right.

Watch For Lures and Traps

Bait advertising in the United States and Canada has been so widely used by retail stores that government officials in both countries moved to protect consumers. The U.S. Federal Trade Commission discovered that low-priced specials were often unavailable and that merchandise on the

An inspector from the New York City Department of Consumer Affairs checks to make sure that all the specials advertised by this supermarket actually are on sale in the store. (*Dr. Lilly Bruck, Director, Consumer Education, New York City Dept. of Consumer Affairs*)

shelves was often not marked down as advertised. The Department of Commerce and Corporate Affairs in Canada prosecuted many businesses for flagrantly misleading advertising. Despite government regulations, however, such practices continue year after year and consumers must continue to be on their guard against them. Government officials advise consumers to compare prices in one store with those in other stores before buying and to report misleading ads to the FTC.

A careful shopper will ask for a "rain-check" when an advertised special is not available, and he will take the newspaper ads along when shopping to make sure that he is not getting charged more than the advertised price. The careful shopper will check to make sure that there is no mispricing or mislabeling, that items to be weighed are weighed properly, and that the measurements marked on packages are accurate. In addition, shoppers must be alert as they pass through the supermarket maze loaded with displays to entice them to buy. The fact is, good retailers have an almost complete control over their customers' purchasing; by means of shelf-position, stack-outs in aisles, special displays, and tie-ins they can sell almost anything, and in volume. One store stocked a shelf with jars marked "Instant Water." Prospective buyers were told to "add hot coffee," and the price was 85 cents a jar![15]

Chain grocery promotional publications are filled with illustrations of sales increases following aisle-end displays, shelf-extenders, dump rack, tower displays, island displays, and snack racks. The average store has fourteen to twenty special display areas where traffic is fifteen times greater than in other parts of a store. Merchandise displays of high-profit items at the check-out counters catch many an impulse buyer. A basket or card display of 10-cent items near the check-out area gives the shopper an impression that it is a low-price store.

In one store twelve items were shifted from floor level to waist level, then to eye level, then down again. When they were moved from floor to waist level, sales increased 34 percent; from waist to eye level, sales increased 63 percent; from floor to eye level, there was an increase of 78 percent. As the items were moved down again, sales dropped off.

When you shop do you want merchandise or do you want merchandise plus atmosphere? The latter is available in luxury stores that endeavor to create a personality image. There are many more of the supermarket self-service discount types of stores where shoppers can purchase merchandise at lower prices with no frills. In between the luxury and the discount stores there are many kinds of retail stores, which follow a variety of selling practices. As advertising encounters increasing difficulty in conveying impressions of differences in merchandise the physical arrangement and design of the store become potent factors in consumer buying.[16]

Lighting is an important selling tool. Fluorescent lighting flattens out merchandise and gives it a monotonous sameness. This is offset by the expensive hot incandescent light and by colored lights. Pink lighting has been designed to make the meat in the display counter look redder, and green tinted lighting to make lettuce look greener.

"Advertising allowance" is a polite term to describe a practice widely used. A manufacturer or distributor may pay a retailer to favor the manufacturer's products by giving them a prominent display in the store windows or a choice location on the shelves. In addition, salesclerks may be paid to recommend the products. This payment is called "pushmoney." If a salesclerk can switch a buyer to the brand that is being pushed, the clerk may be paid an extra sales commission or a flat sum. This is called a "spiff." One manufacturer of electronic products, which Consumer Reports rated below three other brands, paid salesclerks from $10 to $75 to push their products. This practice is prevalent in the retailing of many consumer goods.[17]

"Even expert buyers find it virtually impossible to distinguish between two unknown items (with tags removed) priced at $7.95 and $12.95!"[18] In The Consumer's Guide to Better Buying Margolius tells of a store that advertised a mattress at $39 as a come-on. When prospective buyers came in, salesclerks tried to trade them up to a $79 mattress worth about $44. The only difference was in the ticketing.[19] (For further examples of seller frauds see Chapter 14.)

Avoid Impulse Buying

Experts in retail merchandising say that the profitability of a store depends on its success in stimulating impulse buying. Managers are advised to place impulse items at the foot of the down escalators in department stores. There the items catch the eyes of captive shoppers who are likely to purchase on impulse as they leave the store.[20] Managers of grocery stores with check-out counters place a variety of profitable small items where shoppers cannot miss them. While waiting to be checked out consumers are likely to reach out and pick up cigarettes, candy, or magazines. In some stores aerosol sprays are used to stimulate sales. The simulated aroma of coffee is sprayed near the coffee counter and sets up a complex of physical and psychological reactions that impel shoppers to purchase coffee.

Motivation researchers have concluded that economics textbooks are seriously deficient in recognizing the human factors involved in consumer decisions. People are obviously careless buyers; their motivations are complex and confused and they themselves cannot tell why they buy what they do. They buy not only to satisfy physical and economic needs but also to get others to see them as they wish to be seen. One result of this is impulse buying.

The average consumer buys on impulse half of the time. Shoppers engage in a minimal effort to seek information. Seventy to ninety percent of beer, candy, crackers, cookies, snacks, frozen foods, magazines, and health and beauty aids are purchased on impulse. One third of all purchases in drug stores and variety stores are made on impulse. Impulse buying seems to be increasing, perhaps because of packaging and because shoppers depend on in-store shelf displays as reminders. Sixty percent of all shoppers do not use shopping lists; and twenty percent have only partial lists.[21]

Clothing is likely to be purchased on impulse and according to mood rather than need. One researcher found impulse buying of major goods such as automobiles and appliances to occur only slightly less often than impulse buying of minor goods.[22] Some people even buy houses on impulse!

The tendency of consumers to buy impulsively is exploited by sellers. Aware of impulse purchase traps, the careful shopper buys what is on the shopping list and nothing more.

Watch For Sales

The easy weapon to use against impulse buying is the shopping list, especially for recurring purchases such as food and household items. Family needs should be planned a week or more in advance, just as the purchasing agent for a business firm anticipates the need for supplies. The practice of buying in small quantities every day should be replaced by once-a-week shopping. Modern houses have adequate storage space for canned goods and other food staples. The family having a refrigerator and a freezer can purchase perishable foods when they are on sale and store them indefinitely. It is reported that 80 percent of the sales in food stores are made on Thursdays, Fridays, and Saturdays. Most store managers advertise reduced prices on selected items on those days.

TABLE 16-1. When to Buy Selected Food Items

JANUARY: Beef, broiler-fryers, pork; apples, canned corn, canned figs, canned ripe olives, peanuts, pecans, prunes

FEBRUARY: Beef, broiler-fryers, pork; apples, canned corn, canned ripe olives, pecans, potatoes

MARCH: Beef, broiler-fryers, eggs; apples, canned corn, canned ripe olives, peanuts, pecans, potatoes, rice

APRIL: Beef, eggs, canned corn, canned ripe olives, cottage cheese, dried beans, rice

MAY: Beef, turkey; dairy products; canned ripe olives, salad dressings and oils

JUNE: Beef, canned pink salmon; dairy products; early summer vegetables such as cabbage, cucumbers, corn on the cob, radishes, snap beans, tomatoes

JULY: Locally grown fruits and vegetables; dairy products; orange concentrate

AUGUST: Beef, broiler-fryers, turkey; California plums, frozen concentrated orange juice, summer vegetables

SEPTEMBER: Beef, broiler-fryers; late summer vegetables

OCTOBER: Beef, broiler-fryers, turkey; cheese; apples, cranberries, grapes, pears, potatoes, rice

NOVEMBER: Beef, turkey; sardines; apples, cranberries, grapes, peanuts, potatoes

DECEMBER: Beef, broiler-fryers, turkey; apples, cherries, cranberries, peanuts, pecans

Many food products are produced seasonally. This means that when they are in season supplies are abundant and prices tend to be lower. Conversely, when such foods are out of season supplies are limited and prices are relatively high. Table 16-1, showing when to buy selected food items, is based on information provided by the United States Department of Agriculture, as reported in their monthly publication *Service: USDA's Report to Consumers*. Savings of up to 20 percent of a family's food expenditures can be made by purchasing foods in season. In addition to following this table the alert buyer will also adapt purchases to seasonal variations in supplies of locally produced fruits and vegetables.

Clothing buyers can save money by planning ahead and purchasing when needed items are on sale. Department stores have seasonal peaks, and it is reported that approximately 20 percent of their total annual sales are made in December. As a consequence, sales volume declines in January. In order to dispose of unsold and shopworn merchandise, store managers offer reduced prices in January. A trade practice so generally believed as to be considered a principle is that retailers must mark down prices at least 20 percent. Stores mark down their merchandise anywhere from 10 to 50 percent, according to the type of merchandise and to how long it has been in the store. It takes a long time to process and market clothing items. There is a regular sequence throughout the year—from designers to mills, to cutters, to processors, to retailers, to consumers. In January, after the heavy Fall and Christmas buying, store managers offer bargain prices. These are often advertised as preinventory and storewide clearance sales. Consumer-buyers will find bargains in men's wear, women's wear, shoes, linens, blankets, and large and small electric appliances. In the home furnishings department, they will find draperies, housewares, floor coverings, mattresses, and furniture at reduced prices.

Season-end clearances are offered in February. These are usually advertised as anniversary sales, storewide clearances, and Washington's Birthday sales. Consumer-buyers will find substantial price reductions on winter clothing and furniture. By late March and early April, spring stocks of merchandise are ready for the peak Easter season. Pre-Easter sales offer significant savings on boys' and men's wear. Also the pre-Easter sales feature washers, dryers, luggage, china, silver, and gift items. Volume sales of spring merchandise continue through the month of May. By June some clearance sales are offered, but the best time to buy spring and summer goods is immediately after July 4.

By August stores are stocked with fall and winter merchandise which consumers buy actively through October and November. From the store manager's point of view December is the peak month. After Christmas, sales decline and the annual cycle is completed when store managers offer clearance sales in January and February. Price-conscious consumers who plan their purchases will do most of their buying in January–February and June–July.

In addition to seasonal sales, store managers offer private sales, special purchase sales, anniversary sales, close-outs, one-day sales, dollar-day sales, and one-cent sales. Private sales are usually held a few days before the public announcement of a sale. Regular customers who have charge accounts are notified privately in advance. This practice gives them the advantage of having first choice. Buyers for stores often purchase goods from manufacturers or wholesalers at reduced prices for these sales. Some special purchase goods are standard quality, while others may be substandard or imperfect items. For this reason it is important to look at the merchandise carefully. Good stores mark substandard merchandise as seconds. Often the imperfections are minor and immaterial.

Anniversary sales are usually storewide promotions that offer real bargains. Close-outs feature merchandise that is outdated or out-of-fashion. One-day sales are featured in big cities, usually at the time of a holiday. Dollar Days are valid sales if conducted by established firms. Even so, buyers need to know how to judge quality and whether the presale price was really more than the sale price. One-cent sales offer the buyer a second item for a penny more than the price of a single item.

A word of caution concerning fire sales and going-out-of-business sales. These may be legitimate, but the bulletins of better business bureaus in several cities frequently warn consumers against deceptive practices. Some stores are forever "going-out-of-business." Even if a fire-sale is valid, the buyer must be certain that the merchandise has not been rendered useless by exposure to water or smoke.

When is the best time to buy a new automobile? Many people believe that year-end clearance prices are lower than prices prevailing throughout the year. This may or may not be so. If the dealer or the manufacturer is over-stocked, this would be true, but if cars have been selling well and inventory is low, there is no incentive for discounting the prices very much. In tire merchandising it has become general practice to offer special sales just before Memorial Day, July 4, and Labor Day.

This "Close Out Stock" sign may be a trap for unwary consumers. (*UPI*)

Shop Around

The buyer who never shops around foregoes savings of 10 to 30 percent on food purchases and up to 75 percent on other commodities. It was found that members of lower-income families were less likely to shop in more than one store than buyers for families in the middle- and upper-income groups. Student surveys in many different markets have consistently shown the possibility of saving 20 percent by comparing prices in three or more stores. The practice of shopping around will yield savings in the purchases of all types of consumer goods, from automobiles to wearing apparel. Those persons who habitually buy at one store form the basis of what merchants call "goodwill," which the larger stores may value at millions of dollars. Goodwill is the probability that patrons will continue to make all their purchases at the same store. Consumers who shop around, comparing quantity, quality, and price, are the ones who promote real competition.

A typical family shopper could cut her food bill by 25 percent by shrewder shopping. This could amount to $400 a year or more.

For those who like to believe that you get what you pay for researchers have found that price and quality do correlate but at so low a level as to lack

TABLE 16-2. Calendar of Annual Sales

January	February	March	April
Dresses • Furs • Hosiery • Handbags • Lingerie • House Coats • Active Sportswear • Millinery • Men's Shirts • Haberdashery • Men's Coats • Shoes • White Goods • Housewares • Small Appliances • Refrigerators, Freezers, Clothes Dryers, Water Heaters • Toiletries	Clothes Dryers • Furniture • Rugs • Bedding, Drapes, Curtains • China, Glassware • Air Conditioners • Used Cars • Notions • Stationery	Clothes Dryers • Washing Machines	Dresses • Millinery • Women's, Children's Coats • Men's, Boys' Suits • Clothes Dryers, Washing Machines • Ranges

May	June	July	August
Lingerie • House Coats • White Goods • Washing Machines • TV Sets • Tires • Soaps, Cleaning Aids	Dresses • Piece Goods, Fabrics • Washing Machines • TV Sets • Building Materials, Lumber	Hosiery • Handbags • Lingerie • House Coats • Active Sportswear • Millinery • Men's Shirts, Haberdashery • Shoes • Children's Wear • Refrigerators, Freezers • Toiletries	Furs • Coats • Men's, Boys' Suits • White Goods • Furniture • Rugs • Bedding • Drapes, Curtains • Air Conditioners • Hardware, Paints • Tires

September	October	November	December
Piece Goods, Fabrics • Housewares • China, Glassware • Hardware, Paints • New Cars • Batteries, Mufflers		Women's, Children's Coats • Piece Goods, Fabrics • Water Heaters • Ranges • Used Cars • Seat Covers	Women's, Children's Coats • Men's, Boys' Suits • Children's Wear • Used Cars

Source: Adapted from Sidney Margolius, *The Responsible Consumer,* Public Affairs Pamphlet No. 453, with permission. Reproduction in whole or in part without written permission of the author is not permitted.

significance. Out of forty-eight items surveyed in one study only twelve had a significant price-quality correlation and ten had a negative correlation.[23]

A careful shopper knows that items sold as seconds are frequently good buys. In fact, some so-called seconds are first quality items marked for quick sale to reduce inventory. In others, the defects may be so slight as to be negligible. Some department stores put a new item, such as a dress, in their swank shop at a high price. If it does not sell within ten days, it is moved to another department and marked down in price. If it does not sell there in ten days, it is moved again and marked down still more. Finally, it goes to the basement where it is placed on a rack with good, fair, and poor quality dresses. By that time the price may be as little as one-tenth of the original asking price. A buyer who knows how to judge fabrics can spot the good quality dress and get a bargain. One nationally known store originated the practice of moving its merchandise from department to department to basement in thirty-six days. If it did not sell after five days in the basement, it was donated to a charitable institution. The reason for such a practice is that investments in inventory are costly. It is better to get rid of merchandise at whatever price it will bring than to let it become shopworn. This is particularly true of high-fashion items.

After studying chain store selling practices the Federal Trade Commission wrote that consumers can combat deceptive advertising and pricing by shopping around, comparing prices, and taking advantage of advertised specials.

Bargain for Lower Prices

The One-Price System Most sellers in the United States profess to follow the one-price system, reputedly introduced by Mr. Tiffany. In the operation of his prestige jewelry store in New York City Mr. Tiffany decided that it was not good business to bargain. Once he set a price no one, including himself, could change it.[24] Under this system retailers add their markup to their wholesale cost to determine the price at which they are willing to sell. That price is then marked on the merchandise or on a tag where any prospective buyer may see it. Having free opportunity to examine the merchandise the buyer may then decide whether to buy at that price. In a self-service store the buyer can reach his or her decision without interference from the seller. In defense of the one-price system it is argued that bargaining takes so much time that it slows the marketing process. It would not be possible to have the kind of mass marketing found in supermarket food and variety stores without the one-price system. Even in the Orient the one-price system is used in the marketing of food and variety products.

The assumption underlying the one-price system is that if buyers think prices are too high, they will purchase elsewhere. If large numbers of consumers do purchase elsewhere, the high-price retailer is forced to lower prices. In practice, seller may advertise, stressing quality and service as the reasons for higher prices.

Bargaining in the United States There are some buyers who attempt to bargain in a free economy. Rather than lose the business of such buyers, retailers often bargain in one way or another. As a consequence, the one-price policy has been modified even by sedate department stores in their pricing of appliances, automobile accessories, cameras, clothing, drug items, furniture, home furnishings, sporting goods, and toys. Almost everyone knows that the list price of an automobile is simply the starting price in the bargaining process. Only uninitiated and naive buyers pay the asking price.

Primeaux found three explanations of differences in prices paid for appliances: differences in the buyer's knowledge of retail marketing practices; differences in bargaining ability; and differences in trade-in allowances. Small family-owned and operated appliance stores attempted to capitalize on consumer weaknesses. Among thirty-seven stores surveyed, twenty-three were willing to negotiate prices by bargaining, and seventeen were willing to meet competitors' prices. The range of price differences was from 10 to 45 percent. Special discounts were offered to firemen, police officers, teachers, and clergy. "The evidence clearly revealed that price differences among those purchasing identical products from the same dealer in the market were common."[25]

There are several ways in which price reductions may be obtained. One way is a reduction in list price. This is not as difficult to secure as many buyers believe. By using the same competitive weapons that businessmen use when they buy, price concessions may be secured by the buyer. Normally the buyer need have no compunction in using such tactics, for sellers will not cut their prices to a point too low to cover costs. If a prospective buyer knows about margins and markups, he or she will know how much reduction a seller can give and still make a profit.

The growth of discount stores has led increasing numbers of department stores to engage in bargaining. Lazarus Department Store in Columbus, Ohio, had signs in several departments that read "We will not be undersold." Such stores have comparison shoppers so the salesclerks know what prices are being asked in other stores. If a prospective buyer offers $7.95 for a watch that carries a list price of $11.95, saying that he can buy it for that price at another store, the clerk will sell it to him for the same price.

Price reductions may be secured indirectly by bargaining for a larger allowance where a used article is being traded. In selling such things as typewriters, vacuum cleaners, refrigerators, and automobiles, dealers allow a considerable margin for trade-in allowance. For the careless or naive buyer only a part of this allowance will be made, while the shrewd buyer will bargain until she secures the full amount.

Another way of securing an indirect price reduction is to prevail on the seller to include certain extra items or services not usually included. For example, the buyer of an automobile may secure some extra equipment, and the purchaser of a household appliance may secure free installation. Accepting payment in 30, 60, or 90 days is another "extra" the seller can offer.

A shrewd buyer will attempt to secure a discount from the retail price. In many cases it is possible to secure through employer, professional, family, or friendly connections a discount ranging from 10 to 40 percent. A business firm, hospital, or educational institution buys all needed supplies at wholesale prices. Frequently it is possible to extend the privilege of wholesale buying to employees.

Experienced travelers know that they can often bargain for lower prices for hotel and motel rooms. Managers of hotels and motels would like to follow the one-price system. Some of them may tell a prospective bargainer that they never bargain. But managers of motels and hotels are faced with the same problem of excess capacity that confronts managers of other enterprises. Their prices may be based on an assumption of 60 percent occupancy. A substantial proportion of their expenses continue whether their rooms are occupied or unoccupied. Is it better to insist on a price of $20 and let a room remain unused or to be realistic and accept an offer of $15? Many managers are realistic and readily accept $15 from a traveler who knows the economic facts of pricing.

If the owner of a house decides the time has come to have it painted, he or she should bargain with two or more painters until they reach a satisfactory price. Likewise for interior decorating and plumbing services. If the home-owner decides to repair or remodel his or her house, the same bargaining process is used. In the original purchase of the house a buyer rarely pays the asking price.

While the United States is nominally a one-price economy, actually and in practice, it is a bargaining economy. If the reader is not convinced that this statement is valid let him experiment. This challenge has been made to students in a dozen universities. Invariably the results of the experiments have been positive. Not only do bargainers get lower prices they also find that it is fun to play the game of bargaining. It is a game in which one rarely loses. Bargaining is easier during a recession or depression when sellers have trouble selling their products and services.

If one believes that the type of economic system we have in the United States is preferable, basically an economy where free enterprise and competition play the major roles, then one should realize that sellers should have the right to ask whatever prices they want and that buyers should have the right to offer whatever prices they wish. A transaction can take place only when buyer and seller reach a price that is mutually satisfactory.

Buy in Bulk and Large Quantities

It is still possible to buy some foods in bulk form, especially in rural areas. Apples, peaches, and potatoes are much lower in price when sold by the bushel instead of by the pound. In retail food stores most foods are packaged. Usually the larger packages cost less per ounce than the small ones. For example, a small package of cereal costs 8.1 cents an ounce compared with 3.8 cents an ounce for the 18-ounce package. In one survey it was found that savings of 30 to 38 percent could be made by purchasing eleven items in larger rather than small packages, savings of 20 to 30 percent could be made on six items, and on twelve items the savings ranged from 10 to 20 percent. Milk-drinking families can save $50 a year by purchasing milk in half-gallon cartons in food stores.

Motorists who live in suburban or rural areas can install a 100-gallon storage tank and then buy gasoline for 3 or 4 cents a gallon less than the pump price. In clothing stores sellers often advertise quantity price reductions. For example, five men's shirts may be offered for $20 instead of $25. Several pairs of hose may cost less per pair than a single pair.

In high-school and college supply stores students may purchase paper by the ream at prices substantially less than those charged for tablets or single sheets. Even ballpoint pens priced at 25 cents each may sell for 6 for $1.00. The careful shopper who is willing to experiment and to learn will soon discover the wide range of quantity discounts.

One word of caution: Not all prices for large quantities are lower than prices for small quantities. Shoppers must constantly be alert. They must compare prices per ounce. Once in a while they may find that a store may deceive them into thinking that quantity prices are lower when actually they are not. For example, a chain food store carried one brand of detergent priced at $1.98 for the 5-pound, 4-ounce size and $4.59 for the 10-pound, 11-ounce size. The alert shopper would calculate the price per pound and find it to be 37.7 cents for the smaller size and 42.9 cents for the larger size. The careless or naive shopper would assume the large box to be the better buy, and the seller would make an extra profit of 5.2 cents per pound.

Read Labels, Warranties, and Freshness Codes

The Federal Food, Drug, and Cosmetic Act requires that most foods sold in interstate commerce be labeled to show the ingredients and that the ingredients be labeled properly. Cottonseed oil may *not* be labeled "olive oil." A blend of cane and maple syrup may not be labeled "Vermont syrup." A can labeled "tuna with noodles" must contain more tuna than noodles. The law requires that certain products be labeled with cautionary statements to warn consumers. A few products even show the exact percentage of ingredients. Nutrition information is now being placed on more food product labels and labels should be read carefully and regularly. All the information one might desire to find on a label will not necessarily be there, but use the information that is there to help you make more intelligent choices.

If a product has a warranty, read it and be sure you understand it before you purchase the product. Know what the warranty covers and what it does not cover.

Did you ever wonder how long a particular food has been on the store shelf? Did you suspect that it might be stale? Store management knows through codes on the merchandise. Table 16-3 lists six of the many different codes used by food processors. It is almost impossible for the shopper to know which code dating system a processor has used. The use of code dating by food processors raises a disturbing question, "Why do they feel it necessary to keep such information from consumers?" Open dating is the inclusion on a package of a date for the last day of sale which consumers can understand—for example, July 5, 1977—whereas code dating uses numbers that consumers can't interpret, as in the table below. Even when open dating is used, the consumer needs to know if the date is the *pull date*

The bottom of this package is stamped with an open date, informing buyers of the last date of sale. (*Dr. Lilly Bruck, Director, Consumer Education, New York City Dept. of Consumer Affairs*)

TABLE 16-3. Code Dating

Code	Translation	Last day of sale
0803	08 = month of year; 03 = 3rd day of month	August 3
8K03	8 = month of year; K is meaningless; 03 = day of month	August 3
215	215th day of year	August 3
150	150 days from the end of the year	August 3
HKC	H = August; K = year of decade; C = 3rd day of month	August 3
203C	C = 2nd half of year; 2 = 2nd month of 2nd half of year; 03 = 3rd day of month	August 3

—that is, the last day a product should be offered for sale—the *freshness date*—the last day one can expect the product to be of optimum quality—the *expiration date*—the last day the product should be used—or the *pack date*—the day on which the product was manufactured, processed, or packaged. More and more processors, particularly processors of dairy and bakery products, are "open dating" their products and indicate on the package what the date means. Massachusetts and New York City require open dating on some perishable products.

Check the Quantity

The National Bureau of Standards and state weights and measures officials advise buyers to check the weights and measurements of their purchases. Do not buy unless the weighing and measuring devices, such as scales and gasoline dispensing pumps, have a seal indicating that they have been inspected and approved by state measurement officials. Watch the measurement device when your purchase is being weighed. The scale must start at zero and come to a full stop. On the purchase of an item priced at $1.60 a pound a one ounce shortage costs the buyer 10 cents.

Don't be fooled by the size of a container. Look on the label for the net weight, measure, or count. Shake a package to ascertain whether it is full or only partially full.

Computing measuring devices are very helpful and save time for sellers. But computing devices are not infallible; even if the device is accurate it may be misread. For these reasons it is recommended that buyers themselves calculate the prices of the purchases that are weighed for them by the salesclerks.*

Check Prices and Totals

Many items are priced on the basis of fractional weights and prices. One cannot make the necessary calculations mentally. It is often necessary to use pencil and paper. Even then one must be adept with fractions. Which is the better buy, a $7\frac{5}{8}$-ounce package at 39 cents or a $12\frac{7}{8}$-ounce package at 53 cents? Only by reducing these figures to a comparative basis can one compare prices per ounce. Until unit pricing becomes universal, good shoppers will take the necessary time to make such comparisons.

Some shoppers find it worthwhile to shop with a minielectronic calculator, which greatly facilitates the task of comparing fractional prices and fractional quantities. A number of inexpensive cardboard calculators are available on the market.

No matter how good a reputation a store may have, it is important to check calculations, additions, and totals. Even though there is no intent to defraud buyers, mistakes do occur. Good shoppers are just as quick to call attention to mistakes in their favor as they are to insist on correction of mistakes in favor of the seller. One may be sure that the businesses with which one deals follow the practices recommended here for good shoppers. From the time an order is placed by the purchasing department of a firm until the invoice is approved by the accounting department, quality, price, and amount are checked and rechecked. If such practices are good for business firms, they should be equally good for family buyers.

Pay Cash and Carry

Good shoppers shop in person, pay cash, and carry their own purchases, saving up to 25 percent.[26]

One may use the telephone to secure comparative price information,

---

* See Chapter 23 for more on weights and measures.

but it is usually not considered good practice to order by telephone. Neither is it good practice to send small children to stores alone, even with written orders. It is good practice, however, to allow children to accompany adult buyers so that they can learn proper buying procedure.

Credit costs money. Consumers may pay for credit directly or indirectly, but they always pay. (See Chapter 12 for information on the costs of credit.) The general rule that good shoppers follow is to pay cash. It should be possible for a family whose finances are well managed to pay cash on recurring expenditures. If the family budgets its expenditures, it should also be possible to pay cash for larger, nonrecurring purchases. When credit must be used, good shoppers shop around for the lowest price. There are circumstances in which use of open-account credit may be a convenience that costs no more than if the buyer paid cash. Some stores allow buyers thirty days credit without any specific charge. If one were to pay cash, the price of the merchandise would be no less. If merchandise prices in such stores are competitive with those in cash-and-carry stores, one might as well take advantage of the opportunity to defer payment. One of the costs of doing business is that of losses on bad debts. Credit-granting stores anticipate such losses and mark up the prices on their merchandise enough to offset such losses. This means that in such stores cash buyers help to pay for the costs of credit, whether they use credit or not. One reason why supermarket types of stores usually have lower prices is that cash comes in as the merchandise goes out.

With so many families owning automobiles there is no longer any need for delivery service for small items. Another reason that supermarket prices are usually lower than those of service stores is that shoppers carry their purchases themselves. On larger items that cannot be carried in the family car, it is necessary to depend on delivery by truck. Consumers should recognize that such service must be paid for directly or indirectly. Store managers figure that delivery service costs from 1 to 2 percent of sales.

Keep Records and Receipts

Do not assume that once the purchase has been made, the transaction has ended. After a purchase has been made the buyer may discover that the product is defective, not the right size or right color, or not suitable for the purpose for which it was intended. Therefore, the intelligent shopper will retain sales slips, warranty information, instruction booklets, and all other records that might be needed at some future date. Some stores will make no adjustment if there is no sales slip, and some stores will give a cash refund only if the sales slip is returned. A good filing system can be a real help in keeping records. Then, if a problem arises, the records are available. It is a good idea to get in writing the delivery date of a big item, and it can be helpful to have the name of the sales person to contact if a problem arises.

Know When and How to Protest

In a free economy consumers have the right and the responsibility to protest. Yet many of them never exercise that right. Some consumers exercise their protest function negatively by refusing to make any purchases in an offending store. If enough consumers stopped buying, store managers would know that something was wrong. But unless there is a concerted group boycott, the refusal of one or two or a few consumers to patronize a store will have little effect.

Good shoppers exercise their right of protest positively. They know prices for comparable merchandise in competing stores. If prices in one store are too high, they not only refuse to buy but they tell the store manager why. If a warranted item is defective, it is reported to the seller, who is given an opportunity to make an adjustment. If satisfactory adjustment is not made, a good shopper does not stop with the local manager. The buyer reports his or her dissatisfaction to the owner. If the purchase was made from a local dealer of a large corporation, the dissatisfaction is reported to a top official. When writing to corporate officials it is advisable to indicate on the letter that carbon copies of the letter have been sent to appropriate government agencies such as the Food and Drug Administration, Federal Trade Commission, Office of Consumer Affairs of the Department of Health, Education, and Welfare, or the state consumer protection office. In addition, a carbon copy of the letter should be sent to the better business bureau in the city where the company is headquartered. Complaints will not always be resolved satisfactorily; however, many consumers who have complained to top officials have been both pleased and surprised with the attention they have received for their complaints. A prompt and positive effort to satisfy a buyer is good business practice in the long run; a disgruntled buyer who is converted to a satisfied buyer by prompt and fair handling of a complaint will tell friends that the company was willing to back its product.

QUESTIONS FOR REVIEW

1. "The buyer is the amateur and the seller is the professional." What are the implications of this quotation?
2. If you were to subscribe to one product test reporting magazine, would you choose *Consumers' Research Magazine* or *Consumer Reports?* Why?
3. Would you classify yourself as a careful shopper or a careless shopper according to the standards suggested in this chapter?
4. Are you prone to buy on impulse? If so, how can you become a more rational buyer?
5. In the calendar of annual sales given in Table 16-2 you will notice that

more sales are held in January, July, and August than in other months; why do you suppose sales are concentrated in those months?

6. How do you feel about bargaining for lower prices? Have you ever bargained for anything? Is it a useful practice?

7. What else may a shopper bargain for besides a reduction in price?

8. Is bargaining compatible with our type of economic system?

9. Why should one read labels carefully?

10. Why do you think food processors date their products in codes?

11. What records of your purchases should you keep? Why?

12. What might be the benefits if all consumers who had complaints were to seek redress by writing to company presidents and sending carbon copies of their letters to government consumer protection agencies and the better business bureaus?

PROJECTS

1. Survey five subscribers and five nonsubscribers to *Consumers' Research Magazine* or *Consumer Reports* and get their opinions about these magazines.

2. See if you can find out about any other valuable buying guides not mentioned in this chapter.

3. Order a few publications from the Council of Better Business Bureaus and Household Finance and evaluate them as to their helpfulness to you as a consumer.

4. Read and write a report on one of the books listed under "Books for Consumers" on pp. 386–387.

5. Do an extensive price comparison study of one product in several stores. Were the prices different enough to justify shopping around?

6. Survey a supermarket and try to find out how many products are open dated.

7. If during the term you feel that you have a legitimate consumer complaint, seek redress and report on the results.

REFERENCES

1. Stuart U. Rich and Subhash C. Jain, "Social Class and Life Cycle As Predictors of Shopping Behavior," in Kollat, Blackwell and Engel, p. 438.
2. Ernest Dichter, *The Strategy of Desire* (New York: Doubleday, 1960), p. 175.
3. *Consumers' Research Magazine*, Oct. 1975, p. ii.
4. Ruby Turner Morris and Claire Sekulski Bronson, "The Potential Loss In Money Income to the American People by Haphazard Purchasing," *The Journal of Consumer Affairs* 4, no. 2 (Winter 1970); 111.
5. *Wall Street Journal,* 15 March 1962, p. 1.

6.	Philip Siekman, "U.S. Business' Most Skeptical Consumer," *Fortune* 62 (1960): 159.
7.	Ruby Turner Morris and Claire Sekulski Bronson, "The Chaos of Competition Indicated by Consumer Reports," *Journal of Marketing* 33 (July 1969): 27.
8.	*Advertising Age*, 1 March 1971, p. 12; see also Testimony of Colston E. Warne, President, Consumers Union, before the Subcommittee on Consumer Interests of the Elderly, U.S. Senate Special Committee on Aging, "Hearing Loss, Hearing Aids and the Older American," 19 July 1968.
9.	Sylvia Porter, *Money Book* (New York: Avon Books, 1976), $5.95.
10.	Sidney Margolius, *The Consumer's Guide to Better Buying* (New York: Pocket Books, 1972), $1.25.
11.	*Shopper's Guide, 1974 Yearbook of Agriculture* (Washington, D.C.: U.S. Government Printing Office), $5.70.
12.	John Dorfman, *Consumer Survival Kit* (New York: Praeger, 1975), $3.95.
13.	Christopher and Bonnie Weathersbee, *The Intelligent Consumer* (New York, Dutton, 1973), $10.95.
14.	*Newsletter*, American Council on Consumer Interests, 238 Stanley Hall, University of Missouri, Columbia, Mo. 65201, $15 membership fee.
15.	*New Idea Book* (New York: Progressive Grocer Magazine, 1969), p. 69.
16.	William T. Snaith, "How Retailing Principles Affect Design" in James S. Hornbeck, ed., *Stores and Shopping Centers* (New York: McGraw-Hill, 1962), p. 3.
17.	*Consumer Reports*, Jan. 1971, p. 24.
18.	Snaith, p. 9.
19.	Sidney Margolius, *The Consumer's Guide to Better Buying* (New York: Pocket Books, 1972), p. 182.
20.	Snaith, p. 9.
21.	David T. Kollat, "A Decision Process Approach to Impulse Purchasing," in Engel, pp. 186–197; Leonard M. Guss, *Packaging Is Marketing* (New York: American Management Association, 1967), p. 63; *New Idea Book*, pp. 10–13.
22.	Robert Ferber, "Factors Influencing Durable Goods Purchases," *Consumer Behavior*, Vol. II (New York, N.Y.: New York University Press, 1955), p. 83.
23.	*Journal of Marketing* 33, no. 3 (July 1969): 33.
24.	Walter Hoving, *The Distribution Revolution* (New York: Ives Washburn, 1960), p. 28.
25.	Walter J. Primeaux, Jr., "The Effect of Consumer Knowledge and Bargaining Strength on Final Selling Practice: A Case Study," *Journal of Business* 43 (Oct. 1970): 419–426.
26.	*Changing Times*, May 1970, p. 6.

CHAPTER 17

TO OWN OR TO RENT?

THE URGE TO OWN A HOUSE

Everybody's Dream House

"Be it ever so humble there's no place like home." This line from Stephen Foster's song captures a basic psychological truth. The urge to own a home is a universal one. The U.S. Secretary of Housing and Urban Development stated that even though more and more Americans have been priced out of the housing market by inflation, the government remains committed to fostering home ownership; in her words, "We do not intend to permit the dream of home ownership to end."[1] As the president of a home construction company said, "The average family still dreams of one home on one lot. People will accept less, but not very much less."[2] The psychology of possessiveness is emotional. The world over, people love the land. They also love their homes and the things in their homes. "Home Sweet Home" is still very real. Given the choice and the money, one may generalize, most consumers would choose to own the houses in which they live.*

All age groups have the urge to own, and seem never to lose this urge. The University of Michigan Survey Research Center questioned many people as to their consumer aspirations. They found more than half of the respondents expressed a desire to move to a new house within five years. Most people want to live in a house rather than an apartment. They want to buy rather than to rent. They want a house in the country with woods or a field between their house and the next house. They dream of sunlit, airy rooms, a porch that is cool and breezy in the summer, and a garden in which to dig and to raise vegetables, fruits, and flowers. This is the American dream.

---

* A house or an apartment is a building that serves as living quarters for one or a few families. A home is a family's place of residence. In popular parlance a home is much more than a house. It connotes a social unit formed by a family living together. In the minds of many people it also implies ownership.

(*Hugh Rogers, Monkmeyer*)

Dream Versus Reality

The middle-income family dream house is a single, detached house with three bedrooms and two bathrooms. It has central heating and a two-car garage. There is a family recreation room and the house stands on a half-acre lot in the country. The occupants own the house. Inside they have hot and cold running water, flush toilets, and air-conditioning.

A two-year study by the Harvard–Massachusetts Institute of Technology Joint Center for Urban Studies has established that 6.9 million low- and middle-income American families live in physically inadequate houses. This means that the buildings have such critical defects that they should be extensively repaired, rebuilt, or torn down. Another 700,000 persons reside in overcrowded units, and 5.5 million pay exorbitant rents.[3] In addition, there are approximately 700,000 housing units that are removed from the available supply of housing units each year because they have been torn down or destroyed by fire, flood, tornado, or earthquake, or converted for commercial use.[4] The 1970 census takers found 25 percent of the existing housing units to be structurally unsound or to be lacking one or more essential facilities. Five percent were dilapidated. Such housing is found mostly in rural areas or in rental properties in urban areas, particularly where the elderly live. In rural areas 55 percent of all families were found to be living in dilapidated houses. It is obvious from these figures that we are not attaining our national goal of adequate housing for everyone.* To meet our housing needs, production must be increased from the present level of 1 million units a year to 2.5 million a year.

What Can You Afford to Pay?

Most federal legislation accepts as a standard 20 percent to 25 percent of an individual's income, after federal income and Social Security taxes, as the maximum one can afford to spend on housing. Another formula limits housing costs per month to take-home pay for one week. Still another advises you to take the cost of a house, say $35,000, subtract your down payment, and take 1.1 percent of the remainder. If you paid down 10 percent on $35,000, then 1.1 percent of the balance would be $347, which would be the approximate amount you could afford each month for payments on the mortgage, insurance, taxes, maintenance repairs, heating, and utilities. But experts contend that only one family out of five can afford to buy a $35,000 home.[5] Government statistics revealed that if a family were not earning at least $23,000 a year, it could not afford to buy an average-priced house in the United States. The median cost of a new house in 1975 was $41,300. An annual income of $23,300 would be necessary to handle the high costs of purchasing such a house and meeting interest payments, utility bills, and repair costs. Experts contend that only 15 percent of the population can currently afford even a medium-priced house.[6] The housing crisis has reached such proportions that the question has been raised as to whether it will become necessary for the federal government to provide housing subsidies for 70 million people, one-third of the population. Prospective house buyers should complete Table 17-1 carefully. This table will aid you in deciding approximately how much you can afford to put into a house.

The cost of housing mounts up to a fortune in a lifetime. If you spend the modest sum of $250 a month for housing from the age of 22 to age 76 you will spend a total of $162,000. As your income increases and your housing expenditures increase, you are likely to spend approximately $250,000 or more in your lifetime on housing.

The Cost of Housing

In 1966 the median price of a new, one-family house in the United States was $21,400; by the middle of 1976 it was more than $48,000. Over the past twenty years, the net disposable income of American families has increased only 180 percent, while monthly housing expenses have increased 305 percent.[7] Of the twelve major categories measured by the Con-

---

* Adequate housing means, in addition to a well-built structure, accessibility to schools, playgrounds, parks, hospitals, shopping facilities, and public transportation.

TABLE 17-1. Estimating Income Available for Housing

PART ONE

DEPENDABLE MONTHLY INCOME
Head of Family's Base Pay $____
Head of Family's Other Earnings $____
Spouse's Base Pay $____
Spouse's Other Earnings $____
All Other Dependable Income $____
TOTAL DEPENDABLE INCOME $____

Insurance $____
Taxes $____
Maintenance and Fuel $____
Other Job Related Transportation (If regularly used) $____
Total $____
Other Accounts, Notes, and Installment Payments $____
$____
$____
Total $____
TOTAL MONTHLY OBLIGATIONS AND SALARY DEDUCTIONS $____
Deduct Total MONTHLY OBLIGATIONS AND SALARY DEDUCTIONS from TOTAL DEPENDABLE INCOME. The results will be the amount of income available for HOUSING AND ALL OTHER LIVING COSTS $____

PART TWO

MONTHLY OBLIGATIONS AND SALARY DEDUCTIONS
Federal, State, and Other Income Taxes $____
Personal Property Taxes (Other than real estate and automobiles) $____
Retirement Payments (Including Social Security) $____
Insurance Premiums and Insurance Loan Payments
Life $____
Policy Loan Payments $____
Hospitalization $____
Household and Other Insurance (Excluding home property and automobile) $____
Total $____
Automobile and Transportation Expense
Loan installment Payments $____

PART THREE

PRESENT MONTHLY HOUSING EXPENSE
Rent (or Mortgage Principal and Interest Payments if you own your present home) $____
Mortgage Insurance Premium, if owner $____
Taxes and Any Special Assessments, if owner $____
Hazard Insurance, if owner $____
Maintenance, if owner $____

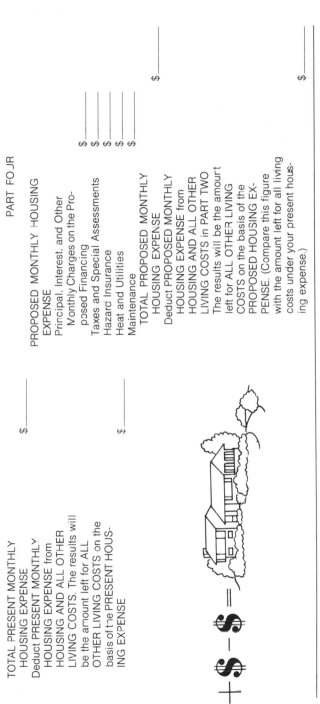

PART FOUR

PROPOSED MONTHLY HOUSING
EXPENSE
Principal, Interest, and Other
Monthly Charges on the Pro-
posed Financing .... $ _____
Taxes and Special Assessments .... $ _____
Hazard Insurance .... $ _____
Heat and Utilities .... $ _____
Maintenance .... $ _____
TOTAL PROPOSED MONTHLY
HOUSING EXPENSE .... $ _____
Deduct PROPOSED MONTHLY
HOUSING EXPENSE from
HOUSING AND ALL OTHER
LIVING COSTS in PART TWO
The results will be the amount
left for ALL OTHER LIVING
COSTS on the basis of the
PROPOSED HOUSING EX-
PENSE. (Compare this figure
with the amount left for all living
costs under your present hous-
ing expense.)

TOTAL PRESENT MONTHLY
HOUSING EXPENSE .... $ _____
Deduct PRESENT MONTHLY
HOUSING EXPENSE from
HOUSING AND ALL OTHER
LIVING COSTS. The results will
be the amount left for ALL
OTHER LIVING COSTS on the
basis of the PRESENT HOUS-
ING EXPENSE .... $ _____

Source: Handbook for the Home: Yearbook of Agriculture (Washington, D.C.: U.S. Government Printing Office, 1972), p. 101

409

sumer Price Index, only the prices of fuel, oil, and coal have increased more since 1967 than the cost of home-ownership. The fuel, oil, and coal price index rose from 100 to 246.2 percent, while the home-ownership index rose from 100 to 189.6. A study of the average selling prices of houses in major metropolitan areas showed that the most expensive single-family houses, on the average, were available in Minneapolis–St. Paul at $57,300; in New York at $54,300; in Los Angeles at $51,200; in Chicago at $48,800; in Philadelphia at $45,000; and in Seattle the average selling price was $40,-900.[8]

The federal government policy of high interest rates has brought housing construction almost to a halt six times in the past thirty years and has resulted in drastic increases in cost. The interest rate charged for home mortgages has increased from an average of 6 percent to an average of 8.75 percent in a decade. This means that the monthly carrying charge on a $30,000, thirty-year mortgage has risen from $180 to $236. That additional $56 per month is due to the higher rate of interest alone.

Why Do Houses Cost So Much?

1. House builders have not been able to develop an assembly-line method of production. The customary procedure in building a house is to gather materials at the building site where the house is manufactured by small-scale builders who construct no more than five houses a year.

Why is it that houses are not built in factories and assembled on the building sites? A few are. But 60 percent of the cost of a prefabricated house is for work done on location. It has been found that prefabs cannot compete in price with conventional houses beyond 500 miles from the factory because of transportation costs. In most areas site fabrication has all the advantages of prefabrication.

Regional differences impede standardization. For example, only 20 percent of houses in the South have basements, compared with 90 percent in the North. In the West stucco finish is preferred, in the South brick facing, and in the North wood frame.

2. A second reason why houses cost so much is consumer attitudes. Many people consider factory-built houses as being too standardized, unattractive, poorly constructed, and subject to faster than normal depreciation. Although such attitudes are irrational and without basis, they are nonetheless real and reflect the power of custom. There is a growing view in the housing industry that the real key to low-cost housing will be found in mass production at the site rather than in prefabrication. Economies of prefabrication are partially offset by delivery expenses and the costs of complying with local building codes. The latter often reflects the combined opposition of local contractors and unions. Real cost reduction will come chiefly from improved organization within the building industry. Mass production at the site yields economies in the purchase of materials and more efficient use of labor and equipment. But mass production, like prefabrication, is ham-

pered by the need for large capital investment, by obstructive building codes, high delivery expenses, opposition from local contractors and unions, and by consumer resistance to standardized housing.

3. The building industry is not well integrated. It consists of a loose collection of related crafts. When an individual signs a contract for construction of a house, the general contractor subcontracts for heating, electrical work, roofing, painting, and other such specialized tasks. As many as 15 craftsmen work with hand tools to assemble thousands of parts. Coordination of their activities is largely a matter of chance.

4. There is excess capacity in the construction industry. Facilities for building houses are 30 percent in excess of those necessary if demand were uniform. Overhead costs on this excess capacity increase all costs of construction.

5. In northern states the building industry is seasonal. Some engineers contend that construction work can be carried on in winter as well as in summer. In fact, there are some who claim that the costs of construction are actually lower in the winter. Yet the industry is still operated on a seasonal basis.

6. There are many hazards involved in building a house. Adequate insurance against these hazards may increase the cost of construction by 7 percent or more.

7. The fee for an architect may range from 6 to 15 percent of construction costs. As a result, not many builders of one-family houses use the services of architects. This may be false economy. Even for a modest sized house architects can achieve savings in design and construction that may pay all or most of their fee.

For those who cannot afford, or think they cannot afford, the services of an architect there are standardized designs that can be purchased for about $50. Most of these plans are designed to meet Federal Housing Administration standards. Yet there are pitfalls for the inexperienced consumer-builder or buyer. An architect can protect his or her client against such pitfalls.

8. In most of the larger cities, workers in the building trades are strongly organized. The fact that unionization has developed along craft rather than industrial lines may result in jurisdictional disputes. This means that the members of one union, for example the carpenters, will contend that part of the work should be allotted to them while the members of another union, possibly the metalworkers, may contend that the work falls within their jurisdiction. No matter which union gets work, the other union may call a strike. This stops work and increases costs. Some unions follow a policy of restricting output. Bricklayers' unions may limit the number of bricks to be laid in a day or painters' unions may limit the width of a brush to be used.

9. The construction or purchase of a house involves a large capital investment. For most families it is probably the largest single expenditure they will ever make. Since few can pay cash, they must borrow. This increases the cost of a home by thousands of dollars. On a $30,000 loan at

8.75 percent interest to be repaid in 30 years, the interest charge would be $54,960.

10. It is amazing that we have as much housing as we do, in view of local governments' rigid building codes, tradesmen's restrictions, union rules, and buyers' idiosyncrasies. In Pittsburgh, one home construction builder reported having to operate under 150 building codes. He stated that when a city increases its required lot size on which to build a house from 80 front feet to 100 feet, this action can force the cost of the house up by $2,000. Another contracter stated, "Every time a city council meets, the cost of housing goes up."⁹ One of the largest single-family home builders in the country reported that there are two areas that have pushed costs up, and where builders can cut costs: labor and restrictive controls on land use.¹⁰ Some codes require roof trusses to be spaced 16 inches apart, instead of 24 inches which is the usual and adequate requirement; some codes require plaster instead of gypsum wallboard; some require metal-covered wiring instead of the commonly used nonmetallic covering. Intended to assure structural strength, protection against fire, and plumbing to safeguard health, some codes have been drafted for the benefit of manufacturers of materials and craft unions. They have become embedded in custom and contract. In some cases they have become devices for establishing local monopolies. Local suppliers may persuade drafters of codes to specify certain materials, even by brand name. There is an urgent need for liberalizing local laws and regulations concerning zoning, building permits, and codes, all of which are burdensome to housing construction and increase costs.

11. The general property tax has long been an important source of revenue for local governments and it is another factor that increases the cost of owning a house. Until the 1971–1972 fiscal year the property tax was the major source of revenue for the nation's cities. In that year for the first time "intergovernmental" revenue became greater than the revenue from property taxes collected by cities. Intergovernmental revenue is money received from federal, state, and county governments. Property tax revenues per person, in a survey of more than 200 cities, varied from a low of $9.77 in Mobile, Alabama, to a high of $449.50 in Hartford, Connecticut. These figures cannot be used to compare total tax burdens because city financing systems differ, but they do illustrate the differences in property taxes per person in different cities.¹¹ The following example shows the cost of property taxes as a housing expense for one family. In one year a total of $784.82 was paid in property taxes, divided as follows: county taxes— $113.83; city taxes—$143.78; and school taxes—$527.21. This was the equivalent of a 4 percent tax on the purchase price of the house. At this rate, the family in a period of twenty-five years would pay in taxes an amount equal to the purchase price of the house. This is an important reason for the continuous scarcity of houses at prices most people can pay.

12. Historically the cost of land has averaged about 12 percent of total property value; it is now 21 percent. The cost of home sites rose an average of 82 percent in ten years, and much more in some cities. These dramatic

increases have been caused by population growth, migration to suburban areas, and growing scarcity of suitable building sites.

13. Consumer-buyers must bear some responsibility for the high cost of houses. Even though the purchase of a house is usually the largest single investment a buyer ever makes, the decision to buy is usually based on a woeful lack of knowledge. The average buyer knows no more about the details of the house he buys than about the engine in his automobile. There are many ways builders can cut costs and yet construct a house that is attractive and appears to be well built. They may use too little cement in the foundation, causing it to crumble. Nails may be spaced too far apart in the flooring. The use of inferior roofing materials may result in leakage. Thin window sashes will cause loss of heat in winter. The use of undersized beams will cause sagging floors and ceilings. Second-hand materials may be used where they will not be seen. Insufficient or poor paint may look good at first, but may not last more than a year. As a result of shoddy construction, maintenance and repair costs are greater than buyers anticipate.

Can House Construction Costs Be Reduced?

If houses were produced on assembly lines as automobiles and trailers are, the cost of production would be reduced. While the average house built during 1976 sold for about $48,000, the average mobile home sold for about $11,750. The selling price of new houses rose so sharply, with so many families priced out of the market, that a new concept in home building evolved — the compact house. The average house of the past, with 1,700 square feet, is now giving way to compact houses of 900 to 1,200 square feet. These smaller houses are in the price range of many more families. They fit in with today's smaller families, and because they are smaller, better insulated, and tightly built, they conserve natural fuels and electricity. The family room is being eliminated. Who needs two living rooms? One dining area is being eliminated. Who needs a dining area near the kitchen and a separate formal dining room? Bedrooms are smaller, and additional money is saved by eliminating halls and extra bedrooms. The base price of the house is reduced by offering as optional such extras as major appliances, air conditioning, and fireplaces. Fewer windows are included, which also saves on heating and cooling costs. More factory-built components are used, saving lumber and time on the job. "The biggest dilemma facing builders today is what to take out to make houses affordable, and what to leave in to make them salable."[12]

Mobile Homes

The soaring cost of conventional houses has created a boom in the mobile home industry. Already more than 9.7 million Americans live in nearly 4.3 million mobile homes. That means that nearly one in twenty Americans lives in a mobile home. According to figures compiled by the Manufactured Housing Institute, mobile homes represented 94 percent of all housing produced in 1974 to sell at less than $20,000, and 70 percent of all housing costing under $30,000. It is estimated that the production of mobile homes will soon exceed 300,000 units annually. As the median price of a new, conventionally built house continues to rise, more American families are being priced out of that market and are turning to mobile homes.[13] The mobile home industry says it can build units for approximately half of what it costs conventional builders—$10.63 per square foot as compared to $21 per square foot. The appeal of mobile homes is particularly high among young married couples and retired couples.

The potential buyer of a mobile home should investigate the purchase very carefully before signing a contract. Buyers should know exactly what the contractual obligations will be in the mobile home park where they place their home. There is a shortage of space in desirable mobile home parks; facilities are often inadequate; many leases are short-term and give park owners every advantage; some parks require tenants to purchase gas, oil, or electricity from the park owner at excessive prices; and rents for park space are rising rapidly. The consumer needs to know what the financing details for mobile homes are, and it is advisable to have a lawyer go over all contracts. Since mobile homes are not considered "real property" by most state governments and most financial institutions, the interest rates charged for financing are usually higher. The interest rate on mobile homes averages approximately 12 percent, about one-third higher than the average interest rate for conventional mortgage financing.[14]

In addition, there are certain safety factors that should be investigated. The National Commission on Fire Prevention and Control flatly states that "mobile homes are the fastest-burning of all homes."[15] Next to fire, the mobile home's worst enemy is a storm. Unless secured by well-anchored, tie-down straps, a mobile home can be blown over by moderately strong winds. The federal government has issued certain standards on construction of mobile homes and mooring requirements that will lessen the problems of fire and storms.

FINANCING THE PURCHASE OF A HOUSE

"Buy Now, Take 30 Years to Pay"

Houses have been sold on the installment plan since the days of Julius Caesar. In a recent year 67 percent of all houses sold were financed with conventional mortgage loans; 12 percent were financed with Veterans Administration-guaranteed loans; and 8 percent were financed with Federal Housing Administration-insured loans. The remaining 13 percent were paid for in cash or financed under some other arrangement.[16] These figures show that the usual method of financing the purchase of a house is to secure a loan from a lending agency, giving as security a mortgage on the property.

A mortgage is a legal instrument that gives the lender conditional title to the property. It is a guarantee that if the mortgager fails to pay interest and principal, the lender may force the sale of the property and obtain the money due him from the proceeds of the sale. Legally this is known as "foreclosing a mortgage." The nominal owner of a $36,000 house who made a down payment of $7,200 has a 20 percent equity in the property. The term "home-owner" is used loosely to include all owner-occupied houses in which the equity ranges from 100 percent to 1 percent. If a no-down-payment mortgage runs longer than twenty-five years, the monthly payments for the first years are almost all interest payments. They are the "rent" one pays for a house one does not really own, yet for which one is fully liable. By contrast an outright renter is free of the risks and the liabilities of ownership. When a borrower makes a small down payment or none at all, he or she has not as much to lose. This is why lenders usually demand a personal note in addition to a mortgage. Then if the proceeds of the sale of the property are insufficient to repay the loan, the borrower is personally liable for the deficiency.

Mortgages are classified as "first," "second," and "third." Third mortgages are not common, and second mortgages have often been replaced by the installment land contract, under which a deed held in trust is security. In case a borrower defaults on payments, the holder of a first mortgage may foreclose and has a prior claim over the holders of later mortgages.

Normally lenders limit loans to 70 or 75 percent of the appraised value of a house, unless the borrower buys mortgage insurance. Such insurance typically costs one-half of 1 percent of the loan the first year, then one-fourth of 1 percent of the principal balance each succeeding year. If a borrower's down-payment is less than 20 percent, the lender may require mortgage insurance. With such insurance a lender may loan up to 97 percent of the appraised value of a house.

There is wide disparity among interest payments on mortgage loans. By the use of fees, dues, points, premiums, commissions, service charges, and discounts the actual rates of interest may be increased. The discount method is one of the most common. Under this plan if a borrower of $5,000 is charged a discount of 20 percent, he or she gets only $4,000 but is obligated to pay back $5,000. In addition the borrower must pay interest on the $5,000. The discount method and the other methods mentioned are used to evade usury laws.

Home-owners who have first mortgages on their property are advised to beware of "money finders" who offer to make debt consolidation loans if the home-owner will give a second mortgage as security. These "money finders" charge excessively for their services and engage in practices that approach the status of rackets. Better business bureaus across the nation have cooperated with state governments in an effort to control this form of exploitation of consumers. In Ohio, for example, cases were investigated in which it was found that consumers had been injured financially by the tactics of some firms. As a result, a law was enacted to regulate the operations of second-mortgage firms.

Four out of five new and existing one-family houses are mortgaged. Two-thirds of the mortgages run for 30 years, and one-third for 35 years. Total mortgage debt on one- to four-family nonfarm houses amounted to $440 billion in 1975.

The Cost of Mortgage Loans

While it is true that the installment purchase plan has made it possible for many families to purchase houses who could not have done so otherwise, it is also true that installment plan buying is expensive. For example, on a twenty-five-year mortgage at 9 percent the cost per $1,000 is $8.40 per month. In 1975 whether a buyer purchased a new house or a used house, the average interest payment would be on the order of 8.5 to 9.0 percent.

How much interest would a borrower pay over a period of years? Answers vary according to the number of years a mortgage runs and the interest rate. Table 17-2 shows the cost of a $20,000 mortgage loan at varying rates of interest over a twenty-five-year period.

Table 17-3 shows the monthly payments required for interest and principal at different rates of interest for periods of twenty, twenty-five, and thirty years. To figure the cost per month of a mortgage, find the appropriate payment period and interest rate and multiply the amount shown by the number of thousands of dollars borrowed. Table 17-4 shows the importance of the down payment. The term "down payment" may also be considered as the buyer's initial equity in the house. On a twenty-five-year 8 percent loan, every $1,000 of down payment decreases the amount of total interest paid by about $1,310. If you repay a loan in twenty-five years instead of

TABLE 17-2. Monthly Payment and Interest Cost on a $20,000 Loan at Varying Interest Rates Over a 25-Year Period

Interest Rate %	Monthly Payment (Principal and Interest)	Total Interest Over 25 Years
6	$129	$18,600
6½	135	20,440
7	141	22,390
7½	148	24,330
8	154	26,280
8½	161	28,200
9	168	30,220
9½	175	32,270
10	182	34,460

Source: *Selecting and Financing a Home,* Consumer and Food Economics Research Division, Agricultural Research Service, Home and Garden Bulletin No. 182, Dec. 1970, p. 21.

TABLE 17-3. Monthly Payments For Each $1000 Borrowed

Interest Rate %	PAYMENT PERIOD, YEARS			
	15	20	25	30
5	$ 7.91	$6.60	$5.85	$5.37
5½	8.18	6.88	6.15	5.68
6	8.44	7.17	6.45	6.00
6½	8.72	7.46	6.76	6.33
7	8.99	7.76	7.07	6.66
7½	9.28	8.06	7.39	7.00
8	9.56	8.37	7.72	7.34
8½	9.85	8.68	8.06	7.69
9	10.15	9.00	8.40	8.05
9½	10.45	9.33	8.74	8.41
10	10.75	9.66	9.09	8.78

Source: Selecting and Financing A Home, Home and Garden Bulletin No. 182, p. 15.

thirty years you will pay about $6,330 less in interest. The trend toward small or no down payments and long-term mortgages results in a rising rate of mortgage foreclosures.

The dramatic and drastic increases in interest charges on mortgage loans for houses to 8 and 9 percent in the latter 1960s not only priced many borrowers out of the market but gave impetus to the idea of variable mortgage interest rates. In an economy in which the general level of prices rises steadily at a rate of 5 or 6 percent a year, we have turned to variable annuities, variable insurance contracts, and to variable interest rates on mortgage loans. The plan is simple. Interest rates would go up on a loan if there were a general rise in interest rates and would fall if there were a decline in interest rates. Adjustments would be made periodically in one of two ways: a borrower could hold his or her payments constant and take a longer or

TABLE 17-4. Effect of Size of Down Payment on Cost of $20,000 Home, With Interest at 8 Percent

Down Payment	MONTHLY PAYMENT—PRINCIPAL AND INTEREST, YEARS			TOTAL INTEREST, YEARS		
	20	25	30	20	25	30
$ 0	$167	$154	$147	$20,110	$26,280	$32,780
500	163	151	143	19,610	25,630	31,960
1,000	159	147	139	19,110	24,970	31,110
2,000	151	139	132	18,100	23,650	29,500
3,000	142	131	125	17,090	22,340	27,860
4,000	134	124	117	16,090	21,030	26,220
5,000	126	116	110	15,080	19,710	24,580

Note: Monthly payment rounded to nearest $1; total interest rounded to nearest $10.
Source: Selecting and Financing A Home, Home and Garden Bulletin No. 182, p. 22.

shorter repayment period or the borrower could accept an increase or decrease in monthly payments on interest and principal. This is standard practice in commercial banking, but very few lenders to house buyers use the flexible or floating type of loan; such variability is not allowed on FHA or VA loans. Supporters contend that borrowers at 9 percent are subsidizing earlier borrowers who are paying 6 percent. Limited experience has shown that borrowers are ready to accept decreases but object vigorously to increases. On a $20,000 mortgage running twenty years a 1 percent rise in interest charge increases principal and interest payments by about 10 percent; on a thirty-year mortgage this would total $5,000.

Shopping Around for Mortgage Money

It pays to shop around for a mortgage loan. Where do you go? If the seller has mortgaged the property, one possibility is to take over the seller's mortgage. Quite likely the interest rate will be lower. But in all probability you will have to arrange for new financing with one of the usual lenders on house mortgages. These include savings and loan associations, which account for 39.3 percent of mortgage loans; mutual savings banks, whose share of the market is 13.6 percent; life insurance companies, whose share is 9.5 percent; commercial banks, 16.1 percent; federal government agencies, 8.0 percent; and other sources, accounting for 13.5 percent of the market.[17] Savings and loan associations are basic in the mortgage market, having 82 percent of their assets invested in mortgages. The Federal Home Loan Bank Board operates to give savings and loan associations needed liquidity.

The conventional lending institutions, which together make 80 percent of all mortgage loans, usually lend up to 75 percent of the value of the property and require a down payment of 25 percent. The usual mortgage term is fifteen to twenty years, but may run to 30, and the rate of interest averages 8 to 9½ percent.

Veterans Administration guaranteed loans are made to eligible veterans by private lenders. VA guarantees repayment of 60 percent of the loan, with a guarantee limit of $17,500. There is no charge for pre-Korean War veterans, but for post-Korean War veterans there is a charge of one-half of one percent. VA does not require a down payment, but the private lender may ask for a ten percent payment. Loans run to thirty years and interest charges vary with the market; in 1976 the effective rate was 8.75 percent.

The Federal Housing Administration insures loans made by private lenders, up to 97 percent of the first $25,000 appraised value, 90 percent on value over $25,000 and up to $35,000, and 80 percent on value over $35,000. No loan over $45,000 can be insured. The down payment requirement ranges from 3 percent to 8.3 percent, and the time for repayment may be thirty or thirty-five years. In addition to the interest charge there is an additional charge of one-half of one percent each year to cover FHA insurance.

Some borrowers think they are protected by state usury laws. Such laws set an upper limit on the rate of interest that can be charged on home loans. In some states these usury laws are unrealistic. For example, in the early 1970s the maximum allowable rate of interest that could be charged in Pennsylvania on a home mortgage was 6 percent. This was so far below the national average – approximately 8.5 percent – that mortgage money flowed out of Pennsylvania to other states and it became difficult for many people to get financing to buy a house in Pennsylvania. A low interest rate ceiling appears to favor home buyers, but it actually hurts them if they cannot find a lending institution willing to lend money at that low rate. Legislation was passed in Pennsylvania that raised the legal rate of interest on home mortgages to close to the national average. This made more loan funds available to Pennsylvania home buyers.

When usury laws set interest rates too low, lenders find ways to circumvent the laws. One way lenders can evade usury laws legally is to charge points, a discount, a fee, or a premium. A point is a one-time charge equal to 1 percent of the loan, which is deducted from the total amount of the loan. To illustrate: a four-point charge on a $20,000 loan means that $800 will be deducted in advance, leaving the borrower $19,200. But the borrower is obligated to repay $20,000. Obviously this increases the real interest charge, but by how much? To ascertain the answer you must make some complicated calculations. An easier way is to refer to tables.* In the foregoing illustration the four-point charge would raise the effective rate of interest from $8\frac{1}{2}$ percent to 9.066 percent.[18]

When shopping for a mortgage loan you would do well to ask at least six lenders the same questions, such as interest charge, point charges, length of loan, or whether the loan can be repaid early without penalty charges. By placing the responses in tabular form one can readily compare them and choose the one that seems most favorable.

Mortgage Lending Practices

There are certain mortgage lending practices that should be known to prospective borrowers. Many borrowers do not know that in addition to passing conditional title to the lender they have signed a personal note, usually called a "bond." In case of default the mortgagee can hold the mortgagor personally liable if the forced sale of the property does not yield enough money to pay the loan. Sometimes mortgage companies require borrowers to purchase insurance coverage at prices higher than market rates.

Another abuse is the inclusion of a clause denying the borrower the right to pay off the loan faster than the mortgage contract provides. If a borrower should inherit $5,000 it would be to his advantage to apply that sum toward reduction of the mortgage and thereby reduce his interest

---

* Carleton Financial Computations, Inc., Box 570, South Bend, Ind. 46642, publishes a complete set titled "Influence of Mortgage Points on Interest Rates." The price is $10.00. In all probability your banker has a copy.

payments. If he had not inquired in advance or had not read his contract, he might find that the lender would refuse to let him reduce the mortgage. This would more likely be true if the borrower were paying a high interest rate.

Once a borrower has signed an agreement, he will find that it is rigid and in favor of the lender. No allowance is made for illness or unemployment, even though borrowers may have an equity of 50 percent or more. In a rapidly changing economy having a high level of unemployment even high-income workers may find themselves unemployed for a year or two or longer. With reduced income they cannot meet their mortgage payments. When they default they find that the loan agreement is rigid. Lenders can foreclose and borrowers lose their equity.

Foreclosure losses could be prevented by the creation of an insurance fund. By the payment of relatively small premiums, borrowers could build up a fund from which mortgagors could draw interest and principal payments for as long as thirty-six months.

Mortgage contracts are lengthy, drawn in legal language, and printed in fine italics. As a result it is estimated that nine out of ten borrowers never read the mortgage loan contract. If everything goes well and all payments are made it may be argued that no one is hurt. But if a borrower defaults, the lender may then point to clause after clause in the contract which are to the disadvantage of the borrower. One expert has written that if the true nature of a mortgage were understood by homeowners there would be fewer homeowners.

IS IT CHEAPER TO OWN THAN TO RENT A HOUSE?

The Real Costs of Ownership

Many potential home owners have grappled with the question, "Is it cheaper to own than to rent?" There is no single answer to this question that will be correct for everyone at all times. Some of the general confusion over this problem is generated by lending institutions that suggest that paying money for rent is like throwing money away. Rent money is no more wasted than money spent for food or medical care.

The decision to own or to rent depends on many factors. These can be grouped into three main areas:

1. *The personal preference aspect.* What kind of shelter meets your preferences and needs?
2. *The cost aspect.* How much is it going to cost and how much can you spend each month for shelter?
3. *The investment aspect.* How can you make the best investment of your money while obtaining shelter that meets your needs?[19]

The installment buyer of a house is responsible for interest and principal payments on the mortgage, for taxes, for insurance, for depreciation, and for repairs and maintenance. For a rented house the landlord is responsible for these expenses. The amounts involved will vary from house to house and from region to region. Obviously if it costs more to build a house in the North than it does in the South, owners in the North will have more expenses. Interest rates vary, as do taxes. Owners in undeveloped areas face the possibility of assessments for sewers, water lines, curbing, paving, and sidewalks.

If the owner has paid cash for his house the interest that he might have received if he had invested his funds elsewhere constitutes an implicit expense of ownership. This means that if he paid $40,000 for his house and could have received 8.5 percent interest on that money if he had invested his savings elsewhere, his house is really costing him $3,400 a year. This may be shown in another way. Suppose he finances his house by means of a first mortgage up to 75 percent of its purchase price. On the $30,000 borrowed from a lending agency he would likely pay 9 percent interest. The $2,700 so spent each year would be considered a cost of ownership. It makes no difference whether he borrows the money from a lending agency or from himself – in either case a cost is involved.

Long experience on the part of lenders as well as buyers provides a formula which holds that the yearly costs of owning a house range from a minimum of 10 percent to 15 percent or more. This means that it would cost from $4,000 to $6,000 to own a $40,000 house. If the owner were to rent the house to someone else he or she would have to receive $4,000 to $6,000, depending on several variables, to earn a fair return on his or her investment after paying operating expenses.

The Cost of Renting

There are very few families who have not rented housing at some time. The decision whether to own or to rent is related to the life cycle. Young married couples may establish their first home in a furnished apartment. The second step is to move to a larger, unfurnished apartment. As income increases after age twenty-five the young couple may rent or purchase a small house. At age thirty-five there is a general move up to larger and more expensive housing. After the children have left home and the parents reach retirement age, the trend is to buy or rent a small house or an apartment.

The market for housing is distinctly local. When there is an oversupply in one market area there may be a shortage elsewhere. A vacancy rate of 8.5 percent of all housing is considered to be the point at which landlords break even. If the vacancy rate is higher than 8.5 percent, rents in a local market will be forced down. The vacancy rate at the national level has been between 4.5 and 6.0 percent for the last few years.

In a period of rising prices or a housing shortage without rent control, rentals may be more flexible than the expenses of ownership. They may rise faster and higher. That is because the financing costs of owners are usually extended over a twenty-five to thirty-five-year period and do not fluctuate with short-run price changes. On the other hand, it may be cheaper to rent if there is a large supply of houses available or if the general price level is falling. Rents bear little relation to the original cost. The renter may pay more or less than is required to cover the landlord's cost. The renter takes advantage of periods of decline in rents and the landlord takes advantage of rises. Moreover, it is not really possible to compare the costs of owning a house or apartment with renting because there are too many variables.

Why Do So Many People Believe It Is Cheaper To Own?

The costs of buying the use of a house or an apartment, whether owned by the occupant or by another person, are essentially the same in the long run. There might be a small margin in favor of ownership equal to the administrative expenses for which the owner hopes to secure reimbursement, but the difference is not great.

One reason so many believe that it is cheaper to own than to rent housing may be found by analyzing the expenses of ownership, as shown in Table 17-5. If a family were to contract to pay $40,000 for a house, the expense of ownership would depend on such variables as the amount of down payment, the length of the mortgage term, the interest rates paid or assumed, taxes, insurance, rate of depreciation, and maintenance expenses. If the family had saved $8,000 and paid that amount to the seller, it would have to borrow $32,000. It could probably borrow $32,000 on a first mortgage at an annual cost of $2,560 to $3,200, depending on interest rates. As savings increased, in the form of principal payments, these figures would diminish but interest on the owner's investment would increase, until eventually the loans were paid. The interest charges would then be the amounts shown in part B of the table — $2,100 to $3,400.

Tax rates range from 1 to 3 percent of an arbitrary valuation. Many buyers are inclined to underestimate the tax burden. The so-called owner is in fact a lessee from the city government. If he fails to pay his taxes, he loses his house, even though it may be free of debt. Some writers think that if the tax rate exceeds 3 percent of the purchase price one should not buy.

A property owner must insure against possible loss caused by fire, lightning, explosion, smoke, vandalism, falling aircraft, windstorm, flood, and other hazards. He needs insurance to cover possible injury to persons on the property, other than members of the family. Adequate annual coverage cost will range from $1/2$ percent to 1 percent of the value of the property.

Many buyers would regard the annual expense of owning a $40,000 house which is being purchased on the installment plan as $5,180 to $7,880, depending on interest, tax, and insurance rates. They would ignore implicit expenses. For reasons already given, however, interest on the owner's investment must be included as an expense.

Houses depreciate in value because of physical deterioration or obsolescence, or as a result of changes in the area where they are located. Many houses built fifty years ago become obsolete. In boom periods houses may

TABLE 17-5. Estimated Annual Expenses Incurred by an Owner of a $40,000 House

	A. Mortgaged			
	Low Estimate		High Estimate	
Explicit expenses				
1. Interest on $32,000 mortgage	8%	$2,560	10%	$3,200
2. Taxes	1	400	3	1,200
3. Homeowner's insurance	½	200	1	400
Totals		$3,160		$4,800
Implicit expenses				
1. Interest on owner's equity of $8,000	5¼	420	8½	680
2. Depreciation	2	800	3	1,200
3. Repairs and maintenance	2	800	3	1,200
Totals		2,020		3,080
Combined totals		$5,180		$7,880
	B. Fully paid for			
Explicit expenses				
1. Taxes	1%	$ 400	3%	$1,200
2. Homeowner's insurance	½	200	1	400
Totals		$ 600		$1,600
Implicit expenses				
1. Interest on owner's equity of $40,000	5¼	2,100	8½	3,400
2. Depreciation	2	800	3	1,200
3. Repairs and maintenance	2	800	3	1,200
Totals		3,700		5,800
Combined totals		$4,300		$7,400

Note: Prospective buyers can apply these percentages to any purchase price.

appreciate in value, and some speculative-minded buyers are impressed by stories of $30,000 houses selling for $50,000. Unfortunately, they do not hear so much about price declines in times of depression, when $30,000 houses sell for $15,000. Neither do they usually allow for the depreciation in the purchasing power of the dollar.

The expenses of maintaining and repairing a house are really explicit, but they are included as implicit expenses because so few families keep records of their expenditures. The money paid out for a new roof, or for painting, or for new gutters or screens is forgotten when annual expenses are considered and is often overlooked by prospective buyers.

The psychological satisfactions of owning a house are so strong that buyers have a tendency to recognize only the minimum expenses of ownership, a tendency which is encouraged by those who have houses to sell. It may be comforting to believe that it costs only $3,160 a year ($263.33 a month) to own a $40,000 house, but it is not realistic. As the figures show, the real cost will range from 10.75 to 18.5 percent, even when the house is fully paid for.

What are the expenses of ownership when a house is fully paid for? The answer will be found in part B of Table 17-5. The main change that has taken place is the substitution of implicit for explicit interest, a change that reduces explicit expenses and strengthens the conviction that owning is cheaper than renting. One cannot expect to rent a $40,000 house for $50 a month or $600 a year, nor would an owner be willing to accept so small a sum. Yet that is what many owners and prospective owners consider their expense to be, and that is why owning is so often considered cheaper than renting. Although owners may ignore their implicit expenses, they cannot escape them. The total annual real expense of ownership will range from $358.33 a month, or $4,300 a year, to $616.67 a month, or $7,400 a year.

For many families the question of whether it is cheaper to own or to rent is rhetorical. The naive view that anyone who can afford to pay rent can afford to own is not supported by the facts. Bankers and real estate firms consider a reasonable rule to be that a family should not pay more than two to two and a half times its annual income for a house. Some lenders and counselors are even more conservative. Such a rule is general, however, and does not take into consideration factors such as family size, inherited wealth, and differing demands on family incomes for such things as education and major medical costs. Lending institutions make it difficult for a family to buy a more expensive house than they believe the family can finance. Those who do spend more are almost certain to find that they cannot keep up their payments. Then the dream of ownership turns to the traumatic experience of a foreclosure. Applying these formulas, prospective buyers would have to have annual net incomes of $16,000 to $20,000 in order to purchase a $40,000 house. The majority of families do not have that kind of income.

Other Factors to Consider

1. Even though ownership may be more expensive than renting, there are other factors to consider. There are times when the only way to secure desirable living quarters is to buy or build a house. In an old community there may be many old houses for rent, but none of them may be equipped with all the modern conveniences. Or it may be that when a family is looking for a house, rents are temporarily so high that it appears cheaper to buy or to build. In such cases prospective buyers would do well to take the long-run view. If rentals are high, it is likely that building costs will also be high. Rentals fluctuate over periods of time. Excessive rentals in one decade may be offset by lower rentals a few years later.

2. Even though it may be cheaper to rent than to own, a family with an adequate income may prefer to incur the added expenses of ownership in order to build exactly the kind of house they want.

3. Probable permanence of employment is an important considera-

tion. If the head of the family is a full or part-owner of a business whose permanence is very certain, there is less risk involved in homeownership. This is true also for professionals, whose job locations are usually permanent. But for those whose tenure of employment is dependent on factors beyond their control, homeownership may result in capital losses. Every year one out of every five families moves. If the heads of these families are employed by corporations that move them from time to time, they may lose or gain when they are forced to sell their houses. If they paid too much for their houses, they are almost certain to lose. If the market is depressed, they will probably lose or they may not be able to sell. Then they become involuntary landlords. In their new locations they must rent or buy housing. As a result, a property owner may find his or her expenditures for housing doubled if the family's former house is unoccupied.

4. Prospective owners must consider the expense of living in the area where they wish to settle as compared with the expense of living elsewhere as renters. One of these items is transportation. Commuting, by whatever means, is expensive.

5. The possible gain of living in the community where one owns or operates a business is another factor to consider. Even though the cost of ownership might exceed the cost of renting or owning elsewhere, the difference might be offset by the goodwill resulting from owning property and living in the area where one is in business. This consideration is probably more important in small communities where personal relationships are more significant. To be able to say that one is a taxpaying property owner often promotes goodwill. This is why managers of chain stores in small towns find it beneficial to become taxpaying citizens of the towns in which their stores are located.

6. Another factor to consider is whether homeownership is a good investment. Many people think that it is. They also think that ownership may result in a capital gain and that ownership is a hedge against inflation. A house to live in is not an income-yielding investment. Housing is a necessity, like other items in the budget. Whether one owns or rents, one must have housing. If a family has enough money to buy a second house, that house could be rented to a tenant for income. The ownership of the second house would be an investment.

Property values fluctuate. In a local market house prices may rise in one period and fall in another period. A curious quirk in the thinking of many people is that a house can always be sold for more than was paid for it. The same people know that automobiles depreciate at a rapid rate and accept that fact, but they refuse to accept the fact of depreciation and decline in prices for houses. They consider the ownership of a house as always being a good investment. If a family owns a second house for which it paid $30,000 and sells it for $40,000, the $10,000 capital gain is real and realized. But the purchase of a house to live in is seldom a good investment.

Is ownership of a house a hedge against inflation? The affirmative argument holds that if a $30,000 house can be sold for $40,000 the owner has an offset to a price level increase of 33⅓ percent. This is more apparent than real, because a family must have a place to live. Another house or apartment would cost about $33\frac{1}{3}$ percent more than it was worth in the base year and rentals would rise. Ownership is a hedge against inflation only when a second property is owned.

On the other hand, mortgage dollars borrowed twenty years ago are worth less today. This is an advantage only if the owner's income keeps pace with or exceeds the rise in the price level.

7. To what extent does the federal personal income tax law favor owners? There is practically no advantage for a family having an income of $10,000 or less. Only those having incomes of $20,000 or more realize any significant tax advantage as a result of owning a house. In the upper-income brackets it is possible to compare the tax advantage as between two families having the same income and the same deductions. The family that buys a house on mortgage can deduct interest payments and local property taxes in figuring net income for tax purposes. The higher the tax bracket, the greater the advantage. In all tax brackets the homeowner is favored over the renter because imputed rent is not considered income for tax purposes. Another tax advantage is available to owners who sell a house and buy another one if a capital gain up to a maximum of 25 percent is realized. The tax can be avoided by the purchase of another house that costs at least as much as the one just sold. The law provides that one must purchase and move into the new house within eighteen months before or eighteen months after formally selling the former principal residence. On custom-built houses the time period is forty-two months—eighteen months before the sale of the old home plus two years after. There is a tax advantage also for the homeowner of age sixty-five or over. If an individual age sixty-five or over sells a house and makes a capital gain of as much as $20,000 that amount may be deducted from the owner's gross income. In order to be eligible for such a substantial advantage, the house being sold must have been owned and used as a principal residence for at least five years during the eight-year period preceding the sale. In Florida, owners over age sixty-five are entitled to a Homestead Exemption, which reduces their property tax liability.

8. If the members of a family are able and willing to do their own maintenance and repair work they can save money by working in their spare time. In such families heating, plumbing, roofing, painting, and other maintenance and repair expenses can be reduced. Instead of spending 2 or 3 percent of the purchase price for maintenance and repair they may spend only 1 percent for materials.

Advantages Claimed for Ownership

Homeownership does much more than provide shelter for families. Its long-range effects in boosting self-respect and encouraging responsible citizenship are immeasurable. "When a man buys a home, he acquires a stake in his community—in his society—that is likely to remain with him for life."[20] Those who favor ownership contend that after twenty-five or thirty-five years the buyer of a house has a 100 percent equity, which represents a good investment. By contrast the renter has only his or her receipts. A second advantage is that ownership encourages thrift. After making monthly payments for twenty-five or thirty-five years, the buyer of a house will have developed the habit of saving. A third advantage is that full ownership of a house assures a permanent residence as long as taxes are paid. Another advantage is that the homeowner has fixed annual expenses in contrast to fluctuating, and probably rising, rent payments. The family which owns its home enjoys a higher credit standing in the community and among business firms. Finally, it is claimed that homeownership develops good citizens who are interested in good schools and good local government.

How valid are the advantages claimed for ownership? It may be true that the homeowner possesses an investment instead of a bundle of receipts. It may be true also that the homeowner may own a liability instead of an asset. In times of deep depression the prices of properties fall but taxes remain constant. That is the kind of situation that has given rise to the term "tax poor." Under the federal income tax law an individual does not have to pay taxes if he or she has no net income. Under the property tax laws, however, taxes must be paid, or title to the property is forfeited, even though the property does not yield any income. It is in this sense that the house may become a liability.

The contention that the homeowner has an investment whereas the renter has only a bundle of receipts tends to be misleading because it implies that less has been received for rental payments than for purchase payments. The renter has the use of the house, just as an owner does. Nevertheless, as a homeowner uses a house, the owner and his or her family gain added psychic satisfaction from the fact of ownership. In the culture of our time the owner has considerably more status than the renter, except when renting a high-rent apartment or house in an exclusive area.

It may well be that ownership encourages thrift, but it may also discourage thrift. If a homeowner has paid too high a price and has incurred payments in excess of his ability to pay, he may become discouraged and default on his payments. There is always the possibility in an urban area that the owner of a $40,000 house may find himself in a blighted area. In such a case, the owner may lose his equity.

There seems to be no offsetting disadvantages to the claim that ownership assures a permanent residence and raises the credit rating of the owner. Before 1950 ownership was often an anchor that chained owners to a job. In recent years more liberal financing has made it easier to sell used houses.

Homeownership may develop interest in good government, but it may also cause owners to be interested primarily in keeping property taxes from increasing. From the social point of view this may retard progress. Many communities today are in serious difficulties with their public school systems because property owners resist tax increases necessary to finance the operation of an expanding school system.

Advantages Claimed for Renting

The chief advantage claimed for renting is that in the long-run renting is cheaper than owning. A second and closely related claim is that if the renter were to invest the difference between cost of ownership and cost of renting in growth stocks the renter would receive a better financial return. The renter does not handicap himself or herself by a thirty-five year debt. Nor does he obligate himself to make fixed monthly payments for half of his lifetime. In case of short-term unemployment or incapacitation resulting from accident or illness he has no equity to lose. His investments in growth stocks will not be affected adversely. Renting can give flexibility and cash savings.

Since the renter has no capital investment in real estate, he does not face the risk of shrinkage in capital value. To him slumps in real-estate prices means gains rather than losses.

The renter has no fear of the spread of blighted areas. Neither is he directly concerned with increases in property taxes. If a better job becomes available in another town, a renter is free to move.

Owners run the risk of damage to or destruction of their houses by hurricanes, earthquakes, and floods. Near the Atlantic coastline property owners may see their houses blown away by hurricanes or washed away by the ocean. On the Pacific coastline in Oregon they may see their houses topple into the ocean. Some houses in the Pennsylvania anthracite coal mining region have been destroyed by mine cave-ins. In Florida sinkholes destroy houses without warning. There does not seem to be any way to anticipate the development of these sinkholes. In Alaska and California earthquakes can damage or destroy buildings. In many sections of the country, floods occur and recur, damaging or destroying houses. The cost of all these hazards must be assumed by property owners. It is impossible to buy mudslide insurance, and brush-fire and earthquake insurance is expensive. The earthquake rate on a $30,000 house in California is about $90 a year, with a 5 percent deductible clause. This means that the owner would have to pay the first $1,500 worth of damage.

If a renter lives in an apartment house, the problem of living is simplified. One check pays for everything – shelter, heat, light, gas, taxes, insurance, depreciation, repairs, and maintenance. It may even include janitor and maid service. As a result of these advantages almost half of the new housing built in recent years has been apartment housing. Young people without children and older people whose children have grown up find that apartment living is less expensive than owning a house. Midcity apartment houses have an advantage in location. Instead of commuting long distances, apartment-house renters can walk to work.

How valid are the advantages claimed for renting? If the cost of ownership runs as high as 17 percent of purchase price, the claim that renting is cheaper than owning is probably valid. But the evidence is limited and unconvincing. In one survey of eight cities it was found that rentals exceeded expenses of ownership in five cities, while the expenses of ownership exceeded rentals in three. The differences were not very great either way, not more than $10 a month. Another comparison showed rentals to be only about two-thirds of the expenses of ownership. There are so many variables involved in such comparisons that it is difficult to be sure. Each family must make its own comparisons in the community in which it lives. Even if it is found that ownership is more expensive than renting, many people believe that more than money is involved.

If we assume, for the sake of argument, that renting is cheaper than owning, two questions must be raised. Will renters save the difference? Or will they fritter it way? If they do save it, is there not equal danger that capital values in other types of investments will shrink?

Is it true that renters need not be concerned over rising property taxes? In the long run rentals on real estate must be high enough to yield a gross return that will cover the owner's expenses and yield a fair return on his or her investment. Otherwise owners will not maintain existent property and investors will fail to build new houses and new apartments. In the long run the tenant actually pays the taxes, whether he realizes it or not. Laboring under the illusion that taxes are none of their concern, renters may be inclined to take their duties as citizens too lightly and to vote for increased expenditures without regard to the probable source of revenue.

Of course renters are free to move. Is this an advantage or a disadvantage? Some critics complain that urban apartment-house renters are nomadic. This is more likely to be true of those who rent furnished apartments or houses. For millions of people the modern apartment is nothing more than a "homette." Obviously such living does not develop the virtues attributed to homeownership.

Which to Choose?

The question of owning versus renting housing is certainly controversial. There is no easy or sure answer. The pros and cons have different appeals for different people. Noneconomic considerations often outweigh the economic ones. Each family must reach its own decision. The consensus of judgment among qualified writers seems to justify the following generalizations. People who are single and live alone would usually do better to rent. Young married couples who are not settled on a reasonably sure job are advised to rent. It is not wise to buy a house for a short time, because very little, if any, equity is acquired. One study concluded that the cost of owning is probably less if occupancy continues for more than four years, and renting is probably the less expensive way to acquire housing if the family is going to stay in the house for three years or less.[21] Moreover, if a move is required the seller of a house must pay a real-estate agent a commission of 6 or 7 percent. For those who move frequently renting is recommended. When you move to a new community, it is usually better to rent for at least a year. That will give you time to familiarize yourself with the housing market and find the area in which you wish to live. Temperamentally, some people abhor a large, long-time debt. Some do not want the responsibilities of ownership, and some are fearful that illness or unemployment would lead to foreclosure. For such people renting is the solution, regardless of cost. Finally, increasing numbers of older couples whose children have left home want less responsibility and find freedom in renting.

It is unlikely that all future buyers of houses will consider the question of ownership as carefully as they should. Those who do consider the pros and cons and then proceed to buy or build a house are much more likely to achieve the satisfaction they yearn for. A hasty, ill-considered purchase of housing that is excessively priced often leads to disappointment.

One final generalization. If you can afford to buy a house, buy it and enjoy it, but do not buy it under the illusion that you are saving money.

If You Do Buy

If, after careful consideration of the advantages and disadvantages of owning and renting, you do decide to buy, the first question will be when. Should you wait for lower prices and lower interest rates? According to the experts you may have a long wait. Prices are likely to become higher rather than lower. A new house that sold for $23,000 in 1965 would command a price of $42,000 in 1975.[22] If the same rate of increase is projected into the future, the 1985 price of the house will be $76,696. At a given thirty-year maturity on a mortgage each 1 percent rise in the interest rate increases the monthly payments on principal and interest by approximately 10 percent. Average construction costs have been rising by about 8 percent a year, and such increases are likely to continue. In May, 1976, the average interest on mortgage loans on new houses ranged from 8.76 percent to 9.03 percent.[23] Whether to buy now or later is a difficult decision which you alone can make. If you make the right decision it could save you several thousands of dollars.

Buying A Coop or Condominium   If you do decide to buy, what shall it be? A new house? A used house? A cooperative apartment? Or a condominium. In a cooperative venture you buy a share or shares in a corporation that owns the building, then lease an individual unit. You pay a monthly charge to cover services, maintenance, taxes, and mortgage on the entire building. A board of directors, elected by the shareowners, determines policies. You must agree to accept increases in assessments if someone else fails to meet his or her payments. You must have permission to remodel, change, or sell your unit.

Housing economists predict that 50 percent of the United States population will live in some form of condominium housing within twenty years.[24] With so many potential buyers of condominiums moving into the market, it is essential that they be aware of the safeguards and pitfalls to look for before signing a contract. The Department of Housing and Urban Development has published a very valuable guide—*Questions About Condomin-*

iums – for prospective condominium owners. Its purpose is to inform possible purchasers about the condominium concept and to encourage – not discourage – condominium ownership.

A condominium owner purchases title to the unit he or she occupies and shares joint ownership of common areas and facilities. Buyers arrange their own mortgage, pay taxes on their units, and makes separate payments for building maintenance and services. Each owner is responsible only for his own unit and his share of overall operating expenses. Along with the other owners, he votes to elect a board of managers. Finally, he has the right to refinance or pay off his mortgage, as well as the right to remodel or sell his unit.

Both cooperatives and condominiums offer some advantages of ownership at a lower cost than for individual houses. Taxes and mortgage interest are tax deductible. Monthly costs are usually less than rental charges for comparable apartments. Many retired persons find one or the other of these forms of ownership desirable.

Buying A House   Beware of bait advertising that offers houses at great bargains. One developer in Philadelphia advertised, "We'll custom-build your dream home . . . and lend you the money to buy it . . . no down payment . . . no closing costs. . . . Long-term permanent financing – if you own a lot. . . . Prices start as low as $69 a month." The Federal Trade Commission charged that this was not a bona fide offer. None of the houses were offered at the advertised price; none were sold or financed without down payments; none were sold without closing costs. The company consented to an FTC order to discontinue such advertising.

To guard against shoddy construction, Federal Housing Administration representatives inspect FHA-financed houses to be sure that builders comply with the minimum standards established by FHA. Even though you do not use FHA financing you can ask the institution financing your house to obtain "conditional commitment" from FHA. FHA representatives will then review the plans to be sure they meet requirements. In addition, FHA representatives will inspect the building three to five times while it is being constructed. The charge for this is only $60. On VA loans, the VA also will appraise a property and supervise construction of a new house.

When purchasing a house, with or without FHA or VA mortgage financing, it is recommended that you have the house inspected by a competent person. Do not pay any money and do not sign a contract until a consultant, a builder, an architect, or an engineer has given you his approval. An expert will examine major structural elements and equipment; he will enter basements, crawl spaces, and attics; he will check the roof, gutters, downspouts, drainage, siding, caulking, and paint. Look in your telephone directory yellow pages for franchised inspection firms, such as Arthur Tauscher, with offices in ten cities, and John J. Heyn, with offices in Baltimore, Philadelphia, and Washington.[25]

For $50 to $100 you can hire an appraiser, who could save you hundreds of dollars. You may also contact an office of the American Institute of Real

Estate Appraisers, or the American Society of Appraisers, or the Society of Real Estate Appraisers. Locally, an insurance company or a mortgage lender may perform appraisal services.

If you are shopping for a house already built or a used house, use a real estate agent. Agents' fees are paid by the seller. The usual fee is 6 to 7 percent of the selling price, but it is usually negotiable. Since the services of the agent cost the buyer nothing, they should be used. An agent can save you time, can help you shop, can bargain for you, and can help place your mortgage. Buyers must be careful, though, to make sure that the agent does not mislead them or oversell them. It is advisable to check on the credentials of an agent before using his or her services.

A panel of appraisers representing thirty-six savings and loan associations in twenty-eight states listed the following mistakes frequently made by buyers of houses. Inexperienced buyers often fail to calculate the total costs of ownership. They fail to realize that a house is a depreciating asset. They are overly optimistic in estimating their ability to do their own repair and maintenance work. Being inexperienced, they often choose the wrong location and the wrong neighborhood. They underestimate commuting costs to and from a house located miles away from their work. They choose houses that are too small or that are odd or unusual types. Being unfamiliar with houses, they often build or purchase houses that have bad floor plans. Used houses may be obsolete and require excessive repair and maintenance expenses. Many communities have zoning restrictions that eager buyers do not learn about until it is too late. Some used houses have been subjected to "overimprovement." This means that the amount of money spent by previous owners for improvements was out of proportion to the basic value of the house.

Builders of new houses know that inexpensive gimmicks can add $2,000 to $5,000 to the purchase price. Indoor flower boxes, wallpaper murals, and incinerators are a few examples of such gimmicks. Certain types of wallpaper can create the illusion of more space. At the same time it can hide defects. The night lighting around sample houses can be softened to conceal undesirable features and brightened to emphasize the more attractive areas. Such gimmicks can be avoided if prospective buyers are well-informed and if they obtain the advice of appraisers, architects, builders, mortgage lenders, or bankers.

How Do You Choose A House?

An estimated 70 percent of the families buying a house choose to buy a used house.[26] Davis and Walker recommend a very thorough inspection of the house you buy.[27] They recommend thorough evaluation of the community and the neighborhood. Are there good schools, churches, shopping areas, public transportation, adequate fire and police protection, and protective zoning laws? An overview of the outside of the house should be made, including a check of the garage, driveways, walks, patios, retaining walls, and outside stairwells, and a complete check on the exterior construction of the house including roofing, gutter and downspouts, foundation, wall structures, windows, doors, porches and stoops, and a check for insect infestation should also be made. A similar inspection of the interior should be made. This should include a check of the walls, floors, ceilings and their finishes. The heating, plumbing, cooling, and electrical systems should be checked out. Checks should be made for leaks in the basement and stains on walls and ceilings. The floor plan should be studied carefully. Will it be satisfactory in serving the family's needs? Is each room adequate for the purpose it is meant to serve? Time spent on a thorough examination of a house will help make you more sure and more satisfied with the final decision to buy or not to buy.

Many a buyer has been shocked when presented with a bill for hundreds of dollars for closing costs. Closing costs may range from less than $100 to over a $1,000. The actual closing costs charged in Seattle on a $25,000 house and lot under different types of financing ranged from $78 to $1,852.75.[28] What are closing charges? They include a charge for placing a mortgage, for the lender's attorney, and for title search and insurance. In addition you may find such items as credit reports, land survey, appraisal fees, and fee for preparing and recording the deed.

Buyers should engage their own attorney to represent them at the closing. There is no set fee for such a service, so one should ask in advance. Depending on location and on attorneys, the fee tends to be around 1 percent of the selling price of the house, but the fee is negotiable. Young attorneys and others who would be interested in getting the buyer's other legal work may be willing to charge by the hour or less than 1 percent. An attorney may easily save the purchaser much more than the cost of the fee.

A young couple buying their first home are often in a state of ecstasy. In their eagerness to own, they may have purchased a house that costs more than they really should pay. Then they are hit by closing costs; after that they have the expense of moving. Experience shows that the typical mover to a house spends 10 percent of the purchase price for furniture, draperies, kitchen equipment, storm doors and windows, landscaping, shrubbery, and lawn and garden equipment. Later there may be assessments for sewers, water, and schools.

Home owners have a yen for remodeling and modernization. This makes them easy victims of door-to-door salesmen who often prey on consumer gullibility and persuade them to sign contracts with itinerant "remodelers." No contract should be signed with a remodeler until his reputation and reliability have been checked out.

Better business bureaus carry on a continuing campaign to protect homeowners in major cities from expensive, unreliable, and dishonest remodelers. The Better Business Bureau of St. Louis gives homeowners the following advice:

1. Check the reputation of a contractor by calling the better business bureau.
2. Insist on a written contract and read every word of it.
3. Do not sign blank papers.

4. Retain a copy of every paper you sign.
5. Do not pay in advance.
6. Beware of a mechanic's lien.

The FHA has issued a publication titled *Precautionary List*. In its forty-five pages one will find the names of firms and individuals known to have done unsatisfactory work on property improvement jobs that were financed by FHA-insured home improvement loans.

One last warning: Beware of using a second mortgage to borrow money for repairs, remodeling, or any other purpose. It is costly and frequently "money-finders" who help you make such mortgages charge excessive fees.

QUESTIONS FOR REVIEW

1. Does it make very much difference to you whether you eventually own or rent your house? If so, why?

2. When building or buying a house to what extent should you consider resale value?

3. Why have housing costs gone up more rapidly than most other costs?

4. Would you be happy living in a house that is the same as all your neighbors' houses? Why or why not?

5. What are the advantages and disadvantages of zoning laws and building codes to the prospective homeowner?

6. What are the pros and cons of mobile homeownership?

7. How can the prices of new houses be reduced?

8. Do you favor or oppose the concept of the variable mortgage?

9. Why are interest costs such an expense in buying a house?

10. What is a second mortgage? Why does it cost more than a first mortgage?

11. Is it cheaper to own or to rent housing? Why is this question so difficult to answer?

12. Explain the differences between explicit expenses and implicit expenses in owning a house.

13. What is a condominium? What are the advantages and disadvantages in owning one?

14. What kinds of problems may an individual have in the purchasing of a house?

PROJECTS

1. Ask ten students if they eventually hope to own a house of their own, or would rather rent.

2. Shop for a mortgage loan. Go to at least five lending agencies. Tabulate your findings and report the recommended lender, with reasons.

3. From your parents secure all the figures comparable to those in Table 17-5 applicable to your parents' home. What is the monthly cost to your parents?

4. Let the class divide according to conviction and debate this question: "Resolved that it is cheaper to own than to rent a house."

5. Interview a realtor and find out what is happening to prices of new and used houses in your community.

6. Interview a better business bureau representative in your home area, asking questions about frauds and misrepresentations in home remodeling. Summarize your findings in a report in class.

REFERENCES

1. *St. Petersburg Times,* 18 Aug. 1975, p. 1A.
2. *Business Week,* Aug. 1975, p. 52.
3. *St. Petersburg Times Parade,* 27 Jan. 1974.
4. Congressional Research Service, Library of Congress, News Release, 28 April 1975, p. 12.
5. *Ibid.,* p. 19.
6. *Ibid.*
7. *U.S. News & World Report,* 2 Feb. 1976, p. 35.
8. *St. Petersburg Times Parade,* 1 June 1975, p. 4.
9. *Business Week,* 25 Aug. 1975, p. 52.
10. *Ibid.*
11. *Changing Times,* May 1974, pp. 8–9.
12. *St. Petersburg Times Parade,* 4 Jan. 1976, pp. 15–16.
13. *St. Petersburg Times,* 13 Oct. 1975, p. 2–1.
14. *Mobile Homes: The Low Cost Housing Hoax* (New York: Grossman, 1974), p. 38.
15. *Ibid.,* p. 127.
16. *Statistical Abstract of the United States,* 96th ed. (Washington, D.C.: Government Printing Office, 1975), p. 714.
17. *Ibid.,* p. 724.
18. *Changing Times,* June 1970, p. 12; *New York Times,* 12 May 1969, pp. 69, 74.
19. *Rent or Buy?* (Washington, D.C.: Government Printing Office, 1974), p. 1.
20. Annual Report of the U.S. Department of Housing and Urban Development, 1968, p. 16.
21. John P. Shelton, "The Cost of Renting Versus Owning a Home," *Land Economics* 14 (1968): 72.
22. *U.S. News & World Report,* 3 Nov. 1975, p. 67.
23. *Federal Reserve Bulletin,* July 1976, p. A45.
24. *Questions About Condominiums: What to Ask Before You Buy* (Washington, D.C.: Government Printing Office, 1974), p. 3.
25. *Changing Times,* Feb. 1970, pp. 11–14.
26. Jack Wren, *Home Buyer's Guide* (New York: Barnes & Noble, 1970), p. 26.
27. Joseph C. Davis and Claxton Walker, *Buying Your House: A Complete Guide to Inspection and Evaluation* (Buchanan, N.Y.: Emerson, 1975).
28. Florence T. Hall and Evelyn Freeman, "Survey of Home Buyers' and Sellers' Closing Costs in the Seattle, Washington Area," *Journal of Home Economics* 64 (1972): 21.

CHAPTER 18

BUYING PROTECTION: PRINCIPLES OF INSURANCE

WHAT IS INSURANCE?

Insurance Is Protection

During our lives we face a multiplicity of hazards and risks, many of which can result in a temporary or permanent loss of income for ourselves or our families. The major hazards threatening our financial security are premature death (that is, death before normal retirement age), incapacitating illness, incapacitating accidents, unemployment, or outliving one's earning power. In addition, there are the constant threats of property loss and liability and automobile loss and liability. Many people simply trust to luck that they will never have a serious illness or accident; others attempt to accumulate sufficient savings to insure against loss of income or property damage. It is obvious that both these methods of dealing with the risks of life have serious defects. Calamities do occur—one cannot wish them away—and most families have such small incomes that they cannot possibly save enough to provide any substantial benefits. For those whose incomes are large enough to make this method of self-insurance possible, there are the constant uncertainties of life itself and health. Any premature stoppage of income obviously will make it impossible to accumulate enough money to provide a substitute income.

One way to safely insure oneself and one's family against these risks is to cooperate with others who face the same risks. By pooling their limited surpluses the members of a group can secure enough money to reimburse the unfortunate few upon whom misfortune does fall. This method substitutes a small, certain loss (the insurance premium) for a larger, uncertain loss. It not only makes it possible for an individual to meet a financial loss if the event insured against occurs, but it also reduces or eliminates the worry caused by uncertainty. This is the insurance method.

There are nearly 4,800 insurance companies in the United States. Some of them sell insurance to cover all types of hazards, but many specialize in one or a few fields. Approximately 2,900 companies sell property and liability insurance, and 1,833 sell accident, sickness, and life insurance. In a typical year consumers pay insurance companies $100 billion to purchase protection.

The Cost of a Lifetime of Financial Protection

It is not far-fetched to estimate that a student graduating in 1976 may pay out more than $100,000 by the time of retirement to protect his or her family from a variety of financial risks. This would include the compulsory payments for Social Security, which provide financial protection in case of permanent disability or premature death, and pension benefits. It would include a life insurance program, a health insurance program, automobile insurance, homeowner's insurance, and it might also include types of insurance protection that have become more popular recently, such as dental insurance or legal service insurance.

Most people, given the responsibility of purchasing something that cost $100,000, would investigate the product or service very carefully before making such a significant purchase. How much thought and care should a person put into purchasing financial protection that is going to cost $100,000? An individual has no choice about paying for Social Security, and his or her employer has no choice about paying premiums for unemployment compensation, but one does have a choice as to how to allocate the money spent for practically all of the rest of your financial protection program. To acquire a reasonable understanding of insurance before the purchase is made is the prudent way to act.

HOW INSURANCE WORKS

Insurance is a cooperative device for sharing risks. It is a device that assures a sum of money with which to meet the uncertain losses resulting from damage to, or destruction of, life or property. Insurance transfers the risks of many persons to an insurance company. This is accomplished by means of a contract between the company (*insurer*) and the individual (the *insured*). In the contract the company promises to pay a stated sum of money if and when the event insured against occurs. The money may be paid to the insured or to persons designated by the insured (*the beneficiaries*). In the contract the insured, or someone who has an insurable interest, agrees to pay periodically a sum of money (the *premium*) to the insurance company.

Property Insurance

To illustrate the way insurance works let us assume that the parents of 1,000 students in your college own houses valued at $40,000 each. Let it be assumed further that the houses are substantially similar and that the annual fire loss for the group averages one-half of one percent. This would amount to $200 per house. For the 1,000 houses the fire loss would amount to $200,000 each year. Statistically, five of the houses will be destroyed by fire. The uncertainty lies in the fact that no one knows which five will suffer fire damage. All owners can protect themselves by paying into a common fund $200 apiece. These premiums would build a fund of $200,000, enough to reimburse the five upon whom the fire loss falls. Insurance is a voluntary communal means of sharing risks and minimizing loss.

What do the 995 property-owners whose houses remain intact obtain for their expenditure of $200? All of them receive the assurance that if their houses had been destroyed their net losses would have been reduced from $40,000 to $200. In the same way, every buyer of insurance of whatever kind gets the assurance that if the event insured against should occur he or she will be reimbursed out of the payments made by those who are insured. One never loses when buying sound insurance because what is purchased is protection, which is delivered day by day and hour by hour.

A contract insuring protection against loss by fire cannot prevent destruction of the property, although the fire prevention program of underwriters may reduce the number of fires and the annual loss attributable to them. What insurance can do is reimburse the owner for personal loss. The $200 that each of the owners pays provides protection for a limited period because total collection is just sufficient to meet total claims, including administrative expenses, for twelve months. It is $200 for the second year, and so on, indefinitely as long as the policy is in effect. This type of insurance is described as a *term policy*. It provides protection at the lowest possible rate based on actual costs for a period of one year. Unlike life, there is no certain end to property. Buildings grow old and need repair, but there is no certain, sudden end to them. For this reason it is not necessary to accumulate a fund of $40,000 to reimburse the owner of each of the 1,000 houses. As long as the average number of fires remains the same, an annual charge of $200 will yield the necessary $200,000 to reimburse the five owners on whom the fire loss falls. Stated more concisely, the annual premium covers the cost because the event insured against may never occur. The premium remains constant year after year. Notice also that the annual premium does not decrease, nor does the contract call for the return of any premiums paid, either singly or in a lump. For $200 every twelve months the owner gets exactly what he or she buys – protection – at the lowest possible price.

Accident and Health Insurance

The protective function of insurance is illustrated by accident and health coverage. On the basis of accident reports and public health records it is possible to predict with a high degree of accuracy how many persons in a group of one million will be sick or injured during any year. Actuaries can predict how long incapacitation will continue. Arbitrary indemnity can then be promised, such as $100 a week for a maximum of 104 weeks of total disability. Or the indemnity may take the form of a lump sum payment, such as $1,000 for the loss of the left hand or $5,000 for death if it results from a certain kind of accident. All of this can be promised with almost perfect assurance that the annual premium will yield a common fund large enough to pay all claims and to cover administrative expenses. Like fire insurance rates, these premiums are constant annual term charges for protection against the hazards named in the contract, because the event or events insured against may never occur. If the insured lives through the year in good health and without injury, he or she is happy. The insurance company did not keep the insured person well or safe; nor could the insurance company guarantee that he or she will escape illness or injury. What the company can do, and does, is to guarantee that if an illness or an accident occurs, the insured would receive financial reimbursement as provided in the contract. The premium paid goes to reimburse the unfortunate ones who did incur illness or injury.

Health and accident insurance is similar to fire insurance in another respect. As a building grows old, if it deteriorates and becomes a firetrap the premium may increase. Ultimately the insurance company may refuse to write further insurance when the risk becomes so great that the premiums would be greater than the protection would be worth. Although accident and health insurance premiums remain constant, it is the practice of many insurance companies to refuse to issue contracts to persons more than age sixty-five because the risk that the events insured against will occur is so great that the rate would equal or exceed the contract benefits.

Life Insurance

Here the event insured against is death, and death is certain. The only uncertainty is when death will occur. Mortality tables show that death is not as likely to occur in early years as in later years, just as health statistics show that ill health is more likely to occur in later years. Actuaries cannot determine which individuals in a large group will die, but they can determine with a high degree of accuracy how many in the group will die. A year-to-year term life insurance policy would cost very little in the early years. In later years, as the certainty of approaching death increases, the annual premium would necessarily be an increasing portion of the indemnity.

To illustrate the operation of term life insurance, let us assume that 1,000 young men, age twenty-two, who will graduate from college next June, wish to assure the college of repayment of a $1,000 loan, in case they should die prematurely. Of course they all expect to repay the loan out of earnings. No one of them anticipates premature death. Nevertheless, mortality statistics show that two of them are likely to die during any one of the next five years. To protect the college against the hazards of premature death during the five-year period, each man pays $4.88 each year to an insurance company.* The $4,880 collected by the insurance company is invested to yield a rate of interest, which, added to the principal, and increased by subsequent premiums, will be sufficient to pay each claim and the expenses of administration. By means of insurance each of these men has substituted a small, certain loss ($4.88 a year) for a larger, uncertain loss ($1,000) to the college. The simplicity of this illustration lessens its accuracy, but the principles are those that life insurance is based upon. If the number is increased from 1,000 to 1,000,000, the law of probability will apply with a higher degree of accuracy.

PRINCIPLES OF SOUND INSURANCE

The Principle of Probability

A basic principle underlying the operation of sound insurance is that the number of objects insured must be large enough for the principle of probability to apply. This principle is also referred to as the law of large numbers. It is possible to predict what will happen in a group numbering one million with great accuracy. On the basis of mortality statistics for large numbers of people, actuaries can predict with assurance that at age twenty-two the probability of death will be 1.86 per 1,000 lives. Using that information actuaries then can calculate the amount of money necessary to yield the amount needed to reimburse claimants.

A Beneficiary Must Incur Loss

If insurance is to operate on a sound basis, it is imperative that the person or persons designated to receive the indemnity must be the ones who would suffer a financial loss if the event insured against should occur. In the language of insurance underwriters, the beneficiary must have an insurable interest in the life or property insured. In accident and health insurance contracts, the insured has an insurable interest because he or she would suffer a loss if the event insured against should occur. In the case of life insurance any dependent possesses an insurable interest in the life of the insured. In the case of property insurance the owner has an insurable interest in the property. As insurance has developed, the concept of *insurable interest* has expanded. Not only dependents but also creditors, business partners, and employers may suffer a financial loss if the life or property insured is destroyed. The reason for limiting beneficiaries to persons possessing insurable interest is to prevent the writing of contracts in favor of anyone who would gain more by having the life or property destroyed than by having it preserved.

* This is the rate quoted by a commercial stock company selected at random.

Indemnity Must Not Exceed Loss

The principle that the amount of indemnity must not exceed the loss caused by the occurrence of the event insured against is closely related to the second principle. Obviously, if a $30,000 house were insured against fire loss for $60,000, the owner would gain if a fire occurred. In such a case the gain would be so substantial that the owner might be tempted to start a fire in order to collect the insurance. Invariably arson increases in times of business recession when some business firms find themselves in financial straits.

How can the principle that the amount of indemnity must not exceed the loss caused by the occurrence of the event insured against be applied when insuring human lives? When companies write contracts to cover loss of health temporarily or permanently, they usually limit the indemnity to a percentage of the insured's earning power. If this were not done, the insured might find it gainful to develop chronic illness. Contracts guaranteeing to reimburse the insured for expenses of hospitalization, surgery, and medical care usually stipulate specific amounts.

The same general rules apply when writing contracts covering accidents. Sometimes arbitrary amounts are specified for losses of certain parts of the body, such as an eye or a foot. Some contracts combine the loss of the right eye *and* the left foot. This of course is an unlikely occurrence and the amounts promised by the insurer are arbitrary. For artists and performers contracts may be written to cover the hazards of one's occupation or the importance of certain parts of the body, such as the fingers of a pianist.

We have noted that a person's life is considered to be worth the capitalized net income attributable to that life. Legally, an individual may insure his or her life for any value. An insured person may name almost anyone as a beneficiary. If a beneficiary applies for a policy, he or she must have a clear insurable interest, such as a close blood relationship or a pecuniary interest. The rule that most companies follow is to limit the amount of insurance on any one life. One company uses a scale that limits the coverage on a single life according to age. A man between ages 20 and 24 is restricted to $200,000. Another company has a maximum limit of $500,000. Policies in excess of these limits are reinsured so as to spread the risk. A $10 million contract on the life of one man was underwritten by several companies.

The Event Insured Against Must Be Determinable

Fundamental in the writing of insurance contracts is the principle that it must be possible to determine when the event insured against has occurred. Before a life insurance company will pay a claim, the beneficiary must present a death certificate issued by a public official. In cases where an insured may be missing, a seven-year waiting period is common. There may be an element of doubt in cases of accident and health insurance. Malingering prevails and persists. To protect themselves, insurance companies depend on the judgment of a physician. If a doctor certifies that the insured is ill or disabled, the insurer will usually pay the claim.

There is no real problem in applying the principle when those insured present claims under property insurance contracts. Physical destruction or damage is evident and measurable. Automobile accidents present the problem of responsibility. In the early days of insurance, responsibility for an accident was a factor to be ascertained and considered.* Nowadays the fact that an accident did occur is the primary fact. Insurance companies pay claims regardless of responsibility for an accident. After paying a claim, however, the legal principle of subrogation permits an insurance company to sue another company or corporation or person for reimbursement in case the party being sued can be proved to have caused the accident.

One reason private companies do not write unemployment insurance contracts is the difficulty in determining when the event insured against has occurred. This type of insurance is written exclusively by government agencies. By requiring registration of those who are collecting unemployment insurance at employment offices it is possible to keep malingering at a minimum.

The Event Insured Against Must Be Uncertain

If a loss is inevitable, there is no risk and insurance does not apply. Because death is absolutely certain, insurance against death as such is not feasible, but because the time of death is uncertain, it is possible to insure against death within a stated period of time. Incapacitating accidents or illness are not certain. It is possible that many people may go through life without having an accident or suffering an illness. Unemployment is not certain. Damage to or destruction of property is not certain. Public liability is not a certainty. Because these hazards are possibilities rather than certainties, it is possible to insure against losses resulting if any of these events occur.

SHIFTING RISKS BY INSURANCE: SOCIAL SECURITY

What Is Social Security?

In the midst of the Great Depression in the 1930s Congress established a social insurance plan. The basic difference between private and social insurance is that private insurance is selective while social insurance is inclusive. It is understood that persons who have reason to believe they may die prematurely or incur accident or illness or suffer unemployment are the ones who would buy insurance. Private insurers consider them poor risks. The good risks are prone to take a chance. To avoid the operation of adverse

---

* For a discussion of no-fault automobile insurance see pp. 498–499.

selection, private insurers required searching physical examinations and investigations of the private lives of applicants for insurance. All undesirable risks were screened and eliminated. Private carriers refused to write certain types of insurance coverage, such as unemployment insurance.

In the case of life insurance, private insurers developed the extra-risk contract. Individuals who could not pass physical examinations because of heart conditions, because they were overweight, or engaged in hazardous occupations were offered contracts at higher premiums. Statistical studies disclosed that men who weigh 25 pounds more than the average for their height and build have mortality rates 25 percent higher than average. Airline pilots and coal miners were at one time denied insurance by private companies. Today only 3 percent of the applications for life insurance are rejected by insurance companies.

A new approach to the problem of adverse selection was developed in 1911 when group life insurance contracts were introduced. It was found that if a large number of lives were insured and all members of a group required to participate, the problem of adverse selection became relatively unimportant. It was also found that the expenses of underwriting and administering group contracts were very much lower than the expenses of underwriting and administering individual contracts. The commission paid to a group life insurance agent is relatively low. Much of the bookkeeping is done by the employer, who also pays a part of the premium.

Social insurance carries the concept of group insurance to its ultimate. Almost everybody who is gainfully occupied in the American economy is required to participate in the Social Security system. The compulsory feature of social insurance eliminates the problem of adverse selection. It reduces expenses to a minimum. There are no commissions. Administrative expenses are only 4 percent of premium collections. By contrast, the selling and administrative expenses incurred by automobile insurers are 52 percent.

In the 1930s the prime purposes of Social Security were to provide unemployment compensation and retirement income. Insurance benefits were available for widows and children. Through the years Social Security has expanded in coverage and in benefits. Disabled workers are covered, and everyone age sixty-five and over is eligible to be included in a hospital care program. For a payment of $7.20 a month, a sum matched by the government, all people 65 and over may purchase medical insurance.

Every few years the Social Security Act has been amended. The gross national product of the American economy in the 1970s exceeds the gross national product of the 1930s many times over. As the economy has grown, Congress has liberalized the benefits and increased the Social Security tax.

What Benefits Does Social Security Yield?

Survivors' Income   If an insured worker who has been earning $833.33 a month dies and leaves a widow and one child under age eighteen, they will receive $668.20 a month until the child reaches the age of eighteen. If there are two or more children, the monthly benefit would be 779.60. Unlike private insurance, there are no lump sum payments except for a sum of $225, which may be used for burial expenses. Although there are no other lump sum payments, the total amount of money payable may be illustrated. In fifteen years a widow with two children under age eighteen would collect a total of $140,328.

A serious defect in the Social Security law is the fact that, from the time her youngest child reaches the age of eighteen, a widow receives no income until she is sixty years old. She may take reduced benefits at age sixty, or if eligible receive disability benefits at age fifty. If a widow were thirty years of age when her husband died at age thirty and had two children ages one and three, she would receive $779.60 a month until she became age forty-five, when the oldest child would reach the age of eighteen. Then her income would drop to $668.20 a month until she reached the age of forty-seven, when the younger child attained the age of eighteen. From age forty-seven until age sixty the widow would receive no benefits. This has been called the Social Security "insurance gap." At age sixty the widow would be eligible for a retirement income of $318.50 a month. The thirteen-year uninsured gap from age forty-seven to age sixty must be covered by private insurance. This is a situation for which term insurance is well suited. One can use term or ordinary life insurance also to supplement Social Security payments so as to provide a monthly income of any desired amount.

One surviving child of an insured worker who had been earning $833.33 a month during his lifetime would receive $334.05 a month to the age of eighteen or to age twenty-two if a student or if permanently disabled.

Disability Income An insured worker who had been earning $833.33 a month would receive a disability benefit of $445.40 a month for as long as the disability continued, until the insured attained age sixty-five when he or she would qualify for pension benefits. A wife and one child would receive $334.20 a month, and the benefit for one child would be $222.70 a month.

Retirement Income An insured worker who had been earning $833.33 a month would qualify for a retirement income at age sixty-five of $445.40 a month. If he retired at age sixty-two, the benefit would drop to $356.40 a month.

A wife's benefit at age sixty-five would be $222.70 per month; at age sixty-two she would receive $167.10 a month.

The maximum retirement income for a husband and wife at age sixty-five would be $668.10 a month, or $8,017.20 a year. If they live out their normal life expectancy of thirteen and a half years, their total retirement income would amount to $108,232.20, tax free. The maximum tax the retiree would pay over a forty-year period, including hospital insurance, at projected rates, would be $38,992.05, an amount matched by the retiree's employer. A self-employed worker would pay $51,538.05.

Hospital and Medical Insurance for the Elderly Nearly all Americans age sixty-five or over are eligible for Medicare. Medicare is a voluntary federal hospital and medical insurance program operated under the Social Security system. Medicare insurance protects 23 million persons, and in just one year Medicare paid medical bills for nearly 13 million people. This means then about 11 percent of all the people in the United States have the protection of Medicare. The hospital insurance program pays inpatient hospital bills except for the first $124 in each benefit period for the first sixty days, and all but $26 per day for an additional thirty days for each benefit period. The medical insurance program pays $4 out of each $5 of reasonable medical costs, except for the first $60 in each calendar year. This includes reimbursement for reasonable charges for the services of physicians and surgeons. In addition, the insured are entitled to outpatient hospital services for diagnosis and treatment and to home health services, including 100 visits a year, even though they may not have been hospitalized. Also included are other medical and health services, such as diagnostic tests, surgical dressings and splints, and rental or purchase of medical equipment. The hospital insurance is financed by payroll contributions which are a part of the Social Security tax. The medical insurance is financed by monthly premiums paid by the federal government and the insured person at the rate of $7.20 each.

What Does Social Security Cost?

The Social Security Act now covers most gainfully occupied workers, including personnel in the armed forces. On annual wages up to $16,500, employer and employee each pays a tax as shown in the schedule in Table 18-1. The contribution rate schedule for self-employed persons increases from 7.90 percent of covered earnings in 1976 to 1977 to 8.50 percent in 1986 and thereafter. The maximum annual tax payable by an employee is shown at the right. The total tax rate for employer and employee will be 12.90 percent of the first $16,500 in earnings received by the employee. In addition, persons over age sixty-five who enroll in the medical care plan

TABLE 18-1. Contribution Rate Schedule For Employees and Employers (each)
Percent of covered earnings

Years	Retirement, Survivors, and Disability Insurance Benefits	Hospital Insurance	Total	Maximum Annual Tax Payable by Employee
1977	4.95%	.90%	5.85%	$ 965.25
1978–1981	4.95	1.10	6.05	990.25
1981–1985	4.95	1.35	6.30	1,039.50
1986–and after	4.95	1.50	6.45	1,064.25

will pay $7.20 a month, a sum that will be matched by the federal government. This rate can be adjusted upward if medical and other expenses covered by the program increase. Since the inception of Social Security, the tax rates have been increased many times. This emphasizes an important difference between social and private insurance. Private insurers cannot legally increase premiums during the life of a contract. By contrast, the federal government can and does increase premiums unilaterally.

Evaluation of Social Security

The original Social Security Act was passed in 1935 when depression still prevailed, and minimum taxes and benefits were included in the law. As the economy has grown, higher taxes and larger benefits have become possible. Hospital and medical insurance for the elderly are now included in the program and coverage is now practically universal.

In an economy in which the price level continues to rise, Social Security payments should be adjusted automatically for changes in the Consumer Price Index. This is now being done. The first automatic increase linking Social Security benefits with the Consumer Price Index came in July, 1975, when benefits were increased 8 percent.

The Social Security tax is a payroll tax and this is a regressive and burdensome method of financing. In the long run, both the employer and employee payroll taxes are probably paid by the workers. Since its inception all payments made in Social Security benefits have been paid from the payroll taxes collected and from earnings on these taxes. It was not until 1975 that Congress voted to allocate general revenue to help meet some of the benefits paid out in Social Security. If a larger portion of the funding of the Social Security program were to come from general revenue, particularly from personal income taxes, it would lessen the impact of the regressive feature – that is, payroll taxing – of the present method of financing the program.

The Social Security program has come under attack in recent years as to the soundness of its future. In 1976, because of the combined impact of years of high inflation and high unemployment, the program paid out about $4.4 billion more in benefits than it collected. Even after this deficit there remained approximately $40 billion in Social Security reserve funds, but such deficits cannot continue very long without jeopardizing the entire program. It seems reasonable to believe that the projected deficits can and will be alleviated by a more realistic procedure for adjusting benefits. Congress is likely to start raising taxes faster and benefits more slowly. Benefits could also be paid out of the income tax and other taxes rather than just out of the Social Security tax. It seems probable that the program will continue to exist since it is backed by the most reliable source of funds – the federal power of taxation.

Medicare

Medicare symbolizes a national commitment to meet medical care needs rationally and effectively. The program has achieved its major aim of freeing the aged from the fear that crushing medical bills will leave them paupers. But the costs have been great. Medicare now accounts for 40 percent of the federal government's health expenditures, cutting into budgets for biomedical research and experiments in new forms of delivering health care. In 1975 Medicare cost $15.6 billion, which was more than 100 percent higher than predicted ten years ago.[1] The soaring costs of health care are creating some real problems for the Medicare program and for those who are insured under it. In the third year of the Medicare program it covered 43.9 percent of the average medical costs for aged persons. By 1974 it covered only 38.1 percent of those costs.[2]

Medicare has made many unscrupulous doctors rich. Their incomes have increased 6 to 8 percent a year since Medicare, which is twice the pre-Medicare rate.[3] There have been many abuses of the program. Unscrupulous doctors and hospitals have unnecessarily hospitalized patients, prescribed unnecessary medicines, and performed operations without medical justification. Congressional hearings turned up evidence that $300 million had been paid out by Medicare for unnecessary surgeries.[4] In 1975 new guidelines went into effect for calculating how much a doctor deserves to be paid for treating a patient. This should save the American taxpayer money, but it may put a greater burden on the patient, depending on whether the doctor accepts the assignment and is paid only what Medicare allows or whether the doctor bills the patient more than Medicare allows, leaving it up to the patient to seek reimbursement from Medicare and pay the doctor the difference out of the patient's own pocket.

Millions of individuals who receive the benefits of Medicare are also buying private health insurance coverage because of the gaps in Medicare.

Medicaid

Medicaid is another part of the Social Security Act. Medicaid is available for certain needy and low-income people – the aged (sixty-five or older), the blind, the disabled, and members of families with dependent children. Medicaid is an assistance program paid for from federal, state, and local taxes. It is a federal-state partnership, with the states designing their own Medicaid programs within federal guidelines. Medicaid programs vary from state to state, with Arizona the only state that does not have a Medicaid program. Medicaid can pay what Medicare does not pay for people who are eligible for both programs, and in one year Medicaid paid medical bills for more than 24 million people.

Unfortunately, extensive fraud has been found in some Medicaid programs. Senate investigations found kickbacks to physicians and to the owners of clinics to be so common that laboratories refusing to pay them "are almost barred from obtaining a Medicaid account." The Senate investigation staff estimated that of the total payout of $213 million for Medicaid, at least $45 million was "either fraudulent or unnecessary."[5]

SHIFTING RISKS BY INSURANCE TO NONPROFIT CORPORATIONS

Mutual Insurance Companies

Since the function of insurance is to share risks, it is understandable that groups of individuals having similar interests and risks should organize themselves into a risk-bearing association. Farmers in a township or county or state may join together for fire protection. In the organizing process a membership fee may be charged to create a capital reserve for contingencies. Fire losses during the year may be paid out of the reserve. The reserve would be replenished the following year by assessing each member of the group an amount sufficient to cover the losses. There is no reason why a mutual insurance association may not operate on a reserve basis and calculate the premium in advance. Then the insured will know exactly what protection will cost.

The distinctive feature of a mutual insurance company is the retention of control by the policyholders, in theory if not in practice. It is their mutual undertaking, with responsibilities and benefits shared mutually. In small local mutuals this retention of control may be realized. Administrative expenses may be lower. Since members of a mutual company are engaged in a cooperative enterprise, they are not likely to cheat themselves or their associates. This practically eliminates such problems as arson and malingering. That this method of organizing for mutual protection is fundamentally sound is indicated by the large number of mutual insurance companies operating in the United States.

Can mutuals implement the principle of probability? By their very nature small local mutuals have difficulty in applying the law of large numbers. Whether the association insures property or lives, the number may be relatively small and the concentration relatively high. Destructive forces of nature may destroy many insured properties at one time. An epidemic may take the lives of many people in a local area.

In evaluating mutual insurance associations one must consider management. When a mutual is small, the management may be more honest and well meaning than efficient. As the association grows larger, management may be more efficient, but who benefits from the efficiency? As the number of policyholders increases, the likelihood that each one will take an active interest in management diminishes and the likelihood that the hired managers will exercise increasing control grows greater.

Accident, health, and life insurance mutuals developed in fraternal orders, labor unions, and among groups of workers with common hazards and occupations such as traveling salesmen, ministers, and teachers. The carly success of property mutuals led to the belief that the same principles could be applied in assuring protection against accidents, illness, and premature death. Since accidents and illness are not certain, the same assessment method can be used if proper regard is given to selection and diversification of risk. On the other hand, death is certain and increasingly certain in later years. A contract guaranteeing $1,000 indemnity at death can be fulfilled at reasonable cost only if a balanced age distribution is maintained. Early assessment mutuals operated with low premiums during the early years of a policy, but unless young lives replace those who have died the premium increases in later years. The record shows that young people are loath to join a group whose premiums increase. Some already included in the insurance plan drop out. As a result, many such insurance organizations have failed, bringing loss and disappointment to members and disrepute on the group and on insurance.

Practically every weakness of small local mutuals is eliminated by the large national and international mutual insurance company. Some of the largest life underwriters, which insure hundreds of thousands of policyholders, are organized as mutuals. Less than 10 percent of all life insurance companies in the United States are mutuals, yet they write 51 percent of all insurance in force and account for 65 percent of the assets of all life insurance companies in the United States.

The number of policyholders is large enough for application of the law of probability. Policyholders' occupations are diversified and their residences are so widely spread geographically that only a national calamity could generate claims beyond their ability to pay.

Theoretically these large mutual insurance companies are owned and controlled by policyholders, but only theoretically. The large number of policyholders and their geographic dispersion, so advantageous actuarially, are fatal to effective control. The result is that control tends to fall into the hands of a small self-perpetuating management group, which sometimes resorts to self-perpetuating, self-serving practices such as unwarranted retention of dividends, failure to notify policyholders of meetings, and general disregard for policyholder rights. For example, one large mutual having 19 million policyholders had only 593 votes cast in its annual election.[6]

Mutual insurance companies' gross premiums are usually higher than those of stock companies. They should be lower, however, because mutuals have no profits to earn for stockholders and competition should have reduced premiums. Actually mutual companies' gross premiums are higher than necessary to meet commitments. Surpluses are spread not in the form of profits but in emoluments of office and in "dividends." Mutual companies emphasize their *low net* premiums over a period of years. A net premium is the gross premium minus dividends. For example, one company quotes a rate of $16.57 per $1,000 for a $10,000 ordinary life insurance policy for males at age twenty-five. Dividends over the preceding twenty-year period totaled $98. Total gross premiums would have been $331.40 (twenty times $16.57). Deducting the dividends of $98 from $331.40 indicates total net premium of $233.40. Dividing that figure by twenty, the total number of premiums, the average net premium is reported as being $11.67. When a policyholder is required to pay $16.57 per $1,000 for insurance instead of $11.67, he is compelled to carry less protection. For an annual expenditure of $165.70 an insured could purchase $10,000 of protection at the higher rate. For an expenditure of $163.38 an insured could purchase $14,000 of insurance at the lower net rate. Lower gross rates are to be preferred over large dividends. The record shows that the gross rates of many mutual insurance companies could be 25 percent lower.

SHIFTING THE RISK BY INSURANCE TO CORPORATIONS FOR PROFIT

Stock Companies

Of the 1,833 life insurance companies, 1,686 are organized as stock companies. Stock insurance companies are profit-seeking corporations that issue capital stock, on which the owners expect to receive dividends as they do on the stock of any other corporation. In legal theory the stockholders control the company. The policyholders are in the same relative position as purchasers of a commodity or service sold by any other commercial company. A flat premium is charged for the insurance coverage. When a policyholder buys a contract, he or she knows what is received and exactly what it will cost through the life of the contract. The holder need not speculate with the company on anticipated earnings, mortality, or management costs. The corporation does all the speculating. If there is any surplus, it is paid to the stockholders rather than to the policyholders. The premium on an ordinary life contract at age twenty-five quoted by a stock company is $11.62 per $1,000, as compared with a mutual premium of $17.82. The difference of $6.20 represents a "loading" charge, part or all of which may be returned to mutual policyholders if claims and management expenses are substantially less than income from premiums and interest. In the illustration just given, the mutual company paid $102.20 in dividends in a twenty-year period. This made the average net payment in that period $12.71, as compared with the actual net premium of $11.62 for the stock company. The difference of $1.90 per $1,000 of insurance coverage could be significant if the insured were purchasing $40,000 or $60,000 worth of insurance. Actually, it is impossible to compare satisfactorily the net cost of protection under the two plans, except historically, because the future dividends of mutuals are uncertain. Any such comparison becomes one of companies rather than of types of companies. Surely the initial cost of protection is lower for the stock companies. For the individual with limited income who wants maximum permanent protection at lower cost, the stock company policy is often the better buy.

With respect to management and control there is little real difference between the two types of companies. The economic doctrine of self-interest applied to stock insurance companies leads to the expectation that owners will hire the most efficient managers to insure larger profits for themselves. Actually, if the number of stockholders is large, the control of the company may fall into the hands of the management group. This is a result of the failure of large numbers of small stockholders to participate in elections.

Promoters of stock insurance companies have found life insurance such a lucrative field that the number of companies has almost quadrupled in thirty years. Yet stock companies have written slightly less than half of the insurance policies currently in force. The relative merits of the two types of companies cannot be resolved in this short discussion. It is important that the consumer-buyer know something about both types of companies. In theory the mutuals appear to have the advantage, but in practice the gains are partially lost because policyholders are unable or unwilling to assume the responsibility of ownership when the group grows unwieldy. Whether one buys insurance from a stock company or from a mutual, the premiums of several companies should be compared. If all other factors appear to be equal, the decisive factor may prove to be price.

Mixed Companies

A combination of the distinctive features of mutual and stock companies results in the so-called mixed companies. Organized as a stock company and owned by the stockholders, this type of company offers both nonparticipating and participating policies. The former is a straight stock company contract, while the latter features the mutual principle of returning to the policyholders the difference between expenses and total income. Because there are two groups to share the surplus, there are plans designed to benefit one or the other. One such plan is the provision that stockholders are limited to 10 percent of the surplus, the remaining 90 percent being reserved for distribution among policyholders. Control of this type of company is certain to rest with the stockholders by means of some restrictions such as granting the right to vote only to holders of policies with a face value of $5,000 and restricting the number of directors which policyholders may elect.

Theoretically this hybrid type of company possesses no real advantage, but in practice it does offer possible gains. This is because a mutual is not as low in cost as it could be and the straight stock company has no way of sharing surplus with policyholders. The mixed company participating policy may prove to be the lowest in cost in the long run. It may even be lower in the short run than the cost of the same protection purchased from a mutual. Here are some illustrative figures taken from a mixed company, selected at random. The premium per $1,000 of an ordinary life insurance policy of $10,000 for males at age twenty-five is $18.60, compared with $13.85 for a nonparticipating policy. This is a difference of $4.75 for exactly the same protection promised by the same company. However, the dividend schedule shows that on the basis of the past twenty-year record, the net cost of the ordinary life policy is $13.24, which is 61 cents less than the nonparticipating premium of $13.85.

TYPES OF LIFE INSURANCE CONTRACTS

Term Insurance

All pure insurance protection is term insurance. This means that the insured is protected against a stated risk for a specified period of time. All property protection and liability insurance contracts are written for terms of one year, three years, or five years. Life insurance terms range from one year to age sixty-five. If the event insured against occurs within the specified term, the insured is entitled to the indemnity specified in the contract. The owner of a house may buy a contract guaranteeing reimbursement for damage caused by fire within the next twelve-month period. The owner of an automobile may buy protection guaranteeing reimbursement if the automobile should be destroyed by fire or stolen within the following twelve-month period. The same individual may purchase a contract that promises to pay specified indemnities if he or she should incur injuries in an accident or be hospitalized by illness. To complete the protection, an individual may purchase a contract in which the insurer promises to pay to a named beneficiary a specified sum of money if the insured should die within the following twelve-month period. If one wishes to have maximum low-cost protection against any hazard for a specified period of time, term insurance provides that protection.

Basically there is only one type of life insurance, and that is *term insurance.* The term may be short or long. There are only two essential expenses incurred by the insurer, those which cover mortality and those which cover operating expenses. All other types of life insurance contracts are combinations of term plus varying degrees of savings. One company quotes a premium of $2.40 per $1,000 for policies for males of $10,000 for five-year, renewable, convertible, term life insurance bought at age twenty-five. At the same age one could buy term life insurance to age sixty-five from the same company for $8.32 per $1,000. For a person of the same age, the same company quotes a premium of $13.12 for a whole life policy. The difference of $4.90 represents a savings feature.

Consider the one thousand young men or women who intend to purchase thousand-dollar life insurance contracts to insure repayment of education loans in case they should die prematurely. Their first jobs will pay relatively small salaries. Within five years they hope to be earning more income, but at first they must consider carefully the usefulness of each expenditure. For a twenty-two-year-old person the five-year, renewable, convertible term contract would cost $5.28 per $1,000. By contrast, an ordinary life insurance contract for the same amount, purchased from the same company would cost $12.02.[7]

It is possible and in some cases desirable to use term insurance for permanent protection. The ordinary life policy and variations of it include an element of forced saving that proves expensive in case of premature death. Young men may purchase a term policy that will remain in effect until age sixty-five. The premiums quoted by typical companies are about

$4.00 per $1,000 of coverage less than for ordinary life policies. If an individual wishes to separate his insurance from his savings, he may purchase term insurance to provide protection for his dependents until he is sixty-five. The difference of approximately $4.00 per $1,000 can be invested in an annuity contract with the same company or in a mutual fund. Such an individual would then be paying the same amount as he would pay for an ordinary life policy, *but with this important difference:* In case the insured should die at any time before age sixty-five the beneficiary would receive the face value of the policy and no more under the ordinary life contract. Under the plan of separating protection from savings, the beneficiary would receive the face value of the policy *plus* the accumulated savings during the intervening years, compounded annually. If the insured outlives the period of time, there is of course no cash value on the insurance contract, but there is a cash value on the annuity contract or on the mutual fund accumulation. On a $30,000 insurance program extending from age twenty-five to age sixty-five, and assuming the death of the insured at age sixty-five, a beneficiary could receive $4,800, in addition to the face value of the policy ($4.00 per $1,000 per year for forty years).

A variation of straight term insurance is decreasing term insurance. The premium on decreasing term insurance is even lower than on straight term insurance. Individuals who purchase decreasing term insurance do so to secure maximum protection for beneficiaries in the early years when there are little or no savings. As the insured's investment program develops and the dollar amounts of his or her investments increase, the need for insurance protection in case of premature death diminishes. As the need for insurance protection diminishes, the amount of term insurance decreases. As will be shown shortly, this is exactly what life insurance companies do in writing the various forms of permanent insurance contracts. In their early years such contracts consist largely of term insurance. As the portion of the premium in excess of the cost of term insurance (savings) increases, the amount of term insurance decreases. When such a policy matures as a result of death or the termination of a period, the payment received by the beneficiary represents some term insurance and a substantial amount of the insured's savings.

A successful life insurance agent who recommends the purchase of term insurance says, "Most insurance companies dislike selling term insurance. They discourage its sale by high premiums and low commission." There are, however, a few really low-cost term contracts available and you should look for them.[8]

This attitude on the part of insurance companies has been changing in recent years, however. Life insurance companies have started to advertise term insurance. Never before to the authors' knowledge has a major company advertised term insurance in major media. On the contrary, the industry has been critical of term insurance and has sold it only when a buyer insisted. This has been attributable to the agent-commission method of compensation. Term insurance is now being advertised quite extensively and particularly as a help to the insured, so that he or she will have adequate coverage to offset the high rate of inflation, which has eroded the value of insurance policies.

Group Term Life Insurance

Group term life insurance accounts for 42 percent of all life insurance in force in the United States. This type of insurance is written on a group of lives rather than on individual lives. The protection expense is minimal because of the use of the yearly renewable term contract. If a group is large enough, an insurance company is safe in foregoing medical examinations of each member of the group. This reduces expenses also. Administrative expenses are reduced by issuing a master contract instead of individual policies. Payment for the premium is made in one check, thereby eliminating hundreds of thousands of individual bookkeeping entries.

The premium per thousand dollars of insurance varies according to the mortality experience of the group. Group insurance is usually written on employees, and the employer pays the variable amount, which is tax deductible. For example, employees may pay a fixed premium of $7.20 per $1,000 a year regardless of age, if under age sixty-five, and without medical examination. If one leaves the employ of the company providing group insurance, it is usually possible, without having to take a physical examination, to convert the amount of individual coverage to another type of contract. All one has to do is to pay the premiums scheduled at the age of conversion. The amount of group life insurance available to an individual is usually related to the person's annual income. It is assumed that in case of premature death the proceeds of a group life insurance policy will yield the same amount that the insured would have provided for his family if he had lived another year. In lieu of salary, the proceeds of a group life insurance policy are intended to help beneficiaries make the adjustments necessary in their way of living.

Constant Premium Contracts: Whole Life Insurance

Many people believe or have been told that term insurance may be inexpensive in the early years but that premiums increase rapidly as the insured grows older. Actually, term insurance premiums do not increase as sharply as some people suppose. A five-year renewable and convertible term insurance contract can be purchased at age twenty-two for $5.28 per $1,000. At age thirty-two it would cost $5.62 per $1,000; at age forty-two, $8.66 per $1,000. At age forty-seven it would still cost less than an ordinary life policy would cost at age thirty-two. Nevertheless, the notion prevails that term insurance premiums increase sharply.

To overcome the objection to the supposedly increasing term rates with advancing age, insurance company actuaries developed the *level annual premium*. Under the whole life plan an insurance company charges an annual premium in excess of the amount needed to meet claims in the early years of a contract. This excess, at age twenty-two, is the difference between the term premium of $5.28 and the whole life premium of $12.02, which is $6.74. This excess premium is invested in a reserve account to meet claims in later years when the annual cost of protection exceeds $12.02. In the illustration being used, the cost of protection would exceed the whole life premium beginning at age forty-eight. The excess premium is invested by the company to yield the maximum interest consistent with security of principal. Using a mortality table and an assumed rate of interest, actuaries can calculate with a high degree of accuracy the uniform annual premium which would yield the reserve needed to pay claims in later years. An analogy would be a plan under which one would pay a doctor more than the actual annual cost of medical care during the years between ages twenty-two and forty-eight with assurance from the doctor that the annual charge would not increase from age forty-eight until death, even though the actual cost would be greater.

This type of contract introduces a new feature into life insurance. No longer is the policyholder buying pure protection at actual cost, except in the long run. The policyholder is now saving involuntarily. His annual saving of $6.74 per $1,000 of insurance creates a fund from which he may borrow in later years or which he may secure by surrendering his policy.

Family Income Rider

This is a decreasing term contract, added to a whole life contract. If an insured has a $10,000 whole life contract, he can purchase a family income rider in the same amount. A twenty-year rider would provide that if the insured were to die within the twenty-year period, his beneficiary would receive a monthly income of $10 for each $1,000 of insurance, for the remainder of the period. At the end of the twenty-year period the beneficiary would then receive the $10,000 payable under the whole life contract. This is low-cost insurance, not only because term insurance premiums are low but also because the amount of the insurance decreases from year to year. At age twenty-five the premium quoted by one company for a twenty-year family income rider is $3.63 per $1,000. In order to qualify for this type of policy one must have a basic level annual premium contract to which the rider is amended.

Contracts Specifying Number of Premium Payments

The whole life concept specifies that the insured shall pay premiums as long as he or she lives or as long as the contract is continued. Some insurance buyers object to the prospect of paying premiums throughout their lives. To meet such objections insurance actuaries designed a contract in which the insured pays a stated number of premiums, for example twenty

This would be described as a twenty-pay life policy. After the twenty payments have been made, the contract would be fully paid for. No matter how long the insured might live, he or she would not have to pay additional premiums. The amount of insurance provided in the contract is not payable, however, until the death of the insured.

In such a contract all that the insurance company does is charge more for each of the limited payments so that the excess reserve, plus interest, will be sufficient to pay the face value of the contract when payments cease. This is evident when the premium for a twenty-pay life contract is compared with the premium for a whole life contract. The premium quoted at age twenty-five by one company is $30.09 for a participating contract. The same company quotes a rate of $17.31 for a participating whole life contract. Both of these contracts promise the insured the same protection. The only difference is that under the limited payment contract the insured pays her bill more rapidly. In one case she knows that she must make only twenty premium payments, while she *thinks* she must pay for the whole life contract as long as she lives. Actually this is rarely true. A participating whole life contract for $1,000 purchased at age twenty-five has a reserve in the amount of $603 at age sixty-five. That amount of money may be taken in cash or it may be used to purchase approximately $800 worth of paid-up insurance. By using either of these methods the insured may have full protection for his or her family for forty years and then stop paying premiums. The insured has a third choice. If he permits the dividends to accumulate, a whole life contract purchased at age twenty-five will have accumulated a reserve at age fifty sufficient to pay the face value of the contract, according to the experience of one company. In other words, a whole life contract may become a paid-up contract in twenty-five years.

It is not always, nor usually, wise to permit an ordinary life policy to run to maturity. When the insured attains age sixty-five, his children will no longer be dependent. His need then is not protection against premature death but against the risks of outliving his income. Depending on circumstances, the insured might then find it wise to discontinue the whole life contract, taking the cash surrender value and using it to purchase an annuity contract, or he may invest it in common stocks or corporate bonds.

For men whose maximum earning power begins to decline at age forty-five or fifty, the limited payment contract has the advantage that they can pay for their protection when their incomes are larger. This is true also for professional athletes, actors, and performers in general. But for clerical and professional workers and business executives, whose maximum earning power is more likely to be attained in the years from forty-five to sixty-five, the limited payment type of contract imposes an unnecessary burden during the years of low income, with no compensating advantage.

Endowment Contracts

Failure to understand that in buying life insurance one is buying protection for dependents in case of premature death gives rise to a common fallacy that "you must die to win." Such a statement indicates confusion in the mind of the insurance buyer. What is it for which "you must die to win"? For those who believe this statement it is the amount they have paid the insurance company in premiums. It would be just as logical to argue that an insured must incur a fire loss in order "to win" on a fire insurance contract. Or that an insured's automobile must be stolen in order "to win" on an automobile theft insurance contract. Nevertheless, many buyers of life insurance believe that "you must die to win." So actuaries have devised a contract to satisfy such uninformed buyers. It is described as an endowment contract. Such a contract in the amount of $1,000 promises not only to pay $1,000 to the insured's beneficiaries if he or she dies prematurely but also to pay $1,000 to the insured if he or she lives beyond the term of the contract. What could be better? Here is a policy for which the insured pays a specified number of premiums and which yields its face value whether the insured lives or dies.

How much does a twenty-year endowment contract for $1,000 cost? When an insurance company writes such a contract, it makes two promises. If the insured dies within the twenty-year period, his beneficiary has a claim for $1,000. If the insured lives twenty years, he then has a demand claim for $1,000. The first obligation is covered by a term contract for $1,000 the first year, and the second obligation is met by compelling the insured to save an amount each year, which, invested at an assumed rate of interest, would yield $1,000 when the contract terminates. The shorter the term, the larger the annual saving required. The second year the company need not include a term contract for the entire $1,000, for if the insured should die his savings would be used in meeting part of the claim. So a one-year term is included which, supplemented by the insured's savings, will meet the contract demands if the policy is terminated. For example, if the one-year term premium is $3.60 while the level annual premium for a twenty-year endowment at age twenty-two is $47.46, the difference of $43.86 represents the first year's savings. In the second year, ignoring interest, the company would include a one-year term for $956.14. In the third year the company would include a one-year term contract for $912.28, in the fourth year for $868.42, and so continue to decrease the protection coverage until it reaches zero in the last year.

It should be clear that under the endowment contract if the insured dies, his beneficiary receives his savings, plus interest, plus the necessary additional sum from a term contract to total $1,000. This so-called insurance policy consists of a combination of term insurance and savings. The longer the contract continues the less the pure protection and the greater the savings. The insured could just as well buy a twenty-year term contract and himself invest the $43.86 each year in an annuity contract with the same company. Or he could invest the $43.86 – which would total $877.20 in twenty years – in a variable annuity that could yield a larger annual return on investment, at the same time participating in capital gain.* If the insured should die during the twenty-year period, the beneficiary of an

---

* See pp. 464–467 for an explanation of annuities and variable annuities.

endowment contract would receive $1,000. If the insured separated his insurance and his saving contracts, the beneficiary would receive $1,000 from the term insurance *and* the accumulated savings, plus interest. To illustrate, let it be assumed that if the insured were to die in the nineteenth year after paying his nineteenth premium, the beneficiary would receive $1,000 from the insurance contract plus the accumulated savings. Disregarding interest, savings would amount to $833.34 ($43.86 × 19).

Indexed Protection Contract

In the past twenty years the Bureau of Labor Statistics' Consumer Price Index has increased more than 100 percent. This development has created a serious problem for life insurance companies. Buyers are unattracted by fixed dollar contracts. Cautiously, a few companies have moved to meet the problem by tying life insurance contracts to the Consumer Price Index. An Indexed Protection Contract moves up as the CPI rises. The dividend structure will keep the amount of insurance in force equal to the cost of living increases if they do not exceed 2 percent a year. If the CPI increases by more than that amount, additional premiums must be paid. If the CPI does not change, or declines, the contract is not changed. The details of this new type of contract are too complicated to explain here, but as a prospective buyer you might wish to investigate further. The advantage of this provision is that it allows one to have the insurance protection increased to meet the erosion in the value of the dollar without having to worry about passing a medical examination, since none is required.

Variable Life Insurance

This form of insurance was in the developmental stage in the early 1970s. The plan provides fixed premiums for contracts whose reserve would be held in a separate portfolio of common stocks. The face amount of the contract will increase or decrease depending on investment results. Historically, common stock indexes have risen as the Consumer Price Index has increased. Therefore, under a variable life insurance program a beneficiary would receive an amount sufficiently large to compensate for the decline in the purchasing power of the dollar. The sharp decline in the early 1970s in the common stock index during a period of a sharply rising Consumer Price Index dampened the enthusiasm for variable life insurance, but in 1975 Equitable Life Assurance Society of the United States, the nation's third largest insurance company, became the first to market variable life insurance. Under the plan, premiums are invested primarily in common stocks, and death benefits fluctuate according to the portfolio's appreciation, though never below the face value of the policy. The premium will be higher than is charged for a typical nonparticipating fixed-benefit policy for the same initial face value because the company will be providing at least the death benefit of the fixed policy and a greater death benefit if investment experience is favorable.

Other Types of Contracts

Insurance company actuaries have devised other types of contracts, such as mortgage payment policies, education policies, and retirement income contracts. On the basis of the preceding explanations, it should now be evident that all such contracts are variations or combinations of term or whole life contracts. One of the largest mutual insurance companies in the United States writes 136 different types of contracts. An insurance company will write a contract containing almost any special feature desired, just as a builder will construct a house to suit the individual preferences of the buyer, *if the buyer is able and willing to pay the price.*

SHOULD ONE USE LIFE INSURANCE AS A METHOD OF SAVING?

Most Experts Advise Saving Separately

In a typical year approximately 33 percent of the premiums paid by purchasers of life insurance contracts are paid as death benefits to beneficiaries. Fifty-eight percent of the payments to policyholders are made to insureds who are still living. This means that many people are using life insurance as a method of saving. There are circumstances in which life insurance may serve as a satisfactory method of saving, but the preceding explanation of different types of policies should have made it clear that combination protection and saving contracts are more expensive than pure insurance contracts. Almost without exception the experts advise insurance buyers to save separately. A man who is himself a life insurance agent has written that *"life insurance is a much better buy as straight protection than as a means of saving."* According to him the myth that people cannot or will not save except by means of life insurance simply is not true. "Even my friends in the life insurance industry admit this is true."[9]

A second objection to the use of life insurance as a method of saving is that, like any other fixed dollar investment, its purchasing power declines as price levels rise. Concluding his analysis of ordinary life insurance, Matteson wrote that as long as rising price levels continue "we do not recommend any other than term insurance for any purpose."[10] The use of term insurance as a hedge against inflation justifies its predominant use in the life insurance program. Almost without exception writers on insurance and investment who are not associated with the life insurance industry recommend that the savings one accumulates in a separate savings program should be invested in common stock as a hedge against rising prices.

But the problem is complicated. Forty years ago Consumers Union advised its members to buy term insurance and save the difference by investing in common stocks. Now CU is not so sure. There are so many unknowns and so many variables. In a hypothetical illustration the cash value of an ordinary life contract at age sixty-five would have been $28,500, compared with the $67,000 available to the insured who bought term insurance and invested the premium difference in equities. But for those who survive, these questions must be answered: Would the insured have saved? Would his investments have yielded as much as in the illustration? Would they have been tax exempt? Would they have appreciated enough to offset price level increases? The answers to these questions are indeterminable.

Before deciding whether to use term or whole life contracts and before deciding whether to use insurance as a method of saving, a prospective buyer would do well to consider the objectivity of the advice he or she has been given. Generally, those connected with the insurance industry gain if they sell the more expensive contracts that include a high percentage of savings. For example, an agent who would receive a commission of $175 on a term contract would receive $1,740 on an ordinary life contract. Denenberg proposes the equalization of commissions "to relieve pressure to favor one life insurance product over another."[11] On the other hand, the experts cited in this chapter and in Chapter 19 have nothing to gain or lose by one's decision.[12]

DO HIGH-COST CONTRACTS PROVIDE MORE PROTECTION?

The Answer Is No

The amount of protection one can buy for a given sum of money will be large or small according to the type of contract purchased. The premiums per $1,000 for policies of $10,000 for eight types of insurance contracts for a man age twenty-five are shown in Table 18-2. The least expensive contract is the ten-year convertible term. This means that after ten years the insured may convert to a permanent form of contract. At age thirty-five the premium would be $6.33; at age forty-five, $11.16; and at age fifty-five, $23.48. The table shows that the least expensive permanent contract is the ordinary life nonparticipating at $13.12. At this price the insured would have a combination insurance and savings contract, whereas the term to age sixty-five contract at $8.32 does not include any savings.

The important thing to be seen in Table 18-2 is that, with the exception of the ten-year convertible term and term to age sixty-five, an insured could pay as little as $13.12 or as much as $47.46 for the same amount of insurance protection. In comparing nonparticipating and participating contracts, account must be taken also of the probable dividends payable on the participating policies. In some companies the net cost after dividends is less than the nonparticipating premium.*

---

* See pp. 475–476 for an explanation of the terms "nonparticipating," "participating," and "dividends."

TABLE 18-2.   Premium per $1,000 For Selected Types of Life Insurance Contracts For a Man at Age 25

1 10-Year Convertible Term	2 Term to Age 65	3 Ordinary Life Nonpar.*	4 Ordinary Life Par.**	5 20-Payment Life Nonpar.
$5.02	$8.32	$13.12	$17.31	$20.77

6 20-Payment Life Par.	7 Life Paid Up to 65 Nonpar.	8 Life Paid Up at 65 Par.	9 20-Year Endow. Nonpar.	10 20-Year Endow. Par.
$30.09	$14.30	$18.66	$42.42	$47.46

* Nonparticipating in dividends.
** Participating in dividends.
Source: Best's Flitcraft Compend (Oldwick, N.J.: A. M. Best, Co., 1975).

The premiums listed in Table 18-2, are those quoted by four companies. If one were to consult a rate book such as *Best's Flitcraft Compend,* one could find other companies whose premiums for all or some of these contracts might be lower or higher.

You should be very careful when comparing costs of various kinds of life insurance policies. There are so many variables that need to be taken into consideration; for example, in Table 18-2 each policy is different. The premium for the ten-year convertible term increases at the end of each ten-year period. The premium for all but the term policies are level, but some must be paid for life and others for twenty years or to age sixty-five. Some of the policies will participate in the distribution of dividends and some will not. The endowment policies will pay a monthly income for life at a stipulated age. You are not comparing identical policies, and it is impossible with the information given to know which is the best policy strictly on a cost basis.

In 1973 the National Association of Insurance Commissioners (NAIC) proposed model cost comparison regulations. This method of attempting to measure the cost of life insurance by the same standard is called the *interest-adjusted index.* Prior to the establishment of this standard the only kinds of policies that one could compare on a cost basis were identical term policies. It was almost impossible to compare costs of identical policies that had cash values because of the participating, nonparticipating aspects and because of the differences in the earnings of the cash value part of policies and how earnings were applied.

Using the interest-adjusted index the Commissioner of Insurance for the State of Pennsylvania published a cost index of many companies operating in Pennsylvania which showed that for a male, age twenty, buying an ordinary life insurance policy the cost index was 2.82 for the lowest cost company at the end of twenty years of payments, while the cost index for the highest cost company was 5.88.[13] Basically what the interest-adjusted index attempts to do is take into consideration all the variables, including the annual premium, accumulated dividends at a given rate of interest, if any, and the cash value of the policy at the given time at which it is being measured. This is not a perfect comparison of costs because of the varying lengths of time that a policy might be in effect, but it is presently accepted as the best method for such cost comparisons developed to date. If the agent does not give you the cost index of the policy or policies in which you are interested, you should ask him for it. Then you can compare his cost index with the cost index of another agent for identical policies.*

HOW TO MEET THE RISK OF OLD AGE WITHOUT EARNED INCOME

Depending on Government Pensions

One of the greatest social upheavals of all times took place in the United States in the 1930s. The idea developed that older people should be treated as persons, not as derelicts. Instead of being sent to institutions, they should be able to live out their last years in their own homes. They should be freed from dependency on children and should not have to undergo the humiliation of depending on charity. The Social Security Act of 1935 included the concept of government pensions for the aged. These were to be paid as a matter of right, not as charity.

The early pensions were meager, but they represented a fundamental break with the past. As the national income increased, it was hoped that the break from dependence to independence for the aged could be accomplished. The benefits have been liberalized during the intervening years. Now it can be said that the current generation of retired persons is more nearly independent than any preceding generation in history.

Depending on Employer Supplemental Retirement Payments

A significant aspect of the social revolution in the 1930s was the vitalization of the labor movement in the United States. Men and women by the millions joined unions, whose representatives bargained collectively with employers. Early negotiations dealt largely with union demands for higher pay, shorter hours, and better working conditions. Soon after the outbreak

---

* Cost indexes of a selected group of policies of the leading life insurance companies of the United States and Canada are included in the *Interest-Adjusted Index: Life Insurance Premium Outlay and Surrender Comparisons* (Cincinnati: National Underwriter Co., 1976).

of World War II, the federal government instituted wage and price controls. Although corporations were making profits and many employers were able and willing to increase wages, they were not permitted to do so. In that situation the concept of fringe benefits developed. Employer and employee representatives found that they could legally increase payments to workers indirectly. One outgrowth of the indirect fringe benefit period was the negotiating of contracts in which some employers agreed to make payments into a fund to be used to supplement the retirement incomes provided by Social Security. One automobile manufacturer agreed to guarantee employees a retirement income of $125 a month. That meant that the employer had to pay the difference between $125 and the Social Security retirement benefit. An unforeseen outcome of that contract was that employers suddenly became interested in supporting union demands for increased Social Security retirement benefits. The more the employee receives from Social Security, the less the employer has to pay. This was one reason why Congress amended the Social Security law from time to time. Every time the law was amended, retirement income benefits were increased.

Depending on Individual Retirement Accounts

The Pension Reform Act of 1974 included a provision establishing Individual Retirement Accounts (IRA). There are 40 million persons in the U.S. who have no way to provide tax-sheltered retirement incomes for themselves. Since millions of employees are covered with company pension programs that are tax-sheltered, Congress passed legislation to provide tax-sheltered retirement provisions for the rest of the labor force. Under the IRA program, a qualified person may put aside 15 percent of his or her earnings, up to a maximum of $1,500 annually, in a personal pension plan, with the money going into banks, federally insured credit unions, savings and loan associations, regulated investment companies, insurance companies, U.S. retirement bonds, or individual stock investments. The amount paid into the program each year along with the interest or dividends earned are exempt from income taxes until retirement, when the person's income tax bracket will be lower. There are a variety of IRA programs being offered by financial institutions and before a choice is made these various programs should be investigated carefully. For some programs, such as through a savings and loan association, there is no charge, but some major insurance companies charge a commission, which can cost as much as 40 percent of the first year's $1,500 investment, and a 6 to 8 percent annual charge after that. A relatively high rate of return promised by a financial institution on an IRA may prove to be a poorer investment than a lower rate where no charge is made. Careful comparisons should be made. For those persons who can take advantage of IRA it can be a worthwhile retirement program with a significant tax benefit.

Depending on Income from Investments

World War II demonstrated that the American economy had a far greater productive capacity than anyone had imagined. During the war and the postwar period the federal government moved from a passive to an active role in the economy. Fiscal and monetary policies were used to stimulate and maintain a high level of production; unemployment diminished; national income increased; and family incomes increased. As family incomes increased people were able to save. For the population as a whole the saving rate remains fairly constant at about 6 percent of national income. As people began to have money to invest they turned at first to the familiar United States government bonds and to life insurance. Increasingly investors put their savings into real estate, mutual funds, and common stock. As the economy continued to boom and as national income increased, returns on investments supplemented Social Security and employer retirement benefit payments. Now many of the 23 million persons over the age of sixty-five are able to live in their own homes where they enjoy considerable dignity and independence. The financial security of many of the elderly has been weakened by the inflation of the 1970s, however.

Depending on Fixed Income Annuities

Probably the most dependable source of continuing income after retirement is an annuity contract. Such a contract guarantees a fixed dollar income to the annuitant. Most annuities are for older people and begin paying at approximately age sixty-five. Of the 10 million annuity contracts in force, 7.5 million are group contracts. Most of the group contracts cover employees and are underwritten by life insurance companies. The monthly income received by Social Security beneficiaries is an annuity that will continue as long as the annuitant lives.

The ordinary life or immediate annuity may be explained by returning to the illustrations of the parents of 1,000 young people who will graduate next June. It is assumed that the parents are now age sixty-five. Their children are independent. Death is certain to occur within a few years, so there is no need for providing a cash income in the event of premature death. It is now more important to assure themselves an income that will not fail, so that they will not be a burden on their children or on society.

One procedure is to convert all assets into cash, using the proceeds to buy an immediate annuity. At age sixty-five the normal expectancy of life for men is five years. A prospective annuitant can buy a guaranteed cash income of $300 a month for $33,937. The annuitant not only buys a safe investment, but he also earns nearly one and a half times the return he could normally expect. If he invested his $33,937 he would do well to secure a 7 percent return, or $2,375 a year. By purchasing the annuity he receives $3,600 a year. There is no magic in this procedure. It is possible because the annuitant is now using principal as well as interest. The insurance com-

pany can afford to guarantee $300 a month because its actuaries have cal-
culated that the principal and interest would yield that amount for fifteen
years at their assumed rate of interest.

If the annuitant dies after ten years, the unpaid portion of his principal
goes to pay some other annuitant who may live seventeen years. This illustrates and emphasizes the fact that annuity contracts, like insurance
contracts, make it possible for a group of people to pool and share their
common risks. People who do not understand this basic principle sometimes object to the type of annuity that stops when the annuitant dies. To
meet that objection insurance actuaries have devised another form of
contract that guarantees to return to the annuitant's beneficiaries or estate
the unpaid portions to which the annuitant would have been entitled if he
or she had lived. Of course, the annuity would be smaller under such a
contract. Or to express the same idea in another way, its purchase price
would be higher. For example, a fifty-five-year-old man buying a refund
annuity of $300 a month would pay $37,113.

Another variation is the twenty-year certain annuity. This contract
guarantees the income for twenty years even though the annuitant dies.
Here again the annuity would cost more. A sixty-five-year-old man buying
a twenty-year, certain annuity of $300 a month would pay $43,380.

It is very common for those buying annuities to wish to provide not
only a guaranteed income per month for life for themselves but also for
their husbands or wives. So it is possible to purchase a joint annuity with
survivor rights. This means that at the death of one annuitant the monthly
annuity payment will continue to be paid to the survivor until death. Where
a company sells a $300-a-month annuity for a male at age sixty-five for life
at $37,800, it will sell a joint and survivor annuity for the husband, age
sixty-five, and wife, age sixty-two, for $46,200. Under the joint and survivor
type of annuity, a monthly income is guaranteed for life for both husband
and wife.

In all of these illustrations if the purchase of a life annuity were postponed to age seventy the same amount of money would purchase a larger
annuity. This is because the annuity table for men shows a life expectancy
at age seventy of approximately twelve years.

Even though insurance companies use the same annuity tables not all
companies quote identical premiums. A prospective buyer will find premium quotations in the *Best's Flitcraft Compend. Annuities from the
Buyer's Point of View* lists selected companies in order of the monthly
income yield on $1,000 for a male age sixty-five. The range for an immediate
nonparticipating life annuity is from $7.62 to $8.84. The range on immediate nonparticipating installment refund annuities is from $6.95 to
$8.15.[14]

Deferred annuities are designed for younger buyers. By the time a man
reaches age thirty-five his income will be large enough to permit a savings
program. By purchasing a deferred annuity contract at age thirty-five a
monthly premium of $10 will buy a monthly income of $43.72 beginning at
age sixty-five.

Depending on Variable Income Annuities

Four decades of rising prices have convinced increasing numbers of people of the need to protect their retirement annuities against continued decline in the purchasing power of the dollar. In terms of goods and services, the current dollar is worth less than half as much as it was twenty years ago. The variable annuity is a device designed to offset in part the decline in the purchasing power of the dollar. This is done by writing a contract that promises the annuitant a variable rather than a fixed number of dollars. Premiums are invested in common stocks, whose value and yield increase in a growing economy subject to mild inflation. The gross national product of our economy is more than twice the dollar value of the goods and services produced ten years ago. Common stock prices and dividends are sensitive to the prospects for success and continued growth in American industry. They reflect the long-term movements of the economy. The average rate of return, including dividends and net capital appreciation, on a representative index of common stocks was 9 percent per year in the first sixty-five years of this century. During the past decade, due to the depth and length of the recession, the average rate of return has been reduced considerably.

Teachers Insurance and Annuity Association pioneered in developing the variable annuity. Approximately one-half of the premiums paid by participants are invested in fixed dollar income yield investments, such as bonds and mortgages. The remaining portion of the premiums is invested in growth common stocks. Annuitants are thereby protected against deflation as well as inflation. When an annuitant reaches sixty-five he receives a guaranteed number of dollars each month on his fixed income annuity, but on his variable annuity he receives a variable number of dollars. If the economy has continued to expand he will receive more. If the economy has been sluggish he will receive fewer dollars. To illustrate the potential of the variable annuity, the value of an accumulation unit under the Teachers Insurance and Annuity Association plan, called College Retirement Equities Fund, increased from $10.52 in 1952, at the end of the first year of the program, to a high of $53.25 at the end of 1972. But since the value of a variable annuity is tied to the market value of stocks, it can go down as well as up. From 1972 to the end of 1974 the value of an accumulation unit dropped from the high of $53.25 to $28.35, but by the end of 1975 it had risen to $36.34.

It must be noted that Social Security retirement benefits provide partial protection against rising prices and complete protection against deflation. When prices decline the fixed dollar income remains constant. The inflation hedge arises out of the fact that periodically Congress increased Social Security retirement benefits by an amount approximately equal to the price level increase in the preceding five-year period and has now built in automatic increases tied to the Consumer Price Index.

Civil Service and military personnel retirees are protected against rising price levels by Congressional acts that provide for automatic increases in retirement pay, based on the Consumer Price Index. If the CPI rises 3 percent and holds there for three months, then retirement pay is adjusted upward by the 3 percent, plus the amount it has increased during the three months, plus 1 percent. During a recent three-month period the CPI went up 3 percent, and during the three-month period it increased another 1.4 percent, so retirement pay was increased by 5.4 percent. Adjustments are made approximately twice a year. A person who retired in 1967 has seen his retirement pay go up about 75 percent in a decade.

The soundness and success of the College Equities Retirement Fund has been demonstrated. By the end of 1974 there were 1,255,000 persons covered by life insurance company variable annuities in the United States, with reserves of $5.2 billion set aside to meet future obligations. The Securities and Exchange Commission was supported by the Supreme Court in its view that variable annuities are securities, similar to mutual funds. As such they are subjected to regulation under the Investment Company Act of 1940.

QUESTIONS FOR REVIEW

1. What is the basic purpose of insurance and how well does it meet this purpose?
2. What are the basic principles under which insurance operates?
3. Why was the Social Security Act passed by Congress?
4. What kinds of benefits might you be eligible to receive under Social Security?
5. What is Medicare? Do you favor it?
6. What seem to be the strengths and weaknesses of the Social Security System?
7. What are differences between mutual and stock insurance companies?
8. What is the difference between a participating and nonparticipating life insurance policy?
9. Discuss the basic differences between term life insurance and cash-value life insurance.
10. Should one use life insurance as a method of saving?
11. What is variable life insurance? How does it work?
12. What is the interest-adjusted index?
13. What are the ways to meet the financial risks of old age?
14. What is an Individual Retirement Account? What are its advantages?
15. What is a basic problem of a fixed income annuity?
16. How does a variable income annuity work?

17. In planning your life insurance program will you build your plan on term or whole life insurance? Why?

PROJECTS

1. Draw up a list of the various kinds of financial hazards to which you and your family could be subjected to and how you and your family might cope with these financial risks.

2. Draw up a chart showing all the potential benefits you and your family could be eligible for over a lifetime from Social Security.

3. Interview a few elderly persons to get their opinions about Medicare.

4. Ask a representative of a mutual life insurance company and a representative of a stock company why you should buy life insurance from the companies they represent. Compare their responses in a written report.

5. Get the opinions of a life insurance agent, a banker, and a stockbroker about buying term insurance and investing the difference versus buying cash-value insurance.

6. Check *Best's Flitcraft Compend* or a comparable rate book in a library and compare the different kinds of policies and rate structures being offered.

7. Develop one life insurance program and then get the interest-adjusted index for it from at least two different agents.

8. Discuss Individual Retirement Accounts with a banker, stockholder, and insurance agent and write a report on their comments.

REFERENCES

1. *St. Petersburg Times,* 14 Dec. 1975, p. 1B.
2. *Ibid.*
3. *St. Petersburg Times,* 28 July 1975, p. 1A.
4. *St. Petersburg Times,* 24 Sept. 1975, p. 23A.
5. *St. Petersburg Times,* 16 Feb. 1976, p. 15A.
6. Dave Goodwin, *Stop Wasting Your Insurance Dollars* (New York: Simon & Schuster, 1969), pp. 46–47; *Best's Review,* April 1970, p. 38.
7. All illustrative premiums have been taken from *Best's Flitcraft Compend,* 1975, A. M. Best Company, Oldwick, N.J., 08858.
8. Goodwin, p. 54; *Life Insurance from the Buyer's Point of View,* American Institute for Economic Research, Economic Education Bulletin 10, no. 6 (July 1970), pp. 6, 21.
9. Arthur Milton, *How to Get a Dollar's Value for a Dollar Spent* (New York: The Citadel Press, 1964), pp. 39, 44.
10. William J. Matteson, *Life Insurance and Annuities from the Buyer's Point of View,* American Institute for Economic Research, Economic Education Bulletin 3, no. 4 (1963), pp. 17–18.

11. Herbert S. Denenberg, "The Decline and Fall of Cash Value Life Insurance," *Best's Review* 71, no. 6 (Oct. 1970): 34.
12. Goodwin; *Life Insurance From the Buyer's Point of View;* The Editors of Consumer Reports, *The Consumers Union Report on Life Insurance: A Guide to Planning and Buying the Protection You Need* (Mt. Vernon, N.Y.: Consumer's Union, 1972).
13. Herbert S. Denenberg, *The Shopper's Guidebook to Life Insurance, Health Insurance, Auto Insurance, Homeowner's Insurance, Doctors, Dentists, Lawyers, Pensions, Etc.* (Washington, D.C.: Consumer News, Inc., 1974), pp. 62 63.
14. *Annuities from the Buyer's Point of View*, American Institute for Economic Research, Economic Education Bulletin 15, no. 8 (Aug. 1975), p. 10.

CHAPTER 19

BUYING PROTECTION: UNDERSTANDING AND USING INSURANCE

INSURANCE IS A COMPLICATED BUSINESS

Venturing into Promise Land

American consumers are insurance-minded. By the mid-1970s 145 million policyholders owned $2.0 trillion worth of life insurance! In one year alone insurance buyers purchased almost $300 billion worth of life insurance! Approximately $110 billion, or about 9 percent of total national income, is being spent each year on premiums for life, health and accident, annuity, property and liability insurance protection.* The amounts of money spent for insurance contracts increase from year to year. In twenty-five years, life insurance purchases increased from a total of approximately $29 billion to $298 billion.

When consumers buy insurance, they buy promises. The promises are written in a contract, usually called a policy. The contract contains an agreement between the parties. It lists the obligations assumed by the insurer. It lists the benefits accruing to the insured if the event insured against should occur. An insurance contract is a formidable document. Its language is technical, legalistic, and confusing to an uninformed buyer. The seller knows the exact meaning of every word. The seller's actuaries have calculated the probability of loss, and they have a measurable margin of safety. If the insurer is a corporation operating for profit it can measure the profit probability.

By contrast, the many buyers of insurance are beginners. It is unlikely that many of them have ever had a formal course dealing with the important subject of insurance. It is equally unlikely that many of them have read a basic introductory insurance textbook. All that most of them know is what they have been told by insurance sellers. According to better business

* These facts and figures will be found in *Life Insurance Fact Book, 1975*, and *Insurance Facts 1976*. These fact books are published annually by the American Council of Life Insurance, 277 Park Avenue, New York, N.Y. 10017, and by the Insurance Information Institute, 110 William Street, New York, N.Y. 10038.

burcaus very few buyers read contracts. It is doubtful that they would really understand them if they did. For example, it has been found that some buyers of twenty-pay life insurance contracts bought those contracts under the assumption that they would receive the face value of the policy at the end of twenty years. Very few insurance buyers know what kinds of coverage they should have. Neither do they know how much insurance protection they should have. Somewhere in their maturing years they have gotten the impression that everyone should have "some insurance." Buying insurance is the thing to do. Such prospects desperately need the assistance of well-trained objective sellers. Some are fortunate enough to find such persons to help them. Others wait until an insurance salesman comes to their home. Most such salesmen represent a single company, and their income consists of a percentage commission on premiums collected. The higher the premiums, the greater their incomes.

As one ventures into the unknown to purchase a much needed service, one should know a little about the way prices are determined.

ACTUARIAL ASPECTS OF LIFE INSURANCE

How Prices Are Determined

The actuarial aspects of life insurance involve more complicated mathematics than the average person can understand. But the fact that the calculation of insurance premiums is difficult is no reason for buyers not to know more than they do about insurance price determination. The insurance business, like any other business, must balance income with expenditures. An insurance company contracts to pay a beneficiary $1,000 if the insured should die. In return for the payment of premiums by the insured, there can be no doubt that insofar as actuaries can determine, the premiums will cover the anticipated claim and all administrative costs. How then are the premiums determined?

The starting point is a mortality table. Most insurers now use the Commissioners 1958 Standard Ordinary Mortality Table. That table has been constructed on the basis of mortality statistics in the United States for the years 1950 to 1954. For a group of ten million persons, the table shows the number who will die each year from birth to age ninety-nine.

The second step is the application of the law of probability. For example, in the assumed group of ten million lives the probability of death during the ensuing year for men age twenty-five is determined by dividing the number living at that age, 9,575,636, into the number who will die that year, 18,481. The result indicates a probability of 1.93 deaths per 1,000.

With this information concerning the probability of death at any given age, an actuary can calculate a price for protection if he or she knows the age of the applicant, the kind of contract desired, and the rate of interest that the company is prepared to guarantee. For example, at age twenty-five the probability of death during the next twelve months is .00193, or 1,930 in one million. By multiplying this decimal by 1,000, the cost of $1,000 worth of protection is found to be $1.93. This can be explained in another way. At age twenty-five there are 9,575,636 persons living, of whom 18,481 will die within the year. If a company were to insure each of 9,575,636 lives for $1,000 for one year, it would have to charge each insured an amount that, multiplied by 9,575,636, would total $18,481,000, the anticipated claims. By calculation this sum is found to be $1.93.

No account has been taken of interest. If it is assumed that premiums are collected annually in advance and that no claims are paid until the end of the year, the company would have $1.04 for every dollar collected as premium, using 4 percent as the rate of interest. The figure for total claims, $18,481,000, bears the same ratio to the amount that the 9,575,636 insureds must pay as $1.04 bears to $1.00. Dividing $18,481,000 by $1.04 gives $17,770,192, which, spread over 9,575,636 policyholders, requires an annual premium of $1.86 instead of $1.93.

All insurance premiums are calculated this way, with necessary variations for age, type of policy, face value of policy, and method of payment. But anyone who has bought insurance knows that premiums are higher than these calculations indicate. The premiums we have just calculated are called *net premiums*, while the premium one pays an insurance company is called the *gross premium*. The gross premium includes the *loading*, a term which covers not only selling, collection, and administrative expenses but also provides a margin for contingencies, such as errors in net premiums that result from a higher mortality or lower interest yield than anticipated.

A customary division of expenses and of the loading to cover them includes 80 percent of the first premium for expenses incurred in securing new business; 10 percent of the renewal premiums for collection expenses; $1\frac{1}{2}$ percent of the face value of the claims to cover settlement costs; $\frac{1}{2}$ percent a year on assets to pay for expenses involved in making investments; and $1 per $1,000 of insurance per year for general expenses. An additional item included in the loading of many mutuals is a margin to create a surplus out of which to pay "dividends." What this means is that the insurance buyer is charged a price higher than necessary. Then insurance companies may return all or part of the overcharge to the policyholder as a "dividend," causing policyholders to believe that, because of good management, their net cost of protection has been reduced.

There is no selling cost charged to persons insured under the Social Security system. The selling cost for group insurance is low, and once a group has been organized and a master certificate issued, there is no selling charge for persons who subsequently join the group. By contrast, the expense for selling individual insurance contracts is high. The charge is 80 percent of the first year's premium and 10 percent of renewal premiums. Insurance agents are paid from 40 to 60 percent of the first premium depending on the terms of the contracts and 5 percent of the next nine premiums. This amounts to practically one full premium per thousand dollars of insurance.

Life insurance companies had an income of $70 billion in 1974, of which $28 billion consisted of premium income! The major portion of the remainder was income from investments. Death benefit payments amounted to $9 billion that year. What the insurance companies call living benefits – those for disability, annuities, matured endowments, surrender values, and dividends – were $12.5 billion. Operating expenses of $12 billion and taxes of $3.2 billion raised the total expenditures of insurance companies to $36.7 billion. This was $14 billion less than premium income and $24 billion less than total income. Some of the difference went into reserves, which were increased at the rate of $16.6 billion in 1974.[1] This excess of income over disbursements is a notable feature of life insurance companies. It has persisted year after year. Even more significant is the fact that the excess of premium income over disbursements is increasing every year.

A breakdown of the insurance dollar may clarify one's understanding of how insurance companies work. For each dollar income in 1974, premiums accounted for 77.5 cents and interest for 22.5 cents. Of each dollar spent by insurance companies in 1974, 52.5 cents were paid to beneficiaries, 23.1 cents went into reserves, and 1.7 cents into special reserves. Commissions to agents accounted for 6.9 cents; the expenses of operating offices amounted to 10.1 cents; taxes took 4.6 cents; and dividends to stockholders amounted to 1.1 cents. These figures show that 52.5 percent of insurance company income was paid as benefits. Of those benefits, only 41.4 percent were paid as death benefits.[2]

Cash Surrender Value Explained

The preceding explanation of how annual premiums are calculated also explains, by implication, the origin and meaning of the cash surrender value of an insurance contract. To avoid increasing rates as the insured grows older, actuaries have calculated a constant premium through the life of a contract. In the early years the constant premium exceeds the actual cost of protection by an amount sufficient to offset the deficit in later years, when the actual cost of protection would exceed the constant premium. For example, the excess would amount to $8.43 on a $1,000 nonparticipating contract at age twenty-five. This sum, invested and improved at 3 percent interest, accumulates a reserve that belongs to the insured. This reserve is held in trust for the insured by the insurer. If, after the contract has been in effect a few years, the insured elects to discontinue the contract, he or she has a legal claim to the accumulated reserve. On a nonparticipating ordinary life contract for $1,000 purchased at age twenty-five the cash surrender value would amount to $169 after fifteen years. This means that the insured has paid a sum, which, with interest, is $169 more than the actual gross cost of protection during the fifteen years. At age sixty-five the cash surrender value would amount to $570.

On the average, approximately 6.5 percent of all insurance contracts in force lapse or are surrendered every year. The lapse rate is higher for contracts that have been in effect less than two years. Lapses and surrenders are related to general economic conditions, tending to increase in times of recession. Surrender rates also vary among companies. A study of the lapse ratios based on the individual ordinary life insurance in force with the 100 largest life insurance companies showed a median lapse ratio of 8.2 percent. The lapse ratio per company ranged from a low of 2.0 percent to a high of 15.9 percent. This means that for one company only one out of every fifty policies lapsed during the year, while the other company had almost one out of every six policies lapse during the year.[3] This suggests that many buyers have undertaken to purchase more insurance than they can afford or that they have purchased higher-priced insurance than they can afford.

There are so many variables built into almost every kind of cash value policy that it is difficult for buyers to know just what rate of return they are getting. Since cash value life insurance is in part sold on the fact that it is a savings medium, buyers should be interested in knowing what rate of return they get on their savings in the cash values. Since banks and savings and loan associations publicize the rates of return they pay on savings accounts, it is reasonable to expect life insurance companies to do the same, but neither the life insurance companies nor the life insurance industry associations tell the buyer what rate is paid on savings in life insurance policies.[4]

When a contract is surrendered for cash, most companies deduct a cash surrender charge. Some charge $18 per $1,000 during the first policy year and $16 in the second year, decreasing by $2 per year until the ninth year, after which there are no deductions. Others deduct a charge on any contracts surrendered during the first nineteen years. There is so much variation in company practice that one of the many comparisons a prospective buyer should make is that of cash values and cash surrender charges.

When a contract is surrendered, the insured may demand cash after a waiting period of sixty days or more. Instead of cash the insured may elect to take a paid-up term insurance contract. For example, after fifteen years each dollar of cash value will purchase $2.46 worth of paid-up life insurance. That means that a cash surrender value of $169 will purchase $415.74 in paid-up life insurance.

How To Borrow on One's Life Insurance Contract

Instead of terminating a policy and taking the accumulated reserve in cash, an insured may borrow the cash value and still continue the contract in force. As security for repayment of the loan, the insured assigns the policy to the company, the amount of the loan becoming a first lien on the proceeds of the contract in the event of termination. This means that if the insured dies before the loan has been repaid, the beneficiary receives the face amount of the policy minus the amount of the loan.

Although the insured is borrowing his own money, the company, having contracted to improve the reserve at a rate of interest ranging from about $3\frac{1}{2}$ to $4\frac{1}{2}$ percent, charges him interest on a policy loan. The interest rates charged by some companies suggest that policy loans are more lucrative than other types of lending. On a loan that is riskless some companies charge as much as 8 percent in advance. That would be an effective rate of 8.7 percent and would be about twice the interest rate guaranteed on the policy reserve. Some companies have adopted a sliding scale, under which the rate of interest declines as the amount of the loan increases. Since there is a range of more than 50 percent in interest rates on loans, this is another factor to consider in choosing a company. *Best's Flitcraft Compend* contains a policy analysis for some 400 companies, including the rate of interest charged on policy loans.

Is it wise to borrow on one's life insurance? The answer depends on the individual. Even a rate as high as 8 percent in advance is less than one would have to pay if the money were borrowed elsewhere. If the insured understands that her insurance protection is reduced by the amount of the loan and if she follows a plan of regular repayment, it may be wiser to borrow from her insurance company. For a person who understands the fundamental principles of insurance, the insurance policy loan is a legitimate means of securing necessary cash to meet an urgent, temporary need. For example, in 1974 when bank interest rates were 9 percent or higher, insureds borrowed substantially more from life insurance companies. The volume of loans rose to 8.7 percent of insurance companies assets, compared with 4.8 percent a decade earlier.[5] But the records show that policy loans are frequently the forerunners of insurance policy lapses.

The Origin and Meaning of Dividends

There is probably no phase of insurance about which policyholders have more delusions than the origin and meaning of "dividends." The use of the word "dividends" in life insurance is a misnomer. That is why the word has been set in quotation marks throughout this discussion. A more accurate descriptive phrase would be "surplus sharing" or "patronage refund." What is the origin of the surplus to be shared?

1. One clue has been given already. Some mutual companies include a percentage in the loading in excess of their estimates for expense. At the end of the year, all or a part of that excess may be paid back to the policyholders. In the words of two insurance experts, "One large source of surplus is the deliberate overcharging of its insureds."[6] Another expert puts it this way: "In computing premiums, liberal estimates of costs of operation are included in the loading. This results in expense savings."[7] Life insurance agent Goodwin would make it illegal to use the word dividend. He would require the following statement on every participating contract: This policy contains an over-charge. At its sole discretion, the company may keep all or part of such overcharge indefinitely.[8]

2. A second explanation is the possibility that insurance companies may earn more on their investments than the amount guaranteed to the

insured. In a fifty-five-year period the net rate of interest earned by insurance companies on their invested funds has ranged from a low of 2.88 percent to a high of 6.25 percent, the current net interest yield.[9] Yet there are many companies that guarantee no more than 2.25 percent interest on reserves, and none guarantees more than 3.5 percent. The most common rate is 3 percent. This gives the companies a margin of 3 percent excess earnings on investments.

3.   A third factor contributing to surplus is a mortality rate lower than anticipated. As a result of selection of risks a company may have fewer claims than the actuaries estimated. Also life expectancy has risen dramatically. For all races, expectation of life at birth has increased from fifty-four years in 1920 to 71.3 years in 1975. This means that insurance companies pay fewer death claims and continue to collect premiums longer.

4.   Another source of excess surplus is possible overloading to cover expenses lumped together under the term "administrative expenses."

5.   Unanticipated capital gains on investments may be realized in boom periods. The laws of many states permit insurance companies to invest portions of their reserves in common stocks, and although not many invest to the limit, those that do may realize greater income if they hold their stocks, or capital gains if they sell at boom prices.

6.   A final source of income not allowed for is gain from forfeitures. Lapses and surrenders of ordinary life insurance contracts have ranged from 2.2 percent to 19.5 percent in the last twenty-five years. On weekly premium contracts the range has been even higher.

It is from these sources that a surplus is accumulated that can be distributed among policyholders. Contracts sharing these dividends are called *participating policies*. Nonparticipating policies carry a lower level annual premium, although their net cost in the long run may be higher. For example, the annual premium quoted by one company for a $1,000 nonparticipating ordinary life contract at age twenty-five, male, is $12.98, compared with the $16.57 charged by a mutual company. Through the years the buyer of the nonparticipating contract would pay $12.98 and would not receive any dividends. The buyer of the participating policy would pay $16.57 each year, but in addition would receive dividends that would reduce his twenty-year average net payment to $10.83.

Dividends may be taken in cash, applied to the payment of premiums, used to purchase more insurance, or allowed to accumulate. In the latter case the individual reserve would accumulate more rapidly and in about twenty-five years an ordinary life contract would become a paid-up contract. Each insured must decide how to use his or her dividends. If he wants maximum protection for his premiums, the dividends should be used to purchase more insurance. If he has enough insurance and wishes to reduce his premium payments, he may take them in cash. In a typical year policyholders use 24 percent of their dividends to reduce premium payments. Twenty-eight percent are left on deposit with the insurance companies. Twenty-seven percent are used to purchase more insurance protection, and twenty-one percent are taken in cash.[10]

WHAT TO DO WHEN A LIFE INSURANCE CONTRACT TERMINATES

What Choices Are Available?

All life insurance contracts, except the endowment forms, are terminated only by death or failure to pay premiums. Upon receipt of proof of death of the insured, the insurer is liable to the beneficiary for the face value of the policy minus any loans secured by it. The insurer usually offers several settlements to the beneficiary. The amount payable may be taken in cash, or the beneficiary may choose to take equal installments of a specified amount to continue until the proceeds of the policy are exhausted. A third choice open to the beneficiary is that of taking installments for a specified period. The size of the installment payments will vary with the length of the period. A fourth choice is that of taking a life income or annuity equal to the income which the proceeds of the policy would purchase as a single premium for the attained age of the beneficiary. A final option is that of leaving the proceeds of the policy with the insurance company at a guaranteed rate of interest, with provision for withdrawal of interest and principal as agreed upon by the beneficiary and the insurer.

Which Option to Choose?

Should the beneficiary take the proceeds of a terminated policy in cash? The only valid answer that can be given is that it depends. It depends on a variety of factors. Most beneficiaries are women who are usually unaccustomed to making investments. Moreover, they are likely to be emotionally upset as a result of their bereavement. Receipt of a large sum of money with full responsibility for its investment places a burden on the beneficiary that often results in loss. Many World War I widows were the victims of unscrupulous operators who persuaded them to put their money into speculative investments. As a result of that experience, the United States government no longer pays insurance policy proceeds in a lump sum. Beneficiaries of insureds under Social Security receive monthly payments for specific periods.

Individual insureds may achieve the same security for their beneficiaries by making the choice themselves while they are still living. The difficulty with this plan is that conditions change. If the price-level continues to rise, beneficiaries need more income. One advantage of having an insured choose the method of settlement before his or her death is that if the proceeds are paid in installments, the payments need not be included by the beneficiary as gross income for tax purposes.

A practice many families have adopted is that of having a qualified insurance counselor help the husband and wife make a choice. The counselor makes an audit of the insured's insurance estate, including recommendations for terms of settlement. If the insured and his beneficiary agree to the recommendations, the counselor then makes the necessary legal arrangements. There are so many possible desirable settlements, depending on the age of the insured at death, the age of the beneficiary or beneficiaries, the burden of indebtedness, and many other factors, that it is futile even to suggest a typical settlement. The important thing is to secure the expert, unbiased advice of an insurance counselor. This need not necessarily involve expense because increasing numbers of well-trained agents, especially those who are Chartered Life Underwriters, perform this service as a part of their selling program.*

For the latest year reported, 93 percent of payments to beneficiaries were in lump sum, 3.3 percent were held at interest, 2.0 percent were placed in annuities with a minimum certain amount to be paid, and 1.0 percent were placed in life income annuities.[11]

IS LIFE INSURANCE SOLD OR BOUGHT?

Historically Life Insurance Has Been Sold

Insurance buyers today are more sophisticated than their ancestors. Nevertheless, many insurance buyers are woefully uninformed. Some of them are even superstitious. Some resist the purchase of life insurance just as they refuse to think about death and burial. The purchase of life insurance has been found to give some people the illusion that they are less likely to die.

These were the prevalent attitudes when the insurance industry was developing. In order to sell insurance, company managements concluded that it was necessary to have large numbers of agents, motivated by the desire to make money. Instead of paying their agents salaries, insurance companies adopted the commission payment system. Simple arithmetic shows that an agent on a 50-percent commission basis will make $24 per $1,000 on an endowment contract priced at $48 per $1,000, compared with $2.50 on a term insurance contract costing $5 per $1,000. The agency system of pressure selling has resulted in the purchase of too much of the wrong kind of high-priced insurance by many insurance buyers. Agents emphasize the savings aspects of insurance. The tendency is to sell all-purpose insurance, covering all members of the family. The basic purpose is to provide protection for beneficiaries in case the insured, who provides the family income, should die prematurely. Such protective insurance can be purchased at low prices. But when all members of a family are included, buyers are promised that they will collect if they live or if they die. The so-called insurance becomes a combination protection plus savings which is expensive, but remunerative to agents.

There are about 385,000 insurance agents selling insurance full time.

---

* A Chartered Life Underwriter (CLU) has passed a series of examinations set by the American College of Life Underwriters, whose purpose is to raise insurance salesmanship to a professional level.

Many others work part time. About half specialize in life insurance; the rest specialize in some type of property/liability insurance. Almost all sell health insurance. How many are qualified to advise buyers in planning insurance and investment programs? Many of them know more about commissions than they do about insurance. There are practically no standards for insurance salesmanship. The standard that dominates and by which the success of an agent is measured is the volume of insurance he or she writes. A person need not know anything about the intricacies of insurance in order to secure an agency contract with many companies. A person may have failed in every previous business or professional venture, yet some insurance company will hand him a ratebook without any question and tell him to "go to it." The result has been the writing of insurance with an eye to the size of commissions rather than to the needs of the buyers.

In spite of all the high pressure selling, 14 percent of American families do not have any life insurance. By the end of 1974, the average life insurance coverage per insured family was $31,200.[12] If you deduct from this amount the insurance coverage on persons in the family other than the chief income earner, the amount of insurance available for dependents at the death of the chief income earner would be even less. With the median income per family in 1974 at about $13,000, and with the recommendation of many life insurance agents that the amount of insurance on the chief income earner should be four to five times his or her annual income, it is easy to see that the average amount of coverage per family is woefully inadequate, and yet one out of every seven families has no life insurance coverage whatsoever.

Government Life Insurance Is Sold

The Vietnam war gave rise to a new federal government life insurance program in 1965. In Public Law 89–214 Congress provided for Servicemen's Group Life Insurance. For the first time private companies are underwriting the military insurance program. Prudential Insurance Company has been chosen as the prime contractor and has formed a syndicate of 500 companies that may write group insurance. This insurance provides coverage for military personnel on active duty, national guardsmen, reservists, and members of ROTC engaged in authorized training duty and while traveling to and from such duty.

Under the plan all military personnel have the option to purchase $5,000, $10,000, $15,000, or $20,000 of life insurance. The premium on the $20,000 policy is $3.40 a month. Note the low premiums on this group life insurance. At $2.04 per $1,000 per year it is very close to the actual cost of protection. The extra hazard cost is paid by the federal government after determination on an actuarial basis.

After discharge servicemen are covered without charge for 120 days. During that time they have two options: They may convert to low cost Veterans Group Life Insurance and then five years later convert this into an individual policy; or they may immediately convert to an individual insurance company contract—without physical examination—at regular commercial premiums for whole life or other cash value contracts, but not term insurance. Unfortunately, military personnel have gotten inadequate information about the conversion options available to them at the end of their tour of service. Legislation was introduced into Congress that would remedy this by requiring the Veterans' Administration to provide veterans with the kind of consumer information that would help them obtain the best policy when they convert their government life-insurance policy to an individual policy with a commercial insurance company.

The maximum amount of insurance available—$20,000—is only twice the amount that was available fifty years ago, even though the price level has tripled during that time. In order to provide the same protection, insureds should be able to purchase at least $30,000 worth of protection. Moreover, the protection should be pegged to the price level, which continues to rise.

Social Security Is Sold by Compulsion

Under the Social Security Act all gainfully occupied workers in occupations covered by the act are required to participate in the Social Security program. They have no choice. Their share of the premiums is deducted from their paychecks by the employer. Together with the employer's compulsory payment, the total amounts are transmitted to the U.S. Treasury.

In the early years many occupations were not included under Social Security. These included the clergy, college teachers, lawyers, physicians, and the self-employed. The law was later amended, however, to permit workers in these occupations to elect coverage. A group such as a college faculty had to indicate its wish to participate by an affirmative vote of three-fourths of the members of the group. Once participation was started, all new employees were required to participate.

As a result of this massive and compulsive social insurance program, more people have more insurance protection in the United States today than would have purchased such protection voluntarily.

Group Life Insurance Is Sold by Ballot

Most of the early group life insurance contracts were negotiated by representatives of unions and employers, with the assistance of representatives of an insurance company. Usually the original contract would be implemented only by an affirmative vote of two-thirds or three-fourths of the workers to be covered. Once adopted, the group plan became compulsory for all new employees. It was one of the conditions of employment. The benefits of group life insurance were so obvious that workers unanimously accepted the coverage.

Many group life insurance programs drawn up between employee and employer are noncontributory, constituting a fringe benefit to the employee. In some programs the employer and employee may share the cost on something like a 60–40 basis. Even though the employee is contributing 40 percent on this basis, he or she gets the benefit of the much lower group rate.

There are over 93 million insurance certificates issued under group policies that primarily cover employees, but many also cover employees' dependents. Master policies covering employer-employee groups average $11,645 coverage per employee.[13] At the end of 1974 group life insurance in the United States totaled nearly $824.6 billion. This amount increased by 17 percent during 1974 and has tripled since 1964. Group protection amounted to 42 percent of all life insurance in force in the U.S. at the end of 1974.

Savings Bank Life Insurance Is Bought

Savings Bank Life Insurance (SBLI) is available to any individual who works or lives in Connecticut, Massachusetts, or New York. Students are eligible while attending school in these states. This unique insurance operation began in the state of Massachusetts in 1908. It was conceived as a plan to permit citizens to purchase low-cost life insurance. In Massachusetts, mutual savings banks are permitted to write life insurance on a person up to a maximum of $1,000 for each bank. Since there are now forty-one insuring banks, individual purchasers may buy $41,000 worth of life insurance.*

Under the SBLI plan there are no agents. Insurance is bought over the counter at cost. By eliminating the expensive selling methods used by commercial insurance companies and by reducing management expenses and lapse losses, net premiums per $1,000 of insurance are less than the premiums quoted by most mutual insurance companies.

After many years of effort, and much opposition from mutual and stock life insurance companies, the New York legislature adopted a modified plan of savings bank life insurance. Among the several points of difference between its plan and the Massachusetts plan was the initial limit of $3,000 on the amount of the insurance New Yorkers could purchase. That limit was written into the law as the result of pressure from mutual and stock companies seeking to avoid full competition with the new system. After years of operation the limit was raised to $30,000 plus not more than $40,-000 of decreasing term insurance for mortgage customers of savings banks.

The third state in which savings bank life insurance is available is Connecticut. The system there is similar to those of Massachusetts and New York, but the maximum that can be purchased by an individual is $5,000

* Eligible persons may secure further information by writing to the Savings Bank Life Insurance Council, 120 Tremont Street, Boston, Mass. 02108; Savings Banks Life Insurance Fund, 200 Park Ave., New York, N.Y. 10017; or the Savings Life Insurance Company, 101 Pearl St., Hartford, Conn. 06103.

worth of protection; however, an additional $10,000 may be purchased through a group plan.

When shopping around for life insurance, people who live, work, or study in Connecticut, Massachusetts, or New York will find savings bank life insurance contracts worth investigating. Once bought, this insurance remains in effect even though the insured moves elsewhere in the future.

ROUNDING OUT A LIFE INSURANCE PROGRAM

Who Should Be Insured?

The original and basic function of life insurance is to provide income for the beneficiaries of the insured if the insured should die prematurely. The answer to the question of who should be insured, then, is that the person or persons who provide the income are the ones who should be insured.

In most families the husband is the income earner. As the chief income earner, the husband is the one who should be insured. In some families wives also are gainfully occupied. If the income earned by an employed wife constitutes a substantial portion of the family income and is necessary to maintain the family's scale of living, then insurance on the life of the wife is also needed.

It has been estimated that in most families, the wife performs services that, if paid for at prevailing wage rates, would be worth about $179 a week, or approximately $9,300 a year.[14] Some insurance agents argue that the imputed services of a homemaker are fully as valuable as if she were gainfully occupied outside the home. If that is true, it is argued, then the husband should buy enough life insurance to yield enough income to replace the wife if she should die prematurely. There are two basic flaws in this argument, however. One is that insurance is expensive and very few husbands can afford to carry adequate insurance on their own lives plus enough insurance on their wives to yield a $9,300 income. A second flaw is the assumption that all the work performed by the homemaker would have to be done by hired help if she were to die. Much, if not most, of the work performed by the homemaker would be assumed in most families by the husband/father and the children. In addition, if the wife dies all her maintenance expenses end, so total family expenses are reduced.

The wife and/or mother should carry life insurance if she works outside of the home and is the sole breadwinner for the family. Life insurance should also be considered if a women works outside the home and contributes a sizable amount to the family's income, so that if she were to die, the family would be forced to lower its level of living sharply. As more and more women are working outside of the home and contributing significantly to total family income, the need for life insurance coverage for them has become more important. In 1964 women made up 34 percent of the total work force. Ten years later the figure stood at 39 percent. In 1964, 21 percent of all life insurance policies were held by women and ten years later it was 26 percent.

If a family finds it financially unfeasible to have adequate life insurance coverage on both the chief income earner and the supplemental income earner, it is vital that all insurance dollars that are available be put where they will do the most good in case of death. The trend for American wives to outlive their husbands is increasing each year. Presently there are about 2,500,000 widows heading households; that is, caring for children too young to support themselves. An estimated 300,000 women of all ages become widows each year. Family income after the death of the husband is reduced, on the average, by 44 percent. This figure includes all benefits and the widow's work income. The average of all death benefits left to widows is $12,000, which includes life insurance, Social Security death benefits, and veteran's benefits.[15]

Should the Lives of Children Be Insured?

Parents love their children and are easily persuaded to purchase goods and services for them that will promote their happiness and welfare. Insurance agents have done an effective job of convincing parents that they should insure the lives of their children. Among the reasons given by two insurance writers, it is argued that parents should have insurance on their children to cover last illness and burial expenses and that the payment of insurance premiums will instill habits of thrift. A third argument is that life insurance can provide funds for college education, for marriage expenses, or for starting a business. Finally, it is argued that if insurance is purchased on children, premiums are low and the children can pass the medical examinations.

How valid are these arguments? Parents must decide for themselves, but in the process of reaching a decision here are some points to ponder. There are many hazards in life, but the average family's income is not large enough to permit the purchase of insurance to cover every contingency. Priorities must be established. Probabilities must be considered. The probability of death from ages one through twenty is minimal. Even if death should occur, there would be no loss of income. Last illness and burial expenses could be paid, and most families pay them, out of current income.

The argument that the payment of insurance premiums instills habits of thrift implies that life insurance is a savings device. This is true also for the arguments that life insurance may provide money for a college education, for marriage, or for starting a business. Children can be taught the habit of thrift by putting their savings into savings institutions. Currently they can earn a higher rate of interest if they invest their savings elsewhere than in life insurance. It must be reiterated that the purpose of life insurance is to provide protection against loss of income in case of premature death. The insurance function and the saving function are basically different.

Finally it is argued that if insurance is purchased on the lives of children at early ages the premiums will be lower and they can pass the physical examinations. One answer to these assertions is that nothing is a bargain if the buyer does not need it. Intelligent consumers do not buy goods or services they do not need even though prices may be low. And increasingly insurance companies are insuring lives without medical examination. Almost without exception every unbiased person who is knowledgeable about life insurance recommends that no insurance be purchased on the lives of children.

How Much Insurance Should Be Bought?

How much is a human life worth? For most people life is precious and priceless. In economic terms a human life is worth its capitalized earning power. Is the life of an individual worth $250 million? Ninety-eight insurance companies, which participated in writing a $10 million life insurance policy on the life of an unidentified "tycoon," thought so. Capitalized at 4 percent, the $10 million policy would indicate that the insured's life is worth $250 million. That is the largest insurance policy ever written on the life of one person.

A number of attempts have been made to measure the value of a life. One researcher estimated that the worth of an individual life is probably above $500,000. A figure that is being used both in and outside of government to justify programs that save lives is based on productivity estimates that place the value of a human life at no more than $250,000.[16] Obviously these figures are far beyond the reach of most people as guidelines for determining how much life insurance to buy. A professor of insurance answered the question how much insurance should be bought in this way: "The objective should be to leave dependents in the same relative economic position they would have enjoyed had the insured person survived."[17]

The life insurance industry reports average family life insurance in the amount of $26,500.[18] This is equal to just about two times the average median family income. In addition, it may be assumed that almost every family is covered by Social Security, and millions of workers are also covered by group life insurance programs. One study showed that most families had $36,000 to $40,000 less life insurance than they should have had for proper coverage.[19]

But the question remains: How much insurance should you buy? There are so many individual variations, such as one's age, health, income, assets, number of dependents, and other insurance coverage, that no definite figure can be given for the "proper" amount of insurance. Few families can afford to buy as much protection as they need and still maintain a desired plane of living. The ideal that they should aim for is to buy enough health and accident protection to maintain income during incapacitation; enough life insurance to yield an income sufficient to enable dependents to maintain their present plane of living; an annuity which, supplemented by Social Security, supplemental pension plans, and income from investments, will provide for maintenance of the accustomed plane of living after retirement; property insurance to cover substantial loss by damage to or destruction of automobile, dwelling, furniture, furnishings, and personal effects; and finally, enough liability insurance to provide protection against legal liability for damage to or destruction of the lives and property of other people.

All this insurance coverage will cost money. A lot of money! Insurance premiums may take from 4 to 10 percent of family income. Assuming a cost of $1,000 a year for years, a typical middle-income family will spend $40,000 for security and peace of mind.

For specific information and recommendations on how much insurance to buy you will find Chapter 5 of *Consumers Union Report on Life Insurance* helpful. (This pamphlet is available from Consumers Union, Mt. Vernon, N.Y.) There you will find a plan and worksheets with which to calculate how much life insurance you should buy. Also Chapter 6 in *Life Insurance From the Buyer's Point of View* (available from the American Institute for Economic Research) presents a plan and worksheets.

Should One Buy Insurance from a Company Agent or a Broker?

Most life insurance agents represent a single company. There are also some independent agents who represent more than one company, and there are brokers who represent many companies. The basic difference between an agent and a broker is that an agent represents a company, while a broker represents the buyer. Both types of sales representatives are paid by the insurance company, but brokers are more likely to help a buyer choose the company that will serve the buyer's needs best.

Whether using an agent or broker, one should consider choosing a salesman who is a Chartered Life Underwriter (CLU). He is a trained specialist in life insurance. To obtain the CLU designation a person must have been an agent for at least three years. It calls for intensive study of a broad range of college-level subjects and successful completion of ten rigorous professional examinations administered by the American College of Life Underwriters. Included in the study program are economics, finance, law, accounting, pensions, taxation, business and estate planning. Most candidates spend four to five years of part-time instruction to complete the study program. More than 34,000 agents have received the CLU designation since 1927, when the American College was founded. In a recent year more than 2,300 representatives were granted CLU status.[20]

In his book *Stop Wasting Your Insurance Dollars*, Goodwin presents eighteen standards to use in rating an agent.[21] He also recommends that you do all your business with one agent because a single agent can give you better service. In his book *Life Insurance: A Consumer's Handbook*, Belth suggests that you ask friends, relatives, or business friends whose judgment you respect for the names of the life insurance agents they regard as the outstanding agents in the community. He suggests you ask your attorney, accountant, or banker for similar suggestions; that you ask agents to show you testimonial letters from some of their policyholders; and that you pay particular attention to their comments about service after the sale. He also suggests that you ask the agent about his or her educational background and qualifications.[22]

How to Choose a Company

The big-name company is not necessarily the one offering the best buys in life insurance. Neither is the big advertiser necessarily a better company than a nonadvertiser. Among the hundreds of insurance companies there are scores of unknowns whose contracts are good buys. These may be discovered by searching one or more of the several good insurance company rating publications.

Just because a company is old does not prove that it is the best. On the other hand, the buyer should be cautious in dealing with a new company. There is no federal regulation of insurance companies, and the effectiveness of state regulatory laws varies.

When choosing a company, a broker can be helpful. In addition to giving advice, brokers can provide prospective buyers with printed information. This might include comparative financial reports and statistics. With the aid of a broker and published information, you should compare the aviation clauses and the war clauses. If special hazards exist, extra premiums may be charged or the coverage may be excluded. It is important to ascertain which mortality table a company uses and what interest rate it is guaranteeing on its policy reserve. Also compare dividend schedules and net premiums over a ten-year or twenty-year period.

Life Insurance From the Buyer's Point of View contains a table (page 21) that lists sixty-eight policies of fifty-five companies in order of their twenty-year net cost per $1,000 according to two types of contracts, whole life and five-year renewable term. It shows a range from $58.06 to $169.54 for continuous premium policies purchased at age thirty-five. These comparisons are followed by some very helpful suggestions for the insurance buyer.

Using the interest-adjusted cost index, the insurance commissioner of Pennsylvania published for statewide distribution statistics on thirty-five companies doing business in the state. The annual premium for a $10,000 ordinary participating life policy for a male at age twenty ranged from a low of $115 to a high of $166. The cash value at the end of twenty years ranged from a low of $1,940 to a high of $2,750. But neither of these measures is indicative of the real net cost of the insurance. The key item that the commissioner included was the interest-adjusted cost index, which is now a widely accepted measure of net cost of life insurance. The interest-adjusted cost index ranged from a low of $2.11 per $1,000 of insurance to a high of $4.72.[23] These differences could amount to hundreds of dollars on large purchases over a period of years.

Some insurance agents emphasize that such simple comparisons of an essentially complex product are misleading and that comparative cost indexes are based on arbitrary assumptions not applicable to all cases. Until some better measure is adopted, however, the buyer of life insurance should find out what the interest-adjusted cost index is for the policies he or she is considering.

Increasing numbers of insurance companies offer quantity discounts. On contracts in the amount of $5,000 or more the discount may be as much as $2 per $1,000 of coverage. Some companies also offer a discount of approximately 4 percent on premiums prepaid five years in advance. For large buyers this feature may offer tax advantages.

In case of doubt, a prospective buyer may always consult the insurance commissioner in his home state. This is especially recommended in case of companies doing business by mail.*

A SUMMARY OF PROCEDURE

In planning an insurance program a young husband and wife should work together. It is important—one might even say imperative—that the wife, as well as the husband, understand the purposes of insurance and the protection being purchased by the premiums they agree to pay. When both have developed some knowledge about insurance, they should then seek the assistance of a competent agent or broker in working out the details of their plan. They will find impartial advisers substantially agreed on the following broad recommendations.

1. An insurance program must be based on the foundation of Social Security. If the insured is included in a group life insurance program, that fact must be taken into account. If the insured has served in the military forces of the United States, he should keep the full amount of government insurance for which he is eligible. It may well be that a combination of Social Security, group life insurance, and government insurance will provide an adequate program. If the insured lives in Connecticut, Massachusetts, or New York, it is recommended that he take advantage of the opportunity to purchase low-cost savings bank life insurance. If eligible for Teachers Insurance and Annuity Association insurance he or she should purchase from that organization. Veterans who are members of the American Legion can buy low-cost group insurance. Increasing numbers of organizations are making group life insurance available to their members.

2. Insurance to supplement Social Security, group life, and government insurance might well be decreasing term and yearly renewable term or term to age sixty-five. Saving for the education of the children and for retirement should be a part of a separate investment program.†

3. All insurance should be on the life of the income-earner. There

---

* For information on mail-order companies see Federal Trade Commission, *Pitfalls to Watch for in Mail Order Insurance Policies*, Consumer Bulletin No. 1 (Washington, D.C.: U.S. Government Printing Office, 1969), 5 pages.

† See Chapter 20.

should not be any insurance on the children. Neither should there be insurance on the life of the wife unless she is a permanent and substantial income-earner.

4.   Many insurance buyers are fascinated with the prospect of double indemnity. This means that if they die in the prescribed manner, the beneficiary will collect twice the face value of the contract. The extra premium for double indemnity is only about $1 per $1,000 of coverage. The double indemnity feature might properly be described as a gimmick. It appeals to the gambling instinct. The probability that the insured will die an accidental death is so remote that the premium can be as low as it is. Accidental deaths are what insurance people call "clean deaths." By that they mean there are no long illness expenses. If the insured could purchase double indemnity if death were caused by such a disease as cancer, the double indemnity clause feature would be helpful. Closely related to the double indemnity clause is "trip insurance." Travelers spend many dollars needlessly for coverage they do not need if they have a well-planned adequate insurance program. Trip insurance is expensive and the probability of the event insured against occurring is remote.

5.   The waiver of premium clause is recommended. For approximately $1 per $1,000 of coverage the insured may add an amendment to the contract under which the insurer promises to continue the contract in force if the insured should become totally and permanently disabled. Such disability might occur as a result of an accident or illness. If the insured could not pay the premiums, the entire program would lapse. The waiver of premium clause will keep it in effect.

6.   If there are any dividends, it is generally recommended that they be applied toward the payment of premiums. The reason for this is that a well-planned insurance program should be adequate. The family budget has allotted the necessary funds for the payment of premiums. Any reduction in the net premium will release money for other family uses. An alternate use of dividends would be to use them to purchase more insurance. In a period of steadily rising price levels this use of dividends would provide some hedge against the depreciating purchasing power of the dollar.

7.   The final step in planning an insurance program is to work out with the beneficiary and with the agent or broker the method of settlement that will assure beneficiaries the protection the insured is seeking to provide. When the plan is completed and put into effect, a family may face the uncertain future with greater confidence and peace of mind.

BUYING INSURANCE TO COVER ACCIDENTS AND ILLNESS

The Cost of Health Care

In the 1960s the right of each citizen to adequate health care was accepted as a national policy goal. In the early 1970s the challenge was to make that right a reality. During the later 1970s the question arose whether it is feasible and economically justifiable for the federal government to assume total responsibility for the fulfillment of the right to adequate health care. The tremendous increases in the costs of health care have raised serious questions as to just how the costs of such care should be borne in the future.

In 1955 Americans spent $17.3 billion on health care; by 1965 the figure had risen to $38.9 billion; and ten years later it was $118.5 billion, or about 8.3 percent of gross national product. Ten years ago it was about 6 percent of the GNP. Americans are now spending about $550 per person per year for health care. In 1965 an appendectomy cost an average of $600; by 1975 it was up to $1,180; a tonsillectomy cost $200 in 1965, and $500 in 1975; and the delivery of a baby cost $425 in 1965, and $1,150 in 1975.[24] By 1975 the average daily cost of hospital care was slightly over $100, and an average hospital stay cost almost $1,000. This was an increase of 102 percent over the 1967 rate for a semiprivate room. During the same period, on the average, physicians' fees increased 51 percent; dentists' fees 47 percent; and eye care costs 39 percent.

One of the problems in the health field is that there are currently between 60,000 to 100,000 surplus hospital beds, and their average maintenance cost is conservatively estimated at about $55 per day. Other costs that are forcing up doctors' fees and other medical charges are the insurance premiums that doctors and hospitals have to pay to protect themselves against malpractice law suits and the costs of additional X-rays and tests that doctors now require in order to protect themselves against malpractice suits. The insurance companies' costs in successfully defending doctors and getting malpractice suits dismissed average more than $6,000 per case. The average judgment in the cases tried to a verdict is about $45,000, but awards and settlements of more than $100,000 account for half of the total claim payments.[25] In addition, the costs incurred to treat persons afflicted with alcoholism, tobacco related illnesses, or drug related sicknesses are constantly increasing.

As medical care costs have gone up, Medicare has covered a smaller and smaller percentage of the total costs of health care. The problem of meeting higher and higher health care costs has become a major economic problem in the nation.

How To Pay For Health Care

There are five basic types of health care coverage available from insurance companies:

1. *Disability income insurance* is the oldest form. It is written by several hundred companies and pays cash for loss of income. The recipient may use the money for any purpose. Benefits range from one-half to one-third of usual income and continue from thirteen to fifty-two weeks for

short term contracts, and for life on the more expensive long-term contracts.

2. *Hospital expense insurance* covers room, food, nursing, and minor medical supplies. Additional expense insurance covers fees for laboratory, X-rays, operating room, anaesthesia, and drugs. Deductibles are typically $50 or $100.
3. *Surgical expense insurance* helps to pay the fee of a surgeon.
4. *Regular medical expense insurance* covers physician calls in the hospital or office. Basic protection covers hospital, surgical, and medical expenses.
5. *Major medical expense insurance* covers catastrophic accidents or illnesses in amounts ranging from $5,000 to $250,000. A typical deductible would be $250 and 20 percent of the first $2,000.

These coverages, and the prices for them, are affected by one's age, sex, physical condition, medical history, occupation, personal habits, moral hazards, and place of residence. Administrative expenses for group policies are considerably less than for individual contracts. As a result, most of the 186 million insured are participants in group plans in which employers pay all or part of the premium. No physical examination is required for group coverage, and the contracts cannot be canceled. Colleges, fraternal societies, consumer cooperatives, and professional associations also make group plans available for their staff and members. Perhaps the best-known group plans are Blue Cross (BC) and Blue Shield (BS), which write almost as much health care coverage as all the 1,500 commercial companies in the field combined. But BC and BS are rated well in terms of returning a high percent of premium dollars in benefits to their policy holders. Premiums usually run over 90 percent of medical costs. One insurance company studied returned only 30 percent of medical costs.[26]

Unlike life insurance, medical care insurance should cover every member of the family. In planning a medical insurance program a family must consider all possible sources of income in case of accident or illness. The most important source of income during illness or disability is Social Security payments. The amount of benefits one is eligible for under Social Security if totally disabled depends on a number of variables, including age, amount of previous earnings on which Social Security taxes were paid, and number of dependents. For example, if a young man became disabled at age twenty-nine or younger and had average yearly earnings of $8,400 over two years, his Social Security disability benefit would be $410.70 a month. If this young man had a wife and two children, family benefits would be $718.70 a month. A disability clause in whole life insurance contracts would pay $10 per month per $1,000 of insurance in case of total and permanent disability. A separate disability policy would cost approximately $35 per year per $100 of monthly benefits. A group health insurance plan at one's place of employment could cover hospitalization charges for a period of thirty days for short-term illness. In addition, many employers have sick-leave plans. Some unions also have group medical care plans. Forty-seven states have Workmen's Compensation Laws under which compensation for hospitalization arising out of accident or illness is fully covered. Veterans of military service may use the services of federal government military hospitals without charge. Most major medical expense insurance is sold under a group contract. Such plans provide protection against catastrophic expenses up to $250,000.

The Medicare provisions of the Social Security law provide for hospitalization and specified services performed by physicians and surgeons. These are described in Chapter 18.

After analyzing the family needs for medical care insurance, one may find that individual accident and health insurance policies will be needed to fill the gaps. Among the several hundred insurance companies selling accident and health insurance contracts, benefits are usually limited to 50 percent or 75 percent of earnings, with a ceiling of $500 or $1,000 a month. There is no standard contract. Definitions of total disability range from inability to do anything to inability to do one's regular job. The length of time before benefits are paid (called the "waiting period") ranges from fourteen days to three months. The longer the waiting period, the lower the premium. Most contracts exclude certain types of illness, and some are very restrictive. Some contracts may be canceled by the company at any time, whereas others may not be canceled. Premiums for cancelable policies are usually about one-third less than for noncancelable policies.

It is not wise to buy an accident and health insurance contract from the first insurance agent who calls. A buyer should shop around. Premiums for the same coverage may vary by as much as 30 percent. It is important to choose a reputable agent or broker. It is equally important to choose a reputable company. Most families can pay for short-term medical expenses out of income. It is the long-term medical care for which insurance is needed. Individual contracts should be noncancelable, and the waiting periods should be as long as a family can afford. Proposed contracts should be read carefully, especially the fine print that lists excluded illnesses.

Dental Insurance

By the end of 1975 more than 25 million Americans were covered by some form of dental insurance, compared to two million in 1965. The American Dental Association predicts dental insurance will cover 60 million persons by 1980.[27] Most of the beneficiaries are covered under union contracts. Many of the plans are paid for entirely by the employer at a cost of about $11 per month for each employee. In other plans the employee pays part of the premium. There is no standard type of dental insurance policy. Some reimburse the person on a fixed schedule based on the dental work done; some pay all costs except for a deductible; and others pay a fixed percent up to a maximum amount per year, with the insured paying the balance.

In commenting on dental insurance an oral surgeon stated, "Only half the population visits a dentist even once a year, and only one of four persons ever visits a dentist for routine care. Anything that improves the attention people give their teeth is bound to be beneficial for the public generally."[28]

Health Maintenance Organizations

For many people a Health Maintenance Organization (HMO) could be an attractive and less expensive alternative to the traditional fee-for-service health care and traditional kinds of health care insurance programs.* A HMO is basically the grouping of a number of health services under one roof for its enrolled members. Instead of charging a fee for each service, the HMO collects a lump sum in advance from subscribers (or their employers). The annual fee for a family is roughly between $600 and $840. That sum pays for comprehensive health care by the HMO's physicians. There are about 200 HMOs in the United States, with more than 7 million persons enrolled. The federal government has encouraged them by granting $325 million to aid formation of hundreds of additional HMOs by 1980. HMOs are a significant alternative to the traditional method of providing health care services.

BUYING PROTECTION AGAINST PROPERTY LOSS AND PUBLIC LIABILITY

Homeowners Insurance

Every 35 seconds fire breaks out in some American home or apartment. Every 45 minutes a fire causes the death of a person in the United States. Fire losses in the United States totaled more than $3.56 billion in 1975.[29]

The typical young couple contracting to purchase a house for the first time is usually blissfully unaware of all the hazards they may be facing and liabilities they could incur. There are literally scores of things that might happen, all the way from fire loss to loss or damage caused by windstorms. The more frequently occurring causes of loss or liability have been grouped together in various forms of insurance contracts, written by mutual and stock insurance companies. For specified premiums, property owners may purchase needed protection.

The homeowners policy is available in five forms: Basic, Broad, Comprehensive, Special, and Contents Broad Form. Table 19-1 shows the perils against which properties are insured under three of these forms. If you live in an apartment or rent the house you occupy, there is a special homeowners policy for you. It is the Contents Broad Form, or Tenants Form (HO-4). It insures your household contents and personal belongings against all the

---

* See *Consumer Report*, Oct. 1974, pp. 756–762, for a detailed discussion of HMOs.

perils included in the Broad Form (HO-2), all eighteen of which are shown in Table 19-1. It also provides coverage for additional living expenses and certain liability coverages.

Many homeowners want the greatest possible protection for their houses, but they do not want to pay for the same extensive coverage on their personal property. Their needs are satisfied by purchasing a Special Form (HO-3), which provides the same coverage for their dwelling and private structures as does the Comprehensive Form (HO-5) while covering their personal property for the same perils as provided in the Contents Broad Form (HO-4).

Comprehensive personal liability is included in all five forms. This coverage protects the insured and all members of the family against liability claims by others resulting from accidents other than automobile accidents that occur on or away from the insured premises. Also included are medical payments up to $500 for persons suffering accidental injury on the insured's premises, or elsewhere if caused by the insured, members of the family, or pets. Guests on the insured's premises are also covered.

TABLE 19-1. Perils Against Which Properties Are Insured Under Homeowners Policy

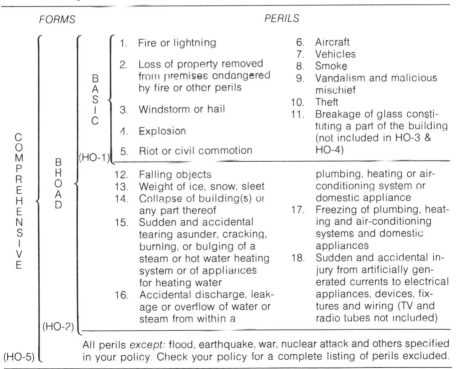

All perils *except:* flood, earthquake, war, nuclear attack and others specified
(HO-5)   in your policy. Check your policy for a complete listing of perils excluded.

Source: A Family Guide to Property & Liability Insurance (9th ed.; New York: Insurance Information Institute, 1976), p. 16.

The liability coverage also includes payments for damage to the property of other people up to a maximum of $250 for any one accident.

In addition, a homeowners insurance policy has been developed for condominium owners (HO-6). This policy covers the eighteen perils listed in Table 19-1 but has slightly different coverages for personal property and additional living expenses. It has the same coverages for comprehensive personal liability, personal property away from premises, damage to property of others, and medical payments.

It is important to know that under the homeowners policy, in order to receive full payment for any partial loss or damage to the house or other structure, the homeowner must insure the house for at least 80 percent of its replacement value, which in the case of a $30,000 house would be $24,000. With 80 percent coverage, if there were a $12,000 fire the policy would pay $12,000. If the house were covered for only 50 percent of its replacement value, or $12,000, and the fire loss were $12,000, only 12/24 or 50 percent of the loss, or $6,000, would be paid by the company, or the company would pay the actual replacement cost minus depreciation, whichever is higher. If 80 percent coverage were carried and the loss—the ratio of the amount of insurance in force ($12,000) to the amount needed to meet the replacement cost provision (80 percent of $30,000 or $24,000)—were $24,000, $24,000 would be paid. Naturally, if the loss were more than $24,000 the payment would be for only $24,000, unless the coverage were for a higher amount. With the rapid rise in the value of houses it is very important that you make sure that as the value of the house goes up, the amount of insurance coverage is increased, so that the house will always be covered for a minimum of 80 percent of its current market value. By 1976 the replacement costs of an average house had gone up 90 percent over the 1967 costs.

In many cases one can plug this inflationary gap by adding an "Inflation Guard Endorsement" to a homeowners policy. This now provides, in most states, for an automatic 8 percent annual increase in policy amounts for the dwelling, personal property, and additional living expenses.

A property insurance contract is a formidable document. There are several hundred lines of legal language in small print. It is important to know, for example, what perils are not included. In lines 11 through 24 of the standard form, ten exclusions are listed. If the insured pays additional premiums he may purchase coverage for some of the excluded perils. Most of the perils are possibilities rather than probabilities. The typical small-income homeowner cannot afford to buy protection against every possibility. The basic homeowners contract provides the necessary protection. The Insurance Service Offices, an affiliation of approximately 500 insurance companies, began marketing a simplified language homeowners policy in six states in 1976.

The calculation of property insurance premiums is so complicated that no attempt can be made to explain the process in this short discussion. Premiums vary according to the type of house, the materials of which it is made, the proximity of fire fighters and water, and many other variables.

There are more than 2,800 companies in the U.S. that sell property and liability insurance, of which 900 do most of the business. *Best's Insurance Guide With Key Ratings* of companies can be helpful in choosing a company and may be available in your local library.* Property insurance does not cost as much as you might suppose. A typical charge for Basic Form coverage of eleven perils, insured to value, would be $60 a year for a $30,000 frame house. The Broad Form, covering eighteen perils, would cost $74, and the comprehensive form, which covers all perils except flood, earthquake, war, nuclear attack, and others specified in the policy, would be $129. All these policies include a $100 deductible clause. The best advice to prospective buyers of property insurance is to search for and find an agent or broker who can be trusted. Before contacting an agent it would be advisable to read *A Family Guide to Property & Liability Insurance*, available free from Insurance Information Institute, 110 William Street, New York, N.Y. 10038.

Automobile Insurance

In the last fifty years more than 1,923,000 persons died in some 634 million automobile accidents in the United States, with the overall cost estimated at a staggering $422 billion. Sharp increases in the costs of automobile repairs and medical and hospital care pushed the economic loss total to a new peak of $36.1 billion dollars in 1975.[30] Automobile traffic on the highways kills and maims at an appalling rate. Every 7 seconds someone is injured in an automobile accident. Every 11 minutes someone dies in a traffic accident.

The costs of insurance claim settlements and court awards resulting from auto accidents have risen steadily in recent years. From 1965 through 1974 the average paid bodily-injury claim rose about 105.7 percent—from $1,202 to $2,472; the average paid property damage liability claim increased approximately 90 percent—from $203 to $397.[31] One car is stolen every 32 seconds. Stolen automobiles have topped the million mark per year, at an estimated total cost to the American consumer of about $2 billion.[32]

Owners and drivers of automobiles are legally liable for loss of life and damage caused in accidents in which they are involved. The responsibility is so great that sensible persons would not dare venture onto the highways without insurance protection. Practically every state either requires that automobile insurance be carried or that drivers be able to show financial responsibility, meaning that if you are in an accident and do not have insurance you must be able to post bond. The requirements of those states that have financial responsibility laws are best complied with by the purchase of insurance.

Bodily Injury Liability and Property Damage Liability   Under this type of automobile insurance, the insurer agrees to pay on behalf of the insured all money that the insured becomes obligated to pay because of a bodily

* It can also be ordered from A. M. Best Company, Inc., Oldwick, N.J. 08858.

injury, sickness, or disease, including a resulting death, sustained by any person in a car accident. In addition, the insurer agrees to pay all sums for which the insured becomes legally liable because of injury to or destruction of property. The amounts that insurance companies agree to pay are specified in the contract. These amounts are usually indicated by three numbers, such as 10/20/5. These figures mean that the insurer will pay a maximum of $10,000 for bodily injury to one person, a maximum of $20,000 to more than one person, and a maximum of $5,000 for property damage in one accident. Coverage as high as 300/500/10 is common. If you wish, you can purchase "liability umbrella" coverage of $1 million, which would cost $50 or $60. The minimum coverage recommended by Consumers Union is 25/20/10. If a 10/20/5 liability coverage costs $100, a coverage of 25/50/10 would cost approximately $130. The premium for 250/500/50 would be approximately $168.

Premiums vary according to the area in which the car is driven, the purpose for which it is used, the age of the driver, marital status, and whether a young driver has taken a driver's training course. In addition, some companies have lower rates for persons who do not drink alcoholic beverages. One insurance company gives a 30 percent price discount on personal injury protection (in states that have no-fault benefits), family compensation, and medical payment coverage if air bags are installed in the car. In New York City the 25/50/10, $3,000 medical payments, $50-deductible comprehensive, and $100-deductible collision cost coverage for an automobile used only for pleasure driving, without any male operators under age twenty-five, is $435. The same coverage costs $259 in Hempstead, which is just outside the city, and only $116 in Keota, Iowa, a town of 700 people. Premiums in other cities range from $211 in Los Angeles to $149 in Dayton, Ohio.[33]

Medical Payments   This coverage pays medical and hospital expenses if the insured is injured in an automobile accident. If the insured dies, funeral expenses are covered. Coverage applies whether the insured is driving his or her own car, a rented car, or a borrowed car. It also applies if the insured is a passenger or walking. Finally, it protects all members of the insured's family and passengers who are guests in the car. Consumers Union recommends a minimum of $500, which would cost approximately $7 a year. For about $9 the coverage could be increased to $1,000, and to $10,000 for $19.

Collision Insurance   Under collision insurance losses incurred if the insured automobile is damaged in a collision or upset are paid. This coverage is expensive and the probability of the event insured against occurring is low. Moreover, if the collision involves another car, the insurance on that automobile may cover the damage. For these reasons the automobile owner should consider carefully the cost of collision insurance as compared with the cost of assuming the risk himself. If it is a new automobile, most owners would be wise to have collision insurance. If the car is purchased on credit, the lender normally requires that it be covered by collision insurance. Many people drop collision coverage when a car gets to be six or eight years old and is only worth a few hundred dollars.

The principle of deductible insurance is used in writing collision insurance. If the insured agrees to pay the first $100 or $250 of damage, the premium declines sharply. This is because so many accidents are minor and involve damages of less than those amounts. If a $100 deductible coverage costs $100, a $150 deductible would cost about $80, and a $250 deductible will cost about $60.[34]

Comprehensive and Personal Effects This coverage reimburses the insured person for losses incurred if the automobile is stolen, damaged, or destroyed by fire, hail, hurricane, flood, or other listed perils. Also included are losses of wearing apparel and other personal effects. The premiums are relatively low. If full comprehensive costs $28 a year, $50 deductible will cost $13, and $100 deductible will cost $10.

Towing and Labor Costs Under this coverage the insurer agrees to pay for towing and labor costs if the insured automobile is disabled, and if the labor is performed at the place where the car broke down. The probability of this event occurring is minimal. That is why the premium is only $3.00 a year. If the insured belongs to an automobile club, he or she already has such coverage.

Uninsured Motorists Insurance against uninsured motorists is included in many contracts. The insurer agrees to pay the insured if he is injured by an uninsured or hit-and-run driver. If the insured dies, the insurer will pay the amount specified in the contract. For $25,000 protection for one person, and $50,000 maximum for one accident, the premium is about $15.

The foregoing summaries of types of automobile insurance are excerpts from a typical family automobile policy. The whole contract, in booklet form, covers sixteen pages. The additional exclusions and qualifications are too numerous to include here, but prospective buyers should study them carefully.

Buying Automobile Insurance: Individual Versus Mass-Marketing

Although group accident, health, and life insurance can be purchased under group plans at a lower cost than under individual contracts, property and casualty insurance companies have been slow in developing group plans. Some group plans have been developed for auto insurance that have rates that are about 15 percent below individual rates. But rates still differ among members of the group, according to their accident records, age, marital status, and personal habits. Buyers should still compare group plans before buying, however, because some group policies offer little or no savings from the insurance company's regular price, while others give substantial reductions.

Prospective buyers can save 20 to 30 percent or more on identical coverage if they shop around. In Pennsylvania, the State Insurance Department published a booklet giving the rates of the major automobile insurance companies in the state. In Pittsburgh the lowest rate charged for the compulsory base insurance program was $76.80, and the highest rate for identical coverage was $177, which is 130 percent higher.[35] In addition to companies represented by agents or brokers, one may secure bids from mail-order firms such as United Services Automobile Association, but when buying automobile insurance through the mail the buyer should be sure to check the financial strength and record of the company.

Fault or No-fault Insurance?

Automobile owners and operators are faced with a dilemma. They must use their cars and they are legally liable for injury to other persons and for property damage, yet insurance premiums rise faster than the price level index, and protection is harder to get and to keep. Many applicants for insurance are rejected, and many policies are canceled. Scores of insurance companies have failed, leaving millions of dollars of unpaid claims. The fault system of compensation leaves many claimants unpaid, and all too frequently overpays on minor claims to avoid costly litigation. Public dissatisfaction over automobile insurance has risen to such a high level that almost half the state governments have instituted reforms and the federal government has investigated the problem and is now considering a variety of remedial measures, including a national no-fault law.

The basic features of no-fault insurance are that victims are paid for medical expenses and income losses from their own insurance company, regardless of who is at fault, and that they lose the right to sue for "pain and suffering" unless they have serious injuries or relatively high expenses. No-fault laws cover only personal injury, leaving property damage to the traditional collision and liability insurance. The provisions vary from state to state. For example, one cannot sue for "pain and suffering" under the no-fault law unless the medical expenses reach a specific threshold, which is $500 in New York, $400 in Connecticut, and $200 (excluding hospital expenses) in New Jersey. Medical bills and income losses are paid immediately. Thus payments tend to be made more on the basis of need and less on the basis of courtroom skills.*

No-fault insurance laws have been in effect too short a time to be able to make an adequate evaluation of them, but some favorable and unfavor-

---

* For an in-depth analysis of no-fault automobile insurance see the basic book on the subject, Robert E. Keeton and Jeffrey O'Connell, *After Cars Crash: The Need for Legal and Insurance Reform* (Homewood, Ill.: Dow Jones-Irwin, 1967), and also Jeffrey O'Connell, *The Injury Industry* (Urbana: University of Illinois Press, 1971).

able aspects have appeared. A reduction in premium rates has been a strong argument for no-fault laws, and rate reductions averaging 15 percent were coupled with no-fault laws in sixteen states. The New York no-fault law saved policy-holders $100 million in its first full year of operation. Faster and more efficient compensation of accident victims is being made, and there has been a reduction in the number of lengthy, expensive lawsuits resulting from auto accidents.

The promise of saving money with lower premiums is disappearing as medical costs and lose of earnings covered increase. Some property and liability insurance companies have run into serious financial trouble since no-fault has gone into effect. One of the larger auto insurers, Government Employees Insurance Company, experienced underwriting losses of $75 million in one year and blamed no-fault laws for part of the loss. Others blamed the management of the company for the loss. Another problem appears to be the low thresholds. Insured parties have padded costs up to the threshold and used the insurance money to hire a lawyer and sue for more.

There is no question that no-fault laws are here to stay and will eventually be in effect in all states, either with or without federal action. The benefits accruing from faster and more equitable compensation for accident victims are too great to be forestalled for long, and where effective no-fault laws have been passed there is little pressure, if any, to repeal these laws.

QUESTIONS FOR REVIEW

1. Why is insurance a complicated business?
2. What is meant by the term "cash surrender value"?
3. Why do you think so many insurance policies lapse or are surrendered?
4. Why is it possible to borrow on one's life insurance contract?
5. What is the purpose of dividends in the insurance business?
6. What are the various options available to the beneficiary of a life insurance policy?
7. Why does life insurance seem to have to be sold instead of bought?
8. Why do you think Savings Bank Life Insurance is available in only three states?
9. What are the pros and cons of a family insuring both husband and wife? Their children?
10. Why does health care cost so much?
11. What kinds of health insurance protection are available?
12. What is meant by HMO?
13. What are the three basic homeowners policies and how are they different?

14. If a person can only afford one form of auto insurance, should he or she purchase liability, comprehensive, or collision insurance? Why?

15. Explain no-fault insurance.

PROJECTS

1. Write a letter to your state insurance commissioner and ask why the state does not require the use of more current mortality tables.

2. Prepare a class debate on cash-value life insurance versus "term insurance and invest the difference."

3. Discuss with your family the various options available to the beneficiary of a life insurance policy and write a brief paper on the choice your family made and why.

4. Ask a life insurance agent and an automobile insurance agent how many people come to them to buy insurance and how many people they contact to sell insurance.

5. Draw up a complete insurance program for a person from twenty-two to sixty-five, who marries, has two children, and owns a house and automobile.

6. Develop a chart showing how a person should determine how much life insurance should be purchased.

7. Read in detail one of the references cited in this chapter and write a report on it.

8. Check out your community library to see how adequately it is stocked with information on insurance.

REFERENCES

1. *Life Insurance Fact Book, 1975*, published annually (New York: Institute of Life Insurance), passim.
2. *Ibid.*, p. 58.
3. *Best's Review*, Sept. 1975, p. 35.
4. *Ibid.*, p. 10.
5. *Life Insurance Fact Book, 1975*, p. 64.
6. Robert I. Mehr and Emerson Cammack, *Principles of Insurance,* rev. ed. (Homewood, Ill.: Richard D. Irwin, 1964), p. 164.
7. Davis W. Gregg, *Life and Health Insurance Handbook,* 2nd ed. (Homewood, Ill.: Richard D. Irwin, 1964), p. 164.
8. Goodwin, p. 141.
9. *Life Insurance Fact Book, 1970,* p. 64, and *1975,* p. 56.
10. *Life Insurance Fact Book, 1975,* p. 48.
11. *Ibid.*, p. 47.
12. *Ibid.*, p. 7.
13. *Ibid.*, p. 31.
14. Florence Turnbull Hall, "The Case of the Late Mrs. Smith, Homemaker: Preparing Testimony for the Court," *Journal of Home Economics* 67 (Nov. 1975): 31.

15. *St. Petersburg Times*, 26 May 1974, p. 11D.
16. *Business Week*, 30 June 1975, p. 116.
17. *U.S. News & World Report*, 28 April 1975, p. 49.
18. *Life Insurance Fact Book, 1975*, p. 9.
19. E. Scott Maynes and Loren V. Geistfeld, "The Life Insurance Deficit of American Families: A Pilot Study," *Journal of Consumer Affairs* 8 (1974): 58.
20. *St. Petersburg Times*, 3 Aug. 1975, p. 21A.
21. Goodwin, pp. 13–15.
22. Joseph M. Belth, *Life Insurance: A Consumer's Handbook* (Bloomington: University of Indiana Press, 1973), p. 113.
23. Denenberg, pp. 62–63.
24. *U.S. News & World Report*, 16 June 1975, pp. 52–55.
25. *St. Petersburg Times*, 27 Dec. 1975, p. 11A.
26. Denenberg, p. 102.
27. *Business Week*, 4 Aug. 1975, p. 28.
28. *U.S. News & World Report*, 8 Sept. 1975, p. 62.
29. *Insurance Facts 1976*, published annually (New York: Insurance Information Institute), p. 33.
30. *Ibid.*, p. 50.
31. *Ibid.*
32. *Journal of American Insurance*, Fall 1975, p. 11.
33. *Money Guide to Automobiles* (Chicago: Time, 1975), p. 11.
34. *The Buying Guide Issue, Consumer Reports*, 1976, p. 381.
35. *A Shopper's Guide to No-Fault Insurance Rates*, Western Pennsylvania ed. (Harrisburg, Pa.: Pennsylvania Insurance Department, Nov. 1975).

CHAPTER 20

BUYING INVESTMENTS: SOME GUIDELINES FOR SMALL INVESTORS

THRIFT OR SPENDTHRIFT?

Most People Are Thrifty

Contemporary American youth is a spendthrift lot, right? Not so, was the response of a national financial services organization based on a survey it made. A key finding showed that 63 percent of the twenty-one- to twenty-five-year-olds list their own home, savings and investments, and life insurance as the three most important items on their financial agenda.[1]

There are numerous difficulties in saving and making investment decisions in a pulsating economy in which the value of the dollar changes markedly in a relatively short period of time and the values of various forms of saving rise and fall sharply. The dollar that bought a dollar's worth of goods in 1967 bought only 60 cents worth of goods in 1976. In recent years the rate of interest paid on some forms of savings programs almost doubled and then dropped by a third. Stock prices dropped as much as 40 percent and then rose by two-thirds. A good investment in 1977 may not be so good in 1980. Great care must be taken in developing a sound investment program, and it must be reevaluated periodically.

Saving is a conscious rational decision to postpone consumption of a portion of one's income. The saver is a thrifty person; spendthrifts spend all their income. They may even spend more than their income, by borrowing or buying on credit. In the United States, saving is a virtue. It has been ever since Benjamin Franklin wrote in Poor Richard's Almanac that "a penny saved is a penny earned." When all those pennies are added together, it is found that during the past decade consumers saved from 5.6 to 8.3 percent of their disposable personal income each year, or $35 to $90 billion dollars.

Family by family, the amount of saving is related closely to the size of family income. A small minority of families have such large incomes that in spite of their lavish living they cannot spend more than half. At the other extreme is a much larger number of families whose incomes are so small that they cannot save any portion of them. In between are millions of families who can and do save.

Why Do Individuals Save?

Regardless of income, consumers seem to have an instinctive urge to save. For many families living on the margin, life is a series of emergencies, such as accidents, illness, death, and unemployment. In popular parlance these emergencies have been called "rainy days," and many people save as much as they can in anticipation of them.

Prudent families anticipate large recurring expenses, such as insurance premiums and taxes. Month by month, money is budgeted for such expenditures and saved in anticipation. Prudent families also anticipate large nonrecurring expenditures. These include the purchase of furniture, appliances, and clothing. Many times they include improvements to the house in which the family lives.

The annual vacation is a highlight in the expenditure patterns of many families. In anticipation, trip money is saved month by month. Christmas is an occasion for an exchange of gifts, the purchase of which involves significant sums of money in small-income families. Many people save month by month from one Christmas season to another. The family car must be maintained and periodically replaced. Prudent families anticipate such expenditures by saving regularly. Many people save in advance for weddings, for a trip to Europe, or for a college education.

Increasingly, older persons are finding it important to save and invest for the purpose of supplementing their Social Security and company pension payments when they retire. Teenagers, too, are substantial savers. The average amount saved by one group of teenagers was 70 percent of weekly income. The three primary reasons for saving were to finance a college education, to purchase clothing, and to purchase a car.

Some people save for the added income their savings will earn. The magic of compound interest is impressive. At an interest rate of $6\frac{1}{2}$ percent compounded annually one's savings will double in eleven years and one month. If savings are invested in real estate or common stock, the capital value may increase in a growing economy.

How Do Individuals Save?

A few people hoard. Having saved some of their income, they hide it. Some hoarders are misers, who live miserably in order to hoard their savings. The Great Depression in the 1930s made hoarders out of many savers. Having lost their faith in all forms of savings institutions and instruments, many well-educated people hoarded cash in safety deposit boxes in banks. In a depression, as the price level declines, the purchasing power of the dollar increases and hoarders gain.

During the severe recession of the 1970s, people's confidence in banking institutions was not shaken but their concern about future economic conditions was such that they saved more money. The percent of savings of total disposable personal income rose from 5.6 percent in 1969 to 8.3 percent by 1975. These savings were placed primarily in banks, savings and loan associations, and government bonds.

People save their money in many different ways. In 1975 the total financial assets held by individuals in the United States, which amounted to $2.3 trillion, were divided among various forms of saving as follows: savings accounts – 30 percent; stocks – 26 percent; pension reserves – 14 percent; checking accounts and cash – 8 percent; life insurance reserves – 7 percent; U.S. government securities – 5 percent; miscellaneous assets – 5 percent; and corporate and tax-exempt bonds – 5 percent.[2]

Millions of people put their savings into Christmas Club programs in banks. Christmas clubs short-term savings for the Christmas season. Many Christmas Club savers are unaware that they could earn interest on these savings accounts. In Pittsburgh, 200,000 savers gave the four largest banks a $750,000 Christmas present by putting $30 million in Christmas Club accounts that paid no interest.[3] If these accounts had been placed with those financial institutions that pay interest, the savers would have had a happier financial Christmas. Some savers prefer to invest their money by buying antiques, art, jewelry, coins, or stamps, hoping for capital gains. The disadvantages of these types of investment are that they cost money to insure and store and do not yield any income.

A selected group of consumers was asked what they would do with additional income if they had it. Four choices were given, among which most respondents favored banks and government bonds over real estate and common stocks.

How Much Should the Prudent Consumer Save?

The American Bankers Association recommends that an individual or a family select a percentage figure for saving. It should be put first in the budget under the heading "This is Mine to Keep." The recommended figure is at least 5 percent of net spendable income. A time-honored formula prescribes no less than 5 percent and no more than 20 percent of family income. Included in savings would be premiums on permanent life insurance and payments on the purchase of a house. Perhaps 10 percent would be a workable figure for the typical family.

Writers on investments generally agree that the head of a family should not attempt to save for the purpose of future income until he or she has provided adequate insurance protection and a quick-recourse emergency fund equal to one-half of the family's yearly income. The emergency fund should be convertible into cash on demand or within 30 to 60 days. Such a fund may be temporarily invested in a savings account or U.S. Government

Bonds. As explained in Chapter 18, holders of permanent types of life insurance may borrow on their insurance contracts.

PUTTING SAVINGS TO WORK

The Meaning of Investment

The term "investment" as used in this chapter means the spending of money for the purchase of property or claims to property that will yield income, or capital gain, or both. Although popular thought distinguishes between spending as the paying out of income for consumers' goods and saving as depositing money in an institution or spending it for the purchase of securities, it is obvious that in either case anyone parting with purchasing power is spending. The difference is in the purpose for which the spending is done. As the terms are used here, the distinguishing feature is that in buying investments one is purchasing other forms of wealth, or claims to wealth, which are expected to yield a subsequent income in cash, either as dividends, or interest, or capital gain.

Types of Investments

There are two general types of investments: those establishing a creditor status (represented by loans) and those establishing a proprietor status (represented by ownership).

The creditor type of investment is illustrated by savings deposits, the purchase of shares in savings and loan associations (unless one buys a paid-up share), and the purchase of bonds or mortgages. In each of these cases the investor is lending his money in the expectation that he will receive interest for its use and eventual return of the principal. The greatest risk involved in such transactions is the possibility that the borrower may be unable or unwilling to return the principal. As a safeguard, lending agreements usually include some type of security in the form of hypothecated wealth. Yet many lending agreements simply pledge the general credit of the borrower.

If an investor were to purchase an independent neighborhood food store, he would find that he had assumed many duties and obligations. He would have to spend time managing his business, arranging for deliveries of supplies, paying bills, paying taxes, keeping his property in repair, hiring necessary help, purchasing insurance to cover risks of customers, employees, and property, and arranging for credit at a bank. In payment for his services, he would receive whatever surplus remained after paying all other bills. In this illustration the risks and responsibilities incurred by the investor are evident. What is not so clear is that if this investor, instead of putting his savings into a food store, were to purchase several shares of stock in a food processing company, the difference in risk and responsibility incurred would be one of degree. As a minority stockholder in a food processing corporation, he would take no active part in the management of the corporation. Hired managers to whom the stockholders had delegated authority would be responsible for managing the operations. If the business should fail, the stockholders would lose not only their anticipated income but also the savings which they had invested.

Concerns of the Small Investor

Aggressive investors have substantial amounts of money to invest. They also have the time to study investment possibilities and alternatives or they can afford to pay for professional investment counselors. The brief discussion of investment policies and practices in this chapter is not intended for aggressive investors.

Defensive investors are those who have smaller amounts to invest and to whom those amounts of money are very important. They wish to avoid serious losses. They do not have the time or the knowledge to study investment possibilities and alternatives.

What are the chief concerns of the small, conservative, defensive investor?

1. *Security of principal* is the primary concern. Security of principal involves not only the preservation and return of the original sum of money but also the preservation or increase of its original purchasing power. The former is called *liquidity*, which is the ability to convert an asset into money without loss. As a rule the less liquid an asset, the higher its monetary return. This creates decision problems for small investors. They would like to have security of principal and high-income yield, but they cannot have both. So they must choose between investments that offer security and low yield and investments that offer high yield and less security of principal. The preservation of purchasing power is accomplished, in the long run, by investing in common stocks, investment company shares, or real estate in times of rising prices. When prices are falling purchasing power is maintained or increased by investing in bonds or keeping cash in savings deposits.

2. *Diversification* is a means of achieving security of principal and stability of income by spreading one's money among a variety of investments. An investor may diversify geographically or by industry, by maturities, or by types of securities.

3. *Stability of income* is important for small investors, particularly those who have retired. Stability of income also involves stability of purchasing power. A steady income of 6 percent is satisfactory if prices are steady or falling, but not when they are rising. Purchasing power stability may be achieved by a shifting ratio of fixed-dollar investments to equities in real estate and common stock. In a period when the Consumer Price Index is rising, a ratio of 40 to 60 is generally recommended.

4. *Increase in the capital value of investments* is important. One's investments should grow at least as much as the economy grows. This would mean a growth rate of no less than 3 percent annually. In addition, one's investments should increase in value enough to offset an annual price level increase. The total growth rate therefore should be no less than 3 percent plus the percentage increase in the Consumer Price Index each year.

5. *Marketability* is the ability to dispose of an asset for money at whatever price may be attainable. This is in contrast to liquidity, which is the ability to convert an asset into cash without loss. Common stocks listed on a stock exchange can always be sold. They are marketable. In contrast, real estate cannot always be sold when a seller needs cash.

6. *The tax status of an investment* affects its net yield. A low-interest-bearing municipal bond may be a good investment because the income from it is not taxable.

A sound investment program yields good results under adverse conditions. It would be easy to invest if one could assume a continuing boom (although one can buy the wrong stock or piece of real estate even then). Since investors cannot foresee the future, they can obtain the best results by following the experience of others, as reflected in the principles listed above. In doing so the individual investor must consider, among other factors, his or her age, number of dependents, amount of life insurance, cash reserve, current income, prospective income, and debt and tax status. Then the investor must decide how much risk he can assume and how much income he needs from his investments. A young single man can properly assume more risk for the purpose of increasing his income, while an older married man is more anxious to provide a smaller, secure retirement income.

All investors face: 1) business risks (decline in earning power); 2) market risks (market psychology which causes a security to decline in price without reference to a fundamental change in its earning power); 3) purchasing power risk (a decline in purchasing power as the Consumer Price Index rises); 4) interest rate risk (a rise in interest rates depresses the prices of fixed income securities); and 5) the political risk (tax increases, price-wage controls, and changes in tariffs or subsidies). Bonds are vulnerable to risks, 1, 3, and 4, while common stocks are vulnerable to risks 1, 2, and 5. Nothing is free of risk; even United States government bonds are vulnerable to risks 3 and 4.[4]

Looking backward twenty years from 1976, the investment picture that emerges is characterized by a boom in 1961 to 1969 (the longest sustained period of prosperity this country has ever experienced, generated by federal expenditures and steady economic and technical growth), occasional mild recessions and one major recession, continuing inflation, sharply rising interest rates, rising taxes, constant war or threat of war followed by some easing of tensions, and recurring balance of payments problems.[5] It is much easier to evaluate the past than to peer into the future and predict accurately. The successful (or lucky) investor is the one who can read (or guess) the road signs for the future.

Investment or Speculation?

Investment is spending money for the purchase of property for income. There is an inescapable conflict between the desire for security and the desire for income. One investor may have a high degree of security if he is satisfied with a modest yield. Another investor may receive a comparatively high yield at the expense of risking her principal. The difference between investment and speculation is that *investment seeks safety of principal and certainty of return while speculation seeks to increase the return by accepting additional risk.* Although speculators are interested in yield, they are usually more interested in the probable market price of a security at a later date. They buy a security or real estate in the hope of being able to sell at a higher price soon. Speculation sometimes verges on gambling, which is the creation of an unnecessary risk where none existed before. No social service is performed by the assumption of an unnecessary or artificially created risk. The records of the New York Stock Exchange indicate that the chances of success in speculation are only one in five, and the risk increases with stocks not listed on the NYSE.

For some people buying gold may be thought an investment, but the magnitude of the fluctuations in the price of gold in recent years places gold-buying in the realm of speculation. December 31, 1974, U.S. citizens were permitted to purchase gold for the first time since 1933, when the U.S. went off the gold standard. At that time gold sold for $20.67 an ounce. European speculators thought that American consumers would be so famished for gold after a forty-year ban on their owning it that they would rush out to buy it. In anticipation of this, gold speculators forced the price of gold up from $114.75 an ounce to $197.50 an ounce by the end of 1974. Unfortunately for the gold speculators, Americans did not rush out to buy gold and the price dropped sharply. By mid-1976 gold was selling for $104.80 an ounce.

A general rule small investors are advised to follow is that securities yielding, or promising to yield, more than twice the return available on U.S. Savings Bonds are too risky. Some writers place the ratio as low as one and one-half times. This means that in a boom period small investors would limit their purchasing to securities yielding a maximum of 9 to 12 percent, depending on which ratio they chose to follow.

Investment and Inflation

Double-digit inflation and the sharp decline in stock market prices during 1973 and 1974 forced many people to reevaluate their investment policies. The Dow Jones Industrial Average of stocks declined from a high of 1,051.70 in January, 1973, to a low of 577 by November, 1974. During the same period the Consumer Price Index rose 23 percent. Stocks did not turn out to be a good hedge against inflation during this two-year period, but they are not meant to be a hedge against inflation in the short run in any case. The situation in the early 1970s has made many investors shy of investing in stocks. In spite of the paradox of the Consumer Price Index going up sharply while stock prices plunge, the small investor concerned with a degree of protection against inflation should still consider stock investments as a hedge against inflation over the long run. One study compared the performances of bonds and a conservative, diversified portfolio of stocks over several overlapping thirty-five-year periods. The results showed that an investor who contributed each year to his or her stock portfolio would earn more than the investor who contributed to bonds in every thirty-five-year period since 1927. This, of course, includes the Depression years.[6] Investors should be careful not to allow themselves to be automatically scared out of the stock market in a declining market, but at the same time they should act with caution.

IS REAL ESTATE GOOD FOR SMALL INVESTORS?

Advantages of Real Estate in Small Towns and Rural Areas

Ownership of real estate is a common form of investment in small towns and rural areas. It is much more common in such areas than ownership of common stock. People often prefer to own real estate because it is tangible and they can see the sale prices of good property increase decade by decade. Pasture land is converted into building plots and some owners become rich because of capital gains. As population continues to grow, the demand for land for business, residential, transportation, and recreational purposes increases. Since the supply of land is constant, prices must increase. Because the population of the United States has grown steadily, land values have increased. But all land does not rise in price; local demand and supply forces vary. Picking land for growth potential is just as risky as picking stocks. And holding land until a price rise is expensive; estimates range up to 12 percent a year to cover taxes and interest on the money spent on land.

Buying land, sight unseen, in Arizona, Colorado, Florida, or elsewhere, is a speculation rather than an investment. Land companies may pay $200 an acre, then subdivide it into lots whose selling price represents a markup of twenty times. Sales agents are paid commissions of 20 percent. Some of them use the "free dinner" method in which the "hard sell is served with the dessert." Buyers are often retirees, escapees from urban areas, and speculators. Fraud and misrepresentation became such a problem and state laws were so ineffective in controlling land frauds that the government passed the United States Land Sales Full Disclosure Act in 1969. The law requires that land companies register with the Department of Housing and Urban Development and that property reports be given to all buyers.[7]

The passage of this act has not stopped fraud in land sales, however.*

* See Chapter 14, pp. 349–350, for examples of fraudulent land sales.

M. S. Paulson, in writing about investment frauds in land, stated that the present value of a tract of land may be hard to determine, and its future value is, of course, unknown. In addition, states Paulson, only a fraction of the nation's land that can be exploited is rising sufficiently in value to make it worth considering as a speculative investment and speculating in land is one of the riskiest and most difficult investment ventures.[8] Holding land for a rise in price is also expensive. In order to have an adequate net return on an investment in land one would need at least a 16 percent appreciation each year in the value of the land, since taxes on the land and interest on the money invested in the land will cost as much as 12 percent or more annually. An appreciation of 16 percent per year means that the price of the land would have to double in less than five years.

The Perils of Real-Estate Ownership

The trick in choosing growth investments is, obviously, to choose the ones that will grow rather than depreciate in value. In the case of real estate, some locations and some properties have become blighted areas. This may happen when a highway bypass leaves a formerly good location stranded. It may also happen in an area into which business enterprises or low-income families move. Elegant brownstone fronts can become tenements and stores. In rural areas, the wealthy man's mansion can become a funeral home.

In addition to the risk of depreciation there are costs of real-estate ownership that continue even though the property yields little or no income. One of these costs is the general property tax, which must be paid annually. If it is not paid, the owner loses his or her property. Another continuing cost is loss of interest on the investment. If a small investor has $10,000 invested in property, his interest cost would be at least 6 percent annually, or a total of $600. If he had put his $10,000 in an insured savings account in a savings and loan association he could have collected $600 in interest annually. After ten years, if such an investor sold his property for $15,000, he would think that he had made a capital gain of $5,000. Actually, he would have lost $7,908—if interest had been compounded annually—and would have paid at least $1,500 in taxes—for a total of $9,408. An investment of $10,000 in real estate would have netted him $5,000 in appreciation, less $1,500 for property taxes, or $3,500. The $10,000 placed in the savings and loan would have netted him $7,908. He would have had a $4,408 greater return from the savings and loan than from the investment in real estate. In this illustration no adjustments have been made for income and capital gains taxes. These taxes would change the net figure because property taxes are an allowable deduction while income taxes have to be paid on interest earned, and there would also have been a capital gains tax on the appreciation in the value of the property. If these are added in, the investor would have netted about $2,000 more by investing in the savings and loan association than by investing in real estate.

Investments in real estate are not liquid. In a declining market real estate may sell slowly, even at reduced prices. Real-estate ownership carries with it responsibilities for managing the property. Management requires maintenance, payment of taxes and insurance premiums, renting, and collection of rentals. For most small investors, too much time is required and the margin of profit is too small to make real-estate investment worthwhile.

For all these reasons direct ownership of real estate is not recommended as a good investment for the small investor. This is the unanimous judgment of qualified experts.[9] Of course, every generalization requires qualifications. In the case of real-estate ownership an exception might be the handyman who can do all of his own maintenance and repair work and who is fortunate enough to keep his properties rented.

ARE BONDS GOOD BUYS FOR SMALL INVESTORS?

What Is a Bond?

A bond is a written promise to pay a certain sum of money on or before a specified date, with interest at an agreed rate. Bonds give investors a fixed return, less risk, and the return of principal at maturity. The various types of bonds are distinguished by certain features.

1. One way of distinguishing bonds is by the *type of debtor.* The two general types are government and corporate, the latter including public utility corporations subject to public regulation.

2. A second basis for distinction is *security.* Many bonds have no specific security for their repayment. This is true of almost all government bonds and of many corporate bonds. (In the latter case they are usually referred to as "debentures.") Many corporate bonds are secured by a pledge of property which is forfeited in case of default, becoming the property of the bondholders, to be disposed of by them with the proceeds used to pay off the bonds. A special type of security is the mortgage bond, which has many variations. A first-mortgage bond is considered stronger security than subsequent property liens, which are of doubtful value in case of forced liquidation. The record of mortgage bonds during severe depression has not been good. In practice, bondholders were unable to foreclose, and when they could, the only buyer for the property was the corporation itself. Consequently, ability to pay is now considered of greater importance, and many of the highest-grade corporate bonds are debentures.

3. A third basis for distinguishing bonds is their *provision for repayment.* While perpetual or long-term bonds are fairly common in Europe, they have not proved popular in the United States. Sinking fund bonds provide that periodic amounts of earnings, when available, be set aside and applied toward their retirement. In the case of such enterprises as mining, where the resource is eventually depleted, this type of provision for repayment offers greater assurance to the investor. Serial bonds are retired in installments at times indicated in the bonds, while callable bonds must be

turned in by the investor when called for by the issuer at previously agreed-upon terms, which usually involve a premium.

4.   A fourth distinguishing basis is the *provision for interest payments*. Most bonds provide for interest at some fixed percentage, default of which makes the principal fall due and enables the bondholders to foreclose. Income bonds contain no provisions for fixed interest. These are usually issued by weak, reorganized companies whose securities are accepted by holders under compulsion.

5.   A final basis for distinguishing among types of bonds is the *special privileges* that some of them carry. For example, some government bonds carry the privilege of tax exemption; corporate bonds may contain provision for conversion into other bonds or stocks or include stock subscription warrants, and in rare cases they may provide voting rights for bondholders or participation in the corporation's earnings.

United States Government Bonds

Federal government bonds are the standard by which all other bonds are judged. They are issued by a sovereign power, their security resting not on a pledge of physical property or on earning power, but on the government's power to raise money by taxation. The value of such bonds depends on investors' confidence in the ability and willingness of their government to repay its debt. In a democratic government such confidence is ultimately a reflection of the citizens' confidence in themselves as a group, for they constitute and compose the final authority.

The fact that federal government bonds are the standard by which all other bonds are judged may be established by another line of reasoning. The nation as a unit is stronger than any individual business enterprise or any one of the separate states, counties, or municipalities. It is a matter of record that investors lose confidence in the bonds of some civil and corporate units while still retaining full confidence in the bonds of their federal government. If U.S. government bonds should become worthless, no corporate security could have value.

Some investment experts advise anyone having $5,000 or less to invest to buy United States savings bonds for their safety, dependable income, and liquidity. Whereas bonds are usually issued in large denominations of $1,000 or multiples thereof, the government has made it possible for small investors to purchase bonds in smaller denominations. The traditional method of paying interest on bonds is to attach coupons to the bond that are negotiable on specified dates for the amount of interest due. The smaller government bonds provide for the payment of interest on an accrual basis. If held five years, a Series E bond now yields 6 percent. Purchases of Series E bonds are limited to private individuals and the maximum amount that can be bought is $10,000 a year.

There is also available a Series H bond, on which owners receive interest checks every six months. These bonds are sold in denominations of

$500, $1,000, and $5,000. An investor may buy up to $10,000 in each calendar year. H Bonds are issued only by the Federal Reserve Bank and the Office of the Treasurer of the United States (Securities Division, Washington, D.C., 20222). The yield is 5 percent the first year, 5.8 percent for the next four years, and 6.50 percent for the second five years, producing an average rate of 6 percent for the ten year period.

One advantage of the Series E savings bond, besides its safety, is that the holder has the option of reporting the interest when the bond is cashed in rather than reporting it annually as it accrues. This provision makes these bonds particularly advantageous as a savings program for retirement, when one's taxable income normally is considerably lower and therefore taxed at a lower rate.

In addition to Series E and H bonds, there are U.S. Treasury Bonds, Notes, and Bills. These are issued in denominations of $1,000, $5,000, $10,000, and $1 million, except for the Bills, which start at $10,000. Original issues of these securities may be purchased from the Treasury only on the occasion of a public offering. Then they may be traded on the various exchanges. In general these securities are not useful investments for the small investor. Under certain circumstances, one might be able to dispose of these bonds only for less than their original cost. If, however, you are interested in getting the benefit of the higher interest rates that these issues usually give over Series E and H bonds, you might investigate purchasing them through the American Stock Exchange (Amex), where they are sold in amounts from $1,000 to $99,000. An order is placed with an Amex broker and the commission fee is negotiated with the firm. For more information on this type of investment ask any Amex member firm for the booklet *Government Securities for the Individual Investor.**

Some investment counselors recommend the purchase of term insurance to age sixty-five to protect dependents and the investment of the difference between term and ordinary life premiums in government bonds. Parents may also use these bonds to build educational funds for their children instead of purchasing expensive educational life insurance policies.

One defect in United States savings bonds is the lack of security of purchasing power. The investor is sure of getting his money back, but he does not know what it will be worth. If the general level of prices has fallen, it will buy more, but if prices have risen, it will buy less. No one knows whether prices will continue to rise, will level off, or will fall. Some investment writers think government fiscal policies indicate a continued long-time rise in prices and recommend that small investors protect their purchasing power by investing part of their savings in common stocks, the prices of which usually rise with the general price level. Some experts advise investors to put half their money into government bonds and half into stocks. Others advise defensive investors to divide their holdings between bonds and stocks, in a ratio ranging from 75/25 to 25/75, depending on current economic trends.

---

* For more information about U.S. savings bonds consult your bank.

Municipal Bonds

Among writers on investments and among bankers no distinction is made between state, county, or city bonds. All are classified as municipals. Included in this classification are the bonds issued by school districts, irrigation districts, sewer districts, water districts, turnpike authorities, port authorities, and any other political subdivision. While there is only one national government, there are fifty sovereign states, all with authority to issue bonds based on public credit. That investors have varying degrees of confidence in the ability and willingness of the several states to repay their obligations is a matter of record. The credit of some states is stronger than that of others, but the disparity is not as great now as it was in the past. In comparing security it is important to remember that a state cannot be sued, even by the holder of a defaulted or repudiated bond. More than a half century has passed since the last repudiation of a bond issued by a state, but as recently as thirty-five years ago three states were in arrears on interest payments on their debts. On the whole, their record has been good since that time. State bonds, for the most part, offer security of principal and stability of income.

Financial experts point out that the safety record of municipal bonds is second only to that of federal government bonds. Even so, an official study shows that since 1938, when the Federal Municipal Bankruptcy Act made it legal for cities to go into bankruptcy, 273 cities have had to go into default and then work out plans to refinance their debts.[10] In the mid-1970s the near bankruptcy of New York City made investors reevaluate municipal bonds as a safe investment. New York City obligations would have defaulted if the federal government had not provided a minimum guarantee.

The market for municipal bonds is largely institutional. Managers of life insurance companies and pension funds like them because interest on the bonds is not taxable by the federal government. Municipal bonds are acceptable investments under state laws, and institutions have investment experts to analyze them. A taxpayer in the 25-percent income tax bracket finds that $1 tax-free is equal to 33 percent more than $1 taxed. Expressed another way, a tax-free yield of 6 percent is equal to an 8 percent yield on a taxable bond.

There are 102,000 state and local governmental units, all of which have the legal right to issue bonds. As one might suppose, there is considerable variation among their bonds. Records show that repudiation has occurred and that default has not been uncommon. Although cities are public corporations, which may be sued, they may also file petitions in bankruptcy. An amateur investor entering the market for the first time might find an excellent county or city bond, but he would be just as likely, perhaps even more likely, to find himself the holder of a bond issued by a local government whose debt is disproportionately large, whose government is corrupt, and whose tax system is bad. The outlook is mixed for the 1970s, so small investors are advised to shun municipal bonds, unless they council with an investment analyst.

Corporate Bonds

A corporate bond is a promise by a corporation to pay a stated sum of money on or before a specified date with interest at an agreed rate. It would seem that a corporate bond resembles a government bond, but there are several differences. Chief among these is the security for repayment. While a corporate bond may be issued on the general credit of a company or on the possibility of its earnings, such bonds frequently are secured by a mortgage on all or a part of the corporate property. They are then designated as first- or second-mortgage bonds.

A second difference is that corporate bonds are repaid out of earnings. If earnings are insufficient, the bonds are repaid out of the proceeds of the sale of the property pledged as security. Whether or not a corporation earns enough gross income to meet its obligations depends primarily on good management, but it may also be the result of many other factors, some of which may be beyond the control of management.

Because of these variations and uncertainties, it is unwise for the average small investor to purchase corporate bonds. If he attempts to do so, he will be as helpless as the average consumer trying to buy a vacuum cleaner or an electric washing machine without some expert advice. He should not buy the bond issues of new or small or unknown mining and oil companies. These ventures are usually risky. Some conservative corporate stocks are safer investments than certain types of corporate bonds. At this point it might be well to remind the prospective small investor again of the general rule that securities yielding more than twice the return on United States government bonds are usually too risky. While a corporate bond promising a return of 12 percent appears very attractive, a prospective buyer must remember that he is purchasing that larger return at the risk of losing all or part of his principal. However, the small investor who is able to invest in multiples of $1,000 and who wishes to invest money for a long period of time may find it worthwhile to place some funds in corporate bonds rated AAA or AA by a rating service such as Standard & Poor's, particularly when such bonds can be had at yields of about 9 percent or better.[11]

Utility Bonds

Certain types of business enterprises, such as those supplying transportation, or electric, gas, or telephone services, have long been recognized as so vested with public interest that they are subject to varying degrees of public regulation. Except for interstate transportation companies, most utilities are subject to state control. In some cases this control has proved efficient; however, situations have developed where the utility companies control the regulating commissions and in some cases almost control the state government. As a rule investment in utility bonds should be avoided by the small investor. It must be remembered that we are now discussing the bonds of private corporate enterprises, whose ability to repay is dependent on their earning power. Analysis of that earning power is a task that requires the services of experts.

Senate investigations revealing fraudulent practices in holding companies' finances confirm the conclusion that small investors should be extremely cautious about purchasing securities offered by holding companies. If they insist on investing their savings in utility securities, they should do so only on the advice of a competent counselor and should consider securities of only those large operating companies serving well-known urban areas.

ARE SAVINGS AND LOAN ASSOCIATIONS RECOMMENDED FOR THE SMALL INVESTOR?

An insured savings and loan association may be the best friend of the small investor. The small investor who places money in an insured S&L will have safety of principal and a choice of savings programs with varying interest rates and degrees of liquidity. In addition, accounts are insured up to $40,000. Table 20-1 shows the maximum rates of return and yields savings and loan associations were allowed to pay in 1977. Savings and loan associations are permitted by law to pay $\frac{1}{4}$ percent more on savings accounts than commercial banks for each kind of account. As indicated in the table, the investor sacrifices a degree of liquidity in order to obtain a higher rate of return. If money is withdrawn from a savings certificate before maturity, there is a penalty clause.

In choosing a savings and loan association to invest in, the small investor should check the earnings rate, the annual percentage yield, how often interest is compounded, whether interest is earned from the day of deposit to the day of withdrawal, and other features that might decrease or increase the amount of earnings paid. The amount earned can vary from one S&L to another.

The public's confusion over differences in the rates of return, yields, methods of compounding interest, and ways of crediting interest to an account among the various savings institutions stimulated the introduction

TABLE 20-1. Savings and Loan Association Savings Accounts

Name of Account	Minimum Deposit	Interest Rate (%)	Effective Annual Yield (%)	Length of Account
Passbook	none	5.25%	5.47%	Day-in/day-out
Savings certificate	$500	5.75	6.00	3 months to 1 year
Savings certificate	$500	6.50	6.81	1 to 2½ years
Savings certificate	$500	6.75	7.08	2½ to 4 years
Savings certificate	$1,000	7.50	7.90	4 to 6 years
Savings certificate	$1,000	7.75	8.17	6 to 7 years

of a "Truth-in-Savings" bill into Congress in 1975. This bill specifies that all significant information must be quoted in the same way by all savings institutions, so that savers know exactly what they will earn and so they can make meaningful comparisons among the various savings institutions. This bill had not passed Congress by the end of 1976.

ARE CORPORATE STOCKS GOOD BUYS FOR SMALL INVESTORS?

Small Investors Do Buy Stocks

About 25.2 million individuals in the United States own stock in corporations or mutual funds. The typical stockholder has an annual income of about $19,000 and has a portfolio of stocks that is worth $10,100.[12] In 1970, 30.85 million persons owned stock. The sharp decline in stock prices during 1973 and 1974 drove millions of small investors out of the market, but many reentered the market in 1975 and 1976 as the market experienced a strong recovery.

What Are Stocks?

A voting share of common stock represents partial ownership and control of the corporation that issued it. In practice there are so many kinds of stocks that it is no longer possible to generalize about the status of stock ownership. Formerly it was possible to say that bondholders were creditors with no control in corporate management and no share in corporate profits, whereas stockholders were owners with voting control and no assured in-

The floor of the New York Stock Exchange. (*UPI*)

come but with the prospect of a share in net earnings. Now one investor may own a preferred share that gives him prior claim to participate in net earnings. Another may hold a 4 percent cumulative preferred share, which means that if he fails to receive his 4 percent dividend one year other stockholders must forgo any share in net earnings the second year until he has received 8 percent on his investment. Still another investor may own a share of Class A nonvoting stock, which means that he has incurred all the risks incident to ownership, yet has no voice in the control of the company.

The income of a corporation depends on several variables over which corporate management may or may not have control. Individual stockholders in large corporations have no effective control over management. From an investment point of view they are in the position of having lent their capital to the corporation without a promise of repayment and without a promise of payment for its use.

There are approximately one million active corporations in the United States. The stocks of 3,000 corporations are listed on the major stock exchanges. The stocks of 25,000 corporations are traded over the counter — that is, sales are handled by brokers without going through the stock exchanges. The stocks of the remaining 972,000 corporations are rarely traded. Consequently, they are not readily marketable. Like the Ford Motor Company for many years, the stocks of closed corporations are held by individuals or family groups.

Advantages of Common Stock

Inflation is more than a fact of life in the United States; it is practically a way of life. Even though the long-run trend of the price level has been upward, people believe this is bad. Consumer attitudes toward rising price levels are emotional. They do not think inflation can be justified in peace time. There can be no doubt that millions and millions of Americans have experienced the best years of their lives in years of inflation, yet they think of higher prices without thinking of their higher incomes.

A slow, steady rising price is the device used to finance the growth of our economy. A growing economy needs more money. This alone explains 1.2 percent of the price rise in recent years. A rising price level of 1.2 percent a year would reduce the purchasing power of the dollar by one-third in twenty years. In thirty-three years it would reduce purchasing power by 50 percent. The Consumer Price Index is a rough measure of the purchasing power of the dollar. It has its limitations — those who use it must be aware of and allow for the inability of CPI to account for quality improvements, a higher average plane of living, and sale prices below list prices.

The CPI indicated that the 1976 dollar was worth 58 cents when compared to the 1966 dollar (1967 = 100). To have as much purchasing power as $10,000 had in 1966, a family would have needed $17,250 in 1976. The experts see a continuing decline in the purchasing power of the dollar in our lifetime; they differ only in their estimate of the rate of decline. Esti-

A sign in New York City tells watchers on March 11, 1976, that the Dow Jones Average has broken through the 1,000 mark for the first time in over three years. (*UPI*)

mates range from a 4 percent to a 6 percent annual rise in the price level. By 1992 you will need an income of $40,000 a year to equal an income of $20,000 in 1977 if the price level rises 5 percent a year during the next fourteen-year interval. How can a small investor meet that challenge? One answer is to purchase corporate shares of common stock. Over a ninety-eight-year period — 1871 to 1968 — common stocks rose in sixty-one years and fell in thirty-seven years. For the entire period, stocks rose 2,989 percent.[13] A $75 savings bond purchased in 1958 yielded $100 in 1968, but the CPI rose 18 percent over the ten-year period so the net yield was $82. In the same period the Standard & Poor's Index of 500 leading stocks rose 90 percent — five times faster than the CPI — and yielded a 5 percent income every year.[14]

Since 1968 the erratic price movements of stocks have raised questions concerning stocks as worthwhile long-term investments. The two key indexes measuring stock prices are indicative of this. Standard & Poor's Index declined 16 percent from 1965 to 1975. The Dow Jones Industrial Average was at 985 in 1968, 631 in 1970, 1,052 in 1973, 577 in 1974, and reached 1,000 again in 1976. Even while the indexes were going down some stocks continued to increase in price.

The investor, in attempting to hedge against inflation by considering stocks, must look not only at the price of the stock but also consider the cash dividends. In a nine-month period while the CPI was going up 7.8 percent, stocks listed on the exchange increased their cash dividends by 6.6 percent, which almost offset the inflation. Steel stocks increased dividends by 21.4 percent, amusements were up 16.8 percent, paper and publishing were up 16.4 percent, petroleum was up 12.8 percent, and utilities were up 11.9 percent. Holders of stocks in the automotive, finance, real-estate, and textile industries were the only investment groups to suffer a decline in dividends during this period.[15] The per share earnings of utility stocks as a group have increased in nineteen of the past twenty years.

The findings of a detailed study of returns from four different kinds of investments were most revealing.[16] Common stocks returned 8.5 percent per year over the forty-nine year period compounded annually and including dividends; without dividends the return was 3.5 percent. Long-term U.S. government bonds returned 3.2 percent compounded annually; long-term corporate bonds returned 3.6 percent compounded annually; and U.S. Treasury Bills returned 2.2 percent compounded annually, which was almost equal to the annual rate of inflation for the forty-nine years.

Traditional hedge theory only requires that the nominal rate of return be equal to or greater than the rate of inflation, but for a stock to be a complete hedge its real rate of return must be greater than its normal required rate of return. For example, if the normal required rate of return is 8 percent and the price level rises 4 percent, a stock must yield 12 percent if it is to be a real hedge. How well do stocks meet this requirement? Comparing stock yields over a thirty-one-year period, Reilly, Johnson, and Smith concluded that "during recent periods of inflation common stocks as a group were not consistent or complete inflation hedges." Nevertheless, this does not mean that common stocks were never complete hedges or that they were not partial hedges for given periods or that specific stocks were not complete or partial hedges. What it does mean is that blanket statements about common stocks as hedges against inflation are invalid.[17] And as was indicated earlier, the fluctuations in stock prices during the last decade, including sharp declines at the same time the Consumer Price Index was rising rapidly, are evidence that in the short run, stock ownership may not only be a poor hedge against inflation, but may, in fact, turn out to be a negative investment.

Some Hazards of Common Stock

There are "winners" and "losers" in the stock market. In a recent year ten companies, which were the "winners," saw their stock prices increase by 260 to 490 percent, while the five worst performers saw prices for their stocks drop 50 to 63 percent.[18] Each day the New York Stock Exchange is open there are companies whose stock prices increase and those that decline. In one day the Exchange recorded price advances for the stocks of 1,067 companies, no change in prices for 429 companies, and price declines for 375 companies.[19] An investment in Eastman Kodak in 1928 grew 2,931 percent in the next forty-seven years, while an investment in Woolworth declined 61 percent in the same period.[20]

New issues of stock are hazardous. The odds are against the small investor. Glamour stocks, such as optics, electronics, solar energy, and scientific instruments, are not for the small, conservative investor. The small investor should avoid fashionable stocks and should resist the temptation to follow the crowd.

A small investor must adopt an investment philosophy and policy and stay with it. The record shows that if you speculate, you will very likely lose your money, and if you follow the crowd, you will buy and sell at the wrong times. Here are nine good rules to follow in buying stocks:

1. Set your goals and stick to them.
2. Investigate before you invest.
3. Seek advice from an established and qualified firm.
4. Don't be a one-stock buyer.
5. Be prepared psychologically for losses as well as gains.
6. If you incur a loss, take it; don't be stubborn.
7. Don't think you can buy low and sell high.
8. Ignore salesmen offering a "sure thing."
9. Beware of tipsters; the cheapest thing in the world is unsolicited investment advice from people unqualified to give it.[21]

On the whole, the ethics and practices of Wall Street are exemplary. But there are manipulators, and their manipulations cost investors hundreds of million of dollars. A favorite operation is the penny stock promotion. The amateur investor is willing to take a chance by purchasing shares of stock at prices ranging from one cent up to one dollar. Another fraudulent operation is the so-called "boiler-room" sales of phony Canadian stocks by telephone. One "sucker list" included a group of ministers with whom the sales representatives "shared a hot tip because they were distant cousins"! Many stock salesmen work only part time. They have no training, but they have a skill in finding gullible and greedy people who hope to make a killing. The ones who make the killing are almost invariably the sellers, not the buyers. The moral of all this is never to buy stocks from telephone salesmen or from salesmen at your door. Never buy new issues. Consider the purchase of stocks at least as carefully as the purchase of real estate or an automobile or expensive jewelry. All these recommendations are made by the Better Business Bureau of New York City in cooperation with the Securities and Exchange Commission, the New York State Attorney General's Office, and representatives of stock exchanges and associations of securities dealers.

HOW TO BUY COMMON STOCKS

Direct Purchase

If a small investor has decided to purchase growth stocks to hedge against rising prices, how should he or she proceed? Writers on investment are almost unanimous in their recommendations that a small investor should first have an adequate insurance program, a substantial savings account in a bank, and some equity in a house. Then he is ready to buy growth stocks, diversified among several industry groups. Most writers would have the investor balance his account by purchasing bonds or making other fixed-dollar investments. It is suggested that small investors might balance their portfolios as big buyers do. In the semi-annual publication *Growth Leaders on the Big Board* you will find a list of eighty stocks that are institutional favorites.* These are the stocks the experts choose. International Business Machines leads the list; 1,230 institutional investors have holdings in IBM. The next nine include Exxon, Eastman Kodak, General Motors, General Electric, American Telephone and Telegraph, Xerox, Texaco, Sears, Roebuck, and Minnesota Mining and Manufacturing.

When an investor starts a stock purchase plan he should buy at regular intervals, and he should hold onto his stock. Buying and selling is not for the small investor. Starting at age thirty the small investor continues his growth stock purchases through the decades. Even at age sixty he should retain his growth stocks because his life expectancy will still be ten or twenty years, during which time the purchasing power of the dollar could depreciate substantially.

One way to save on brokerage fees is to put monthly savings into a savings and loan account paying $5\frac{1}{4}$ to $6\frac{1}{2}$ percent interest. After six or twelve months the accumulated savings may then be used to purchase stock. The experts recommend investing a fixed sum at regular intervals, regardless of price movements, over a long period of time. This is known as "dollar averaging." By using this method the buyer can purchase more shares at low prices than at high prices. As a result, the average cost per share is lower than the average market price. A dollar-averaging plan may be started at any market level or in any phase of an investment cycle. It is essential, however, that the investor have persistence and continue through at least a ten-year period.†

Countless experts have advised small investors to shun in-and-out trading and invest in stocks for the long term. But how long is that—two years? five? twenty? A study covering one hundred years indicated that one is more likely to come out ahead by holding stocks for ten- or fifteen-year periods than three- or five-year periods.[22]

Specifically which stocks should a small investor buy? This is the real question which only skilled professionals can answer. And even they make mistakes sometimes. A small amateur investor who attempts to make his own stock purchase choices is like a doctor trying to be his own lawyer or a lawyer trying to be his own doctor. An investor should choose a reputable and knowledgeable broker. Once you find him, use him and stay with him. How do you find a good broker? You may ask an investment counselor or a banker or a lawyer. You should choose a well-known firm that deals on

---

* *Growth Leaders on the Big Board* is a thirty-two-page pamphlet published by the New York Stock Exchange.

† For details on dollar averaging see Venita Van Caspel, *Money Dynamics: How to Build Financial Independence* (Reston, Va.: Reston, 1975), pp. 139–143.

the major exchanges and has offices in or near the city where you live. You should ask for samples of information provided. For example, one well-known firm provides its clients and prospective clients with a pamphlet entitled "Heirloom Stocks." The pamphlet lists the names of 100 companies that have paid dividends continuously up to 180 years and no less than 40 years. There is a short paragraph describing each company. This is followed by information showing how many years dividends have been paid without interruption, the latest price, the earnings, the price-earning ratio, the dividends, and the yield. With the aid of a reputable broker the small investor can diversify his or her purchases among industries and among companies so as to develop a balanced portfolio.

How much do brokers charge? On May 1, 1975, a Securities and Exchange Commission (SEC) regulation went into effect which ended the 183-year-old practice of stock exchanges fixing the commission rates throughout the country. SEC's prohibition against fixed rates means that the buyer may do comparison shopping among stock brokerage firms for the lowest commission rates and may also negotiate with brokers for special rates. The SEC also adopted a temporary rule that allows brokerage firms to charge customers for investment advice. Commission rates being charged by some of the major brokerage firms run from $47 to $59 for 100 shares selling at $30 per share, and $68 to $80 for 100 shares selling at $50 per share. Discount brokers were selling these at $23 to $43, and $23 to $60.[23]

Investment Clubs

An interesting and effective way of learning the rudiments of investment principles and practices is to participate in an investment club. Investment clubs proved very popular during the 1960s and grew to an estimated 50,000, but the declining stock market during the first half of the 1970s saw the number of investment clubs drop to about 35,000. An investment club is usually composed of fifteen to twenty persons. They may be neighbors, business associates, or members of the same credit union, church, or service club. They meet once a month and each member puts $20 or $25 into the investment pool. In the meetings they discuss the state of the economy, the prospects for growth, the stock market, and particular stocks. They may choose a dozen stocks for careful analysis, each member agreeing to make a comprehensive study and report.

Brokers are interested in investment clubs and are likely to respond affirmatively to an invitation to send a representative to meet with the group. In return they will execute the club's orders for purchases and sale, hoping to develop individual clients as club members' incomes increase and they decide to start their own investment programs. It is reported that investment club members usually purchase about three times as much stock for their personal accounts each month as they do for their club.

Investment clubs have performed reasonably well, even though "too many cooks" may lead to conflict. The average rate of return in investment clubs rose more than the Standard & Poor's Index of 425 industrials in an eleven-year period, or fell less, or rose when the Index declined. The National Association of Investment Clubs reported that during the stock market decline the average portfolio of its member clubs was down 26 percent in value, while the New York Stock Exchange Index was down 44 percent. One investment club consistently out-performed the average for all mutual funds over a decade.[24] The experience of investment clubs confirms the wisdom of buying regularly, reinvesting dividends, and long-term holding of stocks.*

Mutual Funds

Thinking is always hard work. Thinking about an investment problem is doubly hard, so 8.5 million small investors let mutual funds do their thinking for them and pay a high price for the service.

Mutual funds are organized by promoters for the purpose of selling shares to investors, investing the proceeds in the securities of other companies, and managing the investments. The income of mutual funds is derived from dividends and interest received from the operating companies whose shares they own and from capital gains realized from the sale of appreciated securities. Shareholders participate in company income by receiving dividends in proportion to the number of shares owned.

There are over 600 mutual fund companies. The *open-end investment companies* guarantee to repurchase shares at any time at their net asset price, while the *closed-end companies* have a fixed capitalization. No new shares are issued after the original issue has been sold. Open-end companies may issue and retire shares at any time. Ninety percent of all investment companies' assets are in open-end mutual funds. A variation is the common stock common trust fund, of which there are over a thousand, operated by commercial banks and trust companies.

In principle the mutual fund is sound. It offers a way for small investors to diversify their investments. If one security in the mutual fund portfolio declines in price, that decline may be offset by a rise in another security. Similarly, the lower yields of some securities may be offset by higher yields from others. The greater risk of some issues is balanced by the greater security of others. A large company may have in its portfolio stocks and bonds issued by 100 different companies and governmental units. In a period of rising prices, its holdings of common stocks will yield larger earnings and capital gains. In a declining market, its preferred stocks and bonds yield a steady income and maintain principal. The result is that the owner of shares in such funds hopes to have a hedge against inflation and deflation, at least in the long run. In 1972 and 1973, however, confidence in mutual

---

* Anyone wishing to organize an Investment Club may write to the National Association of Investment Clubs, 1515 East Eleven Mile Road, Royal Oak, Mich. 48067, for its *Investment Club Manual: The Handbook for Learn-By-Doing Investing.*

funds was shaken because of the decline in stock prices, and redemptions during that period exceeded sales by almost $3 billion.

As mutual funds grew in popularity, five types of funds emerged: growth funds, income funds, growth and income funds, balanced funds, and money market funds. Some fund portfolios are all common stocks, some are bonds, some are all preferred stocks, and some contain a selection of all three types of securities. The objective of the investor determines which kind of fund is chosen. The primary objective of growth funds is to increase capital, and to achieve that goal investments are made principally in common stocks with growth potential. The primary objective of income funds is to provide current income rather than growth of capital, and investments are normally made in stocks and bonds paying higher dividends and interest. The objective of growth and income funds is to provide for a measure of both current income and long-term growth. A balanced fund has as its objective the "balancing" of the portfolio, generally by including bonds and preferred and common stocks of corporations. The objective of a money market fund is to benefit from high interest rates for current income, generally by investing primarily in short-term securities such as instruments issued or guaranteed by the government, bank certificates of deposits, bankers' acceptances, and commercial paper. In addition, there are some special types of funds. For example, dual-purpose funds, which have two separate classes of shares, are designed for two distinct types of investors—those interested only in income and those interested only in possible capital growth. Income goes to the one group of shareholders, and capital gains go to the other group. Specialty funds deal only in the securities of a certain industry or industries, special types of securities, or in regional investments.*

As fund assets increased from $450 million to nearly $60 billion in thirty years, insurance companies, banks, and retailers, such as Sears, Roebuck & Co., climbed onto the profitable bandwagon by selling mutual funds. The collapse of stock prices in 1973 and 1974 had a "shock" effect on mutual funds sales and assets; the latter dropped from almost $60 billion to about $35 billion.

In the early years of mutual funds they were operated primarily for small investors who appreciated the diversification and professional management the funds offered. But performance became primary, and as fund salesmen played on the avarice of buyers, the basic concept changed from investment to speculation. The "Go-Go" funds developed—funds that were sold in expectation of as much as 20 percent growth annually. The stock market decline in the early 1970s, however, changed the attitudes of investors toward mutual funds. There has been a settling-down in the sale of mutual funds; more emphasis is now being placed on their value as solid, long-term investments.

---

* For further information see the *Mutual Fund Fact Book*, published annually and available free from the Investment Company Institute, 1775 K St., N.W., Washington, D.C. 20006.

What About the Performance of Mutual Funds?

Seeking an answer to this question, the House of Representatives' Committee on Interstate and Foreign Commerce requested the Securities and Exchange Commission to make a major study of mutual funds. The commission contracted with the Wharton School of Finance and Commerce at the University of Pennsylvania to make a study. One major conclusion of the study was the following:

> With respect to the performance of mutual funds, it was found that on the average, it did not differ appreciably from what would have been achieved by an unmanaged portfolio consisting of the same proportions of common stocks, preferred stocks, corporate bonds, Government securities, and other assets as a composite portfolio of the funds. About half the funds performed better, and half worse, than such an unmanaged portfloio.[25]

In a six-year period Standard & Poor's 500 Stock Index rose 139.5 percent. In the same period, the gain shown by 152 mutual funds was 96.7 percent. If allowance is made for the funds' need to keep cash for the repurchase of shares, the comparable Standard and Poor figure dropped from 139.5 to 98.2 percent. Other studies by *Forbes, American Research Council, Wall Street Journal,* and Merrill Lynch, Pierce, Fenner, and Smith confirmed the Wharton study conclusion.

The key sentence for the small investor is that half of the funds performed better than an unmanaged portfolio, while the performance of half of the funds was not as good. This means that the problem is to select a fund whose performance exceeds that of the market. This is just as difficult to do as to select good common stocks. For this reason some writers on investments conclude that the mutual fund does not really solve the selection problem.

A United States senator, who was a member of the Senate Banking Committee, testified that he threw darts at a New York Stock Exchange list to choose a portfolio. Ten thousand dollars invested in the ten stocks hit by the darts grew to $25,300 in ten years, exceeding by $500 the performance of thirty-five so-called "growth" funds![26]

Mutual funds have returned an average of 3.5 percent a year over the past decade. One could have done better by placing one's money in a bank savings account, in high-grade corporate bonds, or in government securities.

The performance of mutual funds during the first half of the 1970s has not been an encouragement to the industry or to its customers. The measure of performance is dependent upon two variables: the particular fund being measured and the years over which it is being measured. The following examples give an indication of what has been happening.

From 1969 through 1973 the average mutual fund lost 16.33 percent, while Standard & Poor's 500-Stock Index went down only 6.08 percent, the Dow Jones Industrial Average was off by only 9.84 percent, and the New York Stock Exchange Index dropped 12.02 percent.[27] Thus the performance of the average mutual fund during this period was less than any of these major indexes.

One study compared the performance of mutual funds with the performance of Standard & Poor's between December 1972 and April 1975. The mutual funds did worse than Standard & Poor's in twenty-six out of the fifty-five time periods compared.[28]

Comparing performance just in 1975 for selected mutual funds and Standard & Poor's, S&P went up 31½ percent while the two best performers in mutual funds went up 184 and 121 percent respectively.[29] Some of the bigger equity funds were up 40 percent or more for the year.

Many mutual funds are sold by high-pressure salespeople. Many of them operate on a part-time basis and many of them begin without any previous experience. They are given a short indoctrination course to show them how to overcome objections and how to appeal to the buyer's emotions. This type of door-to-door selling is expensive. The expense is borne by the buyer through a loading charge that ranges from 7½ to 9½ percent of his investment. This is known as the "load" or "entrance fee." Once in, the investor then pays typically one-half of one percent of his net asset value each year. This is called a "management fee." Most mutual fund contracts call for a monthly payment for a specified number of years. On a ten-year $20-a-month plan, for a total of $2,400, the first-year payment of $240 would buy only $120 in shares. The other $120 would go to the salesperson. This is called "front-end loading." If an investor is unable or unwilling to continue his contract to completion, he loses one-half of his first-year payments. For this reason, contract plans may not be sold in some states. Bills have been introduced into Congress from time to time to prohibit these contractual plans, but none of them have been passed. An investor does have the option of buying either a contractual plan or just purchasing mutual funds from time to time at his option without a contract. The second method avoids the problems inherent in the contractual plan.

There are some "no-load" mutual funds. They do not engage in aggressive selling and there is no selling charge. The only charge is the annual management fee of one-half of one percent of net asset value. This is reasonable. The no-load mutuals represent the mutual fund principle in operation at its best. Small investors who wish to gain the advantages of a balanced portfolio and skillful management may properly do their common stock purchasing through the medium of investment-fund shares. These funds are growing in both size and popularity. There are about 200 no-load mutual funds now in existence, with about one million shareholders.[*] No-load mutual funds held 4.5 percent of total mutual funds assets in 1964, and 21.3 percent by 1974.[30]

The long-term records of the no-load funds compare favorably with those of the load funds. More than half of the no-load mutual funds outperformed the Dow Jones Industrial Average during the first part of 1976

---

[*] For further information on no-load funds write to the No-Load Mutual Fund Association at 475 Park Avenue South, New York, N.Y. 10016.

when the stock market was rising sharply. A number of no-load funds have substantially bettered the DJI over the past five and ten years.[31]

The sales charge on load funds is generally 8.5 percent, and the difference that commission makes in your long-term return can be sizable. Assume you put $10,000 in a load fund and $10,000 in a no-load fund, each of which appreciates by 10 percent a year. At the end of the tenth year, the value of your no-load shares will be $25,937. But the value of the load fund shares will be only $23,733 because an $850 sales charge will have been subtracted from your original $10,000 investment.[32]

As an alternative to no-load funds the small investor may purchase common stocks directly, using the portfolios of one or two good mutual funds and the portfolios of such institutions as the Ford Foundation or the College Retirement Equities Fund of the Teachers Insurance and Annuity Association as guides. These portfolios are published in the companies promotional literature and in their annual reports.

Evaluation of Mutual Funds

Mutual funds grew rapidly in the 1920s, and then many of them collapsed in the 1930s. Failures were due primarily to inept or fraudulent management, lack of public regulation, and a too-rapid growth during a period of unsound values. After the many failures, regulatory laws were passed for the protection of investors. The Securities Act of 1933, the Investment Company Act of 1940, and the Investment Advisers Act of 1940 were designed to prevent the recurrence of the abuses of earlier years.

How effective are these laws today? Congress authorized a study by the Securities and Exchange Commission of the purchase, sale, and holding of securities by institutional investors* to ascertain their stability and effects on the maintenance of fair and orderly markets, the interests of issuers, and the interests of the public. The commission found that institutional trading has had little, if any, effect on large price changes in the securities markets; ". . . institutional trading overall has not impaired price stability in the markets." Nor was there any evidence "that institutions as a group have had significant preferential treatment by issuers of new shares."[33] The SEC did find, however, that stock turnover among mutual funds was 57 percent, compared with 20 percent for individual trust accounts. Also, since these funds held 7 percent of all common stock, their holdings of shares in some companies gave them control of those companies, but there was no evidence that such power was used.

In another study Friend and his collaborators concluded "that mutual funds have little or no influence in stabilizing stock prices, except possibly in the very short run." There was some evidence, however, that fund trading may anticipate or cause subsequent large price movements: "Mutual funds

---

* This classification includes banks, foundations, insurance companies, mutual funds, and pension funds.

and other institutional investors probably stimulated increases in stock prices during the years of their greatest drive to penetrate the equity market." Institutional demand for equities has increased price in the past two decades. There is also evidence of conflicts of interest: "Most funds are controlled by outside investment advisory firms" which are interested primarily in high fees and large turnover of portfolio. There is not enough competition in management fees, sales charges, or in dividing brokerage business.[34]

There are ways of making a fund look good. If fund traders make mistakes, they can "use a whole raft of clever devices to show good performance."[35] By purchasing stocks whose supply is limited, traders can boost their prices. By means of investment letters, traders can buy shares in advance of public issue; then, when the stock goes on the market, the fund managers list it in their portfolios at the quoted price instead of the discounted purchase price and show a capital gain. Traders can make deals with brokers to buy and sell heavily through their firms, thus generating a large volume of commissions, and in return, brokers can let fund traders in on hot issues of new securities. Another trick is to "squeeze the shorts." When a trader finds a stock with a heavy short position, he buys heavily to push the price up, scaring the short sellers into buying to cover their short position, and thereby increasing the price still more.

The Wharton Report did not reveal any fraud or dishonest practices, but abuses arise from the concentration of control in the hands of a small management group. Mutual fund shareholders are so widely dispersed geographically that no shareholders, or at the most a few, attend the annual meetings of the corporations. The board of directors of a fund may rarely meet. They may delegate operating authority to management; 90 percent of the mutual funds are controlled by management groups who own less than 5 percent of the shares of the funds. The management group has several sources of income. They charge the fund a fee for advice, a commission on the purchases and sales of stocks, and split brokerage commissions on the sales and purchases of portfolio stocks. Some funds appear to "churn the portfolio." This means that they deliberately buy and sell shares for the benefit of their broker affiliate—who then collects commissions in and out. There is no correlation between turnover and fund performance. The advisory fee that management charges does not usually decline as the fund grows larger. It is a flat percentage. This is contrary to prevailing practice in the investment advisory field, where a sliding scale is used. Converting the one-half of one percent management fee into a percentage of investment income, it was found that the management charge amounted to 16 percent of investment income. According to the Wharton Report, "This reflects absence of competition." Nonfund clients pay lower management fees, and funds without advisers have lower expenses. All this adds up to a conflict of interest between management and fund shareholders and an absence of arms-length bargaining between fund managers and fund advisers.[36] The magnitude of funds' operations gives funds the ability to fulfill their own market predictions, and it gives them the power to validate their own appraisal of individual issues.[37]

The Need for Reform

The evidence supports the conclusion that mutual fund reform legislation is overdue. The Securities and Exchange Commission recommended a reduction of sales commissions from the present 8.5 percent of payments to 4.76 percent, and from 9.3 percent of the amount invested to 5 percent. A Congressional committee should be formed to eliminate the front-end load and to set "reasonable" fees for management. Mutual fund holding companies should be outlawed. Closer supervision of trading by insiders is needed to prevent managers from taking advantage of inside information. And all surplus commissions arising out of portfolio turnover should be paid into the fund rather than to the brokers.

It is discouraging to report that almost all legislative and SEC efforts to correct abuses were blocked through 1970.[38] One exception was a compromise law that the president signed in 1970. That measure gave the SEC or a shareholder the right to sue to challenge a management fee, and it provided for industry self-regulation of salesmens' commissions and alternative methods of regulating front-end load funds.[39]

The SEC's enforcement files indicate that the inexperience of mutual-fund portfolio managers employed by registered advisory firms was partly to blame for the disastrous declines in some funds' assets. The SEC concluded that one firm lost most of a $21 million investment because it had paid for "speculative, unseasoned" stocks bought "without adequate, independent study."[40] The SEC is seeking additional authority from Congress to use to establish bonding or other financial requirements designed to discourage such slipshod practices.

If the New York Stock Exchange would establish a nonprofit mutual fund that would purchase an equal number of shares of every issue traded on the exchange, the small buyer would in fact have the advantage of a stock exchange average. There would be no sales charge; nor would there be an advisory charge; and there would be no need for a large executive and clerical staff.

Should Small Investors Use Mutual Funds?

Since they find it difficult or are reluctant to pay for the services of expert investment advisers—whose annual fees range from $250 to 1 percent of the account—many small investors find mutual funds meet their needs at prices they can afford and are willing to pay. Mutual fund shares are recommended for anyone who does not have the time and skill to study the market and who has less than $15,000 to invest over a long period of time.[41] In addition to giving buyers professional management and diversification, mutual funds give them a sense of security. Even though fund performance has not been impressive, funds have served a useful economic function. They offer small investors a convenient method of spreading risk at a reasonable cost, and they have raised the average return for small investors, whose only alternative was fixed dollar investments.[42]

As for the experts' opinion of mutual funds, Engel takes a dim view of the funds, as compared with direct purchase of common stock,[43] and Cohen and Zinbarg are cautious, but skeptical. They say the mutual fund investor pays too much for convenience and management, that performance has been exaggerated, and that some odious practices are used in selling.[44] Rutberg was blunt when he said, "The most common mistake investors make about mutual funds is buying them."[45] McAlinden views the role of mutual funds from a different perspective. He believes they have their place in the total investment spectrum, particularly for people with only limited sums to invest, but he believes that even the smallest investor should consider buying some individual stocks.[46]

The final decision rests with each individual. If you do decide to use one or more mutual funds, your next problem is how to select the better ones for your purposes. No final answer can be given as the situation constantly changes, but the factors to consider in choosing a fund are the following:

1. What type of fund do you want—growth or income or both? When you have answered that question you will have eliminated a large number.
2. A fund should not be too small or too large; it should have at least $15 million in assets.
3. What is its investment policy?
4 What is its diversification policy?
5. For marketability, a fund should limit its holdings to shares of companies listed on the New York Stock Exchange and the American Stock Exchange.
6. You should choose an established fund which avoids new shares.
7. What compensation does management pay itself and advisers? One-eighth of one percent of the market value of assets for management, plus $\frac{1}{6}$ of one percent for expenses is reasonable.
8. What is the performance record?[47]

SOURCES OF INFORMATION AND SAFEGUARDS

Published Sources of Information

The naive notions held by many amateur investors and their total lack of precaution are almost incredible. They are more casual in choosing a $10,000 investment than in purchasing a $4,000 automobile or even a major household appliance. Their propensity for "tips" is astonishing. The serious investor, large or small, needs to know something about general economic conditions and business prospects, now, in the near future, and in the long run. He or she needs to know how to identify industries having growth potential and how to locate growth companies in growth industries. Security analysis is a highly specialized field in which thousands of analysts function full time. Even they make misjudgments, but their mistakes arise out of differences in evaluation of information rather than out of emotion or lack of information.*

Basically, an investor must be able to read financial reports. For the uninitiated a simple manual titled *How to Read a Financial Report* may be had for the asking.† Among the other main sources of information are sixteen major reporting services published by Standard & Poor's. Since they are very expensive, small investors can consult them in libraries, banks, or brokers' offices. Moody's Investors Services include reference manuals on industrials, utilities, transportation, governments, and financial institutions, and Moody's Stock Survey and Moody's Bond Survey. Moody's Active Stock Reports are one-page summaries of 1,400 widely held issues. Several services, of which Babson, United Business, and Value Line are typical, publish market advice and stock purchase recommendations.

Informative newspapers and periodicals include *Wall Street Journal, Commercial & Financial Chronicle, Barron's Weekly,* and *The Financial World.* Specialized sources include *Best's Insurance News* and Wiesenberger's *Investment Companies.*

Less objective sources, and less complete analyses, include prospectuses of corporations and their financial reports and also brokers' and dealers' promotional literature.

An investment plan requires accurate records for tax purposes, mechanical supervision to take care of conversions, coupons, maturities, options, and rights, and a place in which to keep securities safely. A small investor can do all this himself or – for a fee – accountants, attorneys, bankers, or brokers will do it for him. Fees range from one-third to two-thirds of one percent of principal, with a minimum ranging from $500 to $1,000.

For those interested only in mutual funds, Doane and Hurll list approximately 230 funds, together with helpful information.** They also list eight outstanding funds, any one of which a beginning investor might safely and wisely select. The authors of *$ Your Investments $* compare 100 funds in size, investment policy, selling charges, income return, and growth. They list the addresses of sixty companies, any one of which can be contacted for detailed information.†† Three specialized publications, usually available in banks, brokers' offices, and libraries, are *Moody's Bank and Finance Manual,* Wiesenberger's *Investment Companies,* and Johnson's *Investment Company Charts.*

---

* For more on the complexity of security analysis see Douglas H. Bellmore, *Investments,* 2nd ed. (Cincinnati: South-Western Publishing, 1966), chaps. 20–32, and especially pages 712–716.

† Write to Merrill Lynch, Pierce, Fenner & Smith, 70 Pine Street, New York, N.Y. 10005.

** C. Russell Doane and Charles W. Hurll, Jr., *Investment Trusts and Funds from the Investor's Point of View,* American Institute for Economic Research, Economic Research Bulletin 11, no. 2 (March 1971), pp. 20–21.

†† American Research Council, *$ Your Investments $,* 18 ed. (New York: McGraw-Hill, 1970).

TABLE 20-2. How Investment Alternatives Compare

	Safety of Capital	Current Yield	Inflation Resistance	Liquidity	Additional Expense Involved
U.S. savings bonds					
First year	Excellent	Poor	Poor	Excellent	None
Held to maturity	Excellent	Fair	Poor	Excellent	None
Insured savings accounts	Excellent	Poor	Poor	Excellent	None
Savings certificates	Excellent	Fair to good	Poor	Fair	None
Government securities					
Treasury bills	Excellent	Fair	Good	Good	May be a sales commission
Medium-term notes	Excellent	Good	Fair	Good	May be a sales commission
Long-term bonds	Excellent	Excellent	Poor	Good	May be a sales commission
Common stocks	Fair	Poor	Good	Good	Sales commission
Preferred stocks	Good	Excellent	Poor	Good	Sales commission
High-grade corporate bonds	Good	Excellent	Poor	Good	Sales commission
Mutual funds					
Growth stock funds	Fair	Poor	Good	Good	Management fee,
Bond funds	Fair	Excellent	Poor	Good	may be a sales commission
Money market funds	Good	Fair to good	Good	Good to excellent	Management fee, may be a sales commission
Real estate					
Land	Good	None	Good	Poor	Maintenance and
Rental property	Good	Varies	Good	Poor	management costs (rental), taxes and interest
Gold					
Bullion	Fair	None	Good	Poor	Sales commis-
Coins	Good	None	Good	Poor	sion, storage fees, insurance

Reprinted by permission from *Changing Times*, the Kiplinger Magazine, Feb. 1976, p. 14. Copyright 1976 by the Kiplinger Washington Editors, Inc.

Changing Times frequently carries articles that deal with a wide variety of investment topics. Table 20-2, taken from *Changing Times*, is a concise and clear picture of the investment alternatives one has to choose among.

Investors Need Protection

Amateurs may be victimized both by themselves and by fraudulent sellers of worthless pieces of paper. Doctors, ministers, teachers, and small business executives are reported to be among the most gullible prospects.

Fraudulent sellers of securities seek to justify their operations by claiming that the buyers of their "securities" are just as greedy as the sellers – both are attempting to get something for nothing. When a consumer is swindled in the purchase of a commodity, it is a misfortune, but usually the amount involved is not large. When an investor is swindled, although the amount may not be large, it probably represents all his savings. If this is true, it is all the more crucial for small investors to investigate before they invest.

Until 1933 the prevailing rule in the sale of new securities was "let the buyer beware." Heavy losses incurred by investors after 1929 resulted in extensive Senate Committee investigations. Those inquiries revealed amazing conditions in the securities markets. The testimony and evidence made it clear that under the practices then governing the marketing of securities, prospective investors were fortunate if they avoided losses.

Just one example of an investment fraud, the Texas attorney general recently issued a statement expressing grave concern about oil and natural gas swindles, which he stated were flooding the nation. He estimated that more than $100 million had been invested by about 50,000 people in more than forty states. One company told potential investors it employed psychics with "supernatural powers" who were able to find underground oil and natural gas almost every time a well was drilled. Another "backroom" operator trained salesmen to "sound Texan" – to swear a lot over the telephone and to attack the masculinity of wavering clients. In a crackdown the SEC ordered eight companies to stop selling shares in thirty wells, and the Texas attorney general sued eighteen companies for alleged fraud. Some of these companies actually had drilled oil wells – sometimes only a few feet deep – and then abandoned them. The investors were then told that their money had gone into a dry well. Most investors, living far away and being naive about the oil business, never showed up to inspect their investments.[48]

Federal Laws to Protect Investors

To protect investors, Congress enacted a series of laws, beginning with the Securities Act of 1933. This law provides that those who issue securities for sale to the public in interstate commerce must file a registration statement containing pertinent information about the issue and the offering. Unless a registration statement is in effect, it is unlawful to sell the securities. If it is found that a registration statement contains misinformation or omissions, the registration may be denied, suspended, or canceled. The fact that a security is registered by the Securities and Exchange Commission does not constitute a guarantee by the commission that the facts disclosed are accurate; nor does registration imply approval of the issue by the commission. Registration does not insure investors against loss. Its sole purpose is to provide information on the basis of which investors may make informed and realistic evaluations of the securities.

The Securities Exchange Act of 1934 requires the filing of registration applications and annual and other reports with national securities exchanges and the commission by companies whose securities are listed on the exchanges. Companies whose securities are traded over-the-counter must file annual reports. Any misstatements or omissions may result in suspension or cancelation of the security for exchange trading. The act also regulates the solicitation of proxies. Officers, directors, and stockholders who own more than 10 percent of the outstanding stock must report their holdings and their transactions.

The Public Utility Holding Company Act of 1935 provides for regulation by the commission of the purchase and sale of securities, properties, and other assets by companies comprised within electric and gas utility holding company systems. The purpose of the act is to protect purchasers of shares in mutual funds.

Finally, the Investment Advisers Act of 1940 requires that anyone selling investment advice or counsel must register with the Commission. Fraudulent or deceptive practices are unlawful.

All the foregoing laws are administered by the Securities and Exchange Commission, whose purpose is to protect the interests of the public and investors against malpractices in the securities and financial markets. This involves surveillance of all persons and companies covered by the several acts and the prosecution of violators. Anyone may direct a complaint or inquiry to the central office of the commission or to the appropriate regional office.* Registration statements and other public documents are available for public inspection.

The commission publishes a blacklist of Canadian firms over which it has no direct control but whose stocks are offered for sale in the United States, often by telephone calls from Toronto. Prospective buyers are warned to beware of telephone salesmen who use high-pressure selling methods to "let you in on a sure thing." The list is available and inquiries are encouraged.

There is ample evidence that these laws, written forty-five years ago, even though patched up with amendments, are inadequate. Moreover, no law can be effective if it is not enforced or is weakly enforced. The Securities and Exchange Commission lacks the money and staff to do its job; some critics say it lacks the will. Drastic reforms are overdue.[49]

The Investment Company Amendment Act of 1970 was a compromise measure that made some changes in management fees and sales commissions.[50]

The Investment Advisers Act passed in 1974 merely requires advisers to fill out a simple registration form and to keep certain records. The number of firms and individuals registered as advisers has grown to more than

* Contact the Office of the Secretary, Securities and Exchange Commission, 500 North Capitol Street, Washington, D.C. 20549 or the regional office in Atlanta, Boston, Chicago, Denver, Fort Worth, New York, San Francisco, Seattle, or Arlington, Va.

3,600, from fewer than 1,400 in 1969, and the investments they now manage or help to manage are estimated to total over $130 billion.[51]

The Securities and Exchange Commission went to Congress in 1976 in the hope of getting a law that would require advisers to tell their clients more about their training, experience, and sources of information. More important, the commission asked Congress for authority to establish qualifications for advisers, as it now does for broker-dealers, for example. What helped bring the issue to a head was the revelation that a sixteen-year-old boy had legally registered with the Securities and Exchange Commission as an investment adviser! The Senate failed to act on the bill. Action is needed from Congress to provide the investor with more protection.

State Investor Protection Laws

Some states have so-called "blue-sky laws" to protect investors in securities traded only within the state. As a general rule, state laws are less comprehensive and less effective than federal laws.

Government agencies can regulate security market practices up to a certain point, but in the final analysis each investor must exercise precaution and good judgment. Those who are gullible or who hope to parlay a one cent share of oil, uranium, or aerospace stock into a fortune will always be found out by slick operators and defrauded.

QUESTIONS FOR REVIEW

1. What motivates people to save?
2. What are the ways that a person can save?
3. Which type of investor—aggressive or defensive—are you, or do you think you would be? Why?
4. What are the differences between investment and speculation?
5. What happened in the economy during the early 1970s that made investors reevaluate some investment principles?
6. Should a small investor invest in real estate? Explain.
7. What are the advantages and disadvantages of Individual Retirement Accounts?
8. Classify and evaluate U.S. government bonds, corporate bonds, and municipal bonds as investment possibilities.
9. What kind of financial program, or coverage, should a person have before investing in stocks?
10. Are common stocks a good hedge against inflation? Discuss.
11. What are the hazards of stock ownership? Bond ownership?

12. What are the advantages and disadvantages of mutual funds for the small investor?

13. What are some of the things an investor should be wary of in investing his or her money?

14. Analyze one source of investment information in the school library.

15. What are some of the reasons why investors need government protection?

PROJECTS

1. Debate the pros and cons of investing savings in coins and stamps or antiques.

2. Trace the price and dividend record of three stocks and three bonds over a decade or two. Evaluate them as investments.

3. Find out the various kinds of accounts, interest rates, yields, method of compounding, and crediting of interest at two savings and loan associations and two commercial banks and compare.

4. Draw up an investment program for a couple with two young children who have inherited $50,000.

5. Find out all you can about one load and one no-load mutual fund at a broker's office.

6. Discuss IRA's with a life insurance agent, a broker, and a banker.

7. Check out your local library as a source for investment information. What does it have?

8. Discuss your parents' or a relative's investment program with them.

9. You receive a gift of $5,000. How would you invest it?

10. Have the class set up an imaginary Investment Club with each member contributing $50 a month over a twelve-month period. How would you set it up and operate it?

REFERENCES

1. *St. Petersburg Times*, 31 Aug. 1975, p. 5D.
2. *U.S. News & World Report*, 10 Feb. 1975, p. 61.
3. Alliance for Consumer Protection, Pittsburgh, Pa., Newsletter, Nov. 1975, p. 1.
4. Jerome B. Cohen, *Personal Finance: Principles and Case Problems*, 5th ed. (Homewood, Ill.: Richard D. Irwin, 1975), p. 636.
5. John C. Clendenin and George A. Christy, *Introduction to Investments*, 5th ed. (New York: McGraw-Hill, 1969), pp. 5–6.
6. *Business Week*, 8 Dec. 1975, p. 64.
7. *Fortune*, July 1969, pp. 160–165; *U.S. Government Organizational Manual 1970–1971*, p. 364.
8. Paulson, pp. 45, 102.
9. Clendenin and Christy, chap. 25; William C. Freund, *Investment Fundamen-*

tals (New York: The American Bankers Association, 1966), p. 43; American Research Council, *$ Your Investments $,* 18th ed. (New York: McGraw-Hill, 1970), pp. 151–152.

10. *U.S. News & World Report,* 18 Aug. 1975, p. 12.
11. See Richard J. Stillman, *Guide to Personal Finance,* 2nd ed. (Englewood Cliffs, N.J.: Prentice-Hall, 1975); and Venita Van Caspel, *Money Dynamics: How to Build Financial Independence* (Reston, Va.: Reston, 1975).
12. *Share-Ownership 1975* (New York: The New York Stock Exchange, 1976), pp. 1, 5, 8.
13. *$ Your Investments $,* p. 20.
14. *Ibid.,* p. 88.
15. *St. Petersburg Times,* 14 Nov. 1975, p. 18B.
16. Roger G. Ibbotson and Rex A. Sinquefield, "Stocks, Bonds, Bills and Inflation: Year-by-Year Historical Returns (1926–1974)," *Journal of Business* 49 (1976): 11–48.
17. F. K. Reilly, G. L. Johnson, and R. E. Smith, "Inflation, Inflation Hedges, and Common Stocks," *Financial Analysts Journal* 26 (Jan.-Feb. 1970): 104–110.
18. *New York Times,* 1 Jan. 1976, p. 23C.
19. *Wall Street Journal,* 4 Nov. 1976, p. 41.
20. *St. Petersburg Times Parade,* 29 June 1975, p. 7.
21. Douglas H. Bellemore, *Investments: Principles, Practices, Analysis,* 2nd ed. (Cincinnati: South-Western Publishing, 1966), p. 3; Jerome B. Cohen, *Personal Money Management* (New York: The American Bankers Association, 1967), pp. 41–42; Louis Engel, ed., *How to Buy Stocks: A Guide to Making More Money in the Market* (New York: Bantam Books, 1967), p. 232; Clendenin and Christy, pp. 111–112.
22. *Changing Times,* May 1975, p. 24.
23. *Consumer Reports,* Oct. 1976, p. 590.
24. *Money,* July 1974, p. 61.
25. *A Study of Mutual Funds,* House Report no. 2274, Serial Set 1243, 87th Congress, 2d Session, 1962, p. x (known as "The Wharton Report").
26. *New York Times,* 16 Aug. 1967, pp. 53, 60.
27. Sidney Rutberg, *The Money Balloon: Inflation and How to Live With It* (New York: Simon & Schuster, 1975), p. 188.
28. *Changing Times,* Sept. 1975, p. 25.
29. *Money,* Feb. 1976, pp. 9–10.
30. Materials received from the No-Load Mutual Fund Association.
31. *Business Week,* 15 March 1976, p. 77.
32. *Ibid.*
33. *Institutional Investor Study,* Report of the Securities and Exchange Commission (Summary Vol.), 92d Congress, 1st Session, House Document 92–64, Part 8, 1971, pp. xxi, xxvi.
34. Irwin Friend, Marshall Blume, and Jean Crockett, *Mutual Funds and Other Institutional Investors: A New Perspective* (New York: McGraw-Hill, 1970), pp. 9, 10, 26, 28, 80.
35. *Finance: The Magazine of Money* 87 (Feb. 1969): pp. 52–53.
36. "The Wharton Report," pp. x, xii, xiii, xxi.
37. "The Wharton Report," pp. xi, xii, xxi.
38. *Investment Company Amendments Act of 1970,* 91st Congress, 2d Session, House Report No. 91–1382, 1970, pp. 3, 19; Friend, Blume, and Crockett, pp. 12, 97–108; Frederick Amling, *Investments: An Introduction to Analysis and Management,* 2nd ed. (Englewood Cliffs, N.J.: Prentice-Hall, 1970), p. 629.
39. *New York Times,* 16 Dec. 1970, p. 69.
40. *Wall Street Journal,* 19 Feb. 1976, p. 36.
41. C. Russell Doane and Charles W. Hurll, Jr., *Investment Trusts and Funds From*

the Investor's Point of View, American Institute for Economic Research, Economic Research Bulletin 11, no. 2 (March 1971), pp. 20–21.

42. Friend, Blume, and Crockett, p. 3.
43. Engel, *How to Buy Stocks,* chap. 29.
44. Jerome B. Cohen and Edward D. Zinbarg, *Investment Analysis and Portfolio Management* (Homewood, Ill.: Richard D. Irwin, 1967), pp. 643–644.
45. Rutberg, p. 187.
46. *U.S. News & World Report,* 5 Jan. 1976, p. 39.
47. Doane and Hurll, pp. 21–22.
48. *St. Petersburg Times,* 26 Jan. 1976, p. 8A.
49. *Business Week,* 31 Oct. 1970, pp. 58–64; and 12 Dec. 1970, p. 76.
50. Public Law 91–547, 91st Congress, S. 2224, 14 Dec. 1970; and *Congressional Record,* 116, Sept. 23, 1970, pp. 9087–9104.
51. *Wall Street Journal,* 19 Feb. 1976, p. 36.

PART FIVE

CONSUMERS NEED HELP: SELLERS AND GOVERNMENT RESPOND

CHAPTER 21

SELLERS' EFFORTS TO HELP CONSUMERS

CONSUMERS NEED HELP

Buying Is a Complicated Process

The proliferation in the number of products and the increasing complexity of products continue to make the task of being an intelligent consumer more and more difficult. The average supermarket carries eight to ten thousand different products, and the newer super-supermarkets carry thousands more. Stereos and mini-calculators are complicated products with so many different characteristics to be aware of and look for that it is almost enough to persuade the consumer to buy without investigating. How well equipped is the buyer to make the necessary decisions when he or she enters the labyrinth of the marketplace? What ability does the consumer have to judge quality, quantity, and price? What abilities are necessary to be a good consumer? These questions should be asked whether the consumer is entering a supermarket, a department or appliance store, or buying home furnishings, an automobile, or a house.

Supposedly the consumer wants to purchase goods and services with the best combination of price, quantity, quality, and service to meet his or her particular needs. The problems involved in reaching this goal at times seem almost insurmountable. The volume of commodities for sale, both as to kinds and varieties, is increasing every day. There are more producers producing more goods, and many of them are marketed under a variety of brand names. Just the companies listed on the New York Stock Exchange introduced 3,500 new products during one year. The computer industry generated 144 new products. Companies selling communications other than telephones introduced 132 products; pharmaceutical firms, 118; photographic equipment firms, 90; toiletry firms, 80; and surgical and medical instrument firms, 52.[1] Not all of these products will be bought by the individual consumer, but many will, and if you add to these products all those new products introduced by the thousands of smaller businesses, the consumer continues to be overwhelmed. The barrage of over $33 billion of advertising blaring forth the virtues of these products adds to the complexity of the marketplace. What are the sellers doing and attempting to do to assist the consumer through this labyrinth—the marketplace?

How Producers Have Reacted

Business executives know that most consumers are not good judges of the quality of the things they buy. Many clerks are unable to judge the qualities of different brands of the merchandise they sell. Indeed, as consumers of goods and services other than those few which they produce, not many producers are able to judge quality.

Classified according to their reaction to this situation, sellers fall into three general groups. There are, first of all, a few who try to capitalize on consumer ignorance by misrepresenting what they have to sell.

A second, larger group seeks to profit from consumer ignorance. They use brands, trademarks, and advertising to lift their products out of competition. They try to make consumers think that their products are the best to be obtained. Much money is spent on advertising to create goodwill and to develop consumer buying habits that will be profitable for these producers.

The third group takes a different attitude. Realizing that consumers are unable to compare the quality of numerous brands of merchandise, they attempt to provide special assurance that their products are as good as they are claimed to be.

COMMON TYPES OF SELLER AIDS

Brands and Trademarks

For those who have been reared in a trademarked world it is difficult to imagine an economy in which the market is not filled with branded commodities. The Federal Trademark Act of 1946 defines a *trademark* as "any word, name, symbol, or device or any combination thereof adopted and used by a manufacturer or merchant to identify his goods and distinguish them from those manufactured or sold by others." The word *brand* comes from the act of affixing a mark—for example, the branding of cattle. In practice the terms are used interchangeably.

Why have brands and trademarks been adopted so completely? They are an outgrowth of the process of the mass production of goods in anticipation of demand by machine methods in large factories. This entails substantial fixed expenses. By marking their products and advertising them, manufacturers hope to lift them out of, or lessen the impact of, price competition. If they are successful, sales are increased and stabilized, the fixed expenses can be spread over a greater volume, and the expense per unit decreased. Advertising is based on the use of trademarks and brands. If it were not possible to identify merchandise, it would be impossible to advertise the products of a particular company. An exception to this is to be found in the advertising campaigns sponsored by a few trade associations, such as the Florida Citrus Commission and the American Dairy Association, which do not advertise a particular company's product, but which advertise the industry's product.

The seller has the problem not only of giving his product a distinctive name to differentiate it from his competitor's products but also of convincing the consumer that there is a "real" difference, whether such a difference exists or not.

Brands and trademarks are valuable aids to aggressive manufacturers and distributors. The adoption and use of such devices create a property right in the user. After use in interstate commerce and compliance with relevant statutes, it is possible to register such a mark. This is valuable in defending the user's right in court against violation by competitors. After continued use and registration, a manufacturer may safely spend millions of dollars annually for advertising. The hope is that shoppers will develop purchasing habits that will turn them into customers, those who habitually purchase the same brands. If this can be accomplished, the manufacturer has lifted his product out of what the economist refers to as pure competition. The manufacturer is then assured a steady market at prices he sets.

Limited evidence suggests that there seems to be a correlation between the amount of education a consumer has and the degree to which he or she depends on brand names – the higher the education level attained, the less dependence on brand names, and vice versa.

Are trademarks helpful to consumers? It is not the primary intent of the sellers of trademarked merchandise to help consumers – any benefit which might accrue to them is secondary and indirect. Trademarks do not give any quality information – in fact, the Trademark Act does not permit the registering of words or devices which seek to describe the goods or to indicate their quality. Nevertheless it is contended that trademarks are a guide to quality because a manufacturer runs the risk of losing repeat sales if his product is unsatisfactory. However, since few consumers can judge quality, the fact that they purchase a certain brand is not evidence of its superior quality. There may be a number of other brands of equal or superior quality, and it is possible that there is merchandise available in bulk form which is as good as, or better than, the branded product.

The trademark provides no price information – in fact, those manufacturers making the greatest use of this device minimize price in their advertising. In many cases similar merchandise carrying unfamiliar trademarks or no trademark may be purchased at lower prices.

It may have been true at one time that trademarked merchandise saved consumers time when they shopped. The argument was that having made purchases of a particular trademarked product and having found it satisfactory, they did not need to spend time shopping around or need to run the risk of making an unsatisfactory purchase by trying other brands. Today a prospective buyer finds himself confronted with scores of brands

of similar products – so similar that they do not have any exclusive selling
argument or appeal. There are so many brands and trademarks that they
are as likely to confuse as to help.

An argument in favor of trademarked merchandise is that once the
buyer has made a satisfactory purchase he can be assured of uniform
quality in the future. But who is to give the assurance, other than the manufacturer? While it may be true that the quality of some products can be
maintained at a desired level of uniformity, it is true also that other products
can and do vary considerably. The use of a trademark does not prevent the
manufacturer from changing the quality of the product if he desires.

Do brands and trademarks increase or diminish competition? An industry spokesman has said they are like surnames, without which there
could be no competition because it would be impossible to distinguish
among products. It has been argued that if they were restricted in use to
their original function of indicating the sources or origins of products, they
could stimulate competition. However, when they are used in conjunction
with advertising, they can become the means of creating partially monopolistic power.

Labels

Labels are closely associated with trademarks. Indeed, from the producer's point of view there may be very little difference between labels and
trademarks, a label frequently being nothing more than a device for applying a trademark to a product.

The form that a label takes varies with the commodity on which it
appears. A label may be stamped on, as in the case of oranges and unpack-
aged meat, or sewed on, as is the custom with clothing. Labels for products
contained in bottles or tin cans are usually pasted on the containers, while
they are printed on the wrappers of some products, such as candy and chewing gum. The vast majority of the items in retail stores are in packaged
form, the labels being pasted or printed on the packages.

The information that labels bear varies considerably. Sometimes it
shows nothing more than the name of the product, the manufacturer, and
the address. Not uncommonly, labels carry directions for use, claims for
what the product will do, or statements of quality. Some labels tell buyers
when the merchandise was packed or the time period within which it
should be used. In many cases the law requires that the quantity contained
in the package be shown by a statement of its net weight, measure, or
count. With the exception of labels covering foods, drugs, cosmetics, woolen
and fur goods, hazardous products, and textiles entering interstate commerce, statements on labels need not be factual.*

In too many cases labels are deceptive. The Federal Trade Commission

---

* For the special provisions regarding labels covering these products, see chapters 22 and 25.

tries to block firms that label merchandise as being imported when it is produced domestically, or as containing materials in whole or in part which it does not contain. Labels often fail to give prospective buyers the information they need in order to make an intelligent selection. These omissions may be more serious than misinformation.

It has been argued that since consumers do not read labels, it is useless to provide informative labels. Maybe all consumers do not read labels, but those who do have a right to know what the ingredients are, whether they may be harmful, how to use the product, the quantity, what company made the product, and other pertinent information. If more and more consumers learn that labels are factual and do give adequate and helpful information, they will realize the value of reading such labels carefully.

Are labels helpful to consumers? Labels on foods, drugs, hazardous products, woolen and fur products, and textiles entering interstate commerce contain factual information on which consumers can rely. Misstatement or misrepresentation makes the manufacturer liable to prosecution and penalty. For other merchandise the label, like the trademark, is of doubtful value. It is not always a reliable guide to quality or an assurance of uniformity. The printing of labels costs very little and the superlatives that many of them contain cost nothing.

The presumption is that only reliable manufacturers will use identifying labels. Their objective will be to secure repeat sales; and in order to accomplish that it will be necessary that the labeled merchandise satisfy buyers. In this way it is the hope of the manufacturer that his label will become a guide which prospective buyers will follow to their satisfaction and to his gain. To the extent that labels contain factual information on which consumers can rely, they may serve this purpose and thus benefit consumers and those producers who use them.

What Good Labeling Could Do

Good, complete, informative labeling should include the brand name of the product; the name and address of the manufacturer; the weight, measure, or count; the drained weight—so consumers can tell how much actual food and how much liquid they are buying; the ingredients—by percentages where possible; directions for the proper use of the product; cautionary measures concerning the product and its use; special care of the product—if applicable; recipes on food products if space is available; nutritional labeling, nutritional guidelines, calorie information, and fatty acid labeling on food products; for perishable products a date showing either when the product should no longer be sold and/or when it should no longer be used and proper storage information; and specific additional information when necessary for certain products. If this type of informative labeling were provided on the containers of most products, *and* if consumers were aware of this, significant changes would take place in the market.

A consumer enters a store to purchase a TV Chicken Dinner. She might see two brands labeled and priced as follows:

Brand A	*Brand B*
TV Chicken Dinner:	TV Chicken Dinner:
Total Weight 12 ozs.	Total Weight 12 ozs.
Government Inspected USDA	Government Inspected USDA
Grade A Chicken—6 ounces	Grade B Chicken—4 ounces
Potatoes—3 ounces	Potatoes—4 ounces
Peas—3 ounces	Peas—4 ounces
Butter, salt, and pepper added	Margarine, salt, and pepper added
Price—89 cents	Price—89 cents
Unit price—$1.18 per pound	Unit price—$1.18 per pound
To be sold by March 15	To be sold by March 15

Nutrition information and cooking instructions should also be on the label. Labels like this would give the consumer the information necessary to make a rational choice based on quality and contents rather than an emotional choice based on the popularity of the brand name. This would do more to force quality improvements than any other measure.

The Food and Drug Administration requires that if nutrition claims are made for a food product in advertising or on labels such information must be clearly listed on the label as prescribed by the FDA. The purpose of this requirement is to prevent nutrition "races" among food processors which might not be in the best interests of the consumer but could be used by the seller for promotional purposes.

The following example shows what food processors must put on their labels, if they choose to give any nutrition information.[2] They are not required to give any nutrition information, but if they do it must be given as required by the FDA.

Net Wt. .... 1 lb. or 454 grams   Cups.......... Approx. 2

INGREDIENTS: GREEN BEANS, WATER, SALT.

NUTRITION INFORMATION—PER ONE CUP PORTION

CALORIES 35   FAT................................. NONE
PROTEIN .... 2 gm   CARBOHYDRATE (avail)....... 6 gm

PERCENT OF STANDARD RECOMMENDED
DAILY ALLOWANCE (RDA) PER ONE CUP PORTION

PROTEIN	2	NIACIN	2
VITAMIN A	20	CALCIUM	6
VITAMIN C	8	IRON	8
THIAMIN (B_1)	2	PHOSPHORUS	4
RIBOFLAVIN (B_2)	4	MAGNESIUM	6

For good nutrition eat a variety of foods.

The need for full disclosure of ingredients on food product labels was emphasized in a report to Congress which showed the number of persons who needed such information for health reasons. For example, officials of the American Heart Association estimate that about 23 million people who have heart conditions should avoid saturated fats, sodium, and caffeine. Over 4 million diabetics and kidney patients must avoid or restrict their intake of sugar and potassium, respectively, and both should restrict their intake of sodium. In addition, allergy physicians estimate that over 7 million people suffer from allergy reactions to ingredients such as milk, eggs, gluten, wheat, corn, tartrazine, nuts, and monosodium glutamate.[3]

How many people are aware of the fact that when they buy ready-to-eat breakfast cereals, they could be buying a cereal that is, by weight, more than half sugar? In a study of seventy-eight ready-to-eat breakfast cereals, eight of the seventy-eight had less than 5 percent of the total weight devoted to sugar. Twelve contained 5 to 10 percent sugar. Twenty-three cereals had 10 to 25 percent sugar. A total of twenty-four contained 25 to 50 percent sugar, and eleven contained more than 50 percent sugar. One of these contained 70.8 percent sugar.[4] But since the law does not require percentage labeling of ingredients there is no way for people to know the sugar content of the breakfast cereals they buy.

Consumers Union tested forty-four brands of cereals, including many heavily advertised to children, a selection of popular hot cereals, and a few so-called "natural" cereals. CU found large differences in relative nutrition. Far and away the most nutritious were Maypo 30-Second Oatmeal, Cheerios, and Special "K." It was noted that none should be relied on for complete breakfast nutrition; juice, an egg, or a meat are also needed.[5]

Warranties

A warranty is an assurance of the quality and service and often of the length of use to be expected from a product offered for sale, usually with a promise of reimbursement. A warranty is usually a written guarantee of the integrity of a product and of the maker's responsibility for the repair or replacement of defective parts. In common usage both terms are used interchangeably. Until 1975 the Federal Trade Commission made no distinction between them and considered them synonymous, but with the passage of the Magnuson-Moss Warranty Act in 1975, the FTC told manufacturers to drop the word "guarantee" in representations to consumers about the performance of their products and instead to use the word "warranty."

Implied warranties are promises that the product is of average salable quality, will do what that product is normally expected to do, and will last a "reasonable" period of time. Depending on the situation, a warranty can be for a very short time or, if the goods are durable and in common understanding are expected to give many years of use, for a long time. Express warranties are specific promises in writing made by the manufacturer or retailer concerning quality, performance, condition, or other characteristics. The major difference is that when one accepts an "express warranty" one often gives up the "implied warranty" as a condition of acceptance.

Then we have a limited warranty—"guaranteed for 90 days"—which frequently tends to be more of a protection to the seller than to the buyer. Lifetime warranty is interpreted by many consumers to mean one's own lifetime, but it usually refers to the lifetime of the good, which might be surprisingly short. Parts warranties specify what parts are guaranteed and for what period of time. An unconditional warranty should mean exactly what it states, but again the realities may be very different. For example, one major mail-order firm advertised that a product was "unconditionally guaranteed," but issued a written warranty containing numerous limitations. A cynic has stated, "The big type giveth and the small type taketh away."

The warranty is an outgrowth of the rule of law known as *caveat emptor*—let the buyer beware. Sellers' quality claims were to be discounted as merely trade puffing. In such a situation, where consumers had no redress, some producers developed the warranty as a device for assuring prospective buyers that they could rely on the statements made by the seller. The purpose of the warranty was to give the warrantor a competitive advantage. Seeing the advantage, unscrupulous sellers adopted the warranty but refused to honor their pledge. Legal action resulted in the growth of a body of doctrine which rendered the warranty comparatively useless.

Warranties may take several forms. Some firms follow the policy that "the customer is always right." While there is no specific warranty covering every transaction, there is an implied and sometimes an explicit warranty that all transactions must be satisfactory to the customer. In case of dissatisfaction, regardless of cause, the merchandise will be replaced or the customer's money refunded.

A second form is that of specific warranties of certain goods, such as automobile tires or household appliances. In some cases these warranties are put into writing and a copy given to the purchaser. This type of warranty is more restricted than the one described above. The rights of the purchaser are stated precisely and technically in written form; beyond that they do not go. For example, a manufacturer may claim that a product warranty has been voided if the product has not been installed properly. To protect himself in this case the consumer needs to obtain a warranty from the installer.

Some manufacturers use a warranty as a protective device for themselves. They set a short time limit, such as 30, 60, or 90 days, on warranties for products that should be usable for a much longer time. Without stipulating a specific time limit, manufacturers sometimes are under pressure "to make good" by some consumers whenever the product breaks down. Establishing a warranty with a fixed time limit gives the manufacturer an "out" when claims are made after the expiration of the warranty.

Another type of warranty is that which seeks to assure the customer on some specific point. A manufacturer may warrant, for example, that his product is 100 percent wool or that the color of the fabric will not fade. These specific warranties may be substantiated by a promise to refund the purchaser's money in case the merchandise does not meet the terms of the promise. A more common method is that of providing adjustment under which the customer is charged a pro rata amount for the use he or she has already had from the product. The consumer must be aware of what is provided in this type of warranty; he is mistaken if he believes that he should receive a new automobile battery free when the battery with a thirty-six-month warranty goes bad after thirty-three months' use. In this case he would receive a refund of one-twelfth of the purchase price. In other cases there is no definite policy in meeting a customer's complaints, and in all cases there is a strong probability that a dispute will arise as to whether or not the terms of the warranty have been met or apply.

The value of warranties to sellers depends largely on the extent to which they follow a liberal policy of honoring them. If buyers find that a seller not only makes but honors a liberal warranty of his products, they may pay higher prices and purchase more from him. If the manufacturer's merchandise is good enough to warrant his warranty, he has nothing to lose and a great deal to gain in following such a policy. Unless he is willing to live up to the promises made to his purchasers, the warranty will prove of slight value, because it will not draw or maintain permanent patronage. Unfortunately for reliable warrantors, there are unreliable and unscrupulous dealers who use the warranty as a competitive device without any intention of meeting its obligations.

The value of warranties to consumers depends on the reliability of the warrantor and the person who has the specific responsibility of making good on the warranty. This is true because in practice and in law the consumer has little recourse. A warranty is usually valid between the retail seller and the consumer buyer and/or between the manufacturer and the consumer buyer. If a warranty is made and the warrantor contests the claim of the dissatisfied buyer, the latter would have to institute suit to recover damages. Business executives know that most buyers are not going to undertake legal action unless the amounts involved are large. Such cases are likely to be rare because the generally accepted legal rule is that the buyer may receive as damages only the difference between the actual value of the article and what its value should have been as warranted. If a buyer has suffered physical injury as a result of consuming a product, she may sue the distributor and, in some cases, the manufacturer for negligence, but this right accrues to her whether or not a warranty has been made.

The scope of the manufacturer's product liability has been expanding in recent years. In the past a person injured by a defective product could recover damages from the manufacturer only if he or she bought the item directly from the manufacturer and could prove that he was negligent. In recent years many state courts have dropped these two provisions and have begun awarding damages for an injury simply if the product is shown to be defective or unfit for its intended use. High courts in some states have adopted the doctrine—known as "strict liability" or sometimes "implied warranty"—and others are moving toward its adoption.

Many department and mail-order stores have developed reputations as reliable warrantors. They follow the practice of satisfying customers as completely as possible, even though such a procedure may entail recognition of some invalid claims. Customers having charge accounts with retail stores are in a stronger bargaining position, which frequently assures them a more satisfactory adjustment than if they paid cash.

Although warranties are related to the use of trademarks and labels, it is doubtful that retail buyers place much reliance on them. Experience has shown that warranties are easily made but hard to enforce. While warranties are not in themselves informational, they may vouch for the validity of information contained on a label or in an advertising statement. Many of them are so vague or so general as to be easily evaded and consequently are of little use to the ultimate consumer. Recognition of this fact led the Federal Trade Commission to issue the pamphlet *Guides Against Deceptive Advertising of Guarantees*, a seven-point guide for sellers to follow. This action grew out of the increasing irritation to buyers and legitimate sellers of abuses of the warranty device by irresponsible sellers. Now sellers must advertise their warranties according to these rules or risk action by the commission. The FTC says advertising of warranties should answer such questions as:

1. What product or part of a product is being warranted?
2. For how long a time?
3. Will the warrantor repair the product, or replace part of it, and charge the owner for labor?
4. Will the warrantor give the buyer a new product?
5. Who is warrantying the product, the manufacturer or the retailer?
6. If products are warranted on a pro rata basis, upon what conditions will adjustments be made?
7. Is routine servicing covered by the warranty?

The Major Appliance Consumer Action Panel* suggests that consumers ask the following questions about warranties:

1. Does the warranty cover the entire product? Only certain parts? Is labor included?
2. Who is responsible for repairing the product? The dealer? A service agency? The manufacturer?
3. Who pays for repairs? Parts? Labor? Shipping charges?
4. How long does the warranty last on the entire product? On individual parts or assemblies?
5. If the product is out of use because of a service problem or if it has to be removed from the home for repair, will a substitute product or service be provided? By whom?

In addition to reading and understanding the operating instructions, you should make sure you can find the answers to your questions about warranties and that you fully understand them.

* See page 563 for a discussion of this organization.

What Do Warranties Guarantee?

A sampling of a few warranties of some well-known companies helps to answer this question. The Hamilton Beach one-year warranty on electrical appliances states: "During the warranty period this product will be repaired or replaced, at Hamilton Beach's option, at no cost to you." This had previously been a five-year warranty. Warranties on some items, such as inexpensive pens and mechanical pencils, are almost worthless when a service and mailing charge is included which are almost equal to the cost of the item. Just because a warranty covers a stipulated period of time should not keep a buyer from attempting to get redress when he believes that the product has not performed as it should. Monsanto Company has a "Wear-Dated" warranty. For more than fourteen years Monsanto has promised that "Wear-Dated" clothing would give a year's normal wear or they would replace the item or refund the full purchase price. It also warrants that its Monsanto upholstery fabric on furniture will be repaired or replaced if it fails to give two years normal wear. Corning Glass Works has a limited warranty. Corning promises to replace the glass part of any Pyrexware item that breaks from heat within two years from date of purchase, when used according to directions.

Automobile warranties change from time to time. Automobile warranties in general are for twelve months or 12,000 miles, whichever comes first. As an added incentive to stimulate sales, car manufacturers have from time to time extended the coverage of a warranty. For example, General Motors had a bad experience with some engines in the early models of the Vega when it was introduced. The results were nearly disastrous for GM, so the company began to warrant the 140 cubic-inch engine for five years or 60,000 miles, whichever came first. Coverage was then extended to the same size engine in GM's Monza, Pontiac Astre, and Sunbird. It warrants to repair without charge the cylinder block, cylinder head, all internal engine parts, intake and exhaust manifold, and water pump if repairs are necessary because of defects in material or workmanship. Chrysler, Ford, and GM, in keeping with the Magnuson-Moss Warranty Act of 1975, now give "limited" warranties. American Motors Corporation cars (but not Jeep vehicles) that carry the AMC "Buyer Protection Plan" carry the full warranty as defined in the Magnuson-Moss Act. Under an AMC warranty a defective car could conceivably be returned for replacement or refund. AMC's general service manager said they could not conceive of a situation where they could not repair a car to the customer's satisfaction under the AMC "Buyer Protection Plan." Each automobile company warrants the emission control system for five years or 50,000 miles, whichever comes first, in accordance with the regulations issued by the federal Environmental Protection Agency.

Like other warranties, the ones for autos are designed primarily to limit manufacturer responsibility. In addition to limitations on time, auto warranties also spell out a list of things for which the manufacturer will not be responsible.

There are also what have been referred to as "secret warranties" – car makers call them "service policies" – under which repairs may be made on cars two, three, or four years old, but owners are not notified about the potential problems being covered. These "extended" warranties are quietly authorized by the manufacturer when a specific defect appears in a number of cars. Then the complaining car buyer will be taken care of, but not those buyers who have the car with that defect who do not complain.

If the Department of Transportation directs a manufacturer to issue a recall notice for a safety problem in a particular car model, the manufacturer is legally responsible for correcting the problem and paying for it, regardless of the conditions of the warranty.

Warranties on Your House

In 1974 the National Association of Home Builders (NAHB) established the Home Owners Warranty (HOW) Program, a voluntary program under which builders can give their customers a ten-year nationally insured warranty on the structural integrity of their new house.

A local warranty council, licensed by the Home Owners Warranty Corporation, an NAHB subsidiary, adopts standards for workmanship and materials. During the first year the builder must make good on any failures to meet construction standards, such as faulty insulation, improper construction, plumbing and electrical defects, at no cost to the homeowner. During the second year of the warranty the builder continues to be responsible for defects in the heating, cooling, electrical, and plumbing systems as well as for structural defects. After the second year a national insurance plan directly insures the homeowner against major structural defects for the next eight years. However, if the builder cannot or will not perform his warranty obligations in the first two years, the insurance company which underwrites the How program backs the builder's written warranty. In addition, if the house is sold before the warranty coverage has expired, the remainder of the coverage passes to the new owner. By 1976 HOW councils covered new houses in 38 states and included 277 state and local homebuilders associations. These councils have insured 58,000 houses.[6] HOW has gained the support of the financial community, and its special feature of providing a conciliation or arbitration program to resolve consumer disputes has had good results. In addition to the HOW program the National Association of Realtors has endorsed warranty contract insurance programs offered by three companies.

The Magnuson-Moss Warranty Act

A congressional staff report on warranties, released in 1974, charged that most manufacturers had escaped their obligations to consumers by offering product warranties with important limitations and ambiguous language.[7] Of the 200 warranties examined, the average length was between 300 and 400 words. The four major American automobile manufacturers offered the longest warranties, one of which exceeded 2,500 words. The staff found that only one of fifty-one companies studied offered a warranty free of "catches." The average number of limitations imposed was between three and four. The report charged that warranties often shroud and effectively cover up the seller's obligation to the purchaser. The report showed no significant improvement in warranties since a 1969 study was issued by a presidential task force. The Better Business Bureau reported that failure to honor warranties was the fifth most complained about practice in 1975. The outcome of this study and general public reaction concerning warranties was the enactment of legislation by Congress which was designed to make sure that buyers would be served better by warranties.

July 4, 1975, the Magnuson-Moss Warranty Act went into effect. This act requires that any manufacturer offering a "full" warranty must agree to correct or replace a defective product free within a "reasonable" time whether the owner is the original buyer or not. Anything less than such unconditional assurance must be labeled a "limited" warranty. The Federal Trade Commission was assigned the responsibility of drawing up specific regulations under the act. The law does not make product warranties mandatory, but it requires all written warranties to disclose their terms and conditions in simple language. The law, in effect, puts all products under implied warranty even where there is no written warranty to cover them.

The act went into effect before specific regulations had been drawn up by the FTC. Unfortunately, the immediate effect was actually to weaken some warranties previously considered models. Some companies switched to the "limited" warranty until the confusion could be cleared up because they were not certain what their legal responsibilities would be if they were to give a "full" warranty.

The FTC then issued three regulations that manufacturers or retailers must abide by if they offer "full" warranties for products costing $15 or more. One regulation requires manufacturers to reveal warranty information to consumers before they buy the product. This can be done by attaching warranties to floor samples, printing them on packages, or displaying them on a sign near the product. Before this regulation went into effect, consumers would take the product home, open the box, and find the warranty inside. The second regulation requires that warranty terms be disclosed in "simple and readily understood language." Among the facts that must be listed are precisely when, how, and by whom a product would be repaired or replaced and who would make a refund. Warranties have often been filled with legal language offering implied instead of explicit promises. The first two regulations took effect January 1, 1977. The third regulation went into effect on July 4, 1976. This regulation establishes a procedure to handle consumer complaints. Under this rule a manufacturer may choose to allow adjudication of disputes before the consumer business arbitration tribunals that have been created by many better business bureaus or to set up its own panel. But a company panel must be composed mainly of nonindustry representatives. In addition, a warrantor of a consumer product that carries a "full" warranty can deduct a cash amount when the item is returned by the purchaser for refund if the consumer made use of the product prior to its return.

There is some concern that the vagueness of the language in the act, and even of the regulations as they have been developed, will encourage many companies simply to stop offering warranties to avoid getting entangled in the new rules. Many companies continue to warrant their products though because a manufacturer's promise to repair defects is a strong inducement to consumers to buy the product.

In addition, the law allows any large group of consumers who have been victimized by a fraudulent warranty to file a federal class-action suit. Such a suit is possible when at least 100 consumers with at least $25 each at stake are involved and where the total amount in controversy has the sum or value of at least $50,000. These conditions, while they sound restrictive, are nonetheless much more liberal than most previous bases for class actions.[8] The FTC also ruled that its *Guides Against Deceptive Advertising of Guarantees* would continue to be in effect.

OTHER TYPES OF SELLER AIDS

Testing Laboratories

There are approximately 1,000 laboratories in the United States that test products used by consumers. These labs may be established with a minimum of effort, and frequently no license is required. As a result, the spectrum of competence of American testing laboratories ranges from high to very low.[9]

Some retailers assume responsibility for the quality and performance of the merchandise they sell by operating their own testing laboratories. Sears, Roebuck & Company has the largest private consumer goods laboratory operated by a retail organization; Montgomery Ward has a Merchandise Development and Testing Laboratory; J. C. Penney Laboratory tests consumer products so as to insure honest tags, labels, and advertising which go beyond the minimum legal requirements. But not many retailers can afford such an expensive service.

Seals of Approval

Surveys have revealed the search of buyers for some dependable assurance as to the quality of the things they buy. "Double-Your-Money-Back" guarantees are useless in their judgment. The promise of "Your Money Back If Not Satisfied" was acceptable, but an "Unconditional Guarantee" was considered better. The phrase "Laboratory Tested" rated high, but the *Good Housekeeping* "Seal of Approval" topped them all.

Good Housekeeping pioneered seals of approval. In 1912, William Randolph Hearst established a Good Housekeeping Institute and a Good Housekeeping Bureau of Foods, Sanitation, and Health. The purpose of those agencies was to aid and protect consumers. To strengthen consumer confidence in the project, Dr. Harvey W. Wiley, whose integrity and professional reputation were nationally known, was appointed director. Readers were told that products advertised in *Good Housekeeping* magazine had been tested and approved. The tests were conducted without charge to the manufacturer, and it was claimed that a large percentage of tested merchandise was rejected. With the exception of certain kinds of goods, a manufacturer whose product had been accepted was permitted to use the *Good Housekeeping* seal of approval in his own advertising and as a label attached to his product. The label was offered to purchasers as assurance that the product was as represented. Magazine readers were guaranteed that if a product advertised in *Good Housekeeping* proved to be unsatisfactory it would be investigated and, if found defective, would be replaced or the customer's money refunded. The Good Housekeeping Institute limited its activities to mechanical devices and articles of household equipment, while the Good Housekeeping Bureau dealt only with foods, drugs, and cosmetics.

In 1939 the FTC charged Hearst Magazines, Inc., with the use of unfair methods of competition and unfair or deceptive acts and practices. The commission announced the following findings: that from 1920 to 1939 *Good Housekeeping* had operated a shopping service represented as free "when in truth and in fact respondents received a commission of from 5 to 7 percent from the sellers of the merchandise purchased through such service"; that *Good Housekeeping* represented that its guarantee was unlimited when in fact it was not; that whoever wished to use the seals was required to purchase them and all plates and certificates from *Good Housekeeping;* and that the tests "generally were not sufficient to insure the fulfillment of the claims made for such products. In some instances seals of approval for services or commercial offerings were issued without even an adequate preliminary investigation," and the FTC found that "many of the advertisements appearing in *Good Housekeeping* magazine contained false, deceptive, and misleading statements and representations." Holding that Hearst Magazines had violated the Federal Trade Commission Act, the FTC in 1941 issued an order against Hearst to cease and desist from: 1) representing in its advertising that statements are true when in fact they are not; 2) from permitting the use of seals of approval unless adequate and thorough tests actually have been made; and 3) from representing that any product advertised in *Good Housekeeping* is guaranteed by *Good Housekeeping* unless such guarantee is without limitation or if limited that such limitations are clearly stated.[10]

In 1941 *Good Housekeeping* adopted a guaranty seal which said: "Replacement or refund of money guaranteed by *Good Housekeeping* if defective or not as advertised therein." In 1946 the words "defective or" were dropped. The Good Housekeeping Institute and the Good Housekeeping Bureau seals were discontinued, as were all other seals of approval. In 1962 the phrase "as advertised therein" in the guaranty seal was deleted.

Good Housekeeping now refers to the seal as the "*Good Housekeeping* Consumers' Refund or Replacement Policy." The seal now states: "A limited warranty to consumers—*Good Housekeeping*—promises replacement or refund if defective." Except for this "Consumers' Policy" of refund or replacement, *Good Housekeeping* makes no warranty or other guarantee, express or implied, with respect to products and services advertised in its pages. This "Policy" does not extend to insurance, realty, automobiles, public transportation, travel facilities, catalogues and merchandise portfolios, "shopping by mail" items, premiums, advertisements for schools, hotels, summer camps, and similar organizations, and institutional advertisements. And it does not assume responsibility for faulty installation or service by dealers or independent contractors for products that carry the seal.

Good Housekeeping has not made public the amount of refunds or the number of replacements that have been made, other than to state that thousands of dollars of refunds are made each year out of its own funds in handling several thousand complaints.

In 1973 a news release put out by the Hoover Company which publicized four new lines of sweepers stated that all were "guaranteed by *Good Housekeeping*." A letter was sent by a friend of the writer to the Hoover Company asking what "guaranteed by *Good Housekeeping*" meant. The Hoover customer relations manager replied, "Unfortunately, I do not have a copy of the *Good Housekeeping* guarantee available for reference." This would lead one to assume that the customer relations manager was not concerned about this "guarantee."

Good Housekeeping has long been pre-eminent among magazines for women, and many housewives have used the seals as one of their guides in buying. Some consumers who question the integrity of an organization such as Consumers Union or Consumers' Research accept the recommendation or the guarantee of *Good Housekeeping* without question. Yet there are questions that should arise in their minds. Assuming that the tests to which products are subjected are valid, the seal simply says to prospective buyers that the article is probably all right in performance. It does not indicate that it is the best available article. The consumer has no knowledge of the standards by which products are tested. Sometimes *Good Housekeeping* investigators go to a factory for a private checkup on new products. Factory demonstrators would be less than human if they did not choose an item known to be in perfect condition. If standards were set very high, the number of potential advertisers would be reduced and the gross income of the magazine might decline. *Good Housekeeping* advertising revenues are over $44 million annually. The November, 1975, issue alone carried over $4.6 million in 162 ad pages. According to its publisher it does refuse some advertising, yet it seeks advertisers aggressively and as an inducement permits them to use the seal in their advertising and on their products. But a seller is prohibited by *Good Housekeeping* from using the seal unless he runs a minimum of two-thirds of a page of advertising during a twelve-month period, at a cost of $17,700 for a black-and-white ad or $22,199 for a four-color ad.[11] By contrast, Consumers Union takes legal action against any firm that it finds trying to exploit a good rating in its magazine by advertising that it has been recommended by Consumers Union.

Parents' Magazine is published by Parents' Magazine Enterprises, Inc. In 1966 the publisher of *Parents' Magazine* consented to a Federal Trade Commission order prohibiting the magazine from misrepresenting the basis on which its seal was granted. The FTC found that the seal was awarded to some products solely on the recommendation of *Parents' Magazine* staff members, who were not qualified technicians or medical experts. Some awards were made on the basis of tests and reports submitted by the applicant for a seal. In some cases use of the seal was permitted by the editorial staff on the basis of the reputation of the applicant. The magazine's seal now reads: "Limited warranty. Refund or replacement guaranteed by *Parents' Magazine* if product or performance is defective and reported within 30 days of purchase." The *Parents' Magazine* seal is granted only to products and services that are advertised in *Parents' Magazine* and that *Parents' Magazine* believes are suitable for families with children.

A lengthy statement is found in the magazine that details the handling of complaints and includes a disclaimer. The use of the seal is not granted in connection with automobiles or public transportation or to insurance companies, banks, or institutional advertisers. The seal may not be used by a seller until the bureau staff and/or consultants have studied the products and the claims made for them. The Nationwide Consumer Testing Institute, Inc., a private commercial organization, is retained to make such tests.*

The magazine's promotional brochure tells prospective advertisers that other advertisers have found that the use of the seal increases sales. The minimum advertisement to qualify has been two-thirds of a page. If complaints are received from consumers, *Parents' Magazine* handles the cases. If a manufacturer fails to settle a valid claim, the magazine settles and then endeavors to collect from the manufacturer. *Parents' Magazine*, like *Good Housekeeping*, does not disclose the number of replacements or the amount of refunds that are made under its limited warranty. They say the total number of complaints is small and each is handled with the manufacturer,

---

* The Nationwide Consumer Testing Institute, Inc. is a wholly-owned subsidiary of the United States Testing Company, Inc. and provides a certification program for manufacturers and marketers of consumer and industrial products. In cases where manufacturers' products meet a rigid qualification test and are included in a continuing quality audit, permission is given for the product to be identified as "certified" by the Nationwide Consumer Testing Institute, Inc. This is done by the Testing Institute for the manufacturer who wishes to have an additional selling point when his product enters the market. Again this is a business relationship and the existence of the Testing Institute is dependent in part on allowing products to be identified as "certified."

and that refunds or replacements are made in the majority of the cases by the manufacturer of the product. The same question of conflict of interests exists with the *Parents' Magazine* seal as with the *Good Housekeeping* seal.

How Safe Are Products Bearing Seals or Certificates?

The Consumer Product Safety Commission confirms that *Good Housekeeping* does do some checking on product safety, especially if there is an obvious safety problem. The commission reported having no information on *Parents' Magazine* as to what it does concerning product safety and the granting of its seal. The *Parents' Magazine* statement about its seal gives no representation that products or services are tested or evaluated. "The program is limited to a dollar and cents guarantee and does not involve any approval or endorsement."[12]

In order for seals of approval to be effective for the seller there needs to be a high level of recognition among consumers. In one study 98 percent of those surveyed recognized the *Good Housekeeping* seal; 97 percent recognized the USDA "Choice" seal; 93 percent recognized *Parents' Magazine* seal; and 20 percent said they recognized a seal which was, in fact, a fictitious symbol.[13] It might be pointed out that even though consumers still think of these seals as "seals of approval" *Good Housekeeping* has been prohibited since 1941 by the Federal Trade Commission from using this terminology.

The Parkinson survey showed that in the absence of other informational cues such as known brands, differential prices, or physical dissimilarities the presence of a familiar seal or certification is a positive inducement toward the selection of a brand.[14] The study points out that seals and certifications do significantly influence consumer choice behavior and that consumers as a whole attribute a great deal more meaning to these symbols than is justified by the seal-granting programs of the donor organizations. Parkinson stated, "It seems logical to assume that the high degree of influence and credibility of seals and certifications is related to some extent to this misunderstanding concerning their meaning"[15] He recommends that the Federal Trade Commission take action to require the seal donors to make greater public disclosure of the true meaning of these symbols in the national media. Such disclosures would include statements explaining what their symbols *do* and *do not* mean and would include disclaimers of liability and any other restrictions on the nature and extent of the guarantee. He also suggests that since these symbols have their greatest impact at the point of sale, where they appear on products, a suitable statement of meaning and a disclaimer could also be displayed in conjunction with the seal or certification where ever it occurs. He concluded that "further efforts must be made in order to educate the public at large and especially the new consumers entering the marketplace each year about the meaning of these symbols."[16]

Consumer Affairs Managers

The last decade has seen considerable growth in the number of corporations that now have formal consumer relations departments. There are now more than 300 companies with such departments, while only a few companies had such departments prior to the resurgence of the consumer movement in the 1960s. In addition, a professional organization has been established for those working in the consumer area of business. The Society of Consumer Affairs Professionals in Business was founded in 1973 and has more than 500 members from business, government, and consumer organizations. Its purpose is to "foster the integrity of business in its dealings with consumers; promote harmonious relationships between business and government and consumers; and advance the consumer affairs profession."[17]

Despite the establishment of such departments, benefits to the consumers have been mixed. There seems to be little question that the consumer affairs departments of some companies are mere "window dressing," while those of other companies have been doing a good job in lessening the tensions that spring up between producers and consumers.

SELLERS' JOINT EFFORTS

Better Business Bureaus

Sellers' joint efforts to help consumers include a number of activities designed not so much to aid consumers as to protect the more scrupulous businessmen from the less scrupulous. Of course, any success in these efforts will benefit buyers as well as ethical sellers. The problem of securing truth in advertising has engaged the attention of many persons for years. As far back as 1912 the Associated Advertising Clubs of the World undertook a campaign to reduce the amount of misrepresentation and fraudulence in advertising. An outgrowth of that activity was the development of better business bureaus.*

Trade Association Standards and Testing Laboratories' Seals of Approval

Both the lack of knowledge and confidence and the ever-increasing complexity of products have almost compelled consumers to depend on something or someone else to assist them in making buying decisions. Among trade associations there is a growing tendency to study the problems of marketing. This interest in consumer relations has led some associations to establish or utilize existing national standards and to test merchandise.

* See pp. 220–221 for further discussion of better business bureaus.

One such program is run by the American Gas Association (AGA), which is the national trade association for the natural gas transmission and distribution companies (it has no manufacturer members). The AGA maintains two laboratories at which, upon the request of a manufacturer, it will test prototypes of a manufacturer's gas-utilizing appliances to determine their conformity to the appropriate American National Standard. If a unit complies, the AGA authorizes and requires the manufacturer to affix its Blue Star Seal (a certification mark registered with the U.S. Patent Office) to each unit manufactured in exact conformity with the design of the prototype. The seal states: "Design complies with National Safety Standards — Certified — American Gas Association."

The AGA conducts periodic inspections at each manufacturer's plant to check the conformity of production with the certified design, but it does not inspect or certify every unit produced. The association also publishes a directory which lists all the models of gas-utilizing appliances and accessories certified by the AGA.

The American National Standards used in the AGA program are prepared by an independent committee operating under the rules and procedures of the American National Standards Institute. Approximately 250 persons with expertise in gas and gas appliance problems, including representatives of approximately ten governmental agencies, participate on the committee and its twenty-six subcommittees.

The International Fabricare Institute (IFI) has three consumer protection seals — "Certified Drycleanable," "Certified Washable," and "Certified Approved." The first two seals are awarded to garments and other textile items which have passed the IFI's tests for drycleanability or washability. These seals mean that the items bearing them will not change in appearance or usability after normal commercial laundering or professional drycleaning and that the product has passed laboratory tests for such characteristics as bleeding, chafing, color fastness, shrinkage, and tensile strength. The "Certified Approved" seal is awarded to personal products, such as deodorants, which have proven harmless to fabrics according to IFI testing. Some manufacturers have complained that IFI standards are too high, but this national trade association of launderers and drycleaners has no plans to lower its certification standards. The seal is not sold but is awarded after the IFI staff satisfies itself that the product merits the seal.

The Association of Home Appliance Manufacturers (AHAM) room air-conditioner certification program is beneficial to consumers buying air conditioners. Before the introduction of this program in the late 1950s buyers had no reliable standard to use in comparing cooling capacities of room air conditioners. Now the prospective buyer can feel assured when he sees the AHAM seal attached to an air conditioner that the information about cooling capacity, amperes, and watts is accurate. AHAM certification seals affixed to refrigerators and freezers confirm that the cubic feet of freezer capacity and cubic feet of refrigeration capacity, as well as square feet of shelf area for upright refrigerators and freezers, are accurate. Certification programs for humidifiers and dehumidifiers provide information on important performance characteristics. Water-removal capacity in pints per twenty-four hours is certified under the dehumidifier program. Water output in gallons per twenty-four hours is certified for humidifiers. AHAM certification seals affixed to these electrical appliances confirm that the information has been verified independently according to AHAM and American National Standards. Certification information also appears in directories published regularly by the AHAM.

The establishment of the Major Appliance Consumer Action Panel (MACAP) was a forward-looking step taken by the Association of Home Appliance Manufacturers, Gas Appliance Manufacturers Association, and the American Retail Federation. This eight-member consumer panel chosen from educators and persons involved in consumer counseling was established to counsel the industry on its relations with consumers, and it is providing a genuinely effective complaint-handling procedure. In addition, MACAP is set up to make recommendations to consumers to help them purchase and secure maximum benefit from their appliances and to take positions on public issues. In its first five years it has handled 15,000 complaints.

Another consumer complaint-handling panel is the Furniture Industry Consumer Advisory Panel (FICAP), which was started by the Southern Furniture Manufacturers Association to handle problems that retailers and manufacturers failed to adjust satisfactorily for consumers. FICAP tries to resolve complaints equitably by contacting the furniture manufacturer. In a six-month period FICAP received 200 consumer complaints. Upholstered furniture headed the list, with fabric complaints the most prevalent.*

Thirty-five AUTOCAPS have also been established across the country. The automobile consumer action panels do more than half their work on warranty problems. These panels normally consist of automobile dealers and members of local consumer groups. They meet periodically to review and study complaints and to prescribe a course of action to achieve customer satisfaction. (Further information on AUTOCAPS may be obtained from the largest of these panels, the Automotive Trade Association of National Capital Area AUTOCAP, 8401 Connecticut Avenue, Chevy Chase, Maryland 20015.)

The UL mark is found on practically all electric products. Underwriters Laboratories, Inc. (UL), founded in 1894, is chartered as a nonprofit organization to establish, maintain, and operate laboratories for the investigation of materials, devices, products, equipment, constructions, methods, and systems with respect to hazards affecting life and property. When a product is "listed" it may carry a listing mark — UL in a circle — when UL is satisfied that the product conforms to established safety requirements. Listed products are not necessarily equivalent in quality or merit. The use of the phrase "UL Approved" is technically incorrect because the word "approved" has certain legal implications that do not apply to UL's listing system. In addi-

---

* For further information write FICAP, P.O. Box 951, High Point, N.C. 27261, and MACAP, 20 North Wacker Drive, Chicago, Ill. 60606.

tion to looking for the UL mark on electrical appliances, the prospective buyer should make sure that the UL mark is for the entire electrical appliance, not for just one part of it.

Only electrical products with the UL label should be purchased by consumers, but even with the UL certification problems of safety crop up. One manufacturer had to warn buyers of more than half a million of its electric coffee pots that the product posed a serious hazard despite certification as "safe" by the presence of the UL label. About 12,000 table-model color television sets produced by one manufacturer posed a possible fire hazard, even though they carried the UL label. The Consumer Product Safety Commission has issued warnings on dozens of unsafe products, many of which have carried the UL label.[18] The UL label is a valuable guide for consumers, but care must still be taken in buying and using products that carry it.

It is to the advantage of gas appliance manufacturers to offer safe, standard, and economical equipment—otherwise consumers would be likely to turn to some other form of heating and cooking device, as they have turned to another form of lighting. This suggests the most serious limitation, from a consumer point of view, of joint promotional consumer activity: whereas competition normally operates among independent firms, the trade association coordinates the firms in an industry, and competition assumes a new form among all the firms of one industry and all those in another. If the producers of gas appliances offer new devices, such as gas dryers, producers of electric appliances confuse consumers with counter-attack advertising that extols the virtues of electricity and either openly or implicitly stresses the dangers of using gas. The operations of such associations are likely to be against consumer interests in other ways. The Antitrust Division of the Department of Justice has suggested that one of the major concerns of trade associations is to establish what they call price stability, which means high or higher prices for consumers.

Unfortunately the consumer must always be alert to outright fraud, even in the use of seals of approval. One discount drug chain advertised and used a "Consumer Protective Institute" seal. The Federal Trade Commission found that the seal was "developed" by an advertising agency, and that there was no institute and nothing had been tested.

ARE SELLER AIDS RELIABLE?

A Qualified Answer

Although the judgments of producers may be biased and their primary purpose to make more profit, this would not justify the conclusion that the efforts of some sellers to help their customers are not sincerely conceived and honestly executed. But the number of those who are sufficiently concerned with their customers' welfare to make some special effort to assure them of quality and fair price is too small. Unfortunately it is difficult for buyers to be sure whether they will benefit from such efforts. Their skepticism is not without justification. Businessmen keep reminding the public that they are not in business for their health; nor are they operating charitable institutions. Taking them at their own word, consumers are justified in concluding that a consumer-aid program will be maintained only as long as it pays measurable profits. They have a right to ask who pays for these special services. It takes money to run testing laboratories and to meet the obligations created by guarantees. Business and tax accounting recognize the validity of charging such costs to operating expenses. Since these firms expect to make a profit, it is evident that those who patronize them pay for such services in the form of higher prices. It may be that the higher price is justified by the greater assurance that the merchandise will prove satisfactory. However, since consumers are paying for such services, considerable duplication may be avoided and greater reliability assured if the laboratory testing and reporting services were performed by a nonprofit association owned, operated, and financed by consumers.

PROFESSIONAL ASSOCIATIONS BENEFITING CONSUMERS

American Home Economics Association

The work of the American Home Economics Association (AHEA) is chiefly educational. Its members, all college graduates, are home economists in every phase of the profession, working as teachers, researchers, extension home economists, dietitians, journalists, health and welfare home economists, and in many other types of positions with associations, agencies, and industry. Throughout all these activities is a concern for educating the individual for family living, for improving the services and goods used by families, for conducting research to discover changing needs of individuals and families, and means of satisfying those needs.

From the very first—at its organizational meeting in 1909—part of the program of the AHEA has been devoted to the buying problems of the consumer. Today the association's program includes the following purposes and responsibilities:

- To provide leadership and direction to consumer information and education programs within the AHEA
- To support programs for consumer protection against misrepresentation, misleading advertising, and fraudulent and unfair practices in buying and selling
- To promote for the benefit of the consumer, the development of standards of quality, safety, and performance as well as identifying marks for consumer goods, and to acquaint members of the Association with standards, especially those of the American National Standards Institute
- To promote informative and descriptive labeling and advertising of consumer goods and services in standardized terms

American Dental Association

The ADA is a professional voluntary association of dentists. The Council on Dental Therapeutics and the Council on Dental Materials and Devices evaluate dental therapeutic agents, dental materials and devices used by the profession and the public, and collect and disseminate knowledge helpful both to the profession and the public.

The Council on Dental Therapeutics provides up-to-date information on all therapeutic products used for dental purposes. Commercial products appropriately classified by the council are listed in *Accepted Dental Therapeutics*. Not all products concerned with dentistry are considered for evaluation by the council. For example, medicated mouthwashes sold directly to the public are not classified, and cosmetic-type dentifrices are not evaluated by the Council, because *none has been shown to be an effective therapeutic agent.*

The council evaluates dentifrices that claim to have inherent therapeutic or prophylactic effect through the inclusion of a biologically or chemically active ingredient and has authorized use of the following statement in commercial advertising for several dentifrices containing fluoride: "[name of dentifrice] has been shown to be an effective decay-preventive (anti-caries) dentifrice that can be of significant value when used in a conscientiously applied program of oral hygiene and regular professional care."

The Council on Dental Materials and Devices has ongoing Acceptance Programs for powered toothbrushes and oral irrigating devices. As of 1976 the council had not found sufficient evidence to support therapeutic claims by any powered toothbrush or oral irrigating device. The council has recognized as "Acceptable" or "Provisionally Acceptable" twelve electric toothbrushes and three oral irrigating devices as effective cleansing devices in a program for good oral hygiene to supplement the regular professional care required for oral health. The Council on Dental Materials and Devices provides up-to-date information on dental materials and devices through the *Guide to Dental Materials and Devices* and through periodic status reports published in the *Journal of the American Dental Association*. In addition, the council plays a leading role in the national and international standardization of dental materials and devices for the protection of consumers.

The American Medical Association

The AMA is the national organization of the medical profession which, as part of its program, promotes better scientific medicine, improved patient care, and better health for all Americans. Through its scientific meetings and publications, the AMA helps the physician keep abreast of the latest developments in medical practice. Through its seventy-seven councils and committees, the association helps raise and safeguard health standards.

Authentic health information is channeled to the public through various means, ranging from the association's popular monthly magazine *Today's*

Health to books, exhibits, motion pictures, pamphlets, and radio and television programs.

Some of the AMA's official positions on controversial issues have not satisfied the society's members, nor many laymen; for example, its opposition to a national health program is not in accordance with the views of some of its members. The conservative position taken by the AMA on some issues has alienated many medical professionals, to the extent that less than 50 percent of all medical doctors are members. This indicates a typical weakness of professional societies — namely, their internal divisions and the differing commitments of their members.

The chief advantage of the services of such professional societies is that they are nonprofit, professional organizations. On the other hand, their inability to reach large numbers of consumers is a defect. Nevertheless, the importance of their work cannot be underrated. They have exercised and continue to exercise a constructive influence in promoting consumer welfare.

CONSUMER-FINANCED TESTING AGENCIES

Consumers' Research and Consumers Union

These organizations, described and evaluated in Chapter 16, are professional nonprofit operations. In their early days they were crusaders operating as amateur testers. Through the years they have developed into professional organizations. This is especially true of Consumers Union, which sponsors pure research and academic conferences in addition to its expanded testing and reporting program.

QUESTIONS FOR REVIEW

1. Why do consumers need help from sellers and government?
2. What would happen in the marketplace if the brand names and trademarks were removed from all products?
3. What are advantages and disadvantages of brand names and trademarks to consumers?
4. There seems to be a correlation between the amount of education a consumer has and the degree to which he or she depends on brand names. Discuss this fact.
5. What information should a good food label include?
6. Why is there an apparent reluctance on the part of food manufacturers to put complete information on labels?
7. Define "implied warranty" and "express warranty."
8. How might warranties become more meaningful to consumers?

9. Are warranties of more benefit to the buyer or the seller?

10. Differentiate between a "full" and "limited" warranty as defined in the Magnuson-Moss Act.

11. What do *Parents' Magazine* and *Good Housekeeping* seals promise the consumer? Is it any more than what the manufacturer promises?

12. What seal of approval do you have confidence in? Why?

13. Do professional associations really benefit consumers?

PROJECTS

1. Collect labels from ten products and evaluate them as to their usefulness to the consumer.

2. Have a class debate on the following: Resolved that the federal government should require complete information on the labels of food products.

3. Evaluate the nutritional information, or lack of such information, found on the labels of ten food products.

4. Evaluate the warranties for five different products, including an automobile.

5. Write to *Good Housekeeping* and *Parents' Magazine* to obtain information on how many dollars' worth of advertising they refuse each year; how much money they spend annually in paying refunds or in making replacements on products with their seals; and how many product complaints they receive.

6. Survey ten adults as to their opinions concerning *Good Housekeeping* and *Parents' Magazine* seals.

7. Interview a medical doctor or dentist about his attitude toward his professional association as a help for consumers.

REFERENCES

1. *Marketing News,* American Marketing Association, 30 Jan. 1976, p. 2.
2. *Food Labeling: Goals, Shortcomings, and Proposed Changes,* Report to the Congress From the Dept. of Health, Education, and Welfare, Dept. of Agriculture, and Dept. of Commerce by the Comptroller General of the United States, 29 Jan. 1975, pp. 18–19.
3. *Ibid,* p. 4.
4. *Pittsburgh Post Gazette,* 7 Dec. 1975, p. 17.
5. *Consumer Reports,* Feb. 1975, p. 76.
6. *Changing Times,* June 1976, p. 38.
7. *Consumer Product Warranties,* House Interstate and Foreign Commerce Committee, Subcommittee on Commerce and Finance Staff Report, 17 Sept. 1974.
8. *Consumer Reports,* March 1975, p. 165.
9. *Preliminary Staff Study (Precis):Self-Regulation – Product Standardization, Certification and Seals of Approval,* Federal Trade Commission, 1972, p. 8.

10. *Decisions, Federal Trade* Commission, vol. 32, Docket 3872, pp. 1440–1463.
11. This information was obtained by the writer in a telephone call to the advertising department of *Good Housekeeping*, Chicago office, 17 March 1976.
12. Statement received by the writer from *Parents' Magazine*, "Information on the Parents' Magazine Seal," undated.
13. Thomas L. Parkinson, "The Role of Seals and Certifications of Approval in Consumer Decision-Making," *Journal of Consumer Affairs* 9 (1975): 4.
14. *Ibid*, p. 5.
15. *Ibid*, p. 13.
16. *Ibid*.
17. Bylaws, Society of Consumer Affairs Professionals in Business, adopted 24 May 1973, p. 1. Available from Society of Consumer Affairs Professionals in Business, 1150 17th St., N.W., Washington, D.C. 20036.
18. *St. Petersburg Times*, 11 June 1974, p. 1D.

CHAPTER 22

STANDARDS AND GRADE LABELS HELP CONSUMERS

THE NEED FOR STANDARDS

Trade Is Based on Standards

Every commercial exchange involves the use of one or more standards of measure. We are so accustomed to their use that we take for granted such standards as those which measure bulk, dimension, time, value, and weight. When you need butter you do not go into a store and ask for some butter. If you do the clerk will ask, "How much?" You would probably say, "One pound." Neither does one purchase some eggs for some money, but asks for one dozen, which may be priced at 79 cents. One does not purchase some milk for some money, but buys one quart for 40 cents. Nor does one purchase some dress or some suit material for some money; rather one asks for a stated number of yards of a specified material priced at a certain number of dollars.

Try to imagine what it would be like to shop where no standards were in existence. In all these cases and in all commercial transactions at least two standards are used, the first of which is a standard of measure, weight, or count. There was a time when weights and measures were not standardized. An ell was a measure of length the standard for which was the length of the king's arm. This resulted in some variation with every change of monarch. Among the nations different standards of weight are found, such as the pound, kilogram, and oka. In the United States the National Bureau of Standards and the various state bureaus of weights and measures maintain standards for both weights and measures, the master standards being in the national capital.

The second standard used in all commercial transactions is that for measuring value. In economic language, value is the power of a good or service to command other goods or services in exchange for itself. Price is a measure of value expressed in terms of money, while money is a universally accepted medium of exchange. The standard for money in the United States is the dollar, which has been defined as being equal to $1/_{42.22}$

an ounce of gold, troy weight. Although the absolute number of grains of gold in the dollar is fixed, the value of the dollar is relative to the values of all other commodities and services and fluctuates within fairly wide limits. The value of the dollar is usually defined as its purchasing power, which is high in some periods and low in others. Many proposals have been advanced for stabilizing the purchasing power of the dollar so that it would function better as a standard of value. Failing adoption of such a plan, the best that can be done with the present monetary standard is to measure changes in its purchasing power by the use of index numbers. This means that we really have two standards—one a theoretically unchanging amount of gold, which we call the dollar, the other a fluctuating amount of purchasing power, measured by deviation from an index base of 100. The Bureau of Labor Statistics in the Department of Labor has the responsibility of measuring the purchasing power of the dollar and reporting its findings monthly under the title "Consumer Price Index." This index was 172.6 in September, 1976, based on a base year of 1967. In July it would have taken approximately $1.73 to purchase the same goods (on the average) that you could have purchased for $1.00 during the base period. In other words the dollar in September, 1976, was worth only 57 cents in comparison with the dollar of 1967.

Missing or Defective Standards

The most serious omission in commercial standards is that for quality. A purchaser has little more assurance when she buys a pair of shoes that their wearing qualities will meet her expectations than she has that she would receive the exact amount she expected if she asked her grocer for "some" sugar. By what standard can the purchaser measure the quality of any one of the numerous items which she must purchase regularly in the market? By implication the price she pays is a measure of quality, but in practice this is not a reliable standard. A high price may mean good quality at one time or in one place, while at another time or at another place a low price might secure merchandise of high quality.

Standards for measuring quality do exist. Either they are not used or, if used, they are not always understood by consumers. Indeed, some so-called standards are more confusing than helpful. When packers of shelled almonds describe the various grades in such terms as "U.S. Fancy," "U.S. Extra No. 1," "U.S. No. 1," "U.S. Select Sheller Run," "U.S. Standard Sheller Run," "U.S. No. 1 Whole and Broken," and "U.S. No. 1 Pieces," how is a consumer to know what the "U.S. No. 1 Pieces" indicates when the designation "No 1" is used for four different grades?

In the olive trade size grading ranges from "Sub-Petite," "Petite" or "Midget," "Small" or "Select" or "Standard," "Medium," "Large," "Extra Large," "Mammoth," "Giant," "Jumbo," "Colossal," to "Super Colossal."

Most grading systems are complicated and irrational. Grade designations are used much more by producers and wholesalers than by retailers, but many of the grade and quality designations are dropped when merchandise passes over the retail counter to the consumer. A perusal of U.S. Department of Agriculture (USDA) grade names for food and farm products makes one wonder if the purpose is to deceive the consumer about grades. U.S. Extra is the grade name for first grade instant nonfat dry milk, but U.S. Extra is the second grade for dry whole milk. U.S. Grade A is first grade for Swiss cheese but second grade for cheddar cheese. U.S. No. 1 is first grade for dry peas but third grade for pea beans. First-grade split peas are designated as U.S. No. 1, while U.S. No. 1 carrots are the fourth grade. Poultry grade U.S. Grade A is the first grade, but U.S. Grade A eggs are second grade.

Some 1,400 different numbers, letters, adjectives, or a mixture of all three are used as grade designations by the USDA to describe 415 products, and in only 25 percent of the cases is No. 1 or Grade A the best grade![1]

A USDA study reported that most consumers knew little about the USDA system. They could not identify correctly the government grades of the products they purchased. The several sets of grade names and designations confuse consumers. The following chart shows ten different top quality grade designations used by USDA for different food categories.[2]

Apple juice, canned	U.S. grade A or U.S. Fancy
Apples, fresh	U.S. Extra Fancy
Beef	USDA Prime
Beets, fresh	U.S. No. 1
Cantaloups, fresh	U.S. Fancy
Carrots, fresh	U.S. grade A
Celery, fresh	U.S. Extra No. 1
Eggs	U.S. grade AA
Peanuts, Virginia in shell	U.S. Jumbo Hand Picked
Peanuts, Virginia shelled	U.S. Extra Large

Too many grade names consist of superlatives that mislead the retail buyer into believing that the products are higher in quality than they are. Why don't the USDA and industry develop standardization in grading by adopting grades of 1, 2, 3, 4, and 5 and/or grades A, B, C, D, and E, which would be readily understood by the consumer?

A serious problem with USDA grade standards is that they generally do not indicate taste or nutritional values in terms of protein, vitamins, or minerals. For example, the grade standard for canned tomatoes sets out four factors of quality: weight of the tomato units, redness of color, amount of peel per pound, and amount of blemishes. The standards are basically established on the criteria of weight, appearance, and superficial qualities. And yet when consumers were asked, "What factors would you most like to see determining quality standards in the USDA grading system?" one survey yielded the following responses: nutrition ranked first, with 72.4 percent choosing it; tenderness ranked second, with 19.6 percent; and appearance ranked last, with 8.0 percent choosing it.[3] In lieu of standards expressed in terms that consumers can understand, producers have substituted brand names and trademarks for which there are no standards.*

Another missing standard is one for size and content of containers. More progress has been made, however, in eliminating this condition by the simplified practice of the United States Department of Commerce. At one time there were 200 sizes of cans in commercial use. The Division of Simplified Practice has succeeded in reducing that number to twenty-seven. In Canada, only eleven sizes are used. One survey showed the most common can sizes to be No. 303, No. 2½, No. 1 Picnic, No. 2, No. 2 Squat, and No. 300. One would scarcely expect to find any great similarity between numbers 2 and 303, yet at a short distance it is difficult to distinguish them. Actually No. 303 is so much smaller that it will fit snugly into a No. 2 can. Four No. 2 cans contain as much food as five No. 303 cans. Yet it is not uncommon for retailers to offer for sale No. 303 cans at the same price or even higher prices than those asked for the No. 2 size.

Increasing varieties of food products are being offered to consumers in packing form. Weights and measures officials estimate that 90 percent of the items in a self-service food store are prepackaged. More often than not the packages contain odd and fractional amounts. A buyer must be adept at fractions or use a mechanical or electric calculator to compare the prices of competing sizes and competing brands. With pocket-size electric calculators selling for $15 to $20, an investment in one should pay for itself within a short time. The savings realized by being able to compute unit prices of competing sizes and brands should prove to be worth both the time, effort, and expenditures. A requirement to standardize packages into subdivisions of a pound—4, 8, and 12 ounces—would also help.†

Some of the customary standards are defective. Should eggs be sold by the dozen or by the pound? There are six USDA sizes for eggs (Jumbo, Extra Large, Large, Medium, Small, and Pee Wee), each based on the minimum weight per dozen. The sizes sold most frequently are Extra Large—at least 27 ounces per dozen; Large—24 ounces per dozen; Medium—21 ounces per dozen; and Small—18 ounces per dozen. Michigan requires that egg sales be based on weight. What other qualities in addition to size and weight should be considered in the purchase of an egg? Age is certainly important, yet in some states "fresh" eggs may not be over fourteen days old, while in others they may be thirty days old. To what extent should egg standards reflect variations in the amount of food nutrients?

Should vegetables be sold by the bunch, basket, pound, or number? Exactly how many radishes constitute a bunch? How many tomatoes are there in a basket? Some states require the sale of fruits and vegetables by the pound. Should coal be sold by the ton or on some other basis, such as the number of British Thermal Units (BTU) it will yield? An investigation revealed that, as between two grades of bituminous coal, the grade that appeared the more expensive actually proved to be more economical if

---

* See Chapter 13 for additional discussion concerning price-quality relationship.
† See pp. 605–608 for a discussion of deceptive packaging.

A consumer weighs eggs on the customer scale in a supermarket to make sure that he gets the grade egg — Jumbo, Extra Large, Medium, or Small — that he pays for. (*Dr. Lilly Bruck, Director, Consumer Education, New York City Dept. of Consumer Affairs*)

judged on the basis of its BTU content; but how are consumers to know this if the information is not made available to them at the point of purchase?

The USDA is well aware of the confusion created by the lack of uniformity in grade names. In 1976 it adopted a policy that established uniform grade nomenclature for grades of fresh fruits, vegetables, nuts, and other special products. The grade names will be adopted in the normal

TABLE 22-1.   USDA Uniform Grade Nomenclature

Grade name	Definition
U.S. Fancy	Premium quality; covers only the top quality range produced
U.S. No. 1	The chief trading grade; represents good average quality that is practical to pack under commercial conditions; covers the bulk of the quality range produced
U.S. No. 2	Intermediate quality between U.S. No. 1 and U.S. No. 3; noticeably superior to U.S. No. 3
U.S. No. 3	The lowest merchantable quality practical to pack under normal conditions

Source: Federal Register Washington, D.C.: U.S. Government Printing Office, Oct. 6, 1975, p. 46115.

process of revising or establishing standards for individual products, but grade names will not be changed otherwise. Table 22-1 lists the revised USDA grade names.

There is no question that this proposal, if adopted, would be a step toward lessening the confusion in grade designations, but it is unfortunate that the USDA is still reluctant to call the first grade U.S. No. 1, and chose instead to designate it U.S. Fancy and to designate the second grade as No. 1.

THE NATURE AND ORIGIN OF STANDARDS

What Is a Standard?

"A standard is a physical, written, graphic, or other representation of a product or a procedure established by authority, custom, or general consent with which other products or procedures of a like nature are compared for identification or measurement or to which they are made to conform."[4]

The Food and Drug Administration establishes standards of identity for certain food products. They set requirements that products must meet if they move in interstate commerce. Once a standard of identity is established by the FDA, it does not require that the ingredients be listed on the label. The FDA may require that optional ingredients be listed, but not basic mandatory ingredients. For example, a standard of identity has been established for mayonnaise. Any product using that name must meet the standard and no listing of ingredients is required if it does comply with the standard. The U.S. Department of Agriculture also establishes grade standards that define levels of quality for various foods. FDA food standards of identity are mandatory or regulatory; USDA grade standards for food are voluntary. In addition, the U.S. Department of Commerce has established similar grade standards for fishery products. Federal law does not require that a food processor or distributor use the grade standards.

Standards for each product established by the USDA describe the entire range of quality. For this reason, the number of grades for a product depends on its variability. While it takes eight grades to span the range of beef quality, only three are required for frying chicken, since the quality of this product does not vary so much as that of beef. In the other extreme, there are thirty-six grade names and fourteen staple lengths for Upland cotton. Marketing and consumer services standardization specialists have developed grade standards for some 300 farm products. They develop new standards as new products are developed or as older products find increased use and standards are needed to facilitate trade. Butter is the dairy product most widely sold on the basis of grades. Butter is graded on the basis of aroma, flavor, body or texture, color, salt, and package. Expert graders score the samples, the highest score being 93. This may then be labeled USDA Grade AA. If the score is 92, the grade is A, and for butter scoring 90, the grade is B. Federal butter grading is voluntary, but in some states grading is mandatory. While the two top grades require a product made of fresh sweet cream, B-grade butter makers may use selected sour cream.

The time-honored recipe of pound for pound of fruit and sugar forms the basis for the FDA standard for jellies and preserves. Products containing 45 or more pounds of fruit to each 55 pounds of sugar constitute Standard acceptable jellies and preserves, while fruit preserves containing less than 45 but more than 25 pounds of fruit to each 55 pounds of sugar must be labeled "Imitation." Moreover, the labels must show just how the product is an imitation and must specify the amount of added fruit acid and artifical color.

The federal standard for sheets stipulates that the material be made of thoroughly cleaned cotton, free from waste. Every sheet must be free from avoidable inperfections and from defects or blemishes that affect appearance or serviceability. There must be at least 74 threads per inch in the warp and 66 in the filler, with a minimum of 4.6 ounces per square yard. Hems must be 2 inches long at each end or 1 inch at one end and 3 inches long at the other. There shall be no less than 14 stitches to the inch, and the breaking strength must be 70 pounds in the warp and 70 pounds in the filling.

Who Determines the Standards?

Standards often originate in the trade and derive their authority from custom. A products standards program for industry was initiated in the Department of Commerce in 1921. Through extensive voluntary cooperation between government and industry, the program provides assistance to American industry in meeting the needs for uniform standards for industry. Over 460 voluntary standards are in effect with a number under revision at any one time, and new standards are developed from time to time.

Some standards are determined by trade associations, with members agreeing on standards of quality and terms for designating variations. For example, the American Society for Testing & Materials has established such grades for asbestos yarns. The grades of plain, metallic, and reinforced asbestos yarn are determined by the percentage of asbestos content by weight. The six grades used for high to low are: AAAA, AAA, AA, A, Underwriters' Grade, and Commercial Grade. Of course, those in the trade become accustomed to such terminology, but they could just as well become accustomed to a straight numerical or alphabetical rating.

The American National Standards Institute (ANSI) is a federation of some two hundred trade, technical, professional, labor, and consumer organizations, and of nine hundred companies. ANSI, which is recognized as an impartial organization functioning in the public interest, does not write standards. Instead it helps identify what standards are required, arranges for competent standard-writing organizations to undertake their development, coordinates their efforts, and establishes timetables for completion of the development work. It approves a standard as an American National (consensus) Standard only when it is convinced that all concerned national interests have had an opportunity to participate in the standard's development or to comment on its provisions. ANSI's Consumer Council represents consumer interests at all institute policy and technical levels. Of the 6000 standards approved by ANSI to date, many help ensure the safety and performance of consumer products. They include standards for lawn and garden equipment, gas and electric appliances, cooking utensils, kitchen cabinets, hearing aids, and textile fabrics for clothing and home furnishings.

Some retail consumer cooperatives have adopted grade-labeling designations for products packaged under the CO-OP brand. The three grade labels are: CO-OP Green (Good) – good quality at lower prices; CO-OP Blue (Better) – high quality; and CO-OP Red (Best) – top quality.

Probably most standards in the United States have been drawn by federal, state, and municipal governmental departments under authority of law. In the federal government there are many agencies that work in one or more branches of the general field of commodity standards. Chief among these is the National Bureau of Standards, whose functions include the custody, maintenance, and development of national standards of measurement and the construction of physical standards.

The USDA's regulations for meat products include these points concerning hamburger. Hamburger, ground beef, or designations of similar character or meaning must be fresh or frozen beef containing not more than

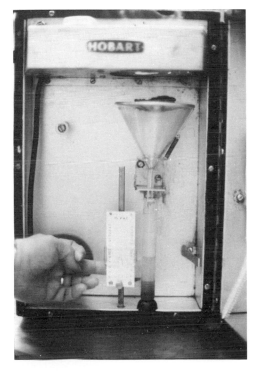

An inspector tests a sample of hamburger to make sure that the fat content is not above the specified USDA standard for chopped meat. (*Dr. Lilly Bruck, Director, Consumer Education, New York City Dept. of Consumer Affairs*)

30 percent total fat and shall be free from bread, cereal, animal blood, and seventeen other listed additives. It may contain monosodium gluta-mate, corn syrup not in excess of 2.5 percent or dry corn syrup not in ex-cess of 2.0 percent, and seasoning which must be declared on the label. Then the regulation for "Ground or Chopped Beef from Specific Portion" stipulates that it may contain no added fat, and the total fat must not ex-ceed 20 percent. No additives are permitted in this product. In New York City, Department of Market inspectors confiscated packages of chopped beef, some of which contained 90 percent fat which had been colored with beef blood. The New York City law is the same as the USDA regulation.

The Food and Drug Administration sets standards of identity, quality, and fill of container for foods — what the food shall contain, what it may contain, the minimum quality, and the amount of food in the container. Industry, consumer, and professional groups participate in the process of drafting standards. The FDA's standards of identity guarantee the com-position of the product. Regardless of whether a standard of identity has been established for a food, the FDA requires that if it contains any arti-ficial flavoring, artifical coloring, or chemical preservative, it must bear labeling stating that fact. Where optional ingredients have not been pre-scribed in a standard they must be declared on the main display panel of the label when used.

The standards for some drugs are set by the United States *Pharma-copoeia*, the *Homeopathic Pharmacopoeia*, and the *National Formulary*, which are published by leaders in the fields of medicine, pharmacy, chem-istry, and dentistry. If a drug is listed in one of these books, it is called an official drug.

Technicians in the USDA have written standards for many agricultural products, including beef, lamb, veal, eggs, poultry, butter, fresh and canned fruits, and vegetables. (See Tables 22-2 and 22-3.) The United States Public Health Service and the Bureau of Dairy Industry have prepared standards for milk. Standard grades for distilled spirits have been made by the Alcohol and Tobacco Tax Division of the Internal Revenue Service, U.S. Treasury Department.

STANDARDS IN USE

Standards Required by Law

Among the standards in use under legal requirement are those govern-ing the sale of merchandise by weight, measure, or count which have been enacted by state legislatures. In most states eggs must be graded and con-tainer labels must show the grade. Many states have established legal weights per bushel for a variety of fruits, vegetables, and grains. Federal law stipulates that packages containing food and drugs must indicate the net weight content if they enter interstate commerce. The Federal Standard

Container Act sets standards of content for various sizes of containers, and the FDA has promulgated standards for many food products.

Many municipalities have enacted ordinances setting standards for milk. Some cities require that all meats sold at retail must be graded and stamped according to standards developed by the USDA.

Optional Standards

Many standards in use have been adopted voluntarily. The USDA has established grades for food products as shown in Table 22-2 and Table 22-3. The grading is done by USDA personnel for packers who request the service and pay a fee for it. In judging eggs, Grade AA eggs have a small spread when broken. The whites are thick and high, and the yolks are firm and high. In use they are the best to fry, poach, or cook in the shell. By contrast a Grade B egg, the lowest grade, has a great spread, a thin watery white, and a flat, easily broken yolk. There is no difference in nutritional value, so that Grade B eggs are good for scrambling and general cooking. Size and weight bear no relation to grade, but are significant in pricing.[5] The buyer has two decisions to make in buying eggs – the grade and the size.

QUALITY STANDARDS AND PRACTICES NEEDED

The General Accounting Office's (GAO) study on food labeling pointed out that in one year the USDA inspected and graded 35 percent of the vegetables processed in this country. But of a sample of 317 products only 4.7 percent were labeled with USDA grades. A USDA official said that requiring all food products to be graded and the grade to be included on their labels was not a practical solution to the problems consumers face in comparing the qualities of products. He stated that the current cost of grading less than 100 percent of only six categories of food products on a voluntary basis was about $183 million annually; but if grading became mandatory, the cost of grading all food products in these same six categories would increase by about $327 million to a total of about $510 million annually. If all food products were graded, the costs would be significantly greater.[6]

The increase in the cost of grading if all these categories were to be graded should be placed in proper perspective. The increased cost would be less than $1.50 per person per year. The benefits would be even greater – providing consumers with more and better information to use in making wiser selections among products and stimulating industry to work for improvements in products. The GAO concluded that although establishing and enforcing a mandatory grading system for all foods could be very costly, revising existing grade designations to make them uniform and easy to understand would assist consumers greatly in using the USDA system. The report's recommendation on grading stated: "To assist consumers try-

TABLE 22–2. USDA Grades at a Glance

Product	1st Grade	2d Grade	3d Grade	4th Grade	5th Grade
Beef	USDA Prime	USDA Choice	USDA Good	USDA Standard	USDA Commercial[a]
Veal	USDA Prime	USDA Choice	USDA Good	USDA Standard	USDA Utility[b]
Calf	USDA Prime	USDA Choice	USDA Good	USDA Standard	USDA Utility[b]
Lamb	USDA Prime	USDA Choice	USDA Good	USDA Utility	USDA Cull
Yearling Mutton	USDA Prime	USDA Choice	USDA Good	USDA Utility	USDA Cull
Mutton	USDA Choice	USDA Good	USDA Utility	USDA Cull	
Butter	U.S. Grade AA (U.S. 93 Score)	U.S. Grade A (U.S. 92 Score)	U.S. Grade B (U.S. 90 Score)		
Cheddar Cheese	U.S. Grade AA	U.S. Grade A	U.S. Grade B	U.S. Grade C	
Colby Cheese	U.S. Grade AA	U.S. Grade A	U.S. Grade B		
Monterey Cheese	U.S. Grade AA	U.S. Grade A	U.S. Grade B		
Swiss Cheese	U.S. Grade A	U.S. Grade B	U.S. Grade C	U.S. Grade D	
Nonfat Dry Milk	U.S. Extra Grade	U.S. Standard Grade			
Instant nonfat dry milk	U.S. Extra Grade				
Dry Whole Milk	U.S. Premium	U.S. Extra	U.S. Standard		
Cottage Cheese	No Grades—May be marked USDA "Quality Approved"				

	U.S. Grade A	U.S. Grade B	U.S. Grade C		
Poultry[a]	U.S. Grade A	U.S. Grade B	U.S. Grade C		
Poultry Rolls and Roasts[b]	U.S. Grade A				
Eggs	U.S. Grade AA Fresh Fancy Quality	U.S. Grade A	U.S. Grade B	U.S. Grade C	
Lentils	U.S. No. 1	U.S. No. 2			
Milled Rice	U.S. No. 1	U.S. No. 2	U.S. No. 3	U.S. No. 4	U.S. No. 5
Brown Rice	U.S. No. 1	U.S. No. 2	U.S. No. 3	U.S. No. 4	U.S. No. 5
Beans	U.S. Choice Handpicked	U.S. Prime Handpicked	U.S. No. 1	U.S. No. 2	
Other Dry Beans, except Limas	U.S. No. 1	U.S. No. 2	U.S. No. 3		
Lima Beans (large and small)	U.S. Extra No. 1	U.S. No. 1	U.S. No. 2		
Dry Peas	U.S. No. 1	U.S. No. 2	U.S. No. 3		
Split Peas	U.S. No. 1	U.S. No. 2	U.S. No. 3		
Processed Fruits and Vegetables and related products[c]	U.S. Grade A (Fancy)[d]	U.S. Grade B (Choice or Ex. Std.)[d]	U.S. Grade C (Standard)[d]		

[a] Three lowest grades are USDA Utility, Cutter, and Canner.
[b] Lowest grade is USDA Utility.
[c] Grades used for these products are usually as listed here, but there are some exceptions.
[d] These terms are being eliminated as the standards are revised.

Source: Originally published in the now out-of-print Shopper's Guide to U.S. Grades for Food (United States Department of Agriculture, Home and Garden Bulletin No. 58 pp. 12–13), these figures were updated by the USDA for the writer in 1976.

581

TABLE 22–3. USDA Consumer Grades and Wholesale Grades Compared

PRODUCT	CONSUMER GRADES		WHOLESALE GRADES			
	1st Grade	2d Grade	1st Grade	2d Grade	3d Grade	4th Grade
Beet Greens			U.S. No. 1			
Potatoes	U.S. Grade A Large U.S. Grade A Medium to Large U.S. Grade A Medium U.S. Grade A Small	U.S. Grade B Large U.S. Grade B Medium to Large U.S. Grade B Medium U.S. Grade B Small	U.S. Extra No. 1	U.S. No. 1	U.S. Commercial	U.S. No. 2
Broccoli (Italian Sprouting)	U.S. Grade A	U.S. Grade B	U.S. Fancy	U.S. No. 1	U.S. No. 2	
Brussels Sprouts	U.S. Grade A	U.S. Grade B	U.S. No. 1	U.S. No. 2		
Carrots	U.S. Grade A	U.S. Grade B	(Topped carrots) U.S. Extra No. 1	U.S. No. 1 U.S. No. 1 Jumbo	U.S. No. 2	
Corn (Husked, on the cob)	U.S. Grade A	U.S. Grade B	(Green-corn) U.S. Fancy	U.S. No. 1	U.S. No. 2	
Cranberries			U.S. No. 1			
Kale	U.S. Grade A	U.S. Grade B	U.S. No. 1	U.S. Commercial		
Parsnips	U.S. Grade A	U.S. Grade B	U.S. No. 1	U.S. No. 2		
Spinach Leaves	U.S. Grade A	U.S. Grade B	U.S. Extra No. 1	U.S. No. 1	U.S. Commercial	
Tomatoes	U.S. Grade A	U.S. Grade B	U.S. No. 1	U.S. Combination	U.S. No. 2	U.S. No. 3

Turnips	U.S. Grade A	U.S. Grade B	(Topped turnips) U.S. No. 1	U.S. No. 2		
Celery	U.S. Grade AA (Stalks)	U.S. Grade A (3d Grade— U.S. Grade B)	U.S. Extra No. 1	U.S. No. 1	U.S. No. 2	
Apples	None	None	U.S. Extra Fancy	U.S. Fancy	U.S. No. 1 U.S. No. 1[a] Early U.S. No. 1 Hail Grade[b]	U.S. Utility

[a] Same as U.S. No. 1 except for color, maturity, and size.
[b] Same as U.S. No. 1 except for hail injury.
Source: Originally published in the now out-of-print *Shopper's Guide to U.S. Grades for Food* (United States Department of Agriculture, Home and Garden Bulletin No. 58, pp. 12–13), these figures were updated by the USDA for the writer in 1976.

ing to use the USDA grading system we recommend that the Secretary of Agriculture revise existing regulations to make grade designations uniform and easier for consumers and industry to understand."[7]

Grading of food products should be of great assistance to the consumer. One may well ask, "Is it?" In a national sample of households, interviews showed that consumers were unfamiliar with USDA grades for food. For the most part, consumers revealed little knowledge of federal grades and significant confusion between grades and inspection marks. The study also indicated that many consumers believe all food items to be graded and frequently reported buying Grade A when no such grade designation existed. Nearly 80 percent of the respondents could not explain the purpose of USDA inspection.

Why Does Industry Oppose Grade Labeling?

What are the industry arguments against a simple, understandable plan of grade labeling based on a 1, 2, 3 or A, B, C system?

- It is argued that it is not practical to think that quality can be measured so objectively that it will stand a court test in case a consumer contends that the article purchased did not meet the grade specified on the label.
- It is asserted that expensive litigation would result from uniform grading.
- Packers assert that consumers would not buy according to grade anyway, but would continue to prefer established, known brand names.
- Sellers, advertising agencies, and media fear that the volume of advertising would decline.
- Some of the huge sums spent to build up goodwill might be lost, since brand names might lose some of their drawing power.
- It is suggested that some packers would not abide by the grades.
- It is feared that consumers, misunderstanding the grading system, would think that any grade below A is undesirable.
- Quality would deteriorate, it is claimed, because canners would meet only the minimum of each grade.
- There would be a tendency also for prices to settle at one level for each of the three or more grades.
- Finally, it is contended that the cost of labeling, inspection, and enforcement would place a financial burden on the industry which would be passed on to consumers.

As a counterproposal, canners have suggested a system of descriptive labeling. It is contended that quality cannot be judged objectively. Rather, pertinent information should be placed on the label so that the purchaser may determine for herself whether the contents of the can possess the qualities she wants. Illustrations of the kind of labeling they propose include such terms as "Medium sweet," "Not tender," and "Thin consistency." Their plan would provide 144 combinations of such "descriptive" terms for a single product – for example, canned, cream-style corn in No. 2 cans. Since corn is also packed in the whole kernel and in several other can sizes, such a labeling scheme would be cumbersome and ineffective. It could lead to greater rather than less confusion.

Proponents of A, B, C or 1, 2, 3 quality grade labeling have answers to these objections. To the canners' contention that it is impractical to test quality objectively the reply is that it is already being done. From growers through processors to retailers, canned products are packed, traded, and priced on the basis of grades. It is only when canned goods are sold to consumers that brand names replace objective quality designations.

Fear of expensive litigation is disspelled by referring to Canadian experience, where the practice of compulsory grade labeling is firmly established. Even if a producer labels his product with a federal grade voluntarily, he must meet the standards prescribed for that grade or be in violation. There have been very few violations involving court action.

Whether or not consumers would buy on the basis of quality grade labeling is, of course, unknown. There is no more reason to suppose that they would ignore grade letters than that they would base their purchases on them. The real fear of the industry may be that consumers *would* base their purchases on quality grades. The contention that the industry would not abide by the grades seems to be self-condemnation by the canners.

Another problem in the establishment of standards for grade labeling is the end use of the product. In textile materials the important characteristics are thread count, tensile strength, bursting strength, shrinkage, color fastness (from sun and washings), and abrasion. The relative importance of these particular characteristics depends on whether the material is to be used in drapes, slipcovers, or clothing. A high rating for color fastness is the most essential for drapes, while abrasion is very important for slipcovers.

USDA Continuous Inspection Plan

Almost forty years ago the USDA started an experiment which has proved successful. Under the USDA continuous inspection plan it is possible for a canner, freezer, or other processor of fruits and vegetables to have a federal government inspector at his plant continuously while products are being processed. The processor voluntarily contracts and pays for the USDA continuous inspection service. Under this plan USDA inspectors observe and make recommendations for compliance with sanitation requirements. They check the quality of the products during the processing. If the sanitation standards and quality of raw materials are satisfactory, the USDA inspector certifies the finished product as to a quality grade, such as grade A (or Fancy), grade B (Choice or Extra Standard), grade C (or Standard). The processor or his distributor is then permitted to use a shield or a statement on his labels indicating that the product has been "Packed under Continuous Inspection of the U. S. Department of Agriculture." The labels on the inspected products may also bear the prefix "U.S." with the quality grade, such as U.S. Grade A (or U.S. Fancy).

Those who have adopted USDA continuous inspection have found it pays and are enthusiastic about it. Many distributors are requiring that certain of their products be packed under the USDA plan. The cost is very small, and with a few exceptions it runs a fraction of a cent per case. The cost per case to the canner depends on the volume packed, the kinds of products, and whether USDA inspection is used all year or only during the short packing season. The percentage of the total supply officially graded varies from one product to another, and ranges from none for some products to 85 percent for fed beef.

MARKS OF FEDERAL USDA INSPECTION

This is the inspection mark used on fresh and cured meat. You are more likely to see it on large cuts, like roasts and hams, than on smaller ones. It assures you that the meat was produced from healthy animals in a plant that is clean and operated in a sanitary manner under constant supervision of a USDA inspector. The number in an inspection seal refers to the establishment that processed the food product.

This mark is used on processed meat products — canned, frozen, dried, or packaged. It means that the product is clean and wholesome. It also means that the label has been approved by the USDA — that it is truthful and accurate.

This is the inspection mark used on poultry and poultry products, whether they are fresh, frozen, or canned. It means the same thing as the meat inspection marks — that the product is clean and wholesome, fit to eat, and that you can depend on the label to tell you what you need to know about the product.

This mark may be used on fruit and vegetable products and a few others like jam and jelly. It is not required by law. But it, too, is assurance of a good clean product, produced under the supervision of a government inspector. Labels bearing this mark must be approved by the USDA as being truthful and accurate.

This is the USDA grade mark used on butter. It is printed on the carton and on the wrappers of quarter-pound sticks of butter. Similar U.S. grade shields may appear on other food products. A grade shield indicates that the product has been inspected by the USDA.

Mandatory Standards of Wholesomeness for Meat and Poultry

With the passage by Congress of the Wholesome Meat Act in 1967 and the Wholesome Poultry Products Act in 1968, a uniform standard of wholesomeness was established by law for meat, poultry, and poultry products regardless of whether the inspection is done by federal or state inspectors. Prior to the passage of these acts it was the responsibility of federal inspectors to inspect meat, poultry, and poultry products moving in interstate and foreign commerce, but the question of whether to inspect such products in intrastate trade was left up to the states. The weakness in, or complete lack of, inspection programs in many states led to the passage of the 1967 and 1968 acts. Now all state standards have to be equal or superior to the federal standards. The USDA handles the federal inspection and supervises state inspections.

There is a difference between USDA inspection and USDA grading of meat and poultry. The inspection mark tells you it is a wholesome product. The grade mark tells the quality. An item may be inspected but not graded, but never graded without inspection. The law requires that all meats, poultry products, and poultry be inspected, but grading is not required.*

Wool Products Labeling Act

After thirty years of confusion in terminology concerning wool products, practically all responsible persons familiar with the situation agreed that the only way to protect consumers and honest sellers was by legislation. An official of the National Association of Wool Manufacturers, speaking in behalf of mandatory fiber identification, said, "We believe that the consumer has a right to know what he or she is buying. We have ourselves supported labeling regulations, knowing that there was a very substantial amount of misrepresentation in the sales of so-called wool products which contained varying amounts of wool."

With the exception of carpets, rugs, mats, upholsteries, and articles whose fiber content is insignificant or which do not enter into interstate commerce, the Wool Products Labeling Act applies to any product that

* See pages 663–666 for a more detailed discussion of meat and poultry inspection.

contains, or in any way is represented as containing, wool of any description and from any source. A label must be affixed to each wool product showing the percentage of the total fiber weight of new wool, reprocessed wool, and reused wool. In addition, if more than 5 percent of any other fiber is contained, that fact must be shown, as well as the percentage of nonfibrous "loading," "filling," or "adulterating" matter. The label must show the name of the manufacturer or the seller responsible for the statement of fiber content, and it must remain attached to the article until sold to the final consumer. The figures showing percentages of various fibers must be plainly legible. The FTC is charged with enforcement of the act, which involves its usual process of complaint, investigation, and cease-and-desist orders. Willful violations are misdemeanors punishable by fines up to $5,000 or imprisonment for up to one year, or both.

When the act went into effect each manufacturer was assigned a Wool Products Labeling (WPL) number. This number has to appear on the label attached to each wool product. Unfortunately the list of numbers with the manufacturers' names is not readily accessible to the consumer who would like to know who manufactured a wool product from which the manufacturer's name has been removed. The name of the manufacturer is frequently removed from famous name brands when the goods are placed on sale at discount or in "bargain basements." If one wishes to play detective he can probably find the WPL number with the manufacturer's name on some other product in another area of the store. There are approximately 46,000 manufacturers, wholesalers, and importers on the list. If a consumer has a problem, a request made to the FTC will secure the name of the business to which that specific number has been issued.

Textile Fiber Products Identification Act

The chief purpose of this law is to eliminate the confusion caused by the increasing number of man-made fiber trademarks or trade names. There are more than 700 such names that must be classified within one or more of the sixteen generic groups defined by the FTC. Some—like "rubber," "glass," or "metallic"—are self-explanatory; and others—"rayon," "acetate," "nylon"—are familiar. But many consumers find little meaning in the remaining ones—"acrylic," "polyester," "saran," "modacrylic," "azlon," "spandex," "olefin," "vinal," "nytril," and "vinyon." When these classifications are understood, they serve as guides to proper washing, drying, pressing temperatures, durability, and storage. The law requires sellers of textile products to attach conspicuous labels showing their generic names and the percentages of constituent fibers, unless a fiber constitutes less than 5 percent of the product. The FTC emphasizes that the full benefits of this law will be realized only if consumer-buyers know what labels must be used and what the names on the labels mean.

Fur Products Labeling Act

Advertising and selling rabbit fur as lapin, woodchuck as marmot, sheep fleece as mouton, weasel as Japanese mink, and muskrat as mink-dyed muskrat are now unlawful. Spurred by a lobby representing 5,000 mink ranchers, Congress passed a law "to protect consumers and others against misbranding, false advertising, and false invoicing fur products and furs." Labels and advertisements must tell prospective buyers of a garment the name of the animal from which the fur was taken; whether it is new or used; whether it has been bleached, dyed, or artificially colored; whether it is made mostly or entirely of paws, tails, bellies, or waste furs; and the country of origin. In this move to standardize practices in a field that was without standards or rules, the FTC was instructed to prepare a Fur Products Name Guide, which is the official list of true English names for the animals in question. The act is administered and enforced by the FTC.

Flammable Fabrics Act

The Consumer Product Safety Commission administers the Flammable Fabrics Act, which prohibits the interstate sale of wearing apparel and fabrics which, when tested, are found to be "so highly flammable as to be dangerous when worn by individuals." This law was passed after a number of persons had been fatally or severely burned while wearing sweaters made of highly flammable materials.*

Truth in Geographic Labeling

The FDA enforces a truth-in-labeling rule for foods with geographic names. Under the rule, Idaho potatoes, for example, must be grown in Idaho and Louisiana hot sauce must be made in Louisiana or from Louisiana peppers. The regulation states that a food is misbranded if its label expresses or implies a false geographical region in words or pictures. Exceptions were made for geographic names indicating a class of food rather than place of origin, such as Swiss cheese, Irish potatoes, and French dressing.

State Labeling Requirements

Factual information labeling is now required by increasing numbers of state legislatures. The Pennsylvania Bakery Law requires that all wrapped bakery products be clearly and legibly marked with the trade name or kind

---

* See pp. 670–673 for further discussion of this commission.

of bakery product, the name and address of the bakery or distributor, and the words "Registered with Pennsylvania Department of Agriculture." This registration indicates that the bakery and/or distributor is inspected regularly, meets specified standards, and is licensed – or registered – to sell its products in Pennsylvania. Before a license can be issued to a bakery located outside of Pennsylvania, the Pennsylvania Department of Agriculture must receive a satisfactory sanitation report from the agency responsible for bakeries located in that particular state or foreign country. Bakery products covered by the act include ice-cream cones, macaroni products, potato chips, and dough products such as pies, cakes, bread, and rolls.

Michigan has a group of state inspectors who have as one of their responsibilities checking labels and labeling for false, misleading, or deceptive statements, illustrations, assertions, or claims. In addition Michigan requires proper labeling or tagging and packaging of fresh fruits and vegetables to prevent fraud or deception by false representation of quality or quantity. In Florida a law demands that all companies selling gasoline in the state must register with the Department of Agriculture the brand names and specifications describing the quality of gasoline, including a minimum octane number below which the gasoline must not fall when offered for sale to the public. Gasoline samples are collected, and if the octane rating falls below the number advertised the seller is held in violation of the law and prosecuted. Reports are published on the department's findings.

A problem is developing for both the consumer and the manufacturer due to the proliferation of state labeling laws and state standards. There is a question of how beneficial standards and labels can be for the consumer if they vary from state to state. It becomes an expensive and complicated task for the manufacturer to manufacture products to meet a variety of different states' standards and labeling regulations. The Pennsylvania Department of Agriculture's registration is strict enough to meet other state standards and is used in other states, but with the high degree of mobility of both people and products, it would seem that the establishment of adequate federal standards and labeling requirements would prove to be of greater benefit to both consumers and manufacturers.

Canada Standard Size

In 1969 the Canadian government launched standard clothing sizes for children and publicized the "Canada Standard Size" symbol. The basis of standard sizes is build or body measurement, not age. To develop standard sizes, body measurement data of more than 150,000 American and Canadian children were analyzed. Dimensional standards were produced for some eighty-three items of children's clothing by a committee of the Canadian Government Specifications Board. To identify clothing that meets the standards, a label was designed bearing the words "Canada Standard

Size." This system is voluntary. It would be a real service to American parents if this standard size program were adopted in the U.S.

QUESTIONS FOR REVIEW

1. What are the differences between a product standard and a product grade?
2. What product standards would you like to see established in the market?
3. How does one explain the confusion in the grades used by the U.S. Department of Agriculture?
4. If all products were grade labeled, would you ever buy any grade other than the first grade? Why or why not?
5. What might be the results if there were no standards for jams, jellies, and preserves, but each label instead showed the percentage of each ingredient in the product?
6. Why has business not been in the forefront advocating understandable grades?
7. What are the differences in responsibilities between the FDA and the USDA in establishing food standards?
8. Does the establishment of a standard ever present a problem for the consumer?
9. What are the industry's objections to standards and grades? Are they justified?
10. What is the USDA Continuous Inspection Plan?
11. Why does industry frequently oppose government standards and grading systems?
12. Is truth-in-geographic labeling necessary? Is it helpful?
13. Would more government standards and grading make our economic system more or less competitive?
14. Who should establish standards for U.S. products?

PROJECTS

1. Interview three students and find out what they know about grades and standards.
2. Bring as many labels as possible to class that indicate USDA grading.
3. Debate the question: Grade labeling of food products should be mandatory.
4. Interview a butcher concerning meat and poultry inspection.

5. Find out what kinds of state labeling requirements there are in your home state.

REFERENCES

1. "Food Grading: Where Do We Go From Here?," unpublished report of the Office of Consumer Affairs, U.S. Dept. of Health, Education, and Welfare, July 1975, p. 7.
2. *Food Labeling: Goals, Shortcomings, and Proposed Changes,* p. 37.
3. *Summary of Food Grading and Labeling Survey Results,* prepared by office of Representative Gilbert Gude, House of Representatives, Washington, D.C., 1975, p. 2.
4. Jessie V. Coles, *Standards and Labels for Consumers' Goods* (New York: Ronald Press, 1949), p. 107.
5. *How To Use USDA Grades in Buying Food,* U.S. Dept. of Agriculture, Consumer & Marketing Service, 1973.
6. *Food Labeling: Goals, Shortcomings, and Proposed Changes,* pp. 38–39.
7. *Ibid.,* p. 41.

CHAPTER 23

MEASUREMENT LAWS HELP CONSUMERS

CONSUMERS NEED HELP

A little girl was upset when a package of candy she had purchased that had a label picturing hundreds of gumballs turned out to contain only seven. Bags of feed marked 50 pounds were found to contain only 45 pounds, a 10 percent shortage to the customer. A sugar company was fined $40,000 for short weighting five-pound bags of sugar. Three-quart containers of milk were found by weights and measures inspectors to be short-filled on the average of 7 fluid ounces, a short weight a little more than 7 percent. In a check of 161 containers of yogurt, inspectors found 73 percent to be short weight, and one of the eight-ounce containers was short weight 3½ ounces. One milk company was selling milk by the "gallon" in containers that could not hold a gallon. Consumers were being short-weighted by nearly 2 ounces per gallon. One state's weights and measures inspectors found 39 percent of all hams produced by a major packer in one county and 76 percent of all turkeys produced by another packer in another county to be short weight. In one county butter weights showed a 22 percent error, with 98 short-weight items out of 447 samples, and fresh poultry had 43 short-weight items among 497 packages checked, for a 16 percent error rate. The Department of Consumer Affairs estimated that New York City consumers bought $25 million worth of nothing in just one year due to short weight!

In every state in a variety of ways buyers are being shorted. Scales may be inaccurate or they may be set to read an ounce or two fast. Inspectors have found ice, water, paper, pencils, and other items on the platters of scales. A scale can be tilted so as to read an ounce or two fast. If the scale is placed above the buyer's eye level, the figures are distorted and appear higher from the buyer's side. Reading the scale on the swing is an easy way for a seller to pick up 2 or 3 ounces. An overnight soaking of hams, chickens, turkeys, and oysters in water or juice can add several ounces to their weight. Failure to allow for the weight of the container is the most common method of shorting. Scales have been found which had a magnet on the scale base that could be moved to show additional weight over actual weight. These are only a few of the many ways consumers are shorted day after day, month after month, year after year.

Almost all items in food stores are packaged and increasingly nonfood items are also being packaged. Modern packing plants have highly sophisticated machinery that can be set to fill packages accurately. Nevertheless, machines sometimes get out of order and an entire lot of packages may be short. The most common method of shorting on random packages is that of weighing the container as well as the product. In every state that has a package program, short weights are reported.

Consumers spend a lot of money for the air blown into an ice-cream mix. A recipe with an original 5 liquid gallons can be made to yield $10\frac{1}{2}$ gallons of finished product by the simple process of blowing it up with air. "Balloon bread" is made by inflating a one-pound loaf of bread with air and baking it in an "extended" pan to make it appear to be a one and one-half-pound loaf. In New York State a baker was apprehended selling "balloon bread" marked 16 ounces that weighed only 13 ounces.

State measurement officials have reported at least seven methods of shorting buyers of gasoline. These include tampering with the pump, failure to set the pump at zero, failure to meet specifications, charging for more gallonage than delivered, and outright stealing. Domestic buyers of gasoline and fuel oil may be the victims of illegal meters or falsified delivery tickets.

A New York City Department of Consumer Affairs inspector checks a gasoline pump to make sure that the price set in the computer inside the pump is the same as the price motorists see on the sign. (*Dr. Lilly Bruck, Director, Consumer Education, New York City Dept. of Consumer Affairs*)

A petition was filed with the Federal Trade Commission charging that consumers were losing up to $219 million annually because the amount and the percentage of propellant in aerosol products does not have to be disclosed on the label, and yet some aerosol cans contain (on a weight basis) 95 percent propellant and only 5 percent product. For example, an aerosol can of Alberto VO5 hair spray, weighing 16 ounces, sells for $1.99 at what seems to be 12 cents per ounce. Alberto VO5 in a nonaerosol pump system sells for $1.99 for 8 ounces. The pump spray costs 25 cents per ounce. The aerosol spray appears to be the better buy, but the amount of propellant in the aerosol can is 65 percent of the total net weight, so the actual cost per ounce of product is 36 cents, three times the original cost estimate and 44 percent more expensive than the nonaerosol package.[1]

The range of products sold by weight, measure, or count is so large that consumers tend to be unaware of the ubiquity of measurements. Paper napkins, paper towels, writing paper, notebook paper, envelopes, tablets, and tissues are sold by count. How accurate are the counts? Who checks their accuracy? How many pills are there in a bottle? A box of toothpicks labeled 750 contained 411—a short count of 45 percent. A box of cough drops labeled 15 contained six; a box of 100 screws contained 60; a pack of paper clips was short by 30 percent. A package labeled 260 cotton puffs contained 205, while a box labeled 150 embossed gummed foil stars contained 288! Hardware items, such as nails, putty, chain, rope, and screening, are sold by weight or count. In many jurisdictions firewood is sold by the cord, but in some states it is sold by the rick or load.

Since short-weighing and short-measuring practices give those who use them a competitive advantage, these practices may be considered a form of quantity competition. At a price of 80 cents a pound, a one-ounce shortage costs consumers 5 cents. At $1 a pound, an overweight of one ounce costs a seller $1,875 a year, figuring 100 weighings a day for 300 days. Attention should be called to the fact that quantity competition is secretive, in contrast to quality competition, which is assertive. Sellers advertise their quality claims but not their quantity claims. Many would not show the quantity claims on their labels if the law did not require it. On many containers consumers have to search for the small-print, hard-to-find quantity declarations.

THE MEASUREMENTS YOU USE

Weight, Volume, Count

Most commodities in the United States, which are sold by weight, are sold by the ounce or the pound. A bulky item such as coal is sold by the pound, while spices are sold by the ounce. These measurements are called "avoirdupois weights." Troy weights are used to measure precious metals. They include the penny weight, the ounce, and the pound. Linear measures include the foot, the yard, the rod, and the mile. Area measures include the square foot, the square yard, the square rod, the acre, and the section. The latter is a measurement of land one mile square. Cubic measures include the cubic foot and the cubic yard. Liquid measures begin with the fluid ounce, then the gill, the pint, the quart, and the gallon. Dry measures begin with the pint, then the quart, then the peck, and the bushel. In the metric system, which is gradually being adopted in the United States, the key measures are the meter for length and area, the gram for weight, and the liter for volume.

In the kitchen, cooks measure by the teaspoon, the tablespoon, the cup. The *Household Weights and Measures* chart shows the equivalents of these measurements in fluid ounces, cupfuls, liquid pints, liquid quarts, milliliters, and liters. A cup of dry beans weighs 6$\frac{1}{2}$ ounces avoirdupois, a cup of flour 4 ounces, a cup of granulated sugar 7 ounces, and a cup of water 8$\frac{1}{3}$ ounces.*

WHO DEFINES AND SUPERVISES MEASUREMENTS?

Federal Measurement Laws

The Constitution of the United States gives Congress the power "to coin money, regulate the value thereof, and of foreign coin, *and fix the standard of weights and measures.*" Yet this is one power that Congress has failed fully to use. The first federal law concerned with weights and measures was passed in 1799, but it remained inoperative for the following thirty-six years because no legal standards had been adopted. The commerce of those times was characterized by the confusing use of the standards of several European nations. It was not until 1828 that the first really effective weights and measures legislation was passed. Eight years later, Congress passed a joint resolution directing the Secretary of the Treasury to deliver to the governor of each state a complete set of weights and measures conforming to those being constructed for use in the federal custom houses. Then nearly thirty years passed with no significant weights and measures legislation. In 1866 Congress sanctioned but did not require the use of the metric system. Then followed another period of twenty-five years in which there was little Congressional legislation dealing with weights and measures. The next important step was the establishment of the National Bureau of Standards, which since 1901 has functioned as a national center for testing and promoting the use of uniform weights and measures. The bureau has no regulatory authority.

Among other federal laws containing weights and measures provisions

---

* The *Household Weights and Measures* chart should be in every kitchen. It is available for 25 cents from the Superintendent of Documents, U.S. Government Printing Office, Washington, D.C. 20402. (Order by SD Catalog No. C 13.10:430.)

probably the most significant is the Federal Food, Drug, and Cosmetic Act of 1938. That law provides that containers for foods, drugs, and cosmetics must not be made, formed, or filled so as to be misleading. Moreover, it provides that all containers must carry labels showing their net contents in terms of weight, measure, or numerical count. In 1966 the Fair Packaging and Labeling Act was passed.* In 1975 a law was passed setting up a federal board to coordinate a voluntary change to metric measurement by U.S. industries. The law does not specify any deadline, however, or even proclaim a goal of an eventual national conversion to the metric system.

From the consumer-buyer point of view the acts mentioned above practically cover the exercise of Congressional power dealing with weights and measures. Although having authority to exercise control, Congress has failed to use it, with the result that there has been an unfortunate hiatus between federal and state weights and measures legislation and enforcement. The Office of Weights and Measures in the bureau has tried to achieve national uniformity in weights and measures legislation by urging each state to adopt a uniform model law, but many state laws are inadequate.

State Laws

Although Congress has a clear mandate in the Constitution to fix the standard of weights and measures, it has never enacted a general inclusive weights and measures law. Since measurement is essential in all economic activity, some of the states began to enact measurement laws. The Massachusetts law dates from the sixteenth century and has been continuously amended. By 1900 only six states had passed general measurement laws. By 1930 basic laws had been passed in twenty-three additional states. Now every state has such a law, the most recent being that of Hawaii in 1965. Some of these laws are good, some of them fair, and some of them poor.

Enforcement of the measurement law is the responsibility of the director of weights and measures, who, with his inspectors, has full police power. Inspectors can enter premises without a warrant, stop the use of inaccurate devices, order sellers to discontinue illegal practices, and seize, condemn, and destroy defective equipment. Enforcement officers are required to test weighing and measuring devices, seal them, and mark them with an approval seal if they are accurate. Violators are penalized by fines or by imprisonment; however, both fines and prison terms are rare. Directors may issue rules and regulations that have the force of law. They may apply to any court of competent jurisdiction for an injunction restraining any person from violating the law. It is the duty of enforcement officials to see that the rules are obeyed. Those guilty of infractions are penalized. Sellers who obey the rules are protected against unfair competition and buyers are protected against cheating.

* See pp. 608–611.

An Ideal Law

The Model State Law on Weights and Measures has been drafted by state and local weights and measures officials who meet each year in the National Conference on Weights and Measures. The conference is sponsored by the National Bureau of Standards of the United States Department of Commerce and it is a quasi-legislative body. Throughout the year its six standing committees' tentative reports are circulated for comment. When the conference meets, open hearings are held at which interested parties may express their support of or opposition to proposed changes. Each committee then prepares final reports for presentation to a plenary session of the conference. After debate on the proposed changes, votes are taken. If a proposal is adopted, all states are urged to implement the new regulation. Manufacturers of measuring devices and other firms affected by weights and measures supervision send representatives to the conference, as do various trade associations. Those representatives have the privilege of the floor, but may not vote.

Since there is no general federal law and since state laws vary so much in content and effectiveness, the business of selling and buying is hampered. The ideal situation would be realized if there were a single effective public law applicable in every jurisdiction and uniformly enforced. Measurement officials in all jurisdictions are keenly aware of the need for unimity. Yet only a few jurisdictions have enacted full versions of the model law. All states have enacted some parts of it—some only sparsely; some adopted parts a long time ago and have not updated their versions; and some have adopted parts of the law very recently.

If you live in a state that has adopted the full version of the model law, you may be reasonably sure that the following requirements govern the sale of commodities.

Concerning devices:

- The Director has the power to inspect and test all weights and measures offered for sale to ascertain if they are correct. Every twelve months all weights and measures in commercial use shall be tested.
- The Director may issue stop-use orders, stop-removal orders, and removal orders for weights and measures devices in commercial use whenever he considers it necessary; no person shall then use or remove from the premises or fail to remove from the premises such a device contrary to the order.
- It is a misdemeanor to use or have in possession for use for any commercial purposes an incorrect weight or measure or device or instrument used to, or calculated to, falsify any weights or measures.
- It is a misdemeanor to use or have in possession for the purpose of commercial use a weight or measure that does not bear the seal or mark showing that the device has been tested and found to be correct.

- It is illegal to dispose of any rejected or condemned weight or measure in a manner contrary to law or regulation.
- It is forbidden to remove from any device any tag, seal, or mark placed upon it by an enforcement official.
- It is illegal to use in retail trade a measuring device that is not so positioned that its indications may be read accurately and the weighing or measuring operation observed from some position which may reasonably be assumed by a customer.

Concerning packages:

- From time to time the Director shall weigh or measure and inspect packages offered for sale to ascertain whether they contain the amount represented and whether they are offered for sale in accordance with law. If packages are found to be in violation, they may be ordered off sale and tagged to show that they are illegal. Owners of such packages may not sell them until they have been brought into full compliance with all legal requirements.
- The Director has power to issue stop-removal orders and removal orders with respect to packages whenever he considers it necessary; no person shall then use or remove from the premises or fail to remove from the premises any specified package contrary to the terms of the order.

A New York City Department of Consumer Affairs inspector checks the customer scale in a supermarket for accuracy. (*Dr. Lilly Bruck, Director, Consumer Education, New York City Dept. of Consumer Affairs*)

- Any commodity in package form offered for sale shall show on the label the identity of the commodity unless the identity is ascertainable through the wrapper or container; net quantity in terms of weight, measure, or count; and the name and place of business of the manufacturer, packer, or distributor.
- Any package which is part of a lot containing random weights, measures, or counts shall show on the outside of the package a declaration of price per single unit of weight, measure, or count.
- No package shall be so wrapped, made, formed, or filled as to mislead the purchaser.
- The contents of the package shall not fall below such reasonable standard of fill as may have been prescribed by the Director.
- Whenever a commodity in packaged form is advertised and the retail price of the package is stated in the advertisement, there shall be closely and conspicuously associated with such statement of price a declaration of the basic quantity of the contents of the package.

Concerning methods of sale:*

- Commodities in liquid form shall be sold only by measure or by weight; commodities not in liquid form shall be sold only by weight, measure of length or area, or by count. Whenever a commodity is sold on the basis of weight it shall be only in terms of net weight. However, if there exists a firmly established general consumer usage and trade custom with respect to the terms used in expressing a declaration of quantity of a particular commodity, such declaration of quantity may be expressed in its traditional terms, if such traditional declaration gives accurate and adequate information as to the quantity of the commodity.
- Whenever any commodity is offered for sale the price shall not be misrepresented. When an advertised price includes a fraction of a cent, all elements of the fraction shall be prominently displayed and the numeral or numerals expressing the fraction shall be immediately adjacent to and at least one-half the height and width of the numerals representing the whole cents.
- All meats, meat products, poultry, and seafood (except shellfish) shall be sold by weight unless they are sold for immediate consumption on the premises or as one of several elements in a ready-to-eat meal.
- When meat, poultry, or seafood is combined with some other food to form a distinctive food product, the food product shall be sold by weight and the quantity representation may be the total weight of the product; it is not necessary to show the quantity of each of the several elements of the product.
- Each loaf of bread offered for sale shall weigh $\frac{1}{2}$ pound, 1 pound, $1\frac{1}{2}$ pounds, or a multiple of 1 pound. Reasonable tolerances are permitted.

* Customary units of weight and measure are required to be used, metric units may be used.

- Butter, oleomargarine, and margarine shall be sold by weight only in units of ¼ pound, ½ pound, 1 pound, or multiples of 1 pound.
- All fluid dairy products shall be packaged for sale only in units of 1 gill, ½ liquid pint, 10 fluid ounces, 1 liquid pint, 1 liquid quart, ½ gallon, 1 gallon, 1½ gallons, 2 gallons, 2½ gallons, or multiples of 1 gallon.
- When in package form and offered for sale, wheat flour, whole wheat flour, graham flour, self-rising wheat flour, phosphated wheat flour, bromated flour, enriched flour, enriched self-rising flour, enriched bromated flour, corn flour, cornmeal and hominy grits shall be packaged only in units of 2, 5, 10, 25, 50, and 100 pounds.
- When a vehicle delivers to an individual purchaser a commodity in bulk and the commodity is sold in terms of weight, the delivery shall be accompanied by a duplicate delivery ticket with the following information clearly stated in ink or other indelible marking equipment, and equal to type of printing in clarity: the name and address of the seller, the name and address of the purchaser, and the net weight of the delivery in pounds.
- All furnace and stove oil shall be sold by liquid measure or by net weight. When deliveries are larger than ten gallons or 100 pounds, the seller shall provide a delivery ticket showing the seller's name and address, the name and address of the buyer, the identity of the type of fuel, and the price per gallon or pound. In cases of liquid volume deliveries the tickets shall show the meter readings of the liquid volume and in case of weight shall show the net weight.
- Berries and small fruits shall be offered and exposed for sale by weight or by measure in open containers having capacities of ½ dry pint, 1 dry pint, or 1 dry quart.
- It is a misdemeanor to sell or offer to sell less than the quantity represented.
- It is a misdemeanor to offer for sale any commodity contrary to law or regulation.

HOW EFFECTIVELY ARE STATE LAWS ENFORCED?

What Constitutes Good Enforcement?

No matter how good a law may be, it is useless if it is not enforced. A national survey of state measurement laws, administration, and enforcement reported many states with weak laws weakly enforced. It also reported some states as having weak laws vigorously enforced and some in which strong laws are enforced feebly.[2]

One standard by which to measure the effectiveness of an enforcement program is the number of prosecutions and convictions in a year. In the survey year there were no prosecutions in twenty-four states. The officials in most of those states believe that "persuasion and cooperation" are more effective than prosecution. Actually, in many states there was no effective enforcement program.

Officials in many states believe that chronic offenders can be curbed only by legal action. The effectiveness of prosecution is open to question. In small communities there were reports of political collusion and favoritism. Court action is slow. Fines are minimal and imprisonment is rare. To avoid the frustrations and delays of court action, increasing numbers of state officials are using their power to order short-weight packages off sale. Such packages must be repacked correctly. The process is expensive and the delay in sale of merchandise is costly. Where this method is being used, violations are diminishing.

Is Effective Enforcement an Expense or an Investment?

How much deliberate shorting goes on? The evidence indicates that there is more deliberate shorting than one would like to believe. Among the state officials who answered this question eleven estimated 2 percent; ten put their estimates at 1 percent; nine estimated 3 to 5 percent; and six put the figure as high as 8 to 10 percent. If we convert the percentage figures into absolute figures, we see the problem in a different dimension. There are approximately 1,500,000 retail store in the United States. If only 1 percent of those are deliberate shorters, the number would be 15,000, and if the figure is 3 percent the total number would be 45,000.

Of all retail sellers, what percent are guilty of shorting because of carelessness? Of the responding state officials eleven estimated in the range of 1 to 5 percent; twelve estimated a range of 6 to 10 percent; seven in the range from 11 to 20 percent; and seven estimated over 20 percent. Obviously careless shorting is deemed a far more serious problem than deliberate shorting. From a consumer point of view it makes little difference whether one is shorted deliberately or carelessly. From an enforcement point of view it is more difficult to ferret out carelessness and prevent it than it is to discover deliberate shorters and stop their practices. The problem is complicated by the possibility that, in the words of one official, "there are some who are deliberately careless." Another state official, who has had many years of experience, divides retail sellers into three groups: "65 percent are real honest, 25 percent are as honest as we make them be, and 10 percent are never honest." As an afterthought he added, "the 65 percent need to be alerted and kept conscious of their responsibility."

How much does all this shorting cost consumers? Missouri estimated $120 per family each year. If that figure is projected to the approximately 56 million families in the United States, the total cost to consumers would be $6.7 billion. Virginia estimated that its enforcement program saved a family $200 a year. If that figure is projected for the nation, the total shortage cost would be $11.2 billion a year. If these figures are adjusted for the high rate of inflation in recent years, they would be $9.7 billion and $16.2 billion a year.

If every state were to spend 35 cents per person, or $1.40 per family, per year for effective weights and measures protection, the cost would be $78 million. If such an enforcement program could reduce the shorting loss by 50 percent, the gain to consumers would be enormous—$4.9 billion or $8.1 billion, depending on which estimate is taken. If we use the larger figure, that would represent a hundred-fold return on investment.

CONSUMER PROBLEMS WITH PACKAGING

The Functions of Packaging

Self-service marketing makes packaging essential. Packages protect the contents from contamination and evaporation, and they provide a means of storing the products and of transporting them. It is hard to imagine the merchandising of most consumer products without some kind of packaging.

From the sellers' point of view packaging is a sales tool. Just as clothes make the individual so packaging makes a product. Packaging identifies the maker as well as the product and carries the brand name and trademark. The labels on packages tell the buyers what the contents are and how to use them. Packaging is a totality and its purpose is to move products; it is the biggest of all advertising media. A nonfunctional change in package design, such as an illustration, can double sales. Packaging encourages impulse buying, identifies the product with the advertising, and establishes a product image. Even the color of an egg carton can and does affect sales; buyers prefer the color aqua, with pink a close second. Sixty percent of fresh produce is now sold in package form and the volume is increasing. Even cabbages can be sold by the unit because growers can now produce standard size cabbages.

The Cost of Packaging

Total packaging costs amount to more than $35 billion annually, and the figure grows each year. This amounts to about $175 for every person, or approximately $700 a year for a family of four. The cost of packaging as a percentage of the manufacturer's selling price ranges up to 10 percent for toys; 13 percent for food; from 20 to 30 percent for stationery and candy; and for motor oil, drugs, cosmetics, and toiletries, the range is from 30 to 40 percent. The container cost for a one-pound package of cereal has been estimated at 12 percent of the retail price, and the cost of a No. 303 can of tomatoes was 25 percent of the retail price. The U.S. Department of Agriculture has estimated that over ten billion dollars are spent annually on packaging materials for food. The Environmental Protection Agency reported that from 1963 to 1971 food consumption on a per capita basis rose 2.3 percent, while the weight of the packaging for that food increased 33.3 percent.

Packaging Promotes Pollution

American consumers are caught in a buy-use-throw-away syndrome that includes everything from diapers to automobiles. Each one of us is responsible for at least 3.75 pounds of trash and garbage to be disposed of every day, and it is estimated that the figure will almost double by 1980. This adds up to 137 million tons of trash each year, a figure which includes 54 billion cans and 26 billion bottles. There were more than six million pounds of trash and garbage left at the Indianapolis Speedway after the running of the "Indy 500" one year. It is now costing cities some $7 billion a year to collect and dispose of all this trash and garbage, and its disposal releases many tons of pollutants into the air.

Packaging Creates Problems for Consumers

In a retail store the consumer has the right to examine a product before buying it. He or she also has the right to compare prices, to purchase the desired quantity, and to get what is paid for. Packaging sometimes negates these rights. Unless a package is transparent, the prospective buyer cannot judge the contents by their appearance. In the absence of quality information on the label the buyer is in effect blindfolded.

Store shelves are filled with packages that contain fractional quantities. No consumer ever demanded such a quantity as $3\frac{7}{8}$ ounces, for example. Confronted with odd sizes the consumer is denied the right to purchase the quantity she wants.

Consumer-buyers are entitled to get what they pay for. But they have no feasible way to check the weight or volume of the contents of packages. The most common method of shorting consumers, as reported by weights and measures officials, is to charge for gross weight rather than for net weight. This means that the heavy wrapping paper on a package of meat or the cardboard carton in which it is packed is sold to the consumer at meat prices. Unless a buyer opens a package and weighs or measures the contents he has no way of knowing whether he is getting what he pays for. Even in states having good laws and good enforcement programs, prepackaged shortages up to 30 percent are reported regularly. Confronted with 171 sizes of potato chip packages, ranging from a few ounces to three pounds, it is almost impossible for a buyer to calculate price comparisons. In the national capital a shopper inspected three markets and found 180 brands and sizes of detergents. Of that number 94 had no size designation on the front panel.

The Director of Weights and Measures for Washington State testified that "we find there is a multiplicity of fractions or decimals of fractions that tend to confuse even weights and measures inspectors." The California Consumer Counsel selected five housewives to participate in a price comparison experiment. All the women had some college training. Each was given $10, with instructions to go to a supermarket and purchase fourteen items on the basis of the largest quantity at the lowest price. It took the women from twenty-five minutes to an hour to make their calculations. All of them succeeded in buying the largest quantity of cheddar cheese at the lowest price, but they all failed in their effort to purchase the largest quantity of rice and toilet soap at the lowest price. Among fourteen choices, not one package of rice weighed an even pound.

Some package sizes and designs exaggerate the contents; essential information that should be on the labels is often hard to find, illegible, or even missing; package contents may be in odd or nonstandard amounts for no technical reason, making price comparison difficult; large "economy" size packages occasionally are priced higher per pound than smaller size packages of the same product; "cents-off" labels proclaim price reductions that may not be genuine; and special prices create confusion as to what the going price is.

Package Hazards

Rodents find it easy to gnaw holes in burlap bags, cardboard boxes, and paper sacks. Feeding on the contents and nesting in the packages, rodents and insects create health hazards for consumers. Most packaging plants and retail stores keep their premises clean. Many, however, are careless. Food and drug inspectors and public health officials are always on the alert for unsanitary conditions. Packaged items stored in warehouses are particularly susceptible to infestation.

Glass containers are impervious to rodents and insects, but are subject to breakage. Sometimes packers attempt to salvage the contents of broken glass containers, and in the process splinters of glass may be mixed in with the contents of a new package. Common law holds processors legally liable for injuries caused to consumers.

A recent and disturbing question concerning packaging is whether the fluorocarbons that are released from aerosol containers pose a threat to life by reducing the protective covering of ozone around the earth which keeps too much radiation from the sun from reaching the earth.

The Food and Drug Administration proposed a ban on certain plastic food packaging and other materials made of vinyl chloride that come in contact with food. Vinyl chloride has been shown to cause cancer when inhaled by humans and is suspected of having a similar potential when ingested.

Deceptive Packaging

The model law and the Food, Drug, Cosmetic Act say that no package shall be so made, formed, or filled so as to be misleading. Neither federal nor state officials have had much success in implementing this provision, however.

One package containing 7 ounces was 2½ inches longer than a competitor's package which also contained 7 ounces. Both were 1 ounce short of an even half pound. A bottle containing hand lotion was designed to give the impression that a five-ounce size was larger than a competing ten-ounce size. Containers for cereals and detergents are often larger than they need to be to hold the net content declared on the label. A great deal of money, skill, and time are spent by package designers to make consumers think they are getting more when in fact they may be getting less.

In the words of a former chairman of the National Conference on Weights and Measures, "The deceptive package has several roommates in trade practices. They are hidden declaration of contents, fine print, camouflage, unexplainable fractions, and glorified illustrations which imply contents that are not contained in the package."

Short-Weight Packages

The Food and Drug Administration sampled net weights of packaged goods among forty-five food groups. Of more than 100,000 packages 15 percent were short-weight. One-half of the lots were short 5 percent or more and the candy packages were short on the average 12 percent. In the third year of a continuing campaign the FDA found even more shorting than before. "We cannot help feeling that some of these incidents were deliberate and not accidents. We were shocked by the results of the campaign. We had all of the law we needed but we did not have enough money to enforce the law."

The inspection statistics of the Bureau of Standard Weights and Measures for Pennsylvania for a twelve-month period showed that 12,482 lots of standard packages were checked and 1,345 lots were rejected for short weight—a rejection rate of 10.8 percent. In random packages, 20,762 lots were checked and 3,717 lots were rejected, for a rejection rate of 17.8 percent. These inspections were conducted monthly in an average of forty-eight counties by seventeen state inspectors. An average of ninety-six different types of commodities were checked in an average of seventy different stores each month. The total value of the products inspected was $3,442,586.57, and the value of the products rejected was $316,634.86; 9.2 percent of the total dollar value of the products inspected were rejected.[3] Pennsylvania inspectors used to work the usual five-day-week schedule until it was discovered that in some stores deliberate short-weighting was being done on weekends since there was no reason to expect to be checked then. Now inspectors are checking stores any time they are open.

Raising Prices by Reducing Contents

There is abundant evidence that many consumers do not read the labels on packages as carefully as they should. Measurement officials know this,

Food and Drug Administration officials know it, and packagers know it. There is nothing measurement officials can do, even though they have tried to educate consumers to read the labels. But there is something packagers can do and they do it. Without changing the size of the package they reduce the net contents and keep the price the same. This is perfectly legal. It can be argued that it is not deceptive since the net weight does have to appear on the label; but it is a questionable practice.

This method of raising prices is popular in a period of rising prices. Here is an example: A package of food marketed by a national manufacturer priced at 37 cents contained 7 ounces, making the price per ounce 5.28 cents and the price per pound 84.48 cents. Three years later the package price had been reduced to 35 cents, but the package contents had been reduced to 5 ounces. That made the price 7 cents an ounce and $1.12 a pound. An apparent price reduction of 2 cents concealed a real price increase of 31.7 percent. A chocolate bar weighing 1 ounce was reduced to $^{13}/_{16}$ of an ounce, but was still selling at the former price. The quantity reduction came to 18.75 percent, and the price increase to 22 percent, or 6.1 cents an ounce.

Prices can be raised by changing packages slightly. A few years ago the canning industry shifted from its No. 2 can, which holds 19.7 fluid ounces, to the No. 303 can, which holds 16.2 fluid ounces. Four No. 2 cans hold almost as much as five No. 303 cans. At a distance of only a few feet very few people can distinguish the two sizes even when the cans are side by side on a store shelf.

A spokesman for a producer of paper products said, "We do not change prices as our costs increase or decrease. We change the number of sheets in a tablet, down or up."

Many products are subject to shrinkage in weight due to evaporation. Some packers like to mark their labels "25 pounds when packed." Such a statement is illegal in thirty-nine states. What happens in the other states? Probably nothing. Too many states do not even have any program for checking the weights of packages. A few states are still using court action in their efforts to regulate shorting. But court action is not very satisfactory. Oklahoma put teeth in its law by requiring that a notice of violation be posted on the main entrance of a store guilty of a second or third short-weight offense. This has proven effective in controlling chronic offenders. Other states are turning to the use of the power to order short-weight packages off sale.

A few states check the weights of packages in the packing plants. Ninety percent of the inventory of a typical store consists of packages packed in packing plants. If the package measurements are correct when they leave the plant, allowing for evaporation, they are very likely to be correct when the final buyer purchases them.

There are two basic weaknesses in state control. One is the inability of states to interfere with interstate commerce. The other is the disparity in the effectiveness of state laws and enforcement programs. By the early 1960s deceptive packaging had become so prevalent that a spontaneous consumer uprising demanded that the federal government strengthen its laws and provide uniform regulation and enforcement.

THE FAIR PACKAGING AND LABELING ACT

Provisions of the Law

After five years of hearings, debates, and delays, the Fair Packaging and Labeling Act (FPLA) became Public Law 89–755 in 1967. Seldom in this century has so complicated a law been passed, with administrative and enforcement responsibility divided among several agencies. The act states that informed consumers are essential to the fair and efficient functioning of a free market economy and food and nonfood packages and their labels should tell consumers clearly what the contents are and help them compare values. In mid-1968 it was predicted that full implementation would not be achieved for years; that prediction still holds. The law contains mandatory, discretionary, and voluntary provisions.

Mandatory Labeling Provisions   A primary objective of the act is to promote uniformity and simplification of labeling. The bill provides that:

- The identity of the commodity shall be specified on the label.
- The net quantity of contents shall be stated in a uniform and prominent location on the package.
- The net quantity of contents shall be clearly expressed in ounces and, if applicable, pounds, or, in the case of liquid measures, in the largest whole unit of quarts or pints.
- The net quantity of a serving must be stated if the package bears a representation concerning servings.

Discretionary Labeling Provisions   The act authorizes the administering agencies to promulgate regulations when necessary to prevent consumer deception or to facilitate value comparisons:

- To determine what size packages may be represented by such descriptions as "small," "medium," and "large"
- To regulate the use of such promotions as "cents off" or "economy size" on any package
- To require the listing of ingredients in the order of decreasing predominance
- To prevent nonfunctional slack fill

Packaging Provisions   The act provides for the voluntary adoption of packaging standards. The act authorizes the Secretary of Commerce to call upon manufacturers, packers, and distributors to develop voluntary standards whenever he finds that undue proliferation of weights, measures, or quantities impairs the ability of consumers to make value comparisons. If voluntary standards are not adopted, the Secretary of Commerce shall report this fact to Congress together with his legislative recommendation.

Enforcement of FPLA

Whether intended or not, the administrative and enforcement procedures prescribed in FPLA divide and confuse. The Food and Drug Administration is responsible for foods, drugs, devices, and cosmetics. The Federal Trade Commission is responsible for all other consumer commodities. The Department of Commerce has no enforcement powers, but is charged with responsibility to obtain from industry agreement on voluntary standards. Finally, the Treasury Department is responsible for imported products, although the FDA makes all decisions whether or not a product may be imported.

No law is self-enforcing. No provision of this law goes into effect until regulations are promulgated. Because final regulations have the force of law, the procedure for their adoption is elaborate and time-consuming. They begin with a notice of proposed rule making. After comments are received, the rules are adopted. Then objections may be filed and public hearings may be required. Eventually a decision is made, but it is subject to judicial review in the United States Court of Appeals. The process of rule making had not been completed after four years. Proposed regulations were delayed by industry requests for exemptions or extensions of effective dates.

It takes money and personnel to enforce a law. The FDA and FTC are short of both. As a result, implementation of FPLA has had a low priority. All of this emphasizes the unofficial role of the states. Although they do not have any new authority or funds under FPLA, it will be state inspectors who police the packages in retail stores, if any policing is to be done. The FDA says, "We expect that the states will have a major part in enforcement of the Fair Packaging and Labeling Act." But the states lack money and personnel, and they look to the federal government for help.

The Department of Commerce reported that package quantity standardization efforts had proceeded at a slower pace than had been anticipated, partly because of industry fears of antitrust violations. Eight industry proposals to simplify quantity patterns were approved, reducing numbers of packages from 11 to 76 percent. For example, the number of package sizes for peanut butter was reduced from thirty to twelve and for paper towels from thirty-three to eight. The determination of what products constitute consumer commodities had not been completed "and will probably have to be determined on a case-by-case basis."[4]

Evaluation of FPLA

Early in 1975 the Comptroller General of the United States released a very detailed report done by the General Accounting Office (GAO) on the implementation of FPLA and related food-labeling laws and the improvements needed.[5] The report stated: "Although most food products comply with federal packaging and labeling laws and regulations, improvements are needed so that labels tell consumers what they need to know to compare and select those products suited best to their needs or wants."[6]

The GAO's report contains specific recommendations in the six areas listed below in which it is felt action needs to be taken if consumers are to secure the benefits that are expressed in the FPLA.

1. *Need for full disclosure of ingredients.* The FDA has established standards of identity for 265 different food products. However, certain ingredients—whether mandatory or optional—in these "standardized" foods are exempt from any labeling requirement. The FDA requires foods without standards of identity to display the common, or usual, name of each ingredient. However, it has been industry practice to list some ingredients in general terms, such as vegetable oils and fats, without specifying whether it is coconut oil, cotton seed oil, or corn oil, or to list artificial coloring without specifying the number and kinds of colorings or combination of coloring.

The GAO recommends that Congress consider amending the FPLA Act to require full disclosure of all ingredients on packaged food products, including standardized products, and to authorize the FDA to require food labels to specifically identify spices, flavorings, and colorings where a proven need of such information exists.

2. *Need for nutritional labeling.* The FDA began a program in 1973 requiring detailed nutritional information on the labels of foods that are fortified or for which nutritional claims are made and encouraging manufacturers of other foods to voluntarily include nutrition information on their labels. The report states that an education program is needed to explain to consumers the purpose and best use of nutritional labeling and to help them understand the FDA's nutritional labeling format.

3. *Need for percentage of characterizing ingredients on labels.* Labels on food products frequently lack information concerning the amount of "characterizing ingredients" in the product—that is, the amount of beef in beef stew, apples in apple pie, or pears in canned pears. Most food labels do not provide consumers with data on the amounts or percentages of such ingredients that have a material bearing on the price or consumer acceptance of the product. As a result, manufacturers can and do vary the percentage of characterizing ingredients and thus vary the value of acceptability of their product without consumers' knowledge. Without this information consumers cannot readily make a value comparison between competing products as FPLA intended.

The GAO review of manufacturers' recipes for twenty-four products in nine nonmeat food categories showed the percentage of characterizing ingredients often differed in four categories by more than 10 percent. For example, the amount of fruit in frozen fruit pies varied from 47 to 65 percent of the total weight for all ingredients. One manufacturer's pies contained 47 percent fruit, while his competitor's products contained 65 percent fruit in apple pie and 54 percent fruit in cherry pie. Officials of the firm reporting 47 percent fruit opposed percentage labeling because it would not permit them to vary product contents without changing labels. They said that during periods of short supply and rising costs, their firm sometimes chooses to vary the percentage of ingredients if they feel the market will not bear an increase in price.

The GAO recommends that the secretary of HEW direct the commissioner of the FDA to identify foods that would be appropriate for percentage of characterizing ingredient labeling and require such foods to include this information on their labels.

4. *Need for uniform quality grading.* Many consumers are unable to compare the value of competing products without opening the container because labels generally do not bear information or grades concerning the quality—that is, color, size, texture, flavor, blemishes or defects, and consistency. When the grades as adopted by the U.S. Department of Agriculture are used this can present problems to consumers because of their confusing terminology. The GAO recommends that existing regulations be revised to make grade designations uniform and easier to understand.

5. *Need for uniform open-dating system.* Because of problems with stale or spoiled foods many consumers favor an open-dating system. The GAO recommends that Congress enact legislation to establish a uniform open-dating system for perishable and semiperishable foods.

6. *Unit pricing.* To compare the value of competing commodities, consumers must be able to readily compare the prices. However, studies of consumer abilities to compare prices showed that—despite FPLA—consumers make inaccurate price comparisons 40 percent or more of the time. The presentation of unit prices—which has been done for years on fresh meats—could facilitate price comparisons of each brand and size of competing commodities. Studies have shown that unit prices can reduce price comparison errors. However, FPLA currently does not require retail grocery stores to provide unit pricing.

The GAO recommends that Congress consider enacting legislation to establish a unit-pricing program, including guidelines for the design and maintenance of unit-pricing information and education of consumers about its use.

THE LAW HELPS THOSE WHO HELP THEMSELVES

Know Your Measurements

The authoritative source of information on weights and measures is the National Bureau of Standards of the U.S. Department of Commerce. Miscellaneous Publication 286 contains the units of weight and measure of the international (metric) system and the traditional U.S. avoirdupois system.[7] For most purposes, however, the essential information is available in a dictionary under the heading of measurements or weights and measures.

In the Third National Survey of state laws one of the questions put to every weights and measures official was this: "What suggestions do you have to offer to consumer-buyers to help them protect themselves?" The following recommendations represent the combined wisdom and experience of fifty-two experts.[8]

Know Your Measurement Law

It is not necessary to know the measurement law of your state in detail but it is helpful to have a general idea of its provisions. Because laws are usually written in legal language, it is difficult for laymen to understand them. Perhaps the summary of the model law on pp. 598–601 of this text will be sufficient for your purposes.

Be a Scale Watcher

As you purchase commodities weighed in your presence, weights and measures officials give you the following suggestions:

- Look for the seal showing that the device has been tested and found to be accurate. Note when it was last checked.
- Observe the position of the scale. If it is to register accurately, it must be flat on the counter. The scale indicators must also be visible. If they are blocked by merchandise, complain to the operator and if he or she fails to remove the obstruction, complain to the manager. If you still do not get satisfaction, notify your measurement inspector.
- Be sure that the scale indicator starts at zero. If it reads over by just one ounce on a $1.60 per pound item, it will cost you 10 cents too much. As prices continue to rise, a short-weight loss costs you more and more.
- Watch the scale as your purchase is being weighed. In the words of one official: "Sellers will give accurate weight if buyers watch them closely."
- "Take the bounce out of the ounce." This means that you should not let the operator weigh on the swing. Be sure that the indicator comes to rest.
- If you are in doubt about the accuracy of a measurement, ask the clerk to reweigh or take the package to one of the other scales in the store and weigh it yourself. Remember, however, the weight of the container must be deducted.
- Some officials recommend that you have an accurate scale in your kitchen and check-weigh your purchases when you get home. In some states your measurement man will test your scale for accuracy.
- If you have any complaints, call the manager of the store or report to your measurement inspector.

Watch Those Packages

- Read all labels. Pay special attention to the weight declaration on loaves of bread. Under the Fair Packaging and Labeling Act, the packager is required to place the weight declaration in the lower third of the front of the package, and the size of the type is specified.
- Know how to read computer scale labels.
- Know the capacity of the various sizes of cans in terms which you understand.
- Don't let the apparent size of a package deceive you. One package may appear to be larger than another but it may not contain as much. Read the label to ascertain net weight. Be alert to deceptive packages. The shape of a package may make it appear larger than it is. A bottle may have a false bottom. There are other forms of deception. Be on the lookout.
- Shake a package to ascertain the amount of slack. After you purchase a package and open it, if you find what you consider to be excessive slack, measure the empty space and report to the store. If you cannot get satisfaction report to your measurement official.
- Avoid fractional sizes. One of the advantages that consumers should ultimately gain from the Fair Packaging and Labeling Act is the gradual elimination of packages with fractional ounces.
- Don't pay for paper; insist on net weight. If there are losses or shrinkages before purchase, those losses should not be borne by the consumer as short weights.
- Do not be misled by vague terms such as "family size" or "giant size." Such terms are without meaning. Read the label to ascertain net contents.
- Watch for packages that are marked as so many cents off. On cents-off deals originated by the manufacturer the cents-off saving is passed on to the retailer, but the retailer may or may not pass it on to the customer.
- When purchasing berries in open containers be sure the berries are firmly packed. In most states small fruits such as strawberries, currants, and cherries are sold by the box, having net contents of $\frac{1}{4}$ pint, $\frac{1}{2}$ pint, 1 quart, or multiples of 1 quart.

Be a Smart Shopper

- Buy by weight. One of the most precise methods of determining quantity in solid items is by weight.
- Purchase by quantity, not by a dollar's worth. Never ask for a "bagful" or a "quarter's worth" or "a dollar's worth." Always purchase by volume, weight, or count and note the price per unit.
- On merchandise packaged in the store, especially at the meat counter,

ask the clerk to write on the package the price per pound, the weight of the package, and the total price.
- Make value comparisons. Compare net weight and price of packaged commodities. For example, 18 ounces for 36 cents would cost 2 cents per ounce, whereas 22 ounces for 48 cents would cost 2.2 cents per ounce.
- Check the prices stamped on the cans or packages.

Be a Pump Watcher

Motorists purchase millions of gallons of gasoline or motor oil. Your measurement inspector gives you the following advice:

- The first thing to do when purchasing gasoline and motor oil is to get out of your car.
- Look for the measurement inspector's seal showing that the pump has been tested and found to be accurate. This act alone will put the operator on guard. For all he knows you may be an inspector. If there is no seal, ask the operator why there is none on the pump.
- Watch the indicator and be sure that it starts at zero. This way you will avoid the "hanging nozzle" trick.
- Order 10 gallons. This will make it possible for you to check the accuracy of the pump. If the price is 56.9 cents per gallon the total should be $5.69. Your measurement inspector says it is a good idea never to run your tank empty. If you start with a full tank, 10 gallons will take you approximately 180 miles, and it is a good idea to stop and take a break after driving that distance.
- If you purchase on a credit card, read the entries before you sign. Draw a line across the blank space so that no subsequent entry can be made.
- If you are purchasing motor oil, watch the dip stick to be sure that the operator inserts it completely. Then after oil has been put into the crank case, ask to have the dip stick inserted again to be sure that your oil is at the proper level and that you have gotten the oil for which you paid.

Observe Fuel Oil Deliveries

In purchasing fuel oil you are heavily dependent on your measurement inspector. It is he who has the knowledge and the equipment to test the accuracy of meters and who knows the ways in which short deliveries can be made. You should watch the delivery truck as the delivery is being made and be sure to get a ticket showing the amount delivered. Your presence alone puts a driver on guard.

Ask Your Weights and Measures Office for Help

Check with your state weights and measures office to find out what information pamphlets are available that tell about the activities of the office and what guidelines they suggest consumers to follow when buying by weight and measure. If you have any problem concerning short weight or measure, contact your weights and measures office and ask for assistance.

THE UNITED STATES IS GOING METRIC—SLOWLY

Arguments for Metrication

The so-called English inch, ounce, gill system of measurement is awkward. It is rapidly becoming passé. The metric system of measurement is used in most of the world.

The metric system is so simple that it can be mastered in an hour. There are no fractions. The metric system divides weights, distances, and volumes into units of 10, 100, and 1,000. These are only three basic units: the gram, the meter, and the liter; which measure weight, length, and volume. There are 1,000 grams in a kilogram, equal to 2.2 pounds. There are 1,000 meters in a kilometer, equal to about $\frac{1}{2}$ mile. A liter is roughly equal to a quart, and there are 1,000 liters in a kiloliter. A metric thermometer measures freezing temperature at zero and boiling temperature at 100°. To compare the complexity of one system with the simplicity of the other, try converting 322 inches to feet, then to yards. You must use long division, and in both cases you will have fractional results. Using the metric system to convert 322 centimeters to decimeters and to meters, you would simply move the decimal point to the left. The result would be 32.2 decimeters, and 3.22 meters. The metric system is so simple that school children can learn it quickly and businessmen, engineers, and scientists can make their calculations rapidly. There is less likelihood of error.[*]

Although the United States is not yet on the metric system, our standard meter is Prototype Meter Bar 27, which is defined in terms of a wavelength of Krypton 86 atom. The standard of mass is Prototype Kilogram 20. The standard for time is the natural vibration rates of the Cesium = 133 atom.

Many drug companies are already on the metric system. Firms exporting to metric system nations put both metric and U.S. measurements on their packages. All armed forces prescriptions are written in metric measurement. All military maps are in metric terms, as are all fire control equipment. The National Aeronautics and Space Agency uses metric measurements for range and projectory calculations. All Olympic Games measurements are in metric. The National Bureau of Standards, the Department of Defense, and the American Geophysical Union all favor the metric system.

[*] The National Bureau of Standards has developed a useful *NBS Metric Kit* which includes a wallet-size metric conversion card, a 15-centimeter ruler, a booklet and other information on the metric system. It is available for $2.00 from the Superintendent of Documents, Washington, D.C. 20402. Specify stock number 0303–01347. The metric conversion card is available by itself for 20 cents.

Metrication Is Coming to the United States

On December 23, 1975, the president signed a bill setting up a seventeen-member U.S. Metric Board, with the responsibility of synchronizing a voluntary switch to the metric system among industrial and business sectors. The passage of this legislation amounts to a formal Congressional recognition of the ongoing conversion and is an endorsement of it.

The U.S. has been slowly converting to the metric system. Several manufacturers, including the "Big Three" automobile makers, have been moving rapidly toward voluntary conversion. The Vega car has already been marketed with metric measurements. Some American cars already have kilometer-per-hour speedometers, and more highway signs are using both conventional and metric measures. Seven-up and Coca-Cola were the first companies to introduce one- and two-liter bottles. By 1978 all states will be teaching their students the metric system. The next generation should be a metric generation.

QUESTIONS FOR DISCUSSION

1. What are some of the ways in which measurement affects your life?
2. How do you account for so much shorting in measurements?
3. "Measurement inspectors aid only consumers." Discuss.
4. List the variety of ways products are measured.
5. What are the different kinds of measurement systems in use?
6. What are some of the key provisions in the Model State Law on Weights and Measures?
7. What constitutes a good enforcement program for measurement laws?
8. On a cost-benefit basis is effective enforcement of weights and measures laws worth it?
9. What are the basic functions of packaging?
10. From your experience and observation can you add any packaging hazards to those mentioned in this chapter?
11. Give examples of deceptive packaging.
12. What are six significant provisions of the Fair Packaging and Labeling Act?
13. How successful has FPLA been?
14. What are ways to protect yourself from being shorted in buying?
15. Draw up a list of pros and cons for adopting the metric system.

PROJECTS

1. Have a dozen products weighed in the science laboratory to see if each contains the same weight as that listed on the label.

2. In your library or from your local weights and measures office secure the latest report of the National Conference on Weights and Measures. Choose five selected articles and summarize them.

3. From your library or local weights and measures official get a copy of the model law and a copy of your state law. To what extent does your state law conform to the model law?

4. Chart the price-per-pound for every box of detergent in a supermarket that does not have unit pricing. Did you find any surprises?

5. Interview a supermarket manager and get his or her opinion about the six recommendations in the GAO report to Congress.

6. Let two or four members of the class debate this question: "Resolved that the United States should make the use of the metric system mandatory in the United States."

7. Interview a plumber, a carpenter, or a machinist about his feelings concerning the adoption of the metric system.

REFERENCES

1. Brief filed in the Matter of Petition for the Promulgation of a Trade Regulation Rule Requiring Disclosure of the Amount of Propellant in Aerosol Products before the Federal Trade Commission by Students Resisting Aerosol Fluorocarbon Emissions, George Washington Law School, filed April 10, 1975, pp. 1–2.
2. Leland J. Gordon, *Weights and Measures and the Consumer: Third National Survey of State Weights and Measures Legislation, Administration, and Enforcement* (Mt. Vernon, N.Y.: Consumers Union, 1970).
3. Letter received by the writer from the Director, Bureau of Standard Weights and Measures, Harrisburg, Pa., dated May 6, 1975.
4. Report to the Congress by the Secretary of Commerce on Activities Under the Fair Packaging and Labeling Act During Fiscal Year 1969 (mimeographed).
5. *Food Labeling: Goals, Shortcomings, and Proposed Changes*, Dept. of Health, Education, and Welfare, Dept. of Agriculture, Dept. of Commerce, by the Comptroller General of the United States, Jan. 29, 1975.
6. *Ibid*, p. i.
7. L. J. Chisholm, *Units of Weight and Measure: International (Metric) and U.S. Customary*, National Bureau of Standards, Miscellaneous Publication no. 286, 1967, 251 pages, $2.25.
8. Gordon, pp. 163–173.

CHAPTER 24

STATE AND LOCAL GOVERNMENTS HELP CONSUMERS

STATE CONSUMER SERVICES

Government and the Consumer

The interests of the consumer and business are not identical. The rational consumer is interested and concerned with getting the best combination of good quality, good service, and low price in a product or service to meet his or her particular need. The primary business interest is to maximize profit. Thus the consumer wants to get as much for as small an expenditure as possible, while business wants to give as little as possible for as high a price as possible. Neither is able to reach fully such a self-interested objective because there are many consumers and many sellers competing in the marketplace. Where there are just a few producers, the benefits of competition are lessened. If the economic system is functioning properly, both parties to a business transaction will benefit. The consumer will be able to secure a satisfactory product at a reasonable price, and the seller will be able to sell products at prices adequate to cover costs and to return a profit that will make it possible for the business to continue operating. Even though the objectives of the consumer and business are not the same, neither can prosper without the other.

One of the functions of government is to see that the rules of the marketplace are fair for both consumer and seller, with equal justice. Governments have at least three approaches to fostering the economic welfare of consumers: 1) to educate consumers so they will be more aware of their options and able to act more effectively in their individual interests; 2) to regulate the sellers to discourage or ban undesirable practices; and 3) to change the legal relationship between the seller and the buyer so that fraud can be made unprofitable and the seller and the creditor bear a greater responsibility for the success of the transaction.

The Problem of Dual Control

Under the American form of government there are, in addition to the federal government, fifty states, the District of Columbia, Puerto Rico, the Virgin Islands, and thousands of county and municipal jurisdictions. Which of these agencies shall regulate economic activities in those areas where regulation is necessary? Federal and state constitutions divide authority, creating jurisdictional problems. Legislative vacuums may be created by the failure of any jurisdiction to act. The federal government is unable to regulate commercial activities confined to a single state, while a state is powerless to regulate interstate commerce. There is a fear among states, also, that too stringent regulation on the part of a state may antagonize business interests, discourage new business, and perhaps encourage established firms to move to other states.

Usually a dozen or more agencies in state governments are involved with consumer problems. The more common among these are agriculture, banking, commerce, conservation, education, health, insurance, pharmacy, public utilities, attorney general's office, universities, and welfare.

Widespread mass production, with products nationally advertised and nationally marketed, means that commerce tends increasingly to become interstate and therefore subject to federal control. The annual reports of the Food and Drug Administration and Federal Trade Commission reveal some cooperation between federal and state regulatory agencies. A major obstacle to greater cooperation is the lack of uniformity in state laws and in the agencies which enforce them.

A comprehensive study of state and local food and drug programs prepared for the Food and Drug Administration in 1965 stated in its "Summary of Principal Findings and Recommendations" that the general food and drug laws of the states fail to have a basic uniformity among themselves and also lack adequate uniformity with federal legislation. In many cases they do not have the breadth of coverage of products and consumer risks that they should have. Differences in laws and regulations are excessive and many laws serve no useful purpose. In varying degrees the states have failed to provide statutory protection against products in which health hazards are present, and in addition they have been slow to modernize their legislation to take into account the newer risks associated with additives, residues, new drugs, and hazardous household products.

An illustration of this problem of conflicting and differing laws was revealed in the study's findings on mislabeling and misbranding provisions of general state food and drug laws pertaining to foods and cosmetics. Of fifteen possible provisions in these areas under the Uniform Act Provision, no state had all fifteen. Several states had thirteen such provisions, but Mississippi had only two. By 1976, however, forty-one states had enacted the model FDA law in whole or in part.

Another illustration of this problem was the case of the stuffed turkeys. The Department of Agriculture ruled that stuffed turkeys should carry labels disclosing total gross weight—turkeys and stuffing combined. New York State wanted to require the label to carry separately the weight of the turkey and the weight of the stuffing. The New York State Extension Service found the amount of stuffing varied from 15 to 30 percent of the total weight. The question to be answered was whether the stricter state law should take precedence over the more lenient federal ruling. The final ruling of the Department of Agriculture stipulated that the total net weight was to be shown on the label along with a statement indicating the minimum weight of poultry in the product.

A study of the activities of the three levels of government in the interest of consumers was a major project of the Intergovernmental Relations Subcommittee of the United States Senate Committee on Government Operations. The purpose of these investigations was to uncover areas of duplication of consumer protection and areas of omission in the protection offered consumers by the combined efforts of the three levels of government. In the area of the regulation of drugs and related products the committee found that one state, Maine, was spending as little as 15 cents annually per 1,000 population for the regulation of drugs and related products, while at the other extreme, in Nevada, the annual expenditure per 1,000 was $209.58.

This committee developed reports on weights and measures, foods and related products, and preneed burial services. Each of these reports outlined what was or was not being done at the various levels of government in the areas investigated.

Policing Business for Consumers

Every state constitution grants to the legislative body broad police power under which laws may be enacted for the protection of public health, morals, and welfare. The scope and coverage of such legislation are greater than is generally realized. There are, for example, laws governing sanitary conditions under which goods and services are produced, such as those requiring sanitary inspection of dairies and restaurants, and laws to compel special treatment of products to make them safer, such as those requiring that all milk offered for sale be pasteurized and all hair and feathers used in mattresses be sterilized. State and local laws forbid adulteration of food and drugs and commonly forbid the sale of food unfit for human consumption. Most cities have sanitary regulations covering stores, bakeries, and meat shops. Among businesses dispensing personal services are barber shops, beauty parlors, and bathhouses, all of which operate under more or less rigid sanitary regulations. Housing regulations have become more strict; most cities fix minimum standards of lighting, air, and sanitary facilities in all buildings leased for residential purposes. Most weights and measures activities are under state auspices, as was shown in Chapter 23.

Since about 40 percent of all foods, drugs, and cosmetics move in intrastate commerce only and since conditions vary among states and cities, state and local laws enforced by state and local agencies are needed to supplement federal control. As we have noted, the Association of Food and Drug officials adopted a model state food, drug, and cosmetic law, which has been amended as necessary to meet changing conditions. A majority of the states have enacted the model bill into law without substantial change. In the food, drug, and cosmetic field, states cannot do the job alone; they need help from the Food and Drug Administration. The failure of some states to pass minimal legislation or, if passed, to enforce it is indicative of a high degree of business influence on the legislature.

Other Legislative Activity in the Consumer's Behalf

The variety of consumer legislative activity possible at the state level is evident in this brief summary of some of the legislation recently enacted by various state governments.

- Charity fund raising came under state regulation in Michigan, North Dakota, and South Dakota.
- Advertising and unfair trade practices were subjected to greater state controls in Georgia, Nevada, and Virginia.
- Automobile repairs were subjected to regulation in Nevada.
- Legislation was passed in Georgia and New York regulating buying and mail order clubs.
- A law requiring item pricing on grocery products was enacted in California.
- Washington mandated free calls, without use of a dime, to the operator from pay telephones by 1980.
- Condominiums came under state regulation in Georgia and South Dakota.
- Landlord-tenant relations were defined by new laws passed in Kansas, New Jersey, and New Mexico.
- Illinois legislators passed a law prohibiting "red-lining" – the arbitrary denial of a mortgage due to the location of a house in an inner city, for example.
- Arizona legislation gave additional protection against land sales fraud.
- New Jersey enacted legislation establishing a statewide building code.[1]

In addition, the Federal Trade Commission urged that all states enact the "Little FTC Act," titled "The Unfair Trade Practices and Consumer Protection Law." The purpose of the act is to afford the public and honest businesses better protection from unfair and deceptive trade practices. Stopping such practices locally before they grow into problems of interstate proportions minimizes the need for federal action, and the people most directly affected will be the ones who decide what constitutes unfair or deceptive practices.

By 1976 the "Little FTC Act" had been adopted in one form or another by every state except Alabama and Tennessee. The forty-eight states' "Little FTC Acts" typically contain authorization for the administering or enforcement official to conduct investigations and to issue cease-and-desist orders or to obtain court injunctions to halt the use of deceptive or unfair trade practices. In forty-one states restitution may be obtained by the administering or enforcement official on behalf of aggrieved consumers. Civil penalties for an initial violation may be assessed in twenty-three states. Class actions by consumers are authorized in fifteen states. This allows consumers to take legal action as a group in cases where they feel that they have been cheated. When the amount involved is so small that it is not worthwhile for any one consumer to take legal action, it may be worthwhile for a large number of consumers, combining the damages they have sustained, to take group action to attempt to recover damages through such legal action. Private actions by consumers, sometimes including minimum recovery of $100 or $200, sometimes including double, treble, or punitive damages, and usually including costs and attorney fees, are authorized in thirty-eight states.

Regulatory Agencies

In a lifetime a consumer spends a considerable amount of money for goods and services provided by legally sanctioned monopolies. These public utilities include those companies that provide electricity, water, gas, telephone, telegraph, and public transportation services. Some of these public utilities are involved in interstate commerce and are regulated by federal agencies. Others are involved in only intrastate commerce and are regulated by state agencies. A few, primarily water companies, are regulated locally, with many of them being municipally owned. The following quotation emphasizes the role of the regulated utility.

> The *raison d'être* of regulation is to provide adequate service to the consumer at a fair price, and at the same time to provide the regulated firm with a fair rate of return. If the regulations show too much favor to the customer or the company then the system of regulation fails to serve its purpose. The rights of both sides must be recognized and protected. It is well to keep in mind that both competition and regulation are directed toward the same objectives, the efficient use of natural resources, and the provision of satisfactory service at reasonable rates. The basic reason given for government regulation is to fill the void made by the lack of effective competition. The intentions of regulation are good. What about the results?[2]

At times regulatory agencies have failed in their responsibility to consumers. Unfortunately there have been cases where regulatory agencies have become the tools of the utilities they are supposed to regulate. Regulatory agencies are caught between the pressures of the industries they regulate and the interests of the consumers for whose benefit they have been established.

Government-Owned Sellers of Consumer Services

Water companies are not the only sellers of consumer services that are owned by government. Many services are owned and operated by the local and state government bodies, with their costs paid out of tax revenues or from fees paid by the users. Police and fire protection are two of the many services provided by local governments free to the persons needing the service, with the cost met out of tax revenues. Water companies, hospitals, and local transportation systems are frequently owned and operated by local governments with fees charged for services rendered. Most park systems are government owned and operated with the costs met by both user fees and tax revenues. Most school systems are government owned and operated with the cost met by tax revenues. The debate continues as to which services owned and operated by government should be financed entirely by tax revenues, entirely by user fees, or by a combination of taxes and user fees.

The government, at the local and state levels, is involved in providing many services for consumers. There is no unanimity as to what areas the government should and should not be involved in providing services in, but some services, such as police and fire protection, clearly do not lend themselves to private ownership or operation.

State Consumer Protection Bureaus

The steady increase in the number of state, county, and city government consumer offices or consumer components within existing government offices has been one of the most significant developments in consumer affairs in recent years. All fifty states, the District of Columbia, Guam, Puerto Rico, and the Virgin Islands have some form of specifically designated consumer office or a consumer division within a state office. The responsibilities and powers of the offices vary widely among the states— from an advisory capacity to actual enforcement of consumer protection laws. In a majority of the states there is a consumer fraud or protection agency or bureau as part of the Office of Attorney General. In addition to state consumer offices there are 139 counties and 66 cities that have established consumer offices with widely varying responsibilities and powers. Some have broad jurisdictional responsibility; others are limited to specific subject areas, such as insurance or consumer credit.[3]

What is the role of these consumer offices? A brief outline of the activities of the Pennsylvania Bureau of Consumer Protection established in 1966 indicates their nature and scope. The specific duties of the Pennsylvania Bureau of Consumer Protection are:

- To provide a center for the receipt and investigation of all complaints received from the public

- To mediate disputes between the consumer and the violator, wherever possible
- To recommend consumer legislation
- To institute a program of continuing education to enable consumers to avoid fraud and to get help if they have been victimized
- To promote business self-regulation
- To cooperate with private agencies, such as chambers of commerce, better business bureaus, and bar associations

The Pennsylvania Bureau of Consumer Protection estimates that over $500 million are lost annually by Pennsylvania consumers through fraud. To meet this problem the bureau has a budget of only $1.5 million, and the seven offices across the state are staffed with only seventy-three persons to service 12 million consumers.

State Consumer Offices and Activities

As in the federal government, farmers, businessmen, and workers have organized and secured representation in the executive departments of state governments. Consumers are entitled to similar representation and they are now getting it.

New York pioneered in state consumer representation when the governor appointed a consumer counsel with cabinet status. The consumer counsel was a trained economist, which enabled her to create and develop a program that became a model for other states. She represented consumers at public utility rate hearings and convened conferences on consumer credit, fraud, and bait advertising. She testified before legislative committees against resale price maintenance and for legislation to regulate installment credit. During her tenure nine laws were passed, all sponsored by the consumer counsel. One law was enacted to protect installment buyers of automobiles. Another law brought sales finance companies under public control and regulated the sales of credit life insurance. Wage assignments in installment sales contracts were forbidden. Bait advertising was outlawed. And the state labeling law was generalized to cover all merchandise. However, with a change in administration, the Office of Consumer Counsel was transferred to the Department of Commerce, where it became moribund.

Subsequently the New York State Assembly passed legislation establishing in the executive department a state consumer protection board. The board is composed of the state superintendents of insurance and banking; chairman of the Public Service Commission; state commissioners of health, agriculture and markets, and commerce; the secretary of state; and an executive director. An impressive program was outlined, but it was never adequately implemented. One executive director of the board released a statement to the press indicating that the lack of support both from the legislature and the governor made the job both useless and impossible, and he resigned from the office.

California's legislature passed a law that created a state Office of Consumer Counsel and that authorized the counsel to advise the governor on matters affecting consumers; to recommend legislation necessary to protect and promote the interests of consumers; to appear before departments, agencies, and commissions to represent consumers; and to cooperate and contract with public and private agencies to obtain needed information and services. The consumer counsel in eight years established an impressive record. The annual reports listed activities that illustrate the services such an office can provide for consumers. With a change in governors, the activities of the office were cut back sharply and merged with the State Department of Professional and Vocational Standards, whose name was changed to the Department of Consumer Affairs. A Division of Consumer Services was created within the department to succeed to the duties and responsibilities vested in the Office of Consumer Counsel. The effectiveness of the former consumer counsel was diminished through this restructuring of operations. But a new governor and the appointment of a new director presented hope that the consumers' interests would be represented better at the state level. During the 1975 to 1976 fiscal year the Division of Consumer Services received a 90 percent increase in its budget, raising it to over $1 million. The office has a staff of fifty, including five attorneys.

The pioneering efforts in New York and California to protect consumers emphasize the importance of personnel. The achievements of both programs were in large part possible because the heads of the consumer agencies had ability, imagination, initiative, courage, and resourcefulness, and also the support of the governors.

The Massachusetts legislature created a Consumers' Council to give the citizens of the Commonwealth a voice in matters that concern the consumer. The council consists of thirteen members. It was established to conduct studies, investigations, and research, and to advise the executive and legislative branches in matters affecting consumer interests. It is to coordinate consumers' services carried on by departments and agencies and to further consumer education. The public is to be kept informed through the council's appearances before federal and state committees, and commission or department hearings. The public is also to be informed of such policies, decisions, or legislation as are beneficial to consumers. In addition the council has the power to initiate legislation, which has been a most valuable asset to its effectiveness. Massachusetts, through the effectiveness of the Consumers' Council, was the first state in the nation to enact a Truth-in-Lending Act, a Unit Pricing Act, and a No-Fault Automobile Insurance Act.

The Michigan Consumers Council was established by state law. The council is composed of nine people, three appointed by the governor, three appointed by the legislature, and three public officials – the Attorney General, Secretary of State, and the Director of Commerce. The council has three objectives: consumer information and education; improved consumer protection legislation; and service to the individual consumer. By way of service, the council accepts complaints from individual consumers and attempts to mediate the complaints. The council has no enforcement authority, however.

Rhode Island became the fourth state to enact legislation providing for a broad consumer voice in government. The Rhode Island legislature, overriding their governor's veto, established a seven-member consumer's council. The act enumerated the powers and scope of activities of the council, which are similar to those of California, Massachusetts, and New York.

In brief we have seen what a few states have done and are doing in attempting to give consumers the protection that is so vitally needed. Again it should be emphasized that a state consumer program can be only as good as the governor, the legislators, and the persons administering the program want it to be. Many state programs which look good when they are passed fail to materialize if there is little administrative support, adequate funding, and strong enforcement.

LOCAL GOVERNMENTS' CONSUMER PROTECTIVE SERVICES

New York City

The Department of Consumer Affairs of New York City is the largest and most forceful local government consumer office. The department's annual budget is about four million dollars. It is headed by a commissioner. It was the first municipal agency charged specifically with protecting the consumer. The activities of the department include consumer protection, information, education, and a volunteer program. In its protection activities the department investigates and resolves consumer complaints; sponsors and supports consumer legislation; tests purchases and checks commodities offered for sale; inspects regularly all weighing and measuring devices in commercial use; investigates false and misleading advertising; licenses over 100 different types of businesses and occupations; and enforces department regulations in licensed operations. Its information program includes weekly food price surveys; timely consumer information by telephone; a traveling information mobile; radio and television broadcasts; and newspaper and magazine articles. Included in its education program are speakers, slide talks, films, consumer education materials, and cooperative programs with community groups. The volunteer program includes New York City volunteers who serve New York consumers. The department's authority to grant or deny, suspend and revoke licenses, and to fine licensees gives it the power to enforce adherence to regulations. Budget cuts have reduced the department's staff by 30 percent, down from 487 in January, 1974, to 341 by 1976, a change which is seriously hampering both its potency and effectiveness.

An inspector from the New York City Department of Consumer Affairs identifies herself at the checkout counter of a supermarket. (*Dr. Lilly Bruck, Director, Consumer Education, New York City Department of Consumer Affairs*)

Nassau County, N.Y.

An illustration of what can be done at the county government level is shown by the activities of the Nassau County Office of Consumer Affairs. The office was established in June, 1967, and was reported to be the nation's first county-level agency created for the specific purpose of protecting and educating the consumer. The law as enacted gave the commissioner of consumer affairs a wide range of powers and responsibilities. Its accomplishments include special, in-depth investigations into unconscionable practices, senior citizen programs, home improvement licensing, weights-and-measures testing and inspection, regulation of fuel oil delivery, and adulteration checks of gasoline.[4] In its eighth year of operations it secured for consumers more than $423,000 in refunds and adjustments on their complaints. It handled more than 17,000 complaints during that year.

Dade County, Florida

Dade County Office of Consumer Services, which serves the Greater Miami area, is also one of the older county consumer offices. It operates on a budget of $275,000, with twenty-one employees. Its cost to the citizens of Dade County is 17 cents per person. It has been instrumental in securing and enforcing county laws which have given consumers more information and greater protection. One law requires that U.S. Department of Agriculture grades be displayed on beef, veal, and lamb. A law requires open-dating on all self-service meat so that the consumer knows when the last day of sale for freshness has expired. Another law requires that self-service meat packages must show 70 percent of the bottom of the package. All the 1,200 taxi meters in the county are checked and sealed twice a year, and the odometers in the 35,000 rental cars are checked on a selective basis periodically. Dade County has also established a Consumer Advocate Office, which is separate from the Office of Consumer Services. The office is staffed by an attorney who operates in the public interest, taking legal action and recommending new laws to assist and benefit consumers.

The above three illustrations indicate what is being done at the local level and what can be done if local elected officials can be made aware of the need for local governmental consumer agencies.

WHAT THE STATE GOVERNMENTS COULD DO

State government action in the consumer's interest is essential. There has been no consensus, however, as to what direction this action should take and how the desirable goals should be attained or what type of governmental organizational structure should be established.

The experience of the first Office of Consumer Counsel in New York State indicates the weakness inherent in establishing such an office by executive action, but the establishment of a Consumer Counsel by legislative action, as was done in California, does not guarantee that such an office would be adequately staffed and funded. The establishment of a consumer counsel, office of consumer affairs, or consumer protection bureau in the office of the attorney general has been the procedure followed by many states. The effectiveness of these consumer offices or counsels has varied considerably from state to state and has also varied with the changes in governors and changes in the personnel in charge of such offices.

The consumer would best be represented at the state level by legislation establishing a state department of consumers. Legislative action should give it permanency, and a cabinet office would give it prestige and stature. A reasonable division of responsibilities among the local, state, and federal governments must be established in order to avoid wasteful duplication or glaring omissions.

Under this department should be placed all state government functions that have as their major purpose the welfare of the consumer. Consumer functions are now found in such varied agencies or departments as commerce, sea and shore fisheries, labor and industries, law and public safety, internal affairs, health, agriculture, pharmacy, and conservation. The department's functions would be:

- To present the viewpoint of consumers within the state in the formulation of policies of the government
- To represent the economic interests of consumers of the state in proceedings before courts and regulatory agencies
- To conduct annually a state consumers' conference, to be attended by experts on consumer education and by representatives of organizations engaged in fostering and protecting the interests of consumers of goods and services within the state, for the purpose of obtaining information, recommendations, and suggestions necessary or desirable for the effective performance of other functions of the department
- To receive, assemble, evaluate, act upon, and disseminate information helpful to consumers of the state in performing their economic function more efficiently, including information concerning commercial and trade practices adversely affecting their economic interests

In those cases where a government agency is not primarily established with the consumer in mind, but where the agency renders some service to the consumer, a representative of the consumer department should be permitted to sit in on the deliberations and express the consumer's position. The department should be established with an adequate budget to do the job assigned.

The major benefit to be gained by consumers from the establishment of a department of consumers is not so much that many new consumer programs would be developed but that many old programs would be centralized, coordinated, and strengthened.

WHAT LOCAL GOVERNMENTS COULD DO

The state governments and federal government cannot and should not be the only levels of the government rendering services and protection to the consumer. It would be well if local governments would also enact ordinances establishing a department of consumers. This need not duplicate state or federal activities; its functions could be quite similar to those suggested for a state department of consumers, but at a local level. The size of the local community would determine the size and scope of such a department. The basic goal should be to let the consumer's voice be heard at the local level. The department should work for the passage of ordinances that are in the consumer's interest and should oppose ordinances that are not in the consumer's interest.

As at the state level, those activities of the local government that are primarily for the consumer's welfare should be centralized in such a department. This should give unity and strength in reaching desirable goals. Once a department of consumers is established, the person in charge should learn rather quickly where his or her energies and the energies of the department personnel should be exerted.

Certain areas of activity that might work best at the local level might include inspection and supervision of milk and dairy plants and eating and drinking places; meat inspection; and regulation of weights and measures, which are often subject to local programs as well as being part of the state and federal programs.

In addition, it is believed by many consumer advocates that the local level is the level at which consumer complaints could best be handled. This would be true only if the local authorities had adequate enforcement powers. This would be especially true when the complaint is between the local buyer and seller. The sheer size of the country and the population make an effective handling of all complaints physically impossible at the federal level. Even at the state level complaint operations can become bogged down easily. In many respects the efficient and quick handling of consumer complaints at the local level could be one of the most important services the local government could render to the consumer. Some coordination at the state or national level would be necessary in order to get effective action when the businesses against which complaints are filed are operating statewide or nationally.

Effective consumer protection can be had only when consumer protection is a responsibility of all levels of government, local, state, and national.

QUESTIONS FOR REVIEW

1. What is meant by "the problem of dual government control" in consumer protection?
2. Would there be any need for state consumer services if the federal government did its job properly?
3. Would it be better for more consumer protection measures to be shifted from the state to the federal government or vice versa? Why?
4. What should be the responsibilities of consumer regulatory agencies?
5. Should the various levels of government increase or decrease their activities as sellers of consumer services? Why?
6. What should be the responsibility of a state consumer protection bureau?
7. What have been some of the weaknesses that have developed in some state consumer protection offices?
8. Why is it generally more effective to have a consumer counsel established by legislative action rather than by executive order?
9. What consumer services might and should a local government provide?

PROJECTS

1. Draw up a proposal for a model state office of consumer protection program.

2. Find out what kinds of consumer legislation have been passed by your state in the past year.

3. Interview an officer of a public utility concerning the problems the utility has with the regulatory agency and with consumers.

4. Interview the local district attorney to find out if he renders any consumer protection services, and if so in what areas and to what extent.

5. Find out if your local community and/or county has consumer protection offices. If there is such an office, find out how it serves consumers.

6. Investigate local and state legislation to see whether any legislation has been passed that went under the banner of consumer protection but was actually not in the consumer's best interests.

REFERENCES

1. *State Government News,* the Council of State Governments, Lexington, Ken., Jan. 1976, p. 7.
2. Stewart M. Lee, "New Dimensions of Competition for the Regulated Utility," *Public Utilities Fortnightly* 76 (11 Nov. 1965): 16.
3. *Directory: Federal, State, County, and City Government Consumer Offices* (Washington, D.C.: Government Printing Office, 1976), p. 6.
4. Kenneth Lasson, *Proudly We Hail: Profiles of Public Citizens in Action* (New York: Grossman, 1975), pp. 200–201.

CHAPTER 25

THE FEDERAL GOVERNMENT HELPS CONSUMERS: THE FOOD AND DRUG ADMINISTRATION

WHY DO CONSUMERS NEED HELP?

A Specialized and Impersonal Economy

At one time the American food supply was processed and consumed almost entirely on the farms and in the rural areas where it was produced. Now food is brought to supermarkets and consumed by millions of people thousands of miles from where it is produced. Every day we consume products that are vital to our health and life, produced by people we have never seen and never will see.

The changes in food and drug technology have made it possible for us to have foods and medicines that our grandparents never knew. But the advances have also created problems. When a family raised its own supply of food, it had control over purity and quality. Today consumers cannot exercise the same kind of control over the purity or quality of the foods, drugs, and cosmetics they consume. Government must do for all of us what no one of us can do alone. This is why Congress passed the original Pure Food and Drugs Act and the Meat Inspection Act over seventy years ago. During the intervening years these laws have been amended to strengthen them and to make them more effective in a rapidly changing technological economy.

In addition, the proliferation of new products and their increasing complexity have made the consumer's job much more complicated, and consumers now need help. As incomes have increased, consumers have been able and willing to buy more and more goods and services; the mere increase in the accumulation of goods in itself creates additional problems. Unable to cope with all these problems consumers have turned to government for help.

Consumers Look to the Federal Government

Consumers' demands for greater protection and services from the federal government in the marketplace are being heard in Washington, and government is responding. The *Guide to Federal Consumer Services* lists thirty-five departments and agencies, with a total of ninety-two programs to protect or advance the consumer's interest.[1] The welfare of the consumer has recently become a politically attractive issue, and legislators and government agencies have responded in varying ways in attempting to meet consumer demands and needs. During the first session of the 94th Congress approximately 500 new consumer bills were introduced.

Consumerism has become a popular issue. The news media have been giving it considerable attention. There is no question that the publicity surrounding the "David versus Goliath" conflict between Ralph Nader and General Motors Corporation caught the attention of the public and furthered the interest in consumerism.*

The federal government has been involved in assisting consumers for many decades, but the degree of involvement became much greater during the 1960s and early 1970s. A brief analysis of the federal agencies that provide services for consumers will indicate the degree of government involvement and the tremendous responsibility these federal agencies have in protecting both the physical safety and the economic safety of American consumers.

Costs of Major Federal Consumer Programs

How much is the federal government spending on its key consumer protection functions? Table 25-1 give you an answer for 1977.

The five federal consumer protection agencies listed in Table 25-1 have

TABLE 25-1. Budgets of Key Federal Consumer Agencies

Federal Agency	Fiscal 1977 Budget Request	Increase Over Fiscal 1976
Department of Agriculture: Consumer Protection, Marketing, and Regulatory Program	$276,000,000	$ 9,000,000
Food and Drug Administration	226,230,000	17,425,000
Federal Trade Commission	52,833,000	5,742,000
Consumer Product Safety Commission	36,999,000	405,000
Office of Consumer Affairs	1,581,000	93,000
Total	$593,643,000	$32,665,000

Source: The Budget of the United States Government: Fiscal Year 1977 (Washington, D.C.: Government Printing Office, 1976), pp. 95, 228, 235, 284, 288.

---

* In the mid-1960s, Nader published a book, *Unsafe at Any Speed*, in which he criticized General Motors' Corvair automobile. General Motors then hired a detective who was instructed to find out something or to do something that would hurt Nader's reputation in the public eye. Instead, the plot was discovered and the president of General Motors made a public apology to Nader on national television before a Senate Investigating Committee, and in an out-of-court settlement General Motors paid Nader more than $300,000 for defamation of character.

been budgeted a total of $593,643,000 for the fiscal year 1977. Based on a total U.S. population of approximately 215 million, the cost of these vital consumer programs was $2.76 per person. When one considers all that is accomplished for each consumer for this $2.76, the conclusion must be that consumers are getting a good return for their money.

The following pages provide an in-depth analysis of the Food and Drug Administration and its importance for American consumers. Other crucial federal agencies, such as the Department of Agriculture, the FTC, the Consumer Product Safety Commission, and the Office of Consumer Affairs, are discussed in detail in Chapter 26.

THE FOOD AND DRUG ADMINISTRATION: HISTORY

The first general food law in the United States was enacted in 1784 by Massachusetts.[2] During the 1800s other states enacted a varied assortment of laws. California passed its pure food and drink law in 1850, one year after the gold rush. For more than a century such laws provided what little protection there was. Meanwhile great changes were taking place in the way people lived. As the country expanded, its industrial economy developed. Technological changes brought new health hazards in foods and drugs, as well as new products. Mass production was in its infancy, and conditions in processing plants were primitive by modern standards. The doctrine of *caveat emptor* was the prevailing philosophy in the marketplace. Products and labeling that might be banned in one state were legal in adjoining states. Varying requirements were a hindrance to nationwide marketing. Increasingly, it became clear that state laws no longer provided enough protection. Between 1879 and 1906 more than one hundred food and drug bills were introduced in Congress. With growing evidence of a great variety of abuses, the public demanded federal government protection. On June 30, 1906, President Theodore Roosevelt signed into law the first federal Pure Food and Drug Act, which established the Pure Food and Drug Administration. The act was popularly named the Wiley Act for the crusading Dr. Harvey W. Wiley who led the battle for its enactment. On the same day the president also signed the Meat Inspection Act.

From 1906 to the present there have been many efforts to strengthen the food and drug law. Most important was the passage of the present law, the Federal Food, Drug and Cosmetic Act of 1938, which replaced the outmoded Wiley Act of 1906. A product of the Depression era and of a bitter five-year legislative battle which pitted consumer interests against industry lobbyists, this law contained many compromises but was far stronger than the original act. Among many changes, it covered for the first time cosmetics and therapeutic devices, authorized food standards, and made it a penal offense to refuse inspection.

Numerous amendments followed over the years to deal with particular problems. A Pesticide Chemicals Amendment, passed in 1954, set up a system of enforceable residue tolerances. The Delaney Amendment (1958), known as the Food Additives Amendment, requires the safety of such additives to be established before they are marketed and prohibits the approval of any food additive if it is found to induce cancer when ingested by humans or animals.

In 1960 two laws were passed. The Color Additive Amendment allowed the FDA to set safe limits on the amounts of colors that may be used in foods, drugs, and cosmetics and required manufacturers to retest previously listed certifiable colors. A separate law, the Federal Hazardous Substances Labeling Act, required prominent warning labels on household chemical products. Beginning with this law, the FDA developed the extensive product safety program now administered by the Consumer Product Safety Commission.

One of the most significant amendments to the Food and Drug Act was the Kefauver-Harris Drug Amendment passed in 1962 to require premarketing proof of drug effectiveness in order to assure a greater degree of safety and reliability in prescription drugs and to strengthen new drug clearance procedures.

Drug abuse control amendments were enacted in 1965 to cope with the problems caused by abuse of three groups of dangerous drugs — depressants, stimulants, and hallucinogens. In 1968 the president transferred the FDA Bureau of Drug Abuse Control to the Department of Justice, forming a Bureau of Narcotics and Dangerous Drugs. In 1970 a Comprehensive Drug Abuse Prevention and Control Act was passed. In 1973, in a reorganization within the Department of Justice, all policing of illegal drug traffic was placed under the newly created Drug Enforcement Administration.

The Fair Packaging and Labeling Act enacted in 1966 spells out in detail how consumer products in interstate commerce must be labeled. The FDA has the responsibility to enforce its provisions as to foods, drugs, cosmetics, and medical devices.

Beginning in 1974 with the passage of the Freedom of Information Act, the FDA, along with other federal agencies, departments, and advisory committees, opened most of their meetings and their files to the general public. Now business firms are required to identify and justify all claims for confidentiality of data submitted to the FDA. It is estimated that under the Freedom of Information Act almost 90 percent of the material in FDA files will be made public, practically reversing the ratio of prior years.

Another important law administered by FDA is the Radiation Control for Health and Safety Act, which protects the public from unnecessary exposure to radiation from medical X-ray and electronic products such as color televisions and microwave ovens.

In the 94th Congress (1975–1976) a number of bills were introduced to strengthen the FDA in the areas of drug advertising, dating, identification, and unsolicited sample drugs; to give the FDA greater protective power in the area of foods in general, particularly fish products, food supplements, milk and dairy products, and food standards and quality grading; and to give the FDA greater control over medical devices. The medical devices bill was the only significant measure enacted into law during that Congress, however.

Additional amendments and changes in the Food and Drug Act will come; how quickly, and how effective they may be, will depend upon consumer interest, the inclinations of Congress, the adequacy of funding for FDA activities, and the effectiveness of the entire FDA operation.

THE FDA AND PURE FOOD

Except for meat and poultry, which come under the jurisdiction of the Department of Agriculture, the FDA has the responsibility to prevent adulteration and mislabeling of food in interstate commerce. The FDA is a division of the Department of Health, Education, and Welfare (HEW) and is headed by a commissioner who reports to the secretary of HEW, who is the official enforcing agent of the various pure food and drug measures.

Definitions and Standards Are Established

The law requires the secretary of HEW to establish reasonable definitions and standards of identity for foods when needed to promote honesty and fair dealing in the interest of consumers. For example, the standard of identity for fruit preserves and jellies requires that they contain not less than 45 parts by weight of fruit or fruit juice to each 55 parts of total sweetening ingredients. Such standards have practically eliminated from the market the type of product which at one time was sold under such names as "raspberry spread." Formerly sold in large volume, spreads were made from a little fruit and much water, pectin, sugar, artificial coloring, and sometimes artificial flavoring, plus a few grass seeds to create the illusion of a fruit product.

The standards of identity developed by the FDA in consultation with industry (and sometimes in the face of great opposition) serve the consumer by establishing minimum specifications for the product and by stipulating that deviations in ingredients from the standard be listed on the label. Once a standard of identity is established, however, it is no longer necessary to list all ingredients on the label, as it is for nonstandard foods. Obviously the consumer does not go shopping with copies of all the standards of identity and would be better served if standardized products were labeled not only with all the ingredients but with the percentage of each ingredient as well.

Standards of quality have been established for some canned fruits and vegetables. These are minimum standards that establish specifications for such quality factors as tenderness, color, and freedom from defects. Under these standards, if a food does not meet the quality specifications it must be labeled "Below Standard in Quality," followed by the statement "Good Food – Not High Grade."

Standards of fill of container tell the packer how full the container must be to avoid deception of consumers and to avoid FDA charges of "slack-filling." Standards of fill are also needed to protect consumers against air, water, or space in containers that could and should hold larger amounts of produce but very few such standards have been established.

A proposal by Consumers Union that the drained weight of canned fruits and vegetables be required on labels was published by the FDA on October 22, 1975. Drained weight is the amount of solid food in the can. Net weight, now shown on labels, includes the water, syrup, or other liquids.

Over 6,000 comments were received by the FDA, mostly from consumers in favor of the change. The FDA particularly asked for data to indicate whether the economic benefits to consumers will outweigh any increases in product cost as a result of adopting the new method of declaring content. The proposal also calls for establishing minimum amounts of solid food that must be contained in most canned fruits and vegetables. Consumers have long complained about excessive liquid inside some of these canned products.

The threat of prosecution has prevented much deceptive packaging, but unfortunately the FDA has met with little success in contested court cases to stop slack-filling. Court decisions have tended to favor industry rather than consumers. The courts have been generally willing to accept

A dairy inspector places butter samples in sterile jars for laboratory tests on the product's keeping qualities. (*USDA Marketing Service, Dairy Division, Inspection and Grading Branch*)

the packers' testimony that fragile food products require protective packaging and that many products will settle in transit. In particular, the courts have ruled that if the correct weight is displayed as prescribed by law, the consumer is adequately protected from deception. One might well question this judgment, however. A check of products will show that generally when the packaging material is transparent, the package is filled to the top; but all too frequently when the packaging material is opaque, "slack-filling" persists. Modern packaging equipment is such that the settling of the product could be done on the assembly line. However, it must be remembered that in today's sales-oriented economy, a packer wants his product to have as much exposure on the grocery shelf as possible, so he wants a big package regardless of how much is in it. Regulations to be drafted under the Fair Packaging and Labeling Act may eventually reduce nonfunctional slack-filling.

Standards also provide that foods labeled "enriched" have actually been improved by the addition of significant amounts of vitamins or other nutrients. Such standards protect consumers from the confusion and deception that might arise if each manufacturer were free to claim that his or her product was enriched in some special way.

In April 1976 lobbyists of the "health food" industry succeeded in getting Congress to restrict the FDA's authority to set standards for vitamin-mineral food supplements. Amendments to the Federal Food, Drug, and Cosmetic Act, attached as a rider to the important National Heart and Lung Authorization Bill, will result in less consumer protection because they prevent the FDA from:

1. Limiting the potency of vitamins and minerals in dietary supplements to nutritionally useful levels
2. Classifying a vitamin or mineral preparation as a "drug" because it exceeds a nutritionally rational or useful potency
3. Requiring the presence in dietary supplements of nutritionally essential vitamins and minerals
4. Prohibiting the inclusion in dietary supplements of useless ingredients with no nutritional value

The amendments were designed to nullify FDA regulations which would have banned irrational "shotgun" formulas widely sold to nutritionally gullible consumers. FDA Commissioner Alexander Schmidt called the bill "a charlatan's dream."

An attempted offset to the regressive legislation was to give the FDA new, but limited, authority over the advertising of vitamin-mineral food supplements. Previously the Federal Trade Commission had exclusive authority over advertising of food. Under the new amendments, the FDA will be required to notify the FTC of a suspected advertising violation, and if the FTC does not act within ninety days, the FDA can then take action.

Health Guards Are Provided

The Pure Food and Drug Law also provides that a food must not be injurious to health. Tolerances for pesticide residues are enforced, and the use of chemical additives is regulated. A food processor offering for sale a food containing added chemicals must use only products cleared for safety. The amount of chemicals that remain in or on food is limited by law. Food containers must be free from any substance that might cause the contents to be harmful. Color additives must be certified for batches tested and certified by the FDA.

Labels Must Be Informative

Under the law, food labels must give the name and address of the manufacturer, packer, or shipper. They must reveal the quantity of contents and the common or usual name of each ingredient if the product is composed of two or more ingredients and if it is not a standardized food. In addition, except for certain dairy products, labels must state clearly whether artificial flavoring, artificial coloring, or chemical preservatives have been used. Labels must be explicit about the nature and content of special dietary foods. The label can help the consumer-buyer get his or her money's worth and protect family health.

Sanitation Is Required

Food must be prepared, packed, and stored under sanitary conditions. It must not be filthy, putrid, decomposed, or otherwise unfit for consumption, nor may it be from a diseased animal.

Deceptions Are Forbidden

Food labels must not be false or misleading. Damage to or inferiority in a food must not be concealed. No substance may be added to a food to increase its bulk or weight or make it appear of greater value. One food must not be sold under the name of another. Imitations and food which is substandard in quality must be so labeled. No substance which is recognized as being a valuable part of a food may be omitted.

The FDA Finds Contamination and Filth

The real test of pure food laws is whether consumers have assurance that their foods are pure. Experience justifies the generalization that consumers have more assurance and more protection than ever before. Nevertheless, the FDA must continue to be on guard. The health of consumers is constantly endangered by food processors and handlers who fail to maintain sanitary safeguards at peak effectiveness. Year after year hundreds of cases of food poisoning are reported. Bacterial contamination may be transmitted by many foods as a result of unsanitary handling or insufficient processing. Inadequate refrigeration and exposure of foods to flies, rats, or mice also cause contamination. Kitchens may be dirty, workers' hands may be unclean, or workers may be carriers of infections. Severe illness is caused by many kinds of bacteria, especially Clostridium botulinum, Type E, Coliform organisms, enterotoxin-producing staphylococci, and Salmonellae.

Clostridium botulinum is a particularly dangerous type of food poisoning. It has been estimated that one teaspoonful of it is potent enough to kill the entire population of the world. Fortunately there have been only five reported deaths in the United States from botulism in commercially canned foods since 1925. In the same period of time, however, about 700 people died from eating contaminated home-canned products.[3] Undercooking is the real culprit in home cooking. In 1974 there were twenty outbreaks of food-borne botulism involving thirty persons – the largest number of such outbreaks since 1935. Of the thirty cases, seven died, and five of these seven deaths were caused by home-canned foods.[4] Ninety-four cases of Salmonellosis were caused by the rare *Salmonella eastborne* in chocolate products. Four recalls were made of these candies. The FDA recalled 11,000 cans of lobster bisque, 1,600 cans of clam bisque, and 200,000 cans of pimentos because of underprocessing which could have resulted in the growth of microorganisms in the can, creating a potential health hazard.[5] Over 244,-000 recall effectiveness checks were made at all market levels to clear stocks of potentially contaminated mushrooms and foods containing them as ingredients. Again it was a case of clostridium botulinum toxin that brought about the recall. An FDA examination of fish from the East coast revealed a high level of infestation of anisakids (roundworms). In a twelve-month period the FDA issued 103 recalls of food products.

The laws under which the FDA receives its authority do not give the agency recall powers, but the FDA can ask a manufacturer to remove dangerous, adulterated, or misbranded products from the market under the threat of legal action, and it can monitor the recall for effectiveness. If industry cooperation and recall are not forthcoming or if the danger to public health is acute and urgent, the FDA can ask the district courts for orders authorizing U.S. marshals to seize and condemn the illegal products. The FDA also has the power to request, but not to require, the U.S. Department of Justice to prosecute the manufacturer, packer, or shipper of such products.[6] Product recalls are effective because thousands of individuals – manufacturers, salespersons, distributors, retailers, and health professionals – cooperate with federal, state, and local officials to protect the public.

Over fifty billion meals are eaten annually in nearly one million restaurants, prisons, nursing homes, and educational facilities in the United States. Prevention of human illness associated with meals outside the home is mainly a function of state and local agencies. The FDA's responsibility in this area is largely to advise and promote cooperation among federal, state, and local agencies, and with the food service industries. Federal inspectors making a limited, random inspection of restaurants in nine large cities found so many health violations that the General Accounting Office (GAO) estimated that 90 percent of America's restaurants prepare food in unsanitary conditions.

An FDA survey indicated that some 14 percent of the nation's food warehouses were out of compliance with federal sanitation standards for the storage of food. Three years earlier the figure had been 60 percent. In 1973 the FDA filed criminal prosecutions against ninety-six food firms; all but two charges were for unsanitary conditions. In one of these cases (a warehouse where food was exposed to contamination by insects, rodents, birds, and cats), the defendents pleaded guilty and paid fines totaling $10,000.[7]

In 1975 the General Accounting Office issued a report on sanitation problems in the food-salvage industry. Food-salvage outlets sell food that has been damaged or subjected to contamination due to mishandling, accidents, or disasters caused by fires, floods, or storms. FDA inspectors visited thirty salvage outlets and found that twenty-three were selling processed food products with absent, misleading, or incomplete labels; twenty-six had food for sale that was insect-infested, or in leaking, rusted, stained, swollen, or badly damaged containers. This survey shows the need for standards and overall guidelines for food salvaging.[8]

FDA inspectors must also be on the alert for dangerous foreign substances in food. There are many ways in which foreign particles such as broken glass, splinters, burrs, or chemicals can contaminate food during the harvesting and processing operations.

FDA inspectors have authority to go into processing plants and examine them for cleanliness. Month after month, tens of thousands of pounds of food are seized and destroyed.* Unfortunately, there are times when the FDA learns about a contaminated food many months after the product has been on the market. With fewer than 1,000 inspectors to cover almost $500 billion of the nation's commerce, the FDA is able to check only a very small part of the total.

Food Additives

A chemical revolution has recently changed the food-processing industry. More than 3,000 additives, of which about 1,500 are flavoring materials, have been approved for use in the preparation and preservation of what we eat. Food processors are spending more than $300 million annually on additives. It is estimated that each of us, on the average, ingests 3 to 4

* See issues of *FDA Consumer* for listings of "Notices of Judgments" on both seizure and criminal actions for food, drugs, medical devices, and cosmetics.

pounds of additives each year. These additives are used because they are cheap and effective nutrients, supplements, nonnutritive sweeteners, preservatives, emulsifiers, stabilizers, thickeners, flavoring agents, or bleaches. Consumer-buyers who read labels will find many such ingredients listed in food products.

The increasing use of chemicals in food poses a purity problem. Of those in use, some are known to be harmless, and some are considered safe within the limits of normal use. The possible long-term effects on the human body of other chemicals in use are unknown. Some are suspected of being cancer-inducing agents. For these reasons, the Food Additives Amendment requires manufacturers to test additives and secure FDA approval before marketing. The law also requires that food-packaging materials, animal feeds, and processes such as irradiation for preservation be inspected. Also the law limits the amounts of additives that can be used and prohibits the use of any additives if tests show possible carcinogenic effects. Product labels must list the chemicals which have been added, specifically preservatives and the presence of any artificial color (except in butter, cheese, or ice cream).

In 1958, when Congress passed a law requiring safety clearance of substances added to food, it exempted from such formal approval ingredients that were at the time "Generally Recognized As Safe" (GRAS) by qualified scientists or which had been sanctioned or approved by the FDA or USDA prior to September, 1958.

Complying with this provision, the FDA published a list of substances believed to be GRAS, including some 675 substances, such as salt, sugar, spices, and commonly used chemicals such as those in baking powder. The law thus created three different categories of food ingredients: food additives, GRAS substances, and previously sanctioned substances. Three categories were established not because the substances on one list were safer than those on the others, but because Congress wished to relieve industry of the burden of proving the safety of substances already regarded as safe.

In 1969, when the artificial sweetener cyclamate was banned because of new research showing that it could cause cancer, the president ordered a review of all the additives on the GRAS list. This was a monumental assignment—both because of the number of substances and because of the difficulty of establishing the safety of many of them because of the lack of scientific data on them.

The basic phases of this project were completed by 1973. In 1974, the FDA began making final decisions on the status of GRAS-listed additives. At the end of that year, 114 scientific literature reviews had been completed, covering 428 substances, and 27 of these reviews had been evaluated, covering 35 substances. The review process resulted in one of three possible actions: 1) affirming the ingredient as GRAS; 2) establishing an interim regulation requiring more data to be obtained; or 3) ordering the use of the ingredient to be discontinued. An "Affirmed GRAS List" was established for those ingredients that had been reviewed and found safe.

The Federal Food, Drug, and Cosmetic Act covers foods and drugs for humans and animals. Practically all commercial feeds contain additives to control animal diseases, to increase meat yield, or to improve meat texture. Any drugs that leave a residue in meat, milk, eggs, or other foods are subject to pre-marketing proof of safety. Congress amended the Delaney Clause to allow the use of carcinogenic substances, such as diethylstrilbestrol (DES), in livestock feed if no drug residue could be detected by analysis of edible tissues from the treated livestock. The FDA's analytical methods and ability to detect DES consequently advanced to the point that they could measure parts per million, and then parts per billion. Thus, in 1973, the FDA banned the use of DES in cattle production because trace amounts had been detected in some beef livers. But the ban was set aside by a court order because the manufacturers of DES had not been provided an adequate opportunity for a hearing. DES is again being added to animal feed in the United States, and the FDA has again proposed to ban it—this time after holding the hearings that the law requires.

Environmental Pollutants

Environmental pollutants became a major FDA problem in the late 1960s, beginning with the disclosure that coho salmon from Lake Michigan contained high residues of DDT. Mercury exceeding 0.5 parts per million was found in tuna fish and over twelve million cans of tuna were removed from retail market shelves. Subsequently, the FDA took the unusual step of warning the public to stop eating swordfish because over 90 percent of the supply contained mercury above the officially safe tolerance. The average mercury level in the swordfish tested exceeded *more than* one part per million, or twice the FDA guideline. Mercury is a toxic metal that is highly injurious to humans if ingested over a long period of time.

Pesticides and Foods

Under Secretary of Agriculture J. Phil Campbell stated:

With pesticides the issue is not whether we will use them or not. We must. Without pesticides there would be no forests as we know them, no food in the quantities we must have, and no fiber in the amounts we need. The quality of the lives of all of us, not just Americans but all the people of the world, depends on the responsible use of pesticides. The real issue—how to achieve a balance between our need to control pests and our need to maintain a safe, clean, and livable environment—has not yet been resolved.[9]

Ten thousand insects are said to be public enemies, together with 1,500 plant diseases, 1,500 species of nematodes (parasitic worms), and 600 weed species. Billions of dollars, millions of hours of labor, and hundreds of millions of pounds of chemicals are used each year to combat the insects, diseases, worms, and weeds that compete with the human population for food. In spite of this massive warfare, the damage to crops and livestock is estimated to be over ten billion dollars annually.

Approximately 33,000 pesticide products are registered with the Environmental Protection Agency (EPA), which has the power to restrict their use, specify their labeling, and set tolerances for residues in foods. The Food and Drug Administration, which formerly set these tolerances, continues to have the responsibility to enforce them. The number of active ingredients in pesticides is much less, around 1,800, including numerous well-known substances such as pepper, alcohol, ammonia, pine oil, kerosene, and so on, which have pesticidal properties. A generation ago lead and arsenic were the dangerous pesticides, highly toxic to humans as well as insects. Today the chlorinated hydrocarbons are the problem chemicals, mainly for environmental and ecological reasons. Several of the most widely used—DDT, aldrin, and dieldrin—have been banned in the United States. Use of others, for example heptachlor and chlordane, has been greatly restricted. Residues of these two were found in 73 percent of all dairy products and 77 percent of all meat, poultry, and fish samples.[10] Without chlordane and heptachlor, the USDA estimates, corn production will be reduced by about 0.4 percent, or roughly 20 million bushels a year.

The Invisible Chemical Warfare

Chemicals are used not only to kill insects and weeds; they are used to control plant diseases, to stop fruit from falling prematurely, and to make leaves drop so that harvesting will be easier. They are even used to make seeds sprout or to keep seeds from rotting before they sprout. To be effective, pesticides must be toxic.

The chemical war against pests is never won. More than one hundred pests have established immunity to poisons which were effective at one time. As a consequence, growers tend to use stronger and stronger poisons.

Effects of Chemicals on Consumers

On the basis of her long study and research, the late Dr. Rachel Carson, author of *Silent Spring*, came to some startling and shocking conclusions: The chemical contamination of our environment threatens the future of the human race. Our environment contains cancer-producing agents injected by man in the form of chemicals. From birth to death every person is now exposed to dangerous chemicals. Not only are there chemical residues on food products, but chemicals seep into the soil and into underground waters. Some of the chemicals that have contaminated fish and domestic food animals are stored in the body. For example, there is a chain of DDT stretching from hayfields to cows to the milk we drink. Every meal we eat contains chemical spray residues. Five hundred new chemicals are produced every year, chemicals to which the human body must adjust or succumb. Gar-

deners and lawnkeepers are insufficiently warned about the deadly sprays
so readily available in all garden supply stores.*

Carson's book *Silent Spring,* published in 1962, alerted Americans to
the pesticide problem, and scientists have subsequently found chemical
residues in human fat of up to 12 parts per million. Worldwide concern
regarding the impact of chemical pollutants on the ecology was further in-
tensified by developments during 1970 stimulating numerous actions by
national and local governments. Particularly involved was the use of DDT
and other persistent pesticides. Steps were taken to greatly reduce, and
ultimately to phase out, the use of such pesticides.

Chemicals do have their beneficial side; they can increase and protect
the production of food and fiber. They may improve health. They are used to
control nuisance insects and weeds. They have freed man from communi-
cable diseases, such as malaria, typhus, and yellow fever. Because they are
relatively inexpensive, they can be used to kill mosquitoes, roaches, and
aphids. Millions of spray cans are sold each year to consumers, who use
them to control house and garden pests. But the dilemma is that the pesticides that are powerful enough to kill the "public enemies" are also powerful enough to harm beneficial plants, animals, and people. Carson suggested
that insecticides and pesticides might more accurately be called *biocides.*
Much of the hazard arises out of the misuse of chemicals. To the extent that
this is true, the problem is one of education and control.

In a typical year FDA inspectors examine thousands of domestic and
imported food samples and find an average of 2 percent having illegal
residues. When illegal residues are discovered, the products are seized or
destroyed. For example, over half a million pounds of frozen spinach were
voluntarily destroyed after FDA analyses showed high perthane residues.
Several hundred shipments of cheese, mainly from southern European
countries, were detained because of excess residues, chiefly of benzene
hexachloride.

A "total diet" study conducted by the FDA showed no significant
change from previous years in the dietary intake of pesticides. It reported
that amounts of pesticides in the American consumer's diet remained at
low, safe levels. The "total diet" investigations provide a continuing safety
check on the use of pesticides in producing the nation's food. With establishment of the Environmental Protection Agency (EPA) in late 1970, the
setting of pesticide tolerances ceased to be an FDA function, but that
agency continued to have the critical job of enforcing the tolerances now set
by regulations of the EPA. At the same time, control of pesticide labeling
was transferred to the EPA from the U.S. Department of Agriculture.

Artificial Colors in Foods

Many food products are colored artificially with synthetic colors. Are
the colors safe? By 1960 there was enough evidence that some colors were

* See Rachel Carson's *Silent Spring* (Boston: Houghton Mifflin, 1962).

not harmless to lead Congress to amend the pure food law so as to strengthen control over color additives. All colors must be approved by FDA, which was given the authority to establish limits on the amount of color used. No color can be used if it has not been found safe or if its use promotes deception of the consumer. The law forbids the use of any colorant which has been found to induce cancer in humans or animals by ingestion or other pertinent exposure.

Until 1976, amaranth, a coal tar derivative known also as "Red No. 2," had been in use as a food color for more than a century. One of the seven colors approved after passage of the original 1906 Pure Food Law, it had become the most widely used color additive in foods, drugs, and cosmetics. No evidence of adverse effects of Red No. 2 on humans has ever been reported, although scientists have expressed doubts of its safety since the 1950s. Over the years, however, animal-feeding experiments have yielded conflicting results. Scientific advisory committees concluded the dye was safe but recommended further research. FDA studies completed in 1975 showed that feeding Red No. 2 at a high dosage resulted in a statistically significant increase in malignant tumors in one strain of aged female rats. On January 19, 1975, the FDA announced its decision to revoke its provisional approval of Red No. 2 under the 1960 Color Additive Amendment. FDA Commissioner Schmidt explained that the action was taken not because Red No. 2 had proven unsafe, but because it could not be proved safe, as the law requires. "Clearly," he said, "the burden of proof belongs not with the government or the consumer, but with those who claim that Red No. 2 has a safe and useful place in our food supply and in our drugs and cosmetics." There was no recall of existing products containing the color, but numerous seizures were made of products manufactured after the ban was announced. An industry suit to reverse the ban was rejected by the U.S. Court of Appeals.[11] Red Dye No. 40, which replaced Red Dye No. 2, passed preliminary FDA tests, but it has not been subjected to the same kind of scientific scrutiny undergone by Red Dye No. 2. In 1976 the FDA banned the use of Red Dye No. 4 in foods and ingested drugs. The use of carbon black was banned in any food, drug, or cosmetic. Red Dye No. 4 had been used in maraschino cherries, while carbon black had been used in candies (such as black jelly beans and licorice), cosmetic products such as eyebrow pencils, mascara, and nail polish, and as a color coating for drugs.

Food Cheats

The FDA describes as "economic cheats" such practices as adulteration, substitution, misbranding, and short weighing. As food prices rise, the incentive to cheat is stronger. Water continues to be the cheapest and the most common of all food adulterants. Some packers of frozen products have found that selling water at frozen food prices is very profitable. Adulteration also takes the form of substituting inferior and cheaper products for better ones. In recent cases one company was charged by the FDA with substituting sugar syrup for honey; another was charged with substituting a product containing less than 80 percent milk fat for butter.[12] A shipment of canned oyster stew was seized because the cans were short-weighted, and a food processor was charged with violating the law because the company's canned tomatoes contained excess tomato peels.[13] It is probable that many more such violations, and more serious ones, would be found out if the FDA gave a higher priority to protecting the consumer's pocketbook, as well as the consumer's health.

PURE, POTENT, EFFECTIVE, AND SAFE DRUGS?

The Drug Revolution

More than five million Americans are alive today who would have died if the 1937 mortality rate had remained the same through from 1937 to the present. Much of the credit for this amazing progress can be given to modern drugs, medical devices, and improvements in medical practice. Most of the prescriptions written today are for drugs that were not even on the market thirty years ago. There are now more than 12,000 drug industry establishments, with total annual sales of more than $15 billion. More than a third of this amount is from sales of prescription drugs. Americans have more than one billion prescriptions filled each year, and they consume an even greater quantity of over-the-counter medication. Unfortunately, about 1.5 million instances of adverse drug effects are estimated to occur each year in hospitalized patients, but reliable statistics are yet to be developed.

A prescription is as personal as one's name. It is intended for one person alone and may be written only by a licensed doctor. Many drugs may be purchased without prescription, and these may or may not help the individual who buys them. Before using nonprescription drugs, the consumer should read the label carefully and he or she should follow the instructions exactly.

Drug provisions of the Food, Drug, and Cosmetic Act were greatly strengthened in 1962 by amendments passed in 1962 following the disclosure that a supposedly safe sleeping pill (thalidomide), which was on sale in Europe but not in the United States, had caused thousands of fetal deformities. The key amendments require that a drug must do what it is stated to do and that more exacting tests must be made on new drugs before their release for general use.

What the Drug Law, as Amended, Provides

An application for approval must be submitted to the FDA before a new drug may be offered for sale. The application must be accompanied by substantial scientific evidence that the drug is both safe and effective for its indicated use. The FDA may approve a new drug application for prescription use only or for direct sale to consumers. After drugs have been cleared, manufacturers must report any information they receive concerning adverse effects in use. If an unforeseen health hazard develops, the approval may be withdrawn immediately. Manufacturers must have adequate controls. If manufacturing methods, facilities, or controls are inadequate, FDA approval may be withdrawn. No testing of drugs on people is permitted unless and until specified safety conditions have been met. A patient must consent to the use of an experimental drug, and physicians must tell patients that a drug is experimental. All drug producers must register annually with the FDA, even though their products do not move in interstate commerce. The FDA must inspect each registered establishment at least once every two years. FDA testing and certification for safety and effectiveness are extended to all antibiotic drugs for humans. The FDA has the authority to designate "established names" for drugs, when that is desirable. The advertising of prescription drugs must include the established (or generic) name as well as the brand name. The advertising must also include the formula and a summary of adverse side effects. Like other provisions of the federal Food, Drug, and Cosmetic Act, these requirements are enforceable by seizure, injunction, or criminal prosecution.

A total of 20,413 advertisements in medical journals was reviewed by the FDA in just one year. As a result, 314 corrective actions were initiated to deal with serious omissions, unsupported claims, and promotionally biased statements that had the potential to seriously mislead the physician and affect the safety of patients. Regulatory measures included requests for cancellation of violative advertisements and publication of corrective advertisements. In most cases these called for the following boxed statement to appear in direct association with the corrective material:

PUBLISHED TO CORRECT A PREVIOUS ADVERTISEMENT WHICH
THE FOOD AND DRUG ADMINISTRATION CONSIDERED
MISLEADING

In some cases the FDA also required the mailing of "Dear Doctor" letters to physicians across the nation pointing out the violative faults in the original advertisement.

The basic 1938 Food, Drug, and Cosmetic Act requires the following:

1. Drugs must not be dangerous to health when used according to printed directions.
2. Containers must not be composed of any poisonous substances.
3. Drug products must not contain any filthy or decomposed substance.
4. Drugs may not be prepared, packed, or held under unsanitary conditions.
5. A drug liable to deterioration must be suitably packaged and informatively labeled.
6. Drugs that do not meet official standards must be labeled to show exactly how they vary from the standard.
7. Drugs listed in the *U.S. Pharmacopaeia* or the *National Formulary*

must comply with all tests and packaging specifications in these compendiums.

8. No substance may be added or substituted to reduce the quality or strength of any drug.
9. A drug must not differ in strength, purity, or quality from its label claims.
10. Color additives must come from a batch certified as safe by the FDA.[14]

Drug Labels Must Bear the Prescribed Information

Labels must give the name and address of the manufacturer, packer, or distributor. They must show an accurate statement of the quantity of contents. They must show a statement of the quantity or proportion of certain habit-forming drugs, together with the statement: "Warning—may be habit forming." The common or usual name of the drug must be given. When the drug is composed of two or more ingredients, the common name of each active ingredient and the amount of certain other ingredients must be shown. Adequate directions for use must be given, as well as warnings against unsafe use by children. Warnings must be given against the use of the drug in disease conditions where caution is necessary to insure against danger. If the dosage or length of time or method of administration may make a drug dangerous to health, such information must be contained on the label in the form of a warning.

It is still a common practice for some drug sellers to attempt to circumvent the labeling requirements by making false claims in other literature. That practice was outlawed when the Supreme Court interpreted the phrase "accompanying labeling" to include any material which serves the purposes of labeling, even though it does not physically accompany the product in interstate shipments. In addition, much false advertising for drugs has been stopped by FDA court cases charging that labels did not contain adequate directions for treating effectively the diseases or conditions mentioned in the advertisements.

Certification

The purity of some drugs is so vital to health and life that Congress included in the basic drug law a requirement that the FDA test and certify each batch of antibiotics and insulin. Batches of these drugs are certified if they possess the characteristics of strength, quality, and purity prescribed by FDA regulations. These certification services are financed by fees paid by the manufacturers. Anyone who ships certification items without certification is subject to criminal penalty and the product is subject to seizure. This testing and certification service is the most comprehensive control of drug quality administered by any government agency in the world. In 1974 the FDA performed approximately 300,000 tests on 20,894 antibiotic patches. Only 156 batches failed to receive certification. Of 403 batches of insulin tested, none was rejected.

Defective, Deficient, and Dangerous Drugs

In spite of the law and FDA inspectors, defective, deficient, and dangerous drugs do reach the market. In 1974 the FDA took action to remove 830 separate, identifiable drug products from trade channels because of deficiences in their effectiveness. Up through 1974, the FDA's drug-effectiveness review under the 1962 amendments removed from the market a total of 6,346 prescription drug products manufactured by 2,836 companies. Many of these drugs have since been replaced by items with revised formulas and labeling. The FDA continues its prescription drug-effectiveness review program.

Another mass review is being conducted on "over-the-counter" (OTC) drugs. For example, a panel of non-FDA scientists reviewed 101 ingredients used in an estimated 25,000 laxative, antidiarrheal, emetic (vomit inducing), and antiemetic drug products sold on the U.S. market without a prescription. The committee found 50 of the 101 ingredients to be safe and effective; 30 as needing further study; and 21 as either ineffective or unsafe. After final review by the panel, ingredients ruled ineffective or unsafe and having false or misleading label claims must be removed from all products. This group is the third category of OTC drugs thus far subjected to an FDA review to upgrade safety, effectiveness, and labeling accuracy of all nonprescription drugs. The first study covered antacids, and its recommendations are how in effect. The second study covered antimicrobial (germ-fighting) products. Further studies will cover analgesics, eye products, sleep aids, dental products, cough and cold products, contraceptives, vaginal products, and antiperspirants.[15]

"Recalls," now a major factor in protecting consumers of all sorts of products, are particularly useful in the drug field. In 1974 the FDA supervised 602 drug recalls, 80 percent involving prescription drugs. Among them, a publicized recall of two OTC arthritis drugs was required because users could receive a serious toxic overdosage of salicylates from them. One lot of cortisone tablets was recalled after bottles containing the cortisone tablets were found to contain also nonprescription asthma tablets. The FDA ordered the J. B. Williams Company to halt distribution and promotion of "Sominex 2" and recall all outstanding stocks of the OTC nighttime sleep-aid because it contained dipehenhydramine, a prescription drug not safe for use without medical supervision.[16]

Abuse of Drugs

The abuse of drugs is a major problem in the United States. Properly used, under the direction of a physician, potent and even addictive drugs can be very helpful. Tranquilizers are useful in the treatment of distressed and disturbed patients, and morphine is a valuable pain-relieving drug, but the nonmedical use of such drugs without prescription is dangerous. The record shows that such use leads to crime, death on the highways, juvenile delinquency, and suicides. Thousands of prosecutions have failed to halt the growth of an enormous, criminal traffic in drugs in this country.

Until 1968 the FDA and the Bureau of Narcotics in the Treasury Department had the major responsibility for policing illegal drug traffic. In 1968 the president combined these activities in the Department of Justice, forming a Bureau of Narcotics and Dangerous drugs. And in 1970 a Comprehensive Drug Abuse Prevention and Control Act was passed in hopes that it would help curb the problem. In 1973 another reorganization took place. The Drug Enforcement Administration was established in the Department of Justice, consolidating law enforcement against drug abuse. Results of these attempts have been discouraging. The continuing abuse of such drugs as marijuana, LSD, and heroin has created a problem verging on a national disaster.

Quack Cures

People who suffer from various chronic or incurable diseases, particularly the aging, constitute a major market for quack products claimed to be scientific breakthroughs. It has been estimated that the victims waste as much as a billion dollars a year and often endanger their health by using quack medicines, quack devices, and vitamin and mineral supplements promoted as cures for disease conditions.

The AMA has said that "health-food" rackets cost ten million consumers more than $500 million a year. Promoters distort facts and claim benefits against diseases that have no relation to dietary deficiency. Even consumers whose health is good are urged to make it even better with a food supplement. Nutrition scientists generally agree that vitamins and minerals are plentiful in a normal balanced diet. Nevertheless, consumers are constantly being bombarded with exaggerated claims made by food faddists, nutritional quacks, and even by supposedly ethical manufacturers. A dietary supplement pill containing alfalfa, watercress, parsley, wheat germ, mint leaves, beets, buckwheat, yeast, and a dozen other such ingredients may cost as much as $20 per month for one person. The FDA warns consumers that vitamins, when taken in excessive amounts, can be harmful.

The FDA's files are filled with cases involving fakes and swindles. These range from phony air-purifiers to "ulcer cures." Here is some official FDA advice:

- There are no drugs, devices, or methods that can truthfully be labeled as a cure for arthritis.
- There are no drugs or treatments that can cure baldness.

- Beware of any product advertised as a treatment for colitis.
- It is practically impossible to purchase properly fitting false teeth by mail.
- Do not expect too much from powders or liquids that are advertised to make dentures stick better.
- Beware of practitioners who have machines supposedly capable of diagnosing or treating different kinds of diseases simply by turning dials and applying electrical contacts to the body.
- Beware of "door-to-door doctors" who are interested only in selling some product at a high price.

Advertising is not a good source of medical advice, and many popular books on dieting are equally unreliable.

The most dangerous quack products are ineffective treatments for cancer. Pain and fear make victims of this disease vulnerable to false promises. A patient who is diverted from seeking effective treatment while trying an unproven remedy can lose his or her life.

Medical history records one fad remedy for cancer after another. Many have become a "cause celebre" to loyal followers who believe the testimonials of patients who thought they were helped. Under the Federal Food, Drug, and Cosmetic Act, however, it is illegal to market a drug until substantial scientific evidence of its effectiveness has been accepted by the Food and Drug Administration. This has greatly restricted the sale of quack remedies in the U.S., but it does not prevent the public from seeking them elsewhere. Currently the FDA is involved in extensive legislation to stop importations of Laetrile, an alleged cancer treatment made from apricot pits.

It is not true that the medical profession or the FDA are suppressing new and effective drugs for cancer, as claimed by quacks. Actually, some 200 drugs have been approved for the treatment of various forms of cancer and the agency is quick to review any product with valid evidence of effectiveness.

CONTROL OF COSMETICS

What the Law Says

The production and sale of cosmetics is a big business. The volume of retail sales is approximately $7 billion a year. The Federal Food, Drug, and Cosmetic Act is intended to assure consumers that cosmetics are safe. A cosmetic is defined as an article (except soap) used for cleansing, beautifying, promoting attractiveness, or altering the appearance of the human body. Some cosmetics, such as hormone creams, skin bleaches, and antiperspirants, are also classed as drugs. Under the law a cosmetic must not contain any substance which may make it harmful to users when it is used customarily or according to directions on the label. Hair dye colors containing coal tar dyes must be labeled with special instructions. Containers for cosmetics must not be composed of any substance that may render the contents harmful. A cosmetic must not contain any filthy, putrid, or decomposed substance. It must be prepared, packaged, and stored under sanitary conditions.

Colors used in cosmetics, except coal tar hair dyes which are subject to special labeling requirements, must be approved by the FDA. Unless exempted every batch of color is subjected to tests in FDA laboratories before it may be used. Colors in cosmetics that may be swallowed, as for example lipstick, are subject to the same safety requirements as are food colors.

Labels must give the name and address of the manufacturer, packer, or distributor together with an accurate statement of the quantity of content. The label of a cosmetic must tell the truth. The law forbids false or misleading claims on the label. For example, a cosmetic may not claim to do the impossible, such as preventing wrinkles or baldness.

A cosmetic that is harmful or falsely labeled may be removed from the market, and shippers of such products may be prosecuted in federal court. FDA inspectors investigate conditions in manufacturing plants and warehouses and collect samples for analysis.

Cosmetics and Safety

In a three-month study of 35,490 participants, made for the FDA, 703 adverse reactions were reported that were believed to have been caused by cosmetics. Of this number, 589, or 84 percent, of these adverse reactions were confirmed by dermatologists as definitely, or most probably, caused by cosmetic products. Eighty-six percent of these were considered minor irritations that did not require medication or a physician's attention; eleven percent were considered moderate reactions which persisted for a prolonged period and caused loss of time from normal activities; and three percent were defined as being painful and severe enough to require a physician's attention and which resulted in a loss of time from normal activities. The overall average rate of 6.9 percent confirmed adverse reactions per 10,000 users for a one-month period constitutes a substantially higher rate of adverse reactions to cosmetics than any data in the past has suggested. The ten categories showing the highest rate of adverse reactions were: deodorant/antiperspirants; depilatories (chemical hair removers); moisturizer/lotion; hair spray/lacquer; mascara; bubble bath; eye cream; hair color; dye lightener; facial skin cream; cleaner; and nail polish.[17]

Two regulations published by the FDA in recent years should help consumers use cosmetics with a greater degree of safety. One requires that cosmetics manufactured after November 30, 1976, must list their ingredients on the product label. If a consumer knows a certain substance has caused a problem in the past, he or she can avoid products that contain it. The second regulation deals with so-called "hypoallergenic" cosmetics.

Many cosmetic products claim to be hypoallergenic, implying that they are safer than normal cosmetics for use by people who have had allergic reactions to cosmetics. In the past, however, the term has had no uniform meaning and there was usually no proof available for the implied lower potential for adverse reactions of products claiming to be hypoallergenic. After June 6, 1977, the regulation would prohibit the labeling of a cosmetic as "hypoallergenic" unless the manufacturer had submitted proof that the product is not likely to cause allergic reactions. Two cosmetic manufacturers have recently entered suit in a U.S. district court against the FDA and this regulation, however, so the effective date may be delayed, or the regulation may even be canceled by court order.

While most cosmetics should be safe if used properly, there is almost always a potential for adverse reactions, even from products that one has used many times before. The best precaution is to read the label carefully and to follow the directions for use, including making a "patch test" if one is recommended or if the user has a history of allergic reactions. Should adverse reactions occur, the FDA urges consumers to notify the manufacturer and the Division of Cosmetics Technology, Bureau of Foods, FDA, 200 C St., S.W., Washington, D.C. 20204, or any FDA regional office.

More Protection Is Needed

Consumers need a provision in the law that specifies that cosmetics must be tested for safety *before* being marketed. The FDA now has the legal power to withdraw cosmetics from the market *after* they have been proven injurious.

MEDICAL DEVICES

Worthless Devices

Therapeutic and diagnostic devices and supplies constitute a large and rapidly growing segment of the health products industry. Retail sales were estimated at $3 billion in 1971, and they are likely to double in ten years.

Long-needed and significant authority to assure the safety and effectiveness of devices prior to marketing was finally provided by the Medical Device Amendments of 1976. Administration will be carried on by a new Bureau of Medical Devices and Diagnostic Products set up by the FDA in 1974.

Because the technology of the device field is complex and highly specialized — with some 12,000 products varying from bone screws to electronic heart pacemakers — the controls needed are also specialized. Under the law three categories of products are established, based on recommendations by panels of nongovernment experts:

- Class I – General Controls: All devices are subject to "general controls," which include the registration of manufacturers and record-keeping requirements. Under the law the FDA can also impose a requirement that manufacturers or distributors report to the FDA any product defect that could cause a health hazard.
- Class II – Performance Standards: Devices for which general controls alone are insufficient to assure safety and effectiveness will be required to meet performance standards established by the FDA.
- Class III – Premarket Approval: All implanted and life-supporting devices will automatically be assigned to this category unless the FDA determines that premarket approval is not necessary. Premarket approval can be required of other devices if general controls or a performance standard are insufficient to assure a device's safety and effectiveness.

"New" devices will automatically be classified into premarket approval status, although manufacturers can petition for reclassification. The law requires that the FDA be notified 90 days before a new product is put on the market, regardless of the kind of device it is or its classification.

The FDA is authorized to quickly ban a device which is deceptive or presents unreasonable risk of illness or injury. Under prior law, removing a hazardous product from the market was often lengthy, expensive, and ineffective. The FDA will also be able to require manufacturers to repair or replace a defective device or refund its purchase price.

A "medical device" is defined under the new law as a health care product that does not achieve any of its principal intended purposes by chemical action within or on the body by being metabolized. A product that does achieve its principal purpose by chemical action will continue to be a drug.

The 1976 device law is primarily designed to regulate "legitimate" products, in contrast to the "quack" devices which were the principal target of the original device section in the basic Food, Drug, and Cosmetic Act of 1938. Although better control of the "quack" devices can be expected, they will doubtless continue to bilk the unwary consumer. An example would be the many gadgets promoted for subtracting from, or adding to, the human physique. As reported by the FDA in 1974, seizures were made of such devices as "Love Legs Instant Leg Shaper," an "Iso-Tensor" breast developer, and a "Neckline Beauty System Chin/Neck Band." All three products were promoted by full-page ads in national magazines, including *Cosmopolitan, True Love,* and *Intimate Story.* The FDA charged, and the court found, that "Love Legs" – rubber stockings to induce perspiration – were not effective in trimming down heavy thighs or in slimming, shaping, or firming the thighs through removal or redistribution of fat, as the advertisements claimed. The FDA also charged, and the court found, that wearing "Love Legs" or performing the prescribed exercises while wearing them could impede venous blood flow and worsen circulatory conditions in pregnant women and other persons with circulatory problems and in some cases could cause thrombophlebitis. Witnesses established that even though the "Iso-Tensor" device exercised the muscles underlying the breasts it had no effect on their size or shape. Trial evidence showed the claims of the "Neckline Beauty System" to be physiologically impossible.

The law covering such medical devices as those mentioned above specifies that a device must not be dangerous to health when used with the frequency or duration described on the label. A label must give the name and address of the manufacturer, packer, or distributor. Adequate directions for use must be given, together with warnings against unsafe use by children, and warnings against uses that might be dangerous to health. Deception is forbidden. It is under the latter prohibition that the FDA takes action against "misbranded" devices.

Quacks will continue to "treat" patients until consumers' money runs out or until they die. The FDA warns that there are no devices or machines recognized for the cure of disease by patients in their homes. All that an electric vibrator can do is shake or massage a part of the body. There are no machines that will diagnose or treat different diseases by applying electrical contact to the body and turning a knob. Such devices are fakes.

What the FDA will accomplish against device quackery under the new law will depend on the priority given to this phase of device regulation.

More Protection Is Needed

Case-by-case litigation as a means to control therapeutic devices is increasingly recognized to be inadequate. Even more important, the advent of hundreds of new, medically legitimate devices, such as heart pacemakers, plastic implants, and metal prosthetic units for repairing fractures, has emphasized the need for standards and premarket testing of such devices.

Medical devices, unlike drugs, have been almost entirely unregulated. The law has provided almost no controls over the premarket testing or quality control of the more than 12,000 medical devices on the market. The FDA can request companies to recall devices, but only *after* they have caused problems. In one year there were sixty-three recalls. The FDA has recalled two types of heart pacemakers, one said to be involved in the deaths of two children. Since 1972, 30,000 pacemakers have been involved in recalls, out of the total of approximately 300,000 pacemakers in the U.S.[18] In most cases the actions called for doctors to notify patients of potential problems and to monitor the devices' operation to assure that problems did not develop. In 1976 the president signed into law a bill that requires premarket testing of about 5 to 10 percent of all medical devices put on the market. Under the current FDA medical device classification process, however, 90 to 95 percent of these devices would not need to have premarket clearance because of the nature of the devices. Patients, physicians, and manufacturers all need such a protective law.

PROGRESS IN RADIATION CONTROL

The FDA has the responsibility to protect the public from excess radiation from such products as medical and dental X-ray units, laser products, television, and microwave ovens and to establish radiation emission standards for these products. There are about 250,000 medical and dental X-ray units now in use in this country, and about 14,000 additional units enter the market each year. X-rays used for diagnostic purposes account for 90 percent of all exposure to man-made radiation. The FDA ordered the recall of 400,000 Panasonic, Penncrest, and Bradford color television sets for suspected radiation hazards in 1975.[19] And in 1976 the General Electric Company agreed to an FDA request to correct defects in 5,300 microwave ovens that could leak microwave radiation as much as ten times the limit allowed by the federal standard.[20] Many other illustrations of corrective action could be cited.

Radiation emissions exceeding the limits in FDA performance standards create significant risks of injury, including genetic injuries.

HOW EFFECTIVELY IS THE LAW ENFORCED?

Inspectors Patrol Plants and Markets

FDA statutes cover more than 100 pages, and the agency's 6,500 employees have the responsibility of enforcing the nation's major consumer protection law. In addition, there are volumes of regulations and interpretations of the law. The FDA is responsible for checking the more than 100,000 establishments that do interstate business in foods, drugs, medical devices, and cosmetics. It is also concerned with 51,500 drug stores, and 359,500 public eating places subject to the law. All this work is accomplished at a cost of approximately $1.05 cents per person per year.

There are three ways to achieve the objectives of a law. One is to educate the regulated groups so they will not do what is forbidden by the law. A second is to educate consumers so they will know the provisions of the law and their responsibility in helping to enforce it. A third step is to take legal action if the law is violated. The FDA uses all these approaches. Educational programs are used to make sure that the managers of regulated establishments know what the laws provide and how to comply. The FDA reports that the most difficult problem in the whole area of consumer protection is to persuade consumers to protect themselves. Better labeling, for example, is useless if consumers cannot or do not read the labels or follow instructions.

When education fails and the law is violated, the FDA may get a court order to seize a product, thereby removing it from sale. Another legal weapon which is used against repeat offenders is the injunction. Injunctions are frequently obtained to prevent the shipment of contaminated foods prepared under insanitary conditions disclosed through factory inspections. The person or firm responsible for violating the law may also be subjected to criminal prosecution. Conviction may result in a fine and imprisonment. If intent to deceive can be proved, the fine and the imprisonment are more severe. Frequently manufacturers are allowed to recall defective products from the market. When this is done promptly and effectively, it is perhaps the quickest way to correct a violation and saves the costs and delays of legal action. Recalls have become a major means of consumer protection and the FDA publishes a weekly list of such actions.

In fiscal 1974 the FDA began using a far-reaching new law enforcement mechanism, the regulatory letter. A regulatory letter is a formal notice to a specific person or firm, charging a specific violation of the law, setting a date for corrective action, and advising the party that a court proceeding will be begun if the violation is not corrected. The purpose of a regulatory letter is to secure compliance and consumer protection in the shortest possible time and with the least expenditure of funds. With the beginning of the issuance of regulatory letters there was an expected decline in the number of new court cases. In the first year, 1,195 regulatory letters were issued, and the total number of new court cases went down from 1,350 to 523.

The FDA was one of the first of the scientific crime-detection agencies. Laws to insure the potency of drugs and the purity of foods would be impracticable and unenforceable without methods of scientific analysis to determine whether products are up to standards. Hence the importance of strong scientific capabilities in this agency.

The Courts Uphold the Laws

When a law is passed, its full effectiveness cannot be measured until the courts have decided issues arising from its provisions and regulations. The Food, Drug, and Cosmetic Act of 1938, as amended, has repeatedly been held constitutional. In one case the U.S. Supreme Court said, "The purposes of this legislation touch phases of the lives and health of countless people who in the circumstances of modern industrialism are largely beyond self-protection."[21] The judicial record shows increasingly sympathetic treatment at the hands of the courts. Most federal judges think of the act as "a working instrument of government and not merely as a collection of English words."[22] Most federal courts have given more weight to the argument that Congress passed the laws to protect consumers than they have given to the technical arguments introduced by lawyers defending alleged violators. Generally, however, the penalties assessed by the courts have been low.

The legal fiction that a corporation is a person made it difficult for a long time for administrative agencies to enforce federal laws. Although corporate officials were responsible for the actions of a corporation, the courts had held that only the corporation was legally responsible. Since it is impossible to put a corporation in jail, the law could not be vigorously enforced. Finally the Supreme Court held in an FDA case that a corporation officer may be held individually liable for violations by a corporation. In 1975 in the case of *U.S. v. Park* the court affirmed and expanded this doctrine of personal responsibility of company officials to insure compliance with the Food and Drug Law.

The Food, Drug, and Cosmetic Act, as amended, is a good law. But it is not perfect. Through the years Congress and the courts have closed some of the more glaring loopholes through which unscrupulous profitseekers frustrated enforcement. Adequate laws, adequate financing, and adequate administration are the essentials necessary to make government agencies truly effective in protecting consumers.

Still More Protection Is Needed

To meet changing conditions and new problems both the law and the administering agency must continually be strengthened. The number of inspectors should be multiplied several times. In 1976 the FDA had approximately 650 inspectors, while there were over 1,100 in 1966! Many food plants operate for years without an FDA inspection.

FDA employment must be continually upgraded as a professional career specialty. A shortage of competent, experienced personnel prevails throughout the agency, and the supply is continually diluted by reorganizations and the demands for new activities. "Management" employees have multiplied, but they do not have competence in law enforcement or science.

The FDA must become more of a scientific institution, but there is a danger that expanded scientific activities will not be sufficiently oriented to the special needs of law enforcement for consumer protection.

In an era of inflation, consumers should demand that the FDA step up its "pocketbook protection" activities. These are being grossly neglected in favor of "consumer safety," a field which can absorb unlimited funds because it includes investigation of unknown dangers. Areas such as short-weighing, cheating on food ingredients, and deceptive packaging have been virtually abandoned to the states for enforcement.

Legislation should be strengthened to insure:

1. Adequate factory inspection authority over foods, cosmetics, devices, and self-medication drugs similar to that provided in 1962 for prescription drugs
2. That scientific data related to the safety and effectiveness of drugs not be considered a trade secret
3. Cosmetic safety through required testing and premarketing approval
4. More informative food labeling through an amendment requiring complete declaration of ingredients on all foods – whether or not they are standardized – percentage ingredient labeling, and drained-weight listing.

The FDA is attempting to meet some of these needs through regulations, but there is a limit to what it can accomplish in this way. The magnitude and dimension of the role the FDA plays in meeting its responsibilities to the consumer may be seen when one realizes that annual personal consumption expenditures in this country have reached $1 trillion and that of every dollar spent by consumers an estimated 38 cents is spent on products regulated by the FDA. The FDA has long been rated a competent federal agency; a Louis Harris poll showed that the FDA is known to 86 percent of the public, which is a higher recognition rate than that of any other similar government organization. The Harris poll also found the FDA at the top of the list of all government agencies in terms of public favor, with a 61 percent positive mark. In fact, the FDA was the only federal agency tested to be judged with favor by more than 50 percent of the persons questioned.[23]

With limited staff and facilities, the FDA has performed a valuable public service. Every consumer is indebted to this group of dedicated public servants. But times, personnel, and conditions have changed. From its beginning the FDA has not been as effective as some have felt it should be. Numerous congressional investigations have probed the administration and the effectiveness of the agency. A widely held belief about government regulatory bodies is that they tend to become captives of those whom they regulate. A widely publicized criticism of FDA came with the publication of *The Chemical Feast*. This was Ralph Nader's "Study Group on the Food and Drug Administration." The report claimed the source of the FDA's problems has been its assumption that business can be trusted. The report denounced past FDA performance, called for revitalization of the food standards programs, and urged the adoption of new laws and procedures requiring food marketers to use labels giving the public more information about food content and quality.

A few years later an FDA commissioner took strong exception to the allegation that the FDA was a captive of those it regulated. In testimony presented before a Senate committee he stated that, "if indeed the industry had been dominating FDA, which of course it has not, we would have seen over the past three to five years a pattern of drug regulation quite different from that which has evolved."[24]

A two-year study by the General Accounting Office (GAO), released in 1976, found that the FDA had conducted only limited inspections to determine whether drug sponsors were obeying the law. The GAO reported that most drug manufacturers were not fully complying with the strict requirements to insure that human test subjects were being protected and that test data were accurate and reliable. The findings led Senator Edward Kennedy to pledge to work for increased financing to correct the FDA's long-term problem of limited resources to carry out endless responsibilities.[25]

A careful analysis of the FDA's record by an objective observer would no doubt show that the FDA has not done nearly as good a job in protecting the American consumer as is needed, nor is it doing nearly as poor a job as a reading of *The Chemical Feast* would indicate. The obvious facts are that it has not had adequate funding to enforce effectively all the laws that Congress has passed, that additional strength is needed in some of the legislation already on the books, and that new legislation is vitally needed in order to strengthen its role in protecting the American consumer.

QUESTIONS FOR REVIEW

1. Are there any reasons why the government should be more involved in protecting consumers today than it was twenty-five or fifty years ago?
2. "An intelligent, educated consumer does not need help from the government." Do you agree?
3. What are some of the basic responsibilities of the Food and Drug Administration?
4. What is meant by a "standard of identity" for a food product?
5. What are recalls and what is their purpose?
6. What are some of the problems and benefits of using food additives?
7. Why are there so many regulations controlling drug products?
8. Why do you think Congress has not passed legislation requiring the pretesting of cosmetics to insure safety?
9. What do you think might be the situation facing consumers if there were no FDA?
10. Why do you think there has been relatively little success with the various attempts to control drug abuse?
11. What are advantages to the consumer of drained-weight labeling?
12. What is botulism and how do you protect yourself from it?
13. What do you believe are additional areas, if any, where the FDA should be more active and/or have more authority?
14. Why do you think it took until 1976 for Congress to pass a medical devices act?

PROJECTS

1. Read Rachel Carson's *Silent Spring* and write a paper on its relevance today.
2. Read an issue of *FDA Consumer* and write a report on its contents.
3. Analyze *The Budget of the United States Government* for the most recent year and compare what is being spent for consumer welfare and other budget categories. What conclusion can you draw?
4. Debate the question as to whether Congress should have restricted

the FDA's authority to set standards for vitamin-mineral food supplements.

5. Discuss the role of the FDA with a pharmacist and/or food processor.

6. Get a farmer's opinion of government regulations and control over pesticides and other potentially harmful drugs.

REFERENCES

1. *Guide to Federal Consumer Services* (Washington, D.C.: Government Printing Office, 1976). Available free from Consumer Information Center, Pueblo, Colo. 81009.
2. *Milestones in Food and Drug Law History,* Food and Drug Administration, DHEW Publication No. (FDA) 75-1005, 1974, pp. 1-2.
3. *Facts About Food Poisoning,* U.S. Department of Agriculture, Washington, D.C., Jan. 1974, p. 4.
4. U.S. Department of Agriculture, News Release, 10 March 1975.
5. U.S. Dept. of Health, Education, and Welfare, HEW News Release, 10 March 1975.
6. *FDA Consumer,* Nov. 1975, p. 23.
7. *FDA Consumer,* March 1975, p. 6.
8. *Need for Regulating The Food Salvage Industry To Prevent Sales Of Unwholesome And Misbranded Food To The Public,* Report To The Congress, by the Comptroller General of the United States, 20 May 1975, p. ii.
9. Statement of J. Phil Campbell, Under Secretary, U.S. Dept. of Agriculture, before the Committee on Agriculture, House of Representatives, 13 May 1975.
10. *U.S. News & World Report,* 3 Nov. 1975, p. 74.
11. Department of Health, Education, and Welfare, HEW News Release, 19 Jan. 1967.
12. *FDA Consumer,* March 1976, pp. 27, 29.
13. *FDA Consumer,* Dec. 1975, p. 38; Jan. 1976, p. 40.
14. Federal Food, Drug, and Cosmetic Act as Amended, U.S. Department of Health, Education, and Welfare, Food and Drug Administration, 1971 revision.
15. U.S. Dept. of Health, Education, and Welfare, HEW News Release, 20 March 1975.
16. *New York Times,* 2 Dec. 1975, p. 5.
17. *FDA Consumer,* March 1976, pp. 16-17.
18. Address given by Alexander M. Schmidt, M.D., Commissioner of the Food and Drug Administration, University of Utah, 22 April 1976.
19. *FDA Consumer,* March 1975, p. 9.
20. U.S. Dept. of Health, Education, and Welfare, HEW News Release, 30 May 1975.
21. *United States v. Dotterweich,* 320 U.S. 277.
22. Daniel P. Willis and William W. Goodrich, "Enforcement and Judicial Progress of the Federal Food, Drug, Cosmetic Act in 1948," *Food, Drug, Cosmetic Law Journal* 4, no. 1, p. 27, 1949.
23. Speech by Alexander M. Schmidt, Commissioner of the FDA, before the Public Relations Society of America, Washington, D.C., 21 May 1975.
24. Annual Report of the Food and Drug Administration, 1974, pp. 3-4.
25. *St. Petersburg Times,* 23 Jan. 1976, p. 3A.

THE FEDERAL GOVERNMENT HELPS CONSUMERS: OTHER AGENCIES

The federal government's concern in assisting and protecting consumers goes beyond its responsibilities represented by the activities of the Food and Drug Administration. In fact, some people contend that every government agency and department serves the consumer in some way. There are certain departments and agencies, though, which have significant responsibilities to consumers. These include the departments of Agriculture and Commerce, the Consumer Product Safety Commission, the Federal Trade Commission, the Consumer Information Center, and the Office of Consumer Affairs in the Department of Health, Education, and Welfare. In addition, the Department of Transportation, the Civil Aeronautics Board, and the Antitrust Division of the Department of Justice have certain responsibilities directly and indirectly related to the welfare of consumers.

HOW PURE IS OUR MEAT, POULTRY, AND FISH? THE ROLE OF THE U.S. DEPARTMENT OF AGRICULTURE

What the Law Says About Meat, Poultry, and Fish

Consumers in this country enjoy safe, clean, nutritious, and attractive food. There are exceptions to this statement, but fortunately they represent a very small percentage of the total. Only by constant vigilance will we continue to be one of the best-fed peoples in the world.

One of the oldest federal laws to protect consumers is the Meat Inspection Act, passed in 1906. Basically the act forbids the interstate shipment of meat and meat products that have not been inspected and that are not stamped with the familiar purple mark that says "U.S. Inspected and Passed."

Standards have been established for many processed meat products, including luncheon meats, meat pies, and soups. These standards establish the minimum amounts of meat in the product. For example, ham salad must contain at least 25 percent meat, pizza with meat must have no less than 15 percent meat, hot dogs are limited to no more than 30 percent fat, and corned beef hash must contain at least 35 percent fresh beef! Poultry stew must have at least 2 percent poultry meat, and poultry pies must contain no less than 14 percent poultry meat!

Labeling must be informative and must not be false or deceptive. To enforce this part of the law all labels are examined in advance and must be approved. In one year USDA labeling specialists examined more than 148,000 label designs for accuracy and completeness as required by law. The first word in a food product's name on a label must identify the ingredient that is present in the largest amount. Certain exceptions are allowed, however. For example, *Pork and Beans, Chicken Noodle Dinner,* and *Turkey and Rice with Vegetables* are exceptions to the rule because the industry argued that the public knew that beans, noodles, and rice were the most important ingredients in these products and there was no need to relabel them. Labeling regulations also require that ingredients statements on products list the ingredients in order of predominance.[1]

USDA labeling and packaging rules eliminated the use of such terms as "all meat" or "all beef" on the labels for hot dogs and similar cooked sausages which have other ingredients besides meat. Use of the terms "all," "pure," and "100 percent" is forbidden on the label of any meat or poultry product containing more than one ingredient.

Packaging materials must also be approved. Likewise imports of meat and meat products must be inspected and passed. Violation of the law invokes heavy penalties, with a maximum fine of $10,000 or two years imprisonment or both. For this protection consumers pay about $1.86 per person annually.

There is a difference between inspection of and grading of meat. The inspection mark tells the buyer the meat or meat product is wholesome. A grade mark tells the buyer the quality of the meat or meat products. A product may be inspected but not graded, but every graded product has been inspected. Inspection is required, but grading is not.

Wholesome Meat   Passage of the Wholesome Meat Act of 1967 was preceded by public indignation at findings which indicated that much meat in intrastate trade was being prepared under filthy conditions or from carcasses unfit, by federal standards, for human consumption. In addition, canned meat was being adulterated with water or cheap extenders such as cereal. Few state meat inspection systems matched the federal one, especially in its insistence on continuous inspection of all slaughtering and processing. Twenty-two states did not require meat inspection of any kind. Over 8 billion pounds of meat received no federal inspection. This does not mean that all or even half of that meat was in any way tainted, or suspected, but it did mean that somewhere there were some packers processing meat from "4-D" animals – dead, dying, disabled, or diseased.

The Wholesome Meat Act closes the loophole that allowed meat not in interstate shipment to be exempt from inspection. This act assures that virtually all meat on sale in the United States is inspected by either the federal government or an adequate state program.

Animals are inspected before slaughter to eliminate those that may be diseased or unwholesome. Carcasses are examined again after slaughter to eliminate any which might be diseased. Inspectors look for residues of pesticides, chemicals, or drugs which might have been ingested with the feed eaten by the animal. All diseased or unwholesome meat is destroyed for food use. Inspectors supervise the preparation of meat and meat products to assure cleanliness and wholesomeness. The use of dyes, chemicals, preservatives, or ingredients which make a product unwholesome, unhealthful, or unfit for human consumption is forbidden.

The key provision of the act gave the states two years to develop a meat inspection program that would be as good as the federal program, with federal funds paying 50 percent of the cost of inspections. It was the intent of the legislation to provide funds and technical assistance that would make it possible for all states to develop meat inspection programs equal to federal standards. However, state-inspected meat cannot be shipped interstate. Eventually thirty-four states were certified as having meat inspection programs equal to federal standards. Gradually the states began to realize that there was little advantage in paying for state inspection unless a state wanted to maintain higher standards than the federal program required. Under state inspection a state pays 50 percent of the cost, but if a state allows the federal government to take over its inspection program, there is no cost to the state. So states began to turn their inspection programs over to the federal government. USDA budget figures for fiscal year 1977 revealed that the federal government had taken over the meat inspection programs in sixteen states and the poultry inspection programs in twenty three states.

The Wholesome Meat Act also raised the quality standards for all imported meats by requiring USDA approval of the meat inspection system of an exporting country. At U.S. ports of entry, USDA inspectors examine shipments as an additional safeguard to see that imported products meet U.S. standards for wholesomeness and proper labeling.

Wholesome Poultry It was not until 1957 that the poultry industry was placed under mandatory federal inspection. That action became necessary because conditions in the growing, processing, and marketing of poultry endangered the health of consumers. The worst hazard was the marketing of diseased poultry. The Hoover Commission reported that one out of every four food-borne diseases was caused by eating defective poultry or poultry dishes.[2] *Salmonellae* infections were especially serious. Diseases common to poultry and humans are significant in number. The mass production of poultry causes a higher disease rate in concentrated broods. Under a voluntary plan financed by fees from users less than 20 percent of the commercial supplies of poultry was being inspected. To meet changing conditions and new problems both the law and the administering agency must continuously be strengthened.

The passage of the Wholesome Meat Act gave stimulus to congressional proponents who were desirous of seeing the inspection of poultry expanded. A Wholesome Poultry Products Bill was introduced into the 90th Congress in 1968. The House debate showed the glaring need for poultry inspection.[3] Thirteen percent, or approximately 1.6 billion pounds, of all poultry slaughtered was not covered by the 1957 Poultry Products Inspection Act. State poultry inspection programs were described as dismal because only twelve states had mandatory inspection programs and only four of these states carried on programs that could be truly described as active. In poultry processing plants that were federally inspected, 4 percent — over 400 million pounds — of the poultry was rejected because it was diseased or contaminated. If the same rate were applied to uninspected poultry, then an additional 64 million pounds should have been rejected at the state level. The need for inspection was emphasized because of the tremendous increase in broiler production. In 1947 U.S. broiler production was 310 million birds, compared with 3.3 billion in 1974.

The Wholesome Poultry Products Act, whose provisions almost duplicate the Wholesome Meat Act, became effective in 1968. In 1971 the GAO released its second report in two years, asserting that many, if not most, of the nation's poultry-processing plants were unsanitary. Contaminated products were observed in thirty-five of sixty-eight plants inspected. Inspectors found dirty equipment, poor sanitation, inadequate pest control, and dirty floors, walls, and ceilings. Many of the sanitation deficiencies appeared to have existed over a long period, indicating a lack of strong, day-to-day enforcement by the federal plant inspectors and a lack of effective supervisory review. The sixty-two page report concluded that in such circumstances consumers are not provided with adequate assurance that they are receiving the unadulterated products intended by the Wholesome Poultry Products Act.

As in the case of meat, poultry may be inspected but not graded, but every graded product has been inspected. Inspection is required, but grading is not. In one year, inspectors of the USDA's Animal and Plant Health Inspection Service examined more than 116 million meat animals and nearly 3.3 billion birds. During later processing, more than 22 billion pounds of processed poultry products and more than 51 billion pounds of processed meat products were inspected.[4] The federal inspection program is growing. There are about 6,000 food inspectors, 1,400 veterinarians, and 600 management, laboratory, and other support personnel working in the USDA meat and poultry inspection programs.

Wholesome Fish?   Consumers now have reasonably pure meat, but what about fish? Sanitary inspection of fish products is voluntary. There are many questionable practices occurring in the fish industry — from the time the fish are brought into the boat until they reach the consumer. Even before the fish are caught, they may be contaminated. The lack of a rigid inspection program creates serious health questions.

The National Marine Fisheries Services (NMFS) in the Department of Commerce is involved with inspection and grading, developing standards and specifications of quality, conditions, quantity, grade, and packaging for fishery plants, fish, and fishery products. NMFS conducts a consumer education program concerning the voluntary fishery inspection service and provides information on the availability of quality fishery products.

When Consumers Union announced in its monthly publication that rodent hairs, moth wings, and insect parts had shown up in samples of almost all the brands of tuna it had tested this was unsettling to consumers and to the fish industry.[5] By 1976 three major packers of tuna in the United States had joined the federal fish inspection program, and their products now carry the official U.S. Department of Commerce inspection seal certifying that their tuna is "safe, clean and wholesome."

There is a need for compulsory inspection of fish and fish products, proper marking, labeling, and packaging, and assistance for the states in administering such programs.

Pesticides

The Department of Agriculture is deeply involved along with the FDA in the pesticide problem. The USDA requires manufacturers to place warning statements prominently on the front panels of pesticide labels. The warnings must include the words "Keep Out of Reach of Children." Also the warnings must contain the word "Danger" or "Caution" or "Warning." The USDA may also require additional toxicity information from manufacturers. Manufacturers must file regular reports on the safety of their product. Safety information must be submitted before the USDA will issue temporary shipping permits for experimental compounds. Finally, reports on the effectiveness of the products in the field tests must be made regularly.

The USDA established a pesticide monitoring system to make regular, detailed, scientific studies. Samples are taken of soil, silt, runoff, water, insects, wildlife, crops, plant life, and fish in check areas. This work is coordinated with other federal agencies and with state departments of agriculture.

In just one year USDA efforts kept 16 million pounds of meat and poultry out of the market because they contained illegal residues.[6]

Other Activities of the USDA

The USDA was one of the early movers in the field of consumer services. There is a USDA Extension Home Economist in almost every county in the United States. As the number of people living on farms has declined, extension economists have become increasingly active in urban areas. Their work involves better nutrition, home improvement, money management, use of credit, budgeting, family relations, and problems of community concern. The extension economists are affiliated with the Land Grant Colleges. The USDA has become one of the major, if not the major, government agency publishing consumer leaflets and pamphlets.

While it is true that significant and impressive consumer services are performed by the USDA, its basic and primary interests are those of farmers, ranchers, and food processors. The department was more concerned with the interests of meat producers than it was with the interests of consumers when it supported the upgrading of certain meats from "Good" to "Choice" and "Choice" to "Prime." The department was more concerned with the interests of turkey farmers than it was with the interests of consumers when it supported the practice of weighing turkeys and stuffing together rather than separately. The department was more concerned with the interests of tobacco farmers than it was with the interests of consumers when it supported the advertising of American tobacco abroad after the Surgeon General's *Report on Smoking and Health* was released. The department has been more concerned with agricultural producers than with consumers in its limited campaign against the perils of pesticides.

In all too many cases the USDA has sided with the agricultural industry instead of with the consumer. Although consumers have been helped by the USDA, the department has found it difficult to serve both the producer and the consumer. In showdown after showdown, all too often it has been the consumer's interest which has been sacrificed by the USDA to the interest of the producer.

THE FEDERAL TRADE COMMISSION'S ROLE IN CONSUMER PROTECTION

FTC Responsibilities

Over the years the significance of the Federal Trade Commission (FTC) as a protector of consumers has been increasing, but the impact of its effectiveness has been questioned a number of times by its critics. The FTC was established by Congress by the passage of the Federal Trade Commission Act in 1914. It was given authority to move against unfair trade practices occurring in commerce wherever such action was deemed to be in the public interest. The basic objective of the FTC is to maintain free competitive enterprise — to prevent it from being stifled by monopoly or corrupted by unfair or deceptive trade practices. The original act has been amended a number of times in order to spell out more specifically the duties of the FTC and to add to the areas in which the commission may act. The commission has no authority to levy fines against violators of trade laws, but it can bring court action through the Department of Justice. The work of the commission is directed by five commissioners appointed by the president and confirmed by the Senate for terms of seven years. The commission works in collaboration with the Antitrust Division of the Department of Justice on mergers, acquisitions, and consolidations of companies which may tend to lessen competition or create a monopoly in a particular line of commerce.

Originally the FTC was not intended to deal with the problem of false advertising. It was intended to work for the efficient enforcement of the anti-trust laws. The key provision of the act was the statement in Section 5 which carried this basic prohibition: "Unfair methods of competition in commerce are hereby declared unlawful." This was interpreted as being applicable to the enforcement of antimonopoly activities, but later broader court interpretations brought many other business practices under the commission's interpretation of Section 5. For example, the commission, in its rule that requires mail-order concerns to fill orders within thirty days or offer customers their money back, stated that not to do so was an unfair method of competition.

This rule-making procedure of the FTC is one of its more effective methods of protecting consumers and ethical businesses. In 1976, the FTC had seventeen rules pending which covered such areas as advertising and labeling of protein supplements, vocational and home study schools, the hearing aid industry, the funeral industry, mobile home sales and services, and advertising of ophthalmic goods and services. A House of Representatives Oversight Subcommittee severely criticized the FTC for the long delays in the processing of trade regulation rules, including a nutrition labeling rule that had been pending for several years. The subcommittee members described the FTC's performance as disgraceful and proof that the commission is a paper tiger. The committee members were upset because the FTC had begun twenty-one investigations since 1974, but only one trade rule and two industry guidelines had resulted.[7]

The commission has moved into many areas to attack fraud in the market. In this book, Chapter 10 describes the work of the commission in protecting consumers against false advertisements, and Chapter 14 deals with the commission's role in protecting consumers from other fraudulent practices.

The effectiveness of the FTC as a protector of consumers came under sharp criticism in a study made by a student group under the supervision of Ralph Nader.[8] This report was so critical of the FTC that the president asked the American Bar Association (ABA) to make a study. The ABA Commission's report substantiated the Nader report.[9] Appointment of a new chairman and a major overhaul in organization and administrative operations of the FTC were then made. Since then the FTC has been more active in protecting consumer rights. The Wool Products Labeling Act, the Fur Products Labeling Act, and the Textile Fiber Products Identification Act, all amendments to the FTC Act, have given the commission more specific legislation upon which to base its actions against unfair practices. See pp. 587–589 for detailed information on these acts.

Over the years the commission has published a series of guides in an effort to make clear to business which practices are prohibited by law and should be avoided. These guides are also useful in educating consumers to the dangers of such tactics as bait advertising, false guarantees, and fictitious bargain prices. Guides, unlike the trade practice rules, may deal with practices common to many industries. There is no necessity for hearings or conferences concerning them. The guides are not intended to cover gaps in the law, but rather they set forth in easily understood language the principles already established by the courts and the commission in cases that have been adjudicated. Their purpose is to give business some knowledge of what the law requires of it. The guides drawn up so far deal with such problem areas as bait advertising, deceptive advertising of guarantees, deceptive pricing, debt collection deception, cigarette advertising, tire advertising, cooling-off period for door-to-door sales,* and care labeling of textile wearing apparel.

Title II of the Consumer Products Warranties–Federal Trade Commission Improvement Act, which was passed in 1974, gave the FTC some very significant additional powers and affirmed its right to make trade regulation rules. For the first time in FTC history, it was expressly authorized to bring suits in the federal courts to obtain redress on behalf of consumers injured by violations of its rules or by unfair and deceptive acts and practices. Since its creation in 1914, the FTC has been limited to obtaining cease-and-desist orders rather than refunds and damages for consumers. The act also enabled the FTC to bring a civil penalty action in federal court, instead of merely instituting an administrative proceeding, once it has defined what the law is, either by trade regulation rule or by its decisions, and the defendant has knowingly violated the law. The fine may be as much as $10,000 per violation per day.

As in most activities of government, the benefits which accrue from the activities of the FTC seem to be determined primarily by the kind of top leadership the agency has.

HOW SAFE ARE PRODUCTS? THE ROLE OF THE CONSUMER PRODUCT SAFETY COMMISSION

The Birth of a New Regulatory Agency

The Consumer Product Safety Act, signed into law by the president in 1972, was the single most important consumer protection measure passed by the 92nd Congress. It represents a dramatic step forward in the federal government's efforts to protect the American public from unreasonable injuries and deaths associated with consumer products.

The reasons behind the establishment of this agency were simple enough. The National Commission on Product Safety published a report in 1970 in which it predicted that each year in this country we can expect 20 million serious injuries requiring professional medical help associated

---

* A "cooling-off" period gives the buyer three business days after he or she signs a contract for $25 or more in his home to cancel it.

with consumer products, plus 30,000 deaths, 110,000 permanent disfigurements and disabilities, and five and a half billion dollars worth of economic loss to the nation.[10]

The act created an independent federal regulatory agency, the Consumer Product Safety Commission (CPSC), with five commissioners, a staff of 750, and a budget of $55 million for fiscal year 1973. Its purposes were:

- To protect the public against injuries associated with consumer products
- To assist consumers in evaluating the comparative safety of products
- To develop uniform standards for consumer products
- To minimize conflicting state and local regulations
- To promote research and investigations into the causes and the prevention of product-related deaths, illness, and injuries

To preserve the existing product safety regulations, which had been developed over the past several decades, Congress transferred to CPSC the authority to enforce the Flammable Fabrics Act, the Poison Prevention Packaging Act, the Federal Hazardous Substances Act, and the Refrigerator Safety Act.

CPSC has jurisdiction over an estimated 10,000 different types of products, 200,000 manufacturing plants, and 2 million retail establishments. The only consumer products over which it does not have jurisdiction are foods, drugs, cosmetics, tobacco, automobiles, firearms, boats, pesticides, and aircraft—all of which are regulated to some extent under other laws by other agencies.

Implementing the Law

CPSC is involved in monitoring the injuries and deaths caused by consumer products, issuing recall notices for unsafe products, setting standards for specific products, and educating consumers in the safe use of products.

The collection and evaluation process of injury statistics is performed by the National Electronic Surveillance System (NEISS). NEISS gathers data from 119 statistically selected hospital emergency rooms located throughout the country. From these data, statistically valid projections of product-related injuries treated in emergency rooms can be made. Each injury report indicates the type of product involved, provides information about the victim and the injury, and reports whether the victim was treated and released or hospitalized or dead on arrival. Products that have been determined by the commission to be frequently involved in injury, or to cause severe injury, are high-priority items for investigations. Death statistics for fatal injuries are collected from all fifty states. Table 26-1 shows the ten leading consumer product hazards.

TABLE 26-1. Consumer Product Hazard Index

Rank	Product Description
1	Bicycles and bicycle equipment, including add-on features (baskets, horns, nonstandard seats, handlebars).
2	Stairs (including folding stairs), steps, ramps, landings
3	Power lawn mowers and unspecified lawn mowers
4	Football, activity, related equipment and apparel
5	Baseball, activity, related equipment and apparel
6	Swings, slides, seesaws, and playground equipment
7	Nonglass tables and unspecified tables
8	Beds (including springs, frames, bunk beds, and unspecified beds; excluding mattresses or box springs, water beds, sofa beds, infant beds, and special beds)
9	Nails, carpet tacks and screws, thumbtacks
10	Chairs, sofas, and sofa beds

Source: NEISS News, Consumer Product Safety Commission, Dec. 1975, p. 3.

In less than three years of operation CPSC judged 25 million items unsafe and called for recalls, repairs, and replacement. Most of these problems were reported to the government by manufacturers themselves, as is required by law. The act requires all manufacturers, inspectors, private labelers, distributors, and retailers to immediately notify the commission whenever they obtain information that a product manufactured or sold by them contains a defect which *could* create a substantial risk of injury. Failure to report such a defect is a violation of federal law and could result in civil and criminal penalties, both to the company and its executive officers.

CPSC has issued recall notices for a variety of products, including defective football helmets, plastic-coated soft drink bottles, disposable lighters, toys, carpets and children's pajamas that failed to pass flammability requirements, Christmas tree lights, television sets, "trouble" lights, electric nose cleaners, and hunting crossbows.

Consumers should be aware that the law requires that the retailer inform them about banned hazardous products and provide full refunds, with the manufacturer ultimately bearing the financial burden.

CPSC has been slow in establishing mandatory safety standards. More than two and a half years after it was created it issued its first standard, which was for swimming-pool slides. Standards have been issued for baby cribs and for bicycles, a product which has consistently ranked number one on the commission's product hazard index. Mandatory safety standards for power lawn mowers were drawn up, but industry has fought this because it felt the stringent standards could price power lawn motors out of the market for many people. Standards for safety matches are being developed.

CPSC has drawn up more than eighty fact sheets on consumer products that are most frequently associated with accidental injuries. These fact sheets show that power lawn mowers cause more than 50,000 injuries each year, bathtubs and showers cause 187,000 injuries, nonglass doors cause

150,000 injuries, and that fireworks caused 6,500 injuries a year until the amount of powder allowed to be used in them was sharply reduced in 1976. In addition, CPSC published a special holiday list of toys and other children's articles that had been banned because they were considered unsafe.[11]

CPSC also established a toll-free "Hotline." In its first year of operation there were nearly 60,000 calls from consumers. Calls to the "Hotline" range from requests for information about product safety to reports of product-related accidents and complaints about the safety of a consumer product. To report a product-related injury or product hazard or to request information on product safety consumers may call the toll free "Hotline" number from anywhere in the continental U.S.: Area Code 800 638–2666. (Maryland residents call 800 492–2937.)

Additional Legislative Power

In 1976 the president signed a bill increasing the power of CPSC, but excluding pesticides, tobacco, and firearms from its jurisdiction in order to eliminate conflict between CPSC and other government agencies. The act expanded the commission's authority by enabling it to issue preliminary injunctions prohibiting the distribution of potentially hazardous products. Previously, CPSC had to hold hearings before banning the sale of a product, pending the results of a full investigation. The act also authorized federal pre-emption of state laws on products and safety in certain circumstances, and it established new procedures and schedules for meeting consumer safety standards.

CONSUMER ACTIVITIES AT THE WHITE HOUSE LEVEL

Office of Consumer Affairs

In 1962 the president submitted the first consumer message ever presented to a United States Congress.[12] In it he called for the Council of Economic Advisers to create a Consumer Advisory Council (CAC) to examine and provide advice to the government on issues of broad economic policy, on governmental programs protecting consumer needs, and on needed improvements in the flow of consumer research material to the public. The council appointed in 1962 was composed of twelve members. The council had no power and was an advisory group to the Council of Economic Advisers, which is also a purely advisory council.

In 1964 the president established the President's Committee on Consumer Interests (PCCI) and made CAC part of it. In addition, the president appointed a Special Assistant to the President for Consumer Affairs, who also served as the PCCI's executive director. PCCI was given a unique task. It was to represent no organized sector of American society, but was charged with the responsibility of representing the millions of individuals – wealthy or poor, young or old, educated or uneducated – who as consumers purchase more than two-thirds of all the goods and services produced by the economy. PCCI had a small budget and staff. The beginnings of consumer representation in the executive office of the White House were small, but a beginning had been made, indicating the growing belief that the voices of consumers should be heard at the highest levels of government as well as the voices of business, labor, and agriculture.

In 1971 the Office of Consumer Affairs (OCA) in the executive office replaced PCCI. Under the reorganization plan, CAC was continued and given the responsibility of advising the Special Assistant to the President with respect to: 1) policy matters relating to consumer interests; 2) the effectiveness of federal programs and operations that affect the interests of consumers; 3) problems of primary importance to consumers; and 4) ways in which unmet consumer needs can appropriately be met through federal government action.[13]

In 1973 the Office of Consumer Affairs was transferred to the Department of Health, Education, and Welfare by executive order, but the OCA's executive director retained the title of Special Assistant to the President for Consumer Affairs.

The OCA operates with a staff of fifty-five and a budget of $1.6 million.[14] Its purpose is to represent the consumer's voice at the highest levels of government. It has been a national focal point for consumer complaints, which number more than 2,500 a month. These complaints are referred to appropriate government agencies and businesses for corrective action. It acts as a catalyst for consumer activity and interests at the national level.

The effectiveness of consumer activities at the White House level is determined by the degree of importance the president gives them. President Kennedy was the first president to submit a consumer message to Congress, and he appointed the Consumer Advisory Council. President Johnson was the first president to appoint a Special Assistant to the President for Consumer Affairs. In addition, he gave his special assistant a rather free hand and was supportive of consumer activity. President Nixon was ready to abolish the office of special assistant, but public reaction changed his mind. He downgraded the OCA, however, by removing it from the executive office and placing it in the Department of Health, Education, and Welfare. President Ford continued both the OCA, CAC, and the office of special assistant, but he felt that too much bureaucracy and too many regulations had been built up. He believed that existing agencies and departments, if they did a better job, would be adequate to the task.

The OCA, CAC, and the office of the Special Assistant to the President for Consumer Affairs basically reflect the attitudes of the president and his staff toward consumerism.*

---

* Many of these are personal observations made by Stewart Lee, who served for six years on the CAC and for two years served as chairman.

OTHER GOVERNMENT ACTIONS IN THE CONSUMER'S INTEREST

Department of Transportation

The Department of Transportation (DOT) has become involved in consumer activities through its National Highway Traffic Safety Administration (NHTSA). NHTSA works to reduce highway deaths, injuries, and property losses. It accomplishes this goal through enforcement of federal performance standards for cars, motorcycles, small trucks, and vehicle equipment; through investigation of reported safety-related defects; through enforcement of laws requiring the recall and free repair of such defects; and through development of various highway safety standards.

Recall campaigns, even when the manufacturer pays for correcting the defect, have not been completely successful. Approximately one-third of the cars recalled are brought in for inspection and correction. The first recall involved about 6.8 million 1965–1969 passenger cars and 1965–1970 trucks with defective engine mounts. The second recall involved about 4.1 million 1970–1971 passenger cars with defective shoulder belt assemblies. The third recall involved 3.7 million 1949–1969 vehicles having defective windshield wiper arms.[15] Between 1966 and the end of 1975, 48.5 million domestic and foreign automobiles were recalled for inspection and/or actual repair. In general, a new model has hardly hit the market before recall notices on it start going out.

You can check whether a car that you are about to buy has been subject to a recall by the manufacturer because of a safety-related defect by sending the vehicle identification number to the Office of Consumer Services, NHTSA, 400 Seventh Street, S.W., Washington, D.C. 20590, or by calling the Office of Consumer Services at Area Code 202 426–0670.

The Department of Transportation also has the responsibility to see that defective tires are recalled. Public notices of recalls are made, but only buyers who have registered their tires will get direct notification from manufacturers in case a safety defect shows up later. The few seconds it takes one to fill out a registration form when buying tires may save a life.

Civil Aeronautics Board

The Office of Consumer Advocate of the Civil Aeronautics Board handles consumer complaints against airlines, attempts to resolve consumer problems by contact with the company involved, publishes monthly statistical reports detailing complaints received by the office, and participates in selected board proceedings as an advocate of air transportation consumers.

During the first seven months of 1976 the office received 9,824 complaints. The three major complaints were cancelled flights, delayed flights, and irregularities in flights with 1,327 complaints. Problems of reservations, including over-booking, had 1,575 complaints, and there were 1,102 complaints for lost, delayed, and damaged baggage.[16]

Consumer Information Center

The Consumer Information Center of the U.S. General Services Administration works with federal agencies to determine what information is available that might be useful to consumers and makes recommendations for new publications of consumer interest. This information is listed in a quarterly catalog, *Consumer Information*. The catalog lists approximately 250 booklets, some of which are free. For a free catalog write Consumer Information Center, Pueblo, Colorado 81009. During fiscal year 1976 approximately eleven million requests for publications were filled. The center operates on a budget of slightly more than one million dollars annually.

Antitrust Activity to Protect Consumers

The record justifies the assertion that while the business community lauds the concept of competition, many business firms try to stifle competition. The record shows that even as you read these words there are probably some business representatives meeting secretly to allocate markets, establish quotas, and set prices. Three or four years from now the Antitrust Division of the U.S. Department of Justice may discover the conspiracy and proceed against it. The Antitrust Division has filed suit against bakeries, steel companies, drug companies, publishing companies, plumbing fixtures companies, electrical companies, a linen supply association, a motorcycle company, a cosmetic company, milk producers and processors, companies making college class rings and graduation invitations, a few leading department stores, a trade association of tour operators, and manufacturers of plywood, veneer, and other lumber products, all of which were rigging prices.

A consumer should keep an eye out for tell-tale signs of price fixing. An antitrust violation may be present if there are large price changes involving more than one seller of a highly similar product, particularly if the price changes are of equal amount and occur at the same time; if competing sellers have identical pricing of the same or similar products and if prices among competing sellers seem to move in the same direction at the same time; or if a seller even tells a consumer, "Oh no, we don't sell in that area; so-and-so is the only firm that sells in that area, according to our agreement."

These signs are not conclusive evidence of antitrust violations. Investigation by trained lawyers would be required to establish proof of a violation. But they may be indications, and the people who enforce the antitrust laws, the Antitrust Division and the Federal Trade Commission, want to hear about them.

SHOULD THERE BE AN INDEPENDENT FEDERAL AGENCY FOR CONSUMERS?

Scattered throughout the federal government are numerous agencies, departments, and offices that have as their primary or secondary purpose serving the consumer interests.

Several government agencies whose work is helpful to consumers have been consolidated in the Department of Health, Education, and Welfare. HEW now includes the Food and Drug Administration, Public Health Service, Social Security Administration, Health Services and Mental Health Administration, National Institutes of Health, Office of Education, the Social and Rehabilitation Service, and the Office of Consumer Affairs.

The Federal Trade Commission, the Consumer Product Safety Commission, and the Civil Aeronautics Commission are independent regulatory agencies which have a responsibility to serve consumers. The Departments of Agriculture and Commerce are actively involved in areas related to consumer welfare.

It has been debated that this fragmentation has not given the consumers forceful and coherent representation at the federal level and that a consolidation of these activities into a Department of Consumers at the Cabinet level would achieve true consumer recognition. In general, the departments and agencies that would be affected by any major realignment or consolidation of consumer activities at the federal level oppose such proposals. Each department and agency attempts to meet such proposals for realignment or consolidation by becoming more active in the consumer area.

The political momentum for the establishment of a Department for Consumers has subsided considerably in recent years and has been replaced with pressure to establish some type of independent consumer protection agency, known as the Agency for Consumer Advocacy, to serve as an advocate for consumers before private industry and other government agencies.

In 1970 legislation was introduced into Congress to establish such a consumer protection agency. It was reintroduced in various forms in the 92nd, 93rd, and 94th congresses. It was not until the 94th Congress that both the Senate and House of Representatives passed such legislation. Under this bill the consumer agency would have as its major function representing the consumer interests before all other agencies and in courts. Business is well represented in government with the Department of Commerce; the Department of Labor represents labor's interest; and the Department of Agriculture represents the farmer's interest. In addition, all these special interest groups have adequately-financed associations and lobbying groups to work for their members. But consumers have not had this kind of forceful representation from within government or outside government.

What this agency would do would be to give the consumer the same voice that business, labor, and agriculture have had for decades in the key stages of policy-making in all federal departments and agencies in which consumer issues are decided. It would serve as the consumer's advocate and watchdog in agencies—from the Federal Power Commission and the Securities and Exchange Commission to the Food and Drug Administration. It would also act as a clearinghouse for consumer complaints.

The bill passed by the 94th Congress budgeted approximately $20 million for the first year of the agency. That represents about 10 cents per person per year, a small price to pay for what could be a potent force for consumer representation at the federal level.

Momentum had been building in Congress for the establishment of such an agency during the six years of debate over this issue, but by the end of 1975 pressures were building to limit the expansion of federal bureaucracy, and the consumer protection agency became a main target of this decentralizing movement in government. Business interests, including the U.S. Chamber of Commerce, the National Association of Manufacturers, and the Business Roundtable, worked diligently for a presidential veto of the bill. Many members of Congress who had originally favored the agency had second thoughts. A growing anti-big-government sentiment hurt the bill's chances of becoming law. Most important, President Ford came out forcefully in opposition to the bill, declaring that he would veto it. There seemed to be almost no chance of the bill being passed over a presidential veto.

The president made his position very clear: He opposed adding another layer of bureaucracy to government at the taxpayer's expense, in spite of the fact that as House Minority Leader in 1971 he had spoken out strongly for an independent consumer protection agency. As an alternative to a new, independent agency, Ford directed each of the seventeen major departments and agencies of the federal government to establish an office to represent the consuming public.

Sides were drawn. Practically all consumer organizations and consumer advocates favored the establishment of an independent consumer agency. In fact the president's own Consumer Advisory Council unanimously endorsed the idea. Those representing the administration argued that reforming all seventeen agencies and departments by modifying their organization was a better way to get the job done. The opponents of the administration's position referred to it as nothing but "window-dressing" and contended that these departments and agencies had not represented consumers adequately in the past so there was no reason to believe that they would change over night. Congress decided not to send the bill to the president for an expected veto, but to reintroduce the bill in the 95th Congress.

DEPARTMENT OF CONSUMER AND CORPORATE AFFAIRS OF CANADA

The primary concern of Canada's Department of Consumer and Corporate Affairs, which was established by an act of Parliament in 1968, is the proper functioning of the marketplace. Its role is to encourage and develop a competitive market system that is fair to all. To accomplish this, the department has been given a wide range of responsibilities under federal jurisdiction. They relate to such matters as product safety, textile labeling, consumer complaints, consumer information, misleading advertising, combines investigation, bankruptcy, federal corporation laws, patents, copyright laws, trademarks, industrial designs, weights and measures, electricity and gas inspections, and inspection of meat, fish, and agricultural products at the retail level for quality and grade standards.

Since its formation in 1967, the department's main objectives have been:

1. To develop new laws, particularly to protect the consumer
2. To develop a coordinated, efficient system across Canada to uniformly administer and enforce the department's legislation and regulations
3. To review, revise, and coordinate existing legislation and programs to meet today's needs
4. To keep Canadians informed on all matters of interest to consumers*

Responsibility for developing programs and legislation is shared by four bureaus covering the areas of consumer affairs, corporate affairs, competition policy, and intellectual property. The Bureau of Consumer Affairs is mainly concerned with consumer protection and consumer information. It does in-depth research to develop regulations and laws that set standards to protect the consumer. The basic aim of these laws is to ensure that correct measures and standards are applied to all products sold in Canada. The bureau carries out an extensive information program through the publication of booklets, fact sheets, and its monthly newsletter *Consumer Contact*. It also provides a focal point for communication between the department and the public through "The Consumer, Box 99, Ottawa," the department's official listening post for consumer complaints and enquiries. The bureau is engaged in research and development projects covering a wide range of subjects of consumer concern.

The Bureau of Corporate Affairs is concerned with much of the general legal framework that governs the orderly conduct of business under federal jurisdiction. It grants charters of incorporation to new businesses and supervises bankruptcy proceedings for insolvent companies and individuals.

The Bureau of Intellectual Property protects the rights of the originators of inventive or creative works by granting patents and registering trademarks, industrial designs, and copyrights.

The Bureau of Competition Policy administers the Combines Investigation Act, which is the Canadian antitrust law, whose purpose is to maintain a competitive market system.

In addition, there is a Canadian Consumer Council to advise and assist

* For further information see *The Department of Consumer and Corporate Affairs: Who We Are and What We Do*, Department of Consumer and Corporate Affairs, Ottawa-Hull, Canada, 1974.

the Minister of the Department of Consumer and Corporate Affairs. The council is an autonomous body of twenty-four members which speaks independently of the views of government or other bodies. The council is designed to bring a wide variety of viewpoints to bear on issues of concern to consumers. The fundamental goal of the council's activities is to improve the consumer environment and to remove imperfections in the system which operate contrary to the most efficient and productive allocation of resources.

The Department of Consumer and Corporate Affairs of Canada might serve as a model for the United States. By incorporating the whole range of consumer affairs in this department, the Canadian Parliament created a strong central consumer agency. A question for debate is whether an independent agency instead of a department might be able to serve consumers better.

QUESTIONS FOR REVIEW

1. What services does the U.S. Department of Agriculture perform for consumers?

2. Do you believe the consumer's interest would be better served if the Food and Drug Administration took over the task of meat, poultry, and fish inspection? Why?

3. What appear to be weaknesses in the meat inspection program?

4. What are some of the provisions of the Wholesome Poultry Products Act?

5. How important is the Federal Trade Commission to consumers?

6. How might the FTC be more effective in protecting consumers?

7. Why was the Consumer Product Safety Commission created and what are its areas of responsibility?

8. How effective is the CPSC in protecting consumers and how might it be more effective?

9. Discuss the development of consumer representation at the White House level.

10. What is the significance of effective antitrust enforcement for the consumer?

11. Would you favor a Department of Consumers at the Cabinet level or an independent Agency for Consumer Advocacy? Defend your answer.

PROJECTS

1. Write an in-depth report about one of the federal agencies serving consumers.

2. Write to one federal agency discussed in this chapter and request materials, news releases, an annual report, and miscellaneous publications relating to consumer protection and welfare. Write a report evaluating the materials you receive.

3. Interview an official of a meat processing plant in your area and get his views concerning pure meat and the activities of the USDA meat inspection program. Write an analysis of the interview.

4. Interview a retail owner concerning his feelings about federal government regulations related to his business. Write an analysis of the interview.

5. Debate the issue: Resolved that there should be established an in-independent Agency for Consumer Advocacy.

6. Write a letter to your senator or representative and try to ascertain what consumer legislation is being considered by Congress and his or her position on such legislation.

7. Do a report on how effective the Canadian Department of Consumer and Corporate Affairs is.

REFERENCES

1. *Fact Book of U.S. Agriculture*, Rev. ed. (Washington, D.C.: Government Printing Office, March 1976), pp. 57–58.
2. *Report on Federal Medical Services*, prepared for the Commission on Organization of the Executive Branch of the Government by the Task Force on Federal Medical Services, Hoover Commission (Washington, D.C.: Government Printing Office, 1955).
3. *Congressional Record*, H 4937-H 4957, 13 June 1968.
4. *Fact Book of U.S. Agriculture*, p. 57.
5. *Consumer Reports*, Nov. 1974, pp. 816–819.
6. *Fact Book of U.S. Agriculture*, p. 58.
7. *Supermarket News*, 1 March 1976, p. 29.
8. Edward F. Cox, Robert C. Fellmeth, and John E. Schulz, *"The Nader Report" on the Federal Trade Commission* (New York: Richard W. Baron, 1969).
9. *Report of the ABA Commission to Study the Federal Trade Commission* (Washington D.C.: Bureau of National Affairs, 1969).
10. *Final Report of The National Commission on Product Safety* (Washington, D.C.: Government Printing Office, June 1970), p. 1.
11. *Banned Products: CPSC* (Washington, D.C.: Government Printing Office, 1 Oct. 1974).
12. *Consumers' Protection and Interest Program, Message From the President of the United States Relative to Consumers' Protection and Interest Program*, 87th Congress, 2nd Session, H. R. Doc. 364, 15 March 1962.
13. Office of the White House Press Secretary, News Release, Executive Order 11583, 24 Feb. 1971, p. 4.
14. *Estimate of Appropriation, Fiscal Year 1977, Office of Consumer Affairs, Office of the Secretary*, Department of Health, Education, and Welfare, p. 41.
15. *The Auto Safety Program: Identifying Defects and Recalling Defective Vehicles*, Report to the Committee on Commerce, U.S. Senate, by the Comptroller General, 11 Feb. 1975, p. 5.
16. Civil Aeronautics Board, News Release, 10 Aug. 1976.

INDEXES

NAME INDEX

SUBJECT INDEX